The MICHELIN Guide

New York City
RESTAURANTS
2014

Michelin Travel Partner

Société par actions simplifiées au capital de 11 629 590 EUR
27 Cours de l'Ile Seguin - 92100 Boulogne Billancourt (France)
R.C.S. Nanterre 433 677 721

© **Michelin, Propriétaires-Éditeurs**

Dépôt légal octobre 2013

Printed in Canada - septembre 2013
Printed on paper from sustainably managed forests

Compogravure : Nord Compo à Villeneuve d'Ascq (France)
Impression et Finition : Transcontinental (Canada)

Dear Reader

W e are thrilled to present the ninth edition of our
MICHELIN Guide to New York City.

*Our dynamic team has spent this year updating our selection to
wholly reflect the rich diversity of New York City's restaurants. As
part of our meticulous and highly confidential evaluation process,
our inspectors have anonymously and methodically eaten
through all five boroughs to compile the finest in each category
for your enjoyment. While the inspectors are expertly trained
food industry professionals, we remain consumer driven and
provide comprehensive choices to accommodate your comfort,
tastes, and budget. Our inspectors dine, drink, and lodge as
'regular' customers in order to experience and evaluate the same
level of service and cuisine you would as a guest.*

*We have expanded our criteria to reflect some of the more
current and unique elements of New York City's dining scene.
Don't miss the tasty "Small Plates" category, highlighting places
with a distinct style of service, setting, and menu; and the further
expanded "Under $25" listing which includes an impressive
choice at great value.*

*Additionally, you may follow our Inspectors on Twitter @
MichelinGuideNY as they chow their way around town. They
usually tweet daily about their unique and entertaining food
experiences.*

*Our company's founders, Édouard and André Michelin,
published the first MICHELIN Guide in 1900, to provide motorists
with practical information about where they could service and
repair their cars, find quality accommodations, and a good meal.
Later in 1926, the star-rating system for outstanding restaurants
was introduced, and over the decades we have developed many
new improvements to our guides. The local team here in New
York eagerly carries on these traditions.*

*We truly hope that the MICHELIN Guide will remain your
preferred reference to the city's restaurants.*

Contents

Peter L. Wrenn / MICHELIN

The MICHELIN Guide

"This volume was created at the turn of the century and will last at least as long".

This foreword to the very first edition of the MICHELIN Guide, written in 1900, has become famous over the years and the Guide has lived up to the prediction. It is read across the world and the key to its popularity is the consistency in its commitment to its readers, which is based on the following promises.

→ Anonymous Inspections

Our inspectors make anonymous visits to hotels and restaurants to gauge the quality offered to the ordinary customer. They pay their own bill and make no indication of their presence. These visits are supplemented by comprehensive monitoring of information—our readers' comments are one valuable source, and are always taken into consideration.

→ Independence

Our choice of establishments is a completely independent one, made for the benefit of our readers alone. Decisions are discussed by the inspectors and the editor, with the most important decided at the global level. Inclusion in the guide is always free of charge.

→ The Selection

The Guide offers a selection of the best hotels and restaurants in each category of comfort and price. Inclusion in the guides is a commendable award in itself, and defines the establishment among the "best of the best."

How the MICHELIN Guide Works

→ Annual Updates

All practical information, the classifications, and awards, are revised and updated every year to ensure the most reliable information possible.

→ Consistency & Classifications

The criteria for the classifications are the same in all countries covered by the Michelin Guides. Our system is used worldwide and is easy to apply when choosing a restaurant or hotel.

→ The Classifications

We classify our establishments using ⚔⚔⚔⚔-⚔ and 🏨🏨🏨🏨-🏨 to indicate the level of comfort. The 🏵🏵🏵-🏵 specifically designates an award for cuisine, unique from the classification. For hotels and restaurants, a symbol in red suggests a particularly charming spot with unique décor or ambiance.

→ Our Aim

As part of Michelin's ongoing commitment to improving travel and mobility, we do everything possible to make vacations and eating out a pleasure.

How to Use This Guide

The Michelin Distinctions for Good Cuisine

Stars for good cuisine

✿✿✿ Exceptional cuisine, worth a special journey
✿✿ Excellent cuisine, worth a detour
✿ A very good restaurant in its category

☺ Bib Gourmand
Inspectors' favorites for good value

Areas or neighborhoods
Each area is color coded...

Average Prices

⊝	Under $25
$$	$25 to $50
$$$	$50 to $75
$$$$	Over $75

Symbols

💵	Cash only
⚐	Wheelchair accessible
⛱	Outdoor dining
🍳	Breakfast
🍽	Brunch
🥢	Dim sum
🍷	Notable wine list
⚱	Notable sake list
🍸	Notable cocktail list
🍺	Notable beer list
🅿	Valet parking
🍽	Late dining
♢	Private dining room

Yellow Dog Café ☺

Americas

The Bronx ▸ Chelsea
Manhattan

A4

1445 Jasmine Court Dr. (at Lee Blvd.)

Phone: 212-599-0000
Web: www.llovegoldens.com
Prices: $$

Named for the owners' beloved yellow Labrador this chic cafe exudes warmth from the welcoming to the lace cafe curtains, and pet portraits in room. Pride of place is evident in the faces servers who are happy to accommodate special You won't be barking up the wrong tree if you specialty of the house: prime rib. It is roasted rare (or whatever degree you prefer) and acco the vegetable of the day and mashed Yukon with garlic. Fish fanciers can choose among di sautéed day-boat scallops, grilled wild salmo fried catfish.

Hearty portions and beef bones available t for your canine buddies bring new meanin "doggie bag."

Jeanine's Uptown

C4

8459 Hart Blvd. (bet. 45th & 46th Ave

Phone: 310-454-5294
Web: www.eatatjeanines.com
Prices: $$$

Carb lovers flock to the Uptown branch o chain for thick-crust pies slathered with sauce and sprinkled with fresh toppin spinach and broccoli, artichoke hearts There's always a line out the door, and the signature pizza, brimming with pe made sausage. Although pizza is the the menu lists a number of traditiona and-white-checked tablecloths and the tables, creating an old-fashion ambience. And speaking of Chianti, here. The chain takes its name from who loves that thick crust, but wo ten-foot pole.

152

Restaurant Classifications by Comfort

More pleasant if in red

X	Comfortable
XX	Quite comfortable
XxX	Very comfortable
XxxX	Top class comfortable
XxXxX	Luxury in the traditional style
📖	Small plates

Map Coordinates

Sonya's Palace ✿ ✿

Italian XXXX

A4 100 Reuther Pl. (at 30th Street)

Dinner daily

Manhattan ▲ Chelsea

Phone: 415-867-5309
Subway: 14th St - 8 Av
Web: www.sonyasfabulouspalace.com
Prices: $$$

David Buffington/Getty Images

Home cooked Italian never tasted so good than at this unpretentious little place. The simple décor claims no big-name designers, and while the Murano glass light fixtures are chic and the velveteen-covered chairs are comfortable, this isn't a restaurant where millions of dollars were spent on the interior.

Instead, food is the focus here. The restaurant's name may not be Italian, but it nonetheless serves some of the best pasta in the city, made fresh in-house. Dishes follow the seasons, thus ravioli may be stuffed with fresh ricotta and herbs in summer, and pumpkin in fall. Most everything is liberally dusted with Parmigiano Reggiano, a favorite ingredient of the chef.

For dessert, you'll have to deliberate between the likes of creamy tiramisu, ricotta cheesecake, and homemade gelato. One thing's for sure: you'll never miss your nonna's cooking when you eat at Sonya's.

153

San Francisco ▲ Nob Hill

Italian 📖

...s.)

Lunch daily

retriever,
waitstaff
e dining
friendly
...quests.
...der the
...edium
...ed by
...inged
...ch as
...pan-

...ome
...rm

...í
...g
...ly
...ne
...am
by
...ged
...n as
...pan-

...ome
...term

...za X

...dinner only

...al pizzeria
...e marinara
...as organic
...etta.
...rave about
...and house-
...action here,
...s well. Red-
...ottles adorn
...n restaurant
...ne of choice
...er's daughter,
...meat with a

107

...meat with a

9

Where to Eat

Manhattan

Chelsea

Restaurants in this artsy neighborhood—the hub of New York City's gallery scene—feature flavors from around the globe, and encompass everything from French bistros and sushi bars, to contemporary Spanish fare. Old World Puerto Rican luncheonettes on and around Ninth Avenue (where patrons are accommodated in English or Spanish, and the *café con leche* packs a heady wallop) provide a striking contrast to the mega-hip places that punctuate Chelsea today. For a heavenly cup of caffeine, thirsty hordes head over to **Cafe Grumpy** for a flavorful roast, each ground and brewed to order.

Meanwhile, FIT students who aren't watching their waistline hover around beloved **brgr** for their lineup of hearty, grass-fed burgers. Speaking of comfort food, **Artichoke Basille's Pizza** is a successful mini-chain complete with simple yet addictive pies. Cochon555 is a national event series that takes place annually in the Lighthouse at Chelsea Piers, and features a massive selection of food pioneers in support of a better food system.

If that's not hip enough for you, there's always the scene at **Buddakan**, that tried and trendy temple of modern Asian fare, courtesy of Philadelphia restaurateur wunderkind Stephen Starr. In the burgeoning area popularly referred to as the West Club District, patrons of nightspots like Mansion and Marquee are grateful for such late-night spots as **The Half King**. This quintessential New York destination dishes up good all-American grub. Named for an 18th century Seneca Indian chief, Half King also sponsors book readings on Monday nights, thanks to co-owner and writer Sebastian Junger, author of *War*, and co-director of the documentary, *Restrepo*.

Chelsea Market

No food-finding excursion to this neighborhood would be complete without a visit to the primo **Chelsea Market**. The 1898 Nabisco factory—where the Oreo cookie was first made in 1912—reopened in 1997 as an urban food market. Interspersed throughout its brick-lined arcades with stores selling flowers, meats, cheeses, artisan-made breads, and other gourmet essentials are cafés, bakeries, and eateries. Drop by to peruse their wares, stock your pantry, and have a bite to eat while you're at it. Treat yourself to organic farm-fresh cuisine and biodynamic wines at **The Green Table** and **The Cleaver Co.** Seafood lovers can pick up a luscious lobster roll or some freshly steamed lobsters at **The Lobster Place**, a leading purveyor of these sea creatures. If you have kids in tow, a stop at **L'Arte del Gelato** is a must. Some welcome additions to the market are **Dickson's Farmstand** for their serious meats and **Lucy's Whey** for tasty cheeses. A trip to the

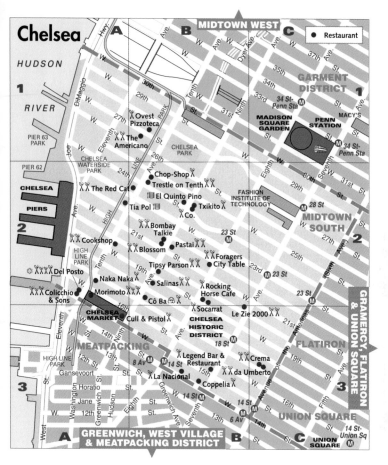

market will nourish you for hours of gallery-hopping on the district's western flank. Upstairs, the Chelsea Market pavilion houses the studios and test kitchens for the Food Network. Continue your stroll north and follow the meaty scents to **Salumeria Biellese** for some great cured products. After these salty snacks, **La Bergamote Patisserie** is the perfect landing spot for sating a sweet tooth. And while in the area, consider dining with a view of Lady Liberty on one of the dinner cruises that departs from Chelsea Piers, an ever-evolving recreational waterfront area located along the West Side Highway. Comprising four historic piers along the Hudson River, this jam-packed complex now houses state-of-the-art sports facilities, including a spa, ice skating rink, and bowling alley. Finally, the **Chelsea Brewing Company**, overlooking the Hudson River, is a glorious spot to close your day. Satiate your palate with one of their unique beers like the Checker Cab Blonde Ale.

The Americano

B1

518 W. 27th St. (bet. Tenth & Eleventh Aves.)

Subway: 23 St (Eighth Ave.) Lunch & dinner daily
Phone: 212-216-0000
Web: www.hotel-americano.com
Prices: $$$

Within its all-mesh metal façade, the Hotel Americano's namesake restaurant is a striking home to contemporary dining in far west Chelsea, just steps from the High Line. A citron banquette seems to pop in the slick setting, which combines floor-to-ceiling windows, glossy walls, and a polished concrete floor.

A talented team behind the line strives—and succeeds—in preparing delicious Latin fare with French flair. Menu options include delicate empanadas stuffed with Oaxacan cheese and wild mushrooms, or succulent lobster fried tempura-style and set on a complex sauce of fruity *chile pasilla* and dried corn. Some classics remain wonderfully familiar, as in the tarte Tatin made from local Golden Delicious apples, topped with a dollop of crème fraîche.

Blossom

B2

187 Ninth Ave. (bet. 21st & 22nd Sts.)

Subway: 23 St (Eighth Ave.) Lunch & dinner daily
Phone: 212-627-1144
Web: www.blossomnyc.com
Prices: $$

Blossom is sultry with just two rows of dim lights, an array of candles, and dark velvet curtains. Yet it remains a fantastic food oasis that is at once convivial yet hushed, and intimate without feeling tight. Whether a fanatic vegan or part-time vegetarian, trust that these dishes are always tasty and gratifying.

Framed mirrors lend an illusion of depth to these close-knit quarters. Shadowing the pleasant hum of diners is Blossom's dynamic cuisine. Nobly clad in black ensembles, servers might present the likes of parsnip *cappelletti*, parsnip and potato "hats" brushed with a shiitake-truffle oil; and pan-seared portobello "shank" rimmed by a tomato broth. Their vegan cheesecake will make you shun the classic version in a heartbeat.

Bombay Talkie

B2

Indian ✗✗

189 Ninth Ave. (bet. 21st & 22nd Sts.)

Subway: 23 St (Eighth Ave.)
Phone: 212-242-1900
Web: www.bombaytalkie.com
Prices: $$

Lunch & dinner daily

Located in a landmarked Chelsea space designed by architect Thomas Juul-Hansen, this Indian spot knows the key to its popularity is in its consistency. Take a seat below the canvases from J.P. Krishna, and pick your meal off a menu boasting sections like "from the roadside" and "street bites." Try a plate of *malai kofta*, dumplings stuffed with cheese and coconut, and bathed in a cashew-yogurt sauce; or *Bombay bhel*, served with wheat flour chips and rice puffs, tossed with a bright lime, mint, onion, and green mango salsa. The cocktail list piques diners' interest, as do the likes of Assam green tea and cardamom coffee.

This double-decker standby offers two stories of seating and a long communal table, but reservations are still recommended.

Chop-Shop

B2

Asian ✗

254 Tenth Ave. (bet. 24th & 25th Sts.)

Subway: 23 St (Eighth Ave.)
Phone: 212-820-0333
Web: www.chop-shop.co
Prices: $$

Lunch Mon– Sat
Dinner nightly

Valued as one of the hippest nooks in town, Chelsea houses everything from art galleries to ethnic food delights. Like its locale, the setting is clean and laid-back, with reclaimed pine, vintage lights, concrete floors, large windows that flood the room with light, and a lovely backyard. Chop-Shop maintains a cool vibe through its delectably fresh and complex Asian menu.

The food meanders this vast continent, beginning with the likes of fresh summer rolls plump with shrimp to juicy pan-fried pork and bok choi dumplings licked with a spicy soy sauce. *Zha jian mian* tosses springy wheat noodles in a spicy ground pork sauce with refreshing cucumber; and a pan-fried sea bass fillet is tender, sweet, and topped with sour vinegar pepper strips.

Co.

B2

230 Ninth Ave. (at 24th St.)

Subway: 23 St (Eighth Ave.)
Phone: 212-243-1105
Web: www.co-pane.com
Prices: $$

Lunch & dinner daily

Go ahead and heave a sigh of relief because Co. is not yet another wood-burning, Naples-aping pizzeria. In fact, it may be lauded as the bake shop that ushered in this Neapolitan-hailing, all-American food frenzy, where owner Jim Lahey (of popular Sullivan Street Bakery a few doors down) is wholly fixated on the art of bread-making.

The menu at this wood-paneled den—decked with mirrors, unconventional lights, and a cozy kitchen—may not be vast but the choices are plenty. A kindly staff presents such fine items as the "Popeye" pizza, served hot and crusty with fresh spinach, spicy crushed tomatoes, and a wealth of cheese. Adored by parents with children in tow is the pizza Bianca spread with olive oil, sea salt, and pickled vegetables.

Cô Ba

B2

110 Ninth Ave. (bet. 19th & 20th Sts.)

Subway: 23 St (Eighth Ave.)
Phone: 212-414-2700
Web: www.cobarestaurant.com
Prices: $$

Lunch & dinner daily

Cô Ba may seem smaller than a bread-box, but this downright warm and friendly Vietnamese spot cleverly presents big, solid flavors and delectable cuisine. Inside, images of rural Vietnamese life, quirky conical rice paddy hats, and charming old photos of the motherland line the walls to decorate the room.

The menu is massive, covers all the familiar hits, and is sure to offer something for everyone, as in *rau nuong*, grilled eggplant with shiitake and okra topped with basil, scallion oil, and a ginger-lime sauce; or Cô Ba beef done three ways (wok-seared with a sweet soy-sake marinade, wrapped inside grilled shiso leaves, or grilled sesame five-spice sirloin rolls). The steamed shrimp-coconut rice cakes with lime sauce are an absolute standout.

Colicchio & Sons

American XXX

85 Tenth Ave. (bet. 15th & 16th Sts.)

Subway: 14 St - 8 Av
Phone: 212-400-6699
Web: www.craftrestaurantsinc.com
Prices: $$$$

Lunch & dinner daily

This stunning, smart Chelsea-meets-Meatpacking outpost highlights the renowned talent of Chef Tom Colicchio. The front "Tap Room" boasts an impressive beer list, small plates with big prices, and cords of chopped wood resting on chrome shelves to fuel the wood-burning oven. The sophisticated back dining room offers moon-shaped leather banquettes, a glass wine hall, and a bird's-eye mural of the neighborhood.

Meals are simple but beguilingly delicious, as in beautifully ridged ricotta cavatelli tossed with silky leeks, *cavolo nero*, and a bit of heat from fiery chili peppers. Desserts might feature a wonderfully firm cream cheese panna cotta with blackberry gelée, cashew brittle, chai ice cream, and a surprising little coriander shortbread.

Cookshop

American XX

156 Tenth Ave. (at 20th St.)

Subway: 23 St (Eighth Ave.)
Phone: 212-924-4440
Web: www.cookshopny.com
Prices: $$

Lunch & dinner daily

The beauty of Cookshop is that it still feels brand spanking new. With sunlight flooding its floors and soft lights by night, everybody looks pretty at this lively scene. Dressed-up with plants and flowers, Cookshop impresses its highbrow neighbors—the Desmond Tutu Center and High Line are in full view.

If you're here stag, settle at the bar to peruse a chalkboard stocked with menu items and their sources. Simple and seasonal is their essence and the outcome is worth it. Marrying soul with pride are such unique dishes as trap-caught Montauk squid with plump, flavorsome beans; fish tacos topped with a spicy jalapeño-cabbage slaw; and Italian plum buckle, a warm, lemony crumb cake filled with fresh plums and crested with buttermilk ice cream.

Coppelia

 B3

Latin American

207 W. 14th St. (bet. Seventh & Eighth Aves.)

Subway: 14 St (Seventh Ave.)   Lunch & dinner daily
Phone: 212-858-5001
Web: www.coppelianyc.com
Prices: $$

Think of ultra-casual Coppelia as a favorite anytime Latin-American diner, ready to please with its enormous menus served 24 hours a day, seven days a week. The space is long and narrow, with a dining counter for solo guests, checkerboard floors, booths, and cheery yellow walls. Late at night, this place is hopping.

Sometimes their dishes can be inconsistent, but nevertheless grow in popularity as the sun goes down. Highlights at this unique spot include *churrasco*, a smoky and perfectly seasoned skirt steak with sweet fried plantains and tender, earthy black beans simmered with aromatics; or snacks like *croquetas de queso*, fried until crunchy and oozing piping hot melted cheese. Dessert might include a fluffy, light, and milk-soaked *tres leches* cake.

Crema

 C3

Mexican

111 W. 17th St. (bet. Sixth & Seventh Aves.)

Subway: 18 St   Lunch & dinner daily
Phone: 212-691-4477
Web: www.cremarestaurante.com
Prices: $$

There seems to be an air of comfort surrounding lovely Crema—especially at dinner. Bare marble tables, warm yellow walls, and a cactus garden surround a front banquette, strewn with pillows and overlooking 17th Street. The bar displays glass vats of sangria and mixes a vast array of refreshing cocktails, like the *delirio* combining gin, cucumber, white cranberry juice, and freshly muddled lime.

From the kitchen, find wonderfully complex Mexican dishes, as in the *caldo de habas*, a thick and rich fava bean soup that is crimson-red, smoky, and very spicy. The *pastel Azteca* arrives as a tall ramekin laying tortillas, shredded chicken, beans, corn, and an array of cheeses with *salsa roja* and a drizzle of truffle oil. The $20 lunch is a fantastic value.

Cull & Pistol

Seafood ✗

75 Ninth Ave. (bet. 15th & 16th Sts.)

Subway: 14 St - 8 Av	Lunch daily
Phone: 646-568-1223	Dinner Mon – Sat
Web: www.cullandpistol.com	
Prices: $$$	

Chelsea Market's Lobster Place has expanded, adding a full-fledged seafood haven replete with reclaimed wood tables, brushed steel chairs, and a zinc-topped raw bar. If that isn't enough, they also boast craft beer and a clever name (a *cull* is a lobster missing one claw, a *pistol* is missing two) to go with a meal that is sure to sate any seafood lover.

Comforting New England classics like chowders and lobster rolls are on offer, but don't pass up the spectacular clams and oysters—a briny, heavenly selection collected from up and down the Eastern seaboard. Other excellent items include *fideos negros* tossed in dark squid ink, braised *seppia*, and garlic aïoli; or copious amounts of clams with caramelized shallots and tasso ham over grilled ciabatta bread.

da Umberto

Italian ✗✗

107 W. 17th St. (bet. Sixth & Seventh Aves.)

Subway: 18 St	Lunch Mon – Fri
Phone: 212-989-0303	Dinner Mon – Sat
Web: www.daumbertonyc.com	
Prices: $$$	

There is a finely tuned harmony to dining at such classic New York restaurants as da Umberto. The Italian menu seems familiar and unpretentious, the kitchen makes no mistakes, and the ingredients are superb; but what actually sets it apart is an ability to serve exactly what you crave without seeming trite or predictable. Even the look is a perfectly conjured mix of dark woods, creaky floors, a lavish antipasto bar, and impeccably timed servers.

The daily risotto special may be glistening with a rich duck ragù beneath a slowly melting slice of Parmesan. When the dessert cart rolls its way to the table, expect a surprising array of excellent house-made sweets, like Italian cheesecake or their legendary tiramisu dusted with cinnamon and fresh berries.

Manhattan ▶ Chelsea

Del Posto ✿

Italian 🍴🍴🍴🍴

85 Tenth Ave. (at 16th St.)

Subway: 14 St - 8 Av
Phone: 212-497-8090
Web: www.delposto.com
Prices: $$$$

Lunch Mon – Fri
Dinner nightly

Joe Vaughn

Classic, dark, and *molto* soigné, Del Posto is New York's fancy Italian favorite for corporate dining. The plentiful service staff dons old-fashioned uniforms and thick Italian accents. The ambience may seem masculine and opulent with stone floors, towering ceilings, and dark wood credenzas, yet it somehow remains youthful and attractive rather than stodgy. But it is always expensive—very expensive.

Chef Mark Ladner demonstrates his wide repertoire and deep understanding of true Italian cooking throughout this menu. Wonderfully fresh pastas may feature springy orecchiette with succulent lamb neck ragù mixed with bright orange carrot cubes and their purée. Most dishes are deliciously straightforward, hearty, and sophisticated without fussy embellishments. Intensely moist pork loin is grilled and then cut from the bone moments before arriving at your table, topped with crisp pancetta-wrapped sage sausage and a spoonful of *ribollita*. Meals culminate in desserts that fascinate and mesmerize. Layered with clear, distinct, concentrated flavors, the caramelized eggplant kissed with bits of mascarpone cheese and coated in chocolate is beguiling.

The wine list and service soar to excellence.

El Quinto Pino

 Spanish

 B2

401 W. 24th St. (bet. Ninth & Tenth Aves.)

Subway: 23 St (Eighth Ave.)
Phone: 212-206-6900
Web: www.elquintopinonyc.com
Prices:

Dinner nightly

Chelsea has enough tapas joints to give the Barcelona metropolis a run for its money, but El Quinto Pino is a worthy member of this crowded landscape. This Lilliputian spot aims to return tapas to its original concept—these are quick snacks rather than sit-down meals. This is an ideal stop for a distinctively authentic *ración* or two and *una copa* or three.

Despite its lack of traditional table seating, this warm and narrow Spanish-tiled bar has been mobbed since its inception thanks to a kitchen of notable repute. But the real credit goes to the small, creative blackboard menu listing tapas like uni panini, squeezed onto bread slathered with Korean mustard oil; or the Menú Turistico, featuring a revolving set of regional Spanish dishes.

Foragers City Table

 Contemporary

 B2

300 W. 22nd St. (at Eighth Ave.)

Subway: 23 St (Eighth Ave.)
Phone: 212-243-8888
Web: www.foragerscitygrocer.com
Prices: **$$**

Lunch Sat – Sun
Dinner Tue – Sat

Chef Nickolas Martinez shows off his impressive pedigree at this Chelsea charmer, where the staff is dutiful and the foodies are leaning iPhones over the counter to get shots of The Action. The style is minimalist and industrial with hardwood tables and unencumbered windows. Foragers City Table may as well be located in California's wine country. Thankfully it's here, and it's delicious.

Start with snacks, like panko-friend spring onions served with tangy and peppery Meyer lemon crème-fraîche. Then, move on to *orechiette* bathed with rabbit Bolognese, fresh fava beans, brown beech mushrooms, and *Parmigiano Reggiano*. Pickled daikon with crushed peanuts and lemongrass aïoli pair beautifully with soft-shell crab. Finish with a minty berry-yogurt parfait.

La Nacional

Spanish

B3

239 W. 14th St. (bet Seventh & Eighth Aves.)

Subway: 14 St (Seventh Ave.)
Phone: 212-243-9308
Web: N/A
Prices: $$

Lunch Mon – Fri
Dinner nightly

Housed on the ground floor of the Spanish Benevolent Society founded in 1868, La Nacional is not merely a cantina for homesick Spaniards, but city dwellers from all walks of life hooked on Iberian classics.

The bar is a fine spot for sangria-sipping while catching up on the latest fútbol match, but the front dining room brings a more subdued experience.

The tapas are tasty, but La Nacional shines in its paella preparations—*paella de la casa* studded with seafood, strips of piquillo peppers, and sweet green peas; *arroz negro* enriched with squid ink and seasoned with *sofrito*; or *fideua* composed of broken thin noodles. Each features excellent ingredients and impressive cooking that produces mouthwatering *socarrat* (golden-crusted rice at the bottom).

Legend Bar & Restaurant

Chinese

B3

88 Seventh Ave. (bet. 15th & 16th Sts.)

Subway: 14 St
Phone: 212-929-1778
Web: www.legendrestaurant88.com
Prices:

Lunch Mon – Fri
Dinner nightly

The chefs manning these stoves are phenomenally well-versed in Sichuan food (one might suspect their skill inspired the name). Legend's superlative Sichuan menu may be laden with missable Vietnamese dishes, but that hasn't kept the masses away from this crowded Chelsea haunt. Happy hour is magnificent here, while the rest of the Asian-accented space caters to the Sichuan-seeking diners.

Vivid colors and a clean décor welcome you inside, while the lower level displays round tables outfitted with lazy Susans; and the orange upholstery pairs perfectly with such zesty offerings as spicy conch topped with slivered scallions; braised, diced rabbit with pickled peppers swimming in a red chili oil; and and rice balls of sesame paste floating in sweet milk.

Le Zie 2000

Italian ✗✗

B3

172 Seventh Ave. (bet. 20th & 21st Sts.)

Subway: 23 St (Seventh Ave.)
Phone: 212-206-8686
Web: www.lezie.com
Prices: $$

Lunch & dinner daily

That austere profile of an elderly woman gracing the awning and menu has no bearing on the atmosphere of this this tiny, warm, and welcoming Italian dining room—perhaps thanks to the provocatively stenciled nudes they juxtapose in the snug front room? Beyond this, an undulating ceiling and carnival-like canopy set a very pleasant mood.

The menu is simple and pleasing, though it does break from tradition: *cicchetti* from the wonderfully ambient wine bar are Venetian in name only. A generous antipasto might include plump, baked sardines stuffed with raisins, onion, pine nuts, and potatoes. Cannelloni filled with white veal ragù showcase an exceptional béchamel. Peruse the ever-changing daily specials for equally satisfying and more progressive options.

Morimoto

Fusion ✗✗✗

A2

88 Tenth Ave. (at 16th St.)

Subway: 14 St - 8 Av
Phone: 212-989-8883
Web: www.morimotonyc.com
Prices: $$$

Lunch Mon – Fri
Dinner nightly

Arriving at Morimoto is a singular experience. The music, the beautiful patrons, and inviting platters—it's all very chic indeed. Know that this culinary citadel will unearth its veritable feast for the senses as you glide through its cascading curtains and into the dusky, Japanese-rooted restaurant.

The adjoining dining levels are a telling commentary on minimalism—from a square, white room and backlit wall, to glass installations, and clear, acrylic chopsticks. Halogen spotlights lend warmth and delicacy to an ambitious lineup of toro tartare capped with caviar; wafer-thin tuna pizza flecked with olives; pork and garlic chive *gyoza* gussied up with crème fraîche; and happily unctuous ravioli stuffed with smoked salmon and trickled with yuzu gelée.

Naka Naka

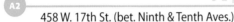

A2

458 W. 17th St. (bet. Ninth & Tenth Aves.)

Subway: 14 St - 8 Av   Dinner Tue – Sat
Phone: 212-929-8544
Web: www.nakanakany.com
Prices: **$$$**

Naka Naka is a quaint, hidden Japanese gem that delivers Tokyo to Chelsea, albeit for a few hours. This infallible cocoon may see a less-than-largely native clientele, yet servers dressed in classic kimonos and faithful accents like Japanese lanterns, chopstick holders, origami "peace" cranes, and paper art deliver a faithful experience.

Dominated by an elevated platform adorned with brocade pillows, find seats at the bar or low-slung tables; jazz standards reveal the American infusion. Extricating this treasure from the rabble are such inventive dishes as *oshinko* tossing cool daikon, cucumbers, and pickled vegetables; a Naka Naka roll crested with crunchy crimson tobiko; and *ika uni ae*, cold, crunchy squid licked with sea urchin sauce and shaved *ohba*.

Ovest Pizzoteca

B1

513 W. 27th St. (bet. 10th & 11th Aves.)

Subway: 23 St (Eighth Ave.)   Lunch & dinner daily
Phone: 212-967-4392
Web: www.ovestnyc.com
Prices: **$$**

Fine fare is rare in these parts, so Ovest Pizzoteca's (of the lauded Luzzo's) is now firmly ensconced into Chelsea's Club Row. Open garage doors cede a glimpse of this chic, modern warehouse with a cement bar, industrial lighting, and a wooden ceiling. From the back of the large, spare dining room, a wood- and gas-burning oven crackles until first light. Ravenous revelers and diners of all stripes follow the alluring aromas of pies and panini, like the Peppino with *prosciutto cotto*, artichokes, and goat cheese. Expect tasty treats like *polpettine*—four plump, juicy meatballs bathed in an excellent, fresh-tasting tomato sauce with a sprinkling of parsley. The well-rounded menu goes on to offer *sfizzi*, antipasti, bruschette, salads, and pasta.

Pastai

 B2

Italian

186 Ninth Ave. (bet. 21st & 22nd Sts.)

Subway: 23 St (Eighth Ave.)
Phone: 646-688-3463
Web: www.pastainyc.com
Prices: **$$**

Lunch & dinner daily

Here at Pastai, Chef Melissa Muller-Daka hits her stride with this second enterprise (after Bar Eolo). This Ninth Ave darling evokes a rustic and airy feel, styled with whitewashed brick, slate walls, and wooden communal tables. Milk bottles serving as water pitchers and bright flower arrangements complete the look.

Freshly made pastas are the main draw, with about ten different varieties made from locally sourced whole grains. Start with a dive into decadent *arancini siciliani*, pork and fontina cheese-stuffed rice balls fried until crisp and set in a pool of tomato sauce. Then, try *piattini di pasta*, such as *bucatini* tossed in saffron and cauliflower ragù, studded with golden raisins and pine nuts, and sprinkled with toasted Parmesan breadcrumbs.

The Red Cat

 B2

American

227 Tenth Ave. (bet. 23rd & 24th Sts.)

Subway: 23 St (Eighth Ave.)
Phone: 212-242-1122
Web: www.redcatrestaurants.com
Prices: **$$**

Lunch Tue – Sat
Dinner nightly

This clever, cozy, and perpetually humming Jimmy Bradley joint is packed wall-to-wall seven nights a week. And no wonder: with its warm, sultry décor, a downright sexy cocktail list, and scrumptious, always inventive American fare, The Red Cat might be called a restaurant triple threat. A jovial red banquette extends along one wall, opposite a bar that dominates the room, lavishly outfitted with flower arrangements and Moorish light fixtures. Take a moment to study the artwork adorning walls and sculpture above the kitchen entrance.

Just remember to book ahead—highly publicized specialties like their deep-fried bacon tempura have only added to the wait. And save room for dessert; chocolate mousse with blackberry-lager sauce is yet another work of art.

Rocking Horse Cafe

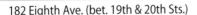

Manhattan ▶ Chelsea

Mexican ✗

B2

182 Eighth Ave. (bet. 19th & 20th Sts.)

Lunch & dinner daily

Subway:	14 St - 8 Av
Phone:	212-463-9511
Web:	www.rockinghorsecafe.com
Prices:	$$

Rainbow flags draped over the awning, the silhouette of a horse's head, and a red garage door that opens to Eighth Avenue are among the first signs you've arrived at the Rocking Horse Cafe. Inside, a shimmering blue mosaic wall and linen-covered tables lend sophistication. Lunchtime is calm when compared to the dinner hours, when music blares and service rushes to keep up with a room that is suddenly cramped with wall-to-wall people. Still, the bar is a fun stop for serious margaritas.

Whether modern or traditional, this Mexican fare satisfies the soul. Expect a succulent, bone-in lamb shank, braised with chipotle and rich with myriad flavors; or fluffy-crisp yucca cake. The freshly grated coconut flan is a perfect rendering of the classic.

Salinas

Spanish ✗✗

B2

136 Ninth Ave. (bet. 18th & 19th Sts.)

Lunch Sun
Dinner nightly

Subway:	18 St
Phone:	212-776-1990
Web:	www.salinasnyc.com
Prices:	$$$

Set on a bustling stretch of Ninth Avenue, 90-seat Salinas is not only a restaurant that delivers more inventive, high-end Spanish cuisine, but also has its own sophisticated and romantic soul. From the front bar to the fireplace in the rear dining room, each space is rustic yet stylish with antique mirrors, crushed blue velvet upholstery, and Moorish glass globes.

The menu may begin with tapas, like thickly sliced bread topped with garlic, tomatoes, excellent olive oil, and marinated anchovies; or Colorado lamb meatballs seasoned with cumin and served with pickled cucumbers. Specials feature the likes of grilled free-range quail with smoky sausage, silky beans, and a sweet muscatel reduction.

In fair weather, the roof retracts for alfresco dining.

Socarrat

B2 Spanish

259 W. 19th St. (bet. Seventh & Eighth Aves.)

Subway: 18 St
Phone: 212-462-1000
Web: www.socarratpaellabar.com
Prices: $$$

Lunch & dinner daily

Tapas bars have been taking over the city, yet Socarrat—named for the delicious crust of rice that forms at the bottom of a pan—is a worthy addition by virtue of its irresistible paella. Like its siblings, this is a friendly and familiar spot, where long communal tables are packed with your newest old friends and tapas-loving locals. Glossy walls reflect the room's gentle light, while mirrors and portraits lend depth and color.

Octopus rounds crowned with spices is a perfect opener for paella Socarrat, a crisp layer of caramelized rice mingled in a fragrant stock with spicy chorizo and briny clams. Happy Hour Mondays keeps everyone beaming by pairing the likes of *croquetas de setas* (mushrooms) or crispy pork belly with sangria, either red or white.

Tia Pol

A2 Spanish

205 Tenth Ave. (bet. 22nd & 23rd Sts.)

Subway: 23 St (Eighth Ave.)
Phone: 212-675-8805
Web: www.tiapol.com
Prices:

Lunch Tue – Sun
Dinner nightly

You can't shake a stick in Chelsea without hitting a tapas joint these days, but Tia Pol sets the standard. Although the bare bones space, a narrow dining room tucked behind a steel-patch door on Tenth Avenue, isn't much to marvel at—one whirl with Tia Pol's affordable Spanish wine list and delicious Basque small plates and you'll be rubbing elbows at the perpetually packed bar in no time.

Kick the night off with a cheese and charcuterie platter loaded with silky hams and garlicky chorizo; then dig into dishes like a chewy, toasted baguette laced with pickled onions and tender veal tongue, cooked *a la plancha*; smoky, paprika-dusted slices of chorizo finished in a sherry reduction; and tender lamb skewers rubbed with fragrant Moorish spices.

Tipsy Parson

✗✗

B2

156 Ninth Ave. (bet. 19th & 20th Sts.)

Lunch & dinner daily

Subway: 18 St
Phone: 212-620-4545
Web: www.tipsyparson.com
Prices: $$

With its masculine bar shelved with books and premium spirits, dining room decorated with bric-a-brac, and French doors looking out on to a garden, Tipsy Parson conjures homey and familiar comfort. Imagine dining at an old friend's house, starting with drinks in the living room and ending on the back porch.

The distinct Southern bent is clear from such beginnings as a trio of spreads including pimento cheese, deviled tasso ham, and black-eyed pea salad with house-made crackers; or devilled eggs judiciously loaded with tarragon. Oysters are marvelously crisp and served with Old Bay mayo flecked with cornichons. For dessert, the Tipsy Parson is a trifle-like and boozy wonder of brandy-soaked almond cake, vanilla custard, and brandied berries.

Trestle on Tenth

✗✗

B2

242 Tenth Ave. (at 24th St.)

Lunch & dinner daily

Subway: 23 St (Eighth Ave.)
Phone: 212-645-5659
Web: www.trestleontenth.com
Prices: $$

Everything is low-key and *très* chic at this Swiss-inflected favorite on a prime corner of western Chelsea. While the exterior looks like some tavern of yesteryear, the inside has a rustic-urban, NY-via-Scandanavia feel, minimally dressed with contemporary art along rough brick walls, blond woods, and clean lines.

Seeking out the *metzgete* ("butcher's affair") in January is a must. Other dishes might include thick, juicy slices of smoked and roasted pork loin atop potato galette and pork jus with a haunting whiff of mustard. The *nusstorte* is a Swiss-style caramel-walnut tart that is an ideal close to any rich, meat-focused meal here.

Through the secret garden in back, discover the Rocket Pig for a carefully packed "pignic" (pork sandwich) to-go.

Txikito

Spanish ✗

B2

240 Ninth Ave. (bet. 24th & 25th Sts.)

Subway: 23 St (Eighth Ave.)
Phone: 212-242-4730
Web: www.txikitonyc.com
Prices: $$

Lunch Tue – Sun
Dinner nightly

First thing's first: they aren't tapas, they're *pinxtos*, and they're outstanding. Give thanks to the gifted Basque chef/owners, Alexandra Raij and Eder Montero, for their superb creations, which represent the duo's deep connection to the region.

Hunker down in the cool, wood-paneled space and order up a frenzy of these tummy-satisfying delights, many of which are made with locally sourced ingredients. The anchovies in any incarnation are a must, but also try the *txipiron encebollado*—long, tender ribbons of squid with sweet onion and pine nuts; *lomo adobado,* house-cured pork loin grilled with sweet-smoky piquillo peppers; or the *pil pil,* fish cheeks finished with a tart-sweet sauce. Drop in for *hamaiketako*–Basque brunch–for poached eggs with chorizo.

Look for our symbol 🍇,
spotlighting restaurants
with a notable wine list.

Chinatown & Little Italy

As different as *chow mein* and chicken cacciatore, these two districts are nonetheless neighbors, though in recent years, their borders have become blurred with Chinatown voraciously gulping up most of Little Italy.

It is documented that New York cradles the maximum number of Chinese immigrants in the country and specifically, Queens, followed by Manhattan, holds one of the largest Chinese communities outside Asia. Immigrants from Hong Kong and mainland China populate Manhattan's Chinatown, each bringing their own distinct regional cuisines.

Chinatown Chow

Chowing in Chinatown can be both delectable and delightfully affordable. Elbow your way through the crowded streets and find a flurry of food markets, bubble tea cafés, bakeries, and eateries both large and small. Feast on freshly pulled noodles; duck into an ice cream parlor for a scoop of avocado or black sesame; or breeze past a market window and gander the crocodile meat and frogs on display (with claws!). **New Kam Man** is one such bustling market that offers everything under the sun from woks and china, to wontons, oyster sauce, and tea. At other storefronts, haggle over the freshest fish and produce before sneaking under the Manhattan Bridge

for a *banh mi*. From Thai chilies to curry pastes, **Bangkok Center Grocery** cradles every ingredient necessary for a Thai-themed dinner at home, along with expat publications and a friendly owner.

Klezmer meets Cantonese at the Egg Rolls and Egg Creams Festival, an annual summer street celebration honoring the neighboring Chinese and Jewish communities of Chinatown and the Lower East Side. Partygoers pack the streets for Chinese New Year with dragons dancing down the avenues accompanied by costumed revelers and firecrackers.

LITTLE ITALY

The Little Italy of Scorsese's gritty, authentic *Mean Streets* is slowly vanishing into what may now be more aptly called Micro Italy. The onetime stronghold of a large Italian-American population (once spanning from Canal Street north to Houston, and from Lafayette to the Bowery) has dwindled to a mere corridor—Mulberry Street between Canal and Broome streets. But the spirit of the origins still pulses in century-old family-run markets, delis, gelato shops, and mom-and-pop trattorias. Speaking of which, **Piemonte Ravioli** has incredible homemade sauces along with dried and fresh pastas, available in all shapes, sizes, and with a variety of fillings. **Alleva Dairy** (known

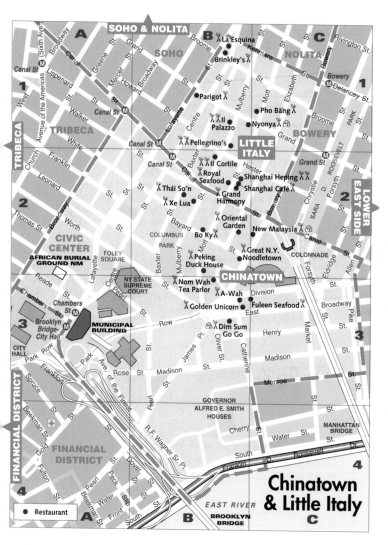

Chinatown & Little Italy

SOHO & NOLITA

SOHO

NOLITA

X La Esquina

Brinkley's X

• Parigot X

TRIBECA

• Pho Bāng X

X X Il Palazzo

Nyonya •

BOWERY

X X Pellegrino's

LITTLE ITALY

X X Il Cortile

X Royal Seafood

Shanghai Heping X X

X Thái So'n

Shanghai Café X

X Xe Lua

X Grand Harmony

LOWER EAST SIDE

X Oriental Garden

New Malaysia X

CIVIC CENTER

COLUMBUS PARK

Bo Ky X

AFRICAN BURIAL GROUND NM

X Great N.Y. • Noodletown

COLONNADE

X Peking Duck House

CHINATOWN

NY STATE SUPREME COURT

X Nom Wah Tea Parlor

X A-Wah

Fuleen Seafood X

MUNICIPAL BUILDING

X Golden Unicorn

Brooklyn Bridge-City Hall

CITY HALL

X Dim Sum Go Go

FINANCIAL DISTRICT

GOVERNOR ALFRED E. SMITH HOUSES

MANHATTAN BRIDGE

FINANCIAL DISTRICT

EAST RIVER

BROOKLYN BRIDGE

• Restaurant

for their homemade ricotta) is the oldest Italian cheese store in the U.S. Nearby at **Di Palo's Fine Foods** find imported *sopressata*, *salumi*, and cheese selections. Loved for its Italian pastries and strong espresso, fans frequent the beloved **Ferrara's Bakery and Café** on Grand Street. During warmer weekends, Mulberry Street is a pedestrian zone, creating one big alfresco party—the Feast of San Gennaro in September is particularly raucous. While these days you can get better Italian food elsewhere in the city, tourists still gather to treasure and bathe in the nostalgia of Mulberry Street.

A-Wah

Chinese ✗

B3

5 Catherine St. (bet. Division St. & East Broadway)

Subway: Canal St (Lafayette St.)   Lunch & dinner daily
Phone: 212-925-8308
Web: www.awahrestaurant.com
Prices: 🍜

A relative newcomer to NYC's diverse Chinatown scene, simple, tiny, and singularly focused A-Wah fires up a vast array of Hong Kong-style comfort foods from ginger chicken feet to sautéed pea leaves. The region's tasty take on *lo mein* is a total departure from the familiar version. Here, find a platter of thin noodles topped with pork or duck, served with a side of delicate, comsommé-like broth for dipping.

However, the biggest treat is the fantastic *bo zai fan*: rice cooked to crunchy perfection in a clay pot, crowned with ginger, scallions, and a mind-boggling choice of seventeen toppings like frog, pork, and preserved vegetables. These dishes and their tasty burnt-rice sides are made even better with a thick and sweet house-made soy sauce.

Bo Ky

Chinese ✗

B2

80 Bayard St. (bet. Mott and Mulberry Sts.)

Subway: Canal St (Lafayette St.)   Lunch and dinner daily
Phone: 212-406-2292
Web: N/A
Prices: 🍜

S

Bo Ky is a total dive... but in a good way. It's the kind of place that everyone wants to know about, where Chinese-born families and savvy locals go for great, cheap food.

The service can seem gruff and the space itself may appear dingy, but no one seems to mind as they gather around large communal tables (set with plastic and disposable dishes), leaning over massive soup bowls brimming with meat, vegetables, and noodles. The menu includes fish ball soup infused with sesame oil, ginger, and scallions, bobbing with flat noodles. Fatty and silky-tender hunks of country-style duck, braised in a briny liquid stocked with star anise, clove, and peppercorns, are so enjoyably tender that they have truly earned their own window display.

Brinkley's

B1

Gastropub

406 Broome St. (bet. Centre & Lafayette Sts.)

Subway: Spring St
Phone: 212-680-5600
Web: www.brinkleysnyc.com
Prices: $$

Lunch & dinner daily

Brinkley's seems to be the provincial "pub" for everyone from students and hipsters to executives looking for a thirst quencher and bite after work. This easy and informal spot wears a boho-chic look with metallic stools lining a zinc-topped bar, a black-and-white checked floor, and burgundy leather booths. The team fits the casual, neighborhood feel of its vibrant yet rather noisy surroundings.

Find such straightforward delights as a pounded chicken and romaine salad with cilantro-yogurt dressing. Then, move on to a deliciously crusty lobster club sandwich filled with bacon and avocado, served with sweet potato fries. A taste of their moist bread pudding crowned with whipped cream will ensure some very simple, homespun bliss.

Dim Sum Go Go

B3

Chinese

5 East Broadway (at Chatham Sq.)

Subway: Canal St (Lafayette St.)
Phone: 212-732-0797
Web: N/A
Prices: $$

Lunch & dinner daily

Winning dim sum and crazy good Cantonese are the stars at this coveted gem, where great quality plus prices equal a thriving formula. This bi-level space is dressed up with contemporary touches like metal chairs, bright white walls, and comfy tables. Additionally, speedy service forgoes the traditional cart in favor of an order sheet, which can be supplemented by anything off the menu.

Treat yourself to delectable dim sum day or night—their vast variety may induce torturous fits of indecision. Still, hunker down for those steaming parcels of pea shoots, shrimp-and-chive, or decadent, fatty duck; followed by excellent pan-fried pork and vegetable dumplings. Other riches include garlic-sautéed baby bok choy, or the famously juicy barbecue pork buns.

Fuleen Seafood

C3

11 Division St. (bet. Catherine & Market Sts.)

Subway: Canal St (Lafayette St.)   Lunch & dinner daily
Phone: 212-941-6888
Web: N/A
Prices: 😊😊

From their variety of hard- and soft-shell crab dishes to the ever-popular snails in black bean sauce or geoduck clams "two different ways," this Cantonese kitchen does impressive things with gourmet ingredients. The large round tables of this Chinatown mainstay are filled with gregarious groups from the local, discerning Chinese community—a testament to its success. Yet all are welcome here, as the polite staff graciously guides you through the menu, making helpful recommendations.

Garlicky, green vegetables are an essential accompaniment to meals here, perhaps complementing a whole fish, presented tableside before being expertly steamed and dressed with ginger and scallions. Landlubbers will unearth plenty of options on the sizeable menu.

Golden Unicorn

B3

18 East Broadway (at Catherine St.)

Subway: Canal St (Lafayette St.)   Lunch & dinner daily
Phone: 212-941-0911
Web: www.goldenunicornrestaurant.com
Prices: $$

This age-old dim sum parlor, spread over many floors in an office building, is one of the few Cantonese spots that actually has the space and volume to necessitate its parade of steaming carts brimming with treats. While Golden Unicorn's system is very efficient and part of the spectacle, arrive early to nab a seat by the kitchen for better variety and hotter items. A helpful brigade of suited men and women roam the space to offer the likes of exquisitely soft roast pork buns, or congee with preserved egg and shredded pork. Buzzing with locals and visitors, it is also a favorite among families who appreciate the kid-friendly scene as much as the delectable, steamed pea shoot and shrimp dumplings, pork *siu mai*, and rice rolls stuffed with shrimp.

Grand Harmony

Chinese

B2

98 Mott St. (bet. Canal & Hester Sts.)

Subway: Canal St (Lafayette St.)
Phone: 212-226-6603
Web: N/A
Prices: ⊜⊗

Lunch & dinner daily

With every seat filled before noon and dim sum carts roaming the sea of famished diners, Grand Harmony's expansive columned hall echoes the commotion of Chinatown. Naturally, they must be doing something right, so snag a seat upon arrival and flag those nimble women as they direct their carts through the labyrinth of tables.

Resting upon these coveted carts is a plethora of solid dim sum. Friendly servers parade the likes of beautifully crisp bean curd skin stuffed with vegetables, shrimp, and pork; congee studded with bits of dried fish and scallions; and juicy shrimp and chive dumplings all at an unbelievably good price. Leave room for what lies on the dessert cart, like fried sweet sesame balls or creamy coconut jelly to finish this feast.

Great N.Y. Noodletown

Chinese

B2

28 Bowery (at Bayard St.)

Subway: Canal St (Lafayette St.)
Phone: 212-349-0923
Web: N/A
Prices: ⊜⊗

Lunch & dinner daily

You don't come for the ambience. With its closely jammed seats, roast ducks hanging in the window, and menus tucked under glass-topped tables, Great N.Y. Noodletown is down-market Chinatown at its drabbest. What you come for is the food—which, served daily from 9:00 A.M.-4.00 A.M—is not only delicious but remarkably cheap. Who could argue with a big bowl of perfectly roasted duck and tender noodles in steaming broth for $4?

Best bets include any of the roasted meats served over fluffy rice; and, of course, duck, in all its crispy, fatty succulence. Don't miss the specials written on the table tents, where you'll find irresistible house delights like salt-baked soft shell crabs (a must-have when in season) and Chinese flowering chive stir-fries.

Il Cortile

Italian XX

125 Mulberry St. (bet. Canal & Hester Sts.)

Subway: Canal St (Lafayette St.)　　　　　　　　　Lunch & dinner daily
Phone: 212-226-6060
Web: www.ilcortile.com
Prices: $$

Beyond this quaint and charming façade lies one of Little Italy's famed mainstays, ever-popular with dreamy eyed dates seeking the stuff of Billy Joel lyrics. The expansive space does indeed suggest a nostalgic romance, with its series of Mediterranean-themed rooms, though the most celebrated is the pleasant garden atrium (*il cortile* is Italian for courtyard), with a glass-paneled ceiling and abundant greenery.

A skilled line of chefs present a wide array of familiar starters and entrées, from eggplant *rollatini* to chicken Francese; as well as a range of pastas, such as *spaghettini puttanesca* or *risotto con funghi*. More than 30 years of sharing family recipes and bringing men to one bent knee continues to earn Il Cortile a longtime following.

Il Palazzo

Italian XX

151 Mulberry St. (bet. Grand & Hester Sts.)

Subway: Canal St (Lafayette St.)　　　　　　　　　Lunch & dinner daily
Phone: 212-343-7000
Web: N/A
Prices: $$

This "palace" on Little Italy's celebrated Mulberry Street rises to every expectation of a good, traditional Italian-American meal. A tuxedo-clad host ushers guests into a long room with stucco walls and linen-draped tables. Beyond, the sunken dining room recalls a winter garden of lush greenery and natural light. Sidewalk seating is beloved among tourists watching tourists.

Old-world dishes reign here, beginning with a basket of focaccia and bowl of *stracciatella alla Romana*. The classics continue with the likes of *vitello alla pizzaiola* (veal scallopini sautéed with tomato, onions, mushrooms, roasted peppers, and fresh basil); or *gamberoni alla scampi* (jumbo shrimp sautéed in a garlic-white wine sauce). Lunchtime frittata specials offer good value.

Manhattan ▶ Chinatown & Little Italy

La Esquina

B1   Mexican

106 Kenmare St. (bet. Cleveland Pl. & Lafayette St.)

Subway: Spring St (Lafayette St.)
Phone: 646-613-7100
Web: www.esquinanyc.com
Prices: $$

Lunch & dinner daily

When La Esquina opened it was a breath of bright air, offering enjoyably fresh cuisine that stood tall among the paltry selection of Manhattan Mexican. Thankfully, the city's south-of-the-border dining scene has evolved since then. However, La Esquina remains a worthy option. More playground than restaurant, the multi-faceted setting takes up an iconic downtown corner and draws a hip crowd to the grab and go taqueria, 30-seat café, and lively subterranean dining room and bar amplified by a nightly DJ soundtrack.

The spirit here is not just alive but kicking with classic renditions of tortilla soup; *mole negro enchiladas* filled with excellently seasoned chicken; as well the likes of *carne asada* starring black Angus sirloin with *mojo de ajo*.

New Malaysia

C2   Malaysian

46-48 Bowery (bet. Bayard & Canal Sts.)

Subway: Canal St (Lafayette St.)
Phone: 212-964-0284
Web: N/A
Prices:

Lunch & dinner daily

Mad for Malaysian? Head to this lively dive, sequestered in a Chinatown arcade. Proffering some of the best Malaysian treats in town, including all the classics, New Malaysia sees a deluge of regulars who pour in for a massive offering of exceptional dishes. Round tables cram a room furnished with little more than a service counter. Still, the aromas wafting from flaky *roti canai* and Melaka crispy coconut shrimp keep you focused on the food.

Capturing the essence of Chinatown are fast (brusque?) servers who deliver abundant yet authentic bowls of spicy-sour *asam laksa* fragrant with lemongrass; *kang-kung belacan*, greens infused with dried shrimp and chili; and *nasi lemak*, the national treasure starring coconut rice, chicken curry, and dried anchovies.

Nom Wah Tea Parlor

Chinese

B3

13 Doyers St. (bet. Bowery & Pell St.)

Subway: Canal St (Lafayette St.) Lunch & dinner daily
Phone: 212-962-6047
Web: www.nomwah.com
Prices:

Possibly the most senior dim sum den along the still, back streets of Chinatown, Nom Wah Tea Parlor endured a face-lift when old man Wally handed over charge to young Wilson Tang. Resembling an old diner-meets-coffee shop, the room features a counter, parade of pleather booths, and tables topped with red-and-white vinyl that spikes a nostalgic sense.

"The original egg roll" is a massive hit (literally) and includes delicious tofu skin wrapped around crunchy vegetables, doused in a tempura batter, and fried to crisp perfection. Cheery servers deliver other dim sum like a rice roll in fried dough splashed with sweet soy; or fried eggplant stuffed with shrimp paste. While the house special pan-fried dumplings are salty, they are some of *the* best in town.

Nyonya

Malaysian

B1

199 Grand St. (bet. Mott & Mulberry Sts.)

Subway: Canal St (Lafayette St.) Lunch & dinner daily
Phone: 212-334-3669
Web: www.ilovenyonya.com
Prices: $$

Nyonya prides itself with a comfortable setting of brick walls and wood tables, but everyone's really here for the food, which is always on the money. The adept staff is eager to steer you through their varied menu—they might even direct you away from such daring (read: delicious) dishes as *asam laksa*, an exceptionally spiced and intensely sour broth floating lemongrass, ground fish, and thick, round noodles. Asians and other hungry locals pack this haunt for seemingly simple yet divine items like *achat* (pickled vegetables tossed with turmeric and peanuts); *mee siam* (noodles stir-fried with tofu, eggs, and shrimp in a fiery chili sauce); or pungent beef *rendang*. Crispy prawns garnished with curry-infused toasted coconut are nothing short of wow.

Oriental Garden

B2 Chinese ✗

14 Elizabeth St. (bet. Bayard & Canal Sts.)

Subway: Canal St (Lafayette St.)   Lunch & dinner daily
Phone: 212-619-0085
Web: www.orientalgardenny.com
Prices: $$

A single room makes up this garden of Chinese delights. Robed in warm shades of beige and red, and packed with tables that expand just as readily as your waistline, Oriental Garden is a precious jewel much sought-after both for daytime dim sum and top-quality Cantonese.

Jammed by noon, dim sum is ordered from carts or the printed menu. The carts carry crowd-pleasers but tune them out and opt for steamy chive dumplings, crisp-baked roast pork triangles, and juicy roast duck. After the dumplings digest, Cantonese takes over. The fish tanks lining the entryway are a good indication of where to start. First-rate preparations of these global swimmers include the seasonal Australian crystal crabs, oysters with ginger and scallions, or lobster "country style."

Parigot

B1 French ✗

155 Grand St. (at Lafayette St.)

Subway: Canal St (Lafayette St.)   Lunch & dinner daily
Phone: 212-274-8859
Web: www.parigotnyc.com
Prices: $$

In the neck of Nolita, Parigot is that hugely favored French bistro teeming with traditional fare. Francophiles come here to be comforted by classics such as mussels Parigot; escargot with garlic-parsley butter; Basque omelette; and *coq au vin*. Smaller groups from around the way might share an *assiette de charcuterie* or *assiette de fromages* served with warm slices of toasted bread, all the while picturing themselves cruising along the glorious Seine.

With French music wafting through a wood-furnished dining room whose cheerful walls are hung with photos of quaint cafés, a meal at Parigot feels like a mini escape to the Côte d'Azur, beautifully capped with a traditional and fresh salad Niçoise, a side of fantastic fries, and a glass of crisp rosé.

Peking Duck House

B2

28 Mott St. (bet. Chatham Sq. & Pell St.)

Subway: Canal St (Lafayette St.) Lunch & dinner daily
Phone: 212-227-1810
Web: www.pekingduckhousenyc.com
Prices: $$

Only rookies open the menu at Peter Luger steakhouse—and the same ought to apply to any restaurant named after a menu item. So, while you may stumble onto a few gems like the sautéed string beans with minced pork, the bird is the word at this group-friendly Chinatown joint.

Despite its rather odd name, the Peking Duck House is a touch classier than her Chinatown sisters, with a contemporary polish that won't frighten your Midwestern cousin. Service may slow down at the more elegant midtown location, but both wheel out the golden brown duck with proper flare, and carve it into crisp-skinned mouthwatering slices. Your job is easy: fold into fresh pancakes, sprinkle with scallion, cucumbers, and a dash of hoisin sauce...then devour.

Pellegrino's

B1

138 Mulberry St. (bet. Grand & Hester Sts.)

Subway: Canal St (Lafayette St.) Lunch & dinner daily
Phone: 212-226-3177
Web: N/A
Prices: $$

Pellegrino's offers a well-done meal that puts her gaudier neighbors to shame. Both regulars and tourists frequent this local mainstay, and on a sunny day the quaint sidewalk tables look upon the pulsating heart of Little Italy. Inside, deep red walls dotted with three-dimensional art take you back in time. The staff is courteous and children are welcome; in fact, half portions are offered for smaller appetites.

The food stays true to its Italian-American roots with heaping portions—grilled portobello topped with caramelized fontina and a drizzle of balsamic vinegar; or fettuccine Giovanni in a cream sauce accented by prosciutto and asparagus. The cannoli is a classic finish, even if it is presented with a rote zigzag of custard and strawberry sauce.

Pho Băng

C1

Vietnamese

157 Mott St. (bet. Broome & Grand Sts.)

Subway: Bowery
Phone: 212-966-3797
Web: N/A
Prices: 😊😊

Lunch & dinner daily

Hangover? Craving? In need of a quick, tasty meal? Pho Băng is where it's at for restorative bowls of bubbling *pho*, served up in a flash and on the cheap. Park it in the simple space and start with a plate of delicious fried Vietnamese spring rolls (*cha gio*) served with lettuce and mint leaves for wrapping; or try the tasty rice "crêpe" (*bahn cuon nhan thit cha lua*) stuffed with black mushrooms, pork, sprouts, and ham—a real treat and rare find here in New York, so don't skip it.

Finally, follow the lead of your fellow diners and slurp up one of seventeen varieties of hearty *pho*. Try the *pho tai gau*— fresh eye of round plus brisket and rice noodles in a flavorful beef broth, served with sprouts, basil, and lemon, all for less than eight bucks.

Royal Seafood

B2

Chinese

103 Mott St. (bet. Canal & Hester Sts.)

Subway: Canal St (Lafayette St.)
Phone: 212-219-2338
Web: N/A
Prices: 😊😊

Lunch & dinner daily

Bright, chaotic, and jam-packed with a multi-generational Chinese crowd, this well-priced favorite has dim sum lovers lined up and waiting in droves. Dinnertime brings a quieter vibe, along with an extensive Cantonese menu. The sizable room is decked with round tables draped in pink linens and kitschy Chinese touches. This communal scene has friends and strangers alike dining side by side.

Join the masses and feast on the likes of steamed dumplings, nicely crafted and filled with mushrooms, vegetables, ground pork and peanut, or seafood and greens. The shrimp wrapped in yellow bean curd skin are crisply fried, not at all greasy, and completely delicious. Pan-fried wontons are thin and delicate yet exploding with flavor from garlic and chives.

Shanghai Café

B2

Chinese ✗

100 Mott St. (bet. Canal & Hester Sts.)

Subway: Canal St (Lafayette St.)
Phone: 212-966-3988
Web: N/A
Prices: 🍷🍷

Lunch & dinner daily

$

Clean, simple, and updated, this café is where one should head when in the mood for well-priced, Shanghai-style food. Appreciably more attractive than its neighbors, Shanghai Café prides itself on a pretty interior featuring a few booths and tables armed with bamboo steamers cradling those classic handmade buns—perhaps filled with tender pork, crab, and ginger with a steaming rich and fatty broth.

Groups gather here with an intent to eat and their tables quickly disappear under the avalanche of dishes like sea cucumber drowned in a brown sauce infused with shrimp roe. A savory soup bobbing with bean curd, dried scallops and thick noodles; chewy rice balls in a clear and delicious pork broth; and spicy beef tendons are favorites of those in the know.

Shanghai Heping

B2

Chinese ✗✗

104 Mott St. (bet. Canal and Hester Sts.)

Subway: Canal St (Lafayette St.)
Phone: 212-925-1118
Web: N/A
Prices: $$

Lunch and dinner daily

Head downtown to Chinatown to fully appreciate the swank Shanghai Heping—a stylish and contemporary restaurant decked in lime green accents, faux-granite tabletops, and tiled floors. Friendly staff and a proficient chef ensure tasty renditions of Shanghainese dishes.

Quality ingredients and great skill shine through menu items like chilled and crunchy-salty bamboo shoots braised in a soy-based brown sauce abundant with Chinese spices; and knots of chewy tofu skin stewed with pork belly cubes in a rich, velvety sauce, wonderfully flavored with cloves, star anise, and ginger. Large slices of green opo squash (long gourd) sautéed in garlic sauce are so tender, delicate, and simply tasty that you might just see them atop every table in the house.

Thái Sơn

 Vietnamese

89 Baxter St. (bet. Bayard & Canal Sts.)

Subway: Canal St (Lafayette St.)   Lunch & dinner daily
Phone: 212-732-2822
Web: N/A
Prices:

Thái Sơn is by far the best of the bunch in this Vietnamese quarter of Chinatown. It's neither massive nor fancy, but it's bright, clean, and perpetually in business. One peek at the specials on the walls (maybe golden-fried squid strewn with sea salt) will have you begging for a seat in the crammed room.

Speedy servers scoot between groups of City Hall suits and Asian locals as they order the likes of *cha gio*, pork spring rolls with *nuac cham*; or *goi cuon*, fantastic summer rolls filled with poached shrimp and vermicelli. Naturally, *pho* choices are abundant, but the real star of the show is *pho tai*—where raw beef shavings are cooked to tender perfection when combined with a scalding hot, savory broth replete with herbs, sprouts, and chewy noodles.

Xe Lua

 Vietnamese ✗

86 Mulberry St. (bet. Bayard & Canal Sts.)

Subway: Canal St (Lafayette St.)   Lunch & dinner daily
Phone: 212-577-8887
Web: N/A
Prices:

For fantastic Vietnamese food, make your way into Xe Lua. Their décor features a basic Southeast Asian tropical theme, but chopstick tins, soup spoons, and enticing condiments decorate the table and return all focus to the food—which is always a winner and delivered at wonderful value.

Efficient servers speed around regulars and suits, but keep your eyes fixed on the laminated menu brimming with pictures. Fried spring rolls (*cha gio*) with ground pork served with lettuce, mint, and *nuoc cham*; or *goi du du*, a spicy papaya salad tossing carrots and cashews in a salty dressing exemplify their tasty repute. *Pho tai* elicits gratified sighs, served as a steaming bowl of spiced beef broth bobbing with noodles, thinly sliced beef, and crunchy bean sprouts.

East Village

This storied bohemia is no longer rampant with riots, rockers, and radical zeitgeist, but remains crowned as Manhattan's uncompromising capital of counter-culture. East Villagers may seem tamer now that CBGB is closed, but they are no less creative, casual, and undeniably cool.

The neighborhood's bars and eateries exhibit the same edge, and denizens craving a nightly nosh have plenty to choose from. **Momofuku Milk Bar** turns out a spectrum of delectable baked goods and soft serve ice cream in seasonal flavors like cereal milk and caramel apple until midnight. Sauces like curry-ketchup and smoked-eggplant mayo heighten crispy Belgian fries from **Pomme Frites**. For burgers, **Paul's** may have the best in town. **Crif Dogs**—open until 4:00 A.M. on weekends—deep-fries their dogs for the perfect post pub-crawl snack.

Many eateries, cafés, second-hand shops, and vendors line these blocks with specialties from pork (**Porchetta**) to macaroni & cheese (**S'mac**) in a distinctly East Village way. Speaking of cheese, **The Bourgeois Pig** draws celebrities on the "down-low" with its pots of fondue; equally stellar is **Luke's Lobster**, a seafood shack offering the freshest of product directly from Maine. Perhaps most

spirited, and in keeping with the kitschy downtown feel, is Japantown—a decidedly down-market and groovier "Harajuku" version of its Midtown East sibling. Along St. Marks Place, look for the red paper lanterns of hip yakitori spots like **Taisho**, or smell the takoyaki frying and sizzling okonomiyaki at **Otafuku**; and explore divey izakayas like **Village Yokocho**. Among the area's sultry sake dens, few can rival subterranean **Decibel**—serving an outrageous selection of sake and shochu in its hideaway setting. Devout bargain-hunters will relish **Xi'an Famous Foods**—their menu is made up of regional Chinese cuisine from the Shaanxi province, an area made famous after the discovery of the Terracotta Army.

Flavor Smackdown

While Japantown may tuck its lounges down a nondescript stairway, everything along the "Curry Row" stretch of East Sixth St. smacks of festivities, with spices as bold as the neon lights that dot the awnings. While these inexpensive spots may cater to NYU students, they also offer a great spread of South Asian food.

For a bit of old-world flavor, an afternoon at **Veniero's Pasticceria & Caffé** is in order. Established in 1894, this friendly staple draws

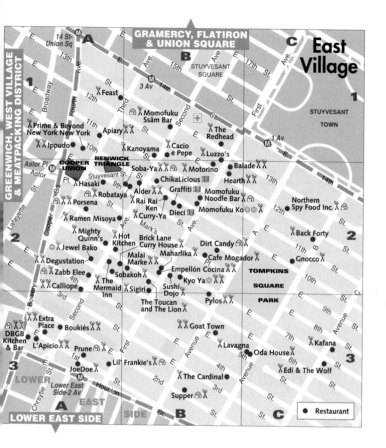

GREENWICH, WEST VILLAGE & MEATPACKING DISTRICT

14 St-Union Sq

13th St.

STUYVESANT SQUARE

STUYVESANT TOWN

12th St.

Feast

3 Av

Momofuku Ssäm Bar

The Redhead

Prime & Beyond New York New York

Apiary

Cacio e Pepe

Luzzo's

Ippudo

Kanoyama

Astor Pl

COOPER UNION

RENWICK TRIANGLE

Soba-Ya

Motorino

Balade

Astor Pl.

Stuyvesant

ChikaLicious

Hearth

Hasaki

Alder

Robataya

Rai Rai Ken

Graffiti

Momofuku Noodle Bar

Porsena

Curry-Ya

Dieci

Momofuku Ko

Northern Spy Food Inc.

Ramen Misoya

Back Forty

Mighty Quinn's

Hot Kitchen

Brick Lane Curry House

Dirt Candy

Jewel Bako

Malai Marke

Maharlika

Cafe Mogador

Gnocco

Degustation

Empellón Cocina

TOMPKINS

Zabb Elee

Sobakoh

Kyo Ya

SQUARE

Calliope

The Mermaid Inn

Sigiri

Sushi Dojo

PARK

The Toucan and The Lion

Pylos

Extra Place

Boukiés

Goat Town

DBGB Kitchen & Bar

L'Apicio

Prune

Lavagna

Kafana

Lil' Frankie's

Oda House

JoeDoe

Edi & The Wolf

The Cardinal

LOWER EAST SIDE

Lower East Side-2 Av

Supper

● Restaurant

long lines (especially around holiday time) for its traditional Italian baked goods. Speaking of baked treats, **Sigmund's** is famed for its handmade pretzels dressed with dips like beet-horseradish mayo. The family-run **Veselka** has been serving Ukrainian treats for over 50 years, representing the area's former Eastern European population. For specialty items, **East Village Cheese** is a premier vendor— find an ample selection here, minus the mark-up of gourmet emporiums.

It goes without saying that liquor flows freely in the East Village. There are many dive bars, but those with an urbane palate will be happy that this area is at the nexus of cutting-edge mixology. Speaking of which, **Angel's Share** (hidden in a Japanese restaurant on Stuyvesant St.); **PDT**, or Please Don't Tell (accessed through Crif Dogs); **Death & Co.** on East Sixth St.; and **Mayahuel** (with its south-of-the-border spin) all offer an epicurean approach to cocktail service garnering them accolades.

Alder

Gastropub

 B2

157 Second Ave. (bet. 9th & 10th Sts.)

Subway: Astor Pl
Phone: 212-539-1900
Web: www.aldernyc.com
Prices: $$

Dinner nightly

Alder is super casual, quite masculine, and very unique. Gathering crowds outside the wood-planked façade are a good sign of the feast that waits inside. The earth-toned space features spindle-back chairs, slat-wood floors, and a hip young staff. A back-lit painted brick wall illuminates the rip-roaring bar.

Food presentations like pigs in a blanket (Chinese sausages wrapped in a thin layer of compressed hot-dog buns and dabbed with biting Japanese mustard) are as precise as they are varied. Your next course might bring a whole head of cauliflower deep-fried until bronze, served in a creamy pool of lemon-almond purée, and crowned with *lardo* and cocoa nib shavings. Try vanilla ice cream drizzled with red pepper oil to fully grasp this complex menu.

Apiary

Mediterranean

A1

60 Third Ave. (bet. 10th & 11th Sts.)

Subway: Astor Pl
Phone: 212-254-0888
Web: www.apiarynyc.com
Prices: $$

Dinner nightly

Bringing a unique elegance and maturity to its East Village locale, Apiary's intimate space is buzz-worthy. Envisioned by Ligne Roset, the sleek and contemporary room features burgundy- and brown-upholstered chairs beneath chandelier-shaped plastic sconces that in turn cast sultry shadows on the walls.

The modern menu follows suit, with the likes of golden brown sweetbreads with deep-crimson romesco sauce—its alluring flavors a wonderful departure from tradition. From the emerald green olive oil and excellent breads to thick-cut, caramelized pork chops with black beans and chunky guacamole, to desserts like a buttery blackberry financier, Executive Chef Scott Bryan keeps the menu concise and tasty. Prix-fixe and tasting menus are also offered.

Back Forty

C2 American ✗

190 Ave. B (at 12th St.)

Subway: 1 Av
Phone: 212-388-1990
Web: www.backfortynyc.com
Prices: $$

Lunch Sat – Sun
Dinner nightly

Chef/owner Peter Hoffman sates city slickers seeking the country life with this popular tavern's array of fresh-from-the-farm themed preparations. The casual setting evokes heartland charm with its tables topped by brown paper mats that display the menu, walls adorned with found objects and agricultural tools, as well as an inviting backyard dining area. Though Back Forty is billed as a grass-fed burger joint, the menu offers much more than spicy homemade ketchup. Starters feature garden-fresh ingredients; while seasonality and sustainability drives the rest of the menu with the likes of Catskill trout and East Coast hake with local clams and salsa verde.

A new SoHo location resides at the corner previously occupied by Savoy (also from the same chef).

Balade

B2 Lebanese ✗✗

208 First Ave. (bet. 12th & 13th Sts.)

Subway: 1 Av
Phone: 212-529-6868
Web: www.baladerestaurants.com
Prices: 🍃

Lunch & dinner daily

Honing in on the cuisine of Lebanon, Balade is a welcoming and tasty Middle Eastern experience fronted by a cheerful red awning. The spotless room is accented with tile, brick, and wood; and each table bears a bottle of private label herb-infused olive oil.

The menu begins with a glossary of traditional Lebanese ingredients and the explanation that *Balade* means "fresh, local." The mezze; grilled meat-stuffed sandwiches; and Lebanese-style pizzas called *manakeesh* topped with the likes of lean ground beef, chopped onion, and spices are all fresh-tasting indeed. House specialties are also of note, like the *mujaddara crush*—a platter of lentils and rice topped by crispy fried onions and a salad of cool chopped cucumber and tomato.

Boukiés

Greek 🍴🍴

A3

29 E. 2nd St. (at Second Ave.)

Subway: Lower East Side - 2 Av
Phone: 212-777-2502
Web: www.boukiesrestaurant.com
Prices: $$

Lunch Tue – Sun
Dinner nightly

Owner Christos Valtzoglou has rejiggered this corner of East Village real estate into a contemporary, inviting, and Aegean-inspired space for sampling inventive meze. White marble, bright-blue rattan furniture, and linen banquettes comfortably convey the geographical focus of Boukiés, where Greek food authority Diane Kochilas has consulted on the menu.

Among the carte du jour's many highlights are claypot-baked chickpeas and eggplant in minty, cinnamon-seasoned tomato sauce; a savory plate of neatly crisped and buttery cigar-shaped mushroom pies; or head-on prawns with a roasted red pepper-and-almond sauce. Semolina cake with caramelized pineapple and sweet vanilla-flecked yogurt is best enjoyed with a dark Greek coffee.

Brick Lane Curry House

Indian 🍴

A2

306-308 E. 6th St. (bet. First & Second Aves.)

Subway: Astor Pl
Phone: 212-979-2900
Web: www.bricklanecurryhouse.com
Prices: $$

Lunch & dinner daily

Located on Curry Row and named after London's own, Brick Lane is a 6th Street standout featuring numerous influences lifted from across the pond. Beers are available by the half or full pint, an Underground map adorns the wall, and meltingly soft cheddar cheese stuffs the tasty *paratha*.

Despite the Anglo-culinary whimsy, Brick Lane's heart belongs to curry with a selection of fifteen varieties that include Goan, spiked with green chilies and a tangy bite. Prepared with your protein of choice, the selection even includes the *phaal*, said to be so spicy it is accompanied by a disclaimer warning guests of "physical or emotional damage" that may result. However, this may also be a reminder of the thoughtful, friendly, and efficient service staff here.

Manhattan ▲ East Village

Cacio e Pepe

B1

Italian

182 Second Ave. (bet. 11th & 12th Sts.)

Subway: 3 Av
Phone: 212-505-5931
Web: www.cacioepepe.com
Prices: $$

Dinner nightly

With its subdued temperament and pleasant service, this casual and charming Italian can be trusted to satisfy, from the warm greeting everyone receives upon entering to the cannoli—a lovely finale to any meal here. The rustic menu of traditional Roman dishes features a house specialty from which the establishment takes its name: homemade *tonnarelli* tossed with pasta water, olive oil, cracked black pepper, and a showering of pecorino cheese. Yet there is much more to be discovered, such as cuttlefish over soft polenta or *bucatini all'Amatriciana*.

The wine list is short but carefully selected to highlight less-familiar producers in the most notable Italian regions. In warm weather, the pretty backyard garden makes for an idyllic dining area.

Cafe Mogador

B2

Moroccan

101 St. Mark's Pl. (bet. First Ave. & Ave. A)

Subway: 1 Av
Phone: 212-677-2226
Web: www.cafemogador.com
Prices:

Lunch & dinner daily

The key to Cafe Mogador's longterm success is its popular array of tasty, crowd-pleasing Moroccan favorites. Open from morning to night, breakfast offers the likes of Middle Eastern eggs, any style, with sides of hummus and *tabouli*. Lunch adds heartier fare like grilled chicken kebob with tart pickles and tahini-slicked Arabic salad stuffed into a warm and tender pita, served with French fries. Dinner focuses on Moroccan specialties like *bastilla*, grilled *merguez*, and a meatball tagine with saffron sauce and couscous.

Opened back in 1983, Café Mogador continues to thrive and has recently received a fresh coat of paint to brighten the laid-back, coffee-house setting.

A second outpost of this beloved café has recently opened in Williamsburg.

Calliope

84 E. 4th St. (at Second Ave.)

Subway: Lower East Side - 2 Av
Phone: 212-260-8484
Web: www.calliopenyc.com
Prices: $$

Lunch Tue – Sun
Dinner nightly

Husband-and-wife team Ginevra Iverson and Eric Korsh have moved into Belcourt's old corner and bring with them an unabashed bistro experience that's easy to love. Oysters, beef tongue with sauce *gribiche*, or Provençal tomato tart are all fine starting points, before moving on to pleasing entrées that may include spoon tender lamb neck braised in a spirited broth of tomato, red wine vinegar, and chili flakes. The *baba au rhum* is a thing of beauty—presented warm, crowned by perfectly whipped cream, and soaked (right before your eyes) with Venezuelan rum.

A communal table supplements seating in the charming dining room that is decorated with vintage mirrors and French doors that make for a relaxed and breezy experience when the weather cooperates.

The Cardinal

234 E. 4th St. (bet. Aves. A & B)

Subway: Lower East Side - 2 Av
Phone: 212-995-8600
Web: www.thecardinalnyc.com
Prices: $$

Dinner Tue – Sun

Southern cuisine continues to make further Manhattan inroads with the arrival of this Alphabet City spot named after the North Carolina state bird. The restaurant's motif is clear, with the state's flag proudly brandishing one wall and a menu of down-home treats built around a brief list of entrées paired with a slew of choices for sides.

The barbecue plate is a meaty delight—spilling over with dry-rubbed pork ribs smoked in-house for six hours, toothsome brisket infused for three times as long, and a link of house-made pork sausage. A trio of sauces is provided to dress-up an already satisfying plate and give equal representation to Tennessee, Texas, and North Carolina. Regional sodas, like Cheerwine, are sure to make some feel nostalgic.

ChikaLicious

Contemporary

203 E. 10th St. (bet. First & Second Aves.)

Subway: Astor Pl
Phone: 212-475-0929
Web: www.chikalicious.com
Prices:

Dinner Thu – Sun

Named for Pastry Chef/owner Chika Tillman, this sweet spot presents an all-encompassing dessert experience that somehow manages to impress without overkill. The chic white space offers counter seating overlooking a lab-clean kitchen where the team prepares elegant jewels that start as butter, sugar, and chocolate. À la carte is offered, but the best way to appreciate this dessert bar is to select the prix-fixe menu. Feasts here may begin with an amuse-bouche of Darjeeling tea gelée with milk sorbet; followed by a mascarpone semifreddo topped with espresso granita; then finish with pillowy cubes of coconut-marshmallow *petits fours*.

Dessert Club across the street tempts with cookies, cupcakes, and shaved ice for a grab-and-go fix.

Curry-Ya

Japanese

214 E. 10th St. (bet. First & Second Aves.)

Subway: Astor Pl
Phone: 866-602-8779
Web: www.nycurry-ya.com
Prices:

Lunch & dinner daily

From the co-owner of Soba-Ya, comes this tasty eatery, specializing in Japan's unique version of curry—*yoshoku*. This culinary icon belongs in the repertoire of Western-style dishes that have become a part of the Japanese palate. Characterized by a mild sweetness and restrained heat, Curry-Ya's rich sauce is garnished with pickled vegetables, short grain rice, and is available with a selection of accompaniments like *panko*-crusted Berkshire pork cutlet, organic chicken, and grilled hamburger. The small menu also offers inspiring starters like a salad of *yuba* and snow peas with green olive dressing.

The bright space, warmed by pale pink walls and blond wood stools, offers seating for 14 at a marble counter set in front of the white-tiled kitchen.

DBGB Kitchen & Bar 😊

French ✕✕

A3

299 Bowery (bet. First & Houston Sts.)

Subway: Lower East Side - 2 Av
Phone: 212-933-5300
Web: www.danielboulud.com
Prices: $$

Lunch & dinner daily

The name of Chef Daniel Boulud's downtown outpost is a riff on the famed punk rock club that once stood just a few doors away. Inside, the spacious setting is accented with polished copper pots and dry goods, drawing further inspiration from its address on Bowery—the neighborhood is a hub for restaurant supplies. Even the bathroom is lined with vintage cookware catalogs.

The menu is inspired, too. Luxe burgers, like the Frenchie, topped with Morbier, and a global lineup of sausages (*merguez, boudin Basque*, Thai pork and red curry) are offered alongside classics like decadent pâté. Be sure to try *spaghetti alla chitarra* with Marky Ramone's (yes, of the Ramones) tomato sauce, enhanced by tender fennel, onions, and a dollop of lemon-zested ricotta.

Degustation

Spanish ✕✕

A2

239 E. 5th St. (bet. Second & Third Aves.)

Subway: Astor Pl
Phone: 212-979-1012
Web: www.degustation-nyc.com
Prices: $$

Dinner nightly

Brought to you by the proprietors of Jewel Bako, this elegant tapas bar is wholly clad in squares of slate. A dark wood counter set with leather placemats seats diners—most of whom tend to be amorous couples—around the chef and his adept team for a memorable dining experience.

Degustation's ever-evolving menu now offers a more edited selection of precisely crafted compositions that are not only tied to Spain, but also imbued with global influences. A small plates spree can include sugar snap peas arranged with *queso fresco* and spongy bits of "aerated" cornbread; or crispy octopus tentacles dressed with Thai red curry foam. A tender Colorado lamb loin and juicy belly with onion purée tells the tale of delightful product mingled with skilled preparation.

Dieci

B2   Fusion

228 E. 10th St. (bet. First & Second Aves.)

Subway: Astor Pl   Dinner nightly
Phone: 212-387-9545
Web: www.dieciny.com
Prices: $$

Dieci fuses Italian and Japanese cuisines for a successful marriage of taste and creativity. Springy ramen clutching spicy lamb Bolognese is a perfect example of this flavorful union. The tiny step-down setting is easy to miss but conquers its spatial challenge with comfortable seats. Find foodies centered around a dining counter that juts out from the kitchen—a handful of small tables also bolster the accommodations.

A unique array of small plates includes buffalo mozzarella with uni and yuzu foam, and steamed buns filled with Berkshire pork belly. Meanwhile, entrées go on to include miso-glazed cod set atop an appealing wild mushroom risotto fortified by a poached egg. Desserts are equally impressive, as in a silky Earl Grey crème brûlée.

Dirt Candy 😋

B2   Vegetarian

430 E. 9th St. (bet. First Ave. & Ave. A)

Subway: 1 Av   Dinner Tue – Sat
Phone: 212-228-7732
Web: www.dirtcandynyc.com
Prices: $$

From her vantage point behind the line, Chef/owner Amanda Cohen keeps a watchful eye on every one of her 18 guests as she skillfully crafts vegetarian fare for a voracious crowd of followers. The room is tiny, but attractively designed with sustainability in mind.

Devotees and skeptics alike can't help but find Dirt Candy's meatless menu intriguing and downright tasty. An entrée simply titled "Beans" brings semi-firm tofu poached in coconut milk, topped by a pyramid of al dente long beans, tempura sea beans, and spiced coconut milk sauce; while "Cauliflower" reveals battered florets arranged on a tender waffle, with horseradish-spiked buttermilk sauce. Eggplant ingeniously finds its way into a tiramisu embellished with rosemary cotton candy.

Edi & The Wolf

C3

102 Ave. C (bet. 6th & 7th Sts.)

Subway: 1 Av
Phone: 212-598-1040
Web: www.ediandthewolf.com
Prices: $$

Lunch Sat – Sun
Dinner nightly

Chefs Eduard Frauneder and Wolfgang Ban, the dynamic duo behind Seäsonal, have brought their wares downtown with the arrival of this *heuriger*—a casual neighborhood wine tavern common in Austria. The dark and earthy den is chock-full of reclaimed materials including a 40-foot rope salvaged from a church, now coiled above the tiny bar.

The crux of the offerings is comprised of small and shared plates such as cured and dried *landjäger* sausage accompanied by house-made mustard and pickles. Entrées fall under the heading of "schnitzel & co." and offer a highly recommended wiener schnitzel, which starts with a pounded filet of heritage pork encased in an incredibly delicate and crunchy coating, finished by Austrian-style potato salad and lingonberry jam.

Empellón Cocina

B2

105 First Ave. (bet. 6th & 7th Sts.)

Subway: 2 Av
Phone: 212-780-0999
Web: www.empellon.com
Prices: $$

Dinner Tue –Sun

This ain't your run-of-the-mill Mexican haunt. Drop in for a dram of the good stuff and linger at the sleek, black circular bar which is stocked with a thrilling offering of tequilas and mescals this side of the Hudson. Empellon Cocina bears a chill vibe and the rock 'n roll soundscape emits an edgy feel. But, the inside remains neatly styled in basic wood and crisp whites.

Alex Stupak's ambitious interpretation generates wildly creative salsas (*sikil pak* with pumpkin seeds and *epazote*) served with masa chips; and guacamole topped with sea urchin and pistachios. Start with snacks like sweetbreads beside refried beans or appetizers (mescal-cured ocean trout?), before sinking into tacos packed with short rib pastrami and pickled cabbage.

Extra Place

Mediterranean ✗✗

8 Extra Pl. (at 1st St.)

Subway: 2 Av   Lunch Sat – Sun
Phone: 212-777-4252   Dinner nightly
Web: www.extraplace.us
Prices: **$$**

Named after its alley location, Extra Place (and its "Heidi" off-shoot) offer two enticing dining options under one roof. The main room has an appealingly earthy look and is perfumed by the open kitchen's wood-fired grill. Each Mediterranean delight emerges with a clever touch, such as fig-sweetened lamb jus to dress an oversized meatball perched in couscous; or a ribbon of house-made carrot pasta to wrap grilled day boat sea scallops with Jonah crab salad.

And then there's "Heidi"—a sliver set just off the entryway, where traditional Swiss cooking inspired by the background of owner Amadeus Bogner (also of Le Philosophe) is served. Try the *kalbsbratwurst mit rösti*, plump veal sausages with red onion marmalade and a divine potato pancake.

Feast

Contemporary ✗

102 Third Ave. (bet. 12th & 13th Sts.)

Subway: 3 Av   Lunch Sun
Phone: 212-529-8880   Dinner Mon – Sat
Web: www.eatfeastnyc.com
Prices: **$$**

This recent arrival with the straightforward but promising moniker is a rustic, textbook amalgam of wood, brick, and tiles.

The kitchen is confidently led by an alum of Veritas who has devised several prix-fixe menus, served family style. These might be based on the farmer's market or even a nose-to-tail meal of lamb, including merguez stew; or a lasagna layering shank, broccoli rabe, and goat cheese. If you're not up for a whole feast, dine à la carte on meaty, ocean-fresh oysters capped by cocktail sauce aspic; or a *nouveau* take on incredibly tender chicken and "dumplings" of liver-stuffed pan-fried gnocchi and wisps of crisped skin. End with the awesome Valrhona chocolate pudding—leaving a single dark chocolate cookie crumb behind is impossible.

Gnocco

C2

337 E. 10th St. (bet. Aves. A & B)

Subway: 1 Av
Phone: 212-677-1913
Web: www.gnocco.com
Prices: $$

Lunch Sat – Sun
Dinner nightly

This charming, mural-lined Alphabet City trattoria lies across from Tompkins Square Park and its panoply of activity— youngsters shooting hoops, strolling dog-walkers, and local characters overcome by the urge to express themselves. The shaded back terrace is a popular hangout come summer.

The namesake *gnocco* are crispy, deep-fried pillows of dough served with a platter of shaved Italian meats. That might be prelude to a thin-crusted pizza; house-made whole-wheat *tubetti integrale* tossed with chickpeas, cherry tomatoes, and diced smoked pancetta; or pork loin braised in milk with rosemary and garlic. After such a hearty meal a light homespun finish is in order, as in a plate of freshly baked almond *cantucci* paired with a glass of chilled *vin santo*.

Goat Town

B3

511 E. 5th St. (bet. Aves. A & B)

Subway: 2 Av
Phone: 212-687-3641
Web: www.goattownnyc.com
Prices: $$

Lunch Sat – Sun
Dinner nightly

This Alphabet City bistro boasts a rustic-chic guise of hand-built, salvaged furnishings awash in a perfectly calibrated glow. Fashioned by a Brooklyn-based design firm, the backdrop is enhanced by a lively crowd and an infectious playlist.

The 50-seat dining room serves a well-made and seasonally influenced selection that might include specials dressed with freshly snipped herbs grown out back. Expect starters such as seared mackerel with olive oil breadcrumbs, and entrées like braised goat shoulder cleverly paired with bread salad punched up by anchovies, dried cranberries, and walnuts. Dessert showcases the evening's sundae special—think dark-roast coffee ice cream draped with caramel, cake bits, and salted pretzel—and is not to be missed.

Graffiti

B2   Contemporary

224 E. 10th St. (bet First & Second Aves.)

Subway: 1 Av   Dinner Tue – Sun
Phone: 212-464-7743
Web: www.graffitinyc.com
Prices: $$

Credibly doted on since it's inception in 2007, this cub of Chef/owner Jehangir Mehta is still going strong and baby boy is quite the dreamboat. Dressed with tightly-packed square communal tables and beaded ceiling lights, petite Graffiti may be dimly lit, but an exposed brick wall glossed with a metallic finish and hugging framed mirrors is all brightness.

Feeding a pack of 20 on newspaper-wrapped tables are Indian-inspired sweet and savory small plates of watermelon and feta salad cooled by a vibrant mint sorbet; eggplant buns spiked with toasty cumin; green mango *paneer*; and a zucchini-hummus pizza. If you forget to order the addictive green chili shrimp, you can hit "Mehtaphor" in the Duane Street Hotel for a taste of this spicy delight.

Hasaki

A2   Japanese

210 E. 9th St. (bet. Second & Third Aves.)

Subway: Astor Pl   Lunch Wed – Sun
Phone: 212-473-3327   Dinner nightly
Web: www.hasakinyc.com
Prices: $$$

 Opened in 1984 and still going strong, this unassuming, no-reservations spot on a tree-lined stretch of the East Village is quietly housed just below street level. The dining room has a clean and spare look, with seating available at a number of wood tables or at the sizeable counter manned by a personable chef.

Hasaki's longevity is attributed to the high quality of its products, which infuses the dining experience with a sense of seriousness and purpose. Skillfully prepared and reasonably priced, delicate sushi and sashimi share the spotlight with shabu-shabu, green tea noodles, and crisp tempura. The menu is supplemented by fascinating daily specials that tend to sell out quickly. Before 6:30 P.M., the generous "Twilight" menu is cherished.

Hearth

B2

Mediterranean ✗✗

403 E. 12th St. (at First Ave.)

Subway: 1 Av
Phone: 646-602-1300
Web: www.restauranthearth.com
Prices: $$$

Lunch Sat – Sun
Dinner nightly

Housed in the happening East Village, Hearth's glass panes allow glimpses into their animated and sophisticated room. Walls padded with fabric panels lend a soft touch to the warm, comfortable space, styled with wine festival prints and maps. Service is either friendly and knowledgeable, or totally checked out.

The dining counter is a great place to absorb the kitchen's controlled chaos as they carefully prepare Italian classics with increasingly contemporary style. Crispy veal sweetbreads finished in a *piccata* sauce reach high levels of artistry. *Lesso misto*, gently cooked chicken, sausage, and veal bathed in tawny *brodo*, is luscious and flavorful. The wine list is as enticing as a carrot cake sundae layered with cream cheese mousse and whipped cream.

Hot Kitchen

A2

Chinese ✗

104 Second Ave. (bet. 6th & 7th Sts.)

Subway: Astor Pl
Phone: 212-228-3090
Web: www.hotkitchenny.com
Prices: $$

Lunch & dinner daily

Hot Kitchen brings a dash of fiery Sichuan cooking to a neighborhood that is already rife with international options. Whitewashed brick walls accented by chili red beams and ebony furnishings detail the tidy space.

Steer clear of the Chinese-American portion of the menu, and partake in Hot Kitchen's offering of classic Sichuan dishes bolstered by a portion of nicely done house specialties. Expect the likes of wok-fried quail liberally seasoned with cumin and salt; steamed whole fish slathered in a deluge of minced pickled red peppers; and shredded crispy duck studded with green onions and fried fresh ginger. Hot Kitchen uses the seasons to influence its roster of specials that have featured an autumnal bowl of braised spareribs with yam.

Ippudo

A1   J a p a n e s e   ✕✕

65 Fourth Ave. (bet. 9th & 10th Sts.)

Subway: 14 St - Union Sq   Lunch & dinner daily
Phone: 212-388-0088
Web: www.ippudony.com
Prices: 🍜

A wall covered in soup bowls is your clue of what to order at this popular outpost of the Japanese chain, opened by the renowned "King of Ramen" Shigemi Kawahara. Ramen-hungry diners are given a boisterous welcome from the energetic staff upon entering; expect the same at the farewell. With most seating arranged at communal oak-topped tables and prominently displayed open kitchen, Ippudo feels laid-back and fun yet sleek. The classic *shiromaru* ramen is a deeply satisfying bowl of rich pork broth and excellent, slender, fresh-made noodles garnished with sliced pork and cabbage.

If left with extra broth, simply tell your server "kae-dama" and for a small charge you'll receive an additional bowl of noodles.

Check out number two in Midtown West.

JoeDoe

A3   C o n t e m p o r a r y   ✕

45 E. 1st St. (bet. First & Second Aves.)

Subway: 2 Av   Lunch Sat – Sun
Phone: 212-780-0262   Dinner Tue – Sun
Web: www.chefjoedoe.com
Prices: $$

Wood and brick construct this rustic and rugged stage sprinkled throughout with whimsical touches. Seating at JoeDoe is bolstered by the comfortable bar-cum-dining counter; speaking of which, don't miss out on their selection of killer beer-based cocktails.

"Aggressive American" is how the chef describes his cuisine and it certainly teems with personality. Chilled pea soup, creamy from yogurt and almonds, is topped with crushed cacao nibs; and succulent beef kielbasa is nestled in a spread of grits and topped with shredded, spicy pickled cabbage.

A meal here begins not with a customary basket of bread, but with fried matzoh dusted with an addictive blend of seasonings. As for bread, check out the chef's takeout sandwich shop, JoeDough.

Jewel Bako ✽

A2

239 E. 5th St. (bet. Second & Third Aves.)

Dinner Mon – Sat

Subway: Astor Pl
Phone: 212-979-1012
Web: www.jewelbakosushi.com
Prices: $$$

Swee Phuah

Except for a tiny window of light, Jewel Bako does little to draw you in, lending an almost furtive, subterranean feel to the narrow entrance. Inside, this long space is lined with intimately spaced wooden tables. The upholstered banquettes are filled with a comfortably casual and convivial crowd, while solo diners seem to adore the dining counter that surrounds the expert team. The chefs here are busy, very passionate, and provide a wealth of culinary entertainment.

Painstaking detail is clear from the colorful glasses to the smiling staff's ability to explain the finer points of each preparation.

Their menu showcases the remarkable quality of each fish, which seem to have arrived straight from Japan. Expect to sample a range of original appetizers like oysters with micro greens and refreshing citrus juice or smooth salmon tartare in crisp pastry. Bluefin tuna, tender octopus, and plump sweet shrimp sashimi are all firm and glossy, with wasabi root grated tableside. Each grain of slightly sticky rice is cooked precisely and combined with barracuda, eel, and scallop for superb sushi. To close, try creamy green jasmine ice cream, sandwiched between crunchy chocolate cookies.

Kafana

C3

Eastern European ✗

116 Ave. C (bet. 7th & 8th Sts.)

Subway: 1 Av
Phone: 212-353-8000
Web: www.kafananyc.com
Prices: $$

Dinner nightly

Translating to "café" in Serbian, Kafana has a heartwarming ambience that beckons one to stay for a while. Exposed brick walls decorated with mirrors, vintage photographs, rough-hewn wood tables topped with votives and flowers, and boldly patterned banquettes outfit the intimate space, attended to by a genuinely friendly staff. In one corner sits the small bar, with a charmingly low-tech antique cash register.

Kafana offers worldly diners an exotic cuisine not often found in Manhattan. The list of hearty Serbian specialties includes a phyllo pie filled with cow's milk feta and spinach; grilled meats; or slow-cooked stews prepared with large, tender white beans perfumed with garlic and paprika, topped with slices of smoky peasant sausage.

Kanoyama

B1

Japanese ✗

175 Second Ave. (at 11th St.)

Subway: 3 Av
Phone: 212-777-5266
Web: www.kanoyama.com
Prices: $$

Dinner nightly

Offering an impressive lineup of excellent quality and deftly prepared fish, this popular sushi den now claims greater capacity following a recent expansion. In a space that is simply done but spotless and well-maintained, the focus here is on a parade of pristine cuts that are bolstered by a passage of daily items such as rich baby shad from Japan and tender, mild American white bonito. Also find a generous listing of oysters; starters such as *wakasagi* tempura (fried baby smelts) sprinkled with green tea-salt; and a handful of cooked entrées. The value-conscious omakase is highly recommended.

Besides being tempting, the website is very informative: it presents diverse fish facts, photos, and recommendations for seasonality and preparation.

Kyo Ya ✿

Kimiko Ukaji/Kyo Ya

B2

94 E. 7th St. (bet First Ave. & Ave. A)

Subway:	Astor Pl	Dinner nightly
Phone:	212-982-4140	
Web:	N/A	
Prices:	$$$	

Within the artsy East Village neighborhood, Kyo Ya remains a secret treasure. Riverstones, slate, and rice-paper lanterns line the long and narrow room, which seems much larger thanks to a wall of windows flooding the subterranean space with light. The modern interior is divided into many distinct nooks, including a front area set with dark tables, counter dining, and a tatami room for small groups. There is a near-obsessive focus on detail that ensures each diner's comfort—even the flower placed upon the table is sure to match the season's color and tone. Consistency and skill are hallmarks of any meal here, and this is equally true of both food and service.

The sushi is excellent, but kaiseki menus are where this chef shines, so be sure to request this when booking your reservation. The opening salvo has featured tempura-fried lotus root stuffed with fishcake and topped with green tea salt. Soups have resembled aromatic dashi with braised mini bok choy in a hand-painted lacquer bowl.

Other combinations can be refreshing and ingenious, as in ripe strawberries beneath opalescent slices of whelk with a tiny cluster of crisp-fried ginger, toasted almonds, and broccoli rabe purée.

L'Apicio

Italian XX

A3

13 E. 1st St. (bet. Bowery & Second Ave.)

Subway: 2 Av
Phone: 212-533-7400
Web: www.lapicio.com
Prices: $$

Lunch Sat – Sun
Dinner nightly

The talented team behind L'Artusi has headed east to open this modern trattoria in a dramatically transformed quarter of the East Village, where luxury rentals now dominate. Rustic yet glossy, L'Apicio provides a chic den for young movers-and-shakers to kick back and unwind after a demanding day. Come for a snack or a meal; the menu's format leaves it up to you. Find the likes of watercress salad with avocado, both roasted and raw carrots, swiped with spiced yogurt and crushed pistachios; or polenta *alla spianatora*, golden-yellow cornmeal topped with a savory stew of rock shrimp, tomato, and bacon. Come dessert, the chocolate *crostata* arrives as a warm ganache in a neatly fluted and wonderfully crumbly cookie crust, paired with *stracciatella* gelato.

Lavagna

Italian X

C3

545 E. 5th St. (bet. Aves. A & B)

Subway: 2 Av
Phone: 212-979-1005
Web: www.lavagnanyc.com
Prices: $$

Lunch Sat – Sun
Dinner nightly

Instantly evidencing Lavagna's popularity is its steady stream of regulars who seem smitten with this delightfully discreet trattoria. Open since 1999, the staff is ever gracious, greeting guests by name, but the same courtesy is offered to first-timers as well. A wood-burning oven flickers in the elfin kitchen thereby elevating Lavagna's sense of snug comfort.
Speaking of snug, the Italian menu offers a terse listing of *pizzette*, perhaps capped with roasted mushrooms, fontina, and white truffle oil. Antipasti unveils cool, shaved octopus massaged with fresh lemon and extra virgin olive oil; while entrées vie for center stage as in an al dente twirl of *fedelini fini* with slow-cooked tomatoes and toasted garlic slices; or oven-roasted fish, flambéed tableside.

Lil' Frankie's

A3

19 First Ave. (bet. 1st & 2nd Sts.)

Subwaу: 2 Av
Phone: 212-420-4900
Web: www.lilfrankies.com
Prices: 💰💰

Lunch Fri – Sun
Dinner nightly

Dinnertime always seems like a party at this offshoot of the ever-popular Frank, featuring a greenery-adorned dining room and a bar area lovingly nicknamed after owner Frank Prisinzano's father, "Big Cheech." The classic East Village space is furnished with a combination of wood- and marble-topped tables, colorful benches, and brick walls with black-and-white portraits, fashioning a shabby-chic backdrop.

Cooked to crispy perfection in a wood-burning oven, Naples-style pizza, with toppings like homemade sausage and wild fennel, star on the menu. Equally impressive is the lineup of antipasti and pastas, handmade with the freshest ingredients. Come with a crowd or expect to wait—reservations are accepted only for parties of six or more.

Luzzo's

B1

211-13 First Ave. (bet. 12th & 13th Sts.)

Subway: 1 Av
Phone: 212-473-7447
Web: www.luzzospizza.com
Prices: $$

Lunch & dinner daily

The reason why decade-old Luzzo's continues to claim top ranking among the city's artisanal pizzerias is the handiwork of Naples-born executive *pizzaiolo* Michele Luliano (also of Ovest Pizzoteca) and his well-trained minions. Fashioned in the Neapolitan manner, these mouthwatering, smoke-kissed pies are made with a blend of flours, slick of San Marzano tomatoes, and creamy blobs of fresh mozzarella (or *mozzarella di bufala*) and baked in one of the city's last remaining coal-fired ovens. Sample from more than 20 variations on offer, or try the crisp, old-fashioned *quadrata* squares and a pizza *fritta* stuffed with cheese, sauce, and ham.

A mirror hung at the front of the slender, rustic space offers a view of the pizza making action in the back.

Maharlika

Filipino 🍴

111 First Ave. (bet. 6th & 7th Sts.)

Subway: Astor Pl   Lunch & dinner daily
Phone: 646-392-7880
Web: www.maharlikanyc.com
Prices: $$

The décor may not be a highlight, but Maharlika's focus on traditional Filipino cooking and a cordial staff shine through the low-tech setting.

The easiest way to describe the food is to say it is hearty and meaty. Prepare yourself for *kare kare*, a stew of oxtail braised in peanut butter-enriched sauce; or Pampangan-style sizzling *sisig*, a hot skillet heaped by a trio of pig parts (ear, snout, and belly) arranged around a fried egg, stirred all together tableside. The chicken and waffle combines crispy pieces of light and dark meat served atop a waffle made with *ube* (purple yam) flour, with contrasting embellishments like anchovy butter and *macapuno* syrup, made from thick, caramelized coconut juice.

Also try the newer offshoot, Jeepney.

Malai Marke

Indian 🍴🍴

318 E. 6th St. (bet. First & Second Aves.)

Subway: Astor Pl   Lunch & dinner daily
Phone: 212-777-7729
Web: www.malaimarke.com
Prices: $$

New on the scene is Malai Marke, where owner Shiva Natarajan has built an appealing room that displays a bit of flash and dispels the notion that Curry Row is not a destination for fine Indian cooking. Polished copper pans hang from brick walls, shiny black tiles accent the space, a dining counter expands seating options, and the kitchen is on view.

The moniker translates to "extra cream" in Hindi tea-stall slang, a rich embellishment that inspires this regionally focused food. A feast here might feature *paneer tikka*, brushed with thick cream and fresh herbs; fish *moilee*, simmered in coconut milk vibrantly spiced with red chili, turmeric, and black mustard seed; *makka roti*, griddled corn flatbread; and coconut rice studded with flecks of *papadum*.

The Mermaid Inn

Seafood ✗

 A2

96 Second Ave. (bet. 5th & 6th Sts.)

Subway: Astor Pl
Phone: 212-674-5870
Web: www.themermaidnyc.com
Prices: $$

Dinner nightly

This laid-back and inviting seafood spot has been a neighborhood favorite since opening a decade ago, spawning locations in Greenwich Village and the Upper West Side. A steady stream of guests lines the bar early for the super-sized "Happy Hour and 1/2" with freshly shucked oysters, snack-sized fish tacos, and other specially priced bites. For a hearty plate after your nosh, try blackened catfish dotted with crawfish butter alongside hushpuppies, or the lobster roll with Old Bay fries. On Sunday night, look out for lobsterpalooza—a whole lobster accompanied by grilled corn on the cob and steamed potatoes.

At the end of your meal there's no need to deliberate over dessert; a demitasse of perfect chocolate pudding is presented compliments of the house.

Mighty Quinn's

Barbecue ✗

A2

103 Second Ave. (at 6th St.)

Subway: Astor Pl
Phone: 212-677-3733
Web: www.mightyquinnsbbq.com
Prices: ⊜⊜

Lunch & dinner daily

Mighty Quinn's luscious treats were previously served only at Smorgasburg, Brooklyn's open-air foodie market, but can now be enjoyed at this permanent stage for Chef/pitmaster Hugh Mangum. The sturdy location features terrazzo floors, whitewashed brick walls, and salvaged spruce tables (repurposed from the renovated Puck building).

Service is totally casual, but that's hardly a complaint. After all, this is a barbecue joint, so you will need to place your order at the counter before sitting. Naturally raised, slow-smoked meats beckon as brisket, sausage, or pulled pork. All are offered by the pound or as a portion, naked or piled high in an egg-yellow bun. Everything is good, but the insanely tender pulled pork sandwich is simply irresistible.

Momofuku Ko ✿ ✿

B2

163 First Ave. (bet. 10th & 11th Sts.)

Subway: 1 Av
Phone: 212-777-7773
Web: www.momofuku.com
Prices: $$$$

Lunch Fri – Sun
Dinner nightly

Noah Kalina

The entry to Chef Chang's lauded destination is shielded by a metalwork façade displaying that iconic peach, and while some may not be enthralled by its typically East Village (read: irreverent) exterior, staunch foodies are fully aware of the storied dining that awaits inside. With little frill and fuss, you will be ushered to your seat at the pristine counter. From that point on, it's all a surprise from the chefs.

The high point here is that kitchen and those sagacious cooks who prepare everything in front of you. Intimacy reigns as chefs present dishes, even if they do not take the time to explain the nuances of each composition. The vibe here is fun and upbeat—as is the music. Cool, laid-back patrons are equally forthcoming as they praise the freshness of a nori-wrapped scallop, or mackerel slivers with spicy seaweed. Other noteworthy dishes have included a delicately puffed egg floating in very clever bacon-dashi broth.

Bento boxes composed of pickled sardines in a crisp tempura batter or 48-hour shortribs, pink at the center and melting in the mouth star in this show. A hollow doughnut filled with ripe banana paste and topped with maple syrup ice cream delivers a knockout end.

Momofuku Noodle Bar

B2

Asian

171 First Ave. (bet. 10th & 11th Sts.)

Subway: 1 Av	Lunch & dinner daily
Phone: 212-777-7773	
Web: www.momofuku.com	
Prices: $$	

This is the one that started it all. David Chang's first-born remains a temple to hipster comfort food and rocks from the time the doors open. Two dining counters and a handful of communal tables furnish the honey-hued room, though the genteel staff deftly maximizes the minimal real estate.

Noodle Bar's gutsy menu is fashioned with Asian street food in mind. Steamed buns filled with tender beef brisket, horseradish mayonnaise, and pickled onion; or a bowl of springy ramen noodles doused with ginger-scallion sauce are just two examples of the crew's signature work. Blackboards display the day's specials and soft-serve flavors, as in the awesomely creamy Ritz cracker and peanut butter swirl, served with a pinch of sea salt and Concord grape compote.

Momofuku Ssäm Bar

B1

Contemporary

207 Second Ave. (at 13th St.)

Subway: 3 Av	Lunch & dinner daily
Phone: 212-777-7773	
Web: www.momofuku.com	
Prices: $$	

Momofuku Ssäm Bar will always be a darling among trendy New Yorkers who can usually be found clamoring at the bar or packing those low-slung tables. This minimalist favorite may be staffed with brisk servers, yet their appetizing menu (especially those steamed buns filled with juicy pork belly) encourages lingering. Lunches are ideal for professionals on the run.

Ssäm Bar's unique blend of Asian and Western flavors accounts for its popularity. Taste the likes of rotisserie duck tucked with duck-and-pork sausage beneath the skin and cooked to crispy perfection. When joined with chive pancakes and sweet hoisin, the dish is elevated to global fame. Best to follow such creativity with a beautifully sweet and salty truffle filled with chocolate-pretzel cake.

Motorino

B2

349 E. 12th St. (bet. First & Second Aves.)

Subway: 1 Av

Phone: 212-777-2644

Web: www.motorinopizza.com

Prices:

Lunch & dinner daily

Mathieu Palombino's Neapolitan-style pizzeria has been successfully churning out a tandem of tasty pies for a few years now. Simply beautified with white marble-topped tables, a pressed-tin ceiling and bold green-and-white striped walls, the room's blackboard specials convey a more complex and product-focused sensibility that is applied here—fresh ramps have been a seasonally tuned topping.

Cold and hot antipasti (an octopus salad tossed with potatoes, celery, and chili oil; or roasted peppers with capers and parsley) bolster the mouthwatering pizza selection topped with the likes of *fior di latte*, caramelized Brussels sprouts, and diced pancetta.

The new Brooklyn location has been sending fans back across the bridge.

Northern Spy Food Co.

C2

511 E. 12th St. (bet. Aves. A & B)

Subway: 1 Av

Phone: 212-228-5100

Web: www.northernspyfoodco.com

Prices: $$

Lunch & dinner daily

Under the steady stewardship of founding partner Christophe Hille, this noteworthy Alphabet City café continues to entice on every level—from the product-driven cooking to the country-chic decor. Reclaimed hickory floors and salvaged wood tabletops fill the petite room, accented in framed mirrors, touches of vintage wallpaper, and a splash of robin's egg blue paint.

The kitchen easily pleases with brunch-like midday meals. Dinnertime really shines, perhaps beginning with pork sticky rolls with parsnip glaze to snack on while awaiting excellent quality farm-raised lamb, prepared two ways. This single dish might feature fanned slices of loin and a collard-wrapped bundle of spoon-tender shoulder, plated with savory granola and a swipe of thick yogurt.

Oda House

C3

Eastern European ✗

76 Ave. B (at 5th St.)

Subway:	2 Av	Lunch & dinner daily
Phone:	212-353-3838	
Web:	www.odahouse.com	
Prices:	$$	

For a taste of something different, this inviting new café serves intriguing specialties from Georgia. That country's proximity to Russia, Turkey, and Armenia results in a vibrant and enticingly unique cuisine that Oda House does proud.

A liberal use of fragrant spices, cheese-filled breads, kebabs, and slow-cooked meats typify the kitchen's preparations. Classic dishes include *satsivi*, boiled chicken served cool in a creamy walnut sauce seasoned with warm spices, accompanied by *gomi*, hominy grits in a mini cauldron studded with morsels of rich, stretchy *sulgani* cheese. Balance out the hearty fare with a fresh, perfectly dressed garden salad.

The vibe is simple and rustic with pumpkin-colored stucco walls, exposed brick, and wood furnishings.

Porsena

A2

Italian ✗✗

21 E. 7th St. (bet. Second & Third Aves.)

Subway:	Astor Pl	Dinner nightly
Phone:	212-228-4923	
Web:	www.porsena.com	
Prices:	$$	

Sara Jenkins' fans gather at Porsena, where her flavorful and approachable style to Italian food shines bright. Casual and rustic, Porsena has an unplanned yet true sense of place. The dining room is divided into two intimate spaces tightly packed with snug tables, in true East Village style. Snagging the coveted chef's table situated before the semi-open kitchen is enough to start a foodie fight.

Expect such sumptuous standards as brandied chicken liver pâté paired with pickles; perfectly cooked octopus infused with smoked paprika and served beside roasted fingerlings; or raw milk curd, a creamy-pungent cheese with a compote of *agretti* and chilies. Massive *anelloni* with spicy lamb sausage, mustard greens, and breadcrumbs is wow-inducing.

Prime & Beyond New York

A1

90 E. 10th St. (bet. Third & Fourth Aves.)

Subway: Astor Pl
Phone: 212-505-0033
Web: www.primeandbeyond.com
Prices: $$$

Lunch Wed – Sun
Dinner nightly

This location of the Fort Lee, NJ original brings great steak to the East Village. Appropriate for the locale, the setting eschews the standard men's club swagger of most steakhouses for a look that's spare and cool. Despite the chillax vibe, expect to see suits; the meat is that good. In fact, it's procured from the same purveyor that supplies Peter Luger and Keens.

Aged in-house for six weeks, the USDA prime Porterhouse is presented hot off the grill but well rested, richly flavored, tender, and juicy. Myriad cuts satisfy all preferences, while sides like kimchi, spicy scallion salad, and fermented cabbage stew are especially appealing and honor the owners' heritage. The lunch menu is pared down but offers Korean-style soups and stews.

Prune

A3

54 E. 1st St. (bet. First & Second Aves.)

Subway: 2 Av
Phone: 212-677-6221
Web: www.prunerestaurant.com
Prices: $$

Lunch & dinner daily

Packed with simple furnishings and attended to by a friendly staff, the popularity of this endearing breadbox of a restaurant never seems to fade. On a warm day when the front doors open, few Manhattan restaurants can match its ambience. From her kitchen in back, Chef/owner (and best-selling author) Gabrielle Hamilton has impressed serious diners since 1999.

The deceptively modest menu changes often but the chef's signature style shines through in items that are fuss-free yet display an undeniable level of skill and talent. A meal here may feature a crisp-skinned fillet of Tasmanian sea trout set atop a bundle of frisée and crowned by a dollop of perfect homemade mayonnaise; or a creamy, sweet, and tart lime custard graced with crumbly oatmeal shortbread.

Pylos

B3

128 E. 7th St. (bet. First Ave. & Ave. A)

Subway: Astor Pl
Phone: 212-473-0220
Web: www.pylosrestaurant.com
Prices: $$

Lunch Wed – Sun
Dinner nightly

Taking its name from the Greek translation of "made from clay," this contemporary taverna features a ceiling canopy of suspended terra-cotta pots and whitewashed walls with lapis-blue insets. The restrained décor produces a chic Mediterranean vibe that perfectly suits its lusty, home-style, deliciously refined cuisine—courtesy of noted Greek food authority Diane Kochilas.

Moussaka, a classic Greek comfort favorite, is beautifully presented here as a dome filled with layers of browned meat and silky eggplant, encrusted in slender potato slices, finished with a layer of golden-browned béchamel. Sides may include *spanakorizo*, wilted spinach rice flecked with feta crumbles; while custard-filled phyllo drenched in mountain honey ends things sweetly.

Rai Rai Ken

B2

218 E. 10th St. (bet. First & Second Aves.)

Subway: Astor Pl
Phone: 212-477-7030
Web: N/A
Prices: ⊜⊜

Lunch & dinner daily

Rai Rai Ken isn't quite what it used to be—it's bigger and much more comfortable. Just a few doors east of its former location, the new room boasts a fresh and tidy look with blond wood seating plus the signature red vinyl stools. An array of pots remain bubbling and steaming behind the counter.

Rest assured the menu's star attraction—those thin, toothsome ramen noodles—are just as delicious, served with four near-addictive, fantastically complex broth variations: *shio, shoyu,* miso, and curry. Each bowlful is chock-full of garnishes, like slices of roasted pork, boiled egg, nori, fishcake, and a nest of springy noodles. Grab a business card before leaving as loyal diners are rewarded with a complimentary bowl after ten visits.

Ramen Misoya

J a p a n e s e

129 Second Ave. (bet. St. Marks Pl & 7th St.)

Subway: Astor Pl

Phone: 212-677-4825

Web: www.misoyanyc.com

Prices:

Lunch & dinner daily

 With 30 locations worldwide, Ramen Misoya now brings its trademark ambrosial bowlfuls to New York City. The earthy dining area dons a bamboo-lined ceiling as well as a TV monitor that is internally looped to broadcast the kitchen's every move.

The ramen offering here differentiates itself by centering on a trio of miso-enriched broths: *shiro* is a white miso fermented with rice *koji* (starter); richer tasting *kome-miso*; and *mame-miso*, a strictly soybean product. The mouth-coating soup is delicious alchemy. Each slurp is a multifaceted distillation of pork and chicken bones with savory-salty-sweet notes, stocked with excellent noodles, vegetables, and the likes of panko-crusted shrimp tempura, fried ginger chicken, or slices of house-made *cha-su*.

The Redhead

A m e r i c a n

349 E. 13th St. (bet. First & Second Aves.)

Subway: 1 Av

Phone: 212-533-6212

Web: www.theredheadnyc.com

Prices: $$

Dinner nightly

At long last, a comeuppance for redheads tired of those endless jokes. This redhead makes its namesake beam with pride. Tucked into a diminutive space, it has cornered the market on charm with a rustic exposed brick-and-bistro table décor. The vibe is laid-back and lures a crowd that packs this little spot and makes it loud, loud, loud. Wait times, even on weeknights, can seem interminable, but the gleaming all-American bar is the perfect antidote.

The address says East Village, but the bold menu says deep South. Selections like hush puppies filled with sour cream and caviar, or buttery oyster pot pies bathed in Pernod show off a North-meets-South flair; while entrées like low country shrimp and grits or roasted duck gumbo keep things civil.

Robataya

 B2

231 E. 9th St. (bet. Second & Third Aves.)

Subway: Astor Pl
Phone: 212-979-9674
Web: www.robataya-ny.com
Prices: $$

Lunch Sat – Sun
Dinner nightly

This latest and fun venture from restaurateur Bon Yagi features a front room with a 26-seat counter lined with salivating diners and platters of ultra-fresh vegetables, fish, and meats to be grilled and served by a paddle wielding team of chefs perched behind the counter.

The *robatayaki* menu offers flavorfully grilled dishes, from silky eggplant to sheets of dried sardines, seasoned with imported salt, brushed with soy, teriyaki, or dressed with miso. The menu shows a plethora of options but is usually supported by cold, warm, and seasonal appetizers; fried dishes like *yuba gyoza*; and iron pots of steamed rice (*kamameshi*) topped with snow crab, perhaps.

Table seating is available in the rear dining room for those who prefer a more serene experience.

Sigiri

 B2

91 First Ave. (bet. 5th & 6th Sts.)

Subway: 1 Av
Phone: 212-614-9333
Web: www.sigirinyc.com
Prices:

Lunch & dinner daily

For a delicious taste of something different, round the corner of 6th Street to First Avenue, and climb to Sigiri's small second floor dining room. This humble Sri Lankan establishment stands above its neighbors for wonderfully prepared, intriguingly fragrant cuisine that needs neither a colorful light display nor boisterous greeter. Instead, the warm, sedate room features sienna walls and simple tables with bright cloths.

Specialties are numerous and include *string hopper kotthu*, a stir-fry of impossibly thin and fluffy rice noodles tossed with eggs, chicken, and vegetables, accompanied by coconut gravy; or spoon-tender chunks of eggplant *moju*, spiced with dried red chili. In lieu of alcohol, fruit cordials or apple-iced tea make for cool offerings.

Sobakoh

Japanese ✗

309 E. 5th St. (bet. First & Second Aves.)

Subway: 2 Av
Phone: 212-254-2244
Web: N/A
Prices: 😎

Lunch Fri – Sun
Dinner nightly

Before entering Sobakoh, stop for a minute to appreciate Chef/owner Hiromitsu Takahashi, sequestered to his temperature- and humidity-controlled glass booth, forming layers of organically grown buckwheat flour dough into first-rate noodles. This ritual is performed several times daily by the smiling chef and is the foundation of the seasonally arranged offerings at this Japan-meets-East Village soba spot. Service can be sluggish, so start with a classic Japanese snack, like the refreshing daikon salad dressed with yuzu, wasabi, and bonito flakes, while waiting for your bowlful of *uni ikura soba*—chilled buckwheat noodles heaped with creamy sea urchin and plump salmon roe.

The inexpensive prix-fixe menu offered nightly is even cheaper before 7:00 P.M.

Soba-Ya 😎

Japanese ✗✗

229 E. 9th St. (bet. Second & Third Aves.)

Subway: Astor Pl
Phone: 212-533-6966
Web: www.sobaya-nyc.com
Prices: 😎

Lunch & dinner daily

In a neighborhood replete with tempting Japanese dining options, Soba-Ya has been sating noodle cravings with awesome buckwheat soba and hearty udon—all homemade daily—for more than a decade. Enterprising co-owner Bon Yagi, also of Curry-Ya, favors authenticity over flash in his establishments, and this popular soba spot fashioning a traditional Japanese aesthetic is no exception.

Sit among the largely Japanese lunchtime clientele to savor and slurp cold, refreshing soba attractively served in a red-black bento box neatly stocked with the likes of dashi-poached vegetables, fresh and deliciously glazed salmon, or crisp shrimp tempura. Complete this meal with a pot of hot broth added to your remaining soy-based dipping sauce for a warming finish.

Supper 😊

Italian ✗

B3

156 E. 2nd St. (bet. Aves. A & B)

Subway: 1 Av
Phone: 212-477-7600
Web: www.supperrestaurant.com
Prices: $$

Lunch Sat – Sun
Dinner nightly

If you lived by Supper, you'd be supping there all the time. Replete with character, warmth, and regulars, this neighborhood spot has it all: its modest menu is deliciously appealing; preparations are simple yet perfect; flavors run large; and its prices are affordable. With three East Village hits in hand, the Frank crew means business.

A substantial menu keeps company with nightly specials and a killer wine list; diners pack the low-lit, sultry front room for a slice of action from the open kitchen. Find more intimacy in the back, or pick the private room for a dinner party starring veal *polpettini* bobbing in *sugo*; roasted chicken massaged with rosemary and garlic; and *spaghetti al limone*, sauced with white wine, cream, lemon zest, and Parmesan.

Sushi Dojo

Japanese ✗

B2

110 First Ave. (bet. 6th & 7th Sts.)

Subway: Astor Pl
Phone: 646-692-9398
Web: www.sushidojonyc.com
Prices: $$

Dinner Tue – Sat

Chef David Bouhadana has reemerged from his stint at Sushi Uo followed by some time in Japan to head up this bright new sushi-ya. A 14-seat counter and a handful of tables outfit the pleasant room, where the congenial chef sends forth an impressive array of morsels.

The chef's choice menu is highly recommended and offers very good value for the masterful skill and high quality of fish. This is immediately clear in the nigiri presentation that has included Tasmanian trout, cherry salmon from Japan, and a trio of *maguro* (lean, medium, and fatty). Beyond the sushi menu, sample dishes like house-made cold tofu served with yuzu salt; and *kaki-age*, a light and crisp tempura-fried combination of delicate *mizuna*, seaweed, squid, and shrimp with green-tea salt.

The Toucan and The Lion

B2

Fusion

342 E. 6th St. (bet. First & Second Aves.)

Subway: 2 Av
Phone: 212-375-8989
Web: www.thetoucanandthelion.com
Prices: $$

Dinner Wed – Mon

A fanciful flourish of creativity and a mighty mash-up of flavors are some of the treasures in store at this clever and current boîte. The space is small, done in a bleached palette and furnished with a quirky smattering of accents including patio furniture and ceiling light pendants that double as terrariums. The overall aesthetic is akin to a crowded urban terrace.

While tables are barely large enough to accommodate one plate, you'll want to order many: excellent quality head-on prawns draped in luscious tamarind and sweet chili sauce, is best accompanied by toasted *bao* for sopping; and goat "pot pie" features a small skillet filled with tender goat meat and root vegetables in delicious coconut-rich Massaman curry, served with warm *roti*.

Zabb Elee

A2

Thai

75 Second Ave. (bet. 4th and 5th Sts.)

Subway: Astor Pl
Phone: 212-505-9533
Web: www.zabbelee.com
Prices: ⊜⊜

Lunch & dinner daily

Proclaim you've found a great new Thai spot, and people listen; announce it's in Manhattan, and crowds race you to the door. This spicy sparkler eschews the high design look common to others in its category, opting instead for a reticent look of pale tones jazzed up by patterned tile and light green shutters.

The food speaks, or should we say shouts, for itself, honing in on Northern Thailand for a vibrant profusion of Isaan specialties. Chef Ratchanee Sumpatboon delivers knockouts such as *som tum poo plara* (green papaya salad with preserved crab and fried pork rind); *pukk boong moo korb* (sautéed morning glory with crispy pork); and *pad ped moo krob* (fried pork mingling with Thai eggplant in a ginger curry sauce fragrant with green peppercorns).

Financial District

Widely considered the financial center of the world, the southern tip of Manhattan is flooded by hard-driving Wall Street types. When it's time to eat, they love a hefty steak, especially when expense accounts are paying the bill. And though expense accounts may be shrinking these days, bigger is still better at stalwarts like **Delmonico's** which opened in 1837 as America's first fine-dining restaurant. The institution that introduced diners to now-classic dishes such as eggs Benedict, lobster Newburg, and baked Alaska, continues to pack 'em in for the signature Angus boneless rib eye, otherwise known as the Delmonico steak.

Reinventing the
Public Market

New is replacing old as the publicly owned Tin Building and New Market Building—home to the former Fulton Fish Market—house tenants in the form of **The New Amsterdam Market**, a seasonal marketplace where butchers, grocers, fishmongers, artisan cheese producers, and other vendors hope to create a regional food system. With a stated mission "to reinvent the public market as a civic institution in the City of New York," this non-profit organization dedicates itself to promoting sustainable agriculture and regionally sourced food, while offering space for independent purveyors to sell on behalf of farmers and producers. Check their website (www.newamsterdampublic.org) for event dates. One of the district's largest tourist draws, South Street Seaport is surrounded by eateries from family-friendly Irish pubs to the historic **Fraunces Tavern**. Innkeeper Samuel Fraunces purchased this three-story, 18th century brick mansion at the corner of Pearl and Broad streets in 1762.

The Financial District has traditionally catered to power-lunchers by day and business travelers by night. However, that's all changing rapidly as the area becomes increasingly residential. What you will discover is a smorgasbord of bars, restaurants, and food services catering to the local residents. These blossoming culinary gems incite buttoned-up Wall Street suits to loosen their collars and chill out over a glass of wine at **Pasanella and Son**—revered by many as "the best wine shop" in town. Front Street has also attracted a spate of eateries, although Hurricane Sandy had a major impact here and many mom-and-pop spots never fully recovered. And yet, Jamaican food cart sensation **Veronica's Kitchen** remains alive, well, and kicking—with a flavorful array of Caribbean eats. If that's not foody enough, the hugely popular Festival Meatopia draws crowds of carnivores to Governor's Island every year. For a quick nosh at a bargain price, follow your nose to **Alan's Falafel Cart** on Cedar

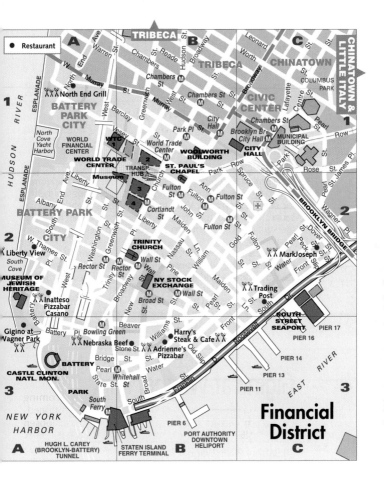

Street. Then for a bit of sweet, head to **Financier Patisserie** on lovely Stone Street, one of the narrow and sinuous streets laid out in the 17th century by New York's Dutch settlers. While here, take your pooch for a drink at **Growler Bites & Brews** and after, wash it down with coffee at one of the myriad street vendors nearby. Despite the destruction incurred by Hurricane Sandy, restaurants downtown are as busy as ever, with Wall Street wonders drowning their worries in martinis and Manhattans, while reviewing their portfolios over hearty burgers and beer. Events like the Stone Street Oyster Festival, sponsored by the same folks who operate Financier Patisserie and Ulysses pub, play to the area's strengths. What better way to lift your spirits and celebrate the local Blue Point harvest in September than by slurping oysters and swilling libations outdoors on Stone Street?

Adrienne's Pizzabar

Pizza ✗✗

B3

54 Stone St. (bet. Coenties Alley & S. William St.)

Subway: Bowling Green   Lunch & dinner daily
Phone: 212-248-3838
Web: N/A
Prices: ⊜⊜

Come midday at Stone Street and Coenties Alley, Adrienne's is abuzz with Financial District business types hungering for delectable pizzas. With their thin-crusts, slightly chunky sauce, and fresh toppings, these pies are a classic—even the square shape is true to the venerable Sicilian-American version.

With increasing residences in this nook, Adrienne's is just as packed at night, when diners linger to appreciate the mosaic-steel bar, stiff-backed leather banquettes, polished marble, or lovely outdoor tables. Choosing between their four hearty ravioli selections can be a challenge, when deciding between lobster, cheese, spinach-cheese, or sausage-broccoli rabe. Desserts are divine, which is no surprise as the owners are also behind Financier Patisserie.

Gigino at Wagner Park

Italian ✗✗

A3

20 Battery Pl. (in Wagner Park)

Subway: Bowling Green   Lunch & dinner daily
Phone: 212-528-2228
Web: www.gigino-wagnerpark.com
Prices: $$

Move over out-of-towners, locals are wising up to this hidden gem, where harbor views, a dedicated staff, and a scrumptious Italian menu make for a fantastic experience. The serenely lit room is outfitted in muted whites, with high ceilings and large windows that peek out at the shimmering water (in warmer seasons, snag a seat on the gorgeous terrace for the best views).

Dine on tasty arugula salad with pear slices, shaved Parmesan, and candied walnuts; *cosciotto di pollo*—tender chicken braised in white wine and vegetable ragù; pan-sauteed artichoke hearts with garlic, flat-leaf parsley, and olive oil; or gnocchi tossed in a veal and beef meatball-laden tomato ragù. Save room for a fresh lemon tart, with whipped cream and slices of strawberry.

Harry's Steak & Cafe

B3

American ✂✂

1 Hanover Sq. (bet. Pearl & Stone Sts.)

Subway: Wall St (William St.)   Lunch & dinner Mon – Sat
Phone: 212-785-9200
Web: www.harrysnyc.com
Prices: $$

Nestled beneath the historic Hanover building, Harry's presents two distinct experiences. The casual café and bar stand at the entrance, packed wall to wall with Wall Street suits haunting their local watering hole. Dining here is both cozy and communal, in an atmosphere that promises a fun time. Harry's Steak sits behind the Cafe, with its own bar and a series of snug rooms for a more intimate evening.

Begin with a classic starter, like mushrooms stuffed with sweet, succulent lobster; but everyone really comes for the steak. Here, a prime hanger steak is perfectly seared, juicy, and tender—impressive for this particular cut—served with homemade béarnaise. There is no room left for disappointment, but maybe enough for the pecan bread pudding.

Inatteso Pizzabar Casano

A2

Italian ✂✂

28 West St. (at 2nd Pl.)

Subway: South Ferry   Lunch & dinner daily
Phone: 212-267-8000
Web: www.inattesopizzabar.com
Prices: $$$

Aside from its convoluted name, everything at Inatteso is delightfully unassuming. The endearing room co-stars a slender though spirited bar at the entrance. Enchanting vistas of the venerable Statue of Liberty and Ellis Island, appropriate lighting, and lattice-like wood paneling augment the overall allure.

The staff within this contemporary, well-designed haunt may not be perfect, but their kindly manner when presenting the likes of a classic and delicious pizza Margherita will win you over. An arugula salad tossed with baked figs stuffed with Gorgonzola *dolce* and wrapped in prosciutto; swordfish *contadina* glistening with an herbaceous olive oil and laid atop broccoli rabe; or sweet vanilla-infused ricotta cheesecake are some of their other big wins.

Liberty View

A2

Chinese

21 South End Ave. (below W. Thames St.)

Subway: Rector St (Greenwich St.)
Phone: 212-786-1888
Web: www.libertyviewrestaurant.com
Prices: $$

Lunch & dinner daily

As befits what is becoming one of the city's most vital and investment-loving neighborhoods, local eateries are cleaning up their act, including this authentic Sichuan option—now more dining scene than just a takeout spot. Long-standing Liberty View, positioned on one of *the* best promenades in the city, offers solid Chinese in a clean and comfortable space.

Scores of surrounding FiDi suits frequent these freshly dressed tables set by windows replete with panoramic views. Don't let their marvelous vista of the Statue of Liberty detract you from the likes of cold beef tripe in a spicy pepper oil; Macau rice cooked with barbecue pork, scallions, and eggs; or Shanghai noodles glistening with mushrooms and shiny soy-glazed mustard greens.

MarkJoseph

C2

Steakhouse

261 Water St. (bet. Peck Slip & Dover St.)

Subway: Brooklyn Bridge - City Hall
Phone: 212-277-0020
Web: www.markjosephsteakhouse.com
Prices: $$$

Lunch Mon – Fri
Dinner nightly

Rising from the shadows of the Brooklyn Bridge in the South Street Seaport Historic District, MarkJoseph's caters to both Wall Street wunderkinds and tourists with deep pockets. The cozy dining room is a notch above the standard steakhouse design, with art-glass vases and pastoral photographs of the wine country adding sleek notes.

At lunch, regulars devour hearty half-pound burgers (though a turkey variety is also offered). At dinnertime, a prime dry-aged Porterhouse, sized for two to four, takes center stage. Classic accompaniments may include crisp salads, seafood cocktails, and sides like creamed spinach. The wine list offers a nice choice of hefty varietals, as well as some interesting old-world selections to accompany that bone-in ribsteak.

Nebraska Beef

B3 Steakhouse 🍴

15 Stone St. (bet. Broad & Whitehall Sts.)

Subway: Bowling Green
Phone: 212-952-0620
Web: www.beststeakhousenyc.com
Prices: $$$

Lunch Mon – Fri
Dinner nightly

It's easy to miss the door that marks the entrance to this beloved Financial District watering hole-cum-steakhouse (look for the red and gold sign out front), but not the raucous happy hour crowd that floods the narrow bar leading to the restaurant. Smile and squeeze through, to discover a much calmer scene inside: a dark, wood-paneled dining room with a clubby, in the know vibe.

This is one Wall Street oasis where the past and present comfortably co-exist—the martinis flow freely, the garlic bread melts in your mouth, and the hand-picked, 28-day, dry-aged ribeye still arrives sizzling, perfectly charred, and juicy as sin. If you're short on time or looking for lunch options, you can also grab a steak sandwich, salad, or burger on the fly.

North End Grill

A1 American 🍴

104 North End Ave. (at Murray St.)

Subway: Chambers St (West Broadway)
Phone: 646-747-1600
Web: www.northendgrillnyc.com
Prices: $$$

Lunch & dinner daily

Brought to you by Floyd Cardoz and restauranteur Danny Meyer, this downtown stunner is quickly becoming the table of choice for Goldman Sachs' tycoons and waterfront-dwelling families. The décor seems sleek with midnight blue banquettes and black-and-white landscapes, but wood salvaged from Wyoming snow fences, impressive service, and over 100 bottles of Scotch whiskey warm the striking setting.

The menu offers a section devoted just to eggs, where one can find quail egg surrounded by celery leaves, slivered celery stalks, and a luxuriant dollop of paddlefish caviar. Also try shatteringly crispy clam flatbread pizza; wood-fire grilled Vermont rabbit; and luscious salted-honey bread pudding with caramel sauce and buttermilk sherbet.

Trading Post

American XX

170 John St. (at South St.)

Subway: Fulton St   Lunch & dinner daily
Phone: 646-370-3337
Web: www.tradingpostnyc.com
Prices: $$

In the historic building that previously housed Yankee Clipper, Trading Post is a massive and stylish reprieve from those nearby pubs and quick-serve joints. It occupies three floors, including a whiskey cellar, first-floor bar, and more upscale second floor with water views, tufted leather banquettes, orange wingback chairs, and an elegant library.

The menu complements the setting with a wealth of top products, found in creamy corn chowder made with briny, tender blue crab; or an heirloom tomato salad nestled among feta and watermelon, finished with balsamic vinaigrette. Also sample more novel items, such as the substantial cornmeal-crusted skate with caramelized pineapple. The coveted crème brûlée is perfectly classic and absolutely delicious.

Your opinions are important to us. Please write to us directly at: michelin.guides@ us.michelin.com

Manhattan ▶ Financial District

C2

Gramercy, Flatiron & Union Square

Gramercy Park, anchoring its namesake neighborhood, is steeped in history, old-world beauty, and tranquility. But, its extreme exclusivity is the stuff of legends among life-long New Yorkers, few of whom have set foot on its pretty yet private paths. This may be where tourists have an advantage, because outside of the residents whose home addresses face the square, Gramercy Park Hotel guests are among the few permitted entrance. The staff accompanies guests to the daunting cast-iron gate, allows them in, and reminds them of the number to call when they wish to be let out again, perhaps to explore this lovely enclave filled with charming cafés and beautiful brownstones. Speaking of hotels, channel your inner Dowager Countess of Grantham at **Lady Mendl's Tea Salon** and nibble on dainty finger sandwiches in the Victorian-style parlor of the Inn at Irving Place. Stroll a few blocks to discover the neighborhood's diverse offerings like Maury Rubin's **City Bakery**—a popular spot revered for its excellent pastries, hot chocolate, and pretzel croissants.

Curry Hill

North of the park is Gramercy's very own "Curry Hill" with an authentic range of satisfying, budget-friendly restaurants. Food enthusiasts should visit **Kalustyan's**—a spice-scented emporium specializing in a mind-boggling wealth of exotic products ranging from orange blossom water to thirty varieties of dried whole chilies. A few blocks to the west, find the very open, tranquil, and welcoming Madison Square Park, which boasts its own unique history and vibe. This was the home of the city's first community Christmas tree in 1912, the original location of Madison Square Garden arena, and site of New York's very first baseball club, the Knickerbockers of 1845. It is therefore only fitting that greeting park visitors is the original and scrumptious **Shake Shack**, serving its signature upscale fast food to a legion of followers from an ivy-covered kiosk. Burgers and Chicago-style dogs are always popular, but the house-made creamy custard has its cultish followers checking the online "custard calendar" weekly for their favorite flavors.

If you wish to hang with the cool kids, head to the reputed Ace Hotel and find them gathered around **No. 7 Sub Shop** for a quick bite, **Stumptown Coffee Roasters** for a cuppa', or just chillin' in the lobby—also a huge hipster common. Barbecue fans adore the Big Apple Barbecue Block Party held in June. This weekend-long event features celebrity pit masters displaying their talents to throngs of hungry aficionados. One of this neighborhood's

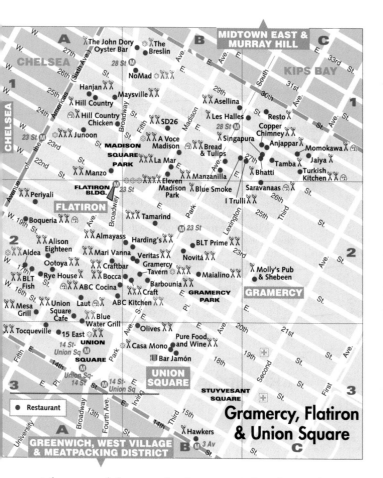

A — B — MIDTOWN EAST & MURRAY HILL — C

The John Dory Oyster Bar
The Breslin
CHELSEA
NoMad
KIPS BAY

Hanjan
Maysville
Asellina
Hill Country
Les Halles
Resto
Hill Country Chicken
SD26
Singapura
Copper Chimney
Junoon
A Voce Madison
Anjappar
Momokawa
MADISON SQUARE PARK
Bread & Tulips
La Mar
Tamba
Jaiya
Manzo
Manzanilla
Bhatti
Turkish Kitchen
FLATIRON BLDG.
Eleven Madison Park
Blue Smoke
Saravanaas
I Trulli
Periyali
FLATIRON
Boqueria
Tamarind
Almayass
Harding's
BLT Prime
Alison Eighteen
Mari Vanna
Veritas
Novitá
Aldea
Ootoya
Craftbar
Gramercy Tavern
Maialino
Molly's Pub & Shebeen
Rye House
Bocca
BLT Fish
ABC Cocina
Barbounia
GRAMERCY PARK
Mesa Grill
Union Square Cafe
Laut
ABC Kitchen
Craft
GRAMERCY
Tocqueville
Blue Water Grill
Olives
15 East
Casa Mono
Pure Food and Wine
UNION SQUARE
Bar Jamón
STUYVESANT SQUARE

Restaurant

Hawkers

Gramercy, Flatiron & Union Square

GREENWICH, WEST VILLAGE & MEATPACKING DISTRICT

most famous and frequented features is **Eataly NY**, founded by Oscar Farinetti and brought stateside by business partners Mario Batali and Joe Bastianich. This massive mecca offers a glamorous marketplace and dining hall replete with diverse Italian products and aromatic food stalls. Nearby Union Square may be known as an historic downtown park with playgrounds and tiered plazas that occasionally hosts political protests and rallies, but today the square is best known for its year-round **Greenmarket** boasting a beautiful array of seasonal produce. Beyond the market, find a bottle of wine to complement that farm-to-table meal from **Union Square Wines and Spirits** or the regionally-specific **Italian Wine Merchants**. Further testament to Union Square's reputation as the center of Manhattan food shopping is the presence of **Whole Foods** and the city's very first **Trader Joe's**, all within blocks of one another.

ABC Cocina

Mediterranean ✗✗

A2

38 E. 19th St. (bet Broadway & Park Ave. South)

Subway: 23 St (Park Ave. South)   Dinner nightly
Phone: 212-677-2233
Web: www.abccocinanyc.com
Prices: $$

Jean-Georges continues to fuel his love affair with sustainable cooking at this aptly named iteration of ABC Kitchen, which reflects the same sensibilities. The cavernous interior is framed by brick walls and softly glowing, mix-and-match chandeliers. The menu is an homage to Spain's vibrant tapas cuisine, listed by cooking technique.

"Golden and crispy" offerings might feature gooey béchamel, cheese, and ham fritters in a panko crust; while "light and bright" means sautéed flowering greens dressed in sherry vinegar and shallots. Under "masa and tortillas" find flaky empanadas stuffed with creamy sweet pea purée alongside chili-spiked yogurt. The "impossible" salted caramel flan layering soft custard and perfectly moist cake is an instant classic.

ABC Kitchen

Contemporary ✗✗

A2

35 E. 18th St. (bet. Broadway & Park Ave. South)

Subway: 23 St (Park Ave. South)   Lunch & dinner daily
Phone: 212-475-5829
Web: www.abckitchennyc.com
Prices: $$

ABC Kitchen's farm-to-table concept touches every heart that walks through the iconic namesake store. There is much to love within the large, stunning space, boasting reclaimed materials aplenty. A boisterous bar leads to a chic dining room outfitted in whitewashed wood floors, glossy laminated tables, and steel-framed chairs. The bucolic décor is a perfect introduction to their organically driven menu starring top-notch ingredients.

Tables are accented with flowers and soy-based candles that cast a gentle glow on fresh tuna sashimi bathed in lime, jalapeño, and ginger. A beautiful fillet of roasted sea bass is kicked up a notch when paired with chili-studded spinach; and a slice of chocolate cake with toasted marshmallow icing is generous and homey.

Aldea ✿

A2

Mediterranean ✗✗

31 W. 17th St. (bet. Fifth & Sixth Aves.)

Subway: 14 St - 6 Av
Phone: 212-675-7223
Web: www.aldearestaurant.com
Prices: $$$

Lunch Mon – Fri
Dinner Mon – Sat

Jerry Errico

For inspired yet focused cooking that sparkles like the Iberian coastline, seek out this impressive dining gem helmed by Chef George Mendes.

Set along a stretch rife with restaurants, Aldea's façade endures as an inviting insignia. The well-tread bar gives way to a cool, contemporary dining room done up in pale wood, soothing shades of blue, and stacks of glass. One of the city's prettiest counters can be found here—six seats under an elegant chandelier offer a view of the white-tiled workspace where, despite a flurry of activity, composure and tidiness prevail.

The chef's Portuguese background effects Aldea's creations replete with seasonal sensibilities. Dine à la carte to enjoy an array of excellent ingredients and complex flavors, or choose the tasting menu for a grander experience. High points include sea urchin toast dressed with mustard seeds and a sprinkle of lime; rich foie gras terrine with cinnamon-dusted brioche, fig and Port compote, and pickled mushrooms; and a block of pressed suckling pig strewn with Littleneck clams. Chocolate tart adorned with pistachios, flecks of gold, crème fraîche sorbet, and red hot candied *piri piri* tenders a show-stopping finale.

Alison Eighteen

Contemporary ✗✗

A2

15 W. 18th St. (bet. Fifth & Sixth Aves.)

Subway: 14 St - 6 Av   Lunch & dinner daily
Phone: 212-366-1818
Web: www.alisoneighteen.com
Prices: $$

Steadfast restaurateur Alison Price Becker has returned with this venture designed by the team responsible for the look of her first operation, Alison on Dominick Street, which served as a launching pad for a notable lineup of culinary talent still working their collective magic today. The feel is fresh yet warm with aubergine-tinted booths, espresso-shaded tables, and walls lined with bespoke toile wallpaper.

The kitchen presents a roster of seasonally inspired, au courant hits. White asparagus tartare is topped with goat cheese and smoked salmon roe; roasted carrots are glazed with lime, pistachios, and Banyuls vinegar; and steamed mussels are deliciously smoky with chorizo.

Alison Eighteen's front kiosk serves weekday morning coffee and pastries.

Almayass

Lebanese ✗✗

B2

24 E. 21st St. (bet. Broadway & Park Ave. South)

Subway: 23 St (Park Ave. South)   Lunch & dinner Mon – Sat
Phone: 212-473-3100
Web: www.almayassnyc.com
Prices: $$

Hot or cold, fresh and flavorful—the extensive choice of meze at Almayass showcases the riches of Lebanese cuisine accented by Armenian influences, thereby reflecting the heritage of this family-run operation with global outposts. A selection from the spreads and dips is a must, as in the *moutabbal*—eggplant seasoned with lemon, sesame paste, and garlic, redolent of smoke, and topped with jewel-like pomegranate seeds. Other items to seriously consider include *subereg* (a baked dish of four cheeses); oven-baked *mantee* traditional; or charbroiled beef kebab laced with sour cherries.

Polished wood accents, vivid artwork, servers attired in candy-hued shirts, and tables sized for feasting produce a distinctly upscale vibe within this delicious dining room.

Anjappar

C1

Indian 🍴

116 Lexington Ave. (at 28th St.)

Subway: 28 St (Park Ave. South)
Phone: 212-265-3663
Web: www.anjapparusa.com
Prices: $$

Lunch & dinner daily

This distinctive Curry Hill settlement is the third stateside location (there are two others in NJ) from a chain of restaurants based in Chennai. Not much to look at from the outside, Anjappar's interior is festive with bold red accents and carved woodwork that pep up the tidy dining room.

South Indian (Chettinad) cuisine typified by non-vegetarian preparations rich in freshly ground and blended spices set Anjappar's specialties in a league of its own. While you may find the usual biryanis and flaky breads, creations like egg masala (sliced boiled eggs sautéed in a pungent onion-and-tomato paste); and chicken *sukka varuval*, stir-fried chicken vibrantly seasoned with curry leaf, ginger, chili, and black pepper have the diners returning time and again.

Asellina

B1

Italian 🍴🍴

420 Park Ave. South (at 29th St.)

Subway: 28 St (Park Ave. South)
Phone: 212-317-2908
Web: www.togrp.com/asellina
Prices: $$

Lunch & dinner daily

From hospitality company The One Group, and housed in the glassy new Gansevoort Park Avenue hotel, Asellina offers a gratifying and updated vision of Italian dining. Bedecked with terra brick walls, concrete flooring, exposed filament bulbs, and sienna-toned leather furnishings, the lofty room glimmers with chic rusticity.

A long list of *antipasti* kicks off the menu with the likes of baked eggplant *tortino* with fresh ricotta and cheese *fonduta*. Pizza topped with nuggets of suckling pig, *robiola*, and tart shallots caramelized in red wine vinegar is one of several flatbread offerings; and more substantial fare features excellent pastas like the hearty but not heavy rigatoni with crumbled sausage, wild fennel, and Pecorino Sardo.

A Voce Madison

Italian

41 Madison Ave. (entrance on 26th St.)

Subway: 28 St (Park Ave. South)
Phone: 212-545-8555
Web: www.avocerestaurant.com
Prices: $$$

Lunch Mon – Fri
Dinner nightly

Evan Sung

Word of mouth alone would be enough to keep this swanky dining room in the good graces of the city's Italian-obsessed denizens, but A Voce Madison's sleek and polished surroundings coupled with its leafy environs (just opposite Madison Square Park) compel a loyal following.

Its vast bar is as appealing as the luxurious tables set with swivel chairs. Though there has been some transition in the kitchen, it remains as solid and sure-footed as ever. The pasta is made in-house daily and thrives as a fresh favorite. Deliciously eggy *spaghetti alla chitarra* is given a zesty gussying-up by San Marzano tomatoes, *bottarga*, and a measured pinch of red chili; while *mezzaluna* stuffed with earthy mushrooms is bathed in a light butter sauce pocked with walnuts and truffled pecorino. Entrées are equally exquisite as in *angello* or accurately cooked Colorado lamb chops served with an herbaceous swipe of salsa *verde*.

Desserts are impossible to resist. Even those proud of their powers of restraint *will* succumb to an enticing *torta di lamponi*, layering an almond paste biscuit, milk chocolate wafer, and bittersweet ganache with plump raspberries and finished with raspberry-lychee sorbet.

Barbounia

 Mediterranean ✗✗

B2

250 Park Ave. South (at 20th St.)

Subway: 23 St (Park Ave. South)
Phone: 212-995-0242
Web: www.barbounia.com
Prices: $$

Lunch & dinner daily

Big and bold, this Mediterranean brasserie highlights the flame-kissed cooking of sunnier climes. Fat columns, arched openings, and pillow-lined banquettes make the sprawling space seem cozy, but Barbounia's most appetizing feature is Chef Efraim Nahon's open kitchen, equipped with a wood-burning oven.

Irresistible bread, served hot from the oven, begins a meal here that should certainly focus on *meze* and hot appetizers like charred octopus. Entrées include brick oven baked branzino with salsa verde, and hanger steak *souvlaki* with black lentil and jasmine rice pilaf. The weekday lunch prix-fixe is a boon to business diners, offering three courses that may end with caramelized milk-coffee gelato crowned by shredded halva and puffed rice brittle.

Bar Jamón

Spanish

B3

125 E. 17th St. (at Irving Pl.)

Subway: 14 St - Union Sq
Phone: 212-253-2773
Web: www.barjamonnyc.com
Prices: $$

Dinner nightly

 A nibble at tiny but terrific Bar Jamón, with its brilliant by-the-glass list of Spanish wines (shared with big sister Casa Mono next door), may convince you that Chef Andy Nusser is the unsung hero of the Batali empire. Though the restaurant is the size of a closet, everything is done deliciously and with panache.

This mouthwatering menu so creatively breaks the tired tapas mold that arrival more than 15 minutes past opening almost guarantees a wait. Luscious slices of *jamón serrano* or the famed Iberico from Spain's *pata negra* (black hoofed) pigs; as well as a long list of cheeses and accompaniments star on their menu of small plates. Wash this all down by more than 600 choices of Spanish wine. A *cuarto* from the impressive list is de rigueur.

Manhattan ▶ Gramercy, Flatiron & Union Square

Bhatti

Indian ✕

100 Lexington Ave. (at 27th St.)

Subway: 28 St (Park Ave. South)
Phone: 212-683-4228
Web: www.bhattinyc.com
Prices: 🍴🍴

Lunch & dinner daily

This Northern Indian eatery is praised for its array of tasty grilled meats and kebabs that emerge from the *bhatti* (open-fire grill). Quality ingredients and a skilled kitchen combine with delicious results as in *haryali choza*, nuggets of white meat chicken marinated in an herbaceous blend of mint, cilantro, green fenugreek, chilies, and hung curd; or the unique house specialty *gilauti kebab*, made from fragrantly spiced lamb ground so fine and incredibly tender that it's almost pâté-smooth. Hearty dishes like *khatte baigan*, silky chunks of eggplant stewed in a tangy onion-tomato masala and garnished with pickled ginger root, wrap up such temptations.

The room is kitsch-free and tasteful with dark wood furnishings set against red-and-gold wallpaper.

BLT Fish

Seafood ✕✕

21 W. 17th St. (bet. Fifth & Sixth Aves.)

Subway: 14 St - 6 Av
Phone: 212-691-8888
Web: www.bltfish.com
Prices: $$$

Dinner Mon – Sat

Now under the domain of ESquared Hospitality, this civilized canteen offers a two-tiered approach to fish-focused dining. The boisterous ground floor Fish Shack embraces an easy breezy look and flavor with its raw bar, lobster rolls, and bowlful of saltwater taffy. Upstairs, the elegant dinner-only setting boasts a retractable glass roof, open kitchen, and mocha-hued furnishings.

Appetizers come both raw, like kampachi sashimi, and cooked, as in Santa Barbara uni risotto. Entrées may feature tomato-based cioppino stocked with Alaskan king crab and Maine lobster; or whole fish for two, priced by the pound. Nightly blackboard specials serve up greenmarket-influenced cooking, as in a decadent broccoli and white cheddar gratin.

BLT Prime

 Steakhouse ✗✗

111 E. 22nd St. (bet. Lexington Ave. & Park Ave. South)

Subway: 23 St (Park Ave. South) Dinner nightly
Phone: 212-995-8500
Web: www.bltprime.com
Prices: $$$

Like its aquatic cousin, this handsome rendition of a steakhouse is also under new direction. Yet, it hasn't missed a beat in sating carnivores with meals of sizzling broiled steaks served in cast iron and glazed by melting herbed butter. Starters such as a heap of baby spinach salad tossed with meaty bacon bits, blue cheese, hard-boiled egg, and a warm bacon-vinaigrette; and an ample choice of sauces and sides offer much in the way of embellishment. In a fitting wave of decadence, dinners are bookended by oversized Gruyère cheese popovers and plates of petite cookies.

A chic yet cozy mien pervades with a warm lighting scheme illuminating the room stocked with earth-toned furnishings, gleaming zebrawood tables, and a lively open kitchen.

Blue Smoke

 American ✗

116 E. 27th St. (bet. Lexington Ave. & Park Ave. South)

Subway: 28 St (Park Ave. South) Lunch & dinner daily
Phone: 212-447-7733
Web: www.bluesmoke.com
Prices: $$

With its distinct roadhouse feel, Blue Smoke is a down-home treat. Carefully calculated rough edges aside, this is a Danny Meyer restaurant where everyone is truly welcome, from serious suits to Björn-strapped young 'uns.

The faint smell of hickory and applewood used to infuse the meat seeps into the dining room and instantly whets the appetite. Pulled pork, beef brisket, and baby back ribs are all irresistible, but don't overlook the applewood-smoked chicken—a revelation of moist, ivory meat under a layer of gorgeously bronzed skin. Dishes are tasty enough on their own, but the tabletop caddy of sauces allows customized embellishment. Save room for their home-spun sweets, like a kick-ass slice of chocolate layer cake, served with ice-cold milk.

Blue Water Grill

Contemporary XX

A2

31 Union Sq. West (at 16th St.)

Lunch & dinner daily

Subway: 14 St - Union Sq
Phone: 212-675-9500
Web: www.bluewatergrillnyc.com
Prices: $$

Facing the Union Square Greenmarket, perennially popular Blue Water Grill is housed in a former, century-old bank, whose grand rooms now bustle with eager guests and a well-trained service team. Still, it retains a stately air with its soaring molded ceiling, gleaming marble, and windows overlooking the terraced dining area, ideal for warmer weather.

The crowd-pleasing menu focuses on seafood, but offers something for everyone. Highlights include a raw bar and sushi or maki selections; as well as fish entrées, simply grilled or accented with international flavors, as in big eye tuna with miso-black garlic vinaigrette. Find live jazz nightly in the downstairs lounge; or private group dining in the Vault Room, a former repository for gold bullion.

Bocca

Italian XX

B2

39 E. 19th St. (bet. Broadway & Park Ave. South)

Lunch Mon – Fri
Dinner nightly

Subway: 23 St (Park Ave. South)
Phone: 212-387-1200
Web: www.boccanyc.com
Prices: $$

It's not the newest kid on the block, but this established Italian claims new fame since the arrival of Chef James Corona. Bocca's Roman-accented cuisine hits the right notes in meals that should absolutely begin with the first-rate *tonnarelli cacio e pepe*. This luscious tangle of pasta is tossed with freshly cracked black pepper and cheese, then dramatically arrives to the table in a giant wheel of hollowed Pecorino Romano. The superb quality of that dish is no surprise, considering the owners also run Cacio e Pepe in the East Village. The *porchetta alla Romana* is just as lovely, crisp-skinned and tender, accompanied by red onion marmalade and rapini.

Parchment-hued walls hung with movie posters conjure Fellini's Roma and frame the pleasant setting.

Boqueria

A2

Spanish 🍴🍴

53 W. 19th St. (bet. Fifth & Sixth Aves.)

Subway: 18 St (Seventh Ave.)
Phone: 212-255-4160
Web: www.boquerianyc.com
Prices: $$

Lunch & dinner daily

Channeling the little bars that surround the legendary *Mercat de la Boqueria* in Barcelona, this upscale tapas spot is among the city's better destinations for an Iberian bite. Despite the crush of occupants each evening, the attractive setting provides a comfortable perch either in the rear room furnished with high tables or at the front counter flaunting plates of *tortilla Española*.

The kitchen is in the capable hands of a Barcelona native who boasts an impresive resume. Treats here have featured crunchy *croquetas* filled with a creamy combination of octopus and tomato; house-made pork sausage paired with crisped yet creamy garbanzo beans and syrupy red wine reduction; and *torrija*, a sensational Spanish rendition of French toast.

Bread & Tulips

B1

Italian 🍴🍴

365 Park Ave. South (at 26th St.)

Subway: 28 St (Park Ave. South)
Phone: 212-532-9100
Web: www.breadandtulipsnyc.com
Prices: $$

Lunch Mon – Fri
Dinner Mon – Sat

Tucked away on the lower level of the Hotel Giraffe, the inspired Italian cooking at Bread & Tulips sets it apart from the host of workaday dining options lining this stretch of Park Avenue South. The windowless room creates an air of seclusion and contemporary good looks through exposed brick, darkly polished woods, and filament light fixtures.

The kitchen shows its chops with a short list of pizzas that emerge charred, moist, and chewy from the brick oven, topped with the likes of hen of the woods mushrooms, pickled ramps, wild watercress, and creamy Taleggio. Nightly specials include house-made pastas and entrées such as Muscovy duck breast seared to a beautiful crisp, and matched with grappa-soaked Concord grapes atop a dollop of dense polenta.

The Breslin ✿

Melissa Hom

B1

Gastropub 🍴

16 W. 29th St. (at Broadway)

Subway: 28 St (Broadway)
Phone: 212-679-1939
Web: www.thebreslin.com
Prices: $$

Lunch & dinner daily

Housed off the lobby of the edgy Ace Hotel, The Breslin's entrance is immediately inviting. The hostess may be too cool for school, but that should not dissuade you. Let the lines do that.

With a no-reservations rule except for special events, most devotees know to arrive early and plan on waiting. Once inside, the room is quirky yet stylish with studded leather banquettes, abundant artifacts, and heavy fabrics. Snug tables sit alongside larger, more luxurious booths—the only option for a more secluded meal. The cheerful staff is friendly and somehow able to keep pace with the kitchen.

Chef April Bloomfield is lauded for her creative genius with gastropub cooking, but the simple truth is that her food is outrageously delicious—the ultra-rich scrumpets are fatty, meaty versions of mozzarella sticks and are an essential beginning to any meal here. Razor clams are cooked *a la plancha* with top-notch olive oil, drowned in garlic aïoli, topped with crisped Serrano ham, and will probably make you want to lick your plate. A seared turbot fillet is balanced with tomato-infused white beans and salty, crunchy potatoes. Malt and stout caramel add serious decadence to a bittersweet chocolate parfait.

Casa Mono 🌼

Spanish ✕

B3

52 Irving Pl. (at 17th St.)

Subway: 14 St – Union Sq   Lunch & dinner daily
Phone: 212-253-2773
Web: www.casamononyc.com
Prices: $$

Peter Siskos

Petite, good-looking, and intensely focused Casa Mono is perhaps this quaint residential neighborhood's most celebrated eatery. It is rustic and yet stunning with antique mosaic-tiled floors and a gleaming open kitchen. Despite the small, even cramped seating, this is a great place to gather with friends and share a bounty of dishes. Every plate arrives as soon as it is ready, yet the pacing is pleasant and never rushed. Service is smooth and engaged. Tables are tiny but smartly designed with a dish repository to ensure that there is always room for more.

Relish the likes of razor clams *a la plancha*, fresh and bursting with salinity, in a perfectly balanced garlic sauce. The house-made chorizo with smoky paprika is hugely flavorful, served with garbanzos, sweet onions, and plenty of bread for sopping up the juices. The kitchen's skill is clear in everything from spicy rabbit kebabs and oxtail-stuffed piquillo peppers, to *pulpo* with fennel and grapefruit. The fried duck egg is a marvel of extraordinary precision: its frilled white barely puffed around the yolk showered with black truffles, fingerling potatoes, and cured tuna.

Excellent wines stand up to the tantalizing cooking.

Copper Chimney

Indian 𝗫𝗫

C1

126 E. 28th St. (bet. Lexington Ave. & Park Ave. South)

Subway: 28 St (Park Ave. South) Lunch & dinner daily
Phone: 212-213-5742
Web: www.copperchimneynyc.com
Prices: 💶

This attractive and sleek dining room with a hip décor and fun vibe impresses with both Northern and Southern Indian cooking that stands well above the array of local options. The appetizer selection may include lovely *malai kofta*, perfectly browned and simmered in a deliciously creamy saffron sauce. Main courses incorporate a wide range of traditional ingredients, while emphasizing refined preparation and elegant presentation. Non-meat eaters will be happy with the ample selection of flavorful vegetarian dishes. Delicately puffed *kulchas*, served hot and dusted with fragrant herbs, is a great foil to any rich, leftover sauce (and the best way to sop them up).

The contemporary setting is further enhanced by a second floor lounge area.

Craft

American 𝗫𝗫𝗫

B2

43 E. 19th St. (bet. Broadway & Park Ave. South)

Subway: 14 St - Union Sq Dinner nightly
Phone: 212-780-0880
Web: www.craftrestaurantsinc.com
Prices: $$$$

This first and most original venture of renowned Chef Tom Colicchio opened back in 2001, yet its look is timeless. Housed in a former department store built in 1886, the setting is masculine yet cozy, lofty yet intimate. Terra-cotta columns, bare-bulb lights, and gleaming copper serving pieces filled with farm-fresh ingredients are among the iconic signatures here. It's still tough to get a reservation, so there is time to save up for your meal.

The menu's laissez-faire conceit allows diners to design their own meal from lists that group ingredients by their method of preparation. Raw bigeye tuna with Meyer lemon zest or roasted quail dabbed with balsamic might lead to a single braised beef short rib coupled with decadent potato gratin.

Craftbar

A2 Contemporary

900 Broadway (bet. 19th & 20th Sts.)

Subway: 14 St - Union Sq
Phone: 212-461-4300
Web: www.craftrestaurantsinc.com
Prices: $$

Lunch & dinner daily

This first Craft spin-off proudly displays its pedigree with simple yet elegant ingredient-focused cooking presented in a chic and lofty domain that respects the bones of its Flatiron locale. With its extensive menu of something for everyone, there is no wonder that this place packs a lively crowd.

Diners nibble on addictive, cheese-flecked breadsticks while perusing a menu that presents snacks, local cheeses, *salumi*, and small plates like a flavor-packed bowl of marinated Montauk squid dressed with a fish sauce vinaigrette, spicy mayonnaise, pickled Fresno chilies, and cool cucumber. A handful of pastas are offered among the large plate selection, such as squid-ink *chitarra* tangled with seafood, red wine *soffritto*, and mustard greens.

Hanjan

A1 Korean

36 W. 26th St. (bet. Broadway & Sixth Ave.)

Subway: 28 St (Broadway)
Phone: 212-206-7226
Web: www.hanjan26.com
Prices: $$

Dinner nightly

The latest from Chef Hooni Kim is similar in scale to his Hell's Kitchen hot spot, Danji. Here, find an entryway bar leading to a clutch of tables surrounding the communal centerpiece. The low-lit room is accented by an array of white ceramic crockery neatly arranged against shades of grey.

Korean small plates headlined under "Traditional" and "Modern" delight palates with vibrant flavors. The scallion pancake stuffed with squid is incredible—this lacy crisp heap is served with a fiery dipping sauce. Skewers of freshly butchered chicken are served hot off the grill with a walnut-and-chili paste; a boneless pig's foot is slowly braised to take on a sweet-salty sheen and is presented with a blend of chopped kimchi and fermented shrimp paste.

Eleven Madison Park

B1

Contemporary ✕✕✕✕

11 Madison Ave. (at 24th St.)

Subway: 23 St (Park Ave. South)
Phone: 212-889-0905
Web: www.elevenmadisonpark.com
Prices: $$$$

Lunch Thu – Sat
Dinner nightly

Francesco Tonelli

Everything at Eleven Madison Park is known by heart and handled with ease—from the name of each reservation to the dramatic presentation of a smoking cloche. In any other hands, this art deco dining room would be serious and heavy. Instead, find a careful study in continuous reinvention: lively yet never too busy; attentive yet never intrusive; minimal yet beautifully adorned; and clever yet never gimmicky.

Dining here is a unique city event with unexpected swirls of dinner theater. This singular experience is a fun, brave, and smart culmination of Chef Daniel Humm's uncompromising personality, technical excellence, and delicious whimsy that never cease to please.

The menu focuses on New York's classics with an imaginative twist. Think you know what a black-and-white cookie is? Think again. Here it may arrive as a savory combination of apple and cheddar. Roasted parsnips actually become more parsnippy, fragrant, and decadent when paired with banana purée and bacon jus. Maine lobster is perfectly poached and served with a grilled leek, blackened onion crumble, and bright dollops of leek and lime purées. To finish, come full circle with yet another sweeter take on the black-and-white.

15 East ❀

15 E. 15th St. (bet. Fifth Ave. & Union Sq. West)

Subway: 14 St - Union Sq
Phone: 212-647-0015
Web: www.15eastrestaurant.com
Prices: **$$$**

Lunch & dinner Mon – Sat

Manhattan ▶ Gramercy, Flatiron & Union Square

Michel Ann O'Malley

15 East is clearly dedicated to quality sushi. Unfamiliar with a certain fish? The personable chef is sure to remove a well-worn book from his shelf so guests may be better acquainted with the nuances of each morsel. The narrow room is modest, with bare wood tables, spotlights, and pops of color through glass portals displaying fish along the sushi counter.

The clientele is equally serious, though it may be comprised of self-proclaimed foodies and poseurs who come here regularly in an attempt to hold court. On those days, the solo diner can feel rushed and has every right to be annoyed. With luck, find yourself relaxing at the counter with nothing more to distract than the chef's sense of humor.

The menu format is not always clear, but the omakase is sure to focus on sushi and sashimi of extraordinary quality. Begin with the likes of amazingly tender octopus that has been "beaten" and braised in a soy-salt liquid. Highlights from the assorted sashimi selection have included utterly creamy toro, or seared *isaki* (grunt fish) that arrives crisp and smoky, alongside freshly grated wasabi. Sushi may reveal briefly marinated Japanese red snapper or scallops topped in shiso-yuzu salt.

Gramercy Tavern ✿

Contemporary ✕✕✕

B2

42 E. 20th St. (bet. Broadway & Park Ave. South)

Subway: 23 St (Park Ave. South)
Phone: 212-477-0777
Web: www.gramercytavern.com
Prices: $$$

Lunch Mon – Fri
Dinner nightly

Ellen Silverman

Cloaked in Americana and the scent of wood smoke, Gramercy Tavern is such an unspoiled rendition of old New York that were it not for the electric bulbs in the iron chandeliers, you might forget we are in the 21st century. The front "tavern" area is always pleasantly bustling and offers one of the city's premium options for solo dining at the bar. Period portraits, wood beams, and velvet curtains accent the series of smaller dining rooms, all staffed by expert yet very friendly servers.

From start to finish, this is a restaurant that bears a steady hand to excel with precision and finesse. Begin with a smooth and silky butternut squash soup, served with braised yet still snappy Brussels sprouts, tangy Granny Smith apple cubes, fresh chives, and enjoyable notes of subtle bitterness from toasted pumpkin seeds.

Perfectly seasonal standouts have shown moist and meaty duck breast set over parsnip purée, crushed hazelnuts, and Puy lentils. Composition and combination are paramount in the tarte Tatin, its flaky and marvelously buttery crust bearing caramelized apples topped with green apple *granite* and batons of fresh apple—the contrast of temperature and flavor offer a knockout finale.

Harding's

Contemporary 🍴🍴

 B2

32 E. 21st St. (bet. Broadway & Park Ave. South)

Subway: 23 St (Park Ave. South)
Phone: 212-600-2105
Web: www.hardingsnyc.com
Prices: $$

Lunch Mon – Fri
Dinner nightly

A bowl of cream-free plum tomato purée drizzled with thyme olive oil, partnered with a grilled cheddar cheese sandwich perfectly portrays Harding's comforting yet up-to-date appeal. Though recently opened, the lofty setting feels more yesteryear than tomorrow, with creaky wood planks underfoot, walls dressed with butter-yellow damask wallpaper, foxed mirror accents, and a giant American flag affixed to the exposed brick wall.

The kitchen keeps up the good work with a menu that includes the likes of a Waldorf salad dressed with blue-cheese buttermilk; or striped bass, slow-cooked then pan seared, plated with shaved planks of roasted fennel and foamy bacon essence. The deconstructed rendering of lemon meringue pie is a sweet and satisfying finish.

Hawkers

Asian 🍴

 B3

225 E. 14th St. (bet. Second & Third Aves.)

Subway: 14 St - Union Sq
Phone: 212-982-1688
Web: N/A
Prices: 💰💰

Lunch & dinner daily

Hawkers takes its cue from the open-air food stalls strutting local specialties that are customary throughout Southeast Asia. The slender room, embellished by a collection of silhouettes and street-theme graffiti art set against a bright red background, showcases a two-sided dining counter and a laid-back crew.

The menu is gently priced and serves up a variety of fresh and tasty snacks such as Thai sausage, chicken *satay* burger, and five-spice pork roll encased in a delicately crisp bean curd skin. Several fried rice and noodle preparations form the heart of Hawkers' offerings: the Maggi, named after a popular brand of instant noodles, features ramen served up as a fluffy stir-fry stocked with sliced tomato, egg, bean sprouts, and green onion.

Hill Country

Manhattan ▶ Gramercy, Flatiron & Union Square

A1

Barbecue ✗

30 W. 26th St. (bet. Broadway & Sixth Ave.)

Subway: 28 St (Broadway)　　　　　　　　　Lunch & dinner daily
Phone: 212-255-4544
Web: www.hillcountryny.com
Prices: $$

This Texas-size roadhouse has won over the hearts and stomachs of smoked brisket deprived New Yorkers. Always a rollicking good time, Hill Country's food stations, dispensing some of the city's best barbecue and country fare, set it above the booming competition.

Here, the crew behind the stoves have clearly honed their skills—successfully fueling Hill Country's massive smokers with cords of oak to recreate a truly Texan Hill Country experience. Grab Flintstone-size ribs by the pound, sausages by the link, stamp your meal ticket, and head to the trimmings counter for home-style sides. Then settle in for some live country music, making this a festive spot for groups and families.

Those seeking a more subdued setting can order takeout or delivery.

Hill Country Chicken

A1

American ✗

1123 Broadway (at 25th St.)

Subway: 23 St (Broadway)　　　　　　　　　Lunch & dinner daily
Phone: 212-257-6446
Web: www.hillcountrychicken.com
Prices:

The city's fried chicken rivalry has gotten more delicious with the arrival of Hill Country Chicken. Like its barbecue-themed sibling, Texas serves as the inspiration for this self-described chicken joint, which can accommodate up to 100 in a country kitchen-style space decked with sunny yellow and sky blue. Service involves lining up to order, but the crew is swift and friendly.

The first order of business is deciding on a variety of naturally raised chicken (classic or Mama El's rocking a skinless, cracker-crumb crust), but there's no wrong choice. Each piece is crunchy, juicy, and very flavorful.

Pimento cheese-topped mashed potatoes; biscuits baked on premises; and a slew of awesome pies prove that this haunt is much more than a one hit wonder.

108

I Trulli

Italian   XX

C1

122 E. 27th St. (bet. Lexington Ave. & Park Ave. South)

Subway: 28 St (Park Ave. South)
Phone: 212-481-7372
Web: www.itrulli.com
Prices: $$

Lunch Mon – Fri
Dinner nightly

I Trulli has been celebrating the wine and food of Southern Italy's Puglia region for the past two decades. From the roaring fireplace to the breezy outdoor garden, this place oozes warmth and the country-chic ambience is always comfortable. Wood furnishings, marble, and white tableclothes outfit the dining room, which is linked through a small hallway to a second dining room and the adjacent Enoteca. Service is engaging and pleasantly old school.

I Trulli takes pride in its pastas, made in-house and on full view in the open kitchen. Selections have included silken rounds of *ravioli d'Olivia* stuffed with ricotta cheese, cloaked in a creamy pistachio sauce. Entrées are appropriately rustic and might feature crispy fried rabbit or roasted chicken.

Jaiya

Thai   X

C1

396 Third Ave. (bet. 28th & 29th Sts.)

Subway: 28 St (Park Ave. South)
Phone: 212-889-1330
Web: www.jaiya.com
Prices:

Lunch Mon – Fri
Dinner nightly

This longstanding Thai jewel serves food worthy of its very fine reputation, thereby drawing a flood of loyal patrons who can be found socializing amid dark wood floors, padded beige walls, and contemporary furnishings. The extensive menu begins with fried appetizers—spring rolls, bean curd, *mee krob*—and follows with savory salads such as grilled eggplant *yum* served warm with baby corn and diced mushrooms, dressed with lime juice and chili.

Find an array of spicy, simmered specialties under the heading Curry Bar; and a trio of entrées listed under the Duck Walk. The tamarind duck reveals the de-boned, crisp-skinned meat, neatly hacked into bite-sized chunks atop bright and leafy greens, drizzled with a subtle, tamarind-based sweet-and-tart sauce.

Manhattan ▶ Gramercy, Flatiron & Union Square

The John Dory Oyster Bar

Seafood ✗

B1

1196 Broadway (at 29th St.)

Subway: 28 St (Broadway)
Phone: 212-792-9000
Web: www.thejohndory.com
Prices: $$

Lunch & dinner daily

Brought to you by Chef April Bloomfield and company, this oyster bar occupies a primo corner spot in the untouchably cool Ace Hotel. The style is vintage with aquatic accents: floor-to-ceiling windows flood the space with light, while black-tiled columns, copper tables, and crayon-bright green and blue bar stools complete the look.

The unpretentious and modern menu showcases impeccable seafood. An assortment from the raw bar might feature whelks with parsley and garlic butter; east and west-coast oysters shucked before your very eyes; and top quality shellfish with a lemon-and-shallot sauce. On the menu, find semolina soup with Nantucket bay scallops, or spicy Spanish mackerel with crunchy cilantro-squid crackers. Sadly, service can be indifferent.

La Mar

Peruvian ✗✗✗

B1

11 Madison Ave. (at 25th St.)

Subway: 23 St (Park Ave South)
Phone: 212-612-3388
Web: www.lamarcebicheria.com
Prices: $$$

Dinner Tue – Sat

Undaunted by the notorious challenge that New York City poses to imported chefs, regardless of pedigree, Peru's own celebrity chef and culinary ambassador, Gastón Acurio, brings his sunny specialties to the former home of Tabla. This grand space features a lounge pouring intoxicating pisco-based cocktails capped by a citron and turquoise-shaded dining room.

The kitchen, helmed by Chef Acurio's devoted deputy, presents pleasingly updated classics like bracing ceviches, as in the *nikei*, made with diced yellowfin tuna awash in tamarind-sparked *leche de tigre*. Entrées might feature the *tacu tacu a la pobre*—grilled hanger steak, crisped cake of rice and lima beans tinted with *aji amarillo*, quail egg, and fried plantain.

Junoon

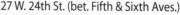

A1

Indian

27 W. 24th St. (bet. Fifth & Sixth Aves.)

Subway: 23 St (Sixth Ave.)
Phone: 212-490-2100
Web: www.junoonnyc.com
Prices: $$$

Lunch & dinner daily

Composition - B Productions

Lodged on a Flatiron block crowded with converted lofts and nighttime attractions, Junoon looms large with its dramatic façade clad in dark interwoven panels. The inside is enormous, impressive, and outfitted with a long counter and bar embellished with two antique *jhoolas* crafted from Burmese teak. Enter the dining room through a 200-year old wooden arch to find carved panels set in a reflecting pool and substantial tables covered in pale linens.

The staff may not be as calm and composed as the setting, but the contemporary Indian cooking does not falter. Turmeric-tinted *tandoori poussin* seasoned with yogurt, fenugreek, and cardamom is beautifully carved, spotted with bits of tasty char from the tandoor. The *Jaipuri bhindi* (deep-fried okra simmered in an appealing sauce of tomato, *amchoor*, and chilies) served with red Bhutanese rice is rightfully adored for its intense flavors and intriguing textures.

The kitchen's skill and ambition shines right through dessert with a very moist and slender cylinder of sticky date-fig *gateaux*—its restrained sweetness is a delicious complement to the swipe of thick caramel, clementine segments, and cinnamon ice cream nestled in black-sesame crumble.

Laut

Asian

15 E. 17th St. (bet. Broadway & Fifth Ave.)

Subway: 14 St - Union Sq
Phone: 212-206-8989
Web: www.lautnyc.com
Prices: $$

Lunch & dinner daily

Arrive early in the evening and the scene here may seem sleepy, but just wait. Sooner than you can say *asam laksa*, crowds will have descended upon this intimate and pretty space, tastefully decorated with the artwork of faraway lands. The ambience is always marked by revelry, as servers zip around with plates of tempting and succulent family-style Malaysian fare. Expect the likes of *mee hoon goring*—wok-fried thin rice noodles spicily sauced with tamarind and shrimp paste, stocked with bits of egg and crunchy vegetables, and sprinkled with fried shallots. Some dishes appear simple, but are deeply satisfying, as in crispy-skinned Hainanese chicken with a vibrant homemade chili-garlic sauce and rice steamed in chicken stock topped with gingerroot.

Les Halles

C1

French

411 Park Ave. South (bet. 28th & 29th Sts.)

Subway: 28 St (Park Ave. South)
Phone: 212-679-4111
Web: www.leshalles.net
Prices: $$

Lunch & dinner daily

Gramercy's long-lived, long-loved French brasserie never lets up—it's open all day and boisterous crowds are the rule, not the exception. Do as the regulars do and dig into luscious beef tartare prepared tableside; a steaming pot of mussels; gut-busting *cassoulet "Toulousain;"* and, of course, a heap of golden and crispy pomme frites. Stick to the classics and you're in for an enjoyable experience.

Known as home base to celebrity Chef-at-large Anthony Bourdain, well-known for his recent bestseller *Medium Raw* and numerous television gigs, the room is dressed in dark tones. Expect carved wood accents, leather banquettes, and checkerboard terrazzo floors that combine to produce an atmospheric room which looks dusky even on the sunniest afternoon.

Maialino

✗✗

B2

2 Lexington Ave. (at 21st St.)

Subway: 23 St (Park Ave South)
Phone: 212-777-2410
Web: www.maialinonyc.com
Prices: $$

Lunch & dinner daily

Danny Meyer's reworking of the Gramercy Park Hotel's dining venue has rendered a chicly casual Italian spot with a rustic theme conceived by the Rockwell Group. Accessed by a separate street entrance, the expanse up front is bright and lively with plenty of counter seating at the bar; while the back area, with its glossy dark wood accents, is furnished with tables dressed in blue-and-white checked tablecloths.

An alumnus of Babbo and Gramercy Tavern rules the kitchen; and the Roman trattoria menu offers a selection of salami and *antipasti*. This is followed by pastas symbolic of the region such as an excellent *tonnarelli cacio e pepe*, and a short list of hearty *secondi* that includes crispy fried suckling pig's foot with braised lentils.

Manzanilla

✗✗

B1

345 Park Ave. South (entrance on 26th St.)

Subway: 28 St (Park Ave. South)
Phone: 212-255-4086
Web: www.manzanillanyc.com
Prices: $$$

Lunch Mon – Fri
Dinner Mon – Sat

Manzanilla hits the Big Apple courtesy of famed Chef Dani García of Calima in Marbella, and Yann de Rochefort of New York City's own Boqueria. A zigzag tiled floor, open kitchen, and dressy crowd make this Iberian brasserie feel enjoyably kinetic.

Chef García's trusted lieutenant guides the team in combining classic flavors and contemporary presentations of dishes that extend well beyond tapas. Expect pretty compositions like salt- and citrus-cured sea scallops, cool and silken, with spoonfuls of *ajo blanco*—a rich purée of garlic and almonds—plated with grapes and crisped Serrano ham for sweet and salty notes. The slow-cooked suckling pig is crisp-skinned, tender, and wonderfully mellow, served with sautéed squash and escarole.

Manzo

200 Fifth Ave. (at 23rd St.)

Subway: 23 St (Broadway)   Lunch & dinner daily
Phone: 212-229-2180
Web: www.eataly.com
Prices: $$$

Eataly New York (brought to you by Mario Batali and friends) is a perpetually bustling emporium brimming with Italian products. The rollicking scene rarely lets up and navigating through the hordes of visitors entranced by the sights and scents of the abundance on offer may prove to be overwhelming for some.

For sit down dining, steer yourself straight toward Manzo, tucked away from the fray. "Beef" in Italian, Manzo offers a meaty take on Italian. Pastas are numerous and impressively prepared; and the weekday lunch prix-fixe is highly recommended—baby artichokes with plump cranberry beans; charred New York strip with Barbaresco vinaigrette; and silken vanilla panna cotta. Pair your meal with a pour from the comprehensive wine selection.

Mari Vanna

41 E. 20th St. (bet. Broadway & Park Ave. South)

Subway: 23 St (Park Ave South)   Lunch & dinner daily
Phone: 212-777-1955
Web: www.marivanna.ru/ny
Prices: $$

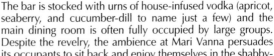

The bar is stocked with urns of house-infused vodka (apricot, seaberry, and cucumber-dill to name just a few) and the main dining room is often fully occupied by large groups. Despite the revelry, the ambience at Mari Vanna persuades its occupants to sit back and enjoy themselves in the shabby-chic room, done in a bleached palette complemented by embroidered seat backs and glowing chandeliers.

Traditional Russian specialties abound with an Olivier salad, *salo* (house-smoked fatback), borscht, and plump *pelmeni* with herbed butter and sour cream. The kitchen's serious effort shines through in entrées like *golubtzi*, featuring two neat bundles of braised cabbage stuffed with fragrant ground beef and rice, then draped with a lush coat of tomato cream.

Maysville

A1 American ✗✗

17 W. 26th St. (bet. Broadway & Sixth Ave.)

Subway: 23 St (Sixth Ave.)
Phone: 646-490-8240
Web: www.maysvillenyc.com
Prices: $$

Lunch & dinner daily

Manhattan now has a Bourbon temple to call its own with Sean Joseph's offshoot of Brooklyn's beloved Char No. 4. Named after the Kentucky port town and birthplace of Bourbon, Maysville tends to exceed expectations in its catalog of American whiskey.

The amber-hued room is sure to sooth any Manhattanite starting to feel culturally overshadowed by that borough across the river. Inside, find a long bar, triptych of charcoal horse sketches, and skilled team led by an ex-Gramercy Tavern sous-chef preparing Southern food. Appetizers are quite interesting as in cubes of crispy grits nestled in Bourbon aïoli and topped with ruffles of salty country ham; or fried, black pepper-flecked veal sweetbreads plated with capers, fingerlings, and fennel.

Mesa Grill

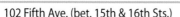

A2 Southwestern ✗✗

102 Fifth Ave. (bet. 15th & 16th Sts.)

Subway: 14 St - Union Sq
Phone: 212-807-7400
Web: www.mesagrill.com
Prices: $$$

Lunch & dinner daily

Responsible for launching Chef Bobby Flay to cookbook and Food Network stardom, Mesa Grill still buzzes nightly even after more than two decades of service—a particularly impressive achievement in this fickle city. The lofty room, colored with Southwest accents, sees its share of tourists hoping to catch a glimpse of the famous celebrity chef and native Manhattanite; but even if the chef is absent, a glass-walled kitchen entertains with views of his team putting a creative spin on Southwest cuisine.

Flay's trademark style results in a solid menu of vibrant preparations that can include a roasted garlic shrimp tamale; grilled mahi mahi with refreshing pineapple-and-onion salsa alongside creamy roasted poblano rice; or a moist, toasted-coconut layer cake.

Molly's Pub & Shebeen

C2

287 Third Ave. (bet. 22nd & 23rd Sts.)

Subway: 23 St (Park Ave. South)   Lunch & dinner daily
Phone: 212-889-3361
Web: www.mollysshebeen.com
Prices: 🅖🅖

A stop at Molly's Pub & Shebeen isn't just for celebrating St. Patrick's Day-style revelry the remaining 364 days of the year. The utterly charming setting, friendly service, and heartwarming fare make it much more than the standard Irish watering hole. First established in 1895, this framework has had various incarnations but has been sating a loyal following since 1964. Wood smoke perfumes the air, rustic furnishings are arranged on a sawdust-covered floor, and a seat at the original mahogany bar couldn't be more welcoming. The ambience of this pub (or *shebeen*, which is an illicit drinking establishment) has few peers.

Stick with the list of house specialties (lamb stew, corned beef and cabbage, and Shepherd's pie) for an authentic experience.

Momokawa 😎

C1

157 E. 28th St. (bet. Lexington & Third Aves.)

Subway: 28 St (Park Ave. South)   Lunch & dinner daily
Phone: 212-684-7830
Web: www.momokawanyc.com
Prices: $$

Fans of Japanese cuisine will cheer at the authenticity of the expansive menu served at this impressive charmer. The location may come as a surprise, tucked away on a busy Curry Hill block, but the sparsely decorated small room is reminiscent of the type of place Tokyo salarymen might frequent for drinks and a delicious bite before the long commute home.

You can opt for one of their set menus (either the $60 prix-fixe or $55 seasonal course menu) or go for the à la carte affair kicking things off with traditional appetizers such as miso eggplant, or soy-marinated rice cake. From there sashimi follows; and then cooked items like simmered beef with daikon, fried sardines with shishito peppers, and beef sukiyaki make for a lovely finish.

NoMad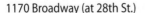

Contemporary 🍴🍴🍴

B1

1170 Broadway (at 28th St.)

Subway: 28 St (Broadway)
Phone: 347-472-5660
Web: www.thenomadhotel.com
Prices: $$$

Lunch & dinner daily

The NoMad

Chef Daniel Humm and Will Guidara have brought their Midas touch to this fashionable dining room set in the boutique hotel of the same name. Built over a century ago, this prime Beaux-Arts specimen has been luxuriously interpreted by noted designer Jacques Garcia to serve as a series of spaces, each with its own character and unique ambience. The atrium is bright and relaxed; the Fireplace room is cozy with its hearth salvaged from a French château; and the regal Parlour is framed by dark oak, claret velvet, and walls lined with pressed herbs.

NoMad's kitchen is doing some astonishing work, producing a range of elegant à la carte creations with their own, singular edge. Snacks to nibble on include a stylish platter of crudité with refreshing chive crème fraîche for dipping; or sweetbreads *en croustillant*. Vegetable dishes are sure to impress, as in roasted broccoli "steaks" seasoned with Mediterranean spices that bring tremendous flavor and heft. Heartier choices include a pressed block of suckling pig confit adorned with cherries and bacon marmalade.

For dessert, the *kouign amann*—a traditional Breton cake utilizing an epic amount of butter—is a standout indulgence when available.

117

Novitá

B2

Italian 🍴🍴

102 E. 22nd St. (bet. Lexington Ave. & Park Ave. South)

Subway: 23 St (Park Ave South)
Phone: 212-677-2222
Web: www.novitanyc.com
Prices: $$

Lunch Mon – Fri
Dinner nightly

This delightfully unpretentious trattoria is located on the ground floor of an art deco residential building that dates back to 1928. Novita may have only opened in 1994, but elegant touches honor its tony Gramercy locale, with flowers dressing up the interior and canvas umbrella-topped tables outside. The dining room combines large, bright windows with pale yellow walls and a warm, autumnal-hued banquette. The staff's air of friendly formality suits the room. Enjoyable house-made pasta might feature *strozzapreti* tossed in fragrant basil pesto. Equally pleasing is a salad of *rucola*, avocado, and warm calamari. Other options include entrées like the black pepper-crusted tuna with lemon sauce, or a bittersweet chocolate speckled semifreddo for dessert.

Olives

B3

Contemporary 🍴🍴

201 Park Ave. South (at 17th St.)

Subway: 14 St - Union Sq
Phone: 212-353-8345
Web: www.olivesnewyork.com
Prices: $$$

Lunch & dinner daily

Todd English's Olives has much to celebrate with its refreshed look. A discernable revamp infused this decade-plus-old dining room at the W Union Square with a more relaxed, current, and carefree manner that expertly unites drinks and dining. A wealth of dark wood complements caramel leather booths, while the marble-fronted open kitchen is attractively set with a wood-burning oven. A communal dining nook sits across the kitchen and looks upon gleaming plate glass windows.

The enterprising chef's brand of interpretive Mediterranean cuisine remains the menu's trademark in items such as diver scallop crudo dressed with segments of crimson grapefruit, slivered red chili, and shaved fennel; and *tagliatelle* draped with a savory, slow-cooked rabbit-and-porcini ragù.

Ootoya

Japanese ✗✗

A2

8 W. 18th St. (bet. Fifth & Sixth Aves.)

Subway: 14 St (Sixth Ave.)   Lunch & dinner daily
Phone: 212-255-0018
Web: www.ootoya.us
Prices: $$

Welcome to this first stateside location of a Tokyo-based chain with more than 300 outlets throughout Asia. A slender dining counter dominates the back section of the rectangular space that also offers table service and a mezzanine seating area. The attractive minimalist design and gracious staff put aside any fears of chain-dining.

Ootoya's angle on Japanese cuisine is hearty portions of comforting *yoshoku*-style (Western-influenced) preparations such as grilled washu beef burger with demi-glace; pork loin *katsu*; and house-made curry sauce. The *teishoku* (set meal) is a fine lunchtime option, especially when it features hefty morsels of excellent quality, deep-fried *buta kurozu* pork dabbed in sweet-and-sour sauce made from aged rice vinegar.

Periyali

Greek ✗✗

A2

35 W. 20th St. (bet. Fifth & Sixth Aves.)

Subway: 23 St (Sixth Ave.)   Lunch Mon – Fri
Phone: 212-463-7890   Dinner nightly
Web: www.periyali.com
Prices: $$$

Bright, airy, and standing strong for over twenty years, Periyali has maintained not only its popularity but a high standard of cuisine and service—quite a feat in NYC. The tranquil, fresh space evokes the Mediterranean with whitewashed walls, colorful banquettes, and billowing white fabric draped across the ceiling. Natural light floods the breezy atmosphere.

Starters include the likes of *fava kremidaki*, an outstanding blend of puréed fava beans with red onion, lemon, and aromatic olive oil. The fantastic rabbit stew (*kouneli stifado*) is served spoon-tender in thick and rich tomato gravy, with perfect little white pearl onions.

Dessert cookies may be honey-drenched and sprinkled with walnuts, little nut-filled cigars, or almond-rich baklava.

Pure Food and Wine

Vegan XX

54 Irving Pl. (bet. 17th & 18th Sts.)

Subway: 14 St - Union Sq

Lunch & dinner daily

Phone: 212-477-1010

Web: www.purefoodandwine.com

Prices: $$

Pure Food and Wine applies upscale sophistication to the conceit of raw cooking. Run by owner Sarma Melngailis, who has positioned herself as a high priestess of the raw movement in this city—with her juice bar/takeout shop, cookbooks, and continuous Twitter posts—a meal here is sure to put the glow back in your cheeks.

To preserve vitamins, enzymes, minerals, and flavors in the food, nothing is heated above 118°F. Despite these constraints, the "cooking" is undoubtedly tempting. These delights include a spicy sesame salad, a slaw of cold-hardy vegetables sprinkled with ground cashew crunch and sparked by wasabi aïoli; or the classic zucchini- and tomato-lasagna, layered with basil-pistachio pesto and dairy-free macadamia nut and pumpkin seed ricotta.

Resto

Contemporary X

111 E. 29th St. (bet. Lexington Ave. & Park Ave. South)

Subway: 28 St (Park Ave. South)

Lunch & dinner daily

Phone: 212-685-5585

Web: www.restonyc.com

Prices: $$

At Resto, the friendly staff is attired in quirky tees flaunting the motto, "Bringing fat back." This heart-on-the-sleeve mentality is utterly appropriate for a menu that proves its nose-to-tail ethos with dishes that have included a wildly flavorful pig's head Cuban sandwich, veal belly gyro, and crispy pig's ear salad. Though the cooking is best described as contemporary, there is a distinct Belgian vibe here, as in *moules frites* paired with an array of flavor-spiked mayonnaise; and Liege waffles flecked with crunchy sugar.

The dining room's gleaming appointments—a marble bar, pressed-tin ceiling, and metal chairs—beckon to a steady stream of residents.

Cannibal, an offshoot next door, also boasts an array of meaty treats washed down by global brews.

Rye House

American

11 W. 17 St. (bet. Fifth & Sixth Aves.)

Subway: 14 St (Sixth Ave.)   Lunch & dinner daily
Phone: 212-255-7260
Web: www.ryehousenyc.com
Prices: $$

As its name would suggest, Rye House offers a tavern-inspired look and easygoing vibe fueled by an impressive selection of amber liquor. The front bar provides a comfortable seat from which to sip a mint julep or single-malt Scotch, but those who wish to dine sacrifice the bar's ambience for the back area's greater comfort and enjoy the kitchen's concise and enjoyably prepared selection of playful pub grub.

The small plate offerings include the likes of crunchy and well-seasoned fried dill pickle slices, Sloppy Joe sliders, and drunken mussels bathed in Belgian-style ale. The list of entrées may be short but items such as roasted chicken dressed with spoonbread, braised greens, and buttermilk-enriched jus prove this is food to be savored.

Saravanaas

C2

Indian

81 Lexington Ave. (at 26th St.)

Subway: 28 St (Park Ave. South)   Lunch & dinner daily
Phone: 212-679-0204
Web: www.saravanabhavan.com
Prices:

With its corner location and attractive two-room setting, Saravanaas emerges from the Curry Hill crowd. The brightly lit room is set with lacquered tables and high-backed ivory upholstered chairs that seem a far cry from the taxi driver cafeterias dotting this strip of Lexington.

The reason this beloved Gramercy location is forever bustling with locals and tourists alike is for vegetarian food that is as good as it is serious, with a wide array of specialties, curries, breads, and weekend-only biryani on offer. However, table-long *dosas*, paired with a plethora of chutneys (think coconut and chili) and fiery *sambar* are *the* main attraction. Don't miss the *aloo paratha*: this butter-drenched, puffy flatbread filled with spiced potatoes is excellent.

Manhattan ▶ Gramercy, Flatiron & Union Square

SD26

B1

Italian ✕✕

19 E. 26th St. (bet. Fifth & Madison Aves.)

Subway: 28 St (Park Ave. South)
Phone: 212-265-5959
Web: www.sd26ny.com
Prices: $$

Lunch Mon – Fri
Dinner nightly

This regional Italian restaurant formerly known as San Domenico now inhabits a 14,000 square foot dining hall replete with a crowd-pleasing array of features—a wine bar, generously sized lounge area, multiple dining rooms, open kitchen, and jumbo *salumeria* station.

The offerings are as wide-ranging as the space, with good value found at both the lunch prix-fixe and small plates served at the wine bar. Given the size and scope of SD26, the service can sometimes flounder but here are three reasons that prove the kitchen gets it right: silky strands of whole wheat fettucine dressed with luscious wild boar ragout; braised beef cheeks, melt-in-your-mouth tender, paired with a dollop of white polenta; and a lovely *baba* with sweet, juicy orange sauce.

Singapura

C1

Asian ✕

106 Lexington Ave. (bet. 27th & 28th Sts.)

Subway: 28 St (Park Ave. South)
Phone: 212-684-6842
Web: www.singapuranyc.com
Prices:

Lunch & dinner daily

Diners craving a dose of spice eagerly fill up this Curry Hill establishment for a taste of something different. Singapura's colorful and decorative accents along with its warm, hospitable spirit give the slender setting a cheerful countenance.

More *sambal* than masala, the emphasis here is on Southeast Asian flavors, particularly Singapore, Malaysia, and Thailand, with some Hakka Chinese specialties thrown in for good measure. *Chili paneer*, cubes of semi-firm cow's milk cheese sautéed with a piquant blend of fried onion, scallions, green chilies, garlic, and lemongrass make for an apt starting point; while heartier plates of *sarawak sambal udang*, shrimp cooked in a tempting mélange of chillies, *belacan*, ginger, and coconut cream are very gratifying.

Tamarind

Indian XXX

B2

41-43 E. 22nd St. (bet. Broadway & Park Ave. South)

Subway: 23 St (Park Ave. South)   Lunch & dinner daily
Phone: 212-674-7400
Web: www.tamarindrestaurantsnyc.com
Prices: $$$

Easy to find on a quiet street, this Indian gem is immediately warm and welcoming. Inside, pass through the long attractive bar, beyond the windowed views into the pristine tandoor kitchen, to arrive in a comfortably elegant dining room. Here, the mood is serene and contemporary, fashioned with marble floors, gleaming skylights, a wrought-iron wall, and regal yet urbane mahogany booths. The clientele is lively and grown-up (no children under five are permitted).

From the menu, each course seems to outdo the next, starting with the exquisitely crisp *lahsani gobi* tossed in a delicious garlic sauce, to lamb *pasanda* in a rich cashew-saffron gravy. *Malai* halibut in a coconut-ginger broth shows terrific skill and pairs superbly with fragrant lemon rice.

Tamba

Indian X

C1

103 Lexington Ave. (bet. 27th & 28th Sts.)

Subway: 28 St (Park Ave. South)   Lunch & dinner daily
Phone: 212-481-9100
Web: www.tambagrillandbar.com
Prices: $$

Slow down in Curry Hill—Tamba is that cozy, sprightly spot one might easily pass, and miss the chance for excellent, wallet-friendly Indian cuisine, as well as great service that soars above other nearby *desi* diners.

Hindi for copper, Tamba showcases Indian delicacies as glorious and gleaming as the copper vessels that carry them. Leaving aside the insanely popular, inexpensive lunch buffet, true gourmands know to branch out and explore the extensive menu of Northern and Southern Indian specialties. From the tandoor oven comes succulent plates like *haryali tikka*—boneless pieces of chicken marinated with mint and coriander. The raita is made with the kitchen's own house yogurt; and Tamba's lemon rice is so popular it deserves its own Facebook page.

Tocqueville

A3

Contemporary ✗✗

1 E. 15th St. (bet. Fifth Ave. & Union Sq. West)

Subway: 14 St - Union Sq
Phone: 212-647-1515
Web: www.tocquevillerestaurant.com
Prices: $$

Lunch Mon – Sat
Dinner nightly

Lovingly run by proprietors Chef Marco Moreira and his wife Jo-Ann Makovitzky since 2000, Tocqueville offers a creative and decidedly upscale approach to seasonal cuisine. The stately dining room, bedecked with starched, linen-draped tables, dove grey furnishings, and butterscotch walls, sits just a block away from the Union Square Greenmarket.

This advantageous locale persuades the skilled kitchen to reveal a bounty of delightful fare that might begin with warm brioche and butter (both house-made). Meals go on to include smooth and zesty tomato soup, elegantly poured tableside over a morsel of fried ricotta; or roasted baby pumpkin risotto with pan-seared wild mushrooms and toasted pumpkin seeds.

Lunch offers particularly good value.

Turkish Kitchen ☺

C1

Turkish ✗✗

386 Third Ave. (bet. 27th & 28th Sts.)

Subway: 28 St (Park Ave. South)
Phone: 212-679-6633
Web: www.turkishkitchen.com
Prices: ☜☜

Lunch Sun – Fri
Dinner nightly

Long heralded for its tasty cuisine and good value, Turkish Kitchen is a jewel-toned mainstay boasting a lively scene and attentive service staff ready to walk newcomers through the extensive offerings. The wide array of appetizers is best tackled with the help of friends, whether starting with vine leaves stuffed with rice, pine nuts, and black currants; house-made yogurt with cucumber, mint, and dill; or phyllo scrolls stuffed with feta.

However, the four course prix-fixe at lunch is a perfectly proportioned and well-priced weekday indulgence. Expect the likes of cool and crisp sheperd's salad; a smear of roasted eggplant with warm flatbread; cabbage stuffed with rice and ground beef; and honey-drizzled semolina cake to end this sumptuous spread.

Union Square Cafe

A2

American ✗✗

21 E. 16th St. (bet. Fifth Ave. & Union Sq. West)

Subway: 14 St - Union Sq   Lunch & dinner daily
Phone: 212-243-4020
Web: www.unionsquarecafe.com
Prices: $$$

This revered dining institution lies in the heart of widely trafficked Union Square. An elder member of the renowned Danny Meyer culinary family, the Cafe is well-loved, never outdated, and does not disappoint. From the warm service to the distinct spaces that feel bright, sunny, and even romantic across the downstairs and mezzanine levels, everything here seems smoother with the years.

The merry bar is as locally cherished as the room's vivid murals and city icons demolishing a yellowfin burger glossed with ginger-mustard. Dining here becomes even more enjoyable over plates of chili-soy-glazed pork belly with tender cuttlefish; a perfectly cooked NY strip with bone marrow mashed potatoes; or sweet, crusty pear dumplings in huckleberry compote.

Veritas

B2

American ✗✗

43 E. 20th St. (bet. Broadway & Park Ave. South)

Subway: 23 St (Park Ave. South)   Dinner Mon – Sat
Phone: 212-353-3700
Web: www.veritas-nyc.com
Prices: $$$

This sophisticated setting is the domain of Chef Sam Hazen where fine cooking is accentuated by a selection of vintages to please any oenophile. The chef isn't shy about venturing out from the back of house; he's often seen chatting with guests and lording over the service team.

Favored by an urbane set, the warm and elegant space is anchored by a lively bar, whitewashed brick walls accented with cork patchwork, and ebony-stained tables. Examples of the chef's wine-friendly cuisine include raw oysters cradling a lightly warmed combination of grilled lemon and diced tomato; grilled beef filet with roasted wild mushrooms, cipollini onions candied in port, and finely grated Roquefort; or apple confit with hot cider and a quenelle of maple ice cream.

Greenwich, West Village & Meatpacking District

Artistic, poetic, and edgy: these ideals are the Village's identity. Thank the Beat Generation for this, because sixty years later, many still seek out this neighborhood for its beloved street cafés brimming with struggling artists, philosophical meanderings, and revolutionary convictions. Perhaps due to the prominence of New York University, local residents still embrace the liberal, intellectual, and bohemian spirit that, in many ways, is the heart of this city. Nevertheless, the belly of this area is equally worthy of attention and praise; even the humble **Peanut Butter and Co. Sandwich Shop** flaunts its creative side with peanut-buttery concoctions like the Elvis, which is grilled with bananas and honey (bacon is optional). Or, pick up a jar to-go, flavored with the likes of maple syrup, white chocolate, and chili powder. Steps away, **Mamoun's** has been feeding NYU students some of the best falafel in town for generations; topping one with their killer hot sauce is a must. In Washington Square Park, savvy students and foodies stand shoulder-to-shoulder in line for **N.Y. Dosas**, delicate and comforting rice- and lentil-flour crêpes, served with character and flair. Peer into the assortment of old-time Italian bakeries and shops along Bleecker Street, where **Faicco's Pork Store** has been offering its specialties for

over 100 years. Take home a sampling of their fresh and perfectly seasoned sausages or a tray of *arancini* (fried rice balls), though etiquette dictates that one must be eaten warm, before leaving the store. Yet the neighborhood's most noteworthy storefront may be **Murray's Cheese Shop**. This is Manhattan's definitive cheesemonger, run by a deeply informed service staff, happy to initiate hungry neophytes into the art and understanding of their countless varieties (enthusiasts note that classes are also available, exploring the meaning of terroir or cheese-pairing fundamentals).

If seeking a more lowbrow spot, try **Dirty Bird To Go** for its sinfully fried or rotisserie chicken. Rest assured that these birds are locally sourced from an Amish farm, and are free-range, vegetarian-fed, and antibiotic free—all necessary qualifications for any self-respecting takeout joint in downtown bohemia. Of course, no Village jaunt is complete without pizza with some of the finest to be found coal-fired and crisp, only by the pie, at **John's of Bleecker Street**. For a quick slice, stop by **Joe's**, another local institution, for their traditional and blistery thin-crust selections. A visit to **Cones** is equally enticing, where uniquely textured Argentine ice cream is available in both expected and unforeseen flavor combinations.

WEST VILLAGE

For a nearly royal treat, stop by **Tea & Sympathy**, offering tea-time snacks or full Sunday dinners comprised of roast beef and Yorkshire pudding. The storefront also sells prized English wares, ranging from teas to pots to jars of clotted cream. No matter where you grab your picnic, one of the best places to enjoy it is Hudson River Park, watching the urban vista of roller skaters and marathoners. Pier 45 is a particularly lovely spot, at the end of Christopher Street, across the Westside Highway. A stone's throw from here is **Il Cantuccio**, a boutique Tuscan bakery that boasts a regional variant of biscotti from Prato.

The influential James Beard Foundation sits in the historic 12th Street townhouse that was once home to the illustrious food writer. While strolling back through chic boutiques and camera-ready brownstones, peek down quaint Perry Street for yet another *very* NY moment: a glimpse at where Carrie Bradshaw (of *Sex and the City*) "lived." For a quick but excellent bite, be sure to stop in at **Taïm** for killer falafels and refreshing smoothies. Then, let the overpowering aromas of butter and sugar lead you to the original **Magnolia Bakery,** the Village's official date night finale. Another sweet spot is **Li-Lac**, dispensing chocolate-covered treats and nostalgic confections since 1923. In the vein of baked treats, **Landbrot**, a sleek German bakery, is hugely beloved for its bratwurst, schnitzel, and strudel.

Late night revelers love the eats at **Rusty Knot**, a "bar's bar" that strives to embody everything a cheap beer and retro juke hope to effuse. Kick back and grab some po' boys or pickled eggs to go with that pint. For a more refined nocturnal scene, expert mixologists can be found creatively pouring "long drinks and fancy cocktails" at the hip and exclusive **Employees Only**. Likewise, bartenders approach celebrity status at **Little Branch**, where an encyclopedic understanding of the craft brings dizzying and delectable results.

MEATPACKING DISTRICT

Further north is the trendy Meatpacking District. Just two decades ago, its cobblestoned streets were so desolate that only the savviest Manhattanites knew that its empty warehouses held the city's edgiest clubs and restaurants. Young hipsters take note: the Meatpacking District has already arrived—repopulated with sleekly designed lounges serving pricey cocktails to the fashionable minions, almost as if in defiance of these cautious times. Luxury hotels have risen, and storied bistros so infamously festive that they once defined the neighborhood have fallen. Completing the picture is the High Line, an abandoned 1934 elevated railway that is now a 19-block-long park. The Standard hotel is the High Line's social hub. In the summer, indulge in beer and sausages at the ever-popular **Biergarten**; and during cooler months, linger at open-air café, **Standard Plaza**, which gets transformed into an ice skating rink.

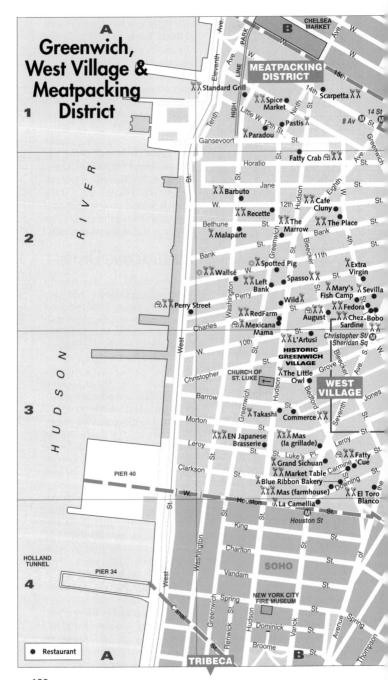

Greenwich, West Village & Meatpacking District

A / **B**

CHELSEA MARKET

MEATPACKING DISTRICT

Standard Grill
Spice Market
Scarpetta
Pastis
Paradou
Gansevoort St.
Fatty Crab
Horatio
Jane
Barbuto
Cafe Cluny
Recette
The Marrow
The Place
Bethune St.
Malaparte
Bank
Spotted Pig
Extra Virgin
Wallsé
Left Bank
Spasso
Mary's Fish Camp
Sevilla
Perry Street
Wild
Fedora
RedFarm
August
Chez Bobo Sardine
Mexicana Mama
L'Artusi
Christopher St / Sheridan Sq

HISTORIC GREENWICH VILLAGE

The Little Owl
WEST VILLAGE
CHURCH OF ST. LUKE
Takashi
Commerce
EN Japanese Brasserie
Mas (la grillade)
Grand Sichuan
Fatty 'Cue
Market Table
Blue Ribbon Bakery
Mas (farmhouse)
El Toro Blanco
La Camellia
Houston St

PIER 40

HUDSON RIVER

SOHO

HOLLAND TUNNEL
PIER 34

NEW YORK CITY FIRE MUSEUM

Spring
Charlton
Vandam
Dominick
Broome

TRIBECA

● Restaurant

A / **B**

128

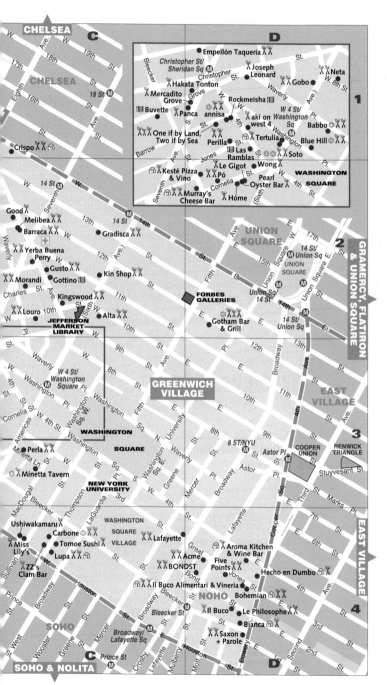

CHELSEA **C** **D**

19th St.

18th St.

*Christopher St/
Sheridan Sq* Ⓜ

X Empellón Taqueria X X

X Joseph
Leonard

X X Gobo

X X Neta

W. 8th St.

X Hakata Tonton

X Mercadito
Grove

🏛 Buvette X Panca

Rockmeisha 🏛

X X X
annisa

aki on
west 4

W. 4th
Washington
Sq

X X Babbo

X X X One if by Land,
Two if by Sea

X Perilla

X Tertulia

Blue Hill X X

X Las
Ramblas

X Soto

**WASHINGTON
SQUARE**

🏛 Kesté Pizza
& Vino

X Le Gigot
X Pó

X Wong

Pearl
Oyster Bar X

X Murray's
Cheese Bar

X Home

Crispo X X

Good X

X Melibea X X

X Barraca X X

X X Yerba Buena
Perry

X Gradisca X X

14 St. Ⓜ

**UNION
SQUARE**

14 St/
Ⓜ Union Sq

**UNION
SQUARE**

X X Gusto X X

X Gottino 🏛

X Kin Shop X X

X X Morandi

X X Louro

Kingswood X X

X Alta X X

**JEFFERSON
MARKET
LIBRARY**

**FORBES
GALLERIES**

🏛 X X X
Gotham Bar
& Grill

14 St/
Union Sq

Ⓜ

14 St/
Union Sq

**GREENWICH
VILLAGE**

**EAST
VILLAGE**

W 4 St/
Washington
Square Pl

8 St/NYU Ⓜ

Astor Pl

**COOPER
UNION**

**RENWICK
TRIANGLE**

**WASHINGTON
SQUARE**

X Perla X X

🏛 X Minetta Tavern

Stuyvesant St.

St. Marks Pl.

**NEW YORK
UNIVERSITY**

**EAST
VILLAGE**

Ushiwakamaru X

X Miss
Lily's

Carbone 🏛 X X

Tomoe Sushi X

Lupa X X

**WASHINGTON
SQUARE
VILLAGE**

X X Lafayette

X X Acme

X X BONDST

🏛 X Aroma Kitchen
& Wine Bar

Five
Points X X

X ZZ's
Clam Bar

🏛 X Il Buco Alimentari & Vineria

Hecho en Dumbo 🏛 X

NOHO

Bohemian 🏛 X X

X Il Buco

Le Philosophe X X

SOHO

Bianca 🏛 X

X X Saxon
+ Parole

Broadway/
Lafayette Sq Ⓜ

C Prince St Ⓜ

SOHO & NOLITA **D**

Acme

Contemporary XX

D4

9 Great Jones St. (bet. Broadway & Lafayette St.)

Subway: Broadway - Lafayette St
Phone: 212-203-2121
Web: www.acmenyc.com
Prices: $$

Lunch Sat – Sun
Dinner nightly

Acme may as well mean "hot spot" in Danish, thanks to Chef Mads Refslund (of Noma) and his seasoned partners. The long front bar is ever-packed and neatly lined with liquor bottles. The wonderfully weathered yet chic arena features head-scratching colors and beguiling flavors.

The cooks display such dedication to seasonal products and you will leave convinced that the chef incited the locavore movement. Expect to find grains cooked risotto-style and enriched with Gruyère and wild mushrooms. If the chocolate ganache verges on disappointing, then ditch it in favor of more savory treats like richly flavored mackerel, salt-cured and cooked rare, accompanied by a bouquet of grilled lettuces drizzled with horseradish-spiked buttermilk.

aki on west 4

Japanese X

D1

181 W. 4th St. (bet. Barrow & Jones Sts.)

Subway: W 4 St - Wash Sq
Phone: 212-989-5440
Web: N/A
Prices: $$

Dinner nightly

Set in a red-brick row house, aki's tiny dining room feels like an intimate parlor. Add to this a warm, polite staff presenting a menu that displays a distinct personality, and it is easy to see why this spot continues to attract a loyal following.

Chef/owner Siggy Nakanishi once served as private chef to the Japanese Ambassador to Jamaica and his menu reflects a sweet and sunny personality. Daily specials are presented as a tabletop photo display; the chef's menu offers a selection of creative preparations that may include the eel napoleon appetizer composed of panko-crusted tofu, delicate eel tempura, and pumpkin purée. Other dishes highlight finely prepared sushi as in the Jamaica roll, stuffed with jerk chicken and hearts of palm, of course.

Alta

 C2

Contemporary

64 W. 10th St (bet. Fifth & Sixth Aves.)

Subway: Christopher St - Sheridan Sq   Dinner nightly
Phone: 212-505-7777
Web: www.altarestaurant.com
Prices: $$

Rusticity reinvented is the order of business at this packed tapas den. Here, you'll need to squeeze your way past the sangria- and rosé-dispensing bar to reach the felicitous back dining room decked with exposed brick, antique Moorish floors, and a wood-burning fireplace.

Alta's nimble kitchen churns out a parade of tastes with a thoroughly creative and contemporary spirit. There's grilled house-made merguez dressed with Lilliputian falafel, gelled red wine, and *lebne*; cavatelli sauced with celery root cream, a dab of wild boar ragù, and Parmesan crumbs; or grape leaves wrapped around jasmine rice and chicken confit with grape molasses. Bronzed apple confit with crushed pralines and vanilla bean ice cream is one among their many divine desserts.

Aroma Kitchen & Wine Bar

D4

Italian

36 E. 4th St. (bet. Bowery & Lafayette St.)

Subway: Bleecker St   Dinner nightly
Phone: 212-375-0100
Web: www.aromanyc.com
Prices: $$

Aroma Kitchen & Wine Bar is a welcoming spot that radiates an amiable vibe from its edge of the Village, thanks to co-owners Alexandra Degiorgio and Vito Polosa. Simple, warm, and rustic, the intimate room's focal point is its dark wood dining counter. On a warm, sunny day, the space opens to provide additional sidewalk seating, thereby alleviating the throng of enthusiastic regulars.

This wine bar menu begins with a host of hearty appetizers like juicy meatballs with a fragrant Neapolitan ragù and *scamorza*, along with expertly prepared pastas like Di Palo ricotta cavatelli tossed in a braised oxtail sugo, studded with zucchini and earthy cremini mushrooms. The unique and fairly priced wine list contains many varietals rarely found outside Italy.

annisa

Contemporary 🍴🍴

D1

13 Barrow St. (bet. Seventh Ave. South & W. 4th St.)

Subway: Christopher St - Sheridan Sq   Dinner nightly
Phone: 212-741-6699
Web: www.annisarestaurant.com
Prices: $$$

Julie Dentities

Beloved annisa is hallowed as one of the most resilient and relished Village options for sophisticated dining.

The frenetic pace of West 4th Street gives way to the tree-lined calm of annisa's site, set amid a charming historic district. The bar up front is always welcoming, never obtrusive, as it graciously pours a rarefied selection that applauds "women in wine"—most of these are crafted by female vintners or vineyard owners. Meanwhile, the elevated dining room is refreshingly serene thanks to thoughtful details like padded walls which transform the hum of enthusiastic chatter into a melodious din. The blush of burnt orange warms this minimalist setting.

One peek at Chef Anita Lo's menu and it is crystal clear how her thought-provoking combinations endure as the hallmarks of annisa's globally influenced cuisine—which is not simply successful but a joy to consume. Find a legion of fans diving into a deliciously silky and smooth red lentil soup ringed by Middle Eastern spices; or meaty, grilled cobia plated with creamy cauliflower purée, shaved florets, caper berries, and a hearty scoop of domestic caviar. Compared to strong savory dishes, her desserts may sometimes disappoint.

August

B2

Mediterranean XX

359 Bleecker St. (bet. Charles & 10th Sts.)

Subwaw: Christopher St - Sheridan Sq
Phone: 212-929-8727
Web: www.augustny.com
Prices: $$

Lunch & dinner daily

One may wonder how August has retained its long-standing popularity as a favored neighborhood destination? Well, it's not that hard to deduce. Wood and stone underscore the lived-in room that is both warm and chic with a wood-burning oven, and yet cooled by an inviting backyard garden. The staff is relaxed and sociable, never missing a step; and the kitchen remains under steady tutelage despite the inevitability of change.

August's farm-driven comfort fare is a little bit Americana and a little bit Euro revealing preparations that may bring crispy-fried squid salad drizzled with yuzu ranch; organic chicken roasted in the wood oven and sided with crinkly fried green beans; and a deliciously gooey warm chocolate cake for a classic and sweet *finis*.

Barbuto

B2

Italian XX

775 Washington St. (at 12th St.)

Subwaw: 14 St - 8 Av
Phone: 212-924-9700
Web: www.barbutonyc.com
Prices: $$

Lunch & dinner daily

Those who wax poetic on the virtues of the perfect roast chicken need look no farther. Located on a quiet stretch of the West Village just steps from MePa, Chef Jonathan Waxman's Barbuto plays up its locale and industrial bones with concrete flooring, painted-over brick walls, and garage doors that open up to create an atmospheric indoor/outdoor vibe.

Still, that chicken is what best expresses Barbuto's refined simplicity—the roasted bird has a coarse pepper-freckled auburn skin and tender ivory flesh moist with flavorful juices, further enhanced by a splash of bright and briny salsa verde. This dish is admirably supported by the likes of grilled octopus salad with fennel and pink grapefruit or a cookie-like chocolate hazelnut *crostata*.

133

Babbo ✿

Italian ✗✗

110 Waverly Pl. (bet. MacDougal St. & Sixth Ave.)

Subway: W 4 St - Wash Sq
Phone: 212-777-0303
Web: www.babbonyc.com
Prices: $$$

Lunch Tue – Sat
Dinner nightly

MICHELIN

After all these years, Babbo is back in the game and better than ever. Its sweet, Washington Square neighborhood home is the same bi-level dining room flaunting an old-world mix of shuttered windows, wrought iron railings, and hefty wooden armchairs. Despite the historical setting and attentive service, its insane popularity and loud music can lead to sensory overload. For better or worse, Chef Mario Batali's classic rock playlist is still thumping through dinner (lunchtime is subdued with smoother jazz). The bar is very lively and sometimes rowdy.

The menu delivers what it has long been hailed for: creative yet rustic Italian food made with stellar skill and extraordinary ingredients. Many dishes have been their own Babbo classics for over a decade, like beef cheek ravioli, a shining signature of succulent meat wrapped in silky pasta sheets and bathed in a subtle *Castelmagno* cheese- and black truffle-reduction. Among the entrées, find beautifully composed poached pork *tonnato* in a delicate yet assertive tuna-and-mayonnaise sauce counterpoised with tart caperberries.

Sweet finales include a delightfully warm and moist rosemary-olive oil cake, with a scoop of melting olive oil gelato.

Barraca

C2

81 Greenwich Ave. (at Bank St.)

Subway: 14 St - 8 Av
Phone: 212-462-0080
Web: www.barracanyc.com
Prices: $$

Lunch Sat – Sun
Dinner nightly

The team behind Latin American Rayuela and Macondo turn their attention towards Spain with this precious spot. Barraca flaunts a rustic air complete with padded wooden banquettes, a beamed ceiling, and bright blue chairs. The staff is enthusiastic and sharply attired in long, dark denim aprons.

At the center of Barraca's menu, find a roster of six paellas for two such as the mouthwateringly fragrant and crisped *roja de carabineros*. Infused with red shrimp stock and scattered with Gulf, rock, and red shrimp, it is the color of terra-cotta. Tapas like chicken and oyster mushroom *croquetas*, flatbreads, and entrées round out the selection that is best washed down by one of the excellent sangrias—think Rioja swirled with Aperol, cherry liqueur, and dried chili.

Bianca

D4

5 Bleecker St. (bet. Bowery & Elizabeth St.)

Subway: Bleecker St
Phone: 212-260-4666
Web: www.biancanyc.com
Prices: $$

Dinner nightly

Curtained windows lead the way to this winsome hideaway which, as evidenced by the always full dining room, enjoys a strongly favorable standing as *the* destination for homestyle Italian dining. Plank floors, an open kitchen, and delicate floral-rimmed china arranged along the walls produce a cherished timeless appeal.

The menu proves simplicity is always satisfying. There is no arguing with a bowl of homemade *tagliatelle* tossed with wild mushrooms sautéed in olive oil and fresh herbs offered as a special; followed by *pollo al balsamico*—chicken poached in balsamic vinegar, set over fresh salad greens, and dressed with a wonderfully restrained sauce. Tiramisu is given a clever and rich twist by a chocolate chip-studded mascarpone mousse filling.

Blue Hill ❀

American 🍴🍴

75 Washington Pl. (bet. Sixth Ave. & Washington Sq. Park)

Subway: W 4 St - Wash Sq
Phone: 212-539-1776
Web: www.bluehillnyc.com
Prices: $$$

Dinner nightly

Thomas Schauer/Blue Hill

The fresh-from-the-farm parade of treats that welcomes diners is an enticing initiation to Blue Hill's serious cuisine. These are of course courtesy of Stone Barns, home to Dan Barber's Westchester outpost, and a small network of suppliers located within a few hundred miles of the city. A veggie slider of say, beets and ricotta sits on an almond bun topped with raw sesame seeds; while house-made charcuterie is superb when paired with warm bread, sweet butter, salted *lardo*, and dehydrated vegetable-tinted salt.

Open since 2000 and occupying a speakeasy turned tucked away landmark location, Blue Hill has grown only more impressive with time. The room is snug, prettied-up by fresh flowers and sultry with the glow of candlelight.

The kitchen brigade applies their remarkable talents and ingenuity to ultra-seasonal product in order to yield such sophisticated items as roasted Brussels sprouts with a cloud of Parmesan cream, mustard, and tart apple; or braised hake with shellfish, silky fennel, and streak of Meyer lemon. Desserts further enhance the sure-footed cooking in a composition of tender diced quince with maple- and cinnamon-scented crumble alongside *fromage blanc* sorbet.

Blue Ribbon Bakery

Contemporary

B3

35 Downing St. (at Bedford St.)

Subway: Houston St
Phone: 212-337-0404
Web: www.blueribbonrestaurants.com
Prices: $$

Lunch & dinner daily

The origin of this very New York bistro begins with the discovery of an abandoned brick oven that brothers Eric and Bruce Bromberg found in the basement of a bodega. This sparked the idea for a bakery, and in 1998 Blue Ribbon Bakery joined the duo's family of popular and impressive dining venues. The sunny corner spot charms with mustard yellow walls and creaky wood-plank flooring; downstairs the heady aroma of freshly baked bread wafts throughout exposed brick alcoves.

Excellent sandwiches star on the roster of lunchtime fare, like shrimp salad with roasted tomato mayonnaise tucked into slices of lightly toasted challah. Dinner brings eclectic possibilities like leeks vinaigrette, grilled sardines, fried chicken, and ice cream parlor desserts.

Bobo

Contemporary

B2

181 W. 10th St. (at Seventh Ave.)

Subway: Christopher St - Sheridan Sq
Phone: 212-488-2626
Web: www.bobonyc.com
Prices: $$

Lunch Sat – Sun
Dinner nightly

This resilient Village paragon continues to reign as a prime spot for fine dining. What's all the fuss about? It could be the relishable show courtesy of a skilled kitchen that divulges delicacies like Niman Ranch pork cheeks Provençal, braised with tomato, olives, and served over succulent lemon-infused cavatelli; sides like broccoli rabe *a la plancha*; or sweets like carrot cake with candied pecans and cream cheese ice cream.

Others maintain that it is most definitely Bobo's charming setting—located in a century-old townhouse—designed to feel warm and very whimsical. If none of these sound appealing, have faith that there's no place finer to spend a sultry evening sipping an excellent cocktail, than in their quaint back garden.

Bohemian

Japanese ✗✗

D4

57 Great Jones St. (bet. Bowery & Lafayette St.)

Subway: Bleecker St
Phone: 212-388-1070
Web: www.playearth.jp
Prices: $$

Dinner nightly

This intriguing den is secreted away down an unmarked hallway and fronted by a thick glass door. Despite its stealthy locale, the staff is welcoming and courteous as they attend to diners seated amid polished concrete floors, white walls, and mid-century furnishings in emerald green, turquoise, and cognac—in a space that once served as a studio for artist Jean-Michel Basquiat.

If that doesn't bespeak creative cooking, a small plate of decadent mushroom croquettes topped with uni will do the needful. But, the true highlight is the exceptional *Washugyu* from Japanese Premium Beef offered in several guises—as a sashimi of short rib; steak of the day; or as luscious mini burgers dressed with lettuce, slow-roasted tomato, and pecorino on tender brioche.

BONDST

Japanese ✗✗

D4

6 Bond St. (bet. Broadway & Lafayette St.)

Subway: Bleecker St
Phone: 212-777-2500
Web: www.bondstrestaurant.com
Prices: $$$

Dinner nightly

The white banner branded with a bold dot marking this edgy and upscale venue is just as swanky as the quintessentially cool, cobblestoned corridor it sits on. This multi-floor brownstone features a ground floor lounge and upstairs dining room, whose minimalist setting suits the chill vibe and very pretty crowd.

Special sushi like Alaskan king crab on crispy rice may sound interesting, but it's best to stick to the straightforward array of good quality nigiri and sashimi arranged by fish type. Cooked items attest to the kitchen's aptitude, as in a dazzling composition of tender and meaty grilled octopus, purple potato, and pink grapefruit; and entrées like pan-seared, sweet and silky Hokkaido scallops with twirls of *ika* soba and frothy uni sauce.

Buvette

C1

French

42 Grove St. (bet. Bedford & Bleecker Sts.)

Subway: Christopher St - Sheridan Sq

Lunch & dinner daily

Phone: 212-255-3590

Web: www.ilovebuvette.com

Prices: 🍪

Wonderfully inviting and proudly French, Chef Jody Williams' *gastrothéque* serves delicious Gallic small plates all day, so there is always a reason for a visit. A white marble dining counter set before polished stemware and bottles of wine dominates the petite, brick-walled room. Everything seems alive with chatter and jazz.

Buvette's snacks focus on French classics, as in silken batons of leek drizzled with stimulating Dijon vinaigrette; or a *croque forestier*, filled with béchamel, oven-dried tomato, wild mushrooms, and Gruyère seasoned with *herbes de Provence*. It goes without saying that a glass of wine is practically mandatory, say a flinty Bourgogne aligoté chosen off the blackboard selection, framed within the outline of France?

Cafe Cluny

B2

Contemporary

284 W. 12th St. (at W. 4th St.)

Subway: 14 St - 8 Av

Lunch & dinner daily

Phone: 212-255-6900

Web: www.cafecluny.com

Prices: $$

A longtime favorite downtown watering hole, Cafe Cluny's mien is a difficult-to-achieve fusion of intimacy, sophistication, and insouciance. The main room is embellished with celebrity caricatures and a wall of shadowy bird cutouts that come alive in the evening candlelight. The back room is a tad more subdued and boasts butterflies behind glass and room-lengthening mirrors.

The kitchen has been shining bright since the pilotage of Chef Phillip Kirschen-Clark. The Corton alum and his inspired team are turning out very fine fare that includes artichokes *barigoule* braised in white wine and miso; and cavatelli abundantly sauced with luscious lobster bisque. Their classic lemon bar is decidedly adult, topped with Chartreuse ice cream and basil ribbons.

Carbone ✿

Italian ✕✕

C4

181 Thompson St. (bet. Bleecker & Houston Sts.)

Subway: Houston St   Dinner nightly
Phone: 212-254-3000
Web: www.carbonenewyork.com
Prices: $$$$

Daniel Krieger

The theme is clear: Carbone is an upscale and infinitely more stylish version of an old timey hangout, complete with jammed tables, black-and-white tiled floors, and curtained windows. If that doesn't make you feel like an extra in a vintage Scorsese flick, peek at the staff donning three-piece burgundy suits and exhibiting saintly patience for such a lustful place. Yes, there is schtick, but the latent sophistication works.

On the one hand, the literally enormous menu follows suit, but that is where the theater ends. There is a modern precision to this cooking, which is a wondrous embracement of those old-school red-sauce joints.Think you've had baked clams? Here, they arrive as an elevated trio, one of which is topped with sea urchin and lemon. *Rigatoni alla vodka* is fiery with red chilies but gently dressed with a cream sauce. The veal Parmesan is a massive chop that harkens back to the spirit of *abbondanza*, yet it is handled with tremendous care and skill. Note the crispness of the coating, the pink center, and freshness of the mozzarella.

Desserts are prepared with an equally expert hand: that massive slice of chocolate layer cake is ethereal and a "cakewalk" to devour.

Chez Sardine

Japanese ✗✗

183 W. 10th St. (bet. Waverly Pl. & W. 4th St.)

Subway: Christopher St - Sheridan Sq
Phone: 646-360-3705
Web: www.chezsardine.com
Prices: $$

Lunch Sat – Sun
Dinner nightly

Restaurateur Gabriel Stulman continues to expand his empire with this distinctive *izakaya*. The petite corner setting rocks a minimalist look with white walls, an arrangement of fish drawings, and a small counter lined with walnut stools. At the bar, a photo of actor Pat Morita from *The Karate Kid* adds a wink of whimsy.

Stulman has partnered with his chef from Fedora to craft these succulent snacks. Ready your taste buds for a pork and barbecued eel hand roll filled with warm rice and wrapped in just-toasted nori. Take heed: the savory confection of maple-and miso-brushed salmon head is best ripped apart with your hands. Additionally, fried monkfish tripe is wow-inducing—crunchy outside, practically gelatinous within, and dressed with ponzu.

Commerce

Contemporary ✗✗

50 Commerce St. (near Barrow St.)

Subway: Christopher St - Sheridan Sq
Phone: 212-524-2301
Web: www.commercerestaurant.com
Prices: $$

Lunch Fri – Sun
Dinner nightly

Commerce sits on a picture perfect West Village block, and although it's only been open since 2007 the lovingly restored space dates back to being a depression-era speakeasy. Belly up to the bar with its backdrop of polished wood veneer; or grab a seat in the convivial dining room that shows off earthy-toned terrazzo flooring and walls accented with glazed ivory tile.

Chef Harold Moore's menu melds seasonal and global inspiration and brings forth items such as BLT soup, a cool, creamy green purée enlivened by buttermilk and stocked with slivered heirloom tomatoes, crushed bacon, and brioche croutons. Entrées have featured a Korean-style pork chop; and desserts are fun—envision a tall wedge of birthday cake, adorned with a candle for deserving diners.

Crispo

Italian ✗✗

C1

240 W. 14th St. (bet. Seventh & Eighth Aves.)

Subway: 14 St (Seventh Ave.)   Dinner nightly
Phone: 212-229-1818
Web: www.crisporestaurant.com
Prices: $$

Its convenient 14th Street address may help draw crowds, but Chef/owner Frank Crispo's impressive Northern Italian fare is what keeps fans returning again and again. The large room fills up easily and is effortlessly comfortable with attentive service and a rustic ambience punctuated by filament light bulbs, mahogany panels, and vintage tile work.

The menu begins with a lengthy list of small plates starring prosciutto, carved in the dining room on the chef's antique Berkel slicers, as well as daily specials like grilled artichokes glossed with a lemony butter sauce. Pastas are expertly prepared and may include a silky twirl of fettucine topped with sweet and plump head-on prawn scampi. For dessert, panna cotta is a voluptuous experience.

El Toro Blanco

Mexican ✗✗

B3

257 Sixth Ave. (bet. Bedford & Downing Sts.)

Subway: Houston St   Lunch & dinner daily
Phone: 212-645-0193
Web: www.eltoroblanconyc.com
Prices: $$

Warm sunset hues shade this Mexican charmer, from the partners behind Lure Fishbar. Polished woods, russet terrazzo flooring, and glossy orange tiles provide a pretty backdrop. So, embrace that beachy state of mind and start with a margarita; followed by Baja-style black bass ceviche; or an open-faced Sonoran cheese crisp. Entrées feature regional specialties as in marinated and fried chunks of Berkshire pork shoulder *carnitas Michoacan* with refried beans and shaved cabbage slaw dressed in bright Serrano chiles and fresh lime juice, complete with a stack of excellent tortillas.

Save room for the dressed-up take on *tres leches*, a sweet milk-sopped round of sponge cake with caramelized banana, a scoop of *dulce de leche* ice cream and dollop of meringue.

Empellón Taqueria

D1

Mexican

230 W. 4th St. (at 10th St.)

Subway: Christopher St - Sheridan Sq
Phone: 212-367-0999
Web: www.empellon.com
Prices: $$

Lunch & dinner daily

Alex Stupak, wd~50's former pastry chef *extraordinaire*, switches gears from sweet to savory at this venture and brings along a temptingly creative and heartfelt rendition of Mexican cuisine with creamy textures, sweet spices, and roasted chiles aplenty. The tasteful setting features dark-stained furnishings in a whitewashed room, infused with pizzazz from a colorful mural and a bar that gets plenty of action.

The kitchen prepares a roster of heavily stuffed and tasty tacos such as shredded chicken with chili- and cilantro-spiked green chorizo. Other treats include a *queso fundido* of braised beef short ribs baked with a blanket of sheep's milk ricotta; or warm and crunchy chips with a duo of smoked cashew and roasted *arbol* chili salsa.

EN Japanese Brasserie

B3

Japanese

435 Hudson St. (at Leroy St.)

Subway: Houston St
Phone: 212-647-9196
Web: www.enjb.com
Prices: $$$

Lunch & dinner daily

Cloaked in darkness and steeped in grandeur, this contemporary West Village *izakaya* is a sexy go-to spot when the urge for sushi, soba, and stone-grilled meats strikes. Sprawling and boisterous, EN sets a swank scene with soaring heights, natural materials, and custom trimmings.

The open kitchen pays homage to authentic Japanese palates, but also reveals ingenuity. Tofu is made fresh hourly and served as a quivering silken scoop drizzled with *wari-joyu* (soy sauce and dashi). This specialty is an absolute must. The chef's sashimi selection may bring Scottish salmon, Pacific bigeye tuna, and Kona kampachi, all incredibly fresh.

For a more private experience, bypass the masses and book your own crowd for kaiseki dinner in a tatami room.

Extra Virgin

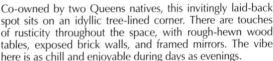

Mediterranean ✗

B2

259 W. 4th St. (at Perry St.)

Subway: Christopher St - Sheridan Sq
Phone: 212-691-9359
Web: www.extravirginrestaurant.com
Prices: $$

Lunch Tue – Sun
Dinner nightly

Co-owned by two Queens natives, this invitingly laid-back spot sits on an idyllic tree-lined corner. There are touches of rusticity throughout the space, with rough-hewn wood tables, exposed brick walls, and framed mirrors. The vibe here is as chill and enjoyable during days as evenings.

Extra Virgin's Mediterranean menu offers crowd-pleasing items like a starter salad of warm pistachio- and breadcrumb-crusted goat cheese with roasted beets, generously showered with crisp, julienned Granny Smith apple. The kitchen's seriousness is evident in touches like the addition of bright and flavorful sweet peas, roasted yellow peppers, and black olives to the rigatoni with sausage; or the apple tart paired with sour cream ice cream and a warm dark caramel sauce.

Fatty Crab 😨

Malaysian ✗✗

B2

643 Hudson St. (bet. Gansevoort & Horatio Sts.)

Subway: 14 St - 8 Av
Phone: 212-352-3592
Web: www.fattycrew.com
Prices: $$

Lunch & dinner daily

Zak Pelaccio's signature dish could be made with mung beans and it would still knock the socks off the uninitiated. Sweet, savory, rich, and deliciously messy, the cooking here expresses a certain alchemy that seems to explode from its cozy little Meatpacking District storefront.

The menu is concise, but there are no misses. Hits included the Malay fish fry, a bowl of Tamaki rice ladled with wondrously funky crab curry and topped with strips of delicate fish deep-fried in turmeric-seasoned batter. A side of braised collard greens sauced with *sambal*, anchovies, and pounded red chili is fantastically strong.

The front patio and small dining room fill up fast, so arrive early for dinner. Come for lunch and have the place to yourself.

Fatty 'Cue

B3   Barbecue   XX

50 Carmine St. (bet. Bedford & Bleecker Sts.)

Subway: Houston St   Lunch & dinner daily
Phone: 212-929-5050
Web: www.fattycrew.com
Prices: $$

This Manhattan sib of the 'Cue brand hatched by Chef Zak Pelaccio and his "Fatty Crew" offers a more comfortable and upscale setting than the Williamsburg original (take note that this location is once again open). The lusty take on Southeast Asian cuisine is built around locally sourced, humanely raised product that's smoked and spiced to the point where flavorful is an understatement.

Start off with a Fatty Manhattan combining rye, sweet vermouth, and smoked cherry cola or go whole hog and flash out with Thai-style bottle service before supping on pork ribs brined in fish sauce and glazed with palm sugar. Thinly sliced brisket with aged Gouda and warm Parker House rolls; or veal sweetbreads dressed with black pepper aïoli garner a loyal clientele.

Fedora

B2   Contemporary   XX

239 W. 4th St. (bet. Charles & 10th Sts.)

Subway: Christopher St - Sheridan Sq   Dinner nightly
Phone: 646-449-9336
Web: www.fedoranyc.com
Prices: $$

Originally opened in 1952, Fedora was recently taken over by Gabriel Stulman. The restaurateur has an affinity for all things vintage, and this freshened-up space has been kept lovingly intact, down to the blazing neon signage out front. The retro setting—polished brass, black-and-white photos, and jelly jars used as votive holders—pours creative libations at a mahogany bar and seats diners along a black leather banquette.

Rich and meaty plates abound as in Wagyu tongue with celeriac remoulade; crispy pig's head with sauce *gribiche*; and a "surf and turf" of fried sweetbreads and seared octopus with port wine-enriched butter sauce. If possible, save room for a creative dessert like the silky cheesecake panna cotta drizzled with passion fruit nectar.

Five Points

D4

American ✗✗

31 Great Jones St. (bet. Bowery & Lafayette St.)

Subway: Bleecker St   Lunch & dinner daily
Phone: 212-253-5700
Web: www.fivepointsrestaurant.com
Prices: $$

The heart of Chef Marc Meyer's first born continues to beat as strongly as when it opened in 1999. This neighborhood favorite blends relaxed ambience, polished service, and seasonal food with a near-Californian sensibility that is utterly irresistible to its nightly stream of food-savvy sophisticates.

Beyond the energetic bar is a quieter back dining room anchored by a tree trunk bedecked with greenery and surrounded by tables wrapped in brown paper. The menu winks at Chef Meyer's take on urbane rusticity as it boasts local, seasonal ingredients. Expect the likes of country-style pâté with house pickles, whole grain mustard, and toast; Montauk Point swordfish with slow-cooked broccoli and fig-almond *anchïoade*; or a Finger Lakes grass-fed beef burger.

Gobo

D1

Vegetarian ✗✗

401 Sixth Ave. (bet. 8th St. & Waverly Pl.)

Subway: W 4 St - Wash Sq   Lunch & dinner daily
Phone: 212-255-3902
Web: www.goborestaurant.com
Prices:

Need a tasty and tranquil timeout from Manhattan's hustle and bustle? Gobo is your place. Sit down, take a cleansing breath and ponder the restful décor. Muted colors and warm wood accents dominate the airy dining room, which offers a view of your meal being prepared from the open kitchen.

Gobo's value-minded menu starts off with healthy beverages like organic juices, soy-milk smoothies, and unfiltered ginger ale. Their "food for the five senses" tempts even those who would disavow any vegetarian tendencies, with starters like scallion pancakes with mango salsa; or house-made hummus with carrots and wonton chips. Larger plates might follow with spicy stir-fried Vietnamese rice noodles with crisp pea pods, bright broccoli, bean sprouts, and tofu.

Good

C2

89 Greenwich Ave. (bet. Bank & 12th Sts.)

Subway: 14 St - 8 Av
Phone: 212-691-8080
Web: www.goodrestaurantnyc.com
Prices: $$

Lunch Tue – Sun
Dinner nightly

Yes, it's true: this charming local fave lives up to its preordained reputation, and has done so since opening in 2000. The pale, earthy, and appealing dining room has a soothing, intimate, and laid-back air, as if to whisper, "Stop by anytime." This echoes through the cozy bar and stretch of sidewalk seating.

The menu displays a greatest-hits list of comfort food favorites that are given a globally inspired turn. Fish tacos are stuffed with the selection of the day; macaroni and cheese is studded with green chilies beneath a tortilla crumb-crust; and grilled lamb sirloin arrives with chickpea polenta and creamed Swiss chard.

Good offers a hearty lunch menu and nicely priced combo specials. Meanwhile, weekend brunch is washed down by clever cocktails.

Gottino

C2

52 Greenwich Ave. (bet. Charles & Perry Sts.)

Subway: Christopher St - Sheridan Sq
Phone: 212-633-2590
Web: N/A
Prices:

Lunch & dinner daily

No matter the time of day, there is an adept team preparing an assortment of snacks in Gottino's inviting space amid picture-perfect baskets of fruit. A white marble dining counter dominates this charming *enoteca*, dolled up with exposed brick and a few knobby wood tables.

The mood is so gracious that it's best to set aside a couple of hours. Nosh on the likes of *farro* salad dotted with roasted and diced butternut squash, a generous showering of finely grated Parmesan, and the deliciously fresh note of celery leaves. Or, go for something heartier—crêpes stuffed with prosciutto and *robiola*, warm and oozing. Be sure to check the wall-mounted blackboard promoting Gottino's all-Italian wine list, offering pours by the glass or carafe.

Gotham Bar and Grill ❦

D2

American

12 E. 12th St. (bet. Fifth Ave. & University Pl.)

Subway: 14 St - Union Sq
Phone: 212-620-4020
Web: www.gothambarandgrill.com
Prices: $$$

Lunch Mon – Fri
Dinner nightly

David Cavallo

This *very* New York destination is a show of professionalism from start to finish. The welcome is warm, service is deft, and the seasonal menu can be both interesting and undeniably excellent. The ambience is equally arresting—note those lofty windows and soaring ceilings dotted with sleek, spherical fixtures. A long line of tables winds its way down the room to a sun-soaked back overlooking a garden. Up a few steps, a large bar serves a slew of enticing cocktails to sip over an extraordinary view of the dining room.

On each table, find a beautiful array of quintessential NYC classics that never seem to falter. Begin with striped bass ceviche boosted by pomelo, green mango, and Thai chili. Or, try a smoked salmon galette bursting with flavor and topped with a lush watercress salad dressed in *raita* made with caperberries, pickled onions, and horseradish. The burger has been raved about for eons and with good reason: the terrific quality beef is cooked to absolute precision and set atop a brioche bun with crispy bacon, Plymouth cheddar, and spicy remoulade.

A Gotham signature since the dawn of time, the chocolate cake thrills with a molten center and salty almond ice cream.

Gradisca

 C2

Italian

126 W. 13th St. (bet. Sixth & Seventh Aves.)

Subway: 14 St (Seventh Ave.)
Phone: 212-691-4886
Web: www.gradiscanyc.com
Prices: $$$

Dinner nightly

Grazie for Gradisca, an Italian trove filled with food like *mamma* used to make. Amid a sea of mediocrity, Gradisca still flickers by virtue of its generosity, first-rate product, and knowledge. All who enter this below-street level dining enclave are struck by their masterful (if pricey) pasta parade. If that doesn't warm you, look around for the cheery Emiliani staff. Parted into three nooks, each dining room flows seamlessly into the other.

Awe-inspiring images of movie stars set against rich red walls lend a romantic vibe and invite you to dine on a rich corn-and-polenta *timbale* with pork sausage; ribbons of *tagliatelle* tossed with wild boar ragù; or brined rabbit with caper berries. Flaunting ace technique is a quivering vanilla-flecked panna cotta.

Grand Sichuan

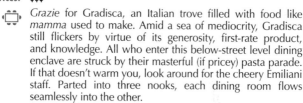

B3

Chinese

15 Seventh Ave. South (bet. Carmine & Leroy Sts.)

Subway: Houston St
Phone: 212-645-0222
Web: N/A
Prices:

Lunch & dinner daily

The popularity of Sichuan cuisine shows no signs of abating, as evidenced by the continued profusion of regionally specific (and similarly named) eateries. This Greenwich Village outpost is part of a burgeoning mini-chain proffering spicy treats throughout the metropolitan area.

The menu is divided into three sections: "American Chinese," "Latest," and "Classic Sichuan." This last heading is especially tempting and should be your focus here. The full roster of specialties includes *dan dan* noodles stocked with spicy minced pork; braised fish with chili sauce; and shredded chicken breast mingling fresh Napa with sour-preserved cabbage.

The inexpensive lunch special is a big draw, and the availability of small and large portions is a thoughtful touch.

Gusto

Italian ✗✗

C2

60 Greenwich Ave. (at Perry St.)

Subway:	14 St (Seventh Ave.)
Phone:	212-924-8000
Web:	www.gustonyc.com
Prices:	$$

Lunch & dinner daily

Gusto may no longer be a hot spot, but it has comfortably settled into life as a preferred hangout for a fine Italian meal. The room retains its chic appeal in contrasting dark, espresso-stained wood furnishings and bright whitewashed brick walls. Downstairs, there is an especially cozy private dining room occupying the stone-walled wine cellar.

Fried food anchors the selection of cooked starters like the impressive *fritto misto* combining calamari and remarkably fresh shrimp given a light-as-air coating, dusted with salt and pepper and a wedge of lemon. House-made pasta is another recommendation, such as the *tagliatelle vongole*—a bowlful of silky ribbons twirled with clam essence, shaved garlic, and broccoli rabe surrounded in plump Manila clams.

Hakata Tonton

Japanese ✗

D1

61 Grove St. (bet. Bleecker St. & Seventh Ave.)

Subway:	Christopher St - Sheridan Sq
Phone:	212-242-3699
Web:	N/A
Prices:	$$

Dinner nightly

A novel cuisine has taken root in New York. Enter this tiny red and yellow dining room to be educated in this other facet of the Japanese culinary repertoire: *tonsoku* (pigs' feet, ears, and the like).

Varied *tonsoku* dishes may include a luxurious slow-roasted pork or *oreilles du cochon* (French in name only) which are an explosion of crunchy, cool, creamy, sweet, sticky, and vinegary flavors. Truer to its Italian roots, *tonsoku* carbonara is made with smoky bacon and is a good choice for wary newbies. A "rare cheesecake" of piped cheese and sour cream is a very smart and absolutely delicious take on the traditional dessert.

The plain-Jane décor sits in stark contrast to the rich and porky fare that diners will come rushing back for.

Hecho en Dumbo

D4

354 Bowery (bet. 4th & Great Jones Sts.)

Subway: Bleecker St
Phone: 212-937-4245
Web: www.hechoendumbo.com
Prices: $$

Lunch Sat – Sun
Dinner nightly

This spirited cantina sports an edgy downtown vibe with reclaimed wood and quirky mismatched chairs. Happy patrons sip on enticing cocktails, and margaritas are obviously a solid option; but, so are other concoctions like *viuda negra* featuring freshly muddled organic fruit and *chelas* (spiced beers).

Antojitos like *picaditas de jaiba*, warmed Dungeness crab and cool avocado drizzled with jalapeño oil and set atop deliciously moist masa medallions, initiate the made-from-scratch menu courtesy of Chef and Mexico City native Daniel Mena. A host of other treats also gratify—perhaps *tacos de Tuétano* stuffed with roasted bone marrow and caramelized Wagyu beef tongue; or seared lamb neck posed over chickpea purée with a *chile guajillo* and cumin sauce.

Home

D2

20 Cornelia St. (bet. Bleecker & W. 4th Sts.)

Subway: W 4 St - Wash Sq
Phone: 212-243-9579
Web: www.homerestaurantnyc.com
Prices: $$

Lunch & dinner daily

This intimate Cornelia Street dining room has persevered through the years and continues to offer great tastes of Americana in a setting that is welcoming and warm—all apt characteristics for an eatery called Home. Everyone seated in their black spindleback chairs or back garden seats, is happy to see this unassuming, unpretentious whitewashed little space thriving.

The kitchen honors sourcing and seasonality in its range of comforting specialties that have included a freshly prepared vegan purée of tomato and sweet basil representing the soup of the day; and a hearty oyster po'boy featuring hefty, briny, cornmeal-crusted Willapa Bay oysters and spice-tinged rémoulade sauce, on a fresh ciabatta roll alongside a tangle of Old Bay-sprinkled shoestring fries.

Il Buco

Italian ✗

D4

47 Bond St. (bet. Bowery & Lafayette St.)

Subway: Bleecker St
Phone: 212-533-1932
Web: www.ilbuco.com
Prices: $$

Lunch Mon – Sat
Dinner nightly

It's hard to find a more charming restaurant than Il Buco. What started as a rustic antique shop in 1994 has evolved through the years into this beloved enoteca that looks as if it was plucked straight from the Italian countryside. The dining room is decorated with polished copper pots, flowers arranged in metal pails, and platters of fruit. An amalgam of farmhouse tables large enough to offer communal-style seating adds to the unabashedly convivial spirit.

Product-obsessed cooking rules the menu here, in a large array of seasonal small plates, house-made pasta and preparations highlighting artisanal ingredients. Expect entrées like stuffed saddle of New York state rabbit set atop rich Anson Mills polenta, with slender gold and orange carrots.

Il Buco Alimentari & Vineria ☺

Italian ✗✗

D4

53 Great Jones St. (bet. Bowery & Lafayette St.)

Subway: Bleecker St
Phone: 212-837-2622
Web: www.ilbucovineria.com
Prices: $$

Lunch & dinner daily

Il Buco's sure-footed spinoff is an enticing option all on its own. Showcasing a tempting store of artisanal products up front and an open kitchen in back, the bewitching room is rustic with terra-cotta tile and pressed copper imported from Italy, wooden communal tables, and the perfume of wood smoke used to fuel the oven and rotisserie.

Italian-inflected and seasonally-driven cuisine is clearly the driving force among the parade of ambrosial small plates. Dishes may include hearty *puntarelle* dressed with anchovy vinaigrette; perfectly cooked spaghetti slicked with a light, pink-tinged cream sauce emboldened with *bottarga di muggine*; or thinly sliced *porchetta alla Romana* seasoned with fennel seeds and topped with amber-like shards of crisped skin.

Joseph Leonard

 Contemporary

D1

170 Waverly Pl. (at Grove St.)

Subway: Christopher St - Sheridan Sq
Phone: 646-429-8383
Web: www.josephleonard.com
Prices: $$

Lunch & dinner daily

Joseph Leonard serves an enjoyable carte of well-prepared contemporary food devoted to the season and bearing a faint French accent in country pâté with pickled onions and baguette; pan-seared Long Island fluke with creamy lemon rice and soy reduction; and a tall wedge of classic carrot cake. Breakfast is served as well and includes the likes of *saucisson à l'ail* with eggs and hashbrowns.

This chicly curated corner setting, owned by Gabriel Stulman, sports weathered wood-plank flooring, rough-hewn walls, and book-filled shelves. The space is installed with a winsome assemblage of vintage pieces, including a zinc bar and fridge that looks like it was lifted from the set of *I Love Lucy*. Both lend an unique air to this always-welcoming establishment.

Kesté Pizza & Vino

D2

271 Bleecker St. (bet. Cornelia & Jones Sts.)

Pizza

Subway: W 4 St - Wash Sq
Phone: 212-243-1500
Web: www.kestepizzeria.com
Prices:

Lunch & dinner daily

A runaway success since day one, Kesté takes the craft of making Neapolitan-style pizza to epic heights. Learned *pizzaiolo* Roberto Caporuscio first opened and established Keste's reputation, though he recently handed over this custom-built, wood-fired, volcanic stone forno to his very capable daughter, Giorgia.

Pizzas are listed under two headings, though every pie (including gluten free) is built upon a nicely salted, faintly tangy, gorgeously puffy crust with a delicately charred *cornicione* (raised edge). Pizza *speciale* feature creative ingredients like pistachio paste or butternut squash purée; while *pizze rosse* are topped with excellent house-made mozzarella, imported tomatoes, and an array of meat or vegetables. Weekday lunches showcase panini.

Kingswood

121 W. 10th St. (bet. Greenwich & Sixth Aves.)

Subway: 14 St (Seventh Ave.)
Phone: 212-645-0044
Web: www.kingswoodnyc.com
Prices: $$

Lunch Sat – Sun
Dinner nightly

Kingswood's mirthful spirit is evident from the moment you step inside. The inviting bar is habitually packed by a good-humored crowd, while beyond, the dining room is abuzz with its own sleek slant and warmth. Bathed in a flattering glow, diners sit at long communal tables and caramel leather banquettes set against a softly lit glass-walled installation and votive candles.

The contemporary menu displays boldly flavored accents while paying homage to its owner's native Australia, as in the house burger with cheddar and sweet chili sauce; Goan fish curry; and beer-battered fish and chips. Here, surf and turf may mean crisp-skinned salt cod and fork-tender pork cheeks dressed in a dark reduction of meaty jus with creamy, smoked mashed potatoes.

Kin Shop

469 Sixth Ave. (bet. 11th & 12th Sts.)

Subway: 14 St (Seventh Ave.)
Phone: 212-675-4295
Web: www.kinshopnyc.com
Prices: $$

Lunch & dinner daily

Chef Harold Dieterle combines an ingredient-driven focus with his love for Thai cuisine at this modern venture, which takes its name from the Thai word "to eat." Salads, noodles, and curries are always creative, so listen for the nightly specials—maybe a coconut milk soup with chili oil or chicken meatballs in green curry.

The inexpensive lunch prix-fixe is offered daily and has featured a stir-fry of aquatic vegetables; and skate braised in a jungle curry of red chilies, funky crab paste, Kaffir lime leaf, and pickled green peppercorns. A scoop of Thai coffee-chocolate ice cream with sweet condensed milk is a perfectly cooling finish.

The exotic dining room boasts whitewashed brick, batik canvases, and a beachy color scheme.

La Camelia

 B4

Mexican

64 Downing St. (bet. Bedford & Varick Sts.)

Subway: Houston St   Lunch & dinner daily
Phone: 212-675-7060
Web: www.lacamelianyc.com
Prices:

 This cheery spot edges out the plethora of workaday Mexican options with a number of advantages: a spacious and cordially attended setting, a comfortable bar stocked with a dizzying array of tequilas, and guacamole made-to-order in the dining room from a station stocked with a heap of ripe avocados among the display of fresh produce.

The selection of pleasing fare includes an array of tacos such as lamb *barbacoa*, braised in beer and chiles, stuffed into a handmade soft corn tortilla; chicken enchiladas draped with decadent and complex *mole poblano*, sided by rice and beans; and *camarones de Camelia* combining jumbo shrimp cooked in creamy goat cheese sauce with *rajas poblano*. Weekend specials bring the likes of pork tamales with *mole verde*.

Lafayette

D4

French

380 Lafayette St. (at Great Jones St.)

Subway: Bleecker St   Lunch & dinner daily
Phone: 212-533-3000
Web: www.lafayetteny.com
Prices: $$

 Chef Andrew Carmellini's latest venture is an homage to French cuisine, proffered in a sexy space conceived by Roman Williams. Counters lined with organic breads and pastries invite patrons to the entryway bakery. From here, the room unfolds into a series of seductive spaces where one finds a rotisserie oven spinning bronzed birds, a backlit bar emitting an amber glow, and columns clad in warm honey and blue tile.

The chef has recruited a remarkable team to direct Lafayette's kitchen as they churn out impressive creations like *pâté maison* bestowed with earthenware crocks of mustard and cornichons; and sea scallops *a la plancha* with a seasonal setup of peas, morels, and turnips. Burnt honey *vacherin* with apricot coulis is nothing short of stellar.

L'Artusi

Italian

B3

228 W. 10th St. (bet. Bleecker & Hudson Sts.)

Subway: Christopher St - Sheridan Sq
Phone: 212-255-5757
Web: www.lartusi.com
Prices: $$

Lunch Sun
Dinner nightly

L'Artusi's façade may be demure, but this attractive dining room offers a fun, buzz-worthy vibe to elevate its upscale rendition of Italian-rooted food, anchored by small plates. The large space, with gray and ivory stripes aplenty, offers three dining counters, table service, and a quieter mezzanine. An open kitchen adds to the lively air.

The impressive Italian wine list, complete with maps, is laid out with a gravitas that demands attention. The well-versed staff is pleased to suggest the best pairings to complement pastas such as buckwheat *pizzoccheri* with Brussels sprouts, fontina, and sage. Salads of chicory dressed in Parmesan, lemon, and anchovies, or crudo plates of beef carpaccio with horseradish *crema* are wonderful ways to start a meal here.

Las Ramblas

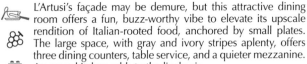

Spanish

D1

170 W. 4th St. (bet. Cornelia & Jones Sts.)

Subway: Christopher St - Sheridan Sq
Phone: 646-415-7924
Web: www.lasramblasnyc.com
Prices:

Dinner nightly

Sandwiched among a throng of attention-seeking storefronts, mighty little Las Ramblas is easy to spot, just look for the crowd of happy, munching faces. The scene spills out onto the sidewalk when the weather allows.

Named for Barcelona's historic commercial thoroughfare, Las Ramblas is a tapas treat. A copper-plated bar and collection of tiny tables provide a perch for snacking on an array of earnestly prepared items. Check out the wall-mounted blackboard for *especiales*. Bring friends (it's that kind of place) to fully explore the menu which serves up delights such as succulent head-on prawns roasted in a terra-cotta dish and sauced with cava vinegar, ginger, and basil; or béchamel creamed spinach topped by a molten cap of Mahón cheese.

Left Bank

Contemporary ✗✗

B2

117 Perry St. (at Greenwich St.)

Subway: Christopher St - Sheridan Sq

Dinner nightly

Phone: 212-727-1170
Web: www.leftbankmanhattan.com
Prices: $$

Although the name may conjure up images of rustic French cooking, the cuisine of this admirable bistro is deftly capricious. Cozily tucked away on a quiet corner, the minimalist space is framed by whitewashed brick walls dressed with a smattering of intriguing artwork and emboldened by a red-painted ceiling.

Find many pleasures within the global scope of Left Bank's carte. Offerings have included a decadent slab of pig's head terrine sided by a supple spoonful of bloomed mustard seeds; impressively prepared pastas like *paccheri* with slow-cooked pork and beef ragù; and mains like a fillet of crackling-skinned wild striped bass propped by wild mushrooms and preserved lemon. For dessert, there's really only one option—the incredible maple syrup pie.

Le Gigot

French ✗

D2

18 Cornelia St. (bet. Bleecker & W. 4th Sts.)

Subway: W 4 St - Wash Sq

Lunch & dinner Tue – Sun

Phone: 212-627-3737
Web: www.legigotrestaurant.com
Prices: $$

Looking perfectly at home on its quaint tree-lined street, Le Gigot is quietly yet confidently alluring. The petite bistro boasts personable and polished service, inlaid wood flooring, olive-colored velvet banquettes, and butter-yellow walls hung with blackboards displaying the day's specials like a lobster salad or bœuf Bourguignon. This intimate setting is a perfect match for the classic French food.

A salad of endive, apple, and Roquefort, studded with toasted walnuts and dressed with sweet vinaigrette indicative of mustard seeds, is simplicity at its most delicious. The duck confit, with its velvety rich meat cloaked with fabulously crisped skin and a bubbling, golden block of potato and celery root gratin, is one of the best in the city.

Le Philosophe

D4

55 Bond St. (bet. Bowery & Lafayette St.)

Subway: Bleecker St

Lunch & dinner daily

Phone: 212-388-0038

Web: www.lephilosophe.us

Prices: $$

The animated scene in Le Philosophe's open kitchen brings to life this modern bistro, framed in a cool aesthetic of grey walls and black-and-white portraits (of famed philosophers, *bien-sûr*). A dining counter offers a view of a former Jean-Georges sous chef leading the team at work.

Blackboard panels display the daily specials and hail the kitchen's purveyors. The cooking is proudly traditional and excels at giving French stalwarts a light touch. The classic duck *a l'orange* is a tender, rosy-fleshed breast under perfectly golden-crisped skin, plated with potato mousseline, baby turnips, and a tawny, citrus-infused sauce that hits just the right note of tartness.

Wine may seem the way to go, but Le Philosophe also has a great beer selection to boot.

The Little Owl

B3

90 Bedford St. (at Grove St.)

Subway: Christopher St - Sheridan Sq

Lunch & dinner daily

Phone: 212-741-4695

Web: www.thelittleowlnyc.com

Prices: $$

Perched on a winsome corner of the West Village, Chef Joey Campanaro's The Little Owl continues to hold a dear place in the hearts of diners near and far who appreciate that simple food and great food can be one and the same. The broccoli soup (a pure, silky purée enriched with a trace of cream and crowned by a crouton of bubbling, aged cheddar) is among the best examples of this.

The small corner room is quaint and despite this establishment's popularity, the service team is completely attitude-free. The wee kitchen is on display, and the focused crew turns out a rousing roster of preparations that bear an affinity for Mediterranean cuisine such as seared cod with *bagna cauda* vinaigrette, and gravy meatball sliders, a hands-down house specialty.

Louro

Contemporary ✗✗

142 W. 10th St. (bet. Greenwich Ave. & Waverly Pl.)

Subway: Christopher St - Sheridan Sq | Dinner nightly
Phone: 212-206-0606
Web: www.louronyc.com
Prices: $$

Louro is a tempting and very creative respite, a world away from Caesar salads and burgers. Here, find truly imaginative cooking through the lens of Chef David Santos. It doesn't hurt that the chef briefly ran an underground supper club; an anti-establishment streak comes through in the exciting menu that may not always score, but always stimulates. Dig into roasted heirloom carrot salad with toasted miso dressing; hand-cut tagliatelle tossed in spicy octopus Bolognese ragù with a hint of tasty goose pancetta; or beautifully seared Spanish mackerel with fresh, crunchy hearts of palm and smoked pineapple purée.

The room's soothing palette showcases foxed mirror panels and trompe l'oeil wallpaper portraying shelves of books lining the walls.

Lupa 😊

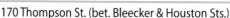

Italian ✗✗

170 Thompson St. (bet. Bleecker & Houston Sts.)

Subway: W 4 St - Wash Sq | Lunch & dinner daily
Phone: 212-982-5089
Web: www.luparestaurant.com
Prices: $$

This ever-popular Roman trattoria has been skillfully sating wolfish appetites for years and continues to fall under the hegemony of culinary heavyweights schooled in the immense bounty offered by the Italian table. Lupa's setting is rustic and charming with that timeless combination of sienna-toned walls, terra-cotta tile flooring, and wood furnishings. The service team is notable for their knowledge and courteousness.

Stop at the bar for a carafe of *vino* from the all-Italian wine list and nibble on house-cured specialties. Then move on to a focused selection of fare such as capon and pork terrine with celery *conserva*; and impressive *primi* like *tonnarelli* dressed with chunks of heritage pork ragù. A short list of *secondi* anchors the offerings.

Malaparte

Italian Italian

B2

753 Washington St. (at Bethune St.)

Subxway: 14 St - 8 Av
Phone: 212-255-2122
Web: www.malapartenyc.com
Prices: $$

Lunch Sat – Sun
Dinner nightly

Tucked away on a quiet, tree-lined street just a short walk away from the Highline and Meatpacking District glitz, Malaparte nails its charmingly rustic ambience. The interior offers an intimate number of seats in a room that is graciously attended.

The food here is anything but an afterthought. In fact, the inexpensive, home-style Italian cuisine is the kind of fare one can return to enjoy regularly. Fresh salads and thin-crust pizzas are fine starters, while the short list of pasta is impressive as in spinach and artichoke lasagna layering fresh made sheets of pasta *verde* with wilted spinach, sliced artichokes, and creamy béchamel sauce. The coffee crème caramel is a lovely finale, especially when sitting outside on a warm summer evening.

Market Table

American 🍴🍴

B3

54 Carmine St. (at Bedford St.)

Subway: W 4 St - Wash Sq
Phone: 212-255-2100
Web: www.markettablenyc.com
Prices: $$

Lunch & dinner daily

Sophisticated cooking is on display at this urbane café brought to you by partners Joey Campanero and Chef Mike Price. The two-room charmer is bright and cheerful during the day, then warm and intimate at night. The décor features red brick walls shelved with wine bottles and pantry staples, wood furnishings, and an open kitchen on display behind an inviting counter.

The team has embraced a fresh face with the arrival of Chef David Standridge, and his spirited, refreshed, and consistently enjoyable menu. Try the incredibly tender octopus *a la plancha* with rich, herbaceous salsa verde and creamy red romesco; or grilled sea bream with olive *nage*. Desserts may include French toast spread with almond butter, set beside ricotta gelato and huckleberry sauce.

The Marrow

European

 B2

99 Bank St. (at Greenwich St.)

Subway: 14 St (Seventh Ave.)
Phone: 212-428-6000
Web: www.themarrownyc.com
Prices: $$

Lunch Fri – Sun
Dinner nightly

Chef Harold Dieterle's popular venture with business partner Alicia Nosenzo is a harmonious pairing of German and Italian cuisines reflecting the talented chef's heritage. This far West Village dining room buzzes nightly and is chicly done in a dramatic palette of red and brown.

Each side of the family receives equal representation in the listing of inspired cooking. Pretzel rolls accompanied by whole grain mustard and olive oil are a perfect prelude to, well, anything. What may follow are the rich *baccala gnudi* cleverly dressed with a buttery sauce, pine nuts, golden raisins, and herbed breadcrumbs; or juniper-braised lamb neck served with rutabaga purée and braised red cabbage. Warm stout gingerbread with honey ice cream is a lovely finish.

Mary's Fish Camp

Seafood

 B2

64 Charles St. (at W. 4th St.)

Subway: Christopher St - Sheridan Sq
Phone: 646-486-2185
Web: www.marysfishcamp.com
Prices: $$

Lunch & dinner Mon – Sat

Yes, Mary's serves lobster rolls. And yes, they are overflowing with succulent chunks of meat, slathered in mayonnaise, and piled onto a buttery, toasty hot dog bun.

However, there are other many other treats to be had at this highly trafficked West Village fish shack, where global accents spice up the seafood. Explore the likes of shrimp toast with scallion ginger sauce; market fish tacos; Portuguese sardine *bánh mì*; and *pozole* with Florida red snapper. The fried clam roll, spread with chunky tartar sauce and piled high with hot and crispy clams, brings things back home. The majority of seating is offered along a curving stainless steel counter facing the kitchen. Hand-scrawled blackboards, red gingham napkins, and scuffed floors set the stage.

Mas (farmhouse)

Contemporary

B3

39 Downing St. (bet. Bedford & Varick Sts.)

Subway: Houston St   Dinner nightly
Phone: 212-255-1790
Web: www.masfarmhouse.com
Prices: $$$

Taking its name from the term used to refer to a country house or farm in Southern France, Mas fully embraces this theme in its menu and décor. Cloistered amid a picturesque West Village locale, the elegant and very popular dining room is shaded in an earthy palette and boasts a wooden communal table and rustic stone accents.

CIA-trained Chef Galen Zamarra, who honed his skills working in David Bouley's kitchen, pays homage to finely sourced ingredients by producing delicious, seasonal feasts. Dinner may reveal a tartlet of trumpet royal mushroom and leek marmalade atop a buckwheat-pecan *sablée*; tidy bundles of seared rainbow trout stuffed with meaty shiitakes and Swiss chard; or oven-warm quince frangipane cake with white chocolate ice cream.

Mas (la grillade)

Contemporary

B3

28 Seventh Ave. South (bet. Leroy & Morton Sts.)

Subway: Houston St   Lunch & dinner daily
Phone: 212-255-1795
Web: www.maslagrillade.com
Prices: $$

Fans of Chef Galen Zamarra are already well-versed in his sophisticated, seasonal, small farm-procured treats. At this fresh venture, he turns up the heat to showcase an array of contemporary creations blazoned with the kiss of fire, fueled by locally sourced hardwoods.

The attractive two-story dining room offers handcrafted millwork, tables elegantly appointed with faux bois china pieces and locally produced pottery, and a bar pouring thematically apt cocktails, as in a Rob Roy made from smoky Islay single malt. From the entirely wood-fired basement kitchen emerge the likes of spit-roasted Rocambole garlic with toast; grilled romaine with lamb bacon and buttermilk blue cheese dressing; and bone-in monkfish tail with smoked celery root purée.

Melibea

C2

Mediterranean ✕✕

2 Bank St. (at Greenwich St.)

Subway: 14 St (Seventh Ave.)   Dinner nightly
Phone: 212-463-0090
Web: www.melibeanyc.com
Prices: $$

An ambitious interpretation of Mediterranean flavors can be found at this beloved darling, where former graffiti artist-turned-chef, Jesús Núñez has teamed up with restaurateur and Spanish compatriot Héctor Sanz (of Rayuela and Macondo).

To drink, a cocktail arranged from under the headings linen, silk, velvet, and leather is recommended while settling down to take in the well-done interior that incorporates beautiful sienna banquettes, Moorish tile, and walnut flooring. And to eat, preparations include petals of salmon and scallop carpaccio dressed with salmon roe and an unexpected yet utterly enjoyable scoop of savory almond ice cream; or a luscious chicken entrée marinated in Syrian spices and plated with lentils and dried figs in lemon gravy.

Mercadito Grove

D1

Mexican ✕

100 Seventh Ave. South (at Grove St.)

Subway: Christopher St - Sheridan Sq   Lunch & dinner daily
Phone: 212-647-0830
Web: www.mercaditorestaurants.com
Prices: $$

Larger of the city's two Mercadito locations, Grove has a devoted following that fills its pastel-painted chairs and corner sidewalk seating nightly. Starters range from a small list of fresh ceviches to flautas filled with chicken and black beans. Recommendations include any of the *platos fuertes* that make up the menu's concise selection like the *adobo*-marinated *pollo a las brasas*, available as a half or whole bird. Tacos are likewise popular and are prepared with homemade tortillas, perhaps stuffed with beer-battered mahi mahi as in the *estilo Baja*. Hungry night owls should note the all-you-can eat taco special late in the evening.

Each dish attests to why Mercadito includes outposts in both Miami and Chicago.

Mexicana Mama 🏮

B2

525 Hudson St. (bet. Charles & 10th Sts.)

Subway: Christopher St - Sheridan Sq   Lunch & dinner Tue – Sun
Phone: 212-924-4119
Web: N/A
Prices: 🏮🏮

Charming and cute, this longtime favorite showcases the authentic and homespun flavors of the Mexican kitchen. The space, virtually unchanged since opening almost fifteen years ago, is painted deep blue and is so small that a trip to the bathroom necessitates a walk through the open kitchen for an up close and personal view of the crew at work, where everything looks tidy.

The menu is tempting, but be sure to take a look at the mouthwatering specials listed on the wall. These might offer a cup of black bean soup seasoned with diced red onion, fresh tomato, and cilantro; or a whole roasted poblano *chile en nogada*, deliciously stuffed with ground pork, draped with creamy walnut sauce. Come dessert, try the homey, sopping moist *pastel de tres leches*.

Miss Lily's

C4

132 W. Houston St. (at Sullivan St.)

Subway: Houston St   Lunch Sat – Sun
Phone: 646-588-5375   Dinner nightly
Web: www.misslilysnyc.com
Prices: $$

Jamaica is the muse at this buzzy Serge Becker boîte. Up front, the look suggests a longtime take out joint, complete with orange Formica booths, linoleum flooring, and a backlit menu board above the open kitchen. Stacks of fresh produce are a bright touch and used for the juice bar preparations. The back room features preferred seating at curved black leather booths accented in red, green, and gold. Reggae record jackets line the walls and a thumping playlist fills the room.

Don't expect much from the service and you won't be disappointed. However, the food is very enjoyable, as in charred and smoky jerk chicken; pasture-raised curry goat; and richly spiced, bright yellow curried vegetables wrapped in warm and tender *roti* hit all the right notes.

Minetta Tavern ✿

Gastropub

113 MacDougal St. (at Minetta Ln.)

Subway: W 4 St - Wash Sq
Phone: 212-475-3850
Web: www.minettatavernny.com
Prices: $$$

Lunch Wed – Sun
Dinner nightly

Ngoc Ngo

To step into Minetta Tavern is to travel back in time—its history dates back to before *The Wizard of Oz* first hit the silver screen. More recently, this distinctive canteen was painstakingly restored and recast as a modern day institution by Keith McNally.

The original oak bar beckons you to sit and sip on a classic cocktail. The back dining room is richly atmospheric with black-and-white checkerboard flooring, red leather banquettes, and a wall adorned with a wraparound mural of Washington Square Park. Note the vintage photos of original owner Eddie "Minetta" Sieveri posing with celebrities.

Despite the departure of McNally's long-trusted co-chefs, Minetta Tavern's kitchen remains under steady stewardship. The food, like the setting, is deliciously timeless. Grilled meats are always high quality and mouthwatering like the excellent bone-in New York strip steak. The kitchen has a way with potatoes, so be sure to include a side like *pommes Anna*, a crisped and buttery cake of thinly shaved spuds. Classic French cooking also shines in items like the wickedly decadent *pied de porc pané*—a deep-fried Berkshire pig's trotter dressed with lentils, sauce *gribiche*, and an herb salad.

Morandi

C2

Italian ✗✗

211 Waverly Pl. (bet. Charles St. & Seventh Ave. South)

Subway: 14 St (Seventh Ave.)   Lunch daily
Phone: 212-627-7575   Dinner Wed – Sun
Web: www.morandiny.com
Prices: $$$

Morandi has all the requisite charm one would expect from a Keith McNally trattoria that recalls Tuscany with all its glorious clichés, antique-tiled floors, brick archways, and walls lined with straw-wrapped Chianti bottles. Dotted with a mishmash of tables, well-dressed patrons shielded by designer shades are bathed in a warm glow even at high noon, thanks to parchment-shaded ceiling fixtures.

They come to pay homage to a rustic menu that begins with seasonal *antipasti* before moving on to a classic panzanella marrying beefsteak and heirloom tomatoes, basil, and red onion. *Spaghetti neri*, squid ink pasta rolling with tender calamari, octopus, shrimp, and mussels; and spongy *budino limone* licked with buttermilk ice cream are favored for good reason.

Murray's Cheese Bar

D2

American ✗✗

264 Bleecker St. (bet. Leroy & Morton Sts.)

Subway: W 4 St - Wash Sq   Lunch Thu – Sun
Phone: 646-476-8882   Dinner nightly
Web: www.murrayscheesebar.com
Prices: $$

If you think a full service sit-down experience from the folks at Murray's Cheese shop sounds divine, you're 100% correct. A few doors away from that all-time foodie fave is this cheesy (that's a compliment) new destination. Flaunting an upscale vibe, the space is decorated with subway-tile walls, whitewashed wood tables, and red lacquered chairs.

The expertly conceived menu is decadently tempting but not for the faint of cholesterol. Indulge in a fondue melding Alpine cheese, pilsner and *piri piri*; gooey mac & cheese baked in cast iron and topped with fried onions; or burger crowned with a choice of pimento cheese, rarebit cheddar sauce, or creamy blue. End with an ethereal slice of lemon ricotta cake drizzled with Earl Grey syrup (and a Lipitor).

Neta

Japanese ✗✗

D1

61 W. 8th St. (bet. Fifth & Sixth Aves.)

Subway: W 4 St - Wash Sq   Dinner Mon – Sat
Phone: 212-505-2610
Web: www.netanyc.com
Prices: $$$$

Find Neta's modest exterior in the primo heart of Greenwich Village. The attractive space may be tiny with scripted servers flitting about, but it has an inviting and easygoing (think downtown) feel. Slim and slender, the space features two large tables in the front as well as a long counter lining the center of this lively space.

Expect to see finance types gobbling up the seafood-centric omakase, perhaps featuring Dungeness crab tossed with cucumber and scallions; mackerel *tataki* with ponzu; or spicy shrimp and lobster, both served on the shell with sautéed onions and tofu. Other distinctive sushi combos might include *tai* and king salmon topped with mustard-mayo sauce; kanpachi with bright and sweet shrimp; or crunchy eel-and-avocado maki.

One if by Land, Two if by Sea

Contemporary ✗✗✗

D1

17 Barrow St. (bet. Seventh Ave. South & W. 4th St.)

Subway: Christopher St - Sheridan Sq   Lunch Sun
Phone: 212-255-8649   Dinner nightly
Web: www.oneifbyland.com
Prices: $$$

Enter this legendary den of romance and try not to get swept away by the dizzying celebration of *l'amour*. This is the place to wine and dine your beloved, whether in the enchanting candlelit dining room amid deep red furnishings, a fireplace and melodious live piano, or the twinkling courtyard. Even the name is poetic (a verse from Longfellow's "The Midnight Ride of Paul Revere"). This is a place where no one dines alone.

Decadent offerings might begin with a cheeky starter of tender, grilled octopus with mint sauce enhanced with bits of apple and ginger, all presented to resemble a dragon swimming through the sea. Share bites of the deconstructed New York cheesecake, topped with warm cherry compote and served with Sevilla orange sorbet.

Panca

D1

Peruvian

92 Seventh Ave. South (bet. Bleecker & Grove Sts.)

Subway: Christopher St - Sheridan Sq   Lunch & dinner daily
Phone: 212-488-3900
Web: www.pancany.com
Prices: $$

Panca's sedate setting is a fine contrast to its highly trafficked location. Citron walls are complemented by a stacked stone bar area lined with bottles of pisco. Tucked away in the corner, find the ceviche station where fresh cuts of fish are transformed into zesty *cebiches* such as shrimp in lime juice with toothsome hominy and barely ripe yet perfectly tart mango. If you choose to sit on the sidewalk, be prepared to give up the dining room's tranquility.

Traditional specialties are a draw here, like *lomo saltado*, slivers of ribeye stir fried with onions, tomatoes, *aji amarillo*, and soy sauce. However, the chicken is a crowd-pleasing favorite—rotisserie-roasted and incredibly flavorful, it fills the room with a mouthwatering aroma.

Paradou

B1

French

8 Little W. 12th St. (bet. Greenwich & Washington Sts.)

Subway: 14 St - 8 Av   Lunch Sat – Sun
Phone: 212-463-8345   Dinner Tue – Sun
Web: www.paradounyc.com
Prices: $$

Paradou offers a bit of Provence and a welcome respite from the spate of gargantuan, too-cool-for-school dining halls populating the Meatpacking District. Here, a casual yet energetic crowd revels in the carefree, distinctly French spirit while relaxing over crisp glasses of champagne and supping on plates of foie gras or bowls of *moules du jour*.

Most guests choose to head to the patio which doubles Paradou's seating capacity, but the intimate dining room is lovely as well. Regardless of your seat, the menu offers classic cooking, as in lamb ribs drizzled with truffle honey; sides such as cassoulet beans showered with herbed breadcrumbs presented in a cast iron skillet; and finales such as warming apple crêpes spiked with Calvados.

Pastis

 French

B1

9 Ninth Ave. (at Little W. 12th St.)

Subway: 14 St - 8 Av
Phone: 212-929-4844
Web: www.pastisny.com
Prices: $$

Lunch & dinner daily

Think what you want about the Meatpacking District, but it's hard to argue its relevance to the herds of fashionistas roaming its cobblestoned streets. Manhattan hot spots come and go (even more rapidly in this neighborhood) but Pastis is one watering hole that still glows. Keith McNally's impressively popular French bistro combines scallop-patterned, mosaic tiled floors, a curved zinc counter stocked with bottles of rosé on ice, and precarious wooden stools to great effect. Closely spaced tables in the back dining room ensure a festive clamor. The menu is good and satisfying, focusing on traditional favorites like *moules frites*, steamed in Pernod and pleasantly enriched with a luxuriant touch of crème fraîche, alongside hot, crisp fries.

Pearl Oyster Bar

 Seafood

D2

18 Cornelia St. (bet. Bleecker & W. 4th Sts.)

Subway: W 4 St - Wash Sq
Phone: 212-691-8211
Web: www.pearloysterbar.com
Prices: $$

Lunch Mon – Fri
Dinner Mon – Sat

It's not hard to find a lobster roll in this city, and for that we can thank Rebecca Charles. This winsome seafood spot—inspired by her grandmother and childhood summers spent in Maine—has been going strong since 1997. Its success has assured many like-minded spin-offs.

The two-room setting offers a choice of counter seating or table service. The wood furnishings and white walls are low-key but beachy memorabilia perk up the space. The classic New England menu offers plates of chilled seafood and smaller dishes like johnnycake topped with thinly sliced smoked salmon. Entrées include that signature roll sided by shoestring fries, or lobster (boiled or grilled) served with corn pudding. A hot fudge sundae is a deliciously nostalgic finish.

Perilla

Contemporary 🍴🍴

D1

9 Jones St. (bet. Bleecker & W. 4th Sts.)

Subway: W 4 St - Wash Sq
Phone: 212-929-6868
Web: www.perillanyc.com
Prices: $$

Lunch Sat – Sun
Dinner nightly

This casually elegant Village fave showcases its unaffected ambience alongside the talent and dedication of partners Chef Harold Dieterle and General Manager Alicia Nosenzo. He is a CIA graduate and the premier winner of the reality television hit *Top Chef*; she hails from San Francisco and has honed her front-of-house skills at impressive restaurants on both coasts.

The kitchen turns globally sparked inspiration into a suite of clever creations that have included crispy lamb sweetbreads with cumin-infused glazed carrots and ginger-spiked sweet and sour sauce; and a roasted bone-in pork chop paired brilliantly with luscious *tonnato* sauce. For dessert, a boozy brunch-inspired block of sour cream coffee cake with rum raisin ice cream is pure pleasure.

Perla

Italian 🍴🍴

C3

24 Minetta Ln. (at Sixth Ave.)

Subway: W 4 St - Wash Sq
Phone: 212-933-1824
Web: www.perlanyc.com
Prices: $$$

Lunch Fri – Sun
Dinner nightly

Although Perla is quietly set along a narrow Village street, she's anything but undiscovered. This restored Italian tavern, named after restaurateur Gabriel Stulman's grandmother, has been a hit since day one. Inside, it boasts a charming backdrop in which to quench your thirst from the well-stocked marble bar or for settling into one of the brass-studded oxblood leather booths for a go at the menu.

Working from the wood-fired kitchen, Chef Michael Toscano churns out an array of pasta such as toothsome nuggets of orecchiette clutching broccoli rabe pesto and crumbles of sweet sausage. Move on to chicken *alla diavolo*, lacquered with a charged reduction of pickled peppers, red chili, and honey; and praline semifreddo in bittersweet chocolate.

Perry Street 🐸

A2

Contemporary ✗✗

176 Perry St. (at West St.)

Subway: Christopher St - Sheridan Sq
Phone: 212-352-1900
Web: www.jean-georges.com
Prices: $$

Lunch & dinner daily

Jean-Georges Vongerichten's far West Village canteen was, like many others, a temporary casualty of Superstorm Sandy. However, Perry Street was quick to bounce back and has returned just as chic, value-driven, and enjoyable as ever. The room is bathed in filtered sunshine and flaunts the same sleek, spare style.

Under son Cedric Vongerichten, the kitchen impresses a savvy clientele, which often includes the elder Chef Vongerichten's family, who live upstairs in the Richard Meier-designed building. A pillow of house-made *burrata* dressed with Meyer lemon jam, cracked pepper, and drizzle of olive oil deserves exultation; meanwhile, Scottish salmon is slow-cooked to perfection. Even chocolate pudding dazzles when topped with crystallized violets and cream.

The Place

B2

Contemporary ✗✗

310 W. 4th St. (bet. Bank & 12th Sts.)

Subway: 14 St - 8 Av
Phone: 212-924-2711
Web: www.theplaceny.com
Prices: $$

Lunch Sat – Sun
Dinner nightly

Set deep within the West Village, The Place is the kind of cozy, grotto-style den that makes you feel all grown-up. Rendezvous-like, guests climb below street level to find a bar aglow with flickering votive candles. Wander back a bit, and you'll find rustic beams and white tablecloth seating; two outdoor terraces beckon when the sun shines.

The guileless name of the "place" and timeless look of the century-old setting is nicely juxtaposed by a wholly contemporary menu that roams the globe: duck confit-filled parcels served with grain mustard and braised red cabbage is a lovely autumnal treat, while entrées please year-round with dishes like a cheddar-capped Shepherd's pie; Long Island duck breast with tamarind sauce; and Cuban-style pork chops.

Manhattan ▶ Greenwich, West Village & Meatpacking District

Pó

D2

31 Cornelia St. (bet. Bleecker & W. 4th Sts.)

Subway: W 4 St - Wash Sq
Phone: 212-645-2189
Web: www.porestaurant.com
Prices: $$

Lunch Wed – Sun
Dinner nightly

This longtime neighborhood favorite, opened in 1993, continues to attract a devoted following for its understated yet sophisticated ambience and creative Italian fare. During the day, the slender dining room is light and breezy, especially in warmer weather when the front door is propped open and ceiling fans swirl overhead. At night, this quaint spot tucked away on tree-lined Cornelia St. feels timeless and utterly romantic.

Egg dishes and panini are available at lunch. The dinner menu features a contemporary slant that may include starters like house-cured tuna dressed with white beans, artichokes, and chili-mint vinaigrette; freshly made gnocchi draped with lamb ragù; and entrées that include grilled skirt steak with Gorgonzola butter.

Recette

Contemporary

B2

328 W. 12th St. (at Greenwich St.)

Subway: 14 St - 8 Av
Phone: 212-414-3000
Web: www.recettenyc.com
Prices: $$$

Lunch Sun
Dinner nightly

At Recette, the atmosphere is quaint and buzzy; the talented kitchen is firing up sophisticated, playful dishes designed for sharing; and the chef's playlist is famous in its own right. Perched on an historic West Village corner, it becomes quickly packed with regulars and newcomers alike. The tiny space is styled with dark wood tables, twinkling votives, and white-paneled floor-to-ceiling windows.

Feast on a fantastic array of generously portioned small plates (you might need fewer than you think). The flow of courses reveals cod fritters nestled in lamb sausage ragù and doused with curry aïoli; exquisite duck breast atop beluga lentils and maitake mushrooms; and "Buffalo" sweetbreads—a twist on wings—complete with Valdeón blue cheese dipping sauce.

RedFarm

B2

  Asian

529 Hudson St. (bet. Charles & 10th Sts.)

Subway: Christopher St - Sheridan Sq
Phone: 212-792-9700
Web: www.redfarmnyc.com
Prices: $$

Lunch Sat – Sun
Dinner nightly

This eclectic Village-meets-MePa gem is tons of fun and reeks of creativity. Everything from its quirkily smart design, stylish staff, to the hipster crowd speaks to a trendy spirit. The vibe is loud and lively and communal seating means rubbing elbows with bright young things.

While for some this may recall those dreaded high school cafeteria scenes, it's a big part of the allure at this foodie hot spot. RedFarm gives Chinese food a slick and sexy makeover. The farmer's market runs head-on into the wok here, as the bustling kitchen sends out a succession of dishes such as lush, spicy jalapeño poppers packed with minced shrimp; duck-and-Fuji apple wraps, *shu mai* shooters, and spicy crispy beef tossed in an addictive glaze of vinegar and Grand Marnier.

Rockmeisha

D1

  Japanese

11 Barrow St. (bet. Seventh Ave. South & W. 4th St.)

Subway: Christopher St - Sheridan Sq
Phone: 212-675-7775
Web: N/A
Prices:

Dinner nightly

Regional specialties hailing from the chef's homeland of Kyushu, the large island in Southern Japan, are the way to go at this laid-back, fun, and tasty *izakaya*.

Like its name, the menu takes on a musical theme in listing its dishes as "goldies" which may reveal *takosu*, thick slices of dense octopus bobbing in a refreshing yuzu-zested soy vinegar sauce. Their "greatest hits" might feature the *tonsoku*, a crispy pork foot that is unctuous to the point of being voluptuous, accompanied by raw cabbage and a dab of citrusy-spicy *yuzu kosho* to cut the richness.

The intimate space is decorated with a touch of kitsch (think poison warning signs), curious little cartoon drawings lining the walls, and rock music pulsing in the background, of course.

Saxon + Parole

D4

Contemporary

316 Bowery (at Bleecker St.)

Lunch & dinner daily

Subway: Bleecker St
Phone: 212-254-0350
Web: www.saxonandparole.com
Prices: $$$

This sexy iteration of the short-lived Double Crown retains its key players in Executive Chef Brad Farmerie and the AvroKO Hospitality Group. Named after two 19th century racehorses, the handsome setting sports a limited use of color, and employs rich wood tones and warm lighting to achieve a suitably clubby atmosphere.

The crowd-pleasing menu, founded on grilled meats and seafood, boasts beginnings like a pot of velvety portobello mushroom mousse capped by a sheen of whiskey and black truffle jelly; and entrées such as whole-roasted branzino stuffed with Parmesan and smoked paprika-seasoned panko, sided by Brussels sprouts in chili caramel. Desserts play a deliciously whimsical note, as in steamed Christmas pudding with hard-sauce ice cream.

Scarpetta

B1

Italian

355 W. 14th St. (bet. Eighth & Ninth Aves.)

Dinner nightly

Subway: 14 St - 8 Av
Phone: 212-691-0555
Web: www.scottconant.com
Prices: $$$

Scarpetta moves to the beat of Chef Scott Conant, who is no stranger to gifted kitchens. Flanked by a MePa neighborhood that seems to have money tucked between the cobblestones to fund its constant development, Scarpetta remains an adored Italian treat. The restaurant is divided into two spaces: a stunning mahogany bar up front offers plenty of seats for the well-heeled patrons; in the main dining room, a retractable skylight crowns the plush tables dressed with a burnt orange motif-fabric.

If nestled at the bar, shoot the breeze with servers about braised duck with tender cavatelli; *capretto* bathed in a shimmering sauce of pancetta, mushrooms, and root vegetables; or a lush almond chocolate torte frilled with white balsamic marshmallows.

Sevilla

Spanish

62 Charles St. (at W. 4th St.)

Subway: Christopher St - Sheridan Sq
Phone: 212-929-3189
Web: www.sevillarestaurantandbar.com
Prices: $$

Lunch & dinner daily

With a long and colorful history since first opening its doors in 1941, charmingly nostalgic Sevilla remains a rarity among Manhattan's dining scene. The roaming menu harks back to traditional Spanish fare, heaping and hearty; the kind enjoyed long before our commonplace exposure to the cuisine became focused on small plates.

The majority of Sevilla's reasonably priced dishes are built around simply prepared seafood and chicken dressed with a number of primary sauces featuring almond, garlic, wine, and the prominent green sauce—parsley-packed and punched with garlic. Starters include the *ajo* soup, a clear chicken broth infused with the nutty essence of roasted garlic and enriched with egg; while the smooth, classic flan is a fitting finale.

Spasso

Italian

551 Hudson St. (at Perry St.)

Subway: Christopher St - Sheridan Sq
Phone: 212-858-3838
Web: www.spassonyc.com
Prices: $$

Lunch Wed – Sun
Dinner nightly

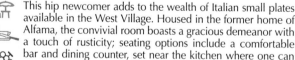

This hip newcomer adds to the wealth of Italian small plates available in the West Village. Housed in the former home of Alfama, the convivial room boasts a gracious demeanor with a touch of rusticity; seating options include a comfortable bar and dining counter, set near the kitchen where one can watch prosciutto being shaved, salads prepped, and gooey chocolate caramel *crostata* sliced and plated.

The kitchen serves up a delightful selection of contemporary Italian food. Bites include antipasti *del mare* and *della terra*. There are plenty of heartier options as well such as *corzetti* with plump razor clams, crunchy spring onions, and fragrant marjoram; and *secondi* like a grilled hanger steak paired with a heart-warming cannellini bean ragù.

Soto ❀ ❀

D1

357 Sixth Ave. (bet. Washington Pl. & W. 4th St.)

Subway: W 4 St – Wash Sq
Phone: 212-414-3088
Web: N/A
Prices: $$$

Dinner Mon – Sat

Tokio Kuniyoshi

Culinary dominance, unmistakable skill, and absolute discipline permeate every angle of this modest storefront. This is not some flashy temple to sushi, but an authentic and visually restrained rendering of a traditional Japanese restaurant. If the sterile look (with little more than blonde wood and bright lighting to embellish) seems too antiseptic, then remember that this is a place that prides itself on precise preparations of raw seafood. Does the staff fear their stern, formidable Chef Sotohiro Kosugi? Maybe.

Knife skills are paramount and every element is at its precise temperature, as these adept cooks coax each morsel of fish into a single bite that vies to be remembered as New York's best sushi. Composed dishes are not only strikingly beautiful, but may prove to be your favorite of the night— finely minced and impossibly rich bigeye tuna with avocado coulis, caviar, minced chives, threads of fried daikon, and nori with a sesame-ponzu sauce. The unctuous uni cocktail combines soy reduction and fresh wasabi with icy-cold sea urchin.

Elegant plates have included ebi tartare, showcasing the fresh flavors of sweet, raw shrimp with ginger, caviar, nori, and shiitake dashi.

Spice Market

B1

Asian ✗✗

403 W. 13th St. (at Ninth Ave.)

Subway: 14 St - 8 Av
Phone: 212-675-2322
Web: www.spicemarketnewyork.com
Prices: $$

Lunch Wed – Sun
Dinner nightly

This former warehouse turned sexy Asian street food lair has spawned offshoots in London and Qatar, further facilitating Chef Jean-Georges Vongerichten's global reach. But here in NYC, the 2004 original is a 12,000 square-foot fantasy glammed up by carved wooden arches, jewel-toned fabrics, a teak pagoda, and sarong-wrapped staff. The scene still thumps nightly, crammed with fun-loving grazers supping on faraway specialties all crafted with the chef's trademark élan. The carte divulges a savory romp: shatteringly crispy shrimp spring rolls; salt and pepper skate; polished copper bowls of pork *vindaloo*; and fried rice crowned by a sunny-side up egg ringed with gingery breadcrumbs.

Come to eat. Come to drink. Spice Market rarely disappoints.

Standard Grill

B1

Contemporary ✗✗

848 Washington St. (bet. Little W. 12th & 13th Sts.)

Subway: 14 St - 8 Av
Phone: 212-645-4100
Web: www.thestandardgrill.com
Prices: $$

Lunch & dinner daily

Classy comfort food is the name of the game at this jaunty grill that draws the "in" crowd. Despite the scene, the cooking is worth every penny. The raw bar or cheese fondue for a crowd make a fine start before moving on to the likes of grilled cobia fillet with a caramelized coating of *chermoula* marinade. Is that lobster Thermidor on the menu? Yes. And high-and lowbrow-desserts include baked Alaska and cookies with local milk.

Perched beneath the Highline, Standard Grill serves up a choice of seating: a bright and airy front lounge, breezy sidewalk, and a knockout dining room—clubby and sophisticated—replete with wood-paneled walls, subway tile-clad vaulted ceiling, comfy red leather booths, and tables sporting menswear-inspired linens.

Spotted Pig

Gastropub 🍴

B2

314 W. 11th St. (at Greenwich St.)

Lunch & dinner daily

Subway: Christopher St - Sheridan Sq
Phone: 212-620-0393
Web: www.thespottedpig.com
Prices: $$

The Spotted Pig

This clone of an English gastropub, reborn and bred as an instant New York classic, is settled within a charming brownstone on a pictorial West Village street. Chef April Bloomfield's esteemed neighborhood fixture may be perpetually packed to the gills, but the scene is worth relishing so plan to stick around for a while.

Dressed-up (or down) with wooden planks, quirky animal knickknacks, gentle lighting, and exposed brick walls, the bar up front boasts a handsome selection of drinks and carousers. Small tables sit close together and are stacked with tantalizing plates like seared, crispy mackerel and smoky pancetta garnished with a smooth, sweet potato purée.

Laid-back servers may look like hipster grad students, but are deeply knowledgeable and committed to their work. They eagerly rhapsodize on any of Chef Bloomfield's favorites, like the moist, meaty, and deliciously crisp pork belly in an aromatic broth brimming with baby turnips, onions, and Swiss chard. Meals may move on to other savory delights, but a wonderfully rich *banoffee* pie made from roasted bananas, cloaked by whipped cream, and served atop a crumbled biscuit base delivers a perfect smack of sweet for the end.

Takashi

456 Hudson St. (bet. Barrow & Morton Sts.)

Subway: Christopher St - Sheridan Sq
Phone: 212-414-2929
Web: www.takashinyc.com
Prices: $$

Dinner nightly

Chef Takashi Inoue's meaty array honors the *yakiniku* (Japanese for Korean-style barbecue) focus of his hot spot and allows diners to tap into their inner pyromaniac by way of tabletop grilling atop striated wood benches.

Start off cool, with say *yooke* (a mound of exquisitely fresh chuck eye steak tartare seasoned with a light, refreshing house sauce and topped with a quail egg) before moving on to sustainably raised cuts of beef which are either seasoned with salt, garlic, and sesame oil, or marinated in Takashi's special sauce. Some nightly specials require the chef's expert preparation, as in domestic Kobe chuck flat steak grilled rare and simply presented with lemon wedges, wasabi, and soy sauce—this well-marbled beauty needs nothing else.

Tertulia 😊

359 Sixth Ave. (at Washington Pl.)

Subway: W 4 St - Wash Sq
Phone: 646-559-9909
Web: www.tertulianyc.com
Prices: $$

Lunch & dinner daily

Hooray for fried food that's totally fun and memorable. Inspired by a *sidreria* or cider house common to Northern Spain, Chef Seamus Mullen's celebrated eatery is a convivial gathering spot. The friendly bar features wooden barrels that dispense Spanish wines, excellent sangria, and of course their ever-coveted ciders.

Cured meats and cheeses bolster the array of tapas like crisp baby eggplant with hazelnut romesco. Open all day, lunch offers a pleasing prix-fixe that may reveal a cool salad of *pardina* lentils mixed with diced cucumber, radicchio, and homemade fresh cheese; or a grilled skirt steak sandwich spread with intense Valdeón cheese alongside spicy pickled veggies and just-fried potato chips. Crispy *churros* are more memorable than a Neruda ode.

Tomoe Sushi

Japanese 🍴

C4

172 Thompson St. (bet. Bleecker & Houston Sts.)

Subway: Spring St (Sixth Ave.)
Phone: 212-777-9346
Web: N/A
Prices: 💰

Lunch Tue – Sat
Dinner nightly

Tomoe focuses on value and quality rather than soigné appearances. Its tile floor has been dulled by a steady stream of sushi aficionados, the simple furnishings aren't conducive to leisurely meals, and the décor is limited to hand-drawn signs displaying specials. Still, regulars enthuse over these supple morsels prepared by the efficient team behind the counter and presented by swift, casual servers.

Characterized by pieces that err on the side of heft, this sushi has a foundation of rich, thickly cut slices of fish, minimal embellishment, and fine technique. The kitchen also prepares a long list of cooked dishes that display a creative hand, as in steamed buns filled with teriyaki-brushed silken tofu, pickled garlic, and a dollop of mayonnaise.

Ushiwakamaru

Japanese 🍴

C4

136 W. Houston St. (bet. MacDougal & Sullivan Sts.)

Subway: B'way - Lafayette St
Phone: 212-228-4181
Web: N/A
Prices: $$$$

Dinner Mon – Sat

Arrive early enough and you may find Ushiwakamaru's tables pre-assigned to reserved guests by way of post-its: most nights, this casual basement *sushi-ya* is packed with regulars craving Chef Hideo Kuribara's skillfully crafted morsels.

Sitting at the counter should influence you to indulge in the omakase, along with most of your neighbors. It is more interactive here than found at more traditional *sushi-ya*, allowing diners to tailor the experience based on their budget. Your *itamae* will send forth the likes of a sweet-tasting slice of giant clam; or wild baby yellowtail perched atop warm, loosely packed rice; and sashimi that may feature silver-skinned horse mackerel; or slivers of toothsome octopus tentacles sided by pepper-flecked sea salt.

Wallsé ✦

B2

344 W. 11th St. (at Washington St.)

Subway: Christopher St – Sheridan Sq
Phone: 212-352-2300
Web: www.kg-ny.com
Prices: $$$

Lunch Sun
Dinner nightly

KGNY

The façade seems so typically "Greenwich Village" that Wallsé might even strive to seal the neighborhood's reputation as a creative hub. Inside, colorful, modern portraits of Chef Kurt Gutenbrunner embellish the bar room and merit attention. The décor is a study in textures, from the Venetian stucco and white brick walls to the long velvet banquette and tables dressed in crisp linen. Carefully arranged flowers and black wood accents strike a moody yet sophisticated balance. The staff is excellent and very much focused; the clientele is affluent and discerning.

Wallsé is named for the chef's hometown outside Vienna, so it is no surprise that each plate reflects both classic and modern flavors of Austria. Meals might begin with a stunning terrine of cool, rich foie gras with chewy bits of Port-preserved figs and beautifully glazed brioche. Then, move on to herb-crusted venison loin, lean and crimson, with woodsy chanterelles and a hearty cheese and potato *schupfnudeln*.

Desserts are always showstoppers as in pear strudel, encasing impeccable little cubes of poached fruit in fine sheets of wonderfully crunchy phyllo, with roasted walnut ice cream and, of course, a dollop of fluffy *schlag*.

Wild

Pizza ✗

B2

535 Hudson St. (bet. Charles & Perry Sts.)

Subway: Christopher St - Sheridan Sq   Lunch & dinner daily
Phone: 212-929-2920
Web: www.eatdrinkwild.com
Prices: $$

A cluster of farm-to-table salads and deliciously distinctive pizzas are the nerve center of this novel Village establishment. The fact that they happily coexist alongside locally roasted coffee, New York State beers and wines, refreshing ginger lemonade, and a gluten-free menu is simply an added bonus. Diners of all stripes delight in items from The Field—maybe a kale salad tossed with smoked tofu, shaved radish, and edamame, drizzled with sublime olive oil and a spot-on hit of salt; or arugula with charred radicchio and roasted yellow tomatoes. The Oven presents pizza with a vegan crust (crafted from wild yeast) that is at once thin, crisp, and light, topped with clouds of mozzarella, blackened chilies, and eggplant; or seared vegetables with pesto.

Wong

Asian ✗

D2

7 Cornelia St. (bet. Bleecker & W. 4th Sts.)

Subway: W 4 St - Wash Sq   Dinner Mon – Sat
Phone: 212-989-3399
Web: www.wongnewyork.com
Prices: $$

Malaysian-born Simpson Wong's eponymous spot is tucked away on one of the coziest blocks in Greenwich Village. Beyond its windowed façade, the cool space is framed by whitewashed brick walls. Diners sit at either communal tables or two counters, one of which overlooks the inner workings of the kitchen.

The menu utilizes local farm products for a concise presentation of contemporary-minded Asian cuisine. Expect the likes of lightly cooked Swiss chard with mildly spiced *sambal*, faintly sweet with gratings of toasted coconut; and novel creations like thick, chewy rice noodles tangled within a hearty, satisfying sauce of finely chopped pork, sea cucumber, and shiitakes. Desserts include roast-duck ice cream with star anise-poached plums—for real.

Yerba Buena Perry

C2 Latin American ✗✗

1 Perry St. (at Greenwich Ave.)

Subway: 14 St (Seventh Ave.)
Phone: 212-620-0808
Web: www.ybnyc.com
Prices: $$

Lunch Sat – Sun
Dinner nightly

Executive Chef Julian Medina mambos his way through the kitchens of not one, but six different restaurants, including Toloache and Coppelia. But, this tiny but oh-so-mighty restaurant takes the cake.

Mixing Cuban, Peruvian, Chilean, and Mexican influences and traditions, upscale Medina delivers a signature flavor. Even familiar dishes have unexpected flair as in the ribeye ceviche dressed with spicy red pepper sauce, and completed with corn kernels and sea urchin lobes. In the hands of this kitchen, even simple shrimp assumes a lobster-like meatiness, complemented with their own Rio de Janeiro-style salsa.

The tightly packed room is comfortable but can feel cramped, so hope to make new friends to share the meaty *parrillada* and a trio of fab fries.

ZZ's Clam Bar

C4 Seafood ✗

169 Thompson St. (bet. Bleecker & Houston Sts.)

Subway: Spring St (Sixth Ave.)
Phone: 212-254-3000
Web: www.zzsclambar.com
Prices: $$$$

Dinner Tue – Sat

Striking while they're hot, ZZ's is yet another reason to love the team of Carbone and Torrisi. Okay, so there's a doorman outside (he's there to prevent curious crowds from spilling into the turquoise-trimmed boîte) and one look at the menu is likely to cause sticker shock. But who's to argue with product this exemplary?

A black leather banquette seats a handful of diners who luxuriate as icy cocktails and clams on the half shell are stirred and shucked before their eyes. Stunning plates reveal kanpachi tartare, chopped into a cloud, studded with raw oysters and caramelized broccoli florets; live sea scallop sliced thin and showered with Sicilian pistachio- and browned butter-breadcrumbs; or *shimaaji* tartare layered with whipped ricotta and caviar.

Harlem, Morningside & Washington Heights

Flanked by beautiful Riverside and Morningside parks and home to stately Columbia University, Morningside Heights is a lovely quarter of the city. It is also known and frequented for some of the best breakfast spots in town. Sandwich shops and eateries line these avenues, where quick, inexpensive meals are a collegiate necessity. Resident academics and Ivy leaguers can be found darting to and from class or lounging at the enticing **Hungarian Pastry Shop** with a sweet treat and cup of tea. Considered a landmark, this old-world bakery has been open for more than three decades now, and is a focal point for students, locals, and visitors alike.

Across the street, Saint John the Divine, a gorgeous Gothic revival and formidable presence on Amsterdam Avenue offers beauty, history, and wonderful community outreach programs. Special occasions call for an evening sojourn at **Lee Lee's Baked Goods**. Rather than be misled by its sterile locale, prepare yourself for a plateful of the most decadent rugelach ever. In the summer, enjoy a drink in the breeze on their alluring outdoor terrace. To the north is Harlem—a true feast for the stomach and soul. Fifth Avenue divides the neighborhood into two very unique areas: West Harlem, an epicenter of African-American culture; and East Harlem, a diverse Latin quarter affectionately referred to as "El Barrio."

WEST HARLEM

West Harlem still retains a kind of sassy edge as it gives way to steady and welcomed gentrification—one of its most visible borders is at **Fairway**, a Tri-State area staple that allures shoppers off the West Side Highway for their mind-boggling offerings and sensational produce. For a taste of the area's history, sift through the impressive literary collection at The Schomburg Center for Research in Black Culture on Lenox Avenue, or spend a sunny afternoon among the quaint row houses in the historic districts of Sugar Hill and Hamilton Heights.

When the sun goes down, slip into famed **Patisserie des Ambassades** whose contemporary yet chic interior and knack for flavors is evident throughout breakfast, lunch, and dinner. They successfully entice with aromas wafting from delicacies like croissants to eclairs au chocolat and plates of cream-filled beignets. Harlem Week is an annual festival that features art, music, and food each August. While here, cool off with a cone of red velvet cake ice cream if the natural ice cream stand is around. Food factors heavily into Harlem culture—both east and west of Fifth Avenue—and the choices are as diverse as the neighborhood itself. From Mexican to Caribbean to West African, the culinary delights abound. To further indulge

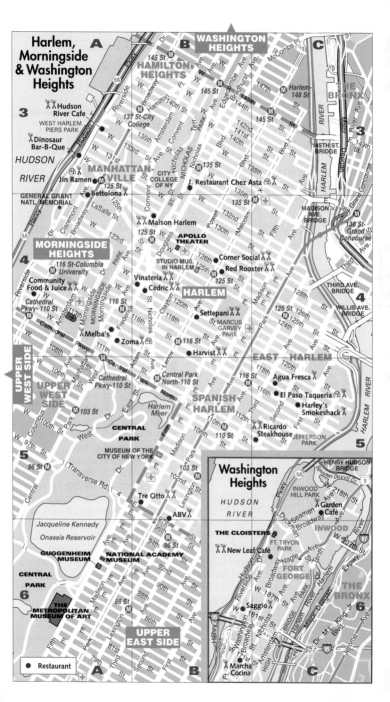

Harlem, Morningside & Washington Heights

A **B** WASHINGTON HEIGHTS **C**

THE BRONX

Hudson River Cafe
WEST HARLEM PIERS PARK

Dinosaur Bar-B-Que

HUDSON RIVER

HAMILTON HEIGHTS
145 St
137 St–City College
145 St
Harlem-148 St
145 St
145TH ST. BRIDGE

Jin Ramen
MANHATTAN-VILLE
Bettolona
CITY COLLEGE OF NY
J. Restaurant Chez Asta

GENERAL GRANT NATL. MEMORIAL
135 St
135 St
MADISON AVE. BRIDGE
138 St–Grand Concourse

Maison Harlem
Apollo Theater
STUDIO MUS. IN HARLEM

MORNINGSIDE HEIGHTS
116 St–Columbia University
Community Food & Juice
Cathedral Pkwy- 110 St

Corner Social
Red Rooster
125 St
THIRD AVE. BRIDGE
WILLIS AVE. BRIDGE

Vinateria
Cédric
HARLEM
MORNINGSIDE PARK
Settepani
MARCUS GARVEY PARK
EAST HARLEM
125 St 126th
125th
124th

Melba's
Zoma
Harvist
116 St
SPANISH HARLEM

Agua Fresca
El Paso Taqueria
Harley's Smokeshack

UPPER WEST SIDE
Cathedral Pkwy-110 St
Central Park North-110 St
116 St
110 St
Ricardo Steakhouse
JEFFERSON PARK

103 St
Harlem Meer
CENTRAL PARK
MUSEUM OF THE CITY OF NEW YORK

96 St
Transverse Rd
103 St

Tre Otto

Jacqueline Kennedy Onassis Reservoir

GUGGENHEIM MUSEUM
NATIONAL ACADEMY MUSEUM

ABV

CENTRAL PARK
THE METROPOLITAN MUSEUM OF ART

UPPER EAST SIDE

Washington Heights

HENRY HUDSON BRIDGE
INWOOD HILL PARK
Garden Café
HUDSON RIVER
INWOOD
THE CLOISTERS
FT. TRYON PARK
New Leaf Café
FORT GEORGE
THE BRONX

Saggio

Marcha Cocina

● Restaurant

your fried food fantasy, entrée venerable **Charles Country Pan Fried Chicken** for Chef Charles Gabriel's acclaimed buffet and sinfully delicious fried chicken. For dangerously spiced Senegalese food, head to **Afrika Kine**; or shop around **Darou Salam Market** for a range of West African groceries. **Harlem Shambles**, a true-blue butcher shop, specializes and offers quality cuts of meat and poultry designed to enhance any dining experience.

East Harlem

In East Harlem, Cuban cuisine fans and culture-vultures should visit **Amor Cubano** for their tasty home-style creations including *lechon*, savored amidst a vibrant atmosphere of live Cuban music. For Caribbean delights stop into **Sisters**; or peruse the taco trucks and taquerias along the Little Mexico strip of East 116th Street in the heart of one of New York's many Mexican communities. A remnant of the former Italian population of East Harlem, **Rao's** is a New York institution. Run out of a small basement and frequented by the likes of Donald Trump and Nicole Kidman, Rao's is one of the most difficult tables to get in all of Manhattan. The original patrons have exclusive rights to a seat here and hand off their reservations like rent-controlled apartments. Better try to get in good with the owner if you can. **Patsy's** is still holding strong in East Harlem, offering a plethora of Italian specialties while burning its coal oven, and sometimes its pizza.

Washington Heights

The diverse Washington Heights offers ample food choices from trucks (**Patacon Pisao** for Venezuelan food?) to restaurants, perfect for the late-night crowd. The Tony award-winning musical *In The Heights* pays tribute to this ebullient neighborhood, where Dominican and Puerto Rican communities have taken root. Latin beats blast through the air; and bright, refreshing Puerto Rican piragua carts can be found selling shaved ice soaked in a rainbow of tropical flavors. Locals line up around the block at **Elsa La Reina del Chicharrón** for their deliciously deep-fried *chicharrón* featuring crispy pork chunks. Then, try *jugos naturales*—juices made from cane sugar and fresh fruits like pineapple and orange—for a healthy treat. On the opposite end of the spectrum, **Carrot Top Pastries** seduces locals with sweet potato pies.

Great fish markets and butcher shops also dot these streets, and less than ten bucks will get you a delicious plate of *pernil* with rice and beans at any number of eateries. Duck into **La Rosa Fine Foods** for fresh fish, meat, and produce; or **Nelly's Bakery** for a creamy cup of *café con leche* and a *guayaba con queso* (guava and cheese pastry). Speaking of standing relics, **Piper's Kilt** in Inwood represents the former Irish and German population of the area. Settle into a booth at the lively "**Kilt**" with some Irish nachos and a perfect pint.

ABV

B5

Gastropub ✗

1504 Lexington Ave. (at 97th St.)

Subway: 96 St (Lexington Ave.)
Phone: 212-722-8959
Web: www.abvny.com
Prices: $$

Lunch Sat – Sun
Dinner nightly

Adam Clark, Michael Cesari, and Corey Cova have leveraged their success at Earl's Beer & Cheese with the more ambitious ABV (alcohol by volume). This Americana gastropub, on a stretch of Lexington Avenue rife with a new development, seems amusingly out of place within posh Carnegie Hill. Just think of the setting as part of the story starring picnic tables, soft lighting, and a giant chalkboard citing beers and specials. The semi-open kitchen can be viewed running on all cylinders, preparing chilled tomato soup spiced with chives, charred edamame, and *cotija*. Emblematic of their fresh vision is a pristine scallop ceviche stirred with horseradish and pea leaves; lamb meatballs in an aromatic tomato-cinnamon sauce; and a standout chocolate *pot de crème*.

Agua Fresca

C5

Mexican ✗

207 E. 117th St. (bet. Second & Third Aves.)

Subway: 116 St (Lexington Ave.)
Phone: 212-996-2500
Web: www.aguafrescarestaurant.com
Prices:

Lunch & dinner daily

Agua Fresca is an out-of-this-world entrance into the sunny, authentic, and delicious flavors of Mexico. Thank Chef Adrian Leon, who also hails from this great land, for his menu's showcase of Nuevo Latin leanings along with solid, traditional fare.

Beyond the rather unimpressive commercial locale, the dining space is cheery—everything seems kissed by bright colors and tastes from strawberry sangria to baked cinnamon churros with *dulce de leche*. Start with the fab guacamole trio: classic; smoky chipotle; and pineapple-shrimp. Other must-haves include *chilaquiles rojos al arbol* (crispy tortilla chips smothered in smoky *arbol* salsa, *queso fresco*, and juicy chicken in tomatillo sauce); or tender pork chop in *pasilla chile* sauce over sweet plantain mash.

Bettolona

A4

 Italian ✗

3143 Broadway (bet. LaSalle St. & Tiemann Pl.)

Subway: 125 St (Broadway)   Lunch & dinner daily
Phone: 212-749-1125
Web: N/A
Prices: $$

 Bettolona has slowly but steadily built a fanfare, courtesy of an Italian team that bestows its authenticity. This hole-in-the-wall is charming, with its mellifluous lighting, red banquettes, and rustic mien. The pizza oven also lends a hand in luring locals for a home-style Regina Margherita with *fior di latte* and San Marzano tomatoes.

Wood tables are tightly set, so this isn't ideal for date-night. Yet familiar, tasty pastas like spinach fettuccine with sweet sausage, peas, and tomatoes in cream sauce; or *penne Siciliane* slathered with ricotta and cubed eggplant in tomato sauce (just like *nonna* used to make) are hugely favored among the Columbia University crowd.

Baby sib Coccola also brings classic Italian food year-round to Morningside Heights.

Cédric

B4

Mediterranean ✗✗

185 St. Nicholas Ave. (at 119th St.)

Subway: 116 St (Frederick Douglass Blvd.)   Lunch & dinner daily
Phone: 212-866-7766
Web: www.cedricbistro.com
Prices: $$

With sensual interior accents like etched mirrors, gold and red splashes, and flashy chandeliers, Cédric oozes almost as much cool as its uptown home—it's impossible not to have a good time here. Stunning florals sit proudly at the bar as if it were a sign that austerity is not their style. While this Harlem sophisticate is hardly dull, the round-the-clock crowd can make the zinc bar and dining room feel snug.

Through the large pane windows, watch happy diners dive into a bowl of excellent mussels plumped with white wine and shallots. Seared salmon fillets quenched with balsamic and paired with ratatouille; or a staggeringly creamy crème brûlée studded with vanilla flecks are other reasons why this darling is so adored and well-attended.

Community Food & Juice

A4   A m e r i c a n   XX

2893 Broadway (bet. 112th & 113th Sts.)

Subway: Cathedral Pkwy/110 St (Broadway)   Lunch & dinner daily
Phone: 212-665-2800
Web: www.communityrestaurant.com
Prices: $$

Community Food & Juice is an accomplished restaurant with a deep understanding of its clientele. As part of the sprawl of Columbia University, this address is a godsend for students, faculty, and nearby residents from morning to night. The weekday blueberry pancake breakfast special complete with bottomless cups of coffee is just one reason why it gets so much love. Executive Chef/partner Neil Kleinberg, also of Clinton St. Baking Company, and his brigade turn out joyful fare, including grilled flatbread pizza, spicy shrimp and grits, and sides like carrot hashbrowns.

The setting is accented by grey slate and ivory seating. Although it's spacious with plenty of outdoor options, expect to wait for a table since reservations are not accepted.

Corner Social

B4   A m e r i c a n   XX

321 Lenox Ave. (at 126th St.)

Subway: 125 St (Lenox Ave.)   Lunch & dinner daily
Phone: 212-510-8552
Web: www.cornersocialnyc.com
Prices: $$

This high-flying neighborhood now boasts some serious restaurant competition, and Corner Social is only enhancing its reputation as a veritable Harlem dining destination. Much more than a tavern, the pub concept is elevated here with attention to ingredients sourced locally and sustainably farmed. This is a cool, welcoming gathering place that locals are proud to call their own.

On the focused menu, find tasty pulled pork sliders awash in cider vinegar and flecked with red pepper flakes, served alongside fresh, cool coleslaw and tart pickle slices. Fried green tomatoes are thick, sturdy slices dredged in cornmeal and pan-fried to perfection. House-made sweet potato cake is heady with spices and frosted with vanilla for a classic wedge of Americana.

Dinosaur Bar-B-Que

A3

700 W. 125th St. (at Twelfth Ave.)

Subway: 125 St (Broadway)
Phone: 212-694-1777
Web: www.dinosaurbarbque.com
Prices: $$

Lunch & dinner daily

Pull the reigns in on any barbecue purists before suggesting a trip to Dinosaur Bar-B-Que. This is not a traditional, Southern spot that seeks to replicate a known, loved style such as Kansas City or North Carolina. This is a fun, welcoming joint for groups craving tasty, well-priced, beer-friendly fare. Everything is pervaded with smoky-rich flavors, as in the ribs marinated in their signature spice rub and slowly pit-smoked. A West Texas rib eye arrives tender beneath an enticingly salty crust. Still, they may save the best for last here, so be sure to try to the sweet potato-pecan pie topped with smoky-sweet nuts. Weekends bring live blues, jazz, and funk music, elevating the already boisterous tone.

Bustling Greenpoint now boasts a delicious sib.

El Paso Taqueria

C5

237 E. 116th St. (bet. Second & Third Aves.)

Subway: 116 St (Lexington Ave.)
Phone: 212-860-4875
Web: N/A
Prices: 🍴🍴

Lunch & dinner daily

Hidden in plain sight is this standout, serving some of Manhattan's best Mexican eats. Beyond the intricately designed wrought-iron gates lies the adorably appointed interior, dressed-up with warming brick walls, ceramic accents, and an inviting back patio.

Begin with the likes of steamed tamales packed with jalapeños and cheese; or the excellent and refreshing beef tripe soup in a tomato-chile *guajillo* broth topped with cilantro and onions. Other highlights might include the *cemita al pastor* of chipotle-marinated pork on a sesame seed bun with Oaxaca cheese, avocado, onions, and pineapple; or classic and delectable *chile rellenos*, cheese-stuffed, egg-battered poblano peppers in a smoky tomato sauce, sprinkled with ample crumbles of *cotija*.

Garden Café

C5

American

4961 Broadway (bet. 207 & Isham Sts.)

Subway: Inwood - 207 St
Phone: 212-544-9480
Web: N/A
Prices: $$

Lunch & dinner daily

This Inwood favorite continues to be an idyllic getaway from the noisy Broadway hustle just outside its doors. Enter to find brick patches peeking beyond pale yellow walls, dark-wood tables, and flower arrangements. A narrow hall leads to the bucolic garden, which is enclosed and warm in the winter, open and airy during the summer, and entertaining with live music on the weekends.

The food here remains as delightful as the surroundings. The menu crackles with such offerings as blackened, sesame-crusted tuna set atop two fluffy black bean corn cakes; or nutty buckwheat penne tossed with wilted baby spinach, portobello mushrooms, garlic, and olive oil. Hearty turkey meatloaf with green beans and mashed potatoes is everything you crave it to be.

Harley's Smokeshack

C5

Barbecue

355 E. 116th St. (bet. First & Second Aves.)

Subway: 116 St (Lexington Ave.)
Phone: 212-828-6723
Web: www.harleyssmokeshack.org
Prices: $$

Lunch & dinner daily

The Harlem barrio is known for heart-thumping Latin eats, so the arrival of barbecue courtesy of Harley's Smokeshack was as refreshing as a glass of cold sweet tea. The exposed brick interior is dressed in cowboy trappings like boots, bull skulls, and leather saddles. It's a sight to behold—and to smell those tantalizingly smoky aromas.

The loud bar is best for those with a game and gulp in mind, while groups head to the back to devour the smoky Southern menu. The food is a mouthwatering, gut-busting homage to this region, as in a barbecue-Frito pie piled with pulled pork, cheddar, and jalapeños. Expect dry-rubbed St. Louis-cut spareribs to carry a delicious dose of charred flavor; or hunks of brisket-stuffed meatloaf glazed with apple-barbecue sauce.

Harvist

American

B4

46 W. 116th St. (bet. Fifth & Lenox Aves.)

Subway: 116 St (Lenox Ave.)
Phone: 646-738-3050
Web: www.myimagestudios.com
Prices: $$

Lunch Sat – Sun
Dinner Tue – Sun

Set off the lobby of the Kalahari condo, this vast ground floor-cum-cultural center houses Harvist. Patronized by art enthusiasts who flock here for the center's live entertainment and film screenings, Harvist is nothing short of respectable. Adorned with a flourishing bar, the handsome space combines sage walls, red banquettes, and ultra-mod panels projecting broadcast events.

The American menu might begin with supremely juicy *sambal*-rubbed barbecue wings glazed with a sweet-sticky sauce; or jalapeño-laced grits paired with a buttery cheddar biscuit. Smoky-tender lamb chops are perfection when finished with spinach-peanut pesto and served over couscous. A red velvet soufflé topped with candied pecans proves that desserts must not be skipped.

Hudson River Cafe

Latin American

A3

697 W. 133rd St. (at Twelfth Ave.)

Subway: 125 St (Broadway)
Phone: 212-491-9111
Web: www.hudsonrivercafe.com
Prices: $$

Lunch Sat – Sun
Dinner nightly

There is nothing more NY than savoring tasty treats while basking in sunny Hudson River views. While the live music and occasional Amtrak rumble may elevate the decibels, lounging on the bi-level patio with a sweet cocktail or beer in hand restores the pleasure. Also lending a soothing aspect is their sleek interior dressed with wooden floors and mosaic tiles. Modern accents prevail with black, white, and red splashes.

Well-crafted fixtures cast a soft glow on flavorful Latin dishes, like *taquitos* stuffed with crispy coconut shrimp, or *costillas de buey*, braised short ribs in a pomegranate-Rioja reduction. Creations like *ceviche mixto* in a Bloody Mary *mojo* and a rich chocolate cake oozing at the center show the kitchen's love for purely fun fare.

Jin Ramen

A3

Japanese

3183 Broadway (bet. 125th St. & Tiemann Pl.)

Subway: 125 St (Broadway)
Phone: 646-559-2862
Web: www.jinramen.com
Prices: 💶

Lunch & dinner daily

Jin Ramen's location at the foot of the 125th subway exit and the owners' ties to Columbia University are not the reasons why this hugely favored establishment sees a constant stream of hungry diners. Nor is their success thanks to the divinely simple space, decked with a smattering of cramped tables and dining counter set beneath warm, wood-textured walls. They just happen to be serving the best ramen anywhere above 59th Street.

Towering windows look upon Broadway, but bubbling stovetops may just be the view of choice here. Steaming bowls of *shio ramen* with bamboo shoots and a soy-flecked egg are churned out routinely by chefs who are all smiles when assembling *tonkotsu*, rich and salty with pork, or the exemplary *nankotsu kara-age* (fried chicken).

J. Restaurant Chez Asta

B3

Senegalese

2479 Frederick Douglass Blvd. (bet. 132nd & 133rd Sts.)

Subway: 135 St (Frederick Douglass Blvd.)
Phone: 212-862-3663
Web: N/A
Prices: 💶

Lunch & dinner daily

♿ 🍽️🕐

Harlem's food scene is exploding, and this sensational Senegalese newcomer is a welcome addition to the party. Enter to find a spirited and generous staff tending to a space outfitted with doily-topped tables, high backed chairs, tile floors, and a massive marble bar.

Exquisitely and authentically prepared dishes range from lamb *mafe*, a rich stew of tender lamb, carrots, and potatoes simmering in decadent peanut butter sauce, served with rice; to the *attiéké*, a tart, fermented cassava root similar in texture to couscous. Senegal's national dish, *thiebou djeun rouge* arrives as a fiery concoction of habanero-stuffed red snapper, yucca, cauliflower, green cabbage, eggplant, and okra, stewed in a tomato-based broth, and served over spicy *jolof* rice.

Maison Harlem

French ✗✗

341 St. Nicholas Ave. (at 127th St.)

Subway: 125 St (St. Nicholas Ave.)   Lunch & dinner daily
Phone: 212-222-9224
Web: www.maisonharlem.com
Prices: $$

Bucolic Paris meets unapologetically cool Harlem at this fun-time spot, where the breezy vibe provides a much needed respite from the phone-toting tourists just east on Lenox. Gorgeous floor-to-ceiling windows, dark red banquettes, and quirky touches like vintage Gallic posters or yellow Mobil T-shirts pinned to the wall, lend a whiff of whimsy.

The bistro-style menu plays around with culinary traditions and the results may include tender duck leg confit, drizzled with orange-cognac sauce, and served with cauliflower gratin; or crispy crab and shrimp cakes atop a green salad. Other playful inventions have revealed grilled daurade fillet matched with an herbaceous lemon sauce and asparagus; or tart lemon curd layered into a rich, buttery crust.

Marcha Cocina

Latin American ✗

4055 Broadway (at 171st St.)

Subway: 168 St   Lunch & dinner daily
Phone: 212-928-8272
Web: www.marchanyc.com
Prices: $$

Owner/chef duo Freddy and Virgilio de la Cruz have staked their territory in Washington Heights with this cool standout, fit for night owls and diners alike. A back-lit bar, bright yellow banquettes, filament bulbs, and white tables create a sleek look, while the engaging staff ensures a friendly atmosphere. Snack on savory *cocas cangrejos*, Catalan flatbread layered with crabmeat, goat and Manchego cheeses, jalapeño, and cilantro; or linger over amazingly crisp *croquetas* of chopped mushroom, cheddar, and herbs over truffled aïoli. *Platos fuertes* may bring a tender skirt steak in a pool of cheese fondue, topped with bright *chimichurri*, and served with fried yucca. Tasty tapas include scallops *a la plancha*, kissed with caramelized onion and Serrano ham.

Melba's

A4   S o u t h e r n ✗

300 W. 114th St. (at Frederick Douglass Blvd.)

Subway: 116 St (Frederick Douglass Blvd.)   Lunch & dinner daily
Phone: 212-864-7777
Web: www.melbasrestaurant.com
Prices: $$

A colorful spirit and Southern classics do much to remind guests of this quickly gentrifying area's flavor, culture, and past. Quaint and lovely Melba's is a place to gather and relax over good food and drinks, from Auntie B's mini-burgers slathered in smoky-sweet sauce to an absolutely perfect fruit cobbler—a golden brown and berry-licious height of the pantheon.

Equally important is the swoon-inducing Southern-fried chicken: darkly bronzed, salty-sweet, and tender. Thick fillets of fresh flakey tilapia may be densely crusted with crushed pecans and topped in white gravy. Expect surprises here, from the spring rolls with black-eyed peas, collards, and red rice, to a complex Italian *semillion* (ideal for pairing with that fried chicken and waffles).

New Leaf Café

C6   A m e r i c a n ✗✗

1 Margaret Corbin Dr. (in Fort Tryon Park)

Subway: 190 St   Lunch & dinner Tue – Sun
Phone: 212-568-5323
Web: www.newleafrestaurant.com
Prices: $$

Located in a 1930s mansion designed by the Olmstead brothers, New Leaf Café was opened as part of the New York Restoration Project. The inside feels like a large cottage with stone walls and arched windows. Alfresco lunch on the flagstone terrace showcases this high, hilly setting with unparalleled views of the Palisades (squint to find the George Washington Bridge).

The American menu features a fried risotto cake with gooey mozzarella over Tokyo turnips and sweet pea coulis; or a hunk of seared tuna with tiny mushroom-filled ravioli. Profiteroles are a particular treat, filled with vanilla ice cream and drizzled with luscious chocolate sauce.

The gorgeous surrounds and jazz concerts make this a sought-after spot for private events after sun down.

Red Rooster

American ✗✗

310 Lenox Ave. (bet. 125 & 126th Sts.)

Subway:	125 St (Lenox Ave.)	Lunch & dinner daily
Phone:	212-792-9001	
Web:	www.redroosterharlem.com	
Prices:	$$$	

So many things make Red Rooster special, not the least of which is Chef Marcus Samuelsson whose head-spinning achievements include inventive world-renowned cooking, penning cookbooks, and bringing the New Harlem Renaissance to Lenox Avenue. Downstairs, find live music at Ginny's Supper Club. Up front, The Nook serves sweets and sandwiches to go. And in the center, the Red Rooster celebrates Harlem, the African-American diaspora, and great food.

Start with a brilliantly simple wedge of crumbly, buttery corn bread. Then, move on to the likes of highly spiced and "dirty" basmati rice with sweet shrimp and swirls of lemon aïoli; or try their interpretation of South African "bunny chow" served as lamb stew on a sesame bun with fried egg and fresh ricotta.

Ricardo Steakhouse

Steakhouse ✗✗

2145 Second Ave. (bet. 110th & 111th Sts.)

Subway:	110 St (Lexington Ave.)	Lunch Fri – Sun
Phone:	212-289-5895	Dinner nightly
Web:	www.ricardosteakhouse.com	
Prices:	$$	

Those brioche-like slices of bread coated with spices and pan-fried with garlic are your first clue this insanely popular steakhouse is grander than the neighborhood at large. Beloved by longtime locals, its vibe is genuine, ungentrified East Harlem. Beyond the polished façade and wood-framed doors, find small tables, happy crowds, and on occasion, a sensational DJ.

Even the open kitchen seems happy to be hard at work. Expect portobello mushrooms stuffed with zucchini, tomato, and mozzarella on a bed of greens. Surf and turf items like medallions of grilled filet mignon and jumbo shrimp are doused with a smoky *mojito* sauce; and banana *fritas* are fried to shatter-crisp perfection.

A few blocks north, Ricardo Ocean Grill is also satisfying crowds.

Saggio

Italian ✕

B6

829 W. 181st St. (bet. Cabrini Blvd. & Pinehurst Ave.)

Subway:	181 St (Fort Washington Ave.)
Phone:	212-795-3080
Web:	N/A
Prices:	$$

Lunch Sat – Sun
Dinner nightly

Washington Heights continues to welcome this Italian stallion with arms wide open—not surprising, given the area's Dominican culinary domination. Its arresting brown-and-white awning beckons from afar, while slim yet tall windows offer glimpses of this burgeoning strip.

Saggio sits on a sloping stretch, but that's where the bend ends. This is straightforward Italian fare further evidenced by rich Mediterranean-style walls, dark parquet floors, and charming wrought-iron chandeliers. The space may be snug, but *lasagna verde* layered with creamy béchamel and salty pecorino; or deliciously moist *polpettone* braised in a rich tomato sauce emits *molto* heart.

While an apple tart streaked with cinnamon may be fairly standard, the genial staff is anything but.

Settepani

Italian ✕✕

B4

196 Lenox Ave. (at 120th St.)

Subway:	125 St (Lenox Ave.)
Phone:	917-492-4806
Web:	www.settepani.com
Prices:	$$

Lunch & dinner daily

Settepani is a breath of fresh Italian air. Set in the Mount Morris Park Historic District and starring a sleek marble bar, ultra-modern banquettes, and fine linen tablecloths, it is lauded as a beacon of Harlem's "second Renaissance." Originally a café, this elegant restaurant now flaunts a stylish interior with slate and concrete flooring, towering windows draped with silk, and sultry lighting.

The backlit bar, premium sprits, and Romanesque-style busts are only part of the fun. Modern and ancient tunes blend happily in impressive classics like *pasta con sarde* perfectly infused with fennel fronds; *coniglio "a Purtusia"*, braised rabbit in an herbed wine broth; or *insalata alla melagrana*, bread salad mingling tomatoes, scallions, and pomegranate seeds.

Manhattan ▶ Harlem, Morningside & Washington Heights

Tre Otto

B5

1408 Madison Ave. (bet. 97th & 98th Sts.)

Subway: 96 St (Lexington Ave.)
Phone: 212-860-8880
Web: www.treotto.com
Prices: $$

Lunch & dinner daily

Find the quaint Tre Otto, exuding its own downtown charm in the heart of burgeoning Carnegie Hill. Set on a busy stretch of Madison Avenue, the kitchen continues to draw with true Italian fare made from a collection of recipes gathered over time. That said, the focaccia is still the highlight and must be enjoyed no matter the mood. Their ample menu is sure to sate any taste.

Tables are tight at this slim yet well-run spot. A display case adorned with panini and black slate bar is tantalizing to say the least. Boasting top products are dishes like *polpette al sugo con crostini*, mini meatballs with grilled crostini; *penne con salsiccia e funghi*, penne tossed with sausage and mushrooms; and *torta di cioccolato*, a classic dark chocolate, flourless cake.

Vinatería

B4

2211 Frederick Douglass Blvd. (at 119th St.)

Subway: 116 St (Frederick Douglass Blvd.)
Phone: 212-662-8462
Web: www.vinaterianyc.com
Prices: $$

Lunch Sun
Dinner Tue – Sun

Adding to Harlem and its hidden charms is Vinatería, an Italian newcomer brimming with wines to accompany each sublime bite. Not only is it cozy, but the attractive slate-toned room etched in chalk with scenes of decanters and menu specials will augment your appetite.

The semi-open kitchen in the back unveils such treasures as house-cured sardines with fiery piquillo peppers and crunchy croutons; or a salad of earthy golden and red beets mingled with yogurt, oranges, arugula, crunchy pistachios, tossed with lemon vinaigrette. Herbs plucked from their copper planters may be featured in an impeccably grilled rosemary-marinated pork blade served with rich mashed potatoes; or desserts like citrus-glazed rosemary panna cotta bathed in chamomile grappa.

Zoma

2084 Frederick Douglass Blvd. (at 113th St.)

Subway: 116 St (Frederick Douglass Blvd.)
Phone: 212-662-0620
Web: www.zomanyc.com
Prices: 💰💰

Lunch Sat – Sun
Dinner nightly

Smart, cool, modern, and always welcoming, Zoma may well be this city's most serious Ethiopian restaurant. The crowded bar emits a yellowish light from below to showcase its premium spirits, and the ambient dining room is filled with locals from this thriving Harlem community.

Attention to detail is clear from the steaming hot towel for cleansing your hands to the carefully folded *injera* bread used for scooping up their chopped salads, chunky stews, and saucy vegetables. Unusual starters might include green lentils with a cold and crunchy mix of onions, jalapeños, ginger, white pepper, and mustard seeds. The *doro watt*—a chicken dish of the Amhara people—is a very traditional chicken stew with berbere sauce of sun-dried hot peppers and ground spices.

Look for the symbol
for a brilliant breakfast to
start your day off right.

Manhattan ▶ Harlem, Morningside & Washington Heights

Lower East Side

Clockwise from the north, this neighborhood is bounded by Houston Street, the East River, Pike Street, and the Bowery. While it has proudly retained the personality of its first wave of hard-working settlers, the area has embraced a steady change to its landscape brought on by artsy entrepreneurs lured to these formerly overlooked parts. A mostly low-lying neighborhood, with the exception of a few high-rise apartments and towering reminders of a recent real estate boom, the Lower East Side feels village-like in its stature with a palpable creative spirit.

Eastern European Eats

Before checking out the scene as it looks today, visit the Lower East Side Tenement Museum for a glimpse of the past. This restored structure dates back to 1863 and depicts what life was like for the swells of immigrant families, primarily Eastern European Jews that settled here in the early part of the last century fleeing famine and war, making this neighborhood the most densely populated area in the country. For a taste of yore, head to **Russ & Daughters** set on Houston Street. Opened in 1914, this beloved institution is a nosher's dream, and is famed for its holiday specialties, selection of smoked and cured fish, hearty bagels, and all things delicious, otherwise known as "appetizing."

ORCHARD STREET

Orchard Street, long the retail heart of this nabe was once dominated by the garment trade with stores selling fabrics and notions. Tailors remain in the area, offering inexpensive while-you-wait service, but boutiques selling handmade jewelry, designer skateboards, and handcrafted denim have also moved in. Shoppers looking to cool their heels should drop by **Il Laboratorio del Gelato** for an indulgent scoop—their gleaming location tempts residents and Houston Street passersby with a seasonally-changing roster of *gelati*.

For purchases with a more daily purpose, the **Essex Street Market** houses numerous purveyors of fresh produce, meat, and fish under one roof. The market is truly a gourmand's delight—it features two cheesemongers, a coffee roaster, a chocolatier, and **Shopsin's General Store**, a crazy joint notorious for its encyclopedic menu and cranky owner. By the 1950s, the melting pot that defined the Lower East Side became even more diverse with a new tide of immigrants, this time from Puerto Rico and other parts of Latin America. This population continues to be the dominant force today. For a sampling of home-style Latino fare (like *mofongo* and *pernil*), try **El Castillo de Jagua** on the corner of Essex and Rivington streets.

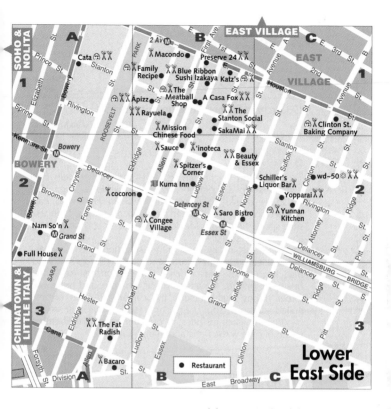

Lower East Side

RIVINGTON STREET

Rivington Street embodies this locality's hybrid of old and new. Located here is **Streit's Matzo Factory**, in operation since 1925; and **Economy Candy**, an emporium that has been flourishing and is coveted for its old-fashioned sweets since 1937. During the day, the mood is pretty chill, perfect for idling in any one of the nearby coffee shops. For a nutritious pick-me-up, **Teanissimo** specializes in vegan vittles served in a café setting. Read: a plethora of teas served alongside a super special brunch on weekends. Come evening, the street fills with meandering groups strolling to

and from a number of popular dining spots. South of Delancey Street, Grand Street is home to well-maintained residential complexes and shops that cater to a cadre of longtime residents. Carb-addicts should be afraid, very afraid, as this street is home to **Kossar's Bialys**, several kosher bakeries, and **Doughnut Plant**, where the owner offers an updated take on his grandfather's doughnut recipe in decadent flavors like Valrhona chocolate. For that quintessential deli accent at home, head to **Pickle Guys** on the corner of Essex Street, and find them stocked with barrel upon barrel of...you guessed it...pickles!

A Casa Fox

Latin American XX

173 Orchard St. (bet. Houston & Stanton Sts.)

Subway: 2 Av
Phone: 212-253-1900
Web: www.acasafox.com
Prices: $$

Lunch Fri – Sun
Dinner Tue – Sun

This bold and bright darling serves superlative Latin fare with fantastic authenticity and a whole lotta love. This is largely thanks to Chef/owner Melissa Fox, who can be seen in the open kitchen or checking on guests in the snug space, filled with Mexican tiles, wide plank floors, and a warming fireplace.

Be sure to begin any meal with a selection of empanadas, as in pulled pork with caramelized onion, chorizo and aged manchego, or the outstanding *carne enchorizada* (seasoned beef with onions, tomatoes, yucca, chayote, and potatoes). Other dishes might include the *camarones a las brazes*, grilled shrimp in sour-orange marinade wrapped in smoky bacon; or chicken *tostones*, its pulled meat on a well-grilled round of corn with *crema* and mango salsa.

Ápizz

B1

Italian XX

217 Eldridge St. (bet. Rivington & Stanton Sts.)

Subway: 2 Av
Phone: 212-253-9199
Web: www.apizz.com
Prices: $$

Dinner Tue – Sun

It's hard not to fall in love with Ápizz. The room (dressed with honey-toned wood furnishings, amber glass votive holders, and slender mirror panels) has a bewitching rosy glow fueled by the star of the restaurant's open kitchen, a wood-fired brick oven. The motto here is "one room, one oven," and this area prettied by polished copper pots, dried flowers, and platters of produce is the command post for the preparations that follow on the menu.

The flame-kissed specialties bear a sophisticated rusticity as in a vibrant pile-up of warm octopus, diced potato, and cherry tomatoes; the L.E.S. pizza topped with chorizo; and *fazzoletti e granchio*—fresh handkerchief pasta with spicy tomato sauce and sweet nuggets of excellent quality lump crabmeat.

Bacaro

 Italian ╳

136 Division St. (bet. Ludlow & Orchard Sts.)

Subway: East Broadway
Phone: 212-941-5060
Web: www.bacaronyc.com
Prices: $$

Dinner Tue – Sun

Steal away to this hidden spot, where crumbling brick walls, aged archways, ornate chandeliers, and soft candlelight give the impression of having stepped back in time. The inspiration is a Venetian *bacaro*—counters where folks stand to graze on small bites and sip wine—yet here one dines with ease, seated at distressed wood tables. A visit to the stunning, dark, wood-carved bar and its display of delicate glassware is a worthy detour before ordering up a series of tasty plates. Starters may feature the *sarde en saor*, with the grilled sardines served over caramelized sweet and sour onions, white raisins, pignoli nuts, and thyme. The *cannolicchi* is a noteworthy special, delivering a fresh burst of salinity with each razor clam in garlic-white wine sauce.

Beauty & Essex

Contemporary ╳╳

146 Essex St. (bet. Rivington & Stanton Sts.)

Subway: Delancey St
Phone: 212-614-0146
Web: www.beautyandessex.com
Prices: $$

Lunch Sat – Sun
Dinner nightly

Chef/partner Chris Santos (also of The Stanton Social) shows off his prowess at creating utterly intriguing small plates at this chic multi-room bôite. The tempting roster offers ginger-glazed General Tso's monkfish garnished with broccoli and rice croquettes; sashimi of tuna, *tonnato*-style; and braised short rib tamales. The extensive menu is also hearty as in dishes like *garganelli* with spicy veal ragù baked in an earthenware crock.

A vestibule fashioned as a pawn shop fronts the dazzling setting which is outfitted in an earthy palette contrasted with metallic touches; upstairs there's a bar arranged against a backdrop of crystal decanters, and a small dining room featuring a collection of vintage lockets hung on the walls.

Blue Ribbon Sushi Izakaya

 Japanese 🍴🍴

B1

187 Orchard St. (bet. Houston & Stanton Sts.)

Subway: 2 Av
Phone: 212-466-0404
Web: www.blueribbonrestaurants.com
Prices: $$

Lunch & dinner daily

This member of the Blue Ribbon family calls the sleek Thompson LES hotel home. Boasting an understandably lounge-y mien the crepuscular setting thumps with beats and chatter. The counter offers more intimacy than the dining room, and the chefs here are not bashful about striking up a conversation. Coral upholstered furnishings accentuate the brightly colored fillets stocking the station along with speckled quail eggs and shelves of wood platters.

The hearty menu offers nigiri such as *Kindai akamai*, along with plenty of cooked tastes, like braised strips of tender tripe in tamari butter; sesame-glazed pork meatball *kushi-yaki*; or a fluffy bowlful of liver, bacon, and onion fried rice topped by a finely grated showering of hard-boiled egg.

Cata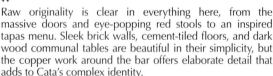

 Spanish 🍴🍴

B1

245 Bowery (at Stanton St.)

Subway: 2 Av
Phone: 212-505-2282
Web: www.catarestaurant.com
Prices: $$

Dinner nightly

Raw originality is clear in everything here, from the massive doors and eye-popping red stools to an inspired tapas menu. Sleek brick walls, cement-tiled floors, and dark wood communal tables are beautiful in their simplicity, but the copper work around the bar offers elaborate detail that adds to Cata's complex identity.

Plates may include the smoked *cana de cabra*, a goat cheese hailing from Murcia, Spain, roasted until gloriously gooey and topped with lemon-thyme honey. Curried cauliflower "couscous" is delicious, aromatic, and ingenious. Paella is prepared with traditional Spanish sausage, *butifarra*, and sinfully addictive foie gras. For a distinctive finale, cleanse the palate with grapefruit sorbet and a selection from their unique gin program.

Clinton St. Baking Company

C1

A m e r i c a n ✗

4 Clinton St. (bet. Houston & Stanton St.)

Subway: 2 Av
Phone: 646-602-6263
Web: www.clintonstreetbaking.com
Prices: ⊜⊜

Lunch daily
Dinner Mon – Sat

Stop by this L.E.S. institution on just about any afternoon and chances are pretty good that you'll be greeted by a crowd waiting patiently for a table and their turn to partake in a menu of brunch-y delights, offered until 4:00 P.M. daily (6:00 P.M. on Sundays). Revered for his skill with carbohydrates, Chef Neil Kleinberg crafts buttermilk biscuits, brioche French toast, *huevos rancheros*, and an assortment of pancakes (think wild Maine blueberry or chocolate chunk) that are, in a word, awesome.

Simple wood furnishings and two small dining counters outfit the room, and the service is as gracious as one would hope. Dinnertime brings a quieter scene and comfort food favorites like fish tacos, spicy shrimp and grits, or buttermilk fried chicken.

cocoron

B2

J a p a n e s e ✗

61 Delancey St. (bet. Allen & Eldridge Sts.)

Subway: Delancey St
Phone: 212-925-5220
Web: www.cocoron-soba.com
Prices: ⊜⊜

Lunch & dinner Tue – Sun

A wide variety of soba offerings served hot or cold, in broth or with dipping sauce, is what one will find at cocoron. Lacking creature comforts, the stall-sized room is cheerily embellished with cartoon figures and smiling service.

Go for something really interesting and order the *natto* soba; the bowlful of chilled noodles and fermented soybeans is presented with refreshing and flavorful elements like diced cucumber, sesame seed paste, daikon, pickled radish, and a quivering egg. Perhaps less adventurous but just as pleasing are the *tororo wakame* and Japanese-style curry dip soba options. Complement your bowlful with an order of the custard-soft tofu dressed with bonito flakes, crisped nori, and grated ginger; miso coleslaw; or daikon salad.

Congee Village

B2

100 Allen St. (at Delancey St.)

Subway: Delancey St
Phone: 212-941-1818
Web: www.congeevillagerestaurants.com
Prices:

Lunch & dinner daily

The menu at Congee Village is vast and its Cantonese focus is clear. The soothing namesake, rice porridge, is well-represented with 30 varieties offering a full spectrum of embellishments, from healthy vegetarian to pig's blood, to name a few. In addition to prized delicacies, find dim sum treats like delicately flaky Hong Kong-style scallion pancakes. Other ample offerings include chicken steamed in lotus leaf with mushrooms and diced Chinese sausage, slicked with soy sauce, ginger, and scallions; bitter melon stir-fried with black bean sauce; or specialties like pork ribs seasoned with shrimp paste and fried until crispy.

From the fringe of Chinatown, the multi-level setting trimmed with bamboo, brick, and stone is well-maintained and inviting.

Family Recipe

B1

231 Eldridge St. (bet. Houston & Stanton Sts.)

Subway: 2 Av
Phone: 212-529-3133
Web: www.familyrecipeny.com
Prices: $$

Lunch Sat – Sun
Dinner nightly

Large windows reveal Family Recipe's simple but chic setting that is framed by blond wood accents, glossy gray tables, and mod black plastic chairs. Lime green seating adds a pop of color at the L-shaped dining counter surrounding the open kitchen where Chef Akiko Thurnauer turns out her heartfelt home-style cooking.

Built upon a range of small plates, the menu offers several specials like mushroom and dried oyster dumplings with a delicate, translucent wrapping; or tempura rolls of thin green tea noodles wrapped around uni and accompanied by sheets of nori tempura. The rock shrimp and squid ink *okonomiyaki* is fantastic, and even Brussels sprouts excite—here they're pan-roasted with capers, pine nuts, and shallots and plated with miso.

The Fat Radish

 A3

Contemporary XX

17 Orchard St. (bet. Canal & Hester Sts.)

Subway: East Broadway

Phone: 212-300-4053

Web: www.thefatradishnyc.com

Prices: $$

Lunch & dinner daily

This is a true downtown spot—fun, hip, and set on a quiet street. Inside, benches, weathered wood boards, and flowerboxes lend a sense of barnyard chic to the dining room, thereby complementing the menu's fresh and seasonal focus. Yet, what makes The Fat Radish distinctive is that it's neither self-consciously cool nor trendy in concept. It's genuinely good.

Expect the opening salvo to be a crunchy-sharp radish tossed in black olive tapenade. Then, move on to such refined dishes as seared Block Island tuna with watermelon, cilantro, mint, and cucumber in a perfectly salty vinaigrette. Dessert may offer a deconstructed chocolate mousse with raspberry compote.

Across the street, The Leadbelly lures legions for its briny oysters and thrilling cocktails.

Full House

A2

Chinese X

97 Bowery (bet. Grand & Hester Sts.)

Subway: Grand St

Phone: 212-925-8083

Web: www.fullhousecafeny.com

Prices:

Lunch & dinner daily

Can't pick between Shanghainese or Cantonese? Just head down to Full House, a bright and modern restaurant that prepares both of these regional cuisines with an equally authentic hand. Dishes here may range from juicy pork and crab dumplings served with black vinegar and grated ginger, to vegetarian mock duck (tofu skin) roll infused with soy-based braising broth, and sautéed fresh eel with shaved yellow leeks in a soy and oyster sauce. Highlights include the sweet sautéed pumpkin, celery, and lotus root coated in garlic sauce.

Illuminated by neon accent lights, the main dining room features comfy booths and spacious tables ideal for families. Up a flight of glass-enclosed stairs is a second, semi-private room that also caters to larger groups.

'inoteca

B2

98 Rivington St. (at Ludlow St.)

Subway: Delancey St

Phone: 212-614-0473

Web: www.inotecanyc.com

Prices: ✇✇

Lunch & dinner daily

This foodie favorite is a beloved dining destination thanks to the winning lineup of owners Jason Denton and Chef Eric Kleinman. Highly coveted wraparound sidewalk seating and knobby wood furnishings perfect the classic wine bar ambience that invites guests to stop by anytime.

Small plates make for an enjoyable repast and feature a range of cheeses, panini, *tramezzini,* and antipasti such as grilled calamari with soppressata and a spicy tomato vinaigrette. An array of heartier items like juicy slices of luscious *porchetta* plated with roasted sweet baby carrots atop a refreshing bundle of parsley flecked with grated horseradish offer highly satisfying sustenance.

Whether it's for a snack or spread, 'inoteca always serves up a reason to drop by.

Katz's

B1

205 E. Houston St. (at Ludlow St.)

Subway: 2 Av

Phone: 212-254-2246

Web: www.katzsdelicatessen.com

Prices: ✇✇

Lunch & dinner daily

One of the last-standing, old-time Eastern European spots on the Lower East Side, Katz's is a true NY institution. It's crowded, crazy, and packed with a panoply of characters weirder than a jury duty pool. Tourists, hipsters, blue hairs, and everybody in between flock here, so come on off-hours. Because it's really *that* good.

Walk inside, get a ticket, and don't lose it (those guys at the front aren't hosts—upset their system and you'll get a verbal beating). Then get your food at the counter and bring it to a first-come first-get table; or opt for a slightly less dizzying experience at a waitress-served table.

Nothing's changed in the looks or the taste. Matzoh ball soup, pastrami sandwich, potato latkes—everything is what you'd expect, only better.

Kuma Inn

B2

Asian

113 Ludlow St. (bet. Delancey & Rivington Sts.)

Subway: Delancey St
Phone: 212-353-8866
Web: www.kumainn.com
Prices: 😊😊

Dinner Fri – Wed

 A veteran of Daniel and Jean-Georges, New York City-born Chef/owner King Phojanakong presents ambrosial pan-Asian bites that reflect the multicultural influences of his Thai-Filipino background.

Come as you are—Kuma Inn doesn't put on airs. The discreetly marked setting is located on the second floor of a nondescript walk-up. The menu is best suited for grazing so bring reinforcements to ensure a sampling of the chef's signature items—perhaps cubes of firm tofu sautéed with earthy wood ears and fragrant Thai basil sluiced by spicy soy and mirin; slices of Chinese sausage bathed in a Thai chili-lime sauce; or drunken shrimp imbibed in chili-sparked sake. Genteel service and a playlist of the chef's favorite tracks add to the mood of this spartan room.

Macondo

B1

Latin American

157 E. Houston St. (bet. Allen & Eldridge Sts.)

Subway: 2 Av
Phone: 212-473-9900
Web: www.macondonyc.com
Prices: $$

Lunch Sat – Sun
Dinner nightly

 Tucked within this bustling stretch of the Lower East Side, Macondo's surrounding never seems to stand still. The front counter opens onto the street and is ideal for a quick bite or cocktail (which can be ordered by the carafe). Beyond this, the dining room has a vague seafaring theme with a few suspended nets, white-washed shelving, and luring dark wood tables.

The rich and dynamic menu may offer dishes that span the Latin culture through *América del Norte*, but everything is prepared with a steady Central American hand. Listed in the "to begin" section, find tender yet crisp calamari tossed with *rocotto* pepper and honey *alioli*. The *tapas del mar* might feature grilled octopus tentacles over a chorizo-studded quinoa salad with mint-basil vinaigrette.

The Meatball Shop

B1

84 Stanton St. (bet. Allen & Orchard Sts.)

Subway: 2 Av   Lunch & dinner daily
Phone: 212-982-8895
Web: www.themeatballshop.com
Prices: ⊕⊕

It is hard to imagine a restaurant truer to its name than this. The focal point of everything here is the mighty meatball, perhaps served as the classic beef with prosciutto and fresh ricotta; spicy pork studded with pickled cherry peppers; chicken flavored with white wine and fennel seeds; a vegetarian option; or daily special. These five incarnations have a choice of five sauces such as classic tomato, spicy meat, mushroom gravy, Parmesan cream, and pesto. Dessert means ice cream—either in floats or sandwiches.

The compact room is a perfect fit for its cool, comfortable locale and is equipped with a communal table, dining counter, brick red walls, vintage photos, and an open kitchen. Their tremendous success has spilled over to three other outposts.

Mission Chinese Food

B1

154 Orchard St. (bet. Rivington & Stanton Sts.)

Subway: 2 Av   Lunch & dinner daily
Phone: 212-529-8800
Web: www.missionchinesefood.com
Prices: $$

The explicit lyrics blasting over the speakers and an abrasive staff may keep some folks away, but judging by the long wait and packed house, not many take offense. Sister to its popular San Francisco original, Danny Bowien's outpost maintains it a similar cool-kid vibe and "it" place reputation. Festooned with Christmas lights and a Chinese dragon overhead, the tiny space is populated with hordes of voracious hipsters sipping One Eyed Jacks (mint, lemon, and rice wine) and nibbling on the likes of mapo tofu.

Tasty options include spicy pickled carrots; smashed cucumber with garlic and chili crunchy pea greens braised in pumpkin broth and tossed with boiled peanuts; and six-egg noodles with poached egg and grated smoky ham.

Nam Sơn

245 Grand St. (bet. Bowery & Chrystie St.)

Subway: Grand St
Phone: 212-966-6507
Web: N/A
Prices: ⊜⊜

Lunch & dinner daily

 Nam So'n will have you wishing you lived closer to Chinatown—enormous praise given the chaos flanking these "mean streets." But if you did, you'd be eating here all the time. This fresh, flavorful Vietnamese spot off the Doyers-Baxter trail may have like neighbors, yet they shine by dint of a pleasant interior and speedy staff.

The value here is incredible. With prices that can't be beat, Nam So'n fills its ample, brightly-lit room with typical faves like *goi cuon*, a summer roll bursting with poached shrimp and pork and rice noodles wrapped in paper. *Cha gio*, well-seasoned pork and vegetable spring rolls with *nuoc cham* for dipping; and *pho tai*, deliciously spiced beef broth floating with noodles are nothing short of a savory triumph.

Preserve 24

177 E. Houston St. (at Allen St.)

Subway: 2 Av
Phone: 646-837-6100
Web: www.preserve24.com
Prices: $$

Lunch Sat – Sun
Dinner nightly

 Preserve 24 may be double-billed as a conceptual art installation, but a nibble of their food makes everything else seem out of place. This is a spot to settle in and feast on excellent cooking. The interior offers two bustling floors dotted with nooks and rooms, a reclaimed oyster boat that serves as a raw bar, amid ropes and oars (now ceiling fans) to exude country-chic.

 The upstairs is a café-cum-bar, but opt to dine downstairs, before the open kitchen and its wood fire. Local ingredients flaunt terrific flavor in a crispy oyster sandwich crafted from brioche, bacon, and rémoulade; ahi tuna with sweet watermelon; or macaroni *rigate* with a fiery tomato sauce and *guanciale*. A lemon pound cake with raspberry coulis is simple yet sublime.

Rayuela

B1

165 Allen St. (bet. Rivington & Stanton Sts.)

Subway: 2 Av
Phone: 212-253-8840
Web: www.rayuelanyc.com
Prices: $$

Lunch Sat – Sun
Dinner nightly

Patrons entering Rayuela first encounter a sleek concrete bar, colorful displays of decorative bottles, sultry lighting, and a gnarly tree majestically rising in the center of the room. The sexy tree-house aesthetic is not the only thrill served at Rayuela. Their vibrant range of Latin American cuisine pops with creativity.

The guacamole arrives studded with crab and shrimp, and should move from nightly special to permanent menu fixture. The *tamal limeño* is a steamed squid-ink-tinted corn cake, thick and moist, topped with lobster and *rocoto* pepper-pisco sauce. The wonderfully inventive *paella verde* reveals herb-infused Valencia rice packed with shellfish, rabbit, and chicken, licked by tomatillo-poblano aïoli, with an enticing soccorat.

SakaMai

B1

157 Ludlow St. (bet. Rivington & Stanton Sts.)

Subway: Delancey St
Phone: 646-590-0684
Web: www.sakamai.com
Prices: $$$

Dinner Mon – Sat

This completely unique newcomer focuses on pairing contemporary Japanese cuisine and sake. The rustic-meets-avant garde space is part restaurant and part lounge, mixing Persian rugs, exposed brick, and plush velvet chairs. The ambience is tied together through lovely touches like dusky lighting, cascading curtains, and floral arrangements.

Each well-crafted dish evokes creativity, like crispy nori wrapped with miso-infused cream cheese; or gently seared uni crostini crested with flakes of salty Parmesan. The Southern-fried chicken confit arrives as boneless, deep-fried morsels smothered in smoked paprika tartar sauce. An excellent lineup of sake matches such top-notch products, as in delightful bits of foie gras in a lush *chawanmushi*.

Saro Bistro

B2

102 Norfolk St. (bet. Delancey & Rivington Sts.)

Subway: Delancey St
Phone: 212-505-7276
Web: www.sarobistro.com
Prices: $$

Lunch Sat – Sun
Dinner Tue – Sun

Inspired by the cooking of his Bosnian grandmother, Chef/owner Eran Elhalal serves cuisine that tours the Balkans from his charming bistro. This petite 22-seat room is not only comfortable, but is also pleasantly arranged with papered walls, wood furnishings, and dried flower arrangements. Tables are set with vintage flatware, mismatched floral-rimmed china, and a glass filled with slender green chilies to spice up your meal.

The menu offers a rich trip through this unique and eclectic region with specialties that include a daily offering of savory pie accompanied by kefir; grilled *cevapcici* kebabs served with zucchini fritters and a quenelle of fresh cheese; homemade linguini with clams; and slow-roasted lamb shoulder with braised cabbage.

Sauce

B2

78-84 Rivington St. (at Allen St.)

Subway: 2 Av
Phone: 212-420-7700
Web: www.saucerestaurant.com
Prices: ⊖⊖

Lunch & dinner daily

Frank Prisinzano (of Supper and Lil' Frankie's) adds this fourth venue focused on nose-to-tail cooking to his clique of simply named restaurants. Already looking well lived-in (even a bit disheveled at times) the décor tilts toward homey with mismatched wallpaper and lacy café curtains dressing the corner setting.

The ingredient-driven menu proudly reads like a red-sauce joint with a range of zesty Italian-American fare. "Sloppy sandwiches" are a tasty lunchtime option, while heartier appetites will be sated by grandmother's tomato gravy ladled over a heap of fresh *cencioni* pasta sided by an order of ragù by the piece—grass-fed beef meatballs, Italian sausage, or braciole. House-butchered meats are showcased in the likes of a gutsy *bollito misto*.

Schiller's Liquor Bar

European

131 Rivington St. (at Norfolk St.)

Subway: Delancey St
Phone: 212-260-4555
Web: www.schillersny.com
Prices: $$

Lunch & dinner daily

Schiller's, like Keith McNally's wildly successful Balthazar and Pastis, touts a magical mix; like the most popular girl in school, this spot knows how to pop in a crowd. However, its components are breezy retro-bistro good looks, comfort food favorites, and a prime location straddling a choice corner of the Lower East Side. The straightforward menu makes things easy with choices like chicken pot pie, fish and chips, or steak with perfect frites.

As to how best to describe the atmosphere that draws locals, day trippers, and low-key celebrities alike, we direct you to the cheeky house wine list, categorized into *cheap, decent,* or *good.* A terrific cocktail selection rounds out the drink list; while pastries from Balthazar Bakery remain a brunch-time hit.

Spitzer's Corner

Gastropub

101 Rivington St. (at Ludlow St.)

Subway: Delancey St
Phone: 212-228-0027
Web: www.spitzerscorner.com
Prices:

Lunch & dinner daily

This modern New York gastropub strives to highlight its honest, local sensibilities; but most importantly, this spot perfectly complements the casual cool of a weekend night on the Lower East. With old pickle-barrel slats for walls and a zinc bar, the multi-room space is effortlessly stylish and comfortable, much to the pleasure of the trendy crowds who pile in, despite the no-reservations policy. Happily, they chill at the bar or settle into a long, sleek bench while nursing a selection from the 40 smartly chosen beers on tap, or the small but studied by-the-glass wine list.

The menu offers a host of salads and sandwiches, but those looking for a proper meal can go with plates of hand-cut French fries, truffled mac' and cheese, and Kobe sliders.

The Stanton Social

B1

Fusion ✕✕

99 Stanton St. (bet. Ludlow & Orchard Sts.)

Subway: 2 Av
Phone: 212-995-0099
Web: www.thestantonsocial.com
Prices: $$

Lunch Sat – Sun
Dinner nightly

A beloved haunt in the Lower East Side, The Stanton Social has a richly tailored design that pays homage to the haberdashers and seamstress shops that once dotted this trendy nabe. Vintage hand mirrors, woven leather straps, and wine shelves laid out in a herringbone pattern outfit the low-lit, dark-wood furnished cave.

This grand boîte is still going strong—a testament to the enjoyable cuisine on offer. The generous order of globally-inspired preparations, executed under the watch of Chef/partner Chris Santos, brings on cooking with gusto and includes sliders, a house signature; hand-pulled chicken arepas kicked with tomatillo sauce and pickled jalapeños; and rounds of crispy eggplant Parmesan finished with mozzarella, micro basil, and basil oil.

Yopparai

C2

Japanese ✕✕

151 Rivington St. (bet. Clinton & Suffolk Sts.)

Subway: Delancey St
Phone: 212-777-7253
Web: www.yopparainyc.com
Prices: $$

Dinner Mon – Sat

Classic Japanese minimalism and reverent service set this sake pub apart from other fun but more boisterous *izakaya*. Press the buzzer to enter and step inside to find a comfortable room in a soothing palette of pale grey and blue. A seat at the counter is the best option, but tables are also available.

The array of small plates is striking, as in "Yopparai-style" sashimi made with toro chopped so finely that the taste is almost cloud-like, mixed with green onion, pickled daikon, and served on ice with sheets of warmed nori for wrapping. *Yaki onigiri* are crisp, golden brown with brushed soy, and deliciously hot from the grill.

And to drink, go with sake. The chefs' backdrop is stacked with *masu* and an arrangement of opened bottles awaiting your selection.

wd~50 ✿

Contemporary ✗✗

50 Clinton St. (bet. Rivington & Stanton Sts.)

Subway: Delancey St
Phone: 212-477-2900
Web: www.wd-50.com
Prices: $$$$

Dinner nightly

Travis Huggett

While it may be known as New York's home to modernist cuisine, wd~50 has refined its distinct style to reflect the creative and bold sensibilities of Chef Wylie Dufresne.

The long and slender room also bears a guise that is very much its own. Picture an amalgam of chunky tables topped with thin plastic mats and modern porcelain, alongside abstract art and comfy leather banquettes. Polished concrete walls and warm coals in the fireplace lend a rustic, Scandinavian feel. Still, the room's focus is a view into the kitchen, and diners are even encouraged to come and take a closer look.

Both prix-fixe menus highlight innovation as in wafer-thin slices of brined, perfectly pink beef tongue, set atop sweet, chutney-like miso with tender oyster mushrooms, baby beets, and crisp quinoa wafers. This might be followed by a playful soup of corn, plump shrimp, jicama-herb oil, and sharply flavored shiso. Sliced duck breast is bound to appear beautifully cooked to rosy pink beneath a layer of sweet fat, perhaps served with spaghetti that is actually squash, and ricotta that is actually parsnip. Desserts combine refreshing passion fruit with pecks of argan oil and tiny Italian meringues.

Yunnan Kitchen

Chinese 🍴

C2

79 Clinton St. (bet. Delancey & Rivington Sts.)

Subway: Delancey St
Phone: 212-253-2527
Web: www.yunnankitchen.com
Prices: $$

Dinner nightly

This classy new Chinese offering hones in on the province of Yunnan, located in Southwestern China and bordering Vietnam, Laos, and Myanmar. The kitsch-free dining room features windows framing the Clinton Street scene. Inside, find a focused menu that might feature such fresh and flavorful creations as wide ribbons of firm tofu tossed with an abundance of fresh cilantro, mint, and smoky chili oil; delicious and delicate potato croquettes dusted with a mouthwatering blend of salt and spices; and spicy pork *shao kao*—pounded nuggets grilled on a skewer.

The day's market bounty is displayed on the carte and has included a bowl brimming with fluffy, minimally-seasoned fried rice stocked with chopped garlic and plump, bright green sweet peas.

Bib Gourmand 😋
indicates our inspectors'
favorites for good value.

Midtown East & Murray Hill

Midtown East is one of the city's most commercial and industrious neighborhoods. Boasting an array of corporate high-rises, hotels, and apartment buildings, the vibe here is always buzzing and never inert. Naturally, this quarter sees a unique blend of suits, students, and longtime New Yorkers. Whether it's your reliable diner around the corner, a gourmet supermarket, or an upscale dining establishment, this area has it all and locals love it. Residents of neighboring Beekman and Sutton are proud of their very own top fishmonger (**Pisacane Seafood**); cheese shop (**Ideal Cheese**); butcher (**Simchick Meats**); bagel and lox shop (**Tal Bagels**); and to complete any dinner party—florist (**Zeze**). While **Dag Hammarskjöld Plaza Greenmarket** around the corner from the UN may by dwarfed by Union Square, it has just the right amount of everything to satisfy its neighbors.

Grand Central Terminal

Started by the Vanderbilt's in the 19th century, then saved from the wrecking ball with the help of Jacqueline Kennedy Onassis in the 20th century, Grand Central Terminal is a 21st century foodie haven. It is a perfect microcosm of its eastern midtown home, because stretching through this neighborhood is the same diversity of shopping and dining. A perfect day at this titanic train station begins with a coffee from **Joe's**. Later, stop by one of Manhattan's most beloved icons, the **Oyster Bar**, tucked into the cavernous lower level. Continue this enticing journey at **Neuhaus**, venerable chocolatiers who craft their decadent goodies with top-notch ingredients; and end at divine **Campbell Apartment**—for those who meet the dress code. This 1920s office of railroad mogul John W. Campbell was restored and re-opened as one of the area's swankier stops for a famously dry martini. No trip here is complete without a visit to the "whispering gallery" where low, ceramic tile arches allow whispers to sound like shouts. At the popular dining concourse, lunch options range from **Café Spice** for Indian; **Eata Pita** for Middle Eastern; and **Mendy's** for kosher. Finish a meal with the sweetest treats including baked goods and cupcakes at **Magnolia Bakery**. For a more deluxe spread, several prized restaurants are situated beneath the celestial ceiling murals. Moving on to the market, Eli Zabar has expanded his territory here to include the freshest fruits, vegetables, and flowers, available at **Eli Zabar's Farm to Table**; as well as bread, pastries, and coffee cakes at **Eli Zabar's Bread & Pastry**. Follow this up by a visit to **Oren's** for their first-rate coffee beans. Fishmongers, produce stands, butchers, florists, and possibly the best spices in the city can all be found here at one of the market's better-kept secrets,

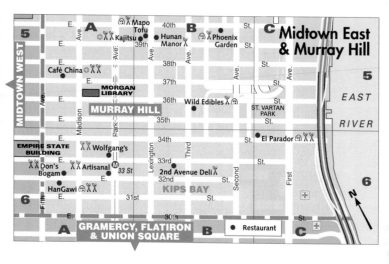

Map: Midtown East & Murray Hill

Spices and Tease, a boutique store specializing in exotic teas and spice blends.

Japantown

Within these busy commuter, residential, and internationally focused midtown nooks, is a very sophisticated Japantown. Scores of *izakayas* and a few hostess clubs now line this stretch east of Lexington. Find Japanese suits sippin' and suppin' at **Riki**; while expats linger on the late-night at **Shochu Bar Hatchan**. The younger working set may prefer a light lunch from **Cafe Zaiya** or **Dainobu** (deli-cum-markets); while others flock to **Onya** for their steaming bowls of udon. Replicate these dishes at home by visiting the **Japanese Culinary Center** for tabletop items, kitchenware, and unique ingredients.

Murray Hill

Assuredly younger and quieter than its northern neighbor, Murray Hill has its own distinct restaurant vibe. Here, faster and casual finds thrive by dint of hungry twenty-somethings craving pizza or cheesesteak. Afterwards, they move on to their favored watering holes like **Bar 515** or **Wharf Bar and Grill** to hoot and holler with buddies over Bud Lights while catching the snowboarding finals. Those in need of more than just booze and a bar should head to Tex-Mex hot spot **El Rio Grande** for their myriad *especiales* or **Baby Bo's** *cantina* for flavor-packed classics like burritos, quesadillas, tacos, and more. Extra jalapeños? Of course. But, this is only one Murray Hill. The other rises with the sun over pristine brownstones and apartment towers, awakening young families who can be seen gathering amid blooming flowers at St. Vartan Park. These are the (slightly) senior locals of Murray Hill—they love it here and will remain faithful residents until well after the frat party has ended.

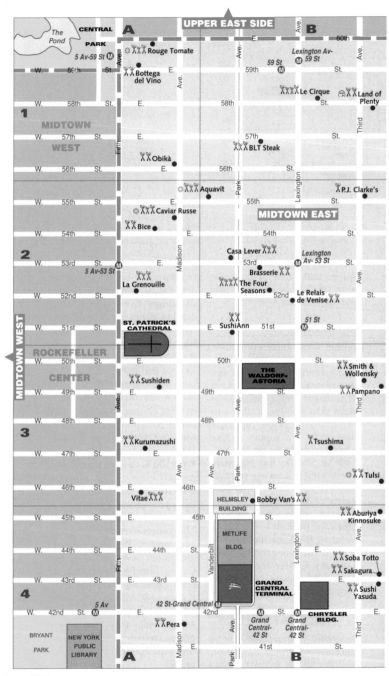

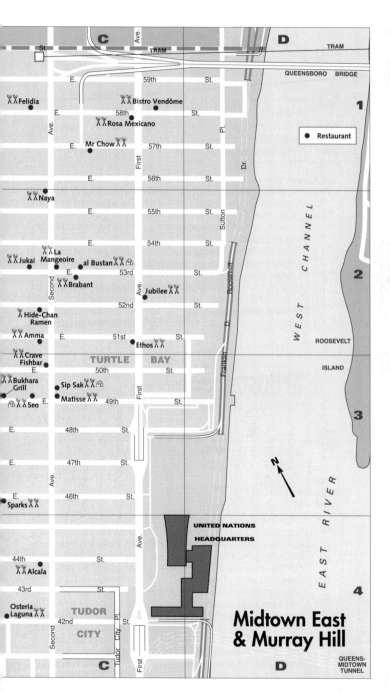

221

Aburiya Kinnosuke

B4

213 E. 45th St. (bet. Second & Third Aves.)

Subway: Grand Central - 42 St   Dinner nightly
Phone: 212-867-5454
Web: www.aburiyakinnosuke.com
Prices: $$$

Every bit as authentic in style as in cuisine, Aburiya Kinnosuke offers its elite diners a trip to Tokyo without the tariff. So book ahead for those private nooks or tables separated from the main room by *shoji*. Towards the back, a gleaming action-packed counter wraps around the fiery robata and almighty young cooks.

The staff is good if sometimes amiss as they gush on about an omakase to their global clients. You may be better off sharing a range of enticing items with equally pleasing sips of sake. So, let the kitchen coddle you with terrific toro and sea urchin sashimi; tofu in a light soy bath; or *tskune*—chicken meatball brushed with teriyaki, and set beneath a creamy egg yolk. If *hamachi kama* (fatty, grilled yellowtail) is on offer, grab it.

al Bustan

C2

319 E. 53rd St. (bet. First & Second Aves.)

Subway: Lexington Av - 53 St   Lunch & dinner daily
Phone: 212-759-5933
Web: www.albustanny.com
Prices: $$

Lebanese specialties are fired up with aplomb at this enticing retreat, where a moneyed Middle Eastern crowd dominates the space along with a stream of locals including diplomats from the UN. Inside, chandeliers hang from a beam-lined ceiling, while neat white leather chairs and glass partitions impart an air of elegance.

The expansive menu boasts a slew of meze, house specials, and knockout dinner prix-fixe. Let the feasting begin with *samboussek jibneh*, a baked pastry bubbling with salty feta and crisp *fattoush*, tossing crunchy romaine lettuce, cucumber, tomato, and sumac. And that's not all: add on the hugely flavored *sujuk*—spicy beef sausage—sautéed, sliced, and kissed with lemon for that perfect smack of flavor.

Alcala

 C4

Spanish ✗✗

246 E. 44th St. (bet. Second and Third Aves.)

Subway: Grand Central - 42 St
Phone: 212-370-1866
Web: www.alcalarestaurant.com
Prices: $$

Lunch Mon – Fri
Dinner nightly

Located steps away from the UN, this chirpy Spanish establishment draws an international clientele whose exuberance often reverberates throughout its cozy quarters. The interior combines buttery yellow walls, hand-painted ceramics, and a petite bar stocked with Spanish wines.

The kitchen focuses its attention on northern specialties that include chilled *esparragos*—plump, white asparagus from Navarra and roasted piquillo peppers dressed with scallion vinaigrette dotted with minced green olives and hard-cooked egg. Beyond tempting tapas, taste the perfectly seasoned grilled lamb chops sided by a lighter take on potato gratin prepared with olive oil. For dessert, a slice of warm *tarta de Arrese* filled with dense custard is pure decadence.

Amma

 C2

Indian ✗✗

246 E. 51st St. (bet. Second & Third Aves.)

Subway: 51 St
Phone: 212-644-8330
Web: www.ammanyc.com
Prices: $$

Lunch & dinner daily

Make your way up a few stairs to enter Amma's home, an elegant parlor arranged with close-knit, white-robed tables set atop carpeted floors. This is indeed Indian food—brought to you in a colonial-style townhouse in frenzied midtown. Amma's "living room" feels bright with big windows, saffron-tinted walls, chaste artwork, and a chandelier twinkling upon an affluent set.

Brimming at lunch with delicacies like *prawn masala* steeped in coconut, Amma becomes romantic at night. In keeping with its mien, warm yet vigilant servers present you with Indian hospitality at its finest—in the form of *tandoori* sea bass with plantain dumplings; *bagharey baingan* (eggplant stuffed with a spicy peanut sauce); and *bhindi ka raita*, all soaked up by a basket of breads.

Aquavit ❁

Scandinavian 🍴🍴🍴

B2

65 E. 55th St. (bet. Madison & Park Aves.)

Subway: 5 Av - 53 St
Phone: 212-307-7311
Web: www.aquavit.org
Prices: $$$$

Lunch Mon – Fri
Dinner Mon – Sat

Evan Sung

Known for its distinct, modern Scandinavian style, Aquavit is undeniably cool. Inside, the lounge features funky leather chairs for post-work drinking. The dining room has Star Trek-like seating, dark plank flooring, and high-minded design of a Swedish furniture show room—but in a really good way. The crowd is a pleasant mix of old, young, and anyone looking for a little Nordic purr; servers favor black-framed spectacles and are polite, professional, and wondrously synchronized.

Whether choosing one of the prix-fixe menus or selecting courses à la carte, all ingredients and combinations remain very true to Scandinavian flavors. Begin with an oversized shell artistically displaying Nantucket bay scallops, lobes of sea urchin, cucumber beads, chives, and vibrant dill oil. This might be followed with an umami-rich array of sautéed mushrooms set over a silky poached heirloom chicken egg, polenta emulsion, and crisp grains. Mild, tender rabbit confit is paired with toasted garlic chips, tart lingonberry, and cured egg yolk.

Desserts promise ambition, skill, and pleasure, as in the orange crème brûlée with rum *muscovado* ice cream, caramel truffles, and pistachio brittle.

Artisanal

A6 French ✗✗

2 Park Ave. (entrance on 32nd St.)

Subway: 33 St
Phone: 212-725-8585
Web: www.artisanalbistro.com
Prices: **$$**

Lunch & dinner daily

Terrance Brennan's much-loved restaurant serves a whole roster of bistro delights (think chicken paillard, tuna niçoise, and steamed mussels), but the real fans of Artisanal treat the place like their own private cheese club. Brennan has a passion for the stuff, and the restaurant has oodles of varieties as well as an on-site cheese cave—that you can enjoy it in a lively, upscale brasserie only makes it even more fun.

Choose a glass of wine from the extensive list, and get to work on a perfectly prepared basket of *gougères*, followed by one of the house fondues; or an irresistible *croque monsieur*, sporting tender prosciutto, soft Gruyère, and a delicious lick of browned béchamel, paired with a crunchy stack of house-made chips.

Bice

A2 Italian ✗✗

7 E. 54th St. (bet. Fifth & Madison Aves.)

Subway: 5 Av - 53 St
Phone: 212-688-1999
Web: www.bicenewyork.com
Prices: **$$$**

Lunch & dinner daily

This swanky midtown fixture has been at it for over twenty-five years, and it's not the only Bice to have a long run. The original Milan outpost opened in 1926, sprouting locations all around the world from Tokyo to Dubai. The successful formula? Generous portions of well-made, authentic Italian favorites.

Take a seat near the front of the restaurant and join the well-heeled crowd for a bowl of classic, creamy risotto with porcini mushrooms and a dash of excellent truffle oil. The grilled sea bass arrives perfumed with smoke from the wood-burning oven, along with grilled seasonal vegetables drizzled with olive oil. Sate the sweet tooth with deeply flavored vanilla panna cotta, topped with caramelized banana, fresh berries, and banana sauce.

Bistro Vendôme

C1

405 E. 58th St. (bet. First Ave. & Sutton Pl.)

Subway: 59 St
Phone: 212-935-9100
Web: www.bistrovendomenyc.com
Prices: $$

Lunch & dinner daily

Bistro Vendôme brings a breath of fresh air to stuffy Sutton Place with this sunny and quaint multi-level townhouse. Bright and airy (they also have a picturesque outdoor terrace), this classic New York restaurant nails the European bistro look and feel. While neighborhood denizens (of a certain age) with their dashing beaus may crowd the place, it remains surprisingly family friendly, especially on holidays.

The kitchen delivers classics exactly as they were conceived. From the escargot bathed in a rich and fragrant parsley and garlic-butter, to mussels Provençale with crispy frites; tailed by floating islands of meringue in crème anglaise with toasted almonds and spun sugar—each dish is solid, traditional, and just as it should be.

BLT Steak

B1

106 E. 57th St. (bet. Lexington & Park Aves.)

Subway: 59 St
Phone: 212-752-7470
Web: www.e2hospitality.com
Prices: $$$$

Lunch Mon – Fri
Dinner nightly

Pass the lengthy bar and Mondrian-style panels to reach the heart of this power lunch spot, beloved more by jackets than jeans. The handsome floors and polished striated tables at BLT Steak offer an idyllic stage for that steady din of corporate chatter. Augmenting the machismo are black-and-white pics of immortal NYC scenes including the "Charging Bull" invoking images of power and money...and meat.

Hanger steak moistened with maitre'd butter is a darling among expense accounts, while the "B" in BLT may as well stand for their double-cut smoked bacon. Tuna tartare becomes highbrow when paired with *gaufrettes*; and the mashed potatoes are deeply gratifying, so don't hold back. Same for the peanut butter chocolate mousse licked with banana ice cream.

Bobby Van's

Steakhouse ✗✗

B3

230 Park Ave. (at 46th St.)

Subway: Grand Central - 42 St
Phone: 212-867-5490
Web: www.bobbyvans.com
Prices: $$$$

Lunch Mon – Fri
Dinner Mon – Sat

This scene is so powerful that it intoxicates. A regular flock of bankers and brokers (entering through the passageway beneath the Helmsley Building) seek this clubby and boisterous haunt for its crowd, pricey wines, and those towering shellfish platters, served with flourish and perhaps a gruff edge.

After starters like the popular steakhouse Iceberg wedge salad with fried onions and bacon, arrives the meaty main attraction. These steaks are cooked exactly as ordered and carved tableside, with sides like fried zucchini served family-style.

After work, the bar is adorned with addictive homemade potato chips and offers a lighter menu as it comes alive with well-shaken martinis.

Bobby Van's has four other locations in Manhattan, plus BV's Burger.

Bottega del Vino

Italian ✗✗

A1

7 E. 59th St. (bet. Fifth & Madison Aves.)

Subway: 5 Av - 59 St
Phone: 212-223-2724
Web: www.bottegadelvinonyc.com
Prices: $$$$

Lunch & dinner daily

Amidst a sea of overpriced, mediocre, and stuffy Italian-feigning restaurants, Bottega del Vino is a welcome relief tendering some genuine Italian fare. Naturally, such authenticity comes at a price, and a costly one at that. The primo location, off Fifth Avenue, makes this a magnet for shoppers, tourists, and boutique investment bankers.

Up front, the menu covers panini, cappuccino, and pastries; while Bottega del Vino's back quarters are close-knit with nooks and banquettes. Dark wood and engravings lend warmth to this European-loving oasis whose classic Italian menu unveils *insalata di mare* with shaved celery in a light lemon dressing; *risotto del giorno* gleaming with asparagus and mascarpone; and a flawless version of the oft-clichéd tiramisu.

Brabant

C2

316 E. 53rd St. (bet. First & Second Aves.)

Subway: Lexington Av - 53 St

Phone: 212-510-8588

Web: www.brabantbelgianbrasserie.com

Prices: $$

Lunch & dinner daily

Rejoice Belgian beer aficionados, Brabant has the goods. Pouring an impressive brew selection and serving a decadent menu of pots of mussels alongside *frites* aplenty, this East Side newcomer could tempt the most disciplined teetotalers and dieters off the wagon. Inside, dark wood wainscoting, linen-topped tables, and a lovely marble bar create a bistro feel.

Sip on a fizzy Troubadour and dip a spoon beneath the crisped Gruyère-and-Fontina crust of the steaming grande *fromage* onion soup, with crisp sourdough *croûte*. Move on to an incredibly rich Belgian mac and cheese gratin pocked with ham and scallions, before closing with the heavenly (and shareable) Brussels-style Belgian waffle—light, fluffy and drizzled with bittersweet chocolate sauce.

Brasserie

B2

100 E. 53rd St. (bet. Lexington & Park Aves.)

Subway: Lexington Av - 53 St

Phone: 212-751-4840

Web: www.patinagroup.com

Prices: $$$

Lunch & dinner daily

Sleek, mod Brasserie is an eye-catching spot for corporate lunches, dinner dates, and drinks in between. Guests arrive by descending a short catwalk-like staircase into a room impressively dressed with polished wood panels, slanting green partitions, and white furnishings. And if you're waiting for someone, just keep your eyes on the screens over the bar, which project everyone's entrance.

The menu may be inspired by France but is prepared with contemporary flair. Velvety lobster bisque has the distinct, concentrated flavors of shellfish and is merely dabbed with crème fraîche rather than laden with cream. At dessert, the peaches and cream may arrive as a simple, light, and summertime combination of flaky biscuits and roasted peaches.

Bukhara Grill

C3   Indian 🍴🍴

217 E. 49th St. (bet. Second & Third Aves.)

Subway: 51 St   Lunch & dinner daily
Phone: 212-888-2839
Web: www.bukharany.com
Prices: $$

Blazing Bukhara Grill's dusky space exudes sophistication, drama, and a dash of kitsch. The upper level leans contemporary; while the rustic and timbered first-floor dining room is dressed in tables carved from tree-trunks, Indian artwork, and stoneware. Sink into a booth and gaze at the imposing cooks manning fiery tandoors.
Waiters in traditional garb are gruf in their presentation of foods from India's Northwest Frontier. Bite into juicy chicken *malai kebab* marinated in ginger, garlic, and spices; *aloo bukhara korma* starring saucy lamb chunks dancing with apricots and potatoes; and the beloved *kurkuri bindi*—crispy okra tossed with onions, spices, and coriander. Piles of puffy bread, straight out of the oven, reveal a committed chef and kitchen.

Casa Lever

B2   Italian 🍴🍴🍴

390 Park Ave. (entrance on 53rd St.)

Subway: Lexington Av - 53 St   Lunch & dinner Mon – Sat
Phone: 212-888-2700
Web: www.casalever.com
Prices: $$$$

The modernist design and crowds of corporate denizens give this loud, lively favorite a *Mad Men* feel. Housed in the basement of the iconic Lever House, the sexy, low-lit space is decked with tufted charcoal bucket seats circling red cocktail tables, wood panels, honeycomb-shaped wine racks, and Warhol-esque artwork. The gracious staff is top-notch.
The elegant, Northern Italian menu offers the likes of perfectly roasted, thinly sliced *vitello tonnato* in that unlikely yet incredibly delicious sauce of tuna, capers, and mayonnaise.

Linguine with sea urchin, crab meat, crushed tomato, and *peperoncino* is generous and beautifully calibrated. To finish, the contemporary *millefoglie* layers delicate pastry, vanilla Chantilly cream, and raspberry *granite*.

Café China

Chinese ✗✗

A5

13 E. 37th St. (bet. Fifth & Madison Aves.)

Subway: 34 St - Herald Sq   Lunch & dinner daily
Phone: 212-213-2810
Web: www.cafechinanyc.com
Prices: $$

Yiming Wang

On the outside, Café China is devoid of pomp, displaying an artless façade with wood-framed doors and red calligraphy. Inside, this is a high-minded dining home to some of New York's most elusive celebrity residents (if only at dinner). The décor reflects the bygone but glorious 1930s Shanghai, with thoughtful touches like dramatic sea green walls, high ceilings, and brass chandeliers. A marble-and-walnut bar, brilliant red seats, and portable typewriters set the highly stylized Sichuan scene.

It should be no surprise that the cooking here sets an equally high bar of fragrant, complex, and utterly irresistible dishes. Sample three-pepper chicken with meat so tender, skin so crispy, and peppers so fiery, that diners have been known to swoon. Sliced beef tendon arrives in a spicy chili sauce that brings mind-numbing heat; and butternut squash peppered with ginger is wholly luscious. Every taste and texture in the tea-smoked duck with hoisin is just as it should be; while tender fish fillets with pickled cabbage and greens, dried red chilies, and peppercorns is its own intense feast.

Even the desserts exceed expectations as in piping-hot and panko-crusted fried sweet potato pancakes.

Caviar Russe

A2

538 Madison Ave. (bet. 54th & 55th Sts.)

Subway: 5 Av - 53 St
Phone: 212-980-5908
Web: www.caviarrusse.com
Prices: $$$$

Lunch daily
Dinner Mon – Sat

Caviar Russe

Manhattan ▶ Midtown East & Murray Hill

This slightly obscure second-floor location (ring the bell to enter) is an extremely ornate, intimate room with massive flowers, murals, and marble aplenty. By day, it is populated by wealthy Russian families and affluent New Yorkers. Come nightfall, this just might be the perfect place to hide an affair, even if you can't pay in Euros. It sounds expensive because it is—wildly so. However, it is also a fitting home to luxuriate in an assortment of caviar that is as impossibly elegant as a champagne bubble, and a singular experience in this city. Yet to ignore the rest of the menu would be an enormous mistake.

Both timeless and modern, the solid European cooking is crafted from the best ingredients money can buy, then doused with heart-stopping extravagance. Risotto is not only perfectly cooked, but is ultra-creamy with the addition of sea urchin fillets and a generous dollop of lush, briny caviar on top. The excellent turbot arrives with tender, crisp squid in a light sauce and is then showered in samphire, micro-herbs, clover, and shaved black truffle.

Desserts test the bounds of decadence with layers of dark chocolate, salted caramel, tiny edible lavender flowers, and gold leaf.

Crave Fishbar

Seafood

C3

945 Second Ave. (bet. 50th & 51st Sts.)

Subway: 51 St
Phone: 646-895-9585
Web: www.cravefishbar.com
Prices: $$

Lunch Mon – Fri
Dinner nightly

This petite cottage is a little mod and a lot chic. Tastefully designed with raised tables up front and plaid-covered booths, Crave Fishbar bespeaks style and singularity in shades of blue, gray, and green. A 25-foot marble-topped bar is ideal for solo dining while tables in the back are perfect for larger parties.

The staff is polite and learned as they present a serious, never-tedious affair, showing the chef's skilled hand in a house-smoked bluefish salad tossed with dill dressing; or olive oil-poached cod, pearly white and bathed in brown butter vinaigrette. Pan-roasted prawns arrive flavorful with a sweet kick of gypsy chili and kabocha squash purée; desserts are as pleasing as a warm chocolate chip cookie, not with a scoop of vanilla ice cream.

Don's Bogam

Korean

A6

17 E. 32nd St. (bet. Fifth & Madison Aves.)

Subway: 33 St
Phone: 212-683-2200
Web: www.donsbogam.com
Prices: $$

Lunch & dinner daily

For a fun, festive night with family and friends, head to Don's Bogam. The food here is fantastic and it is no wonder that it is perpetually packed. Be sure to reserve ahead as every seat is filled, from the front bar and two-tops to the elevated level of traditional, sunken tables with powerful grills and enormous vents. Go hungry and order platters of immaculate beef and oodles of *soju*.

Novices can rest easy as the gracious staff will guide and grill your way through their classic Korean menu featuring dishes like *japchae*, stir-fried sweet potato noodles in sesame oil with beef, vegetables, and soy sauce; or deep-fried pork *mandu* with a sesame- soy- and scallion sauce. Thinly sliced beef *bulgogi* with mushrooms and carrots is utterly memorable.

El Parador

C6

Mexican ✗✗

325 E. 34th St. (bet. First & Second Aves.)

Subway: 33 St

Phone: 212-679-6812

Web: www.elparadorcafe.com

Prices: $$

Lunch & dinner daily

This neighborhood mainstay can boast over fifty years of success. With their fantastic menu, killer margaritas, and dedication to hospitality, El Parador is worthy of its status as a beloved destination. The intimate space is decked with ornate wood chairs, red banquettes, and wood plank ceilings, while white brick walls are hung with artwork and artifacts. The bountiful menu offers favorites like taco trays and nachos in three varieties, as well as a rotating menu of daily specials (be sure to try the fish of the day). Fill up on *aguachile de camaron*, deliciously classic shrimp ceviche in lime juice and jalapeño; and tender, falling-off-the-bone baby-back ribs, grilled and served with tequila-chili *huajillo* salsa, cabbage slaw, and braised *camote*.

Ethos

C2

Greek ✗✗

905 First Ave. (at 51st St.)

Subway: 51 St

Phone: 212-888-4060

Web: www.ethosrestaurants.com

Prices: $$

Lunch & dinner daily

Ethos not only brings pizzazz to this rather mundane quarter (just across from Beekman and its ritzy residents), but it also presents an authentic picture of Mykonos with whitewashed walls, cozy cushions, and light wood trim. Glossy china, glassware, and an upbeat soundtrack finish off the polish and transport you to the Greek islands... for a night.

While the meze makes for a delicious meal on its own, Ethos' menu remains appealing with the likes of *avgolemono* (the Greek version of grandma's chicken soup) with egg, lemon, and orzo; or a standout *spanakopita* composed of phyllo triangles filled with spinach and feta. The staff is hit or miss, but when gifted with *keftedes* (savory meatballs in tomato sauce) paired with lemon potatoes, all is forgiven.

Felidia

Italian ❌❌

C1

243 E. 58th St. (bet. Second & Third Aves.)

Subway: Lexington Av - 59 St
Phone: 212-758-1479
Web: www.felidia-nyc.com
Prices: $$$

Lunch Mon – Fri
Dinner nightly

Felidia's burnt-orange awning, red brick patio, and tiny olive trees instantly make it the most attractive spot on the block. Inside, the space is bright and warm with a long wood bar, cherry red leather chairs, and colorful Venetian glass sconces. Expect to glimpse owner and matriarch Lidia Bastianich, herself, adding to the friendly ambience.

The consistent menu is filled with top ingredients handled with straightforward care, as in fresh *burrata* topped with a fried egg—its warm, runny yolk drips down to meet perfectly blanched asparagus and crisp bacon; or *cacio e pere* featuring tender ravioli filled with pear purée and finished with showers of pepper. Classic desserts get a fantastic twist, as in tiramisu flavored with limoncello rather than coffee.

The Four Seasons

American ❌❌❌❌

B2

99 E. 52nd St. (bet. Lexington & Park Aves.)

Subway: 51 St
Phone: 212-754-9494
Web: www.fourseasonsrestaurant.com
Prices: $$$$

Lunch Mon – Fri
Dinner Mon – Sat

Resolute in its embrace of power and privilege, The Four Seasons is one of Manhattan's most iconic dining rooms. Opened in 1959, this time capsule of mid-century swagger still remains the choice table for the panoply of today's movers and shakers. Whether it's lunch in the Grill Room or dinner in the Pool Room, design aficionados will revel in the beauty of the Picasso curtain, the walnut paneling, and Mies van der Rohe furnishings.

This ambience comes at a price, but the food is refined, skillfully prepared, and made with exceptional ingredients. Expect dishes to highlight classical elements, as in luscious Nantucket Bay scallops with a black truffle sauce and wild mushrooms; or Dover sole, filleted tableside and presented with a lemon-caper sauce.

HanGawi

Korean ✗✗

A6

12 E. 32nd St. (bet. Fifth & Madison Aves.)

Subway: 33 St
Phone: 212-213-0077
Web: www.hangawirestaurant.com
Prices: $$

Lunch Mon – Sat
Dinner nightly

Don't worry about wearing your best shoes to HanGawi; you'll have to take them off at the door before settling in at one of the restaurant's low tables. In the serene space, decorated with Korean artifacts and soothed by meditative music, it's easy to forget you're in Manhattan.

The menu is all vegetarian, in keeping with the philosophy of healthy cooking to balance the *um* and *yang*. You can quite literally eat like a king here starting with vermicelli delight (sweet potato noodles), perfectly crisp kimchi and mushroom pancakes, devastatingly delicious tofu clay pot in ginger sauce, and the regal kimchi stone bowl rice made fragrant with fresh veggies. Of course, you'll have to rejoin the crowds outside. Still, it's nice to get away...now and Zen.

Hide-Chan Ramen

Japanese ✗

C2

248 E. 52nd St. (bet. Second & Third Aves.)

Subway: Lexington Av - 53 St
Phone: 212-813-1800
Web: N/A
Prices:

Lunch & dinner daily

Hide-Chan may as well be called Killer Ramen. Up a narrow flight of steps on a sleepy midtown block, this hideaway has been drawing epicures for their impeccable ramen and authentic vibe. Sedate at lunch, the mood gets livelier at night, when the beers flow faster.

The menu features plenty of pork-centric additions like steamed buns folded around *char siu* (barbecued pork) and Kewpie mayo; or Japanese fried chicken (*tori kara*). Just get a double-order of *gyoza*—it's that good. However, ramen is the rightful focus of any meal here, served in a rich, complex broth brimming with excellent roast pork. Delve into the likes of *kuro-ramen*, highlighting black garlic paste and a host of your own embellishments, from egg and extra nori to pickled mustard leaf.

Hunan Manor

B5

339 Lexington Ave. (bet. 39th and 40th Aves.)

Subway: Grand Central - 42 St
Phone: 212-682-2883
Web: www.hunanauthentic.com
Prices: 😎

Lunch & dinner daily

Located only steps from the bustling Grand Central Terminal, Hunan Manor (baby sibling of Flushing's Hunan House) is a terrific addition to the Sichuan scene. Forever busy at lunch, make sure you get here early enough to snag a spot. Even when this tight-knit space is packed with an obvious blend of local suits and zealous foodies, the staff remains adept and affable.

Like its surrounds, presentations and prices are delightfully modest. The Manor's menu is massive, so bring friends to share plates of Hunan-style spicy pickled cabbage; probably *the* best scallion pancakes in town; outstanding and silky *mai fun* in a spicy-sour broth of string beans and ground pork; or white pepper-smoked duck, fantastically fragrant with dried turnips and chilies.

Jubilee

French ✕✕

C2

948 First Ave. (bet. 52nd & 53rd Sts.)

Subway: Lexington Av - 53 St
Phone: 212-888-3569
Web: www.jubileeny.net
Prices: $$

Lunch & dinner daily

Jubilee has been and remains a longtime neighborhood favorite among Beekman and Sutton Place residents alike. The character-rich décor straddles the border between nautical and residential with sisal carpets, blue-and-beige splashes, leather settees, and a wall of painted anchors with blackboards listing nightly specials worthy of serious consideration.

The menu is packed with crowd-pleasing, Belgian-inspired classics like eleven varieties of *moules* paired with perfectly crisped house frites; or an asparagus "napoleon" starring tender asparagus layered with crispy speck and florets of Parmesan foam. The chef adeptly demonstrates classic skills in his fish soup, rich in texture and flavor, paired with *croûtes*, *rouille*, and grated Gruyère.

Jukai

 Japanese ✗✗

237 E. 53rd St. (bet. Second & Third Aves.)

Subway: Lexington Av - 53 St
Phone: 212-588-9788
Web: www.jukainyc.com
Prices: $$

Lunch Tue – Fri
Dinner Mon – Sat

 With its furtive location, Jukai is a subterranean hot spot that instantly transports you to Tokyo...on a dime. Styled with woods and bamboo, this lair is packed with Japanese expats lingering over elaborate meals attended to by an amicable staff.

The menu is traditional, though the chef's unique influences are well expressed in a massive oyster "sashimi" quartered and served with ponzu; or mixed greens mingled with rich foie gras terrine and sliced duck. First-timers should opt for a fixed menu as it allows for sampling of bites like dried cod roe and *tamago*. Shabu-shabu is par excellence with top quality beef, thinly sliced, swished in dashi until perfectly tender, and then served with noodles, tofu, and two delicious sauces for dipping.

Kurumazushi

Japanese ✗✗

7 E. 47th St., 2nd fl. (bet. Fifth & Madison Aves.)

Subway: 47-50 Sts - Rockefeller Ctr
Phone: 212-317-2802
Web: www.kurumazushi.com
Prices: $$$$

Lunch & dinner Mon – Sat

 The second-floor location up a steep set of stairs may seem pure Tokyo, but the business clientele and foreign tourists have no problem finding their way to this stalwart of traditional, Edo-style sushi. The room is simple (if outdated) but a warm welcome to your seat at the sushi bar before the extraordinary Chef Toshihiro Uezu is all that's needed. A *washitsu* room is available for private parties.

While à la carte may suffice, Kurumazushi is regaled for its omakase (though there are dramatic variations in pricing, so be sure to communicate a budget). Each taste of this precious sushi—from kampachi and sea scallop to sweet shrimp, giant clam, and uni—holds its place within the upper eschelons of New York sushi dining. The toro is a worthy specialty.

Kajitsu ✿

Japanese 🍴🍴

B5

125 E. 39th St. (bet. Lexington & Park Aves.)

Subway: Grand Central - 42 St
Lunch & dinner Mon – Sat
Phone: 212-228-4873
Web: www.kajitsunyc.com
Prices: $$$

Chihiro Kimura

There is an ancient art to *shojin ryori* (Zen vegan temple cuisine). The chef's movements are measured, there is a contemplative quiet to dining, and each ingredient reflects time and season. Kajitsu adheres to much of this wisdom from its second-floor dining room in a Murray Hill townhouse. Note the silence of the servers' soft shoes (interrupted by the chef's clogs on slate), the Zen-minimalist design, and harmony in the procession of dishes.

Each plate is sure to be visually striking, as in a light starter of *wakame* soup showcasing a scoop of homemade tofu mixed with green peppers, bathed in soy, topped with crumbles of tempura-fried basil, alongside cubes of *tomato-fu* and fresh fava beans. This might be followed by a cylinder of yuba wrapping bits of *hijiki* and morel mushrooms, with cooked nori that is blended to form a deep black, shimmering pool. Sukiyaki is a savory, subtle mix of sweet and punchy flavors. Summer black truffle rice is pure and balanced, with pearly steamed rice, pickled asparagus, peppers, *umeboshi*, deep brown dashi, and lemony mountain vegetables.

Downstairs, Kokage serves an excellent, traditional lunch and is under the same ownership, but is not vegan.

La Grenouille

French 🍴🍴🍴

A2

3 E. 52nd St. (bet. Fifth & Madison Aves.)

Subway: 5 Av - 53 St	Lunch & dinner Tue – Sat
Phone: 212-752-1495	
Web: www.la-grenouille.com	
Prices: $$$$	

A warm, discreet welcome proves proper breeding in gorgeous La Grenouille, which recalls an Old World where true beauty and elegance went hand-in-hand. Imagine handsome suits and coiffed updos amid rich fabric walls, lavish velvet banquettes, accoutered tables, and glorious florals. (Yes, scenes from *Mad Men* have been filmed here, without a single change to the set.) The staff is famously gracious and unobtrusive.

The very classic French kitchen sets a standard for the Old Guard, assuring that even the tiniest dab of tarragon purée is well placed in *les ravioles de homard a l'estragon*, silky pasta filled with lobster in a rich butter sauce. *Quenelles "Lyonnaise"* in béchamel are prepared with total precision. *Ouefs à la Niege* are feather-light and divine.

La Mangeoire

French 🍴🍴

C2

1008 Second Ave. (bet. 53rd & 54th Aves.)

Subway: Lexington Av - 53 St	Lunch Sun – Fri
Phone: 212-759-7086	Dinner nightly
Web: www.lamangeoire.com	
Prices: $$$	

Cozy and warm, La Mangeoire is the French bistro that everyone dreams of having in their neighborhood. Housed on a harried street, this delightful farmhouse feels at once updated and modern with sunlight drenching its floors and French artifacts dotting its walls.

As if to prove their authenticity, they also have a fully French staff who are adept, friendly, and even flirty in their relaying of the classic menu. *Rilettes* of smoked salmon are delicious and rustically served in a little jar with toasted baguette. Still, the roast chicken should be the stuff of culinary legends: gorgeously dark and crisp-skinned, juicy, served with an accompanying pitcher of *jus* to pour as desired. A rich yet lightly textured milk chocolate mousse is decadence incarnate.

Land of Plenty 🐕

B1

204 E 58th St. (bet. Second & Third Aves.)

Subwalk: 59 St
Phone: 212-308-8788
Web: www.landofplenty58.com
Prices: $$

Lunch Mon – Fri
Dinner nightly

The exceedingly elegant and fully decorated Land of Plenty features an attractive interior, beautifully augmented by a handsome and inviting bar as well as intimate tables. The selection of offerings can boast not only surprisingly delicious Sichuan cuisine, but these fiery delights are brought to you at the hands of a remarkably fast and well-humored staff.

If your wisecracking waiter lists Sichuan *douhua* as a special, be sure to get it—the soft tofu is topped with chili oil, fried soybeans, and crushed Sichuan peppercorns. Showcasing excellent products and solid techniques are crunchy jelly fish strips tossed in a spicy oil and citrus vinaigrette; tender poached chicken in peanutty chili oil; and a bubbling vat of savory beer-braised duck meat.

Le Cirque

B1

151 E. 58th St. (bet. Lexington & Third Aves.)

Subway: 59 St
Phone: 212-644-0202
Web: www.lecirque.com
Prices: $$$$

Lunch Mon – Fri
Dinner Mon – Sat

At this NYC citadel, also lauded as Sirio Maccioni's cathedral of contemporary cuisine, menu classics are showcased with both a description and date of birth ("Flounder Le Cirque, est. 1974") that serve as further testament to Le Cirque's culinary eminence. This ultra-chic stalwart never ceases to stun, beginning with its limousine-lined central courtyard entrance.

The décor is a classy and tasteful throw-back of sorts that manages to invent a "circus-chic" aesthetic through rich fabrics, handsome paneling, and many, many monkeys. Speckled with glitterati, the dining room seduces with a warm artichoke soup finished with tarragon; excellent *lasagnette* of lamb braised with aromatics and fresh herbs; and gingerbread profiteroles atop fluffy whipped cream.

Le Relais de Venise

B2

Steakhouse ✗✗

590 Lexington Ave. (at 52nd St.)

Subway: 51 St
Phone: 212-758-3989
Web: www.relaisdevenise.com
Prices: $$

Lunch & dinner daily

There is no menu at Le Relais de Venise L'Entrecôte, a Parisian restaurant with a prime location set along thumping Lexington Avenue. There is only one $26.95 option, but it is a delightful option indeed—green salad with tangy mustard vinaigrette and walnuts, followed by juicy steak served in two parts (because you wouldn't want the rest of it to get cold, would you?) laced in the house's mouthwatering secret sauce, with all the crunchy frites you can eat.

With a Parisian décor and waitresses darting around in saucy French maid get-ups, this is a lively joint—all the more reason to pluck a glass of *vin* off the extremely affordable list, sit back and relax. By the time the dessert menu rolls around, you'll have forgotten how stressful decisions can be.

Mapo Tofu

B5

Chinese ✗

338 Lexington Ave. (bet. 39th & 40th Sts.)

Subway: Grand Central - 42 St
Phone: 212-867-8118
Web: N/A
Prices: 🍜

Lunch & dinner daily

Just when you think you're sated, this Sichuan Shangri-la bestows you with another boon. At Mapo Tofu it's not just about tofu, but their sumptuous feast. Their forte also includes the expert marriage of spices, wafting into a simple though neat room adorned with tables and slapdash servers. Their genius locale and superior spread hoists it into a league of its own.

Start this Sichuan safari with sliced conch steeping in roasted chili vinaigrette; string beans with bamboo shoots and pork are an incredible item; and braised fish, tofu, and cellophane noodles carry a fiercely flavorful chili broth. Camphor tea-smoked duck; *dan dan* noodles with pork; and wok-tossed prawns with spiced salt and Sichuan peppercorns are stunning, flavor-ridden plates.

Matisse

C3

924 Second Ave. (at 49th St.)

Lunch & dinner daily

Subway: 51 St
Phone: 212-546-9300
Web: www.matissenyc.com
Prices: $$

Matisse might be smack dab in midtown, but this tightly packed, sun-filled bistro looks and feels more downtown. Informal without being casual, this single room restaurant with a front row seat to the action of Second Avenue has that typical New York lack of elbow room, but forever lively and whizzing spirit.

Young and old area denizens are lured by the simple and classic French cooking with a reasonable price tag. The menu presents an appealing range of comfort foods, such as a caramelized onion tarte and *croque monsieur*. Sunday brunch delivers the goods with omelets and French toast alongside other usual suspects.

Some of the dishes are presented on delightfully rustic wooden boards and exude charm thereby displaying Matisse's stylish flair.

Mr Chow

C1

324 E. 57th St. (bet. First & Second Aves.)

Dinner nightly

Subway: 59 St
Phone: 212-751-9030
Web: www.mrchow.com
Prices: $$$$

Oh Mr Chow, how you hook the hordes with your flavorful fusion and fancy prices! Perhaps it's the retro scene decked in black-and-white, lacquered Asian-accented chairs, and glinting mirrors. Or, maybe it's the noodle guy's theatrical display of hand-pulling? Whatever the hype, Mr Chow still has it and Sutton suits along with their wealthy wives party here like it's 1999.

Attentive service and flowing drinks keep everything moving as fans nibble away on the well-priced Beijing duck prix-fixe with four starters plus entrées. Tender orange chicken satay and water dumplings with seafood are tasty, but Dungeness crab sautéed with egg whites, and *ma mignon*, cubes of tender fried beef tossed in a sweet-spicy sauce laced with scallions truly get the crowd going.

Naya

C2

Lebanese

1057 Second Ave. (bet. 55th & 56th Sts.)

Subway: Lexington Av - 53 St
Phone: 212-319-7777
Web: www.nayarestaurants.com
Prices: $$

Lunch & dinner daily

Amid this bland stretch of cheap booze and loud beats lies Naya, a tiny and mod neighborhood spot with tasty Lebanese fare. Inside, the streamlined décor feels smart and attractive, with white pleather booths contrasting against shiny dark tables. This sleek aesthetic runs to the back where a large table is best for suit-donning groups.

Most love Naya for its vast choice of Lebanese meze and daily specials featuring home-style food with modern flair. It is clear that this is no amateur show, as obliging waiters present you with the likes of a "quick Naya" lunch special unveiling generous portions of *fattoush*, *labné*, and *baba ghannouj*. A chicken shawarma sandwich reaches epic scopes when paired with their deliciously tangy homemade pickles.

Obikà

A1

Italian

590 Madison Ave. (at 56th St.)

Subway: 59 St
Phone: 212-355-2217
Web: www.obika.it
Prices: $$

Lunch daily

Conveniently located in the glass atrium of the IBM building, Obikà exudes an elegant yet casual style that attracts slim suits and sleek shoppers alike. Plentiful sunlight lends an airy feel to the space, which offers counter dining and table seating, smartly separated from the building's lobby with planters.

The focus here is the truly exceptional mozzarella—fresh *bufala*, hauntingly smoked, or tangy *burrata*—which can be paired with a *tagliere* of cured meats and/or grilled vegetables for a perfectly light lunch. The menu ventures on to offer an exceptional rendition of lasagna *tradizionale*, made with delicate layers of pasta, hearty beef ragù, béchamel, and a showering of Parmesan. Come dessert, the tiramisu is another classic.

243

Osteria Laguna

C4

Italian ✕✕

209 E. 42nd St. (bet. Second & Third Aves.)

Subway: Grand Central - 42 St
Phone: 212-557-0001
Web: www.osteria-laguna.com
Prices: $$

Lunch & dinner daily

A little bit corporate (it is midtown, after all) and a little bit casual (daytrippers from nearby Grand Central), Osteria Laguna has nailed its audience and delivers a perfect blend to suit both worlds. Inside, it's delightfully rustic, complete with the requisite Italian ceramic plates and wooden chairs with rush seating.

Crowd-pleasers like pastas, pizzas from the wood-burning oven, *antipasti*, salads, and grilled meats and fish dishes comprise the menu at this better-than-average Italian. The friendly service can be spotty, but the perfectly crisped wood-fired pizzas are always spot on. The portions are abundant, perhaps even too much given the tiny tables, but the prices aren't, so you can treat your out-of-town friend and keep the change.

Pampano

B3

Mexican ✕✕

209 E. 49th St. (bet. Second & Third Aves.)

Subway: 51 St
Phone: 212-751-4545
Web: www.richardsandoval.com
Prices: $$$

Lunch Sun – Fri
Dinner nightly

Pampano is a proven pick among corporate types craving upscale, seafood-centric Mexican food. An army of hostesses may greet you at the entry but leave you feeling cool. No matter, they might as well have escorted you to Acapulco, otherwise known as a table upstairs—think whitewashed ceilings, giant wicker chairs, and overhead fans. While the bar is very popular at happy hour, the mediocre downstairs "botaneria" seating and menu should be skipped in favor of the superior upstairs setting.

Expect the likes of red snapper-packed *quesadillas de pescado* oozing with Oaxaca cheese and spicy salsas. *Huarache de hongos* topped with mushrooms and goat cheese; or a dark chocoflan with candied peanuts are tasty studies in presentation and texture.

Pera

Turkish

A4

303 Madison Ave. (bet. 41st & 42nd Sts.)

Subway: Grand Central - 42 St
Phone: 212-878-6301
Web: www.peranyc.com
Prices: $$

Lunch & dinner daily

This perennially-packed Mediterranean brasserie attracts a loud lunchtime crowd of office workers, while at nighttime the scene is populated by intimate pairs. The establishment, named after an upscale neighborhood in Istanbul, warms the heart with its chocolate-brown color scheme and grand display kitchen boasting an open flame grill station.

The expert cooks churn out a throng of mouthwatering fare, like fig *pidette*—a dense flatbread spread with strips of Turkish-style dried beef, *rucola*, dried figs, and cumin-infused yogurt drizzles; the cubed watermelon and feta salad massaged with fragrant basil oil is a warm weather must; and roasted whole fish is offered to be de-boned and comes delightfully dressed with blistered tomatoes and candied lemon.

Phoenix Garden

Chinese

B5

242 E. 40th St. (bet. Second & Third Aves.)

Subway: Grand Central - 42 St
Phone: 212-983-6666
Web: www.thephoenixgarden.com
Prices:

Lunch & dinner daily

This fuss-free and no-frills basement shows Chinatown that delicious Chinese food for a great value can exist outside of its borders. Forgo ho-hum lunch deals and pop in at dinnertime for a delectable selection of authentic Cantonese cooking.

The vast menu can take some navigating, so chat up the servers for their expert advice in order to get the goods. Highlights include exquisite salt-and-pepper shrimp, shell-on, butterflied, flash-fried and tossed with sliced chilies and garlic; sautéed snow pea leaves in an egg-white sauce of sweet crabmeat, carrots, and snow peas; sizzling eggplant casserole studded with minced pork and ham; and crispy Peking duck sliced tableside, rolled up in pancakes, and layered with hoisin, cucumber, and scallions.

P.J. Clarke's

 B2

915 Third Ave. (at 55th St.)

Subway: Lexington Av - 53 St
Phone: 212-317-1616
Web: www.pjclarkes.com
Prices: $$

Lunch & dinner daily

Old time and on the ball, P.J. Clarke's drips with New York history—ad men and business execs have patronized this pour house for generations, and with good reason. Besides a dazzling medley of drinks, the kitchen sends out a crowd-pleasing menu showcasing solid technique. Following its repute, the distinct décor spotlights notable artifacts, worn floors, and smartly dressed tables.

Weekends draw a touristy set, but who's complaining with an amazing Bloody Mary so close at hand? Highlights include potato chips with an outrageously gooey blue cheese gratin; braised short rib spring rolls with horseradish-tinged sour cream; and tuna tartare tacos filled with scallion and sesame seeds. The cheeseburger is as classic and on-point as the staff itself.

Rosa Mexicano

C1

1063 First Ave. (at 58th St.)

Subway: 59 St
Phone: 212-753-7407
Web: www.rosamexicano.com
Prices: $$

Lunch Sat – Sun
Dinner nightly

Rosa may have spread her wings, but one thing remains gospel: her original location is the "wind beneath" and the only one where the food is not just good, it's great. Despite the expansion, Rosa upholds her excellence by virtue of a titanic roster of delicious dishes, those stellar margaritas, and hospitable ambience. Warm and worn in a distinctly Mexican style, find the front room flocked with booths, tables, and a bar packed three deep.

The tortilla lady and her *comal* live in an adjacent room, while the back space whispers intimacy. Lights are low here but the flavors are as bright as *guacamole en molcajete*. Captivating plates of *queso fundido* with *chorizo y rajas*; *plantanos* topped with *crema*; and *budin de pollo*, complement their unhurried service.

Rouge Tomate ✿

Contemporary   🍴🍴🍴

A1

10 E. 60th St. (bet. Fifth & Madison Aves.)

Subway: 5 Av
Phone: 646-237-8977
Web: www.rougetomatenyc.com
Prices: **$$$**

Lunch & dinner Mon – Sat

Thomas Schauer

Rouge Tomate is happily located in one of the most affluent blocks in town, right off Fifth Avenue and all its glitzy shopping. Conceived by architectural firm Bentel & Bentel, this contemporary beauty features sleek glass walls, flattering lights, tables crafted from reclaimed coconut shells, and a curved walnut-and-oak bar. The courteous staff guides guests through the stunning bi-level space, while detailing its history and cuisine with great enthusiasm. Everything seems exquisite from their earthy backdrops and meticulous cutlery, to the well-timed courses.

This isn't just a pretty, health-minded restaurant committed to using sustainable ingredients—the food is carefully composed, very unique, and always delicious. Expect starters like seasonal toasts with cranberry tapenade and curried cabbage, or sweet spaghetti squash and meaty Maryland crab. Then, move on to superbly grilled venison à la plancha laid atop braised sunchokes and sweetened with poached quince, farro folded into a verdant purée, cocoa nibs, and cranberry jus.

Lovely desserts are offered in small sizes like a tiny pear with chocolate and hazelnuts. Don't forget about the juice bar for tasty, thirst-quenching sips.

Sakagura

B4

211 E. 43rd St. (bet. Second & Third Aves.)

Subway: Grand Central - 42 St
Phone: 212-953-7253
Web: sakagura.com
Prices: $$$

Lunch Mon – Fri
Dinner nightly

Without changing, Sakagura continues on as a sought-after sake den. Buried in the basement of an office building, this very Japanese gem requires reservations. The staff is vigilant, but lingering is the name of the game in their vast dining room, elegantly adorned with a counter and lush booths.

Here, lunch is cherished for its fantastic choice and notable value. Nibble your way through perfectly fried chopped shrimp and shredded vegetable *kakiage*, served with radish and dipping sauce; a tasty seaweed salad tossed with ponzu; and *sake ikura don set*—rice topped with salmon sashimi and roe alongside chewy soba with scallions, pickles, and dashi. Dinner is a different ball game with pages upon pages of little bites for savoring with carafes of sake.

2nd Avenue Deli

B6

162 E. 33rd St. (bet. Lexington & Third Aves.)

Subway: 33 St
Phone: 212-689-9000
Web: www.2ndavedeli.com
Prices:

Lunch & dinner daily

While the décor may be more deli-meets-deco and there's a tad less attitude, this food is every bit as good as it was on Second Avenue. Ignore the kvetching and know that this is a true Jewish deli filled with personality, and one of the best around by far.

The menu remains as it should: kosher, meat-loving, and non-dairy with phenomenal pastrami, pillowy rye, tangy mustard, perfect potato pancakes, and fluffy matzoh balls in comforting broth. Have the best of both worlds with the soup and half-sandwich combination.

Carve a nook during midday rush, when in pour the crowds. The deli also does takeout (popular with the midtown lunch bunch), and delivery (grandma's pancakes at your door). Giant platters go equally well to a bris or brunch.

Seo 😊

C3

Japanese ✕✕

249 E. 49th St. (bet. Second & Third Aves.)

Subway: 51 St
Phone: 212-355-7722
Web: N/A
Prices: $$

Lunch Mon – Fri
Dinner nightly

For home-style Japanese food in a delightful setting, head to Seo. This hospitable hideaway wears no airs; its kitchen is wholly dedicated to the cooking and conservation of their little lair. While Westerners may misconstrue it for a sushi bar (glimpse the long wraparound counter), Seo is anything but. Make your way beyond a steamy kitchen to a small dining room neatly attired with a few tables and a glass wall overlooking a traditional and very tranquil Japanese garden. Amid this serenity, eat your way through crunchy, salty edamame followed by tender *inaniwa udon* or superb salmon sashimi atop rice with wasabi and shiso. Like its Zen backyard, a lick of the red bean-green tea ice cream will deliver you far from the maddening midtown streets.

Sip Sak 😊

C3

Turkish ✕✕

928 Second Ave. (bet. 49th & 50th Sts.)

Subway: 51 St
Phone: 212-583-1900
Web: www.sip-sak.com
Prices: $$

Lunch & dinner Mon – Sat

It's as if Chef/owner Orhan Yegen treats Sip Sak like his personal design project—primped, preened, and never left alone. Yet this is working. Everything here feels warm with Turkish artifacts on mellow-toned walls and an imposing floral arrangement. The lights are low, but cast a pretty glow upon marble-topped tables, bistro chairs, and small front bar. With the master on set, the staff is nimble (if sometimes robotic) in delivering a recital of their tasty eats. Appetizer platters are ideal for groups, and throw in a Shepherd salad featuring spicy cubanelles. If the stuffed cabbage stars, try it. Otherwise, a deliciously restorative red lentil soup; feta-packed *borek*; and soft *manti* floating in yogurt and filled with spiced beef are equally delightful.

Smith & Wollensky

B3

797 Third Ave. (at 49th St.)

Subway: 51 St
Phone: 212-753-1530
Web: www.smithandwollensky.com
Prices: $$$$

Lunch Mon – Fri
Dinner nightly

Long before Manhattan's steakhouse craze reached epic proportions, there was Smith & Wollensky. The New York flagship opened in 1977, and over 30 years later, it is still jumping—it's historic green and white façade is a welcome beacon to neighborhood power players during the week; while families and tourists keep busin ess booming over the weekends. Now you too can have your "Devil Wears Prada" moment as they deliver to your desk, no assistant required!

The owners may have plucked the names Smith and Wollensky out of a phone directory, but they were considerably more careful choosing their USDA Prime beef, which they dry-age and hand-butcher on premises. The result, paired with mouthwatering mashed potatoes or hashbrowns, is steakhouse nirvana.

Soba Totto

B4

211 E. 43rd St. (bet. Second & Third Aves.)

Subway: Grand Central - 42 St
Phone: 212-557-8200
Web: www.sobatotto.com
Prices: $$

Lunch Mon – Fri
Dinner nightly

It's a jam-packed lunchtime affair here at Soba Totto, where business folks gather and quickly fill this popular space. As the name suggests, everyone arrives in droves for the tasty homemade soba. Dinnertime brings a mellower vibe, and a crowd of beer- and sake-sipping patrons ordering tasty plates of spicy fried chicken and yakitori galore.

Midday features several varieties of lunch sets. Tasty appetizers may unveil a salad of assorted pickles and simmered daikon in a sweet ginger dressing. Skip over the fried seafood in favor of the *soba totto gozen* set, which includes the wonderful soba in fragrant *dashi*; or try one of the many delicious *dons* topped with tasty tidbits like sea urchin and salmon roe or soy-marinated tuna, grated yam, and egg.

Sparks

C3

Steakhouse ✗✗

210 E. 46th St. (bet. Second & Third Aves.)

Subway: Grand Central - 42 St
Phone: 212-687-4855
Web: www.sparksnyc.com
Prices: $$$$

Lunch Mon – Fri
Dinner Mon – Sat

Sparks isn't contrived or outdated. This venerable steakhouse lives up to its reputation and very little has changed—even their service team remains as efficient as it is obliging. This place is a loud and loveably gruff slice of NYC history that was the backdrop of an historical mob hit. Today, suits and regulars seem to grab the spotlight. The main dining room meanders into cozy corners but still reeks of the Old World with dark wood and rich carpets.

This is straight steakhouse fare with some salads (a Caesar topped with salty anchovies) and seafood (flavorful baked clams combined with shrimp scampi in lemon, butter, and garlic) to start. Get a perfectly cooked sirloin drowned in its own juices, paired with an side of excellent creamed spinach.

SushiAnn

B2

Japanese ✗✗

38 E. 51st St. (bet. Madison & Park Aves.)

Subway: 51 St
Phone: 212-755-1780
Web: www.sushiann.net
Prices: $$

Lunch Mon – Fri
Dinner Mon – Sat

Lucky are those who wander into this large, peaceful den helmed by one of the best sushi teams in town—even luckier are those regulars at the counter, who know that despite the Americanized menu options, there is a depth of authenticity rare in these parts. Such standby sushi classics as SushiAnn know just how to balance tradition, pleasure, and expectation. For an adventure, sit at the counter (where there is a $30 minimum) and don't hesitate to express interest in the more authentic dishes. This is just the right place to go for the omakase: fresh mackerel served with ponzu and minced ginger; fatty bluefin fanned over shiso leaf and kelp; smoky slices of grilled giant clam; or rich torched sardine—all carefully explained by the knowledgeable staff.

Sushiden

Japanese ✗✗

19 E. 49th St. (bet. Fifth & Madison Aves.)

Subway: 5 Av - 53 St
Phone: 212-758-2700
Web: www.sushiden.com
Prices: $$$

Lunch Mon – Fri
Dinner Sun – Fri

Forget everything you think you know before stepping into this traditional *sushi-ya* in the heart of midtown—there won't be a California roll in sight. Be sure to reserve ahead, as tables are buzzing with businessmen at lunch, though treating yourself to omakase at the sushi bar is the best way to watch and appreciate the sushi magic.

Soothing wood accents keep perfect company with their soft-spoken, kimono-clad staff and quiet, expert chefs. Menus may reveal such outrageously fresh fish as four silky slices of bonito sashimi (*hagatsuo*); a fresh, live scallop sliced into three rounds with a touch of freshly ground wasabi; mild and delicate branzino nigiri; and *benisake*, deep orange Sockeye salmon, sweet in flavor and pleasantly rich in texture.

Sushi Yasuda

Japanese ✗✗

204 E. 43rd St. (bet. Second & Third Aves.)

Subway: Grand Central - 42 St
Phone: 212-972-1001
Web: www.sushiyasuda.com
Prices: $$$$

Lunch Mon – Fri
Dinner Mon – Sat

Attention rule breakers: this glorious sushi spot ain't for you. Late for your reservation? It will be forfeited. Lingering too long after eating? You will be informed that time is up. Sushi-loving diehards can handle the tough love though, and come back time and time again for their spectacularly fresh fish. Left in the capable hands of Mitsuru Tamura after Naomichi Yasuda's departure, this beloved spot still maintains its loyal following.

Grab a spot on the sleek bamboo sushi counter and give over to the chef's superb recommendations, which will be circled on the menu. Tasty slices of kanpachi (amberjack) and *aji* (mackerel) are brushed with soy and served over rice; while the exquisite *hotate* (scallop) is sprinkled with a touch of sea salt.

Tsushima

Japanese

B3

141 E. 47th St. (bet. Lexington & Third Aves.)

Subway: Grand Central - 42 St
Phone: 212-207-1938
Web: N/A
Prices: $$

Lunch Mon – Fri
Dinner nightly

This Japanese lair below-street level is jam-packed with business diners and neighborhood dwellers seeking fantastic value (especially at lunch) and terrific quality. Be warned though: the sign is subtle and one could easily walk right by. It's not big, but it is bright and upbeat with a long, narrow space that is stylish in a spare Tokyo-meets-Manhattan way. Service is speedy, which is perfect for those who need to get back to a meeting after slurping some soup and nibbling some sushi—options are authentic but will nod if needed to spicy tuna-craving Americans. Lunch specials are generous, plentiful, and inexpensive. The omakase for dinner is well worth the extra expense, when the sushi chefs are less rushed and the quality is turned up big time.

Vitae

Contemporary

A3

4 E. 46th St. (bet. Fifth & Madison Aves.)

Subway: Grand Central - 42 St
Phone: 212-682-3562
Web: www.vitaenyc.com
Prices: $$$

Lunch Mon – Fri
Dinner Mon – Sat

Vitae may be the epitome of *Mad Men*-chic, from the lively bar scene and sunken dining room to the retro-woven walls and patterned carpets. Thus, it seems only right to begin the night with a Kentucky flip—a roasted peanut-infused cocktail of Bulleit Bourbon, honey, cream, egg yolk, and nutmeg that is even creamier and warmer than it sounds.

Once settled into a teal banquette or boxy white leather chair in the glamorous dining room, move on to feather-light yet rich Parker House rolls. Starters may show a tasty personality, as in the pan-roasted quail over Marcona almond couscous, tender carrots, chopped Castelvetrano olives, and preserved cherries. Pastas are wonderfully satisfying as in *chitarra* with tender chicken and ricotta meatballs.

253

Tulsi ✿

B3

Indian ✗✗

211 E. 46th St. (bet. 2nd & 3rd Aves.)

Subway: Grand Central - 42 St
Phone: 212-888-0820
Web: www.tulsinyc.com
Prices: $$

Lunch Mon – Sat
Dinner nightly

Melissa Ham

Tulsi sits in a busy neighborhood amid heavy-hitting steakhouses and loud construction sites, yet it stands out with soft-spoken and serene grace. It's hard to pass their vibrant awning and not glance inside, where colorful silks and translucent, billowing fabrics separate private dining booths. Silk light fixtures and artifacts echo the elaborate nature of this cuisine with a look that is somehow glittering yet very tasteful.

The kitchen skillfully brings a delicate, sophisticated, and very authentic touch to each dish, which can be a reminder of what is at the heart of true Indian cuisine. Start with *vevichathu*, giant shrimp cooked in a Kerala-style coconut curry fantastically balancing heat and flavor, served over tomato basmati rice. The *baghare baingan* arrives as reconstructed Japanese eggplant: its flesh has been stir-fried with complex masala, stewed with peanuts, coconut, and onion, then artfully served in the hollowed, roasted eggplant shell. Breads like onion and potato *kulcha* or puffy *parathas* are excellent and ample in size.

Seasonal desserts are a highlight as in an upscale version of mango *falooda* in sweet-spiced milk studded with toasted pistachios and tapioca pearls.

Wild Edibles

Seafood

B5

535 Third Ave. (bet. 35th & 36th Sts.)

Subway: 33 St
Phone: 212-213-8552
Web: www.wildedibles.com
Prices: $$

Lunch & dinner daily

Wild Edibles is just plain neat: this utterly charming Murray Hill fish shop is absolutely flooded with warmth. With a counter in the Grand Central Market, the fabulous retailer remains unequalled—notice a smattering of dark wood tables, subway tiles, and a bar joined to the seafood counter unveiling the freshest (and finest) treats.

Relish the quiet at lunch, and do as the regulars do in seeking out straight-from-the-source specials. Take off with an outstandingly warm seafood salad mingling fennel, arugula, and creamy white beans; and then fly high with the Canadian club oyster flight with three pours of wine or beer. The New England (or New Orleans) mussels are sumptuously sopped up by Old Bay fries. Rushed? Take your 'catch' and sauce to-go.

Wolfgang's

Steakhouse

A6

4 Park Ave. (at 33rd St.)

Subway: 33 St
Phone: 212-889-3369
Web: www.wolfgangssteakhouse.net
Prices: $$$$

Lunch & dinner daily

What started for the fomer waiter of the esteemed Peter Luger has evolved into now seven locations going strong—a decision that has yielded mouthwatering results. Housed in the former Vanderbilt Hotel dining room, this 1912 landmark space is dressed with elegant tables and showcases a gorgeous terra-cotta tiled ceiling courtesy of famed architect, Rafael Guastavino.

The setting is handsome, but the steak's arrival refocuses all attention on the strapping Porterhouse (for two, three, or four) served sizzling and paired with fried onion rings; sautéed mushrooms; and German potatoes...extra crispy please! If you really want something to knaw on before the meat makes its way, order a perfect martini and slice by slice of Canadian bacon—you're not here for a diet.

Midtown West

This New York is a city of incomparable diversity, as evident in every tree-lined neighborhood, ethnic enclave, and luxury high-rise. The truth remains, however, that there is only one street in all five boroughs to be boldly hailed Restaurant Row. Considering that its famed location—where celebrity chefs prepare all-you-can-eat pasta alongside promising sushi bars—is in a neighborhood named Hell's Kitchen is further testament to its dedication to great food.

Restaurant Row

Still, this is an area that insists on reinvention. Hence, Restaurant Row (perhaps due to its uneven reputation) is becoming known as Little Brazil near Sixth Avenue, where samba and street food are celebrated late summer each year on Brazilian Day. A few steps farther west and the city's eclectic identity comes to life again, where a walk down Ninth Avenue offers a world of goods. A wonderful start (or finale) can be found at **Amy's Bread**, whose crusty baguettes supply countless restaurant kitchens, while colorful cakes or cookies tempt passersby. Meanwhile across the avenue, **Poseidon Bakery** is rumored to be the very last place in America to still make its own phyllo dough by hand—a taste of the *spanakopita* will prove it. Regardless of its name, **Sullivan Street Bakery**'s one and only retail outlet is actually on 47th, between 10th and 11th avenues (a location so perilously far west in the Manhattan mindset that its success proves its worth in gold). A sweet side-trip is the **Little Pie Company**, whose treasured wares are rolled, filled, and baked in its glass-paneled display kitchen. While this stretch of Hell's Kitchen is rich with markets and restaurants, those highlights familiar to any theater-going tourist or Lincoln Tunnel-bound commuter who has been stuck in its traffic, include "the hamburger you must try before you die" at **The Counter**. And then there's **City Sandwich**, stuffed with fantastic components and typified by a warmed Portuguese-style roll. While **La Boîte**'s exotic spice blends are ever-luring, **Sergimmo Salumeria**'s first-rate *salumi* and *formaggi* will warm the soul. Travel south of Port Authority Bus Terminal and unearth a string of pleasures starting with **Ninth Avenue International Foods**. These olives, spices, and spreads are serious business, but it is the renowned *taramosalata* (as if prepared by the gods atop Mount Olympus themselves) that finds its way into city restaurants. Stop by **Giovanni Esposito and Sons** meat market for a sampling of Italian sausage. Truffle fiends will find a spectacular selection at **Urbani Truffles**, happily located on West End Avenue and 60th Street.

Street Eats

While this is an area often choked by traffic and hungry office workers, New Yorkers demand outstanding food, no matter the venue. Under the guidance of the Vendy Awards and the blog Midtown Lunch, discover a moveable line of fast, satisfying street food vendors. Hell's Kitchen is rife with Mexican treats from delis stocked with dried chiles, herbs galore, and fresh produce, to exquisitely cooked eats. **Guelaguetza** on 47th Street offers a handful of seats at the back of its tiny setting; while just steps away from each other on 10th Avenue are **Tehuitzingo**, which prepares 17 varieties of tacos to be enjoyed at slender counters along the wall; and **Tulcingo del Valle**, which has a proper dining room adjacent to the grocery. Those seeking a more stable location to grab a juicy burger, fries, or milkshake will not be disappointed at Le Parker Meridien's **burger joint**. Foodies in need of a rarer treat know to head south to K-town—the type of neighborhood that sneaks up and floors you. Its instant, unmistakable Asian vibe owes largely to the prominence of karaoke bars, authentic grocers, and countless spots for fresh tofu or handmade dumplings.

Tucked into the basement at Macy's is **De Gustibus**, a cooking school and stage for a range of culinary legends. Throughout Midtown West, it is clear that equal attention is paid to cuisine as to arranging storybook holiday mannequins behind the velvet ropes of Saks Fifth Avenue. As if to illustrate the point, the Japanese bakery **Minamoto Kitchoan** channels elegance and subtlety in its beautiful rice cakes, bejeweled with plum wine gelée. The stylish packaging makes these the penultimate hostess gift. French-influenced **Petrossian Boutique** offers caviar and croissants to their patrons; after which an espresso shot at **FIKA** (where the Swedes display their passion and skill for the Italian elixir) tastes nothing short of divine. Wind up the affair with a stirring cocktail at the chic **Empire Room** housed in the Empire State Building.

TIME WARNER CENTER

No visit to this locality is complete without a tribute to the gargantuan feat that is the Time Warner Center, presiding over Columbus Circle. Here, world-renowned chefs indulge both themselves and their patrons with earth-shattering success. Find a range of pleasures here from **Bouchon Bakery**'s classic French macarons, to the eye-popping style and sass of **Stone Rose Lounge**. Located on the fourth floor, **Center Bar** by Michael Lomonaco (of Porter House) is a sophisticated perch for enjoying a traditional and lovely small plate while taking in the incredible views of plush and pretty Central Park.

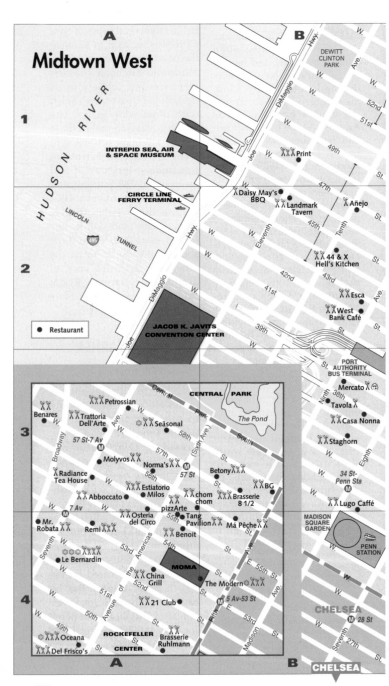

Midtown West

HUDSON RIVER

INTREPID SEA, AIR & SPACE MUSEUM

CIRCLE LINE FERRY TERMINAL

LINCOLN TUNNEL

JACOB K. JAVITS CONVENTION CENTER

● Restaurant

DEWITT CLINTON PARK

Print

Daisy May's BBQ
Landmark Tavern
Añejo

44 & X Hell's Kitchen

Esca
West Bank Café

PORT AUTHORITY BUS TERMINAL

Mercato
Tavola
Casa Nonna
Staghorn

34 St-Penn Sta

Lugo Caffé

MADISON SQUARE GARDEN

PENN STATION

CHELSEA

CENTRAL PARK
The Pond

Benares
Petrossian
Trattoria Dell'Arte
Seäsonal
Molyvos
Norma's
Radiance Tea House
Estiatorio Milos
Abboccato
pizzArte
chom chom
Brasserie 8 1/2
Betony
BG
Osteria del Circo
Tang Pavilion
Má Pêche
Benoit
Mr. Robata
Remi
Le Bernardin
China Grill
MOMA
The Modern
21 Club
Oceana
Del Frisco's
Brasserie Ruhlmann
ROCKEFELLER CENTER

5 Av-53 St

CHELSEA

258

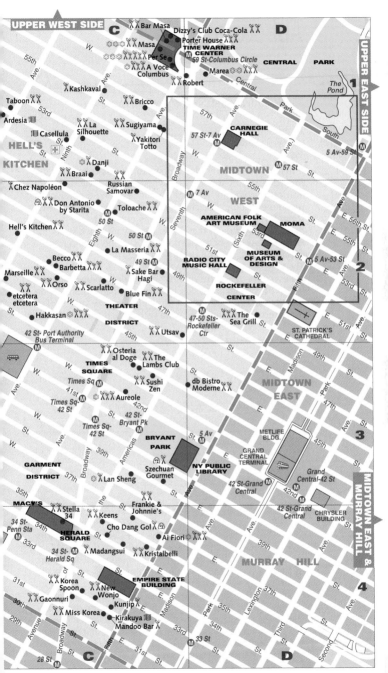

Abboccato

A3

136 W. 55th St. (bet. Sixth & Seventh Aves.)

Subway: 57 St
Phone: 212-265-4000
Web: www.abboccato.com
Prices: $$$

Lunch Mon – Sat
Dinner nightly

It may seem like everyday a new Italian restaurant opens in Manhattan, but Abboccato (owned by the Livanos family, also of Molyvos and Oceana) continues to be a noteworthy recommendation. Adjacent to the Blakely Hotel, the lower street-level dining room is a soothing contrast to the bustling midtown commotion outside. Inside, cream-toned walls and leather furnishings complement inlaid stone flooring and a comfortable bar, set off on its own.

The regional spread begins with an array of shareable small plates (*cicchetti*), such as *nonna's* meatballs or polenta-coated *fritti*. The cannelloni is luscious, house-made pasta sheets heartily stuffed with braised pork. Entrées may bring grilled skewered wild shrimp *oreganata* with shaved fennel salad.

Añejo

B2

668 Tenth Ave. (at 47th St.)

Subway: 50 St (Eighth Ave.)
Phone: 212-920-4770
Web: www.anejonyc.com
Prices: $$

Lunch Sat – Sun
Dinner Tue – Sun

Fact: things are sprouting fast in NYC's Mexican food realm and heart-stopping, buzz-worthy Añejo is at the head of the pack. The keyed-in kitchen keeps this delicious trajectory alive and well. Adding sensory fuel is the hand-painted Day of the Dead mural in the rear. Sturdy communal tables are chockablock so after one (or three) of their excellent cocktails, your neighbor may be a new best friend.

The rustic room is softened by chandeliers and puts you in the right mood for such notable food as fluffy corn dumplings floating in a meaty porridge of chorizo and Oaxaca cheese. The guacamole trio starring tomatillos and roasted pineapple is a salty addiction; while mushroom-*huitlacoche* tacos raised a notch by smoky mayo elicit countless "oohs" and "aahs."

Ai Fiori ✿

Italian 𝕏𝕏𝕏

C4

400 Fifth Ave. (bet. 36th & 37th Sts.)

Subway: 34 St - Herald Sq
Phone: 212-613-8660
Web: www.aifiorinyc.com
Prices: $$$$

Lunch Mon – Fri
Dinner nightly

Evan Sung

Keep your expectations high while climbing the winding staircase to the second floor of the lovely Langham Place Hotel Fifth Avenue, and you will not be disappointed. Far above typical hotel dining, Ai Fiori is an elegant destination, impeccably decorated with brown velvet banquettes, windowed walls, and gilded place settings. The crystal glasses and polished flatware seem right at home in the hands of this posh crowd, and the staff who tend to their every need. The space exudes class and finesse, right down to the plate.

Each skillfully prepared and delicious bite honors the repute of Chef Michael White. Meals begin with beautifully layered crisp sheets of "panzanella" tucked with glossy, pickled sardines, black olives, and an excellent tomato confit dotted with basil. Expect outstanding pastas like spaghetti scented wtih saffron, kissed with blue crab and tomato, and tarted up with lemon and *bottarga*. Balance and talent are on display in the bay-crusted Atlantic cod, pan-roasted, served with a buttery sauce of chorizo and Manila clams; each flavor shines yet never overwhelms.

Come dessert, *La Religieuse* is a sort of chocolate snowman that evades description but delivers pure pleasure.

Ardesia

C1

510 W. 52nd St. (bet. Tenth & Eleventh Aves.)

Subway: 50 St (Eighth Ave.)
Phone: 212-247-9191
Web: www.ardesia-ny.com
Prices: $$

Lunch Sat – Sun
Dinner nightly

Ardesia's talented ladies, owner Mandy Oser and Chef Amorette Casaus, have fashioned such a sophisticated, comfortable, and welcoming wine bar that anyone living outside Hell's Kitchen is right to be jealous. Dominated by a white marble counter, the intimate setting feels open amid plate glass windows and high ceilings.

A lounge area accommodates those who come with friends in tow. Be sure to peruse the impressive selection of wines by the glass, listed on the chalkboard-gray walls. Nibbles may feature spiced lamb skewers with mint yogurt sauce, or chicken liver mousse with apple compote and sage. Highlights include slices of perfectly fatty house-cured pastrami atop sauerkraut, braised until it verges on creamy, and excellent toasted rye bread.

Barbetta

C2

321 W. 46th St. (bet. Eighth & Ninth Aves.)

Subway: 50 St (Eighth Ave.)
Phone: 212-246-9171
Web: www.barbettarestaurant.com
Prices: $$$

Lunch & dinner Tue – Sat

Standing proud since its 1906 opening, Barbetta proves that the "new" in New York need not be taken literally. From its gilded furnishings to its candelabra and crystal chandeliers, this dining room celebrates an old-world aesthetic. At the ornate tables, find true-blue New Yorkers who, as regulars, have been treated like family here for more than century (though outsiders may detect a hint of indifference from the service staff).

Consistency is the theme here, and some of the menu items, such as *minestrone giardiniera*, have been served since the very beginning. Good, traditional Italian food with a few throwbacks, capped off by a selection from the dessert trolley, prove that this just might be your grandfather's favorite Italian restaurant.

Aureole

Contemporary ✗✗✗

C3

135 W. 42nd St. (bet. Broadway & Sixth Ave.)

Subway: 42 St - Bryant Pk
Phone: 212-319-1660
Web: www.charliepalmer.com
Prices: $$$$

Lunch Mon – Fri
Dinner nightly

Eric Laignel

Throughout its home on the ground floor of the Bank of America tower, Aureole's earth-toned venue is brought to life by the constant stream of patrons. Inside, find a casual yet chic bar room where suits and tourists alike come to devour a great burger or enjoy the lunchtime prix-fixe. The formal back dining area is more of a destination. It boasts a mezzanine dedicated to displaying their impressive wine selection; and a cozy room furnished with upholstered banquettes, shimmering pillows, and the finest in cutlery and stemware.

Few restaurants are able to maintain Aureole's consistency: from start to finish dining here is a joy. Global influences factor heavily in the contemporary menu, with such creations as pan-seared veal sweetbreads plated with chestnut purée, cranberries, and a perfectly salty hit of Iberico ham. New Zealand venison is beautifully cooked to a deep garnet, presented with vanilla-scented sweet potatoes and sautéed black trumpet mushrooms.

Dessert lovers won't be disappointed by the range of finales. Seasonally themed treats have included ginger-poached pear composed with warm chocolate ganache and caramel ice cream tucked in a nest of coriander *nougatine*.

A Voce Columbus ✿

C1

Italian 🍴🍴🍴

10 Columbus Circle (in the Time Warner Center)

Subway: 59 St - Columbus Circle
Phone: 212-823-2523
Web: www.avocerestaurant.com
Prices: $$$

Lunch & dinner daily

Bruce Buck

Despite the flawlessly contemporary design of this spacious room, flaunting dark mosaic tiles, lots of metal, and leather-topped tables, that wall of windows facing Central Park actually steals the scene. Every single seat manages to have a view, against which even this bustling display kitchen cannot compare. Service is often disorganized—a surprise since such a sharp and powerful crowd dominates the room—but all is forgiven in light of the formidable cooking.

Many dishes here are based on solid traditions, as in the handmade *mischiglio* pasta, made so each deliciously chewy morsel bears the telltale shape of having been dragged across a wooden spoon. Yet this pasta becomes as contemporary as its surroundings when dressed with butter, orange rind, coriander, chili, and mussels. Other highlights include the juicy *bistecca*, beautifully charred and perfectly cooked to order, served with paper-thin rounds of beets, grilled onion, and crushed black olive vinaigrette.

Desserts provide a solid finish as in a seasonally spiced chocolate *torta* with toasted nuts and whipped mascarpone; or an intensely flavored almond cake topped with warm pineapple and a quenelle of smooth vanilla ice cream.

Bar Masa

Japanese 🍴🍴

355 ...

10 Columbus Circle (in the Time Warner Center)

Subway: 59 St - Columbus Circle
Phone: 212-823-9800
Web: www.masanyc.com
Prices: $$$

Lunch & dinner Mon – Sat

Bar Masa is practically an elder of the Time Warner Center—the mall that many NYers derided but is now a gourmet harbor attracting moneyed foreign tourists and locals alike. Booming with banter, Bar Masa fills with shoppers craving a modern and more American take on Japanese cuisine. Dining here is a decidedly different experience from its eponymous neighbor.

Limestone floors and wood accents warm the space with a convivial aura; a row of tables sit behind billowing fabrics and relaxing perches are set at the bar. The chefs offer no showmanship here: from behind curtains, a masterpiece of oysters bathed in a citrus-mirin sauce, dancing shrimp sprinkled with chili salt, and squat glasses of cocoa- and black sesame-ice cream magically appear.

Becco

Italian 🍴🍴

355 W. 46th St. (bet. Eighth & Ninth Aves.)

Subway: 50 St (Eighth Ave.)
Phone: 212-397-7597
Web: www.becco-nyc.com
Prices: $$

Lunch & dinner daily

Designed for the throngs of tourists, Becco may verge on brusque but is all about business. Given the bold and big-named eateries lining Restaurant Row, the competition rages on and Becco reigns supreme with one secret behind its success: Lidia Bastianich. Amid dishes piled high and a bread basket that could choke an *anatra*, patrons are visibly content throughout her multi-nook arena.

Ms. Bastianich deserves accolades for this well-oiled machine. Expect the likes of mozzarella in *carrozza*, deep-fried bread slices sandwiching mozzarella and served over pesto; grilled swordfish covered with sautéed onions and poised atop roasted sweet potatoes; and *strudel di mele*, an apple purée studded with raisins in bread-like pastry and cinnamon ice cream.

Benares

240 W. 56th St. (bet. Broadway & Eighth Ave.)

Subway: 59 St - Columbus Circle · · · · · · · · · · · · · · · · · · · Lunch & dinner daily
Phone: 212-397-0707
Web: www.benaresnyc.com
Prices: **$$**

Christened after the holy city set on the banks of the Ganges, seafood-centric Benares brings a slice of sacred India to Hell's Kitchen. With scarce competition and a sultry mien, the polished eatery soars to great peaks—picture turmeric-toned chairs and walls dressed in vibrant Benarasi saris. Large green plants feel lush and gold-veined tiles lend a bit of glitz. Accoutrements include a lively kitchen and tasty repertoire of vegetarian dishes like Kashmiri soup with roasted turnips.

Meat and (especially) fish seekers can rest easy, as these play prominent roles in the *safed gosht*, a Rajasthani special featuring marinated lamb in a cardamom-almond sauce; or *sevai kurma* brimming with seafood.

A new FiDi outpost is perfect for suits in need of spice.

Benoit

60 W. 55th St. (bet. Fifth & Sixth Aves.)

Subway: 57 St · Lunch & dinner daily
Phone: 646-943-7373
Web: www.benoitny.com
Prices: **$$**

What started as the Manhattan outpost of a century-old Parisian classic has grown, matured, and indeed come into its own as an elegant French bistro with genuine New York style. One step inside reveals layer upon lovely layer of red accents, polished brass, frosted glass, and modern chairs that combine to make this a very special place.

Be sure to begin with a range of hors d'oeuvres that showcase the kitchen's potential, from lentil salad topped with quail eggs to the excellent rillettes and *baccalau*. While some dishes are touched with innovations, others highlight good quality and tradition, as in the hand-cut steak tartare. Desserts are not to be missed—the rum *baba*, topped tableside with rum and dollops of whipped cream, is simply outstanding.

Betony

B3 — Contemporary 𝕏𝕏𝕏

41 W. 57th St. (bet. Fifth & Sixth Aves.)

Subway: 57 St
Phone: 212-465-2400
Web: www.betony-nyc.com
Prices: $$$

Dinner Mon – Sat

This elegant new dining room (named after a medicinal herb) brings sure-footed elegance to a highly trafficked stretch of midtown. Posh in the daylight but sultry in the evening, the space is richly appointed with carved wood panels, engraved limestone, parquet flooring, and chocolate brown velvet banquettes.

Betony's kitchen flaunts a noteworthy pedigree, resulting in wonderful cooking that is fresh, light, and beautifully minimalist. A lovely, delicate salad combines toasted grains, sprouts, and a rich swipe of *labne*. Entrées have included poached black bass punched with a bright dollop of tomatillo purée and a scattering of almost buttery toasted pine nuts. The coconut *bombe* oozing with salted caramel-rum sauce is a smashing sweet.

BG

B3 — American 𝕏𝕏

754 Fifth Ave. (at 58th St.)

Subway: 5 Av - 59 St
Phone: 212-872-8977
Web: www.bergdorfgoodman.com
Prices: $$$

Lunch daily
Dinner Mon – Sat

The inviting and inventive *carte du jour* is never lost on its discerning clientele at posh and stunning BG. Afternoon tea is all the rage within this Parisian-style brasserie that oozes panache with its ornate seats and hand-crafted wallpaper. If tea's not your taste, stop at the bar for an excellent *croque monsieur* dressed with béchamel and organic greens; then lose yourself in those Central Park vistas.

BG's setting is exquisite and certainly not a secret, especially among its bevy of Bergdorf blondes. Neither are their heavy-hitting chefs who employ the finest ingredients in the main event, like a Gotham salad tossing chicken, Gruyère, and beets; or lobster Napoleon featuring fresh pasta frolicking with meaty lobster, mushrooms, and truffle butter.

Blue Fin

C2

1567 Broadway (at 47th St.)

Subway: 49 St   Lunch & dinner daily
Phone: 212-918-1400
Web: www.bluefinnyc.com
Prices: $$$

The ocean's bounty awaits in the heart of Times Square where Blue Fin is anchored on the ground floor of the W Hotel. Stylish yet never kitschy, the décor plays up the kitchen's aquatic theme with pale blue, gently rippled walls, and a school of fish suspended overhead in the two-story space. As expected at the W, lounge music and dimmed lights color the scene.

Find towers of chilled shellfish, sushi, and satisfying entrées. Seared halibut might be presented with pan-crisped herbed-potato gnocchi, jumbo lump crab meat, and a bouillabaisse-inspired sauce redolent of saffron, red pepper, and orange zest. Desserts can include salted caramel *tres leches* cake with nut brittle and fresh berries; or take-away chocolate chip cookies for rushed theater-goers.

Braai

C1

329 W. 51st St. (bet. Eighth & Ninth Aves.)

Subway: 50 St (Eighth Ave.)   Lunch & dinner daily
Phone: 212-315-3315
Web: www.braainyc.com
Prices: $$

From its ground floor townhouse home, Braai is adored for its tantalizing South African cuisine. Two tables sit up front in a snug patio, which dovetails into a long and slender dark wood space. Drawing inspiration from its region, wide planks make up the flooring while the arched ceiling is thatched with straw. Yet the African décor in the dining room, set with marble-topped communal tables, is anything but kitschy.

The menu is resplendent with new and balanced flavors that are at once evident in *frikkadel*, a classic dish of baked meatballs in broth; or calamari drenched in a lovely wine-lemon emulsion. Speaking of mainstays, *bunny chow*, a street treat of lamb curry ladled into a bread bowl, is a favorite here as well as at nearby sibling Xai Xai.

Brasserie 8 1/2

B3

Contemporary 🍴🍴🍴

9 W. 57th St. (bet. Fifth & Sixth Aves.)

Subway: 57 St
Phone: 212-829-0812
Web: www.brasserie8andahalf.com
Prices: $$$

Lunch Sun – Fri
Dinner nightly

Nestled into the unique Solow building, the sweeping, tangerine-colored staircase that delivers you into Brasserie 8 1/2 is a bit more theatrical than the menu's predictable performance, but this Patina Group restaurant impresses nonetheless. Settle into the main dining room—with its eye-popping hues and original artwork of Henri Matisse and Fernand Léger—to find solid, contemporary, and prettily plated offerings. From the seasonal game menu, expect the likes of stuffed pheasant with apples, foie gras, cabbage, and an apple cider reduction.

Though its thoughtful design and well-spaced tables will impress company, it also caters well to solo guests, whether at the handsome, elevated mezzanine or one of the two sleek bars anchoring the room.

Brasserie Ruhlmann

A4

French 🍴🍴

45 Rockefeller Plaza (bet. Fifth & Sixth Aves.)

Subway: 47-50 Sts - Rockefeller Ctr
Phone: 212-974-2020
Web: www.brasserieruhlmann.com
Prices: $$$

Lunch daily
Dinner Mon – Sat

Named for the French designer, Émile-Jacques Ruhlmann, this stunning brasserie is the work of Jean Denoyer (also of Orsay). Just across from Rockefeller Center's Sunken Plaza, Brasserie Ruhlmann is a glamorous draw for both business and pleasure. Atop the bold mosaic-tiled flooring, the space is elegantly wrapped in a glossy faux-ebony veneer, enhancing the glowing silver sconces and red velvet furnishings.

The commendable kitchen honors its classical conceit, yet flirts with contemporary global cuisine. The menu features raw bar treats in addition to beef carpaccio "vitello tonnato-style." NY steak *au poivre* is perfectly seared to specification, presented in a hot cast iron pan, and accompanied by Cognac cream infused with briny green peppercorns.

Bricco

C1

Italian 🍴🍴

304 W. 56th St. (bet. Eighth & Ninth Aves.)

Subway: 57 St - 7 Av
Phone: 212-245-7160
Web: www.bricconyc.com
Prices: $$

Lunch Mon – Fri
Dinner nightly

It's a bit of a challenge to spot this cozy nook in the swirling hubbub of nearby Columbus Circle, but it's well worth the effort. Romantic little spots like Bricco are a rarity in this neck of the woods, and owner, Nino Catuogno, knows it—those autographed lipstick kisses lining the ceiling and popular, female-friendly bar prove it.

Couples can head back to the intimate main room for a comforting menu of delicious pizzas (maybe prosciutto, arugula, and creamy mozzarella?) visibly made to order in the brick oven; fat ribbons of whole wheat pasta in meaty ragù; or tender filet mignon dancing in brandy and cream, and sprinkled with crunchy peppercorns. Save room for a fragrant dessert of deep purple pears, poached in wine and liqueur.

Casa Nonna

B3

Italian 🍴🍴

310 W. 38th St. (bet. Eighth & Ninth Aves.)

Subway: Times Sq - 42 St
Phone: 212-736-3000
Web: www.casanonna.com
Prices: $$

Lunch Mon – Fri
Dinner nightly

Quaint sounding Casa Nonna is actually a behemoth of a restaurant run by an international dining group. A boon to garment district workers and suburban commuters, this sprawling, multi-room space is just a few blocks away from bustling Penn Station and the Port Authority bus terminal.

There is a dish for every taste at Casa Nonna, whose attractive menu is replete with satisfying and well-prepared Roman and Tuscan fare. Panini and Neapolitan-style pizza are popular during lunchtime, while dinner serves a hearty lineup of *primi* such as *tagliolini frutti di mare*, with fine breadcrumbs clinging the vibrant tomato sauce to the pasta. Entrées feature grilled Cornish hen, spiced *alla diavola*-style with garlic, lemon, and hot pepper.

Casellula

C1

 American

401 W. 52nd St. (bet. Ninth & Tenth Aves.)

Subway: 50 St (Eighth Ave.)
Phone: 212-247-8137
Web: www.casellula.com
Prices: $$

Dinner nightly

 Casellula oozes with warmth in both look and feel. Dark wood tables, exposed brick, and flickering votives are a sight for sore eyes, while the delightful staff is so attentive and friendly, that you may never want to leave.

Small plates are big here, while medium plates feature yummy sandwiches (crunchy *muffulettas* stuffed with fontina and savory cured meats) and tasty shrimp tacos splashed with salsa verde. Pity the lactose intolerant, as dessert (pumpkin ice cream "sandwich" pecked with brown butter caramel?) along with cheese (and lots of it) are part and parcel of the special experience at this petite place. Feeling blue? They've got that and much more with over 50 different varieties, perfectly complemented by an excellent and vast wine list.

Chez Napoléon

C2

French ✗

365 W. 50th St. (bet. Eighth & Ninth Aves.)

Subway: 50 St (Eighth Ave.)
Phone: 212-265-6980
Web: www.cheznapoleon.com
Prices: $$

Lunch Mon – Fri
Dinner Mon – Sat

When a restaurant affectionately refers to its matriarch as "Chef Grand-mere," you can expect a virtual time warp into that ageless gastronomy of tried and true dishes like Dover sole and soufflés. Chez Napoléon may not be nouvelle, yet the Bruno family continues to work their magic in this old-school cream sauce favorite.

From the bartender's bellowing French accent to the décor featuring green walls dotted with sepia photos and historic maps, the snug bistro feels well-worn and beloved. Staying true to its tune, the food is equally authentic: think *escargots de Bourgogne*, meaty snails in garlicky parsley-butter; *rognons Dijonnaise*, hearty and deliciously seasoned veal kidneys; and *pêche Melba* with vanilla ice cream and raspberry coulis.

China Grill

Asian ✗✗

60 W. 53rd St. (bet. Fifth & Sixth Aves.)

Subway: 7 Av
Phone: 212-333-7788
Web: www.chinagrillmgt.com
Prices: $$$

Lunch Mon – Sat
Dinner nightly

Opened more than 20 years ago, this first China Grill continues to be a perennial favorite and serves as the flagship of Jeffrey Chodorow's international restaurant organization. The sprawling interior, designed by Jeffrey Beers, is housed on the ground floor of the CBS building and features a multi-level dining room of soaring 30-foot ceilings accented with white canopy light fixtures. The long bar area is a popular spot to unwind after a long day at work.

Large tables provide the perfect spot to dine with a group; the food is good, fun, and is best enjoyed when shared. Served family style, the Asian-influenced menu may include perfectly fried rice topped with creamy, diced avocado; or delicate pancakes generously filled with tender lobster.

Cho Dang Gol

Korean ✗

55 W. 35th St. (bet. Fifth & Sixth Aves.)

Subway: 34 St - Herald Sq
Phone: 212-695-8222
Web: www.chodanggolny.com
Prices: ⊖⊖

Lunch & dinner daily

K-town may boast its barbecue joints, but Cho Dang Gol has its own calling in tofu, that creamy little bean curd that sets hearts a-jumping. The restaurant is named for a South Korean village famous for this specialty; one imagines those locals would approve of this fresh, silky house-made version. Here, tofu finds its way into more than two dozen dishes, including hot and crispy pancakes, filled with ground pork and vegetables; or a cast iron pot, loaded with sweet and spicy octopus. A spicy prime rib casserole is perfect for sharing.

At first glance, Cho Dang Gol is warm and sentimental with cute Korean artifacts and rustic wooden tables, but don't expect like-minded service. When the house gets packed, servers respond with brusque efficiency.

chom chom

Korean XX

40 W. 56th St. (bet. Fifth & Sixth Aves.)

Subway: 57 St
Phone: 212-213-2299
Web: www.chomchomnyc.com
Prices: $$

Lunch & dinner daily

Somehow, chom chom landed well north of its K-town compatriots to happily bring its soul-shaking Korean cuisine to a neighborhood away from the clamor. The vibe at this Korean corridor is mod and folksy (vertically cut trees drape the walls), but the food is flavorfully faithful. Sip a *soju* at the bar before diving into a menu that favors fun over tradition.

Chom chom wears many hats, but everything is crested with serious ingredients. Begin with a few "kapas" (Korean tapas) like spicy pork buns; succulent sweet potato *japchae* with paper-thin beef and vegetables; and *bo ssäm* with braised and seared pork belly, spicy batons of root vegetables, and fresh Boston lettuce. Simpler dishes highlight amazing quality, as in broiled wild salmon.

Daisy May's BBQ

Barbecue X

623 Eleventh Ave. (at 46th St.)

Subway: 50 St (Eighth Ave.)
Phone: 212-977-1500
Web: www.daisymaysbbq.com
Prices:

Lunch & dinner daily

Trek to the ends of the earth (known to some as Eleventh Avenue), and the barbecue gods will reward you. Welcome to Daisy May's BBQ—where Chef/owner (and cookbook author) Adam Perry Lang's smoky, succulent 'cue served up in a big old dining hall (think school lunchroom-meets-barn) counts everyone from Oprah to bike messengers to midtown suits as fans.

Three chalkboards list the pig specials: a whole pig for up to 12 people (should you be blessed with so many friends); half a pig; and a few daily specials. The house pulled pork, a mound of tender, glistening sweet and smoky meat, is a fan favorite for good reason. A limited selection of beer and wine is available to wash it all down, but our money's on the irresistibly sweet and minty iced tea.

Danji ✿

Korean 🍴

346 W. 52nd St. (bet. Eighth & Ninth Aves.)

Subway: 50 St (Eighth Ave.)
Phone: 212-586-2880
Web: www.danjinyc.com
Prices: $$

Lunch Mon – Fri
Dinner Mon – Sat

James Park/2be Photography & Design

This slender shrine to Korean food is a complete and total departure from its Hell's Kitchen surrounds. Upon entering, go for a seat at the bar, or try a communal table away from the door (especially on blustery days).

Flattering lights, spare furnishings, undulating silk panels, and a striking display of spoons do much to attract a slew of trendy urbanites to this small, well-designed space. Service ranges from rushed if seated at the popular bar, to engaged at the lovely communal tables. No matter: an endless dinner queue alludes to the serious flavors that wait inside.

In the kitchen, Chef Hooni Kim brings classic culinary training and precision to his very refreshed take on Korean food. Start with *golbaengi moochim*, whelks steamed in a sumptuous blend of rice wine, garlic, and aromatics, tossed with fiery cayenne-spiked oil, and served with cooling cucumbers, cilantro, and a beautiful nest of soba. Thick fillets of pearly white sablefish are poached to perfection, then placed in a pool of sharply flavored and umami-loaded sauce. A tray of *bossam* arrives as succulent braised and caramelized pork belly with hot sauce, scallion salsa, dehydrated kimchi, and cabbage for wrapping.

db Bistro Moderne

D3 Contemporary XX

55 W. 44th St. (bet. Fifth & Sixth Aves.)

Subway: 5 Av
Phone: 212-391-2400
Web: www.danielboulud.com
Prices: $$$

Lunch & dinner daily

This stylish Daniel Boulud bistro is an ideal upscale spot for drinking and dining pre- or post-theater—after 9:00 P.M., try the champagne and dessert pairings. Its moneyed European clientele and service that is beyond reproach befits the sophisticated space, which now flaunts a new face courtesy of noted designer Jeffrey Beers.

Boulud's French-inflected menu showcases consistency and formidable skills in dishes that somehow become richer and more decadent with each bite. Outstanding products embellished with mouthwatering touches are to be expected. Yet most famously, the humble burger is reinvented when ground sirloin is filled with braised short ribs, foie gras, and black truffles on a Parmesan bun.

Del Frisco's

A4 Steakhouse XXX

1221 Sixth Ave. (at 49th St.)

Subway: 47-50 Sts - Rockefeller Ctr
Phone: 212-575-5129
Web: www.delfriscos.com
Prices: $$$

Lunch Mon – Fri
Dinner nightly

Prime, aged, corn-fed beef is the main attraction at this sprawling, outrageously successful outpost of the Dallas-based steakhouse chain. Portions range from the petite filet to a 24-ounce Porterhouse to make any Texan proud. The menu begins with a suitably rich feast of cheesesteak egg rolls or white clam flatbread; but then does an about face with knife-and-fork Caesar salad. Lunch is an affordable way to sample their classics.

Complementing its McGraw-Hill Building home, Del Frisco's flaunts a masculine look with its large L-shaped bar, dramatic wrought-iron balcony, wood accents, and floor-to-ceiling windows. The mezzanine dining area, accessible by a sweeping staircase, enjoys a quieter ambience.

Also try Del Frisco's Grille in Rockefeller Plaza.

Dizzy's Club Coca-Cola

C1

10 Columbus Circle (in the Time Warner Center)

Subway: 59 St - Columbus Circle   Dinner nightly
Phone: 212-258-9595
Web: www.jalc.org
Prices: $$

It's probably one of the better ways to spend a night on the town: reserve a modestly priced ticket, request a perch at the bar or stage-facing table, and you will start to understand what all the fuss is about at this modern and swanky "club." From the alluring lights and cars dotting Columbus Circle, to a dizzying show of Southern staples and jazz artists, the audience is entranced at this formidable home to America's equally formidable art form.

And can there be anything better than crispy Louisiana hot wings, roasted duck with a salty side of andouille étouffée, and a buttery pecan pie to go with such serious tunes? Everybody is here for the top performances, taking in the dreamy views of Central Park along with a Genever splashed with white cranberry.

Don Antonio by Starita 😃

C2

309 W. 50th St. (bet. 8th and 9th Aves.)

Subway: 50 St (Eighth Ave.)   Lunch & dinner daily
Phone: 646-719-1043
Web: www.donantoniopizza.com
Prices: $$

Get on your knees and thank the pizza gods for this divine addition to the Neopolitan pie scene. The place has serious street cred—the original in Naples has been open since 1901, and its current owner, Antonio Starita, is a renowned instructor. The dark, narrow space rocks a polished but raw style, with deep reds, exposed brick, and spider-like light fixtures. It's also packed, so expect a wait.

The delectable offerings include the *girella*, a homemade mozzarella-filled crust topped with pecorino, *prosciutto cotto*, grape tomatoes, and arugula; and *montanara Starita*, fried pizza dough crowned with smoked buffalo mozzarella and tomato sauce. Though pies are the main draw, appetizers like potato croquettes are always tasty. Gluten-free crust is on offer.

Esca

 B2

Seafood

402 W. 43rd St. (bet. Ninth & Tenth Aves.)

Subway: 42 St - Port Authority Bus Terminal
Phone: 212-564-7272
Web: www.esca-nyc.com
Prices: $$$

Lunch Mon – Sat
Dinner nightly

The spicy Gaeta olives and white bean bruschetta here could sustain a foodie for days, but lucky for us, Esca also proffers a swarm of seafood that vows to nourish for years. This butter-colored and wood-planked outpost via Dave Pasternack is divinity for fish lovers. Wine cabinets at every turn and excitable servers dressed in neckties are sure to lure the trendsters.

Most dishes are delightfully literal letting the *pesci* shine. It's best to bring helpers to sample their schools of crudo (amberjack glazed with olive aïoli and sea salt) and antipasti like seared monkfish liver with logs of soft-cooked rhubarb. But, it's not all about sharing as crisp, golden brown flounder fillets accentuated simply with sautéed mushrooms and leeks are all yours.

Estiatorio Milos

 A3

Greek

125 W. 55th St. (bet. Sixth & Seventh Aves.)

Subway: 57 St
Phone: 212-245-7400
Web: www.milos.ca
Prices: $$$

Lunch & dinner daily

Estiatorio Milos is a Greek restaurant with such deliciously singular focus on the sea that it may best be described as sunbleached. Beyond a giant urn stationed at the entrance, there are no shawarmas or moussakas in sight; however, the gleaming dining room is dramatic, amid 30-foot ceilings and a swarm of hovering suits that part like the Red Sea at the hostesses' command. Then, of course, there are the iced beds of fish: pink, gold, clear-eyed, and flecked with silver, they are a tableau of the Agean's bounty.

The dining room casts a spare glow on such tasty portions as grilled St. Pierre, wonderfully fleshy and crisp with a squeeze of lemon and hint of smoke; or the Lavraki and Petropsara soup, a classic treasure hailing from Santorini.

Manhattan ▶ Midtown West

etcetera etcetera

C2

352 W. 44th St. (bet. Eighth & Ninth Aves.)

Subway: 42 St - Port Authority Bus Terminal
Phone: 212-399-4141
Web: www.etcetcnyc.com
Prices: $$

Lunch Wed & Sun
Dinner nightly

Hip and modern, etcetera etcetera is a breath of clean, fresh air in the often-staid Theater District. The modern and contemporary design punctuated by pops of bright orange has a Milan-meets-Miami sensibility, but the crowd here is never too cool for school.

The kitchen turns out seriously solid and well-prepared meals. Pasta and risotto dishes, such as the homemade basil spaghetti with jumbo lump crab and sweet roasted peppers, can be halved and served as tasty appetizers. Entrées (crispy Cornish hen or braised lamb shank) are hearty and offer beautifully balanced flavors and textures. Etcetera etcetera proves that looking good does not always mean spending a fortune—the $38 prix-fixe, three-course dinner is an exceptional value.

44 & X Hell's Kitchen

B2

622 Tenth Ave. (at 44th St.)

Subway: 42 St - Port Authority Bus Terminal
Phone: 212-977-1170
Web: www.44andx.com
Prices: $$

Lunch & dinner daily

There's a sophisticated kind of charm about this casual, delicious, and affordable neighborhood haunt. Maybe it's the carved wooden bar set with intricate wrought-iron bar stools, the gorgeous chandeliers against the crisp white ceilings, or the stunning fresh flower arrangements? Perhaps it's those quirky religious statues perched away from the merry-makers at the bar? Whatever it is, it works, and everyone seems to love it.

Snag a seat on the spacious sidewalk patio and get nibbling on Maryland lump meat crab cakes over sun-dried tomato vinaigrette and roasted vegetables; or a persimmon salad with toasted walnuts, pomegranate seeds, and blue cheese. Mains include an excellent crispy sea bass over braised artichoke hearts and chanterelle mushrooms.

Frankie & Johnnie's

Steakhouse ✕✕

C4

32 W. 37th St. (bet. Fifth & Sixth Aves.)

Subway: 34 St - Herald Sq
Phone: 212-947-8940
Web: www.frankieandjohnnies.com
Prices: $$$

Lunch Mon – Fri
Dinner nightly

You get a slice of history with your perfectly-seared ribeye at this storied Garment District steakhouse. The renovated townhouse—with its masculine sensibility and cozy wood-paneled library-turned upstairs dining room—used to belong to the actor John Drew Barrymore, and it is the second of three sibling restaurants that began in 1926 (the first restaurant is a stone's throw away and the third location resides in Rye, New York).

Served by a professional, all-male brigade, the food is pure steakhouse bliss: think silky Clams Casino, topped with crispy bacon and scallions; tender, bone-in ribeye, seared to rosy perfection; irresistibly crunchy hashbrowns; and buttery, flaky apple strudel, delivered with a side of fresh whipped cream.

Gaonnuri

Korean ✕✕

C4

1250 Broadway (at 32nd St.)

Subway: at 32nd St.
Phone: 212-971-9045
Web: www.gaonnurinyc.com
Prices: $$$

Lunch & dinner Mon – Sat

Don't let the security checkpoint, the bland lobby, or the fact that you'll need to take the express elevator up 39 floors dissuade you. A grand entrance and charming hostess await. The modern space is beautifully designed with round windows to emphasize the skyline views from every table, each of which is equipped with its own barbeque and downdraft vent (this is no smoke-filled barbecue joint).

The very fine cuisine is fragrant, approachable, and harkens back to traditions with classics like their sizzling *bibimbap*—rice that develops a tantalizing crust, served in a hot stone bowl topped with tofu, fresh vegetables, kimchi, and a raw egg. Fish dishes include the black cod *jorim jungsik*, simmered until tender, with daikon in a tangy-spicy sauce.

Hakkasan

C2

311 W. 43rd St. (bet. Eighth & Ninth Aves.)

Subway: 42 St - Port Authority Bus Terminal Lunch & dinner daily
Phone: 212-776-1818
Web: www.hakkasan.com
Prices: $$$$

Daniel Krieger

Enter through an unmarked, understated façade and make your way down a long, spare corridor to arrive at beautiful, cool Hakkasan. The stunning décor mixes dark wood, marble, low lights, and little dining nooks to divide the expansive space, making it feel intimate and secluded. Some seats even afford a view of their top-of-the-line kitchen, although drinking is an equally serious business around the sleek bar. Servers are knowledgeable, friendly, and elegant in their bright red, slim-fitting DVF dresses; the food is even prettier.

Dim sum presentations are painstakingly formed, cleverly presented, outstandingly delicious, highlighting chive flower dumplings; sticky rice studded with tiny, tender pieces of chicken wrapped in a lotus leaf; a meaty duck-stuffed pumpkin puff; and prawn *cheung fun* coated with slices of silky bean curd. Other immaculate works of edible art include moist, fleshy Chilean sea bass encased with crunchy daikon and black bean sauce; or steamed and then quickly sautèed *gai lan* cooked to perfect crispness and color, flavored with a delicate amount of chicken stock, salt, and garlic.

Desserts, like the signature tarte Tatin are excellent and surprisingly adept.

Hell's Kitchen

C2 Mexican

679 Ninth Ave. (bet. 46th & 47th Sts.)

Subway: 50 St (Eighth Ave.) Dinner nightly
Phone: 212-977-1588
Web: www.hellskitchen-nyc.com
Prices: $$

This progressive Mexican eatery continues to be a go-to spot for smart south-of-the-border dining. Intimate in scale and tastefully done with dark stone flooring, colorful glass tiles at the bar, and polished copper accents, the dining room often fills up quickly.

Delightful preparation is the key to the success at Hell's Kitchen. This isn't a chips and salsa kind of place; instead, diners are served wedges of cornbread and black bean purée to ward off hunger. The evening's specials may offer a *tlacoyo* trio of griddled masa rounds topped with earthy *huitlacoche*, chorizo crumbles, and shrimp dressed with tomatillo salsa. Entrées have included perfectly caramelized and maple-glazed pork loin sided by roasted *poblano chilaquiles* and spicy salsa.

Kashkaval

C1 Mediterranean

856 Ninth Ave. (bet. 55th & 56th Sts.)

Subway: 50 St (Eighth Ave.) Lunch & dinner daily
Phone: 212-581-8282
Web: www.kashkavalfoods.com
Prices: $$

Taking its name from a sheep's milk cheese popular throughout the Balkans, this inviting wine bar is also a gourmet shop offering more than 100 kinds of cheese, various accouterments, as well a refrigerated glass display case stocked with take-away meze. Venture towards the back and the room offers a cozy seat and a tile-topped bar where labels ranging from California to Lebanon are poured.

An array of spreads and dips followed by a pot of fondue such as cheddar and ale, make Kashkaval ideal for groups. Or dine solo at the bar and dig into abundant platters like marinated and grilled chicken kebabs dressed with *tzatziki*, then paired with Greek salad and bulgar pilaf.

The owners of Kashkaval recently opened similarly themed Balkanika, across the street.

Keens

Steakhouse 𝓧𝓧

C4

72 W. 36th St. (bet. Fifth & Sixth Aves.)

Subway: 34 St - Herald Sq
Phone: 212-947-3636
Web: www.keens.com
Prices: $$$

Lunch Mon – Fri
Dinner nightly

Dating back to 1885, Keens is imbued with a palpable sense of history that sets it apart from the average midtown chophouse. A collection of dining rooms build the setting, each arranged with dark wood furnishings, linen-draped tables, and chock-full of Gilded Age charisma. A vestige of Keens' men-only, smoker's club days is displayed in their collection of long-stemmed, clay churchwarden pipes lining the ceiling.

Mouthwatering slabs of broiled meat star here; and the hand-selected prime cuts of beef are dry-aged in house. Icy platters of juicy oysters and bananas Foster are classic bookends to any feast.

The Pub Room offers lighter fare, and the bar pours one of the most extensive selections of single malt Scotch around.

Kirakuya

Japanese 🍜

C4

2 W. 32nd St. (bet. Broadway & Fifth Ave.)

Subway: 34 St - Herald Sq
Phone: 212-695-7272
Web: www.sakebarkirakuya.com
Prices: $$

Lunch Mon – Fri
Dinner Mon – Sat

Via its large pane windows hung with iridescent drapes, Kirakuya offers a rich view of K-town, vibrant with revelers and travelers. Set on the second floor of a nondescript building, this little sake bar excels for its expertly prepared mix of Japanese classics along with a few Korean favorites. The room is long, spacious, and great for groups eager to explore the array of sake and small plates. Hefty banquettes draped with red tapestries add a stamp of color.

The calm, sultry vibe is perfect for enjoying plates of pickled vegetables—each bite furnishes big flavor and fresh crunch. Arriving in ceramic vessels, other prized items include *nasu dengaku*, creamy-smoky grilled eggplant spread with sweetened miso; or thin slices of Berkshire pork tempura.

Korea Spoon

C4   Korean   ✗✗

39 W. 32nd St. (bet. Broadway & Fifth Ave.)

Subway: 34 St - Herald Sq   Lunch & dinner daily
Phone: 212-560-9696
Web: N/A
Prices: $$

Dining along Korea Way is an experience all to itself, too often involving loud, threadbare, 24/7 hot spots that seem beaten down by the crowds. Enter Korea Spoon. Its popularity does not lend serenity, but this dining room is a pretty, modern, earth-toned departure from the norm. Picture yourself snacking on daikon kimchi and other *banchan* in a West Elm catalog shoot.

The traditional array of Korean cooking highlights inexpensive specials to fortify the lunch and dinner groups. Sample a whole broiled fish, *johgi gui* with *soondooboo*, accompanied by a bowlful of bean paste, seafood, and chilies; or the hearty and spicy *budae chigae* stew of kimchi, noodles, sausage, and tofu. Also find a full roster of Korean-style barbecue prepared on tabletop grills.

Kristalbelli

C4   Korean   ✗✗

8 W. 36th St. (bet. Fifth & Sixth Aves.)

Subway: 34 St - Herald Sq   Lunch Mon – Sat
Phone: 212-290-2211   Dinner nightly
Web: www.kristalbelli.com
Prices: $$$

Turning up the heat in the dreary Garment District, Kristalbelli is a sexy harbinger of this fast-changing neighborhood. Outside, the gray slate and marble façade and impressive wooden door imply opulence; inside, crystal barbecue grills set on grey marble framed by a jolly gold monk bring tabletop dining over-the-top. The fun and bling continues upstairs in the young, hip, and hopping lounge.

Yet amid all this glitz and glam is a well-trained service team and very talented kitchen. *Banchan* opens with a superlative assortment that might include green chilies with fermented bean paste, marinated mushrooms, cold egg custard with scallions, and kimchi. A sparkling signature crystal bowl does not distract from the deeply flavored, almost buttery ribeye.

Kunjip

C4

9 W 32nd St. (bet. Broadway & Fifth Ave.)

Subway: 34 St - Herald Sq
Phone: 212-216-9487
Web: www.kunjip.com
Prices: ⬭

Lunch & dinner daily

One of K-town's better recommendations, this ever-bustling restaurant is open 24-hours a day, seven days a week. Prepare yourself to be immersed in a noisy setting, wafting with food aromas, where orange-shirted servers whiz by, balancing trays heaped with plates of *banchan*, sizzling stone bowls of *bibimbop*, or empty dishes from instantly re-set tables.

You may feel compelled to order right away as the line out the door makes for a less than leisurely ambience, but relax. The staff is pleasant and the vast menu is worth perusing. Find specialties like *mae woon dduk boki*—a saucy stew of pan-fried rice cake tossed with softened white onion, plenty of scallions, mung bean noodles, and fish cake all tossed with spicy, sweet, and rich *gochujang*.

La Masseria

C2

235 W. 48th St. (bet. Broadway & Eighth Ave.)

Subway: 50 St (Eighth Ave.)
Phone: 212-582-2111
Web: www.lamasserianyc.com
Prices: $$

Lunch & dinner daily

La Masseria is a popular and bright Theater District spot, but it is also a wonderfully cozy place where stone, stucco walls, and exposed wood beams add farmhouse-inspired warmth. The restaurant's convenient location ensures that the large dining room is a routinely full house, and spot-on service delivered by a smartly attired team keeps the conviviality stoked.

When it comes to the food, La Masseria chooses simplicity over theatrics in its Puglia-influenced menu. There are no distractions on a plate of roasted baby artichoke hearts draped with Taleggio *fonduta*, or in a bowl of *grannato* cooked risotto-style stocked with white beans and shellfish. Pasta is *fatta in casa*; and entrées include oven-roasted rabbit with herbs and wine sauce.

The Lambs Club

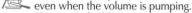

 C3

American 🍴🍴

132 W. 44th St. (bet. Broadway & Sixth Ave.)

Subway: Times Sq - 42 St
Phone: 212-997-5262
Web: www.thelambsclub.com
Prices: $$$

Lunch & dinner daily

With its rich red leather seats, warming fireplace, and black-and-white photo-filled walls, The Lambs Club is reminiscent of its roots as a flourishing theater club. The dining room is dark, moody, and masculine; in contrast, the staff is friendly and all-around professional—it's easy to feel special here even when the volume is pumping.

This iconic building was envisioned by Stanford White, and renowned Chef/restauranteur Geoffrey Zakarian's American cuisine does the setting justice. Talent and care are palpable at this sequestered spot, in such dishes as grilled quail set over farro and tart-sweet cranberry *gastrique*; Heritage pork chop in a delicious sherry jus with crispy pork hash; and a lush lemon *baba* with limoncello and raspberries.

Landmark Tavern

 B2

American 🍴🍴

626 Eleventh Ave. (at 46th St.)

Subway: 50 St (Eighth Ave.)
Phone: 212-247-2562
Web: www.thelandmarktavern.com
Prices: $$

Lunch & dinner daily

Step inside and sense the history. Originally built in 1868, the setting is warm with penny-tile flooring, mahogany woodwork, and stained glass panels. The pub is located in one of the last remaining wild stretches of the island, too far west to attract attention...though gleaming residential towers, boutique hotels, and creative agencies have recently started popping up. Still, service is friendly and speaks with a genuine Irish accent.

The tavern's highly enjoyable pub grub presents bangers and a fluffy mound of mashed potatoes dotted with sweet peas and ladled with brown onion gravy; beer-battered fish and chips; or corned beef with boiled potatoes. End your meal with a boozy coffee, fortified with a wee nip of Irish whiskey or Bailey's.

Lan Sheng ✿

C3

Chinese ✗

60 W. 39th St. (bet. Fifth & Sixth Aves.)

Subway: 42 St - Bryant Pk
Phone: 212-575-8899
Web: www.lanshengrestaurant.com
Prices: $$

Lunch & dinner daily

MICHELIN

Located deep within bustling midtown, Lan Sheng is a comfortable and warm respite from the surrounding clatter. The dining room features plush, high-backed banquettes, wood-carved wall hangings, and blue-hued lighting that lends an elegant glow.

The service is competent, focused, and always courteous. Be forewarned: peak lunch hours bring long lines from nearby offices. That said, everyone agrees that a meal here is worth it.

Keep a bowl of rice nearby, because the spice levels here can verge on incendiary. Even before the first peppercorn has passed their lips, hearts are all set on fire with anticipation of the tongue-numbing fish pots. Restorative, hot, and beautiful, these tall, silver cauldrons arrive bubbling with strips of supremely flavorful and firm sea bass that glistens with crimson-red chili oil. The broth itself is a rich, clear, and enticingly sour combination of Chinese celery, cilantro, Sichuan peppercorns, cabbage, bamboo, noodles, star anise, lily bulb, and many, many aromatics. *Mapo* tofu arrives amid plumes of billowing fragrance and tastes of superb quality. The camphor tea-smoked duck is perfectly cooked with crisped skin and meat that is tender and juicy.

La Silhouette

French ✗✗

C1

362 W. 53rd St. (bet. Eighth & Ninth Aves.)

Subway: 50 St (Eighth Ave.)
Phone: 212-581-2400
Web: www.la-silhouettenyc.com
Prices: $$$

Lunch Mon – Fri
Dinner nightly

With its sprawling interior that includes three distinct dining areas and a terrace, La Silhouette may seem like a surprising discovery to those unfamiliar with its tucked away Hell's Kitchen location. Bold red and white stripes accent the tastefully subdued dining room where fine service further heightens the elegant atmosphere.

The kitchen has welcomed a new chef and is sending out deftly crafted fare that possesses a strong French accent, but also has a contemporary attitude. Sit back and savor the likes of pistachio- and currant-studded country pâté accompanied by Dijon mustard-spiked celery root rémoulade; seared sea bass and diver scallop in red miso and yuzu broth; and velvety mocha semifreddo atop a *feuilletine*-flecked chocolate base.

Lugo Caffé

Italian ✗✗

B3

1 Penn Plaza (entrance on 33rd St.)

Subway: 34 St - Penn Station
Phone: 212-760-2700
Web: www.lugocaffe.com
Prices: $$

Lunch Mon – Fri
Dinner Mon – Sat

Snagging a seat at the long, semi-circular bar is *the* best way to carouse at this spirited café, set in an otherwise drab locale. Everyone loves Lugo and awe prevails as one meanders through this vast, well-dressed space. Keeping company with quirky touches like coffee cans and Italian newspapers are more handsome elements like sky-high ceilings, massive windows, and cocooned booths.

Diners at this airy *ristorante* are here for the mood and food. Set with placemats that read like menus, tables tender the likes of irresistible homemade mozzarella paired with fiery peppers and *soppresata*; fried artichokes licked with lemon aïoli; *rigatoni all'Amatriciana* revealing salty pancetta; and classic rosemary chicken *al forno* with root vegetables and jus.

Le Bernardin ✿ ✿ ✿

A4

Seafood ✗✗✗✗

155 W. 51st St. (bet. Sixth & Seventh Aves.)

Subway: 50 St (Broadway)
Phone: 212-554-1515
Web: www.le-bernardin.com
Prices: $$$$

Lunch Mon – Fri
Dinner Mon – Sat

Lyn Hughes

From first glance, this is a spectacular home to fine dining. Everything is done to the highest standard, yet never appears showy. The room itself feels very posh and spacious, with intricate teak panels, brown leather armchairs, and a stunning seafaring triptych covering the back wall. Even the servers (dressed in full black and white livery) remain discreet, anticipatory, and personable. The clientele is an upscale mix of grown-ups celebrating special occasions or business deals.

Chef Eric Ripert's menu promises to take the taste buds on a rousing tour of seafood-centric dishes that are sure to cover vast areas of the globe. This might begin with "flash marinated" hamachi with sea beans, daikon, black garlic ponzu, and a liberal sprinkle of *pimente d'Esplette*. Tuna may seem shockingly simple but sublime, thinly pounded like a ruby red carpet, draped over brioche toast with a touch of foie gras and drops of emerald green olive oil. The roasted cobia is opaque and buttery, in a well-spiced curry and light coconut-lime broth. Overall, the elements are subtle rather than basking in the complex power of East Asian ingredients.

Desserts are surprising, fun, and a consistent highlight.

Madangsui

Korean

C4

35 W. 35th St. (bet. Fifth & Sixth Aves.)

Subway: 34 St - Herald Sq   Lunch & dinner daily
Phone: 212-564-9333
Web: www.madangsui.com
Prices: $$

The air is calmer here than at other K-town spots, and it's much fresher too—thanks to a good ventilation system that keeps the smoky scent of Korean barbecue sizzling on those tabletop grills at bay. Upon entering, find shelves displaying numerous cuts of meat, a kitschy yet authentic touch in an otherwise pleasant setting. The staff is genuinely friendly.

Soy-marinated ribeye *bulgogi*, a thinly sliced brisket *chadol-baegi*, and fresh pork belly *saeng sam gyeop sal*, are some of Madangsui's grilling options. Additionally, find a full roster of traditional Korean specialties here, like *nak ji dol sot bibimbob*, a hearty portion of fluffy rice served in a viciously hot stone bowl topped with a saucy-spicy mixture of diced bits of octopus and vegetables.

Mandoo Bar

Korean

C4

2 W. 32nd St. (bet. Broadway & Fifth Ave.)

Subway: 34 St - Herald Sq   Lunch & dinner daily
Phone: 212-279-3075
Web: N/A
Prices:

Whether steamed, fried, spicy or not, Mandoo is always Korean for "dumpling," and every kind you can dream up is served here as unique, tidy little bundles. This postage stamp-sized K-town favorite keeps its massive number of customers happy with an array of freshly made, unassuming Korean fare, dished out fast enough to keep weekend shoppers on the move.

Meals may begin with the likes of pan-fried dumplings filled with pork and vegetables (*goon mandoo*); bite-sized and boiled baby *mandoo*; or the combo *mandoo*, with fillings of seafood, vegetables, and pork. Korean-style spicy beef soup (*yuk kae jang*) and acorn or buckwheat flour noodle dishes tossed with citrus vinaigrette, sesame seeds, scallions, and cilantro are fine and worthy accompaniments.

289

Má Pêche

Fusion 🍴🍴

B4

15 W. 56th St. (bet. Fifth & Sixth Aves.)

Subway: 57 St
Phone: 212-757-5878
Web: www.momofuku.com
Prices: $$

Lunch Mon – Sat
Dinner nightly

Since the arrival of Má Pêche, Momofuku-mad foodies no longer have to venture below 14th Street for a taste of the gutsy brilliance—here churned out by Chef Paul Carmichael. Rather austere in comparison to the edgier East Village originals, this soaring blond-wood furnished room is wrapped in canvas warmed by a peachy glow and boasts a lounge, raw bar, and branch of Milk Bar. Reservations are accepted—a unique convenience.

Skill, talent, and judiciously sourced ingredients prevail throughout, especially in items like raw, thinly sliced scallops from New Jersey mingled with sweet plantain, yuzu and sesame; soft-shell crab buns with fiery Calabrian chilies; or an entrée of fried catfish *étouffé*-style with meaty mussels and broken vermicelli.

Marseille

French 🍴🍴

C2

630 Ninth Ave. (at 44th St.)

Subway: 42 St - Port Authority Bus Terminal
Phone: 212-333-2323
Web: www.marseillenyc.com
Prices: $$

Lunch & dinner daily

Marseille marries the charm of a classic French bistro with the inimitable style of New York City. The sexy, soft golden glow, convivial spirit, and superlative Theater District location make it a popular choice for everyone from tourists craving a taste of Broadway to colleagues cooling off after a day's work. The skilled and truly professional kitchen prepares an impressive cuisine bursting with pronounced, balanced flavors. From salads and seasonal specials to more French-formed entrées like steak frites, there is something for everyone. Hungry diners appreciate that the portions lean toward American sensibilities; while the budget-conscious value the prix-fixe lunch and dinner menus. Don't skip out without the frites—they may be the best in the city.

Marea ✿ ✿

D1

Seafood XXX

240 Central Park South (bet. Broadway & Seventh Ave.)

Subway: 59 St – Columbus Circle
Phone: 212-582-5100
Web: www.marea-nyc.com
Prices: $$$$

Lunch & dinner daily

Noah Fecks

This gorgeous restaurant clearly points to the sea, from the sheen of its high-gloss, wood-grain panels that almost seem to be undulating, to sleek table lamps that cast a gentle glow upon large decorative shells. This is also the source of Chef Michael White's culinary inspiration. Servers are observant, prompt, neat, and slightly hip—a perfect match for the publishing houses that seem to unleash their young and fashionable staffers into the room. The swanky leather chairs are packed and the mood is high-spirited.

Of course, the food is worthy of its attention; even the bread (green olive-studded focaccia) sparkles from its patterned plate. Each dish puts a hearty focus on the ocean, as in ribbons of barely cooked, snappy cuttlefish tossed like pasta in a micro-*brunoise softrito* with grated *bottarga di muggine.* This may be followed by the sweet meat extracted beautifully from lobster shells in a verdant composition of *burrata* and basil seeds with dabs of "eggplant *funghetto.*" Lightly breaded fillets of New Zealand John Dory are tender, moist, and delicious, served atop earthy vegetables and puffed quinoa with a whiff of juniper.

A rich panna cotta merits saving room for dessert.

Mercato 😬

Italian ✗

B3

352 W. 39th St. (bet. Eighth & Ninth Aves.)

Subway: 42 St - Port Authority Bus Terminal   Lunch & dinner daily
Phone: 212-643-2000
Web: www.mercatonyc.com
Prices: $$

By virtue of its location on spirited 39th Street, Mercato sees a torrent of visitors filling its invitingly rustic domain. But address aside, the inviting trattoria is routinely mobbed for its very nice and well-priced cuisine prepared with a delicious *Pugliese* accent.

Mercato's look includes a high-ceilinged front bar leading to a cozy back room, all furnished with rustic woods, polished concrete, and exposed brick. The extensive antipasti selection includes decadent fresh *stracciatella* cheese served with speck; fava bean purée with chicory and extra virgin olive oil; and grilled whole sardines with *salmoriglio*. The long list of excellent pasta has featured a special of house-made fusilli tossed in slow-cooked pork ragú with *cavolo nero*.

Miss Korea

Korean ✗✗

C4

10 W. 32nd St. (bet. Broadway & Fifth Ave.)

Subway: 34 St - Herald Sq   Lunch & dinner daily
Phone: 212-594-4963
Web: www.misskoreabbq.com
Prices: $$

Miss Korea ain't no pageant queen; she is in fact a sleek, smart restaurant churning out seriously tasty Korean fare. Its unique façade of rocks encased in wiring carries to the interior, which is equally striking with massive cut-stone walls. In fact, you may feel as if you are inside an ancient castle softened by greenery and a highly convivial spirit.

The deep room is enlivened by four-tops set with billowing branches shrouded with ivy and birds. Floating in a wood frame, rosy bulbs cast a gentle glow on *haemul-pajeon*, crispy seafood-scallion pancake; *samgyupsal*, pretty pink strips of barbecued pork belly kissed with salt and delicious sesame oil; and a richly complex *bullak-jeongol*, hot pot of kimchi broth filled with octopus, tofu, and *bulgogi*.

Manhattan ▸ Midtown West

Masa ✿ ✿ ✿

C1

Japanese XX

10 Columbus Circle (in the Time Warner Center)

Subway: 59 St - Columbus Circle
Phone: 212-823-9800
Web: www.masanyc.com
Prices: $$$$

Lunch Tue – Fri
Dinner Mon – Sat

Masa

Dining here is an experience that may seem unprecedented. Located on the fourth floor of the behemoth Time Warner Center, the entrance feels like a forgotten passage into a hushed and spartan yet very relaxed room. Its focal point is the precious *hinoki* wood sushi counter, though the eye is equally drawn to an enormous forsythia tree. The staff assures your every comfort without ever seeming stiff. Even the angle of the counter's footrest seems perfectly relaxing, if not revelatory.

Still, a seat at the counter can feel like a high-stakes club for people who each seem to know Chef Masa Takayama better than the next. Is he serving you directly? If not, no matter. The food is just as elevated, theatrical, and extraordinary without the backslapping.

An exhaustive list of superlatives could be applied to any of the highly seasonal omakase meals here. The rice alone is worth its weight in stars. Suffice it to say this: the famed sea urchin risotto; barely opaque Ohmi beef with shaved white truffle; and toro caviar are even better than they sound. The sushi—from Thai sea bream to grilled freshwater eel—will leave you convinced that you have tasted the sea for the first time in your life.

The Modern ✿

9 W. 53rd St. (bet. Fifth & Sixth Aves.)

Subway: 5 Av - 53 St
Phone: 212-333-1220
Web: www.themodernnyc.com
Prices: $$$

Lunch Mon – Fri
Dinner Mon – Sat

Ellen Silverman

Welcome to one of Gotham's best restaurant locations, set inside the magnificent MoMA—even the door looks like a piece of art. Once inside, the scene endures with a bar that is a worthy destination in its own right: sometimes loud, always fun, and populated by everyone from real-life Carrie Bradshaws to the baristas who make their gourmet coffee in the morning. Beyond this, a fine dining area showcases stunning views of the sculpture gardens through floor-to-ceiling windows.

While The Modern's visual appeal is dramatic, it pays equal attention to maintaining friendly service, a stylish yet celebratory vibe, and outstanding food.

Homemade bread with goat's milk butter is a sublime prelude to starters like foie gras terrine, coated in poppy seeds with mango purée and a dab of Balsamic vinegar. Then, move on to a slow-poached farm egg served with squid ink spätzle, topped with a bit of black truffle. Meat courses may highlight a beautifully pink roasted rack of lamb with olives, fine herbs, and bacon fondue. Sweet dishes are sure to soothe as in a brittle filled with mango mousse, served with citrus mousseline and passion fruit sorbet. The chocolate sculptures are truly a site to see.

Molyvos

A3

Greek ✗✗

871 Seventh Ave. (bet. 55th & 56th Sts.)

Subway: 57 St - 7 Av
Phone: 212-582-7500
Web: www.molyvos.com
Prices: $$

Lunch & dinner daily

Mighty Molyvos is both an attractive and applauded choice among Greek gourmands and Carnegie Hall patrons. This slender yet deep space is bright albeit warm and subdued; while the décor, void of themed clichés, exudes style in the form of wood paneling, ceramics, and an elaborately patterned coffered ceiling.

From your post at a large table, glimpse a gallery of smiling family photos. Carrying this congenial spirit is Molyvos' beloved menu. The kitchen's vision and devotion can be tasted in *keftedes me saltsa domates*, spicy meatballs in cumin-infused tomato sauce; tender and meaty lamb ribs glossed with thyme and ouzo; and a toasted almond-vanilla cake served with vanilla-yogurt ice cream. A pre-theater menu and loaded bar keep the scene lively.

Mr. Robata

A4

Japanese ✗✗

1674 Broadway (bet. 52nd & 53rd Sts.)

Subway: 50 St (Broadway)
Phone: 212-757-1030
Web: www.mrrobata.com
Prices: $$$

Lunch Mon – Fri
Dinner nightly

In an amusing and unexpected feat, humble Mr. Robata somehow thrives within the strip-clubby netherworld of touristy Times Square. Among discerning and discreet of-age adults, this is clearly an entertaining locale. And among foodies, it's a great stop for fusion Japanese. Inside, find two attractive dining areas: one that offers an inviting counter and an auxiliary room decked with well-sized tables.

The food is tasty but less than authentic. Still, Mr. Robata entices with friendly, adept service. Oversized platters shine with powerful flavors, as in fried tuna tacos tossed with crunchy sesame seeds. Wagyu sliders are a generous crowd-pleaser, while the "never too late" maki with soft shell crab and *robata*-grilled mushrooms and eggplant are fun finds.

New Wonjo

C4

23 W. 32nd St. (bet. Broadway & Fifth Ave.)

Subway: 34 St - Herald Sq
Phone: 212-695-5815
Web: www.newwonjo.com
Prices: $$

Lunch & dinner daily

Smack in the middle of Koreatown, New Wonjo offers a savory respite among the sensory overload of this jam-packed quarter. The simple, well-maintained space offers seating for small parties on the ground level, and a second floor reserved for barbeque-seeking groups to huddle around platters of marinated slices of beef brisket (*chadol baeki*) or spicy squid with pork belly (*o-sam bul goki*) sizzling on table top grills.

Non-barbecue options feature tasty Korean favorites, with starters like *mandoo*, *jap che*, and *pajun*. Sample satisfying stews like *gamba tang*—a bubbling red chili-spiked broth floating slowly simmered and very meaty pork bones with chunks of potato, cabbage, greens, and onions, that is wonderfully flavorful but not incendiary.

Norma's

A3

119 W. 56th St. (bet. Sixth & Seventh Aves.)

Subway: 57 St
Phone: 212-708-7460
Web: www.parkermeridien.com
Prices: $$

Lunch daily

Going strong for almost 15 years and serving heaping platters of breakfast well into the afternoon, Norma's may have been derived from the most humble diner, but she is no greasy spoon. A table at this Le Parker Meriden dining room is highly sought after by suits already wheeling and dealing over the first meal of the day.

Upscale touches welcome guests with tables wide enough for a laptop *and* your plate, a polished staff, and gratis smoothie shots. The whimsically worded menu (think "egg cellent" or "Benny sent me" sections) covers all bases and then some: house-made granola; thickly sliced and crunchy brioche French toast drizzled with warm caramel sauce; and poached eggs nestled in barbecued pulled pork hash. Savory delights appear after noon.

Oceana

A4

Seafood XXX

120 W. 49th St. (at Sixth Ave.)

Subway: 47-50 Sts - Rockefeller Ctr
Phone: 212-759-5941
Web: www.oceanarestaurant.com
Prices: $$$

Lunch Mon – Fri
Dinner nightly

Paul Johnson

Smack dab in the midst of cavernous midtown, Oceana is always a gratifying spot for indulging in spectacular seafood. Located on the ground floor of the McGraw-Hill building, the grand dining room is soothing yet dramatic with its spacious layout, plentiful windows dressed with sheers and aqua-blue drapery, dark woodwork, navy banquettes, and seasonal flowers. The private, glass-enclosed room and chef's table by the kitchen are attractive options for the power crowds seeking a more exclusive experience.

A lounge area and raw bar display of pristine shellfish chilling on ice welcomes diners and underscores the restaurant's seriousness of purpose. The superbly fresh items never falter in finding just the right global accent, as in *carnaroli* risotto infused with shrimp stock, studded with diced shrimp and pumpkin, and enlivened with slivered bits of sage. The grouper *"chraime"* is a plump block of steamed fish plated with a spicy, North African-inspired tomato sauce, diced eggplant, and blistered shisito peppers. Desserts offer a refreshing finale, as in a bar of delectable olive oil-enriched cheesecake paired with a quenelle of tarragon sorbet and pale pink watermelon *granité*.

Orso

Italian ✗✗

C2

322 W. 46th St. (bet. Eighth & Ninth Aves.)

Subway: 42 St - Port Authority Bus Terminal   Lunch & dinner daily
Phone: 212-489-7212
Web: www.orsorestaurant.com
Prices: $$

This intimate little restaurant—with its knowledgeable, friendly staff and antique photos—is the late-night haunt of Broadway players in search of a post-show meal. It shows off their good taste too, for the food at this Restaurant Row darling rises well above the competition.

Occupying the ground floor of a charming brownstone, Orso offers a daily menu of simple, delicious Italian classics like *raviolone* with crab, tomato, and capers in brown butter; or oven-roasted quail with a Marsala reduction. The $24 *contorni* selection of five vegetable dishes like roasted potatoes and garlic; or the tasty mélange of sweet-sour eggplant, yellow squash, and peppers is a meal in itself.

Be sure to call ahead; their pre-theater prix-fixe books quickly.

Osteria al Doge

Italian ✗✗

C3

142 W. 44th St. (bet. Broadway & Sixth Ave.)

Subway: Times Sq - 42 St   Lunch & dinner daily
Phone: 212-944-3643
Web: www.osteria-doge.com
Prices: $$

Tucked into one of those theater-dominated cross streets that define this jumbled area of Times Square, the first thing Osteria al Doge has on the competition is its good looks: think sunny yellow walls, wrought-iron chandeliers, and bright Italian ceramic plates. Not to mention a long marble and wood bar where solo diners can settle into a comfortable padded stool and enjoy a little people-watching before the real show.

Back on the plates it's delicious Italian food tended to with love, like a plump tangle of fettuccine *verdi* in a silky lamb ragù dotted with lemon rind and pitted black picholine olives; thin slices of tuna carpaccio drizzled with citrus olive oil, a dash of crunchy sea salt, and herbs; or a fresh lemon tart topped with strawberries.

Osteria del Circo

Italian ✗✗

A3

120 W. 55th St. (bet. Sixth & Seventh Aves.)

Subway: 57 St
Phone: 212-265-3636
Web: www.circonyc.com
Prices: $$$

Lunch Mon – Fri
Dinner nightly

Ever fantasized about running away to join the circus? Fulfill that dream without all of the acrobatics at Osteria del Circo. This restaurant, run by the Maccioni clan of Le Cirque fame, offers a tasteful take on the Big Top. Its tent-like ceiling is complete with streaming fabric in a riot of colors and is punctuated by spinning circus performers and animal sculptures. There is a palpable buzz here—just one of the reasons there are so many regulars.

However, this menu isn't about peanuts and popcorn. Instead, look forward to deftly prepared Italian dishes like grilled branzino and milk-fed veal chops from the professional kitchen. The staff is warm and engaging—not surprising given the Maccionis' reputation for throwing open their arms to guests.

Petrossian

French ✗✗✗

A3

182 W. 58th St. (at Seventh Ave.)

Subway: 57 St - 7 Av
Phone: 212-245-2214
Web: www.petrossian.com
Prices: $$$

Lunch & dinner daily

Petrossian is not hip. It is classic, continental, and a rare breed in the city. With such exemplary attributes—location, historic setting, and refined staff—this French bastion smacks of bourgeois indulgence. The exterior is unique with detailed stonework that features frolicking cherubs and griffins; a forbidding wrought-iron door guards the entrance. But, the dining room is typical with pink and black granite, a mirrored bar, and crystal sconces.

This costly (or stuffy?) *paradis* clings to the fabric of New York dining with pleasant, comforting offerings like a tasting of foie gras terrine and smoked fish. Affluent regulars adore the pan-roasted lobster risotto with porcini and Parmesan; and a classically rich almond-apple torte with vanilla ice cream.

Per Se ⁂

Contemporary XXXXX

C1

10 Columbus Circle (in the Time Warner Center)

Subway: 59 St - Columbus Circle

Phone: 212-823-9335

Web: www.perseny.com

Prices: $$$$

Lunch Fri – Sun
Dinner nightly

Deborah Jones

It is hard to imagine a more dramatic departure from the soulless Time Warner Center mall than passing beyond those iconic blue doors to enter Per Se. An upscale sense of calm—the kind that only money can buy—instantly pervades the atmosphere. The words *plush* and *luxe* are sure to come to mind, whether admiring the spacious tables, corner banquettes, or stunning views. The crowd is impossibly elegant, moneyed, special, and could probably take it down a notch. Service is professional and intuitively understands the needs and personality of each table.

Note that the salon is often empty, which is confounding since much of the menu is available for ordering à la carte. Somehow, Chef Thomas Keller continues to raise the bar here with meals that convey an even stronger sense of seasonal artistry that finds inspiration right down to the day. The kitchen is particularly adept with vegetables, which may arrive as a savory little avocado cookie, or sweet corn sorbet with Bing cherry relish, corn shoots, corn consommé, and black truffles.

Desserts are contemporary, light, and lovely, as in floating islands of Swiss meringue, lime tapioca, and ginger ice cream with roasted golden pineapple.

pizzArte

A3   Italian ✕✕

69 W. 55th St. (bet. Fifth & Sixth Aves.)

Subway: 57 St   Lunch & dinner daily
Phone: 212-247-3936
Web: www.pizzarteny.com
Prices: $$

If there were one dish universally loved, it would be pizza, that slice of Neapolitan bliss. While it is many things to many people, NYers rejoice at pizzArte, where pizza is baked to perfect pliability with a bit of char and topped with immaculate ingredients. Unlike its chaotic surrounds, this bi-level establishment is all opulence with whitewashed walls, marble, a well-set bar, and manicured stools.

Beyond its gentle hum of music and regal Neapolitan paintings, the handsome pizza oven is buried in the back. Here, a *pizzaiolo* stands sentry, churning out a deliciously charred Margherita with milky mozzarella. While pizza is their art, *paccheri al baccalà* with tomatoes and olives; and *penne Ferdinando* with eggplant and basil will not disappoint.

Porter House

C1   Steakhouse ✕✕✕

10 Columbus Circle (in the Time Warner Center)

Subway: 59 St - Columbus Circle   Lunch & dinner daily
Phone: 212-823-9500
Web: www.porterhousenewyork.com
Prices: $$$$

At Porter House, one feasts on Brooklyn-born Executive Chef Michael Lomonaco's impressive work served amid polished cherry wood, tobacco brown leather, stainless steel, and stunning Central Park views.

The name alone is enough to conjure images of charred meaty satisfaction but a nicely marbled, 45-day aged ribeye given a ground chili rubbing down seals the deal. This is best accompanied by thick-cut buttermilk onions rings, or a crisped and decadent cake of cubed potatoes. Though steaks and chops receive top-billing, the real draw here is their well-rounded menu. Other items to enjoy may include slow-roasted organic Scottish salmon; porcini risotto with black truffle butter; and great down-home desserts like a tall wedge of 7-layer coconut cake.

Print

B1

653 Eleventh Ave. (at 48th St.)

Subway: 50 St (Eighth Ave.)
Phone: 212-757-2224
Web: www.printrestaurant.com
Prices: $$

Lunch & dinner daily

At Print, located in the West Side's hinterlands, a touch of Californian sensibility blooms. Its home, off the lobby of the Ink48 hotel, has an easy breezy layout that unites lounging and dining in a room that is pleasantly dark and cozy.

The talented team behind this locavore dining room takes its mission seriously: there is a full-time forager on the payroll, water is poured into recycled glass, the kitchen composts, and the menu highlights the provenance of the ingredients. Seasonality and simplicity are on show in creations like grilled octopus with Pennsylvania potatoes and house-made chorizo (made from Berkshire pork raised upstate); goat-cheese gnocchi with zucchini and cherry tomatoes; and grilled sea bass with wild mushrooms and shell beans.

Radiance Tea House

A3

158 W. 55th St. (bet. Sixth & Seventh Aves.)

Subway: 57 St - 7 Av
Phone: 212-217-0442
Web: www.radiancetea.com
Prices: $$

Lunch & dinner daily

Tea drinking is synonymous with Asian hospitality; the respect and harmony this tradition conjures is part and parcel of the experience had at Radiance Tea House. Open the doors and climb a few steps to enter this tranquil sanctum whose pin-drop silence is broken only by the gentle sip of tea-drinkers.

This sweet book and tea shop may offer a rather limited menu (a bit larger at dinner), but the tea selection is truly vast. The room is airy with a semi-open kitchen and wing devoted to a well-chosen book selection. Servers may be hushed but are happy to answer your queries about *unagi-don* with broiled eel and pickled radish; sticky rice and pork wrapped in lotus leaf; or a fresh salad of "tropical" salmon with mango, avocado, and five-spiced pecans.

Remi

A4   Italian   ✗✗✗

145 W. 53rd St. (bet. Sixth & Seventh Aves.)

Subway: 7 Av   Lunch & dinner daily
Phone: 212-581-4242
Web: www.remi-ny.com
Prices: $$

A convivial buzz winds through this Italian restaurant, from the lively back dining area to the glass-roofed atrium in the front that offers a gourmet breakfast and great salad selection to-go. At its center, find whimsical flying buttress archways, murals, mirrors, and glass chandeliers that recall the Veneto region.

Yet this well-orchestrated production's true draw is its delicious menu that highlights easygoing, rustic Italian specialties as in house-made pasta with lamb ragù, crowned with pillowy-soft lamb meatballs, and topped with aged buffalo milk *Parmigiano*. The nice offering of Remi classics is always spot-on, as in seared tuna with poppy seeds, roasted vegetables, and balsamic reduction; or *garganelli* with garlic, shrimp, and fried zucchini.

Robert

D1   Contemporary   ✗✗

2 Columbus Circle (bet. Broadway & Eighth Ave.)

Subway: 59 St - Columbus Circle   Lunch & dinner daily
Phone: 212-299-7730
Web: www.robertnyc.com
Prices: $$

Behold the sweeping views of Central Park from this bright, sexy setting on the 9th floor of the Museum of Art and Design. Be sure to request seating near the north-facing, floor-to-ceiling windows. The interior is almost as pleasing to the eye: cheery splashes of fuchsia and orange perk up a sleek space, where transparent bucket seats, clear-topped tables, and contemporary art installations beautifully reflect the museum to which it belongs.

Drop in for lunch, afternoon tea, or dinner for the likes of tuna carpaccio pizza sprinkled with trout caviar, spicy aïoli, and cucumber; *tagliatelle* with juicy lamb meatballs, fresh mint, and grated *ricotta salata*; or sweet- and sour-braised veal breast atop mashed cauliflower dabbed with quince relish.

Russian Samovar

Russian 🍴🍴

C2

256 W. 52nd St. (bet. Broadway & Eighth Ave.)

Subway: 50 St (Broadway)   Lunch & dinner daily
Phone: 212-757-0168
Web: www.russiansamovar.com
Prices: $$

Which came first: the vodka or the celebs? It's hard to say when it comes to this hot spot, which caters to hockey players, Russian intellectuals, and vodka aficionados alike. Our bets are on that beautiful vodka selection, available in all kinds of flavors, qualities, and sizes (shot, carafe, or bottle). Nestled into the bustling Theater District, Russian Samovar is both quirky and elegant—with low lighting, glass panels, and musicians playing the piano and violin. The staff, both attentive and sweet, can walk you through delicious fare like fresh salmon caviar blini, prepared tableside; *pelmeni*, tender veal dumplings served with sour cream and honey mustard; or milk-cured Baltic herring, paired with pickled onions, potatoes, and carrots.

Sake Bar Hagi

Japanese 🍴

C2

152 W. 49th St., B1F (bet. Sixth & Seventh Aves.)

Subway: 50 St (Broadway)   Dinner nightly
Phone: 212-764-8549
Web: N/A
Prices: 💷

This basement *izakaya* can be a challenge to locate—its name is slyly marked on a door that opens to a flight of stairs. Descend to find an unremarkable, brightly lit, and boisterous room tightly packed with wood furnishings and a strong Japanese following.

The space may be small but the menu is vast, so bring friends to ensure a fulfilling experience. Their spot-on small plates are designed to be washed down by beer, sake, or distinctly Japanese cocktails like cassis with oolong tea or soda, or a Calpico sour. Be sure to include the wasabi-spiked *shu mai* stuffed with ground pork; *takoyaki*, deep-fried octopus croquettes with daikon and grated ginger root; spicy cod roe fried rice; or grilled hamachi collar that only needs a light squeeze of lemon.

Scarlatto

C2   Italian   ✗✗

250 W. 47th St. (bet. Broadway & Eighth Ave.)

Subway: 50 St (Eighth Ave.)   Lunch & dinner daily
Phone: 212-730-4535
Web: www.scarlattonyc.com
Prices: $$

Dip down below street level and find a lovely exposed brick interior displaying rows of wine bottles and glass beaded wall sconces to match the sparkly tiara crowning Audrey Hepburn in a framed still from *Roman Holiday*.

The menu doesn't offer many surprises but this is cooking that—just like a little black dress—never goes out of style. Among the array, search out *polpette al pomodoro*, house-made meatballs in tomato sauce, or bean soup with fresh pasta. Their *pollo Parmigiana* is a "red sauce" classic, made with breaded and fried chicken breast draped in bright tomato sauce beneath a bounty of grated and caramelized Parmesan, served atop a mound of al dente spaghetti.

Theater-goers take note: a prix-fixe dinner menu is offered throughout the evening.

The Sea Grill

D2   Seafood   ✗✗✗

19 W. 49th St. (bet. Fifth & Sixth Aves.)

Subway: 47-50 Sts - Rockefeller Ctr   Lunch Mon – Fri
Phone: 212-332-7610   Dinner Mon – Sat
Web: www.patinagroup.com
Prices: $$$

With its dining room overlooking Rockefeller Center's iconic ice-skating rink, The Sea Grill boasts one of the city's most famed locations. A wall of windows frames that view, while sand-colored carpeting and gleaming terrazzo cover the floors. This cool aqua-accented setting is the kind of room to dress up for. Understandably, tourists flock here but it is also popular among business folks, especially at lunch when the bar is seated with sharp-looking suits dining on iced lobster tail and tending to business.

As for the food, the kitchen turns out enjoyable cuisine to complement the setting. Offerings are built upon quality seafood dishes such as Block Island golden snapper *a la plancha* dressed with tangy cherry tomato vinaigrette.

Seäsonal ❀

Austrian 🍴🍴

132 W. 58th St. (bet. Sixth & Seventh Aves.)

Subway: 57 St - 7 Av

Phone: 212-957-5550

Web: www.seasonalnyc.com

Prices: $$$

Lunch & dinner Mon – Sat

Seäsonal Restaurant & Weinbar

Arrive at lunch and prepare to be blown away by one of midtown's greatest dining secrets. Seäsonal may appear to be an attractive albeit rather straightforward little sleeper of a restaurant—the entrance might even be obstructed by scaffolding. But, the staff is cordial and observant, the room is sophisticated, and the food is downright excellent.

Starting with a plate of whole-grain bread with piped rosettes of pumpkin seed and paprika-chive butters, each dish is served with striking artistry. A modest pork belly arrives as a linear composition of the cubed, glazed, slow-cooked meat seasoned with mustard seed and set atop kale purée, garnished with dots of fried sweet potato and pink grapefruit beads. Fluke may be pressed into a cylinder, draped with rich veal reduction, and accompanied by quenelles of winter squash, a crisp shard of speck, and a twirl of house-made parsley fettuccine.

These Austrian desserts are as intense as their reputation. So, anticipate the likes of a moist, slim, and very dense Sacher cake, flaunting the strong taste of almonds and more delicate flavors of chocolate, infused with a fruity layer of jam, iced with shiny ganache and clouds of whipped cream.

Staghorn

315 W. 36th St. (bet. Eighth & Ninth Aves.)

Subway: 34 St - Penn Station
Phone: 212-239-4390
Web: www.staghornsteakhouse.com
Prices: $$$

Lunch Mon – Fri
Dinner Mon – Sat

Does the word "steakhouse" conjure up images of old-school, slightly brusque waiters in white aprons and no frills good-old-boy décor? Well, think again. Staghorn steakhouse takes the bull by its, ahem, horns, and turns it completely on its head. The less-than-thrilling neighborhood may leave something to be desired, but inside this former warehouse is a wondrous space with an Asian-Zen ambience.

The look is modern but the food is classic, with typical sides like mashed potatoes and creamed spinach. Start with tasty baked clams or the Staghorn salad bursting with Roquefort and tomatoes. From well-aged Porterhouse steaks that ooze with juice to thick and meaty Kansas City bone-in sirloin, it's all about the beef to the chic carnivore at this temple.

Stella 34

Italian ✗✗

151 W. 34th St. (entrance at 35th St & Broadway)

Subway: 34 St - Herald Sq
Phone: 212-967-9251
Web: www.patinagroup.com
Prices: $$

Lunch & dinner daily

You can find just about anything your heart desires at Macy's flagship Herald Square store, but *pizza Napolitana*? Oh yes, as well as many other Italian delights at this recently installed trattoria accessed by a dedicated elevator for the six story ride. Step inside to find a spacious layout with large, bright windows and a lush color scheme. A winding counter fronts the open kitchen equipped with three wood-burning ovens. Run by the Patina Restaurant Group, this dining room tempts with much more than great pizza. Enjoy a rousing array of starters like escarole wilted on the grill; and a fantastic pasta lineup, like *strozzapreti con seppie*, squid-ink tinted twists and tender cuttlefish coated in creamy red pepper sauce sprinkled with breadcrumbs.

Sugiyama

C1

251 W. 55th St. (bet. Broadway & Eighth Ave.)

Subway: 57 St - 7 Av
Phone: 212-956-0670
Web: www.sugiyama-nyc.com
Prices: $$$

Dinner Tue – Sat

On the outside, nothing screams unique about this spot. But, it is sage to never judge a book by its cover, so stay awhile. Amid construction sites, parking lots, and traffic, find warm and demure Sugiyama. Make your way inside its narrow hallway to a warm, welcoming earthy-toned haven replete with rock gardens.

Transporting you further into Japanese comfort are bamboo lamps hanging from boughs and an open kitchen starring the master Nao Sugiyama as he moves in slow, steady precision. Perhaps observe him preparing a modern kaiseki including monkfish liver, braised baby squid, and a snow crab-radish roll. Smoky toro and creamy uni are presented beside a fragrant red snapper dashi and followed by wonderful Wagyu beef paired with garlic chips.

Sushi Zen

C3

108 W. 44th St. (bet. Broadway & Sixth Ave.)

Subway: 42 St - Bryant Pk
Phone: 212-302-0707
Web: www.sushizen-ny.com
Prices: $$$

Lunch Mon – Fri
Dinner Mon – Sat

Sushi Zen's peaceful interior and intimate scale is a welcomed contrast to its high traffic location. High ceilings and pale earthy hues combine for a soothing look that is accentuated by wood flooring, stone, and an artful tangle of branches.

From behind the u-shaped bar, Chef Toshio Suzuki's team doles out a wide-ranging assortment that might kick off with refreshing wilted spinach *oshitashi*, cooled in dashi and topped with toasted sesame seeds. A colorful seaweed salad is dressed with nasal passage-clearing pickled wasabi skin and *tosazu*, combining rice vinegar, dashi, and soy sauce. The daily nigiri platter has featured generous slices of Spanish mackerel, raw scallop, and black sea bass; as well as very tasty diced tuna and scallion *gunkan-maki*.

Szechuan Gourmet

C3

Chinese ✗

21 W. 39th St. (bet. Fifth & Sixth Aves.)

Subway: 42 St - Bryant Pk

Phone: 212-921-0233

Web: N/A

Prices: $$

Lunch & dinner daily

It doesn't matter that Szechuan Gourmet is buried among storefronts, because half of Manhattan knows to come here for its devilish repertoire of Szechuan specialties. The entryway is used to corral waiting guests and take-away orders. Separated by a glass wall, the dining area has its own energy and is sparingly embellished with red lanterns, white tablecloths, and a highly trafficked carpet.

Focus on the regional specialties and you will eat very well. Picture heaps of *dan dan* noodles clutching wok-fried ground pork in pools of chili oil. Plump and tender prawns are stir-fried with asparagus and green onion, dressed with more pork and chili oil; while camphor tea-smoked duck, neatly hacked into nibble-sized pieces, is absolutely mouthwatering.

Taboon

C1

Middle Eastern ✗✗

773 Tenth Ave. (at 52nd St.)

Subway: 50 St (Eighth Ave.)

Phone: 212-713-0271

Web: www.taboononline.com

Prices: $$

Lunch Sun
Dinner nightly

This far western neighborhood gem offers an always pleasant vibe and enticing air courtesy of the brick-walled, wood-burning oven (*taboon*) that greets entering guests and sets the whitewashed interior aglow. The crackling logs, fronted by neatly arranged platters of produce, exude a rustic mien and fuse deftly with the food and philosophy.

Fresh from *taboon* to table, rip into the house-made focaccia and await the lot of enticing specialties. Linger abroad with the likes of charred octopus confit with hearth-roasted apples and pickled cucumber; or succulent osso buco of lamb glossed with a meaty reduction, atop a pile of bulgur wheat. A solid dining feat, Taboon is a pioneer of sorts in fusing Middle Eastern and Mediterranean flavors.

Tang Pavilion

Chinese ✗✗

65 W. 55th St. (bet. Fifth & Sixth Aves.)

Subway: 57 St
Phone: 212-956-6888
Web: www.tangpavilionchinese.com
Prices: $$

Lunch & dinner daily

It's not easy to be a favorite spot in a city of constant change, and Tang Pavilion has been succeeding for decades. This Chinese classic raised the bar when it first appeared on the scene and hasn't changed course since. In fact, they've garnered quite a following, but Tang shines thanks to its tasty Shanghainese fare.

Snub the regular offerings and request their menu of "Shanghai specialties," faraway and well above the passé standards. Mauve walls and banquette rows spill into a large room graced with jacketed servers carrying around plates of steamed lamb jelly infused with five-spice and other aromatics; ribbons of dried tofu tossed with crunchy soy beans and sweet, tender pork; and a giant, buttery sea cucumber frilled with dry shrimp roe.

Tavola

Italian ✗

488 Ninth Ave. (bet. 37th & 38th Sts.)

Subway: 42 St - Port Authority Bus Terminal
Phone: 212-273-1181
Web: www.tavolahellskitchen.com
Prices: $$

Lunch Mon – Fri
Dinner nightly

This Clinton pizza and pasta spot is housed in the former Manganaro's Grosseria Italiano, a family-run emporium dating back to 1893. A year after its closing, Chef Nicola Accardi has respectfully repurposed this setting as a convivial destination for an under-served area.

Bright and clean but boasting the patina of its long existence, the dining room now greets guest with a wall of Italian products and skylit pizza station. Here, a wood-burning pizza oven crafted from volcanic clay (from Mt. Vesuvius) produces ten varieties of thin-crust pizza, like the *Calabresa bona*— sporting crushed tomato, fresh mozzarella, dabs of creamy ricotta, basil, and hot slices of *soppressata* from neighboring Esposito's. Pastas include a very fine lasagna *della casa*.

Toloache

Mexican ✗✗

251 W. 50th St. (bet. Broadway & Eighth Ave.)

Subway: 50 St (Broadway) Lunch & dinner daily
Phone: 212-581-1818
Web: www.toloachenyc.com
Prices: $$

Mexican dining is at its hottest in New York, with many thanks to the unstoppable team behind the uniquely authentic Toloache, Yerba Buena, and their other rapidly expanding outposts. Here in midtown, this two-story restaurant is decked in Talavera tiles, wood-beam ceilings, and stunning copper and tin lanterns.

A pleasure from start to finish, try the outrageously good house specialty, the *chapulines* taco, filled with Oaxacan-style dried grasshoppers. Tamer tastes can chose from an array of brick oven-fired quesadillas or ceviches, perhaps followed by flan with coffee-caramel sauce and fresh berry pico de gallo.

A serious list of divine margaritas and over 100 tequilas is on offer—all worthy bar mates to more than a dozen varieties of mescal.

Trattoria Dell'Arte

Italian ✗✗

900 Seventh Ave. (bet. 56th & 57th Sts.)

Subway: 57 St - 7 Av Lunch Mon – Sat
Phone: 212-245-9800 Dinner nightly
Web: www.trattoriadellarte.com
Prices: $$$

There's a downright contagious exuberance to Shelly Firemen's always-packed Carnegie Hall classic, Trattoria Dell'Arte. It might be the smart, confident service staff, or the overflowing, recession-be-damned antipasto bar. Perhaps it's the cheeky welcome motto ("What's Italian for Carnegie Hall? Trattoria Dell'Arte."), or the Tuscan-styled rooms lined with mahogany wine racks and dripping candles? Whatever it is, people keep returning time and again.

Expect to pay—maybe a bit too steeply—for this kind of *io non lo so*, but the flaky, thin-crust pizzas and heady dishes of finely sauced pastas do not disappoint. Save room for irresistible Italian desserts like an airy cheesecake wrapped in chocolate sponge cake and topped with piping-hot chocolate ganache.

21 Club

American ✗✗

21 W. 52nd St. (bet. Fifth & Sixth Aves.)

Subway: 5 Av - 53 St
Phone: 212-582-7200
Web: www.21club.com
Prices: $$$

Lunch Tue – Fri
Dinner Mon – Sat

The fabled 21 Club has been in business for over 83 years, but there's nothing slowing it down. Opened originally as a speakeasy, this NYC institution has wined and dined everyone from movie stars and moguls to moneyed city folk. From its lantern-holding jockeys and townhouse exterior to its leather and wood-paneled dining room that feels like a step back in time, 21 Club is a classic through and through.

The menu is a perfect accompaniment to the setting with choices like seared foie gras tinged with mango chutney and spread atop toasted brioche; or a splendid and classic rendition of steak tartare paired with a green salad. Upstairs and in the back, the feel is formal—so for a casual bite with prettier prices, head off the main entrance to Bar 21.

Utsav

Indian ✗✗

1185 Sixth Ave. (entrance on 46th St.)

Subway: 47-50 Sts - Rockefeller Ctr
Phone: 212-575-2525
Web: www.utsavny.com
Prices: ⊜⊜

Lunch & dinner daily

Meaning "festival" in Sanskrit, Utsav is an upscale hideaway perched on a suspended corridor between two office buildings. The ground floor features a bar and small plaza with outdoor seating, while the second floor dining room is spacious and has walls covered with floor-to-ceiling windows. Swathes of gold fabric along the ceiling embellish the well-maintained space.

The wallet-friendly and overflowing lunch buffet brings office workers in by the droves, and the early evening prix-fixe is popular with the pre-theater crowd. To whet the appetite, start with a small bite like potato croquettes drizzled in tamarind. Then, move on to *murg xaccutti*, a coconut-rich chicken curry from Goa; or *bhindi subju*—okra simmered with tomato, onion, ginger, and cumin.

West Bank Café

American ✕✕

B2

407 W. 42nd St. (bet. Ninth & Tenth Aves.)

Subway: 42 St - Port Authority Bus Terminal
Phone: 212-695-6909
Web: www.westbankcafe.com
Prices: $$

Lunch & dinner daily

Nowadays, the Theater District is a sea of glass-wrapped condo towers, new hotels, and flocks of families on their way to a Disney production. This beloved neighborhood mainstay has kept its head above the choppy waters of Manhattan's dining scene since 1978 by offering its distinctly comforting and progressive American food at honest prices.

The vibe is lively and warm so settle into a plush leather banquettes and enjoy the pleasant hum of jazz (check for live entertainment downstairs). Come for brunch and try the stack of light yet richly flavored lemon ricotta pancakes, with perfectly ripe berries and real maple syrup. At dinner, choose from a trio of pastas or entrées like grilled Scottish salmon with lentils and chorizo vinaigrette.

Yakitori Totto

Japanese ✕

C1

251 W. 55th St. (bet. Broadway & Eighth Ave.)

Subway: 57 St - 7 Av
Phone: 212-245-4555
Web: www.tottonyc.com
Prices: $$

Lunch Mon – Fri
Dinner nightly

As if it were hiding from its brassy surrounds, Yakitori Totto is discreetly set up a narrow, steep flight of stairs. Inside, this faithful *yakitori-ya* is buzzing with diners, polished wooden tables, and a soundtrack ranging from J-pop to jazz. Two glassed-in private rooms shield subdued groups from the sultry and hip vibe.

Yakitori Totto is devoutly devoted to grilled meats and treats. Tended by prompt servers, the front counter and grill station dominates with parcels of *gyoza* and *tako waso*, octopus massaged with salty wasabi. Best to arrive early for authentic and irresistible treats like *sunagimo*, *reba*, *kawa*, *bonchiri* (gizzard, liver, and skin crested with sea salt); *ton toro* (pork neck skewers); and *momo*, juicy chicken thighs with soy *tare*.

SoHo & Nolita

SoHo (South of Houston) and Nolita (North of Little Italy) prove not only that New York has a penchant for portmanteaus, but also that the downtown "scene" lives on now more than ever. What remains new and ever-changing are the subtle transformations that redefine these neighborhoods block-by-block. Despite the retail invasion that has taken over some of SoHo's eastern corners, it remains true to its promise of sun-drenched restaurants and open-air cafés filled with European sophisticates and supermodels lingering over salads. There are also plenty of tourists to admire them.

Shopping in SoHo

Those fortunate enough to live in what were once artists' lofts (now multimillion dollar condos) know that there are still a few foodie gems in this area. For your at-home tapas needs, **Despaña** offers Spanish foods (and rare wines next door) as well as delicacies from oil-packed tuna to mouthwatering *bocadillos*. They will even prepare a traditional tortilla Española with advance notice. A visit to **Pino's Prime Meat Market** (that carries some of the best meat in town) or **Parisi Bakery**, (their prosciutto rolls are par excellence) should be followed by a visit to the original **Dean and Deluca**, filled with the cities favorite cakes, pastries, and coffees. Some others may opt for **Little Cupcake Bake Shop** on Prince Street for a mind-boggling array of sweets. For international home accessories, head to **Global Table** whose exquisite selection emphasizes simple lines and vivid finishes. On Hudson Square, **City Winery** gives urban wine enthusiasts a place to make their own private-label wine by providing the grapes, the barrels, the storage, and the expertise.

NOLITA

Farther east is Nolita—an area as cool as its name. This is where a slightly hipper and hungrier downtown set flock. These locals aren't living the typical midtown nine-to-five life and shun the *je ne sais quoi* of SoHo in favor of small spots that begin with the word "café." At the top of this list is **Café Habana**, offering its casual crowds a gritty diner vibe and amazing Mexico City-style corn on the cob (also available for takeout next door at **Café Habana To Go**). Equally coveted hangouts rife with hip hordes include **Café Gitane**, serving French-Moroccan cuisine. The ethos in Nolita is focused: do a single thing very well. This may have been inspired by **Lombardi's**, which claims to be America's very first pizzeria (founded in 1905) and still has lines outside the door. **Hoomoos Asli**'s setting and service may be basic, but they clearly put much effort into the outstanding hummus,

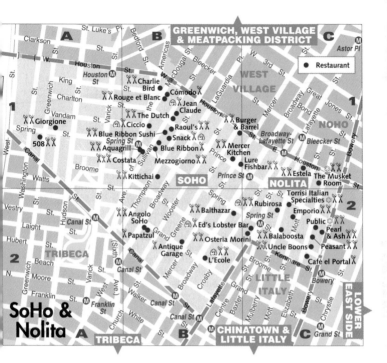

SoHo & Nolita

- GREENWICH, WEST VILLAGE & MEATPACKING DISTRICT
- Restaurant
- WEST VILLAGE
- NOHO
- SOHO
- NOLITA
- TRIBECA
- LITTLE ITALY
- LOWER EAST SIDE
- CHINATOWN & LITTLE ITALY

Charlie Bird • Cómodo • Jean Claude • Rouge et Blanc • The Dutch • Giorgione • Blue Ribbon Sushi • Raoul's • Snack • Burger & Barrel • Broadway-Lafayette St • 508 • Aquagrill • Blue Ribbon • Mercer Kitchen • Costata • Mezzogiorno • Lure Fishbar • Estela • The Musket Room • Kittichai • Rubirosa • Torrisi Italian Specialties • Angolo SoHo • Balthazar • Emporio • Public • Pearl & Ash • Papatzul • Ed's Lobster Bar • Balaboosta • Peasant • Antique Garage • Osteria Morini • Uncle Boons • Café el Portal • L'École • Ciccio

fluffy pitas, and crispy falafels to accompany those tart, fresh lemonades. **Pinche Taqueria** is where you should head for the best fish tacos this side of California, but if whiling away the afternoon in an aromatic bakery better suits your mood, then sojourn at **Dominique Ansel's Bakery** where the pastry chef who worked with Daniel Boulud is now fulfilling his own dessert dreams with deliciously addictive cronuts—crafted from equal parts doughnut and croissant! Date-night duos might seal the deal at stylish **Pappabubble**, whose candies are created with an eye-popping sense of design. With equal ingenuity and old-school flair, **Rice to Riches** serves its celebrated bowls of decadent rice pudding with creatively named toppings, like "Mischief" (buttery graham crackers) or "Nudge" (chilled espresso and cocoa). Cheesecake connoisseurs take note that **Eileen's Cheesecake** has been chasing those Junior's fanatics back to Brooklyn. Even between feedings, this locale promises to nurture your inner epicurean with a visit to the Bowery for its throng of unrefined kitchen supply stores. One of the greater challenges Nolita poses is the decision of where to end the day. Tucked into these streets are snug bars, each with its own sleek city feel, *sans* the masses besetting other neighborhoods. Date-like places such as **Pravda** with its thrilling range of vodkas or **Sweet & Vicious** for stellar libations, are a fitting finale.

Angolo SoHo

Italian ✗✗

331 West Broadway (at Grand St.)

Subway: Canal St (Sixth Ave.)
Phone: 212-203-1722
Web: www.angolosoho.com
Prices: $$

Dinner nightly

 With its stylish layout and impressive cuisine, Angolo SoHo is excellent from any angle. This sparkling room features a fetching white marble bar with wood stools and cocktail tables dotted with bright orange chairs on one side; the other side is a dining room spotlighting snazzy artwork and a tufted black banquette running the length of the wall.

Take the time to indulge in the likes of griddle-seared sweetbreads with blueberry compote and piney rosemary over parsley root purée; or fresh fusilli tossed in a perfectly braised pork ragù and finished with basil chiffonade. The grilled bone-in pork chop is a hefty and juicy sensation, served over caramelized baby fennel, drizzled with honey vinaigrette, and surrounded with hot cherry peppers.

Antique Garage

Turkish ✗

41 Mercer St. (bet. Broome & Grand Sts.)

Subway: Canal St (Broadway)
Phone: 212-219-1019
Web: www.antiquegaragesoho.com
Prices: $$

Lunch & dinner daily

 Let the sultry sounds of live jazz lure you into this little Bohemian hot spot, performed by a trio of old-school jazz cats—and absolutely free. The seduction continues inside, where exposed brick walls, high ceilings, low lighting, and a collection of charming antiques and photos make the perfect setting for a rendezvous or a quiet meal.

A nice selection of cocktails as well as Turkish white and red wines pair up perfectly with the likes of *circassian* chicken (shredded and served with tangy walnut sauce); *sarma* (thick slices of halloumi cheese topped with tomatoes and thyme and wrapped in pickled grape leaves, then grilled); or to end, dry and sweet apricots, stuffed with cream, *kaymak*, and almonds. Food is served up with genuine happiness.

Aquagrill

Seafood ✗✗

B1

210 Spring St. (at Sixth Ave.)

Subway: Spring St (Sixth Ave.)
Phone: 212-274-0505
Web: www.aquagrill.com
Prices: $$

Lunch & dinner daily

Aquagrill is a SoHo fixture that keeps out of the spotlight. Despite its ordinary façade and snug interior, it is *the* best place in town for impeccably fresh oysters. And if that doesn't float your boat, find prawns, clams, and sea urchin on their excellent "Seafood Plateau Royale." Unique Loire valley whites complement this bivalve-centric menu that is widely adored by all who flock to this sophisticated space.

Every item of décor pays homage to the menu's focus—seafood and oysters. While it can get cramped inside and on the enclosed deck, patrons continue to queue up for steamed sumptuous whelks with a cayenne aïoli; bouillabaisse with poached Casco cod and lobster in a garlic-saffron-tomato bath; and pumpkin pie with *schlag* for a spicy finale.

Balaboosta

Middle Eastern ✗✗

C2

214 Mulberry St. (bet. Prince & Spring Sts.)

Subway: Spring St (Lafayette St.)
Phone: 212-966-7366
Web: www.balaboostanyc.com
Prices: $$

Lunch Tue – Sun
Dinner nightly

This bright, friendly Middle Eastern café keeps its keen eye on Sephardic Jewish traditions. The room feels cozy and rustic, with windows framing Mulberry Street sidewalks, inlaid wood tables, and walls lined with books and wine bottles. A bar mixes cocktails and pours an inexpensive yet interesting list of organic wines.

The dynamic, all-female kitchen is on full display as they deep-fry green olives and set them atop *labne* with drizzles of harissa oil; toss ribbons of deep-burgundy beet pasta; or blend smoky-creamy eggplant with spices and tahini, then slather it over toasted sour dough with a vividly green herb salad. The hearty Moroccan fish *cazuela* may arrive as a rich and fiery tagine with pepper-paprika sauce, preserved lemon, and chickpeas.

Balthazar

French **×× ×**

B2

80 Spring St. (bet. Broadway & Crosby St.)

Subway: Spring St (Lafayette St.)   Lunch & dinner daily
Phone: 212-965-1414
Web: www.balthazarny.com
Prices: **$$$**

With its legendary red awning and brassy good looks, Keith McNally's ageless downtown darling has been a joyous zoo ever since it opened its doors in 1997.

All of this means that reservations are highly recommended, though there are a few ways to dodge the prime-time problems. Bar tables are open to walk-ins; breakfast hours are lovely; and the bakery next door serves scrumptious salads, sandwiches, and pastries to-go (not to mention devastating hot chocolate). At the restaurant, classic bistro fare abounds in a rotating list of daily specials, from trout on Monday to Sunday's *choucroute*. Of course, anyone seeking that timelessly Balthazar experience should attempt the towering feast of chilled oysters and *fruits de mer*—a true must-have.

Blue Ribbon

Contemporary **×**

B1

97 Sullivan St. (bet. Prince & Spring Sts.)

Subway: Spring St (Sixth Ave.)   Dinner nightly
Phone: 212-274-0404
Web: www.blueribbonrestaurants.com
Prices: **$$$**

Every New Yorker without a 9-5 job knows that Blue Ribbon serves food until 4 A.M. and is hailed as a chef's canteen for good reason. This classic bistro is genuinely hospitable, lacks pretense, and deserves every bit of its success. The tiny, square space has remained relatively unchanged through the years, and bar seats are still a hot commodity.

The food here is somewhat simple, very memorable, and reliably excellent. Start with the likes of shellfish in smoky dashi broth, bobbing with enoki mushrooms, cilantro, and cubes of white fish spiced with jalapeño. Their fried chicken with silky mashed potatoes and collard greens is a crowd-pleasing platter of pure comfort. The flourless chocolate cake is moist, decadent, and everything you want it to be.

Manhattan ▶ SoHo & Nolita

Blue Ribbon Sushi

Japanese ✗✗

B1

119 Sullivan St. (bet. Prince & Spring Sts.)

Subway: Spring St (Sixth Ave.) Lunch & dinner daily
Phone: 212-343-0404
Web: www.blueribbonrestaurants.com
Prices: $$$

Set below street level and just down the block from its eldest sibling, Blue Ribbon Sushi is the famous and successful stalwart whose formula has been reproduced many times over. A sushi bar displays colorful sake bottles and premium spirits as it dominates the space outfitted with polished tables and low, wood-covered ceilings.

While the staff is happy to explain each dish and more Americanized options are available, this is absolutely a place where the $85 omakase is a downright steal. The menu proudly divides its offerings into the *Taiheiyo* ("Pacific") such as the spotted *kohada* atop gently vinegared rice, or a sweet and briny giant clam; and the *Taiseiyo* ("Atlantic"), perhaps featuring fluke fin or spicy lobster knuckle encasing savory egg.

Burger & Barrel

American ✗✗

B1

25 W. Houston St. (at Greene St.)

Subway: Broadway - Lafayette St Lunch & dinner daily
Phone: 212-334-7320
Web: www.burgerandbarrel.com
Prices: $$

It should come as no surprise that Burger & Barrel is busier than a barrel of monkeys. After all, it comes from the same owners that have worked their magic with the lovely Locanda Verde and Lure. Inside, it's as tight as it is cool with a classic pub feel. You won't be able to have a private conversation, but the eavesdropping is fantastic!

Renowned burgers (like the Puebla) deserve the headline, with tasty toppings like red onion relish, roasted chili peppers, and creamy *queso fresco*, though there is more to this menu than meat. Comforting favorites go on to include fried chicken and sides like corn pudding or polenta fries. Desserts are to drool over—the salty peanut butter-brownie sundae is a perfect way to round out a heart-stopping meal here.

Café el Portal

C2

174 Elizabeth St. (bet. Kenmare & Spring Sts.)

Subway: Spring St (Lafayette St.)   Lunch & dinner Mon – Sat
Phone: 212-226-4642
Web: N/A
Prices:

 Be thankful, Nolita natives. Given the mass of hip, overpriced joints around, it's a minor miracle that this well-run charmer firing up excellently economical Mexican food continues to thrive. Inside, find bright kitschy walls, thumping tunes, and sweet service; so snag a spot at one of the few tables and get noshing.

Comforting *sopa de pollo* with vegetables, cilantro, and tortilla strips is a fine way to start; followed by *tacos de camaron* stuffed with shrimp, shredded lettuce, *queso*, and onion. The fiery *tinga* quesadilla will set your taste buds ablaze with beef marinated in smoky chipotle sauce and tucked into corn tortillas with *tomatillo* sauce.

Spawned from the same team, Peix bar de Mariscos is a popular spot for seafood "tapas" and more.

Charlie Bird

Italian

B1

5 King St. (at Sixth Ave.)

Subway: Houston St   Dinner Tue – Sun
Phone: 212-235-7133
Web: www.charliebirdnyc.com
Prices: $$

Simply put, Charlie Bird is an excellent restaurant. Located on the outer edge of SoHo, this "Italian influenced, American executed and entirely New York" establishment couldn't have picked a more fitting headline. The bi-level newcomer has a full bar and comfy tables on the lower level; yellow banquettes straddle the slightly elevated area. Huge windows, street art, and retro tunes appeal to the hip crowds.

On the menu, find clever dishes like *chitarra nero*, squid ink pasta tossed in a creamy crab sauce spiked with *peperoncino*; and spring peas simmered in butter with salty, fatty *guanciale*. Rigatoni with veal ragù proves the kitchen is serious; and grilled black bass with olives, fennel, and *olio santo* has flavors so bright, they may come to life.

Manhattan ▶ SoHo & Nolita

Ciccio

✕

B1

190 Sixth Ave. (bet. Prince & Vandam Sts.)

Subway: Spring St (Sixth Ave.)   Lunch & dinner Tue – Sun
Phone: 646-476-9498
Web: www.ciccionyc.com
Prices: $$

Chef and owner Giacomo Romano defines this brilliant little *alimentaria* as a place where patrons can find an ever-changing menu day or night. Here, that wonderful formula might mean pastry and *caffè* in the morning, ribollita at lunch, or fresh pasta for dinner. Step inside to find a sun-drenched space outfitted with blonde wood tables, white-washed brick walls, and wood beams.

Expertly prepared dishes include *polpo e ceci*, tender, charred octopus atop chickpea-thyme purée served with fresh bread; a trio of crostini with toppings like lentil and mushroom pâté or tomato, garlic, and oregano; or homemade *tagliatelle* with *polpettine* (tiny meatballs) in tomato ragù. For a fantastic conclusion, try the almond-chocolate tart with mascarpone cream.

Cómodo

✕

B1

58 MacDougal St. (at King St.)

Subway: Houston St   Lunch & dinner Tue – Sun
Phone: 646-370-4477
Web: www.comodonyc.com
Prices: $$

After a year of hosting Thursday night "pop-up dinner parties" at their TriBeCa apartment, Chef Felipe Donnelly and his wife, Tamy Rofe, seamlessly transferred their labor of love into this storybook enterprise. Quarters are small and cozy, as diners and staff chat with warm familiarity, lending to the welcoming vibe.

Squeeze into one of the communal tables and get started with juicy lamb sliders on Brazilian cheese bread with chipotle cream sauce; or warm kale and quinoa salad tossed with shiitake mushrooms, dried blueberries, feta cheese, and aged balsamic. Dive into the fantastic three-potato *ajiaco* soup with pulled chicken, sweet corn, avocado, capers, and cilantro; or the *picanha*, a dry-aged Newport steak atop rice and stewed greens.

Costata

B1

Steakhouse

206 Spring St. (bet. Sixth Ave & Sullivan St.)

Subway: Spring St (Sixth Ave.) Dinner nightly
Phone: 212-334-3320
Web: www.costatanyc.com
Prices: $$$$

Prolific Chef Michael White has returned to the spot where he first made it big. Marking a moderate departure from his Italian-focused directive is this steakhouse set in what once was Fiamma. This multi-level setting has been recalibrated to shield patrons in a wood- and stone-adorned dining room complete with colorfully captivating artwork.

Aged for 40 days, Black Angus beef is the anchor of the menu which also offers cuts like the *tagliata* (a bone-in NY strip) paired with porcini sugo—a pleasing feast for two. Anyone familiar with Chef White's handiwork knows his tremendous skill with pasta; so relish in fresh *rigatoni alla contadina* tossed with a smooth tomato basil sauce and *polpettine*, subtly sweetened by mortadella and prosciutto.

The Dutch

B1

American

131 Sullivan St. (at Prince St.)

Subway: Spring St (Lafayette St.) Lunch & dinner daily
Phone: 212-677-6200
Web: www.thedutchnyc.com
Prices: $$$

Chef Andrew Carmellini's ode to New York in The Dutch is as truly American and distinct as the three rooms it fills nightly. Expect to see Keith Haring among other iconic artists on the walls, handrails inspired by famed local horse stables, and seasonal accents like a vibrant cornucopia strewn throughout. The front rooms are hopping and lure with an oyster bar, while the reservation-only back dining room is warmed with a wood-burning fire.

Start with pleasing appetizers like crisp flatbread paired with creamy-smoky eggplant dip spiced with za'tar, before moving onto a perfect plate of fried chicken with honey-buttered biscuits and cool slaw. Their daily pies are not to be missed, as in the fragrant apple-concord grape in a supremely flakey crust.

Ed's Lobster Bar

Seafood

C2

222 Lafayette St. (bet. Kenmare & Spring Sts.)

Subway: Spring St (Lafayette St.)
Phone: 212-343-3236
Web: www.lobsterbarnyc.com
Prices: $$

Lunch & dinner daily

The delicacy and purity of seafood is epitomized in cute and convivial Ed's Lobster Bar. A sunny yet cool space with a good mix of food-savvy NYers, Ed's is that ideal sanctum for anyone who wishes to escape to New England for an hour.

As if to ease the no-reservations policy, this saltwater gem offers a fine choice of seafood-friendly wines and beers that go down as smoothly as the oysters. The narrow space is dotted with tables, but true cheer is found at the marble bar. While side dishes are all enticing, faves like perfectly fried calamari; creamy and luscious chowder with succulent clams; and the stellar buttery lobster roll (piled with juicy meat tossed in mayo, celery, and dill) aside crispy fries and Ed's homemade pickles are sheer decadence.

Emporio

Italian

C2

231 Mott St. (bet. Prince & Spring Sts.)

Subway: Spring St (Lafayette St.)
Phone: 212-966-1234
Web: www.auroraristorante.com
Prices: $$

Lunch & dinner daily

Although Emporio neighbors other exciting spots, it remains a well-loved alternative to the countless cafés that dominate these SoHo blocks. This noisy yet attractive restaurant showers its pretty patrons with a warm welcome and heaps of attention. Decorative touches include a profusion of reclaimed wood, subway tiles, and a seductive glow. The requisite wood-burning oven sits in the back room outfitted with a skylight and beautiful open kitchen.

Forever focused on organically driven dishes, the kitchen turns out the likes of *le pappardelle*, ribbons of chestnut pasta tossed with mushrooms and *pecorino Sardo*; *la passera*, roasted fluke crested with fennel and Brussels sprouts; and a silky *torta di latticello* frilled with berries and maple syrup.

Estela

C1

47 E. Houston St. (at Mulberry St.)

Subway: Broadway - Lafayette St

Phone: 212-219-7693

Web: www.estelanyc.com

Prices: $$$

Dinner Mon – Sat

Chef Ignacio Mattos is back from Brooklyn and makes his debut at this second-floor SoHo spot. Estela's exterior is fashionably scuffed and above a bar; inside, the minimalist dining room features white globe lights above neat wood tables, wild flowers, and a copper tub set with ice and bubbly. The white marble bar is lively and the kitchen can be boisterous.

Begin with contemporary bites like poached egg with meaty *gigante* beans and wonderfully fishy tuna floating atop a warm, savory broth. Then, relish a thick fillet of cod, crisped on the edge, laid atop garlicky mashed potatoes and fresh lettuce. Finish with a deconstructed, deliciously boozy *baba* layering cubes of brandy-soaked cake with excellent crème anglaise and crunchy cocoa nibs.

508

A1

508 Greenwich St. (at Spring St.)

Subway: Spring St (Sixth Ave.)

Phone: 212-219-2444

Web: www.508nyc.com

Prices: $$

Lunch Mon – Fri
Dinner nightly

This western edge of SoHo teems with trading tycoons mingled with music moguls—think Jay-Z arm-in-arm with Beyoncé and Blue Ivy. From cobblestoned streets dotted with delightful watering holes to luxury condominiums, this otherworldly locale seems to have it all, including 508, a contemporary and intricate little American favorite.

It's all very quaint and casual inside with a modest décor of exposed brick, communal tables, and cozy armchairs. However, their beer list is anything but meek, and couples perfectly with a flatbread pizza spread with homemade spicy tomato sauce and wild boar smoked sausage. Goat "sloppy joe" sliders are wonderfully tender, but reach epic status when matched with short rib-stuffed peppers capped with creamy Manchego.

Giorgione

Italian ✗✗

307 Spring St. (bet. Greenwich & Hudson Sts.)

Subway: Spring St (Sixth Ave.) Lunch Mon – Fri
Phone: 212-352-2269 Dinner nightly
Web: www.giorgionenyc.com
Prices: $$

Owned and founded by jovial Giorgio Deluca (of Dean & Deluca), this long-time resident of Spring Street has become a SoHo destination, maintaining a loyal following and impressive longevity.

Excellent pastas and knock-out pizzas are spot on, but save room for the glorious array of house-made desserts. Start with a fresh fava salad tossed with crispy escarole, mint, pecorino, lemon, and olive oil; then roll up your sleeves for a choice of seasonal fresh pastas, like *garganelli con ragù di coniglio*, with its fragrant ragù of tender rabbit, tomatoes, earthy mushrooms, white wine, and the unmistakable scent of juniper berries. Finish off with a divine *crostata di albicocca*— flaky crust topped with poached apricots, almond cream, and mascarpone.

Jean Claude

French ✗

137 Sullivan St. (bet. Houston & Prince Sts.)

Subway: Spring St (Sixth Ave.) Dinner nightly
Phone: 212-475-9232
Web: www.jeanclauderestaurant.com
Prices: $$

With its tight-knit tables, lived-in good looks, and soft French music quietly thrumming in the background, this romantic little bistro could be straight off of Paris' Left Bank. Luckily for Manhattan, though, the infinitely charming Jean Claude is smack in the middle of SoHo.

In winter, the room is decidedly cozy; while summer finds the front windows thrown open and couples lingering over the reasonably priced wine list, which boasts a nice carafe and half-carafe list. The French cooking is straightforward and delicious, with a solid lineup of bistro staples like tender *moules marinieres* and frites; seared hanger steak in a thyme, red wine and shallot reduction, paired with a sinful *gratin dauphinois*; and a spot-on rendition of crème brûlée.

Manhattan ▲ SoHo & Nolita

325

Kittichai

Asian ✗✗

B1

60 Thompson St. (bet. Broome & Spring Sts.)

Subway: Spring St (Sixth Ave.)
Phone: 212-219-2000
Web: www.kittichairestaurant.com
Prices: $$$

Lunch Sat – Sun
Dinner nightly

When Kittichai hit the scene at SoHo's ultra-hip Thomson Hotel, it was all the rage. Its popularity may have leveled and the Thai menu may cater to the western palate, yet the food remains impressive. The space itself is an absolute knockout. From its trendy lounge, theatrical silk accents, pond with floating candles, and handsome tables, Kittichai flaunts first-rate finesse.

Allow yourself to be diverted from the décor for a moment to contemplate the sweetness of Nantucket bay scallops with cucumber-galangal espuma and cilantro pearls. Or, try the sensational risotto folded with sweet, creamy uni, brilliantly strewn with pickled mussels and cucumber ribbons. Fresh snapper sashimi is lively and light, with grassy-green vinaigrette, cashews, and roe.

L'Ecole 😊

French ✗✗

B2

462 Broadway (at Grand St.)

Subway: Canal St (Broadway)
Phone: 212-219-3300
Web: www.lecolenyc.com
Prices: $$

Lunch daily
Dinner Mon – Sat

Inspired and led by the dedicated students of the International Culinary Center, L'Ecole's creations are naturally insightful; even a dish that feels over-the-top illustrates their desire to succeed. It is a lovely room–welcoming and affable–with an earnest staff. Decorated with colorful walls, black-and-white photos, and circular fixtures, the space feels festive. The large glass windows overlook a bustling intersection, and people-watchers vie for these seats.

The menu features delicious classics, as promised by the surrounding "oohs and aahs." Pretty tables are set with finery, enhancing that roasted spiced monkfish atop green lentils; cured Spanish mackerel beside a warm potato salad; and a gooey chocolate almond cake laced by lemon cream.

Lure Fishbar

Seafood ✕✕

B1

142 Mercer St. (at Prince St.)

Subway: Prince St
Phone: 212-431-7676
Web: www.lurefishbar.com
Prices: $$$

Lunch & dinner daily

Housed in the basement of the popular Prada showroom, Lure Fishbar easily has some of the best digs in town. Outside, SoHo's streets might be covered in beautiful, old-school cobblestones and teeming with young gorgeous gazelles, but down here a tiki-trendy-meets-maritime motif (think tropical prints, angular porthole windows, and cozy booths) and fat seafood plates reign supreme.

A mean-looking sushi counter and raw bar lets you know how seriously they take the food, though. A plate of yellowtail carpaccio arrives fresh as can be, topped with garlic-chili sauce, sesame oil, thin slices of avocado, and crispy, deep-fried shallots; while a wickedly fresh branzino is served whole, perfectly de-boned and laced with pesto, scallions, and crunchy shallots.

Mercer Kitchen

Contemporary ✕✕

B1

99 Prince St. (at Mercer St.)

Subway: Prince St
Phone: 212-966-5454
Web: www.jean-georges.com
Prices: $$$

Lunch & dinner daily

From its home in the elegant Mercer Hotel, Jean-Georges' mainstay has been sexing up SoHo for over a decade. Once a stronghold for the famous and the fabulous, Mercer Kitchen still draws a well-heeled, mostly European crowd. The bi-level space splits into a café on the top floor and a dining room and lounge on the lower level, where bare tables, sultry lighting, and brick archways lend an air of swank.

Try a refreshing salad mixing plump, steamed shrimp, avocado, white mushroom, and tomato, tossed in a Champagne vinaigrette; or their classic sashimi-grade tuna spring roll, tucked with a layer of tender Napa cabbage and served with a spicy soy bean purée. Bubbly, crisp pear-and-sour cherry crumble, dolloped with crème frâiche, is divine.

Mezzogiorno

Italian Italian ✗✗

B1

195 Spring St. (at Sullivan St.)

Subway: Spring St (Sixth Ave.)　　　　　　　　Lunch & dinner daily
Phone: 212-334-2112
Web: www.mezzogiorno.com
Prices: $$

Although Mezzogiorno's striking blue awnings arrived on the scene back in the 80s, this pleasing local stalwart has been consistently occupied by pretty people and continues to be a tasteful, timeless SoHo fixture. Those seated inside are charmed by the wood-burning oven, deep-toned wood bar, and walls lined with 100 collages—each one a local artist's unique interpretation of the restaurant's logo.

An Italian-American accent pervades the kitchen's stylish cooking that bursts with flavor. Meals here might include an exceptional *vitello tonnato*, with tuna caught off the coast of Favignana draped with a lusciously creamy sauce, mayo-rich with wonderfully tart, sour capers; and *fiocchetti* pasta stuffed with a beguiling combination of cheeses and pear.

Osteria Morini

Italian ✗✗

C2

218 Lafayette St. (bet. Kenmare & Spring Sts.)

Subway: Spring St (Lafayette St.)　　　　　　　Lunch & dinner daily
Phone: 212-965-8777
Web: www.osteriamorini.com
Prices: $$

True to its roots, simple, and unassuming, Osteria Morini is Chef Michael White's homage to regional Italian cooking, in all its vast and mouthwatering glory. The ambience is cozy and rustic touches abound in exposed bricks, plank ceilings, and wood curios from afar.

The food here is uncompromising and far from commonplace, so expect dishes to be bold and extremely hearty. Taste an ode to Emilia Romagna in the *tortellini in brodo*—each little cap of pasta is perfectly encasing its porky- garlicky- and nutmeg-spiked center. *Porchetta* here arrives as an enormous slab of meat with a crunchy exterior, ultra-soft and succulent center, all folded over sage, rosemary, and garlic, then served alongside acorn squash cubes with crumbled amaretti cookies.

The Musket Room ⁂

Contemporary 🍴🍴

C1

265 Elizabeth St. (bet. Houston & Prince Sts.)

Subway: Broadway - Lafayette St   Dinner nightly
Phone: 212-219-0764
Web: www.themusketroom.com
Prices: $$$

Emily Andrews

In the bourgeois Bohemia that is Nolita, find this clever little spot with a contemporary take on the cuisine of New Zealand. The Musket Room's whitewashed door frames and 19th century name immediately casts it as a reprieve from the neighborhood's ongoing fiesta. Inside, the uniquely urban and modern farmhouse décor combines bright white paint with rough brick walls and views out to the blossoming backyard herb garden, illuminated with string lights. The crowd is hip and more sophisticated than young. Service is so friendly and warm that it seems almost surprising, considering the downtown norm. Their sense of enthusiasm extends right down to the food.

A cold-smoked scallop starter arrives with the sweet meat pulled and shredded into strands, with neat cubes of juicy pear, cucumber rosettes, briny sea beans, and black garlic lending a mellow, pungent note. New Zealand red doe is seasoned with the "flavors of gin" delivered through salted juniper meringues, roasted and puréed fennel, and licorice jus.

Desserts may express a unique beauty and sense of grace, like an artistically presented, fragrant peach with fennel ice cream, dabs of lavender yogurt, puffed rice and candied nuts.

Papatzul

Mexican ✕✕

B2

55 Grand St. (bet. West Broadway & Wooster St.)

Subway: Canal St (Sixth Ave.)   Lunch & dinner daily
Phone: 212-274-8225
Web: www.papatzul.com
Prices: $$

Since its inception, Papatzul has remained a sought-after spot for tasty Mexican food. Just about every table holds a heaping bowl of creamy guacamole, so forget all notions of a diet. It's easy to spot this tiny SoHo storefront—look for a blue banner with the white logo fluttering above the door. Make your way through the glass doors to arrive in the cozy bar, packed with friends sipping sangrias, margaritas, and beers.

The dining room widens beyond the bar, revealing well-spaced wood tables and whitewashed walls adorned with masks. Expect such hearty fare as *sopes con calabaza* (masa cakes with zucchini and mushrooms, topped with goat cheese); *ensalada de nopalitos* with artichokes and fava beans; and churros served with a rich *cajeta* mousse.

Pearl & Ash

Contemporary ✕✕

C2

220 Bowery (bet. Prince & Spring Sts.)

Subway: Bowery   Dinner Mon – Sat
Phone: 212-837-2370
Web: www.pearlandash.com
Prices: $$$

This newest resident of the historic Bowery House is mad stylish. The narrow, dark space is decked with long, intensely populated tables nestled under a wall made of over six-hundred stacked wooden crates displaying antique knickknacks and vintage vases.

The menu is meant for sharing, so bring along your cohorts and nibble on the likes of raw *ama-ebi* with smoked lime yogurt, radish, and bee pollen; and tender skirt steak simmered with ale and onions, and served with sea beans. Brussels sprouts and pearl onions coated with five spice, caramelized, then tossed in buttermilk and lemon juice; or octopus cooked in rice wine and fried to a perfect crisp are equally delightful. Wash this all down with a glass of Red Hook Winery's excellent Cabernet Franc.

Peasant

Italian

C2

194 Elizabeth St. (bet. Prince & Spring Sts.)

Subway: Spring St (Lafayette St.)　　　　Dinner Tue – Sun
Phone: 212-965-9511
Web: www.peasantnyc.com
Prices: $$

Chef and owner Frank DeCarlo keeps getting it right at Peasant—the wine bar downstairs is a perfect mix of cozy and communal, thereby capturing the feeling of being in an authentic *osteria*. But, whether seated upstairs or down, the scene is wholly rustic and genuine, showcasing whitewashed brick walls, bare wood tables, and a roster of expert culinary delights.

Try not to fill up on the terrific bread—save it for sopping up the heavenly razor clams *al forno* simmering in garlic sauce. Every bit of the *maltagliati con coniglio* is a perfect ratio of pasta to braised rabbit and fava beans. *Porchetta arrosto*, their excellent rotisserie suckling pig, is wondrously juicy with hints of garlic and rosemary, served with fingerling potatoes.

Raoul's

French

B1

180 Prince St. (bet. Sullivan & Thompson Sts.)

Subway: Spring St (Sixth Ave.)　　　　Dinner nightly
Phone: 212-966-3518
Web: www.raouls.com
Prices: $$$

Whether by charm or talent, this beloved bistro has survived 30-plus years in one of the fussiest parts of town, somehow remaining popular, sophisticated, and stylishly unpretentious. The authentic French fare is prepared simply, but remains impressive with top ingredients and delicious flavors—as in the steak tartare with quail egg, or seared foie gras with Concord grape purée. The menu, exquisitely handwritten on chalkboards and presented by the amiable waitstaff, still appeals to savvy diners and connoisseurs hungry for meaty steaks and crispy duck fat fries.

The energetic atmosphere in the dimly lit main room is intoxicating, but those seeking a calmer spot for quiet conversation should try the bright upstairs space or tiny covered garden.

Public ✿

C2

Fusion ✗✗

210 Elizabeth St. (bet. Prince & Spring Sts.)

Subway: Spring St (Lafayette St.)
Phone: 212-343-7011
Web: www.public-nyc.com
Prices: $$$

Lunch Sat – Sun
Dinner nightly

Yuki Kuwana

After more than a decade in operation, this gorgeously re-tooled former factory has still got it. Public's meticulous look embraces a sultry, industrial mien that's hard to beat.

Chef Brad Farmerie deserves high praise; few chefs are able to pull off fusion so successfully. His menu is abuzz with creatively interlaced Asian and Mediterranean flavors. Starters include a trio of marinated anchovies nestled atop crisp croquettes made of quinoa and dressed with saffron aïoli. Entrées showcase impressive preparations like Ora King salmon with a wonderfully crisped skin, plated with cauliflower—turmeric-tinted whipped purée and roasted florets seasoned with cumin—as well as charred leeks and pink grapefruit segments. Desserts veer off into a more traditional direction with dark chocolate mousse, and a spot-on rendition of a classic British sticky toffee pudding, served warm, syrupy, and sweet with dried fruit, crowned by Armagnac ice cream.

The drinks program deserves a concentrated once-over for its collection of Australian and New Zealand wines, sake, and offering of mixed drinks and alcohol-free concoctions. The Daily is Public's cozy lounge serving finely crafted cocktails and nibbles.

Rouge et Blanc

Contemporary ✗✗

B1

48 MacDougal St. (bet. Houston & Prince Sts.)

Subway: Houston St
Phone: 212-260-5757
Web: www.rougeetblancnyc.com
Prices: $$$

Dinner Tue – Sun

Rouge et Blanc features a menu that stirs together the conceits of Vietnamese and French cuisines served amidst a backdrop of Indochine-influenced décor—a burlap-covered ceiling, red lacquered chairs, handcrafted pottery, and plants.

The talented kitchen impresses with salacious specialties like green papaya salad, that ubiquitous favorite, here elevated with homemade green curry vinaigrette and crunchy-fried head-on shrimp. Other items have included cool rice vermicelli dressed with sweet onion sauce and coarse-ground pork sausage; as well as a spicy claypot of tofu and minced chicken braised in rich veal stock. A fine selection of French wines complement the menu, but the chestnut ale from Corsica, on draught, is a great thirst quenching option.

Rubirosa

Italian ✗✗

C2

235 Mulberry St. (bet. Prince & Spring Sts.)

Subway: Spring St (Lafayette St.)
Phone: 212-965-0500
Web: www.rubirosanyc.com
Prices: $$

Lunch & dinner daily

A no-nonsense approach and unapologetic pride in Italian-American culture leads Rubirosa to success on every level. The rustic wood floors creak with authenticity, the curved marble bar is perfect for people-watching, and the classic menu tastes as if it were passed down through generations of hard-working *nonni*.

Beneath the barrel-vaulted, pressed-tin ceilings, success seems evident on every plate, like the Rubirosa sandwich of fried chicken cutlets with sweet roasted peppers, slathered with excellent pesto. Piping hot and hearty "grandma's braciole" is wonderfully tender beef wrapped around breadcrumbs, cheese, and herbs in a chunky and garlicky tomato sauce that begs to be mopped up with a heel of bread. Grab a slice of pizza from 4-5 P.M. daily.

Snack 🐶

Greek ✗

B1

105 Thompson St. (bet. Prince & Spring Sts.)

Subway: Spring St (Sixth Ave.) Lunch & dinner daily
Phone: 212-925-1040
Web: N/A
Prices: 🍸

Snack may not be that quaint, laid-back Santorini *taverna*, but there is much to love in this bustling slip of a restaurant tucked into SoHo's quiet, leafy Thompson Street. The old black-and-white photos and shelves of Greek groceries fail to conjure far-off lands; ignore the slightly erratic interior and strive to snag one of the four dining room tables. The Hellenic fare is authentic enough to transport at first bite. Just don't stop at the meze—entrées are equally satisfying.

Despite the moniker, most of the portions here are hearty, including a generously-sized shredded lamb sandwich, topped with ripe tomatoes, roasted red onions, a smear of aïoli, and fresh arugula; or a Greek salad bursting with creamy feta, kalamata olives, and oregano.

Uncle Boons

Thai ✗✗

C2

7 Spring St. (bet. Bowery & Elizabeth St.)

Subway: Bowery Dinner Tue – Sun
Phone: 646-370-6650
Web: www.uncleboons.com
Prices: $$

Matt Denzer and wife Ann Redding are displaying a skilled hand at Uncle Boons and bringing a welcome change to Nolita's cocktail-slinging and small bites spots. While the attractive space is below street level, large windows make it feel like a hideaway. A wood bar lined with eclectic stools and mirrored tile ceilings draw affluent crowds, but flavorful food and authentic sips (like Singha beer slushies) outdo the scene.

Yum kai hua pli, chicken in coconut milk, crowned with banana blossoms is spicy yet balanced. *Lon pu kem* is a dip mixing salted black crab, pork, and coconut cream that is perfect for sharing. From the charcoal rotisserie, try blowfish tails (*pak pau*) flavored with charred lime, garlic, and a chili dipping sauce.

Torrisi Italian Specialties ❀

C2

Italian ✗✗

250 Mulberry St. (at Prince St.)

Subway: Spring St (Lafayette St.)
Phone: 212-965-0955
Web: www.torrisinyc.com
Prices: $$$

Lunch Fri – Sun
Dinner nightly

Ryan Lee

Few restaurants succeed in creating such a distinct personality: sophisticated yet never stuffy, upbeat, diverse, and always interesting. Gone are the days when everyone promptly arrived at 5:00 P.M to score a table—reservations are now accepted for the prix-fixe menus. Still, it's packed by 5:30 P.M.

The intimate room is closely set but comfortable, with bare wood furnishings and high-backed banquettes atop a penny-tiled floor. Shelves of ingredients reveal something new each time like Manhattan Special, canned tomatoes, and Stella d'Oro cookies. Even the presentation of each dish on floral-patterned china or in a mini paper cup flaunts whimsy.

This extends to the plate, perhaps beginning with *antipasto* like pork terrine with crisped rye toasts, spicy-sweet mustard, and lightly pickled apple. Pastas may headline delicate bowties, black with squid ink, tossed with tender lobster in cream sauce strewn with fragrant tarragon. Duck breast is sure to be rosy-fleshed yet seared to a crisp golden skin, spooned with a ruby-hued Maraschino liqueur and almond sauce. Refined desserts beguile with their simplicity, as in a lemon cake layered with buttercream, as rich and moist as custard.

TriBeCa

Catering to its local clientele of creative types, trendy TriBeCa is, quite simply, a cool place to eat. Here, splurge on meals in pricey restaurants (whose reputations and namesake celebrity chefs precede them), or go for more modest gastropub fare. On sunny days, snag an umbrella-shaded table outside—TriBeCa's famously wide sidewalks are hugely accommodating and among the city's top spots for star-gazing. This stretch of cobblestoned streets, galleries, design stores, and historic warehouses converted to multi-million-dollar lofts was named in the 1970s by a real-estate agent hoping to create a hip identity for the area. The acronym—which stands for Triangle Below Canal—describes an area that is not a triangle at all, but a trapezoid bounded by Canal Street, Broadway, Murray Street, and the Hudson River. Greenwich and Hudson streets are its main thoroughfares for dining and nightlife.

Drinking and Dining

In keeping with its independence and artistic spirit, TriBeCa offers a gourmet experience for any palate (or price tag). On West Broadway, **Bubble Lounge** gives urban wine and champagne enthusiasts a place to celebrate special occasions in style. With such a massive list of hors d'oeuvres and a premium bar, it successfully seduces scores of revelers. Also beloved by wine connoisseurs is **Chambers Street Wines**. Those looking for something to enjoy with their wine will rejoice in the monthly events sponsored by **New York Vintners**, which may include free cheese tastings or lessons on making mozzarella. Luxury spa AIRE now offers rituals where one can soak in olive oil, cava, or red wine. The only downside? You can't drink it. The neighborhood is also loaded with wonderful bakeries, the most popular of which include **Sarabeth's** and **Duane Park Patisserie** for pastries and seasonal specialties; and **Tribeca Treats** for decadent and delicious chocolates. Part of the City Bakery family is **Birdbath**, a neighborhood green bakery, which is not just admired for its eco-friendly philosophy and practices, but also for its unique repertoire of breakfasts and lunches to-go, as well as desserts and specialty drinks offered all week long. **Puffy's Tavern** is a friendly hangout displaying five flatscreens for sports fans, happy-hour drinks, and hearty lunchtime Italian sandwiches. Speaking of local delights, **Bubby's** will cater to your homestyle food cravings; **Dirty Bird To Go** is a mainstay; and **Zucker's Bagels & Smoked Fish** will remind you of *bubbe's* grub. Like every New York neighborhood TriBeCa claims its own culinary treasures. **All Good Things** is a lovely marketplace and **Korin** boasts an array of Japanese chef

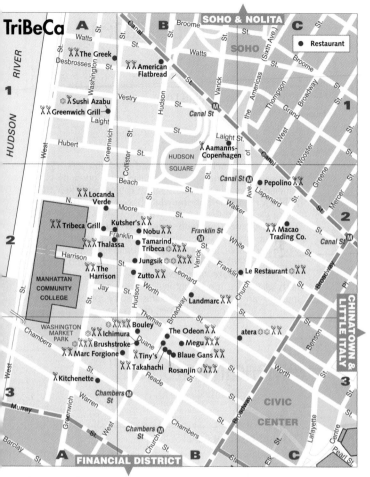

TriBeCa

HUDSON RIVER

Legend:
● Restaurant

Watts St.
The Greek
Desbrosses St.
Washington St.
American Flatbread
Canal St.
Broome St.
SOHO
Watts St.
Vestry St.
Sushi Azabu
Greenwich Grill
Laight
Hudson St.
Canal St
Varick St.
the Americas (Sixth Ave.)
Thompson St.
Grand
Broadway
Broome
Hubert
Greenwich St.
Collister St.
Laight St.
Aamanns-Copenhagen
HUDSON SQUARE
of
Canal
West St.
Wooster St.
Greene St.
Beach St.
Canal St M
Pepolino
Lispenard St.
Mercer St.
Locanda Verde
Moore St.
Walker St.
Tribeca Grill
Kutsher's
Nobu
Franklin St M
Macao Trading Co.
Canal St M
Franklin St.
Thalassa
Tamarind Tribeca
White St.
Harrison St.
Jungsik
Le Restaurant
Broadway
The Harrison
Zutto
Leonard St.
Franklin St.
Church St.
MANHATTAN COMMUNITY COLLEGE
Jay St.
Worth St.
Landmarc
WASHINGTON MARKET PARK
Thomas St.
Bouley
Ichimura
Duane St.
The Odeon
atera
Chambers St.
Brushstroke
Megu
Marc Forgione
Tiny's
Blaue Gans
Benson St.
Kitchenette
Takahachi
Rosanjin
Reade St.
Worth St.
Chambers M St
Warren St.
CIVIC CENTER
Murray St.
Chambers M St
Chambers St.
Lafayette St.
Centre St.
Barclay St.
Greenwich St.
West St.
Church St.
Broadway
Elk St.
Pearl St.

CHINATOWN & LITTLE ITALY

knives and restaurant supplies. Speaking of Asian heaven, round up some friends to sample unique Japanese treats at **Takahachi Bakery**. Under the "dinner and a movie" category, the 2001 film *Dinner Rush* used TriBeCa as a stage. In fact, director Bob Giraldi shot this mob- and food-themed movie at one of his famed eateries— **Gigino Trattoria**. The plot tells the story of a night in the life of a chic TriBeCa restaurant, delving into sidelines such as food critics and ambitious chefs. Today this area is still associated with films of many stripes, thanks to the annual Tribeca Film Festival, created by Robert DeNiro to revitalize the area after 9/11. This world-famous springtime extravaganza hosts twelve days of great films and plenty of community camaraderie. Throngs of locals, tourists, and film fiends flock here during this time to see the movies.

Aamanns-Copenhagen

B1

13 Laight St. (at St. Johns Ln.)

Subway: Canal St (Sixth Ave.)   Lunch & dinner Tue – Sun
Phone: 212-925-1313
Web: www.aamanns-copenhagen.com
Prices: $$

After much anticipation (followed by Hurricane Sandy delays), this striking spot has finally flung open its glass-paneled doors. Phrases like "Danish Eatery" and "RUGBØD PORK" are tattooed on the white-brick façade. The interior cuts a clean and sleek design with its white walls, free form art murals, bare wood tables, and fresh Nordic touches.

The sour, chewy, sweet, and nutty brown bread alone is worth a trip here. Inspired dishes go on to include tangy kale tartare topped with white endive, diced apples, and walnuts; and pan-fried hake *smørrebrød* with green remoulade and herb salad. The trio of herring is a revelation, prepared in mustard-tarragon cream with radish; spicy tomato compote and endive; and pickled juniper, capers, egg, and onion.

American Flatbread

B1

205 Hudson St. (at Canal St.)

Subway: Canal St (Sixth Ave.)   Lunch & dinner daily
Phone: 212-776-1441
Web: www.americanflatbread.com
Prices: $$

This TriBeCa outpost of the Vermont favorite is the first Flatbread to cross its state's border since its inception. The expansive downtown space is impeccably designed with wraparound windows, plenty of sunlight, and wood-burning ovens put to heavy use.

While they pride themselves on their unique, perfectly formed flatbread crust, the toppings (house-made and organic everything) are the real draw—each ingredient is vibrant, fun, and well balanced. The Mopsy's Kalua Pork is decked with house-smoked shoulder meat, their own mango-barbeque sauce, red onions, pineapple, and Vermont chevre and whole-milk mozzarella. The New Vermont is layered with juicy maple-fennel sausage, sundried tomatoes, fresh herbs, and a host of other delicious toppings.

atera

Contemporary 🍴

C3

77 Worth St. (bet. Broadway & Church St.)

Subway: Chambers St (Church St.)
Phone: 212-226-1444
Web: www.ateranyc.com
Prices: $$$$

Dinner Tue – Sat

Nathan Rawlinson

This thinly populated street flaunts the unmarked office-building entrance of a new-world speakeasy, atera, that at times may not be the easiest to spot. However, its many charms are instantly presented at the door, thanks to a staff that is gracious, engaging, and keeps the small room more lively than serious. Seats are centered around a black cement U-shaped counter that surrounds the stage-like kitchen area. Beyond this, find a vertical herb-garden and slab walnut table for groups. Downstairs, a lounge provides a moody lair for exploring the cocktail list.

The chef is furiously talented, extremely ambitious, and creating a very personal cuisine. Meals begin with snacks that explore a range of earthy flavors, like mushroom meringues or lichen crisps that resemble rocks. Lamb tartare is beautifully cut and balanced with the flavors of crispy black malted crackers. Squid masquerades as al dente ramen, served in a wonderfully strong and aromatic chicken broth. An aged beef tenderloin is juicy, tender, and excellent. Desserts present a mind-boggling simulation as in a cracked-egg, meringue-like shell filled with egg yolk "jam;" or white chocolate birch "leaves" atop birch ice cream.

Blaue Gans

Austrian XX

139 Duane St. (bet. Church St. & West Broadway)

Subway: Chambers St (West Broadway)　　　　　Lunch & dinner daily
Phone: 212-571-8880
Web: www.kg-ny.com
Prices: $$

Blaue Gans is revered for its winning trifecta of food, drink, and vibe. This venerable space is endowed with snug tables and banquettes, while its hospitable bar is popular among the FiDi set. Find a cozier perch beside looming windows, perfect for a beer and sausage. Embellished with movie posters and a marvelous soundtrack, Blaue Gans feels at once Euro and downtown. If that doesn't scream unique, check their menu of fine wursts and schnitzels.

A bibb salad bathed in pumpkin oil offers a perfect prelude to *käsekrainer*, a fatty, cheesy sausage matched with sauerkraut; or fried *jäger schnitzel* drowned in a mushroom-bacon sauce. You'll want to save room for dessert—maybe a *schwarzwälder kirsch torte* with sour cherries and amaretto crunch ice cream.

The Greek

Greek XX

458 Greenwich St. (bet. Desbrosses & Watts Sts.)

Subway: Franklin St　　　　　Dinner nightly
Phone: 646-476-3941
Web: www.thegreektribeca.com
Prices: $$

TriBeCa may offer more highfalutin dining halls than intimate ethnic eats, but one step inside this newcomer immediately transports you to a rustic, cozy den of Greek hospitality. Beyond the impressive mahogany bar and mounted wine barrels, head toward the rear dining room and bask in the relaxed vibe of this very comfortable neighborhood spot.

Start with a trio of excellent, traditional meze, or a whole roasted eggplant drizzled with olive oil. Revel in the land's bounty with the mixed grill, served as a cornucopia of marinated meats like pork and chicken souvlaki with thinly sliced ribeye. End the meal with *kataifi*, shredded phyllo layered with semolina custard, pastry cream, and toasted pistachios, or just sip another glass of Greek wine.

Bouley ✿

Contemporary XXXX

B3

163 Duane St. (at Hudson St.)

Subway: Chambers St (West Broadway)
Phone: 212-964-2525
Web: www.davidbouley.com
Prices: $$$$

Lunch & dinner Mon – Sat

Nicole Bartelme

Through a discreet entrance filled with fragrant apples, find this Grande Dame of TriBeCa. Bouley may flaunt more stone, moldings, and carvings than a North Jersey McMansion, but here it all seems elegant, upscale, and European in style. It's where high-rollers come for special occasions—if they want to splurge. This is a level of opulent fine dining that few restaurants strive for anymore, in an atmosphere that remains humming and pleasant. Tuxedoed servers are professional, though they may time meals with a stopwatch. Classic French cuisine is at the heart of Chef David Bouley's menu, demonstrating a highly skilled kitchen. A commitment to superb ingredients and presentations with flourish is clear upon viewing the *chariot de pain* (or the other trolleys for cheeses and digestives). Bread this good deserves to arrive on its own chariot. Move on to the likes of foraged mushrooms in a contemporary presentation with grilled toro, coconut foam, sweet garlic, florals, and "special spices." Hudson Valley squab is flawlessly roasted with thyme jus and salsify.

A Valhrona chocolate soufflé is warm and cake-like, with a white coffee cloud, coffee ice cream and scoop of decadent mousse.

Brushstroke ✿

Japanese ✕✕✕

B3

30 Hudson St. (at Duane St.)

Subway: Chambers St (West Broadway)
Phone: 212-791-3771
Web: www.davidbouley.com
Prices: $$$$

Dinner Mon – Sat

Nicole Bartelme

Brushstroke is instantly attractive and inimitable, in an unexpected confluence of Japanese country and urban TriBeCa styles. Ceilings tower over unusually spacious tables laden with ceramics and rife with open views into the multigazillion dollar kitchen. While everything appears pleasant and inviting, service is… well… not really what it should be. On the menu, celebrated Chef David Bouley offers his own take on a kaiseki menu. This is by no means a traditional experience, but a meal that luxuriates in high-end ingredients, often in copious portions. Buyer, beware of those supplemental charges, which can add up quickly.

Begin with crunchy winter bamboo shoots dressed in white miso-mustard, presented with *ankimo, tosazu* gelée, and elderberry reduction topped with a sesame cloud. Highlights include a rich presentation of yuzu-perfumed and grilled *akamutsu* blanketed with fried gobo shards. That salver may go on to include more *akamutsu* sashimi with monkfish liver, giant clam, uni, and a dollop of osetra caviar. Seared Crescent duck breast infused with *hojicha* tea, served beside sweet potato sauce and vanilla salt is a demonstration of this kitchen's skill and technical aptitude.

Greenwich Grill

A1

Fusion 🍴🍴

428 Greenwich St. (bet. Laight & Vestry Sts.)

Subway: Franklin St
Phone: 212-274-0428
Web: www.greenwichgrill.com
Prices: $$

Lunch Mon – Fri
Dinner nightly

Within earshot of the *whooshing* Holland Tunnel but on a lovely cobblestone street, find this fantastically intriguing (as in Japanese-accented Italian-French fusion) cuisine. Its location above one-starred sister restaurant Sushi Azabu is testament to the exceptional quality, creativity, and wonder found in each dish. This upper level offers varied seating in the sultry front room with tufted leather booths, and rear dining area with skylights and stone accents.

On the menu, explore the likes of sweet and fragrant Thai curry tossed with chicken, peppers, and silky fettuccine; or daily specials like "healthy grilled fish"—a lovely snapper fillet atop cannellini beans in a prosciutto-studded sauce, served alongside arugula dressed in ponzu vinaigrette.

The Harrison

A2

Contemporary 🍴🍴

355 Greenwich St. (at Harrison St.)

Subway: Franklin St
Phone: 212-274-9310
Web: www.theharrison.com
Prices: $$

Lunch Wed – Sun
Dinner nightly

Justifiably admired by locals and astute visitors, The Harrison is stunning in that downtown hip sort of way. The softly lit dining room is sensual and slightly jazzy, as "ribbons" of red beveled glass trim the top of every window and lend a sultry air when sunlight filters in. In keeping with the neighborhood spirit, even the floral ensembles are elaborate and fun.

The service is well-orchestrated, with the bar clearly ruling the room. Dressed with fine china, tables showcase homemade ricotta *cavatelli* enriched with braised duck, tomato and chevre; sharp eggplant croquets with tomato chutney; and tender bites of lamb Milanese paired with sautéed greens. And whether they serve you birthday cake or not, custard-filled éclairs are a total treat.

Ichimura ⸙

Japanese 🍴🍴

B3

30 Hudson St. (at Duane St.)

Subway: Chambers St (West Broadway)   Dinner Mon – Sat
Phone: 212-791-3771
Web: www.davidbouley.com
Prices: $$$$

Brushstroke

As if to prove that great things are worth seeking out, Chef Eiji Ichimura's eponymous home is hidden beside Brushstroke's racket, in its own peaceful nook. The staff is professional, unobtrusive, and as gracious as the chef himself, who may be alone in serving the immense eight-seat counter. The tiny space is ingeniously designed with a wall made of books, rice-paper windows, and Japanese ceramics to conjure that distinct *wabi-sabi* look. Everything is immaculately maintained and of extraordinary quality, especially the food. The omakase-only menu draws inspiration from what is undeniably among the freshest array of fish in the city. Sashimi courses are creative and present a clear view of the chef's personal style. One platter might arrive with bites of marinated toro topped with thinly sliced *myoga* or chunks of albacore bathed in ginger and soy. Meanwhile, an incredibly simple yet deeply flavorful sushi parade includes fluke, Hokkaido ocean trout, toro, and salmon roe, all majestic in appearance and flawless in composition. *Chawan mushi* is delicately steamed and enriched with black truffle, thickened dashi, and Florida golden crab.

In lieu of dessert, treat yourself to more uni.

Jungsik ✿ ✿

B2

Korean 〤〤〤

2 Harrison St. (at Hudson St.)

Subway: Franklin St   Dinner Mon– Sat
Phone: 212-219-0900
Web: www.jungsik.kr
Prices: $$$$

Why Not Smile

Jungsik is a restaurant with impact. The stylish room is a brilliant combination of contemporary and comfortable, with lighting that is bright enough to see your food yet soft enough to hide any flaws from across the table.

Cream-colored velvet banquettes and flower arrangements reflecting the seasons surround each table. The hip, sophisticated ambience reflects its TriBeCa home. The staff could not be more gracious.

Here, luxury is more than eye-candy, extending to the plate and palate with the kitchen's formidable talents. Chef Jung Sik Yim is not merely preparing excellent food, but presenting his own, very unique reflection of modern Korean cuisine. Sweet and creamy sea urchin may be served resting on cool shreds of lettuce over warm sticky rice cooked with dark, inky seaweed. Move on to the beautiful presentation of Seoul duck, the breast served pink beneath crisped skin, tender confit of leg spiced with *gojuchang*, and the elusive flavor of sesame leaf. Lobster is coated in a lush and complex curry-like sauce that perfectly blankets the sweet meat. A very contemporary and impressive strawberry dessert combines intensely foamy purée with green pistachio sponge and stewed berries.

Kitchenette

A3

156 Chambers St. (bet. Greenwich St. & West Broadway)

Subway: Chambers St (West Broadway) Lunch & dinner daily
Phone: 212-267-6740
Web: www.kitchenetterestaurant.com
Prices:

With its steady stream of moms and financial types looking for a strong cup of fresh brewed coffee, unassuming Kitchenette is a beloved anytime stop for homey food and amazing layer cakes. Everything feels a bit quirky, with sawed-off doors doubling as tables, picket fences lining the pink-striped walls, and a time-worn cupboard.

Their famed breakfasts feature egg dishes and freshly baked treats, but the separate milkshake menu (peanut butter-blondie served in a mason jar) is earning equal attention. At other times, find satisfying bowls of chicken noodle soup, or succulent fried chicken drizzled with honey. Desserts here are not to be missed as in moist, fragrant sprinkle cakes slathered in cream cheese frosting and...you guessed it...sprinkles aplenty.

Kutsher's

A2

186 Franklin St. (bet. Greenwich & Hudson Sts.)

Subway: Franklin St Lunch & dinner daily
Phone: 212-431-0606
Web: www.kutsherstribeca.com
Prices: $$$

Who knew herring could be hip? Zach Kutsher, that's who. The name might sound familiar to a certain set of New Yorkers (it was a longtime vacation spot in the Catskills à la Dirty Dancing), but it's now becoming known more for chopped liver than campfires.

At this self-proclaimed modern Jewish bistro, you can expect your *bubbie's* food, but finished with downtown oomph. The menu showcases some serious chops (Jeffrey Chodorow is a partner) via perfectly comforting potato latkes topped with sour cream; hugely addictive duck fries double-fried in duck *schmaltz*; and simply delectable crispy artichokes. Chopped liver, pickled herring, and *kreplach* stray from the classic preparations with modern interpretations, perfect for the moneyed Bugaboo set.

Landmarc

B2   French ⅩⅩ

179 West Broadway (bet. Leonard & Worth Sts.)

Subway: Franklin St   Lunch & dinner daily
Phone: 212-343-3883
Web: www.landmarc-restaurant.com
Prices: $$

Saunter into this bi-level beauty to find cool steel touches and warm woods mingling with slate and lavender hues, the space set a-twinkle with soft track lighting. An open fire grill cozies up the place, and on warmer days, the serene second level expands out into a breezy balcony.

Choose a half bottle of wine from the terrific selection, and absorb yourself in the comfort and pleasures of rich foie gras terrine, served with pickled red onion and toasted points; warm and savory goat cheese profiteroles, plump with chevre, herbs, and diced red peppers; or a delectable special such as a generous oven-roasted *boudin blanc* over celery root slaw and braised red cabbage. Top it off with a decadent chocolate-iced éclair, bursting with Chantilly cream.

Locanda Verde

A2   Italian ⅩⅩ

379 Greenwich St. (at N. Moore St.)

Subway: Franklin St   Lunch & dinner daily
Phone: 212-925-3797
Web: www.locandaverdenyc.com
Prices: $$$

Chef Andrew Carmellini may be a busy man, yet his rustic and gratifying Italian idol remains as trendy as ever. Locanda Verde is coveted as much for its incredible setting as its well-versed lineup of tasty fare. Breakfast verges on divine—think lemon pancakes and apple-cider donuts. No matter the time of day, this Italian brasserie (of sorts) is abuzz and everyone looks beautiful amid low lights, handsome floors, and walls adorned with wine bottles.

Expect to see bare tables packed with diners waxing poetic about marinated beets strewn with pecorino and crushed walnuts, or green fettucine with white Bolognese. Nobody should leave here without sampling one of their superb sweets: a sticky fig-honey upside down cake with fig *sorbetto* shows much flair.

Le Restaurant

Contemporary 🍴🍴

102 Franklin St. (at Church St.)

Subway: Franklin St   Dinner Thu – Sat
Phone: 212-925-5081
Web: www.allgoodthingsny.com
Prices: $$$

Amanda Brown

Seek out the boutique food hall called All Good Things and venture past the flowers, locally sourced meats, and handmade chocolates to reach the secreted doorway where a metal staircase leads you to Le Restaurant.

This subterranean stunner throws together an oh-so-now-rusticity and Scandi-minimalism to achieve that idiomatic milieu. The abundantly staffed display kitchen is a scene of wood-fueled cooking. Guests take in the scents and sounds from their blonde wood seats flatteringly set aglow by globe pendants.

A prix-fixe menu is the only option, and although it is not presented beforehand, the spot-on staff will always inquire about your food issues upfront. Sharply honed skill and astounding creativity are the forces behind Le Restaurant's procession of surprises that include a quivering globule of white asparagus-tinged tapioca bursting with caviar; freshly shucked sweet peas and tendrils ringed by trout roe, sorrel ice, and bacon dust; or sweet-and-sour halibut dressed with braised endives, raisins, and citrus. Dessert may be a complex but wonderful fruity mash up of black cherry *cremeux*, passion fruit gel, and vanilla- and pepper-poached carrot with iced homemade crème fraîche.

Macao Trading Co.

Macanese ✗✗

C2

311 Church St. (bet. Lispenard & Walker Sts.)

Subway: Canal St (Sixth Ave.)
Phone: 212-431-8750
Web: www.macaonyc.com
Prices: $$

Dinner nightly

A red light marks the entrance to this playful spot, where just beyond the black velvet curtains, a smart clientele packs the dimly lit bar and downstairs dining area. The upstairs space seems to flaunt the opium den-chic of old Macao. Wooden crates sealed in chicken wire hold a collection of decorative items, while dark furnishings and high ceilings complete the look.

The menu is divided into subsections by ingredient and style (Portuguese or Chinese) and includes tasty bites like tetilla cheese-stuffed meatballs in smoked-paprika tomato sauce, topped with chorizo and served with bread chunks for sopping. Seared cuttlefish with sesame noodles may be followed by Chaozhou-style cod, delicately steamed and set atop braised *choi sum* with "sizzling" broth.

Marc Forgione

American ✗✗

B3

134 Reade St. (bet. Greenwich & Hudson Sts.)

Subway: Chambers St (West Broadway)
Phone: 212-941-9401
Web: www.marcforgione.com
Prices: $$$

Lunch Sun
Dinner nightly

Make your way up a few steps from the street and walk past an industrialized patio to arrive at the warm and pleasurable Marc Forgione. Strikingly large windows, exposed brick walls broken up by gleaming mirrors, wood plank flooring, and sultry lights merely set the scene for a memorable meal in the main dining room.

The rustic yet elegant visual marries impeccably with the kitchen's innovative American fare. This is a place where foodies savor the decadent flavors of a foie gras torchon with Concord grapes atop duck fat-slathered English muffins; or a foil packet full of meaty mushrooms infused with truffle oil to get their taste buds going. Craving pure comfort? Opt for the crispy skinned chicken roasted under a brick with lush amounts of garlic.

Megu

Asian

B3

62 Thomas St. (bet. Church St. & West Broadway)

Subway: Chambers St (West Broadway)
Phone: 212-964-7777
Web: www.megurestaurants.com
Prices: $$$

Dinner nightly

One peek at Megu's menu and you can expect a pleasurable affair. A stunning blend of beauty and style, this space comes with a pretty price, but trust that it's worth it—imagine an omakase of seven courses and the rest of the puzzle will fall into place. Descend the slate stairs into the large, lofty dining room dramatically decorated with an ice Buddha and a giant bell.

As expected, Megu is perpetually packed with sake-sipping trendsters grooving to the thumping music while clamoring for inventive Asian fare. Expect such well-balanced dishes as Kobe beef skewers paired with soy-wasabi, miso, black sesame, and soy-garlic sauces; *hoba* leaf-wrapped lamb chops grilled to tender perfection; and crab fried rice tossed with garlic mayonnaise.

Nobu

Japanese

B2

105 Hudson St. (at Franklin St.)

Subway: Franklin St
Phone: 212-219-0500
Web: www.myriadrestaurantgroup.com
Prices: $$$$

Lunch Mon – Fri
Dinner nightly

Everything is exactly as it should be at this longtime TriBeCa success story. And yet, the décor doesn't seem aged at natty Nobu, a seasoned Japanese gem still favored for both casual and corporate gatherings. While suits with Blackberries favor their fast and friendly service, the vibe at night attracts good-looking locals. Two-tops may be packed but booths along one wall and the sushi counter are far more inviting.

Lunch serves a pared down menu, while dinner unveils almost twice as many of Nobu's signature courses. Most of these flirt with Western accents and may include bigeye and Bluefin toro tartare in a drinkable bath of wasabi-soy; squid "pasta" with crisp vegetables; sweet and tender miso cod; and excellent shiitake or eggplant tempura.

The Odeon

American ✗✗

145 West Broadway (at Thomas St.)

Subway: Chambers St (West Broadway)   Lunch & dinner daily
Phone: 212-233-0507
Web: www.theodeonrestaurant.com
Prices: $$$

Classic and dry, The Odeon's martinis are among the best in town. Then again, the stylish art deco feel, cascading flowers, and red leather banquettes do just as much to endear this favorite local bistro. In fair weather, the huge, columned space opens to the sidewalk where a handful of tables are set not far from their ice cream cart. It may be thirty-some years young, but the mood is always either fun or ebullient.

The brasserie menu is straightforward and very good, offering crowd-pleasers like hearty onion soup beneath thick slices of bread and a gooey canopy of bubbling Gruyère. Or, try NY strip steaks cooked exactly to order and served with a house-made béarnaise sauce with hints of tarragon. Skip the fries in lieu of crème brulée for dessert.

Pepolino

Italian ✗✗

281 West Broadway (bet. Canal & Lispenard Sts.)

Subway: Canal St (Sixth Ave.)   Lunch & dinner daily
Phone: 212-966-9983
Web: www.pepolino.com
Prices: $$

Head upstairs to the second floor of this bi-level fave, where diners and staff are on a first name basis and Chef Enzo Pezone amicably makes his way through the dining room. A fine array of pastas and fish specials draws crowds of locals in the know.

To whet the palate, savor the complementary tomato-basil pâté (one of the tastiest openers around), before moving onto the irresistible *tagliolini gratinati*, long flat noodles loaded with shredded *prosciutto cotto*, fontina, Parmesan, and béchamel sauce with hints of rosemary. Other hits include braised salt cod in tomato sauce with capers, peppers, garlic, and parsley; and the homemade ricotta cheesecake, mousse-like and ethereal with touches of lemon and vanilla, which makes for a superb finale.

351

Rosanjin ⌘

Japanese 𝕏𝕏𝕏

141 Duane St. (bet. Church St. & West Broadway)

Subway: Chambers St (West Broadway)   Dinner Mon – Sat
Phone: 212-346-0664
Web: www.rosanjintribeca.com
Prices: $$$$

Peter Dressel

Elaborate and genuine, Rosanjin offers its patrons an extraordinary opportunity to experience a leisurely kaiseki meal. From the moment guests enter, their every comfort is taken into account. The well-spaced yet cozy room is cloaked in lacquered woods and brushed silks, amid inspired floral arrangements and vibrant upholstery. Each vessel, bowl, and chopstick that appears on your table can only be described as harmonious. Servers double as real-time mind readers: they know what you need or want slightly before you do.

Dinners here are limited to set menus; the most basic of the three options is very reasonable given the craft and supreme ingredients that comprise each dish. The sashimi course alone resembles a gift—an elegantly draped fish is presented on a wooden tray and may include Japanese yellowtail, fluke, or golden-eye snapper with delicately pickled ginger and a tiny glazed pot of their own soy sauce. Cooked dishes go on to present grilled yuzu-marinated pike with a cool mound of grated daikon; or simmered salmon cake with chrysanthemum petals.

The tempura is past perfection, while seasonal rice dishes may be a delicious hot pot of flaky red snapper and shimeji mushrooms.

Sushi Azabu

Japanese X

428 Greenwich St. (bet. Laight & Vestry Sts.)

Subway: Franklin St

Phone: 212-274-0428

Web: www.greenwichgrill.com

Prices: $$$

Lunch Mon – Fri
Dinner nightly

Sushi Azabu

Sushi Azabu is located beneath the fusion restaurant Greenwich Grill, so expect the hostess to guide the stars to the subterranean dining room. The space is snug and has a distinctly Japanese feel, fashioned with handmade chopsticks, bamboo ceilings, and an oversized print of a giant fish looming large over the sushi bar. A few banquettes are available, while most solo guests prefer the counter. The clientele is a mix of Japanese salarymen, TriBeCa locals, and foodies with iPhones. Service is either excellent or a confused circus of good intentions.

The menu offers a number of options, from sushi platters to omakase. However, faithful renditions of traditional sushi are a highlight here. Sashimi may be presented on a black stone tray, laden with an array of horse mackerel, yellowtail, and pink, creamy tuna with accouterments. Sushi courses may bring Spanish mackerel topped with vinegary gelée, or an absolutely perfect morsel of Japanese uni. Cooked dishes might include tender Wagyu beef *tataki* with grated radish, or *chawan mushi* with crab and mushrooms.

Matcha meringue roulade tucked with strawberries and bananas typifies Azabu's ace technique with modern interpretation.

Takahachi

B3

Japanese

145 Duane St. (bet. Church St. & West Broadway)

Subway: Chambers St (West Broadway)
Phone: 212-571-1830
Web: www.takahachi.net
Prices: $$

Lunch Mon – Fri
Dinner nightly

Pop into this quiet neighborhood favorite for an *Oceans 13* or *Perfect Storm*, to name a few of their signature maki. Here, those cinematic titles mean non-traditional rolls featuring excellent products that don't hold back, as in eel, mango, tuna, and salmon, drizzled with spicy mayo and tobiko; or shrimp tempura, cream cheese, and cucumber with black tobiko. Sidle up to the black sushi bar and get started with *beni toro carpaccio*—salmon belly sashimi topped with marinated red onion and cilantro. Follow with a belly-warming bowl of *nebeyaki* soba, full of buckwheat noodles, veggies, and shrimp tempura.

Inside, friendly hosts greet guests behind a wavy white counter, while the serene sounds of water trickling down a stone wall create a calming atmosphere.

Thalassa

A2

Greek

179 Franklin St. (bet. Greenwich & Hudson Sts.)

Subway: Franklin St
Phone: 212-941-7661
Web: www.thalassanyc.com
Prices: $$$

Dinner Mon – Sat

It's fair to say Greek cuisine is part of Thalassa's history—this sprawling venue was once a warehouse used to store Greek food products. Today, it sports classic TriBeCa bones like soaring ceilings and leather seating spread across multiple levels. Sultry candlelight and delicate flowers soften the look. Starched white linens and the suited captain staff are clues to the seriousness of this sleek spot.

Whole fish displayed on ice tempts diners and steers them toward tasting the kitchen's gift with seafood. Portuguese octopus is beautifully grilled with end bits crisped to a tantalizing crunch and simply dressed with red wine vinaigrette. Whole black bass is ultra-fresh, neatly deboned, and plated with tangy herb emulsion and fantastic lemon potatoes.

Tamarind Tribeca ⌘

Indian 🍴🍴🍴

B2

99 Hudson St. (at Franklin St.)

Subway: Franklin St

Phone: 212-775-9000

Web: www.tamarindrestaurantsnyc.com

Prices: $$$

Lunch & dinner daily

Tamarind Tribeca

Enter dramatic Tamarind Tribeca and be captivated with its unique beauty, from the pristine marble bar to the arresting glass-fronted wine room. Lofty windows draped in lavish silks, teak floors, and muted shades extend through two levels of crisply dressed tables. The mezzanine offers a bird's-eye view of the flawless tandoor, while the back is more intimate. Irrespective of locale, the ambience is always fantastic and very luxurious. Service is as polished as the gleaming cutlery.

The menu is ambitious and ever-tempting. Phenomenal curries take center stage from the start with *kolambi pola*, giant prawns in a rich gravy of coconut, lemongrass, and red chili, atop a chickpea flour cake. Chunks of tender lamb braised in a thick, fiery red *vindaloo* are enlivened by coconut vinegar. Venison chops are marinated in pickling spices, roasted chickpea flour, and yogurt before being superbly cooked in the tandoor, resulting in meat that is appetizingly caramelized, juicy, and deep pink. For sopping up the cashew-saffron sauce in *nargisi kofta*, order a broccoli-cheese *naan*.

Blemishes at lunch will be a fading memory after a whiff of the light and cool cardamom-scented sweet potato pudding.

Tiny's

American

B3

135 West Broadway (bet. Duane & Thomas Sts.)

Subway: Chambers St (West Broadway)
Phone: 212-374-1135
Web: www.tinysnyc.com
Prices: $$

Lunch & dinner daily

The impossibly charming Tiny's is housed in a quiet TriBeCa enclave that bears the distinction of cradling some of the most soaring and pricey lofts in the city. Perched at the bottom of a pink-painted, Federal-style residence and amid ultra-chic shops, it is a welcome relief from the hectic city bustle. Inside, pressed-tin ceilings, white terra-cotta floors, antique wood banquettes, and a wood-burning fireplace make for an enchanting atmosphere.

The kitchen's talents are clear in sensational offerings like sweet potato and apple soup with brioche croutons and maple cream; mozzarella-stuffed meatball marinara with crostini; and smoky duck breast over cashew-miso purée and wok-finished broccoli. Save room for the moan-inducing chocolate pretzel tart.

Tribeca Grill

Contemporary ✗✗

A2

375 Greenwich St. (at Franklin St.)

Subway: Franklin St
Phone: 212-941-3900
Web: www.myriadrestaurantgroup.com
Prices: $$$

Lunch Sun – Fri
Dinner nightly

Tribeca Grill is hallowed for its proficient and well-paced service; and disciples in the know (wealthy patrons from around the way) love to seek their expert sommelier for counsel on a wine list—replete with impressive German and Austrian selections. Less suited for intimate affairs, the Grill exudes a classic quality and is a reliable destination among the elite and beautiful people of NYC.

Diners hold court amid exposed duct work, wall-to-wall windows, and a mighty bar posed in the center. To delight the palate, find rustic veal and mushroom terrine served with raisin-walnut bread and violet mustard. Seared scallops with squash-bacon risotto, subtly spiced pumpkin cheesecake, and a well-plated cheese course unveil a real love for seasonal ingredients.

Zutto

B2

77 Hudson St. (bet. Harrison & Jay Sts.)

Subway: Franklin St
Phone: 212-233-3287
Web: www.zuttonyc.com
Prices: $$

Lunch & dinner daily

Zutto is at the helm of serious Japanese *izakaya* entrenching themselves in the city's scene. A welcoming space with a practical yet pleasing aesthetic, this "Japanese-American pub" as the owners like to call it, has long been a TriBeCa fixture. Contemporarily fit with wooden communal tables and exposed brick, there is ample space to lounge here, likely to a background beat of Billboard's best.

While the menu meanders, a taste of such varied dishes as *chuuka manjuu* (*baos* filled with tender, fatty pork belly and miso); or *shoyu ramen*, a dish native to the north of Japan and enriched with tofu and *menma*, will have you smitten.

From pristine sushi like soft shell crab decked with fresh roe to *negi toro* with pickled daikon, the chef reveals fine pedigree.

Look for **red** symbols, indicating a particularly pleasant ambience.

Upper East Side

The Upper East Side is a massive, mainly residential neighborhood with many faces ranging from prominent New York families to fresh-from-college prepsters. Closest to the park are posh spots catering to the Euro crowd and ladies who lunch. Walk further east to find young families filling the latest, casual *sushi-ya* or artisanal pizzeria. Along First and Second avenues, pubs are packed with raucous post-grads keeping the party alive.

The most upper and eastern reaches were originally developed by famed families of German descent who built country estates in what has now become Yorkville. **Schaller & Weber** is one of the few remaining butchers carrying Austro-German products including fantastic wursts for winter steaming or summer grilling, and the pungent mustards to match them. The Upper East Side has a greater concentration of gourmet markets than any other area in the city. Each shop may be more packed than the next, yet has made processing long lines an art of inspired efficiency. **Agata & Valentina** specializes in everything Italian, while **Citarella** pumps its mouthwatering aroma of rotisserie chickens out the storefront to entice passersby. **Grace's Marketplace** is also a longtime gem, loved for its cramped corners and cascading displays. Insiders frequent their trattoria replete with quality ingredients carried in the store. However, the true champion of everything uptown and gourmet, is Eli Zabar and his ever-expanding empire. **E.A.T.** is a Madison Avenue gem selling baked goods and takeout foods alongside its casual café. Later branches include his **Vinegar Factory** and mega-mart **Eli's**. Still, there are smaller purveyors to patronize here. **Lobel's** and **Ottomanelli** are among the best remaining butcher shops offering the finest meats. **William Greenberg** bakes New York's favorite cookie, the black-and-white, along with tasty *babka*. Paris' venerable **Ladurée** makes this nook even sweeter with its rainbow of pastel macarons; and **Glaser's Bake Shop** looks and tastes of everything Old World. On the high end, **Lady M**'s boutique cakes blend right in with this chic locale.

In the mood for a cocktail? It doesn't get more classic than supper and a show at the storied hotel's **Café Carlyle** or at **Bemelmans Bar**. **Bar Pleiades** at The Surrey is a more contemporary offering but as elegantly uptown as one would expect with its quilted walls and lacquer finishes.

For any foodie, **Kitchen Arts & Letters** has the largest stock of food and wine publications in the country, and owner Nach Waxman is as good a source of industry insight as any book or blog.

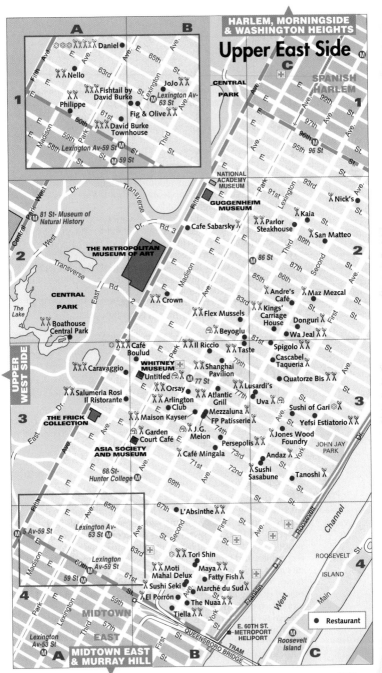

SPANISH HARLEM

CENTRAL PARK

A / B

Daniel

Nello

Fishtail by David Burke

Philippe

JoJo

Lexington Av-63 St

Fig & Olive

David Burke Townhouse

Lexington Av-59 St

59 St

Inset map labels

81 St-Museum of Natural History

NATIONAL ACADEMY MUSEUM

GUGGENHEIM MUSEUM

Cafe Sabarsky

Nick's

Kaia

Parlor Steakhouse

San Matteo

86 St

THE METROPOLITAN MUSEUM OF ART

CENTRAL PARK

The Lake

Boathouse Central Park

Crown

Andre's Café

Maz Mezcal

Flex Mussels

Kings' Carriage House

Donguri

Beyoglu

Wa Jeal

Café Boulud

Il Riccio

Taste

Spigolo

Cascabel Taqueria

Caravaggio

WHITNEY MUSEUM

Untitled

Shanghai Pavilion

Quatorze Bis

Salumeria Rosi Il Ristorante

77 St

Orsay

Lusardi's

THE FRICK COLLECTION

Arlington Club

Atlantic Grill

Uva

Sushi of Gari

Maison Kayser

Mezzaluna

FP Patisserie

Yefsi Estiatorio

Garden Court Café

J.G. Melon

Persepolis

Jones Wood Foundry

Andaz

ASIA SOCIETY AND MUSEUM

Café Mingala

Sushi Sasabune

Tanoshi

JOHN JAY PARK

68 St-Hunter College

UPPER WEST SIDE

L'Absinthe

ROOSEVELT ISLAND

Lexington Av-63 St

Tori Shin

5 Av-59 St

Lexington Av-59 St

59 St

Moti Mahal Delux

Maya

Fatty Fish

Sushi Seki

Marché du Sud

El Porrón

The Nuaa

Tiella

MIDTOWN EAST

Lexington Av-53 St

E. 60TH ST. METROPORT HELIPORT

QUEENSBORO BRIDGE TRAM

Roosevelt Island

Channel

West

Main

● Restaurant

Andaz

Indian ✗

C3

1378 First Ave. (bet. 73rd and 74th Sts.)

Subway: 77 St
Phone: 212-288-0288
Web: www.andazny.com
Prices: $$

Lunch and dinner daily

For an admirable array of traditional regional favorites, Andaz is a prudent Indian recommendation. This Yorkville treat is understated in its appearance, but the room is well-maintained and politely staffed.

Northern specialties abound in the variety of preparations including a silky mélange of fragrant but mildly spiced house-made cheese and spinach in the *saag paneer*. Southern India is well-represented with classics like a Kerala fish curry wherein pieces of flaky white tilapia are bathed in a complex sauce of tamarind water, cumin seeds, curry leaves, and enriched with coconut powder. Jumbo prawns, minced lamb rolls, and other treasures emerge from the tandoor; and a selection from the full roster of puffy breads is strongly advised.

Andre's Café

Eastern European ✗

C2

1631 Second Ave. (bet. 84th & 85th Sts.)

Subway: 86 St (Lexington Ave.)
Phone: 212-327-1105
Web: www.andrescafeny.com
Prices:

Lunch & dinner daily

This charming café details deliciously old-fashioned baked goods from a bakery of the same name established in Queen's in 1976. Tiny, tidy, and welcoming, the exterior proudly boasts this establishment's Hungarian heritage with a red, white, and green awning. A temptingly arranged display of sweet and savory strudels, tortes, and cakes greet guests upon entering. Table service is available in the rear, and before delving into dessert, there is a full menu of hearty old-world fare offered daily.

Weekday meal specials come complete with a salad or soup and choice of three desserts, and can include home spun traditional favorites like chicken *paprikash*, swathed in a luscious paprika cream sauce and accompanied by freshly made *nokedli*.

Arlington Club

Steakhouse ✕✕

B3

1032 Lexington Ave. (bet. 73rd & 74th Sts.)

Subway: 77 St
Phone: 212-249-5700
Web: www.arlingtonclubny.com
Prices: $$$

Dinner nightly

Chef Laurent Tourondel has teamed up with the Tao Group to serve steaks and sushi in this Upper East Side lair. Born and bred in France, he displays an almost wicked flair for both flesh and fish in this handsome, clubby, and cozy dining room, equipped with an oak bar, vaulted brick ceiling, and tufted leather booths.

A hot Gruyère popover is a decadent welcome and classic Tourondel touch, but pace yourself because the kitchen gives plenty of reason to stuff yourself silly. Start light as in a refreshing chopped vegetable salad dressed with Parmesan and lemon vinaigrette; or maki, perhaps with yellowtail, jalapeño, and avocado. Finally, move on to broiled, dry-aged USDA Prime cuts and American Wagyu skirt steak, accompanied by one of the great sides.

Atlantic Grill

Seafood ✕✕

B3

1341 Third Ave. (bet. 76th & 77th Sts.)

Subway: 77 St
Phone: 212-988-9200
Web: www.atlanticgrill.com
Prices: $$

Lunch & dinner daily

Swimmingly similar to its growing family including the Blue Water Grill, this handsome haunt hooks a very New York clientele with a vast, Asian-accented menu focused on the sea. True to its name, Atlantic Grill's menu highlights seafood options like sushi, caviar, and raw bar offerings. Entrées can be a simple grilled salmon or a more involved affair like Mediterranean bronzini with artichokes *barigoule*, saffron potato, and Italian salsa verde.

The alluring space is frequented by a fun-loving crowd occupying two rooms—one features a nautical blue-and-white theme; and the other is sunny with a terrazzo floor and wicker chairs. Fair weather sidewalk seating is in high demand as is weekend brunch, and an efficient staff holds court at this corporate gem.

Manhattan ▶ Upper East Side

Beyoglu

B2

Turkish

1431 Third Ave. (at 81st St.)

Subway: 77 St
Phone: 212-650-0850
Web: N/A
Prices: $$

Lunch & dinner daily

Sharing may not come naturally to everyone, but when dining at Beyoglu, arrive with a crowd and prepare to pass your plates to fully experience the delicious range of Mediterranean meze that earns its praise. Most of the recipes—and some wine and beer offerings—come from Turkey, though Greek and Lebanese accents can be found throughout. Warm and tender pita bread makes a delightful accompaniment to anything on the menu. Thick homemade yogurt with spinach and garlic; grilled shrimp; and marinated octopus are a short sampling of the wide selection.

If grazing doesn't satisfy, choose from a list of larger daily specials, perhaps including *tavuk izgara*, char-grilled breast of free-range chicken, and *kilic sis*, swordfish kebabs served with rice pilaf.

Boathouse Central Park

A2

American

The Lake at Central Park (E. 72nd St. & Park Dr. North)

Subway: 68 St - Hunter College
Phone: 212-517-2233
Web: www.thecentralparkboathouse.com
Prices: $$$

Lunch & dinner daily

This unique locale offers Manhattan's only lakeside dining experience. Built in 1954, Loeb Boathouse is a pleasant multi-venue operation that includes a charming outdoor bar perched along the water and a lovely glass-walled dining room offering views of the lake, greenery, and skyline beyond—there isn't a bad seat in the house.

Highlighting American ingredients and sensibilities, the menu features an updated approach in items like steak tartare dressed with a Parmesan tuile; Muscovy duck breast with leg confit, wild rice-apple pancake, and Calvados sauce; or roasted Scottish salmon with root vegetables and pinot noir sauce.

While lunch and brunch are served year-round, note that dinner is only offered during warmer months (April through November).

Café Boulud

B3

French 🍴🍴🍴

20 E. 76th St. (bet. Fifth & Madison Aves.)

Subway: 77 St
Phone: 212-772-2600
Web: www.danielboulud.com
Prices: $$$$

Lunch & dinner daily

Bill Milne

Intimate and a little less luxurious than Chef Daniel Boulud's sanctified dining temple to the south, this café is, dare we say, more casual in mien. Yet, we are still in the Upper East Side, so the utmost civility reigns. Settled in The Surrey, Café Boulud enjoys a similar vintage 20s-era demeanor via low ceilings, eye-catching art, and mirrored surfaces. Tables are tight-knit, tapping into the establishment's DNA as a convivial meeting spot.

The menu is divided into four categories: La Tradition; La Saison; Le Potager; and Le Voyage. With each item exuding copious amounts of temptation, diners are sure to work up an appetite as simply as the eyes and stomach flit between categories.

Stand firm in your decision as Café Boulud seldom disappoints. A perfectly crisped fillet of salmon is served with earthy beans, bacon, and mustard jus; while fontina and black truffle *arancini* routinely tickles the palate before such "soulful" plates as celery root-stuffed agnolotti embellished with *mimolette* and celery leaves, or pan-seared duck breast over sauce *albuféra* and Minnesota wild rice. Desserts like a coconut-pineapple *vacherin* are followed by warm madeleines for a bonus indulgence.

Café Mingala

Burmese

B3

1393B Second Ave. (bet. 72nd & 73rd Sts.)

Subway: 68 St - Hunter College
Phone: 212-744-8008
Web: N/A
Prices: 🍴🍴

Lunch & dinner daily

Don't let the well-worn exterior or nearby construction craze deter you from visiting the only Burmese spot in all five boroughs. Know that Café Mingala is well worth the stop. Inside, colorful murals depicting the country's landscape deck the walls; while floral turquoise-colored booths line one side of the narrow space, and wooden tables the other.

The traditional Burmese dishes really soar; *mohinga* is especially spot-on featuring rice noodles in a thick broth of puréed fish, lemongrass, and legumes, served with garnishes of deep-fried shallots, crispy yellow lentils, cilantro, and lemon. Another must-have is the *keema*—a rich ground beef-and-potato curry draped atop a dense "thousand layer" pancake. Lunch specials are a great money saver.

Café Sabarsky

Austrian

B2

1048 Fifth Ave. (at 86th St.)

Subway: 86 St (Lexington Ave.)
Phone: 212-288-0665
Web: www.kg-ny.com
Prices: $$

Lunch Wed – Mon
Dinner Thu – Sun

In addition to the renowned art displayed at the intimately scaled Neue Galerie, find Chef Kurt Gutenbrunner's charming café modeled after a late 19th century Viennese *kaffehause*, complete with dark wood-paneled walls and formally attired servers. The museum, housed in a 1914 Beaux-Arts mansion, was conceived by cosmetic mogul Ronald Lauder and art dealer Serge Sabarsky to display their collections of early 20th century Austrian and German art.

The traditional menu features savory fare like sautéed bratwurst over riesling sauerkraut, along with an indulgent listing of classic sweets like apple strudel. Beverages include a very interesting selection of German and Austrian wines by the glass, tremendous coffee offerings, and divine hot chocolate.

Caravaggio

Italian

A3

23 E. 74th St. (bet. Fifth & Madison Aves.)

Subway: 77 St   Lunch & dinner daily
Phone: 212-288-1004
Web: www.caravaggioristorante.com
Prices: $$$

Nestled among Madison Avenue boutiques and commanding a rather formal air, this highbrow Italian dining room is a good reason to dress up and splurge. The slender setting is adorned with silk-lined walls, sleek leather seating, and evocative artwork. The well-dressed staff is serious, but their hospitality is genuine.

The team of highly experienced co-chefs is equally intense in turning out their skilled cooking. Antipasti might include an elegant, warm octopus salad with baby artichoke and crispy potatoes, while heartier options may feature house-made *cavatelli* with jumbo crabmeat and sea urchin. Lunch offers a more pared-down experience, but a bowlful of velvety *pasta e fagioli* stocked with plump *borlotti* beans is a perfect post-shopping tonic.

Cascabel Taqueria

Mexican

C3

1538 Second Ave. (at 80th St.)

Subway: 77 St   Lunch & dinner daily
Phone: 212-717-8226
Web: www.nyctacos.com
Prices:

Tasty Cascabel Taqueria continues to be massively popular for its delish tacos. The menu is concise and in keeping with the focused taqueria theme, with selections that include double layered corn tortillas filled with house-made chorizo and smoked paprika onions; roasted wild shrimp with fresh oregano, garlic, and chili oil; or chipotle-braised Amish chicken topped with chicken *chicharrón*. Interesting (and deliciously healthful) sides include a bowl of fluffy organic quinoa topped with Cotija cheese and cilantro.

The daylight-flooded space is complete with a TV-equipped bar; dining room done in zesty shades of lime green and lemon yellow; and tables topped with caddies of salsas.

Upper West Siders check out the buzzing Broadway location.

Crown

Contemporary ✕✕

24 E. 81st St. (bet. Fifth & Madison Aves.)

Subway: 77 St
Phone: 646-559-4880
Web: www.crown81.com
Prices: $$$

Lunch Sun
Dinner nightly

Restaurateur John DeLucie brings his downtown brand (as in The Lion) uptown at Crown located in a 1930s mansion between Fifth and Madison avenue. Elegant beige and brown don the multi-room setting bedecked with a zinc bar and window-walled rear dining room offering spectacular views of the block's privileged backyards. A secret room fronted by a swinging bookshelf offers very private dining.

The menu displays verve in its offering of fresh handkerchief pasta draped with a decadent white Bolognese sauce; and fantastic specimens of Maine diver scallops, seared golden brown, and sided by plump escargots. Even if this crowd shuns dessert, you shouldn't, with treats like espresso-infused panna cotta with *fior di latte* ice cream and crushed cacao nibs.

David Burke Townhouse

Contemporary ✕✕✕

133 E. 61st St. (bet. Lexington & Park Aves.)

Subway: Lexington Av - 59 St
Phone: 212-813-2121
Web: www.davidburketownhouse.com
Prices: $$$

Lunch & dinner daily

David Burke's refreshed Upper East Side restaurant is housed in a quaint brick building. An elegantly appointed, white-furnished lounge is dressed with handsome red banquettes amidst tall white walls adorned with Roman shaded mirrors and bright artwork.

The immaculately attired service staff might kick things off with a warm Gruyère and poppy seed popover; and then move on to Burke's classic brand of bold, contemporary cuisine that may reveal sea scallop "Benedict" with a quail egg, potato cake, and lobster foam; or a trio of duck preparations—glazed with soy and honey, meatloaf, and foie gras dumplings—accompanied by gingered spinach. Desserts include an over-the-top signature cheesecake lollipop tree gilded by bubblegum-whipped cream.

Daniel ✿ ✿ ✿

A1

60 E. 65th St. (bet. Madison & Park Aves.)

Subway: 68 St - Hunter College

Dinner Mon – Sat

Phone: 212-288-0033
Web: www.danielboulud.com
Prices: $$$$

Eric Laignel

A sense of modern romance is deeply set within this celebrated room, on a picture-perfect block lined with trees and multi-million dollar brownstones. Thick carpets, custom chandeliers hanging rings of Limoge tiles and a see-through wine wall adorn the sunken dining room, surrounded by archways and elevated tables layered in elegant linens topped with a simple calla lily. Professional servers ensure that pretentious billionaires perhaps experience far better service than young couples preparing to pop the question.

This is a place for serious dining and undistracted pleasures. The food is worldly, expert, and very memorable. Guinea hen arrives beautifully plated—its confit of leg nestled into a carved cup of hollowed-out purple potato, the breast lean and tender. The dish is finished tableside with a subtle yet distinctive jus seasoned with a *vadouvan* spice blend of turmeric, curry leaves, and coriander.

Desserts feature a *tranche* of peanut butter *feuilletine*, slicked with dark chocolate ganache and chocolate curls; alongside a quenelle of *turrón* (honey nougat) ice cream set in chocolate crumbs; and a bit of gold leaf for the sake of opulence. The precious *mignardises* are extraordinary.

Manhattan ▶ Upper East Side

Donguri

Manhattan ▶ Upper East Side

Japanese

C2

309 E. 83rd St. (bet. First & Second Aves.)

Subway: 86 St (Lexington Ave.)   Dinner Tue – Sun
Phone: 212-737-5656
Web: www.dongurinyc.com
Prices: $$$

The ongoing construction of the Second Avenue subway may have obscured Donguri's already unassuming location, but this intimate Japanese hideaway still draws a devout following. Its steady clientele of high-powered international bankers, neighborhood couples, and Japanese expats longing for a taste of home speaks to its sophistication and authenticity.

Owned by Ito En (known for green tea products), Donguri specializes in the Kansai regional specialties of Osaka and Kyoto. Savory starters like fried sesame tofu or *tako tataki-kyuri* (octopus and cucumber in a spicy sauce) lead to heartier plates such as roasted duck breast with *yuzu-kosho* pepper paste. Soba and udon noodles round out the offerings, with sashimi as an appetizer or entrée.

El Porrón

Spanish

B4

1123 First Ave. (bet. 61st & 62nd Sts.)

Subway: Lexington Av - 59 St   Lunch & dinner daily
Phone: 212-207-8349
Web: www.elporronnyc.com
Prices: $$

&

A sleek looking sliver of a spot, El Porrón brings mouthwatering tapas to a traffic-clogged Upper East Side stretch. Dark colors give the space a cloistered feel, amid black-and-white portraits of people drinking from *porróns*—blown-glass wine vessels with tapered spouts.

The kitchen churns out a graceful, all-encompassing array of savory small plates, hearty entrées, and scrumptious paellas that are absolutely worth the 40-minute wait. Sample tapas may include the *puerros del Monasterio*, combining leeks and wild mushrooms softened in garlic and olive oil sauce; or the delicate *empanada del dia*. *Callos Madilenos* is a lusciously unctuous and ambrosial stew of diced beef tripe and pig's foot, *morcilla*, and chorizo served in a bubbling hot *cazuela*.

Fatty Fish

International

B4

406 E. 64th St. (bet. First & York Aves.)

Subway: Lexington Av - 63 St   Lunch & dinner daily
Phone: 212-813-9338
Web: www.fattyfishnyc.com
Prices: $$

Tucked away near the edge of the Upper East Side, Fatty Fish is a beacon for home-style fare that successfully melds traditional western cooking methods with eastern ingredients. The result? An eccentric array of preparations that are not easily typified. One will find sushi, *gyoza*, fish and chips with ponzu aïoli, and seared salmon with coconut rice and carrot-ginger sauce among the offerings.

Come lunch, the restaurant presents a gently priced list that may offer a thick and hearty green split-pea soup with buttery croutons; tasty *yakisoba* studded with slices of Kurobuta pork sausage; and house-made almond cookies.

The graciously attended setting is low-key, unlike the bold orange accent wall that matches the attention-grabbing awning out front.

Fig & Olive

Mediterranean

B1

808 Lexington Ave. (bet. 62nd & 63rd Sts.)

Subway: Lexington Av - 63 St   Lunch & dinner daily
Phone: 212-207-4555
Web: www.figandolive.com
Prices: $$$

Fig & Olive's exceptional devotion to a single product (olive oil) sets it apart from the nearly countless supply of Mediterranean options. Its burgeoning popularity has enabled expansion, now boasting several branches, including Westchester and Los Angeles.

This original location sits close to fine shopping and offers a sophisticated respite. Rattan seating, a pristine marble dining counter, and warmly lit arrangement of olive oil bottles are squeezed into the slender setting.

Dinners begin with an olive oil trio to sample (though your helpful server will choose which ones you try). One can graze on small plates—crostini, cheeses, or carpaccio—or wholeheartedly dig in to the likes of chicken tajine with preserved lemon and plump figs.

Fishtail by David Burke

Seafood

B1

135 E. 62nd St. (bet. Lexington & Park Aves.)

Subway: Lexington Av - 63 St
Phone: 212-754-1300
Web: www.fishtaildb.com
Prices: $$$

Lunch Sun
Dinner daily

This fitting addition to Chef David Burke's oeuvre features an elegant setting through two levels of a cozy townhouse, lending a ritzy, residential feel. The first floor is an oyster bar and lounge popular with the after-work crowds, while the upstairs is a deep red dining room with accents that colorfully convey the ocean theme.

The menu focuses on fish and much is caught by the company-owned boat. Dishes are stamped with the chef's unique touch, whether as salt-baked American red snapper with smoked tomato sauce; shellfish towers; or more creative interpretations like pretzel-crusted crab cakes with lemon-poppyseed mayonnaise. Sunday nights bring a luxe but affordable lobster-themed menu. Regardless of your choice, every item shows ample skill.

Flex Mussels

Seafood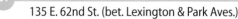

B2

174 E. 82nd St. (bet. Lexington & Third Aves.)

Subway: 86 St (Lexington Ave.)
Phone: 212-717-7772
Web: www.flexmusselsny.com
Prices: $$

Dinner nightly

Despite its strong name, Flex Mussels is actually a fun, casual, and intimate seafood shack with uptown polish. Usually packed to the gills, the slim bar area features pretty touches like flowers, slender mirrors, and a dining counter. The back dining room is spare, contemporary, more subdued, and fills up quickly.

The menu features the namesake bi-valve, hailing from Prince Edward Island, priced by the pound, steamed in more than twenty globally inspired guises, like the "PEI" featuring lobster stock and drawn butter; or "San Daniele" with prosciutto, caramelized onions, white wine, and garlic. No matter the choice, your best accompaniment is a side of piping-hot, hand-cut skinny fries.

Flex also has a downtown sibling in the West Village.

FP Patisserie

French

B3

1293 Third Ave. (at 74th St.)

Subwary: 77 St
Phone: 212-717-5252
Web: www.francoispayard.com
Prices: $$

Lunch daily
Dinner Mon – Sat

This enticing emporium marks Francois Payard's return to the Upper East Side, where sophisticated sweet-tooths can either grab a box of handmade chocolates or macarons to take home, or stay for an enjoyable meal in the *salon de thé*. Popular among the ladies, this petite room carries a sunny color scheme.

Salads paired with freshly baked bread comprise their fine lighter fare; while heartier appetites will enjoy a choice of *croque monsieur*, or perhaps foie gras- and mushroom *duxelles*-stuffed chicken breast dressed with an intense mushroom jus. It goes without saying one must save room for dessert. Walk up to the sparkling display case and select any one of the fabulous creations, like the simply stated caramel tart for a salt-flecked piece of heaven.

Garden Court Café

Asian

B3

725 Park Ave. (at 70th St.)

Subwary: 68 St - Hunter College
Phone: 212-570-5202
Web: www.asiasociety.org
Prices: $$

Lunch Tue – Sun

Tucked into the glass-enclosed, plant-filled lobby of the Asia Society, this café is a far cry from your garden-variety museum restaurant. Though it doesn't generate much fanfare, it is worth seeking out—not only for its quiet ambience, but for the light Asian dishes that expertly fuse East and West.

Serving lunch only, from Tuesday through Sunday, the menu draws Asian inspiration in its offerings that may include herb-crusted salmon with lemongrass, Thai basil, and mint. The bento box features two chef selections along with rice and salad.

Everything here is done with quality, right down to the careful presentation and very good service—plus the museum's entry fee is not required. Don't miss the museum gift shop for its wonderful wares.

Il Riccio

Italian ✗✗

152 E. 79th St. (bet. Lexington & Third Aves.)

Subway: 77 St
Phone: 212-639-9111
Web: www.ilriccioblu.com
Prices: $$

Lunch & dinner daily

This low-key Italian, and its smiling cadre of charming staff, is just the right spot to recharge after an afternoon of perusing the fabulous neighborhood boutiques or meandering through nearby Metropolitan Museum of Art. Inside, the space offers a cozy feel with warm ochre walls, simple furnishings, and an assemblage of photographs, though regulars know to head back to the enclosed garden to enjoy their meals.

The cooking here is fuss-free, pasta-focused, and lovingly dedicated to the Amalfi Coast. Dishes may include an arugula-and-roasted red pepper salad with salty marinated anchovies; spaghetti with crab meat and fresh tomatoes; grilled fish dressed simply with olive oil and lemon; and a straightforward selection of dessert pastries.

J.G. Melon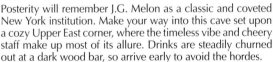

American ✗

1291 Third Ave. (at 74th St.)

Subway: 77 St
Phone: 212-744-0585
Web: N/A
Prices:

Lunch & dinner daily

Posterity will remember J.G. Melon as a classic and coveted New York institution. Make your way into this cave set upon a cozy Upper East corner, where the timeless vibe and cheery staff make up most of its allure. Drinks are steadily churned out at a dark wood bar, so arrive early to avoid the hordes.

The focus at this multi-generational saloon is the burger—perhaps paired with a lip-smacking Bloody Mary at brunch? The warm toasted bun topped with meat cooked on a griddle to rosy pink is coupled with onions, pickles, and crispy crinkle-cut fries. Be forewarned: you will go through the entire stack of napkins before finishing. Other simple pleasures include standards like salads, steaks, and eggs. Seal the meal with a chocolate chip-studded layer cake.

JoJo

B1

Contemporary ✕✕

160 E. 64th St. (bet. Lexington & Third Aves.)

Subway: Lexington Av - 63 St   Lunch & dinner daily
Phone: 212-223-5656
Web: www.jean-georges.com
Prices: $$$

If only everybody could have a neighborhood home like this. Lodged in a lovely townhouse in an affluent area of town, JoJo sees a routine following of ritzy revelers. Two velvet-covered stools sit by the terra-cotta-covered entrance beside an antique desk where the host holds court; and fitted below the front window is a bar mixing an array of potions. Every well-heeled tourist rubbing elbows with the local crowd agrees: tiny JoJo oozes charm, snugly packed tables and all.

Keeping company with such pretty patrons is a menu of contemporary creations including roasted butternut squash purée gilded with chives; slow-baked salmon poised atop sweet corn pudding and crested with pickled onions; and a spiced pear tart drizzled with a hot milk chocolate sauce.

Jones Wood Foundry

C3

Gastropub ✕

401 E. 76th St. (bet. First & York Aves.)

Subway: 77 St   Lunch & dinner daily
Phone: 212-249-2771
Web: www.joneswoodfoundry.com
Prices: $$

The moniker of this pleasing Yorkville pub refers to when the neighborhood was merely a stretch of heavily forested land. Although that bucolic ideal has been replaced by tower-lined corridors, the eatery offers a taste of the Old World tucked away from the fray. A narrow wood bar area welcomes guests, while a pretty courtyard dining room and larger rear space offer plenty of breathing room.

Chef/partner Jason Hicks garners inspiration from his childhood in England to beget a spot-on lineup of enjoyable pub grub. A "toast" list includes a soft-boiled farm egg and soldiers; steak and kidney pie is presented as golden brown pastry stuffed with a stew of chopped beef and vegetables; and a delightfully boozy sherry trifle caps off any meal here.

Kaia

C2

1614 Third Ave. (bet. 90th & 91st Sts.)

Subway: 86 St (Lexington Ave.)
Phone: 212-722-0490
Web: www.kaiawinebar.com
Prices: $$

Dinner nightly

This South African wine bar takes its name from the word for shelter. It is owned by a native South African who chased her dreams of stardom to New York City, while building an impressive resume of work in some in the city's finer dining rooms. The space has a comfortable appeal, spotlighting a lively dining counter as well as high and low wood tables. Discover a plethora of wines not just from South Africa, but also South America and New York. To accompany your glass, select from the interesting small plates like "spear and shield" of bacon-wrapped asparagus with melting cheddar-stuffed mushroom caps; or *vark ribbetjies en vark pensie*, pork ribs glazed with honey and *rooibos* tea and pork belly braised in Indian pale ale dressed with candied kumquats.

Kings' Carriage House

C2

251 E. 82nd St. (bet. Second & Third Aves.)

Subway: 86 St (Lexington Ave.)
Phone: 212-734-5490
Web: www.kingscarriagehouse.com
Prices: $$

Lunch Tue – Sun
Dinner Tue – Sat

Picture the mist rolling in when dining at this bona fide facsimile of an Irish manor, warmly run by Elizabeth King and husband Paul Farrell (of Dublin). Since 1994, this elegantly countrified setting has been an old-world rarity, complete with creaky floors, murals, linen-draped tables with lacy overlays, antique china, and vintage silverware accenting the multiple dining rooms. A collection of china teapots is even available for purchase.

The nightly prix-fixe menu offers an updated take on classically prepared cuisine that complements the romantic ambience beautifully, as in the roasted filet mignon with a medallion of tarragon-Cognac sausage and port wine demi-glace. Afternoon tea is quite popular, so be sure to reserve in advance.

L'Absinthe

French ✗✗

B4

227 E. 67th St. (bet. Second & Third Aves.)

Subway: 68 St - Hunter College   Lunch & dinner daily
Phone: 212-794-4950
Web: www.labsinthe.com
Prices: $$$

A true charmer, L'Absinthe is a uniquely enjoyable neighborhood bistro that can claim few peers. The warm and amiable setting boasts an authentically continental elegance that is enhanced by an understated, sophisticated clientele.

The flawless menu offers a culling of preparations that are seasonal and contemporary in theme, but the real draw here are Chef Jean-Michel Bergougnoux's "brasserie classics" like the *choucroute royale Alsacienne*, presented as a heaping platter of expertly prepared pork: garlicky sausage, *boudin blanc*, belly, and ham. Also await caraway-spiced braised cabbage and boiled potatoes. Another standard, the *baba au rhum* is deliciously done—a boozy moist cake slathered with *crème pâtissière* and *brunoise* of tropical fruits.

Lusardi's

Italian ✗✗

C3

1494 Second Ave. (bet. 77th & 78th Sts.)

Subway: 77 St   Lunch Mon – Fri
Phone: 212-249-2020   Dinner nightly
Web: www.lusardis.com
Prices: $$$

A neighborhood mainstay since 1982, brothers Luigi and Mauro Lusardi continue to run an impressive operation. Tastefully appointed with pumpkin-colored walls and deep-toned woodwork, the dining room is warmly attended to by a beaming staff that suits Lusardi's comfortable elegance and old-world vibe.

Fresh ingredients and careful preparation go into the Northern Italian fare such as *crespelle Fiorentina*, a cylinder of pan-fried eggplant filled with a fluffy blend of spinach and ricotta, then bathed in bright and creamy tomato sauce. Many of the preparations feature an appetizingly rustic presentation as in the *fegato alla Veneziana*—chunks of chicken liver sautéed with sweet onions and white wine, then piled on to a nest of coarse ground polenta.

Manhattan ▶ Upper East Side

Maison Kayser

French French

 B3

1294 Third Ave. (at 74th St.)

Subway: 77 St
Phone: 212-744-3100
Web: www.maison-kayser-usa.com
Prices: $$

Lunch & dinner daily

Maison Kayser is the US flagship of French baker extraordinaire Eric Kayser whose skill with flour and water has yielded him a collection of *boulangeries* that spans the globe. Arrive to find a small retail area stocked with temptation and a bustling café that comforts guests in an oak-floored, mirror-paneled room staffed with servers sporting Breton tees. Get the ordering out of the way to speed up the arrival of the bread, made from organic New York-grown grain and studded with walnuts or dried fruit, rustically presented in a burlap sack.

From the menu, enjoy the likes of shrimp- and lump crabmeat-topped guacamole; traditional bœuf Bourguignon presented in a cocotte; or pistachio éclair. All are worthy complements to the array of bread.

Marché du Sud

French

 B4

1136 First Ave. (bet. 62nd & 63rd Sts.)

Subway: Lexington Av - 59 St
Phone: 212-207-4900
Web: www.marchedusud.com
Prices: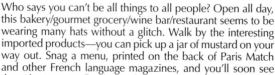

Lunch & dinner daily

Who says you can't be all things to all people? Open all day, this bakery/gourmet grocery/wine bar/restaurant seems to be wearing many hats without a glitch. Walk by the interesting imported products—you can pick up a jar of mustard on your way out. Snag a menu, printed on the back of Paris Match and other French language magazines, and you'll soon see that *Alsatian tarte flambée* is de rigueur here. Go for tradition and you'll enjoy this thin, flaky crust topped with Gruyère, bacon, and onions; or go house-style with crème fraîche, duck confit, and black truffle-foie gras.

Chef/partner Adil Fawzi hails from Morocco, so the *Marocaine*, topped with hummus, harissa, merguez, cheese, and lemon confit is a sure bet. Don't worry *cherie*, there's dessert too.

Maya

Mexican ✗✗

1191 First Ave. (bet. 64th & 65th Sts.)

Subway: 68 St - Hunter College
Phone: 212-585-1818
Web: www.richardsandoval.com
Prices: $$

Lunch & dinner daily

Maya continues to impress as one of the city's finest examples of upscale Mexican cuisine. And if that isn't luring enough, it now offers increased potential for margarita-fueled revelry with its inviting Tequileria Maya, pouring more than 200 bottles. The room is nicely attended to and features dark furnishings contrasted with soft orange-splashed walls.

Here, Mexican flavors are captured with modern flair and combine seamlessly in delicious *especialidades* such as mahi mahi *"a la talla"*—a plump piece of adobo-marinated fish set atop slivered Napa cabbage, tomato, and dressed with chipotle aïoli. *Cazuelas* like beef short ribs spread with tamarind *mole* are served with warm tortillas, and even sides excite as in the poblano chile-and-potato gratin.

Maz Mezcal

Mexican ✗

316 E. 86th St. (bet. First & Second Aves.)

Subway: 86 St (Lexington Ave.)
Phone: 212-472-1599
Web: www.mazmezcal.com
Prices: $$

Lunch Sat – Sun
Dinner nightly

This family-run, longtime favorite still draws its legions of Upper East regulars for satisfying and traditional Mexican fare. Welcomes are personalized and the dining room is filled with guests chatting up the staff about their latest news. The narrow front room is bright with sienna and turquoise walls quirkily decorated with watermelon-themed artwork. The back feels cozier and the bar area seems tucked away.

Commendable specialties have included *camarones en pipian rojo*, shrimp sauced with a blend of dried chiles, ground nuts, and sesame seeds. Family-friendly combination platters can pair tender fried poblano *chile rellenos* abundantly stuffed with mild cheese, and a crisp, chorizo-filled *flauta* with tomato-tinted rice and dollop of refried beans.

Mezzaluna

Italian ✗

B3

1295 Third Ave. (bet. 74th & 75th Sts.)

Subway: 77 St
Phone: 212-535-9600
Web: www.mezzalunanyc.com
Prices: $$

Lunch & dinner daily

After more than 25 years in the business, this old Upper East Side cat could show the new crop of wood-burning ovens popping up across the city a thing or two. Mezzaluna (named for the crescent-shaped knife, which you'll find rendered 77 different ways on the restaurant's art-strewn walls) manages to feel both fresh and comforting to the throngs of loyal patrons who keep it packed day and night.

What's their secret? Simple, unfussy Italian food that's made with pristine ingredients and careful attention to detail. Add to that a wood-burning oven that turns out perfectly bubbling pies; a thoughtful wine list; and a convivial staff bolstered by a hands-on owner who can often be found milling about his dining room, and feel like you're in paradise.

Moti Mahal Delux

Indian ✗✗

B4

1149 First Ave. (at 63rd St.)

Subway: Lexington Av - 63 St
Phone: 212-371-3535
Web: www.motimahaldelux.us
Prices: $$

Lunch & dinner daily

This tempting newcomer marks the first American location of a fine dining chain that began in Delhi and now boasts outposts throughout India, Nepal, and London. Here in NYC, it's a corner spot with a sidewalk atrium and main dining room decked with stone floors and leather banquettes. The cuisine features a northern accent and traces its origins back to the kitchens of the Mughal Empire, which brought Muslim influences to the Indian subcontinent.

Tasty *tandoori* preparations factor heavily on the menu, as in the delicate *ajwaini machchi tikka* marinated with mustard and carom seeds. Simmered specialties are not to be missed, like their signature *murgh mahkani* (butter chicken) or *dum ke phool*, broccoli florets decadently slow-cooked in saffron-yogurt sauce.

Nello

Italian XX

A1

696 Madison Ave. (bet. 62nd & 63rd Sts.)

Subway: 5 Av - 59 St

Lunch & dinner daily

Phone: 212-980-9099

Web: www.nellorestaurantnyc.com

Prices: $$$$

Fashionably perched among pricey boutiques and astronomical real estate, Nello struts a chic and polished yet satisfying Italian dining experience. The bright and airy room (resplendent with marble, ivory walls hung with black-and-white safari scenes, and thick linen-covered tables dressed with white flowers) is overseen by a well-orchestrated, suit-clad service team. Everything here radiates privilege and optimism. Even the menu's typeface appears elegant...and expensive.

While high prices and celebrity sightings do not ensure an enjoyable meal, the flavorful offerings like San Daniele prosciutto and melon; neat mounds of perfectly prepared pasta; and hearty entrées of osso buco should bring enough pleasure to help ease the potential sticker shock.

Nick's

Pizza X

C2

1814 Second Ave. (at 94th St.)

Subway: 96 St (Lexington Ave.)

Lunch & dinner daily

Phone: 212-987-5700

Web: www.nicksnyc.com

Prices:

Due to a blockade of equipment needed for the ongoing construction of the Second Avenue subway line, Nick's may be a bit harder to spot but still ranks highly on Upper East Siders' short list of pizza favorites. This Manhattan location of the Forest Hills original, named for owner Nick Angelis, has cozy environs with tables overlooking the dough-tossing *pizzaiolos* and jovial service staff.

In addition to the excellent, bronzed, and crackling thin-crust pizzas, a variety of Italian-American pastas (referred to as "macaroni") and entrées are available as full or half portions for family-friendly dining. Offerings may include veal scaloppini with lemon and butter; or an enjoyable tangle of linguini with white clam sauce infused with roasted garlic cloves.

The Nuaa

Thai   🍴🍴

1122 First Ave. (bet. 61st & 62nd St.)

Subway: 59 St   Lunch & dinner daily
Phone: 212-888-2899
Web: N/A
Prices: $$

The Nuaa brings a certain sexy vibe to a rather blah, trafficky stretch of First Avenue. The room's deep dark palette, with brown leather seating and carved woodwork, pops against abundant gold accents.

The thumping playlist won't be to everyone's liking, but fans of Thai cuisine will find much to enjoy from the well-executed menu. A few nicely pungent salads and noodle dishes give way to creations like char-grilled tiger prawns, served head-on, slicked with ambrosial house-made citrus red curry, plated with stir-fried morning glory; or crispy whole fish with roasted cashew nuts, herb salad, and chili-herb emulsion. Do not miss the braised rice with blue crab, generously stocked with lump meat, green onion, and lemongrass presented in a lotus leaf.

Orsay

French   🍴🍴

1057 Lexington Ave. (at 75th St.)

Subway: 77 St   Lunch & dinner daily
Phone: 212-517-6400
Web: www.orsayrestaurant.com
Prices: $$

This Lexington Avenue corner is a classy scene through and through. The art nouveau look is so well done it may as well be an authentic tableau of hand-laid mosaic tiles, mahogany paneling, and a pewter-topped bar. When the weather warms, the chic crowd spills out onto the sidewalk, protected by a wide awning.

Chef Antoine Camin, formerly of La Goulue, has brought his celebrated cheese soufflé with him, as well as his deliciously signature touches brightened with au courant flourish. The ladies who lunch here happily devour the likes of *Japonais* tartare—a cylinder of chopped tuna moistened by toasted sesame oil and flecked with tempura bits and wasabi cream. Classics like the golden brown, creamy, cheesy *croque monsieur* do this brasserie proud.

Parlor Steakhouse

Steakhouse ✗✗

C2

1600 Third Ave. (at 90th St.)

Subway: 86 St (Lexington Ave.)
Phone: 212-423-5888
Web: www.parlorsteakhouse.com
Prices: $$$

Lunch & dinner daily

This sexy, contemporary Upper East Side steakhouse, straddling a busy corner of Third Avenue and 90th Street, has managed to remain under the radar. But what a shame, for this neighborhood find boasts clubby, welcoming good looks (think plush fabric and masculine dark stripes); first-class steaks cooked to juicy perfection; and a mean Belgian beer selection.

Kick your night off with one of the rotating daily specials, such as a starter of soft shell crabs, delicately fried and served with a punchy gherkin-spiked rémoulade; and then move on to the succulent bone-in ribeye, topped with roasted garlic cloves and accompanied by a bevy of traditional sauces (béarnaise, horseradish, herb fresh lime, and red wine reduction) to choose from.

Persepolis

Persian ✗✗

B3

1407 Second Ave. (bet. 73rd & 74th Sts.)

Subway: 77 St
Phone: 212-535-1100
Web: www.persepolisnyc.com
Prices: $$

Lunch & dinner daily

Silky-smooth spreads, homemade yogurt, grilled meats, and fragrantly spiced stews have solidified Persepolis' reputation as one of the city's finest Persian restaurants. Reddish wood furnishings, linen-draped tables, and landscape paintings fashion a setting that is attractive enough to dress up for (or not). Gracious service enhances the convivial scene.

The kitchen's seriousness and skill is revealed in one bite of the house tabbouleh. It arrives as a neatly stacked tower of bulgar wheat and diced vegetables sparked by a bright balance of lemon, garlic, and a vibrant green profusion of fresh parsley and mint. The chicken *kubideh* is a hot, juicy kebob of highly seasoned ground chicken alongside fluffy basmati flecked with dried dill and fava beans.

Philippe

A1

Chinese 🍴🍴

33 E. 60th St. (bet. Madison & Park Aves.)

Subway: Lexington Av - 59 St
Phone: 212-644-8885
Web: www.philippechow.com
Prices: $$$

Lunch Mon – Sat
Dinner nightly

This luxe Chinese is elegant but not too fancy to be delicious. Inside, the stage is set with linen-draped tables, chopsticks in wooden boxes, and celebrity sightings. The staff pairs white jackets and mandarin collar uniforms with red canvas sneakers—this whimsical departure from formality is juxtaposed by the monochromatic color scheme throughout the multi-room space.

The satisfying menu features masterfully prepared noodles and pick-your-protein lettuce wraps. Entrées, like nine seasons spicy prawns with sweet-and-sour sauce are sized to share, but half-portions are also offered. A supplemental listing of healthier steamed dishes includes chicken and broccoli with brown rice.

Enthusiasts can visit Philippe in Los Angeles and even Mexico City.

Quatorze Bis

C3

French 🍴🍴

323 E. 79th St. (bet. First & Second Aves.)

Subway: 77 St
Phone: 212-535-1414
Web: N/A
Prices: $$

Lunch Tue – Sun
Dinner nightly

With its lipstick red façade and sunny yellow awning, Quatorze Bis easily stands out along this high-rise stretch of the Upper East. The pleasant interior, frequented by a mature, well-dressed crowd, displays a continental flair with framed vintage posters, mirrored panels painted with the wine list, and comfortable red velvet banquettes. The friendly waitstaff greets patrons with a small blackboard to present the day's specials.

The menu's roster of satisfying French classics is executed with savoir faire, as in the terrine *maison* and a savory tart of bacon, leek, and Gruyère. Grilled sirloin with light and crispy frites and decadent sauce béarnaise followed by the excellent hot apple tart is testament to the timelessness of true bistro cooking.

Salumeria Rosi Il Ristorante

Italian XX

A3

903 Madison Ave. (bet. 72nd & 73rd Sts.)

Subway: 77 St
Phone: 212-517-7700
Web: www.salumeriarosi.com
Prices: $$$

Lunch & dinner daily

This larger and more formal station of the Upper West Side's Salumeria Rosi, is brought to you by rosemary-scented Chef Cesare Casellla and Italy's Gruppo Parmacotta. Designed by Academy Award-winning Dante Ferretti, the elegant scene is set by deep red walls, sleek leather furnishings, and faux-Roman statues. If that doesn't bespeak singularity, the sharply attired and Italian-accented staff adds to the vibe.

Of course, a selection from the range of meats is highly advised. Find *bresaola* with *stracciatella* and wild Puglia onions; or prosciutto *Toscana*, rubbed with black pepper, juniper, and presented paper-thin with pecorino knobs. Chase this down with a hearty pasta like *pasticcio all'Amatriciana*; or go meatless with grilled cauliflower "steak."

San Matteo

Pizza X

C2

1739 Second Ave. (at 90th St.)

Subway: 86 St (Lexington Ave.)
Phone: 212-426-6943
Web: www.sanmatteopanuozzo.com
Prices:

Lunch Fri – Sun
Dinner nightly

Upper East Siders have been counting their blessings since this convivial pizza newcomer moved into the neighborhood. The space is tiny and rustic, but also very inviting and gracious.

More than 20 varieties of Neapolitan-style pizza temptingly emerge from the hand-built, wood-fired oven. Add to this a unique regional specialty hailing from Campania called *panuozzo*. Simply stated, it is a cross between a calzone and *panino*, comprised of a puffy plank of freshly baked pizza dough stuffed with an array of fine quality ingredients such as roasted pork, fresh mozzarella, and baby arugula for the *panuozzo di Bartolomei*.

The boys of San Matteo can now be found slicing *Prosciutto di Parma* at their new Il Salumaio, housed a few doors away.

Shanghai Pavilion

Chinese ✗✗

 B3

1378 Third Ave. (bet. 78th & 79th Sts.)

Subway: 77 St
Phone: 212-585-3388
Web: N/A
Prices: 🍜

Lunch & dinner daily

Shanghai Pavilion may be considered upscale neighborhood Chinese, yet it rises above its many peers with attractive surroundings and service with a smile—these are your first hints that there is an underlying seriousness to the cooking here. The polished, unobtrusive staff does much to draw these well-heeled local residents, but the list of celebration-worthy, order-in-advance specialties earns their devotion.

Shanghainese and Cantonese regional favorites abound, as with the slurp-inducing steamed juicy dumplings. While enjoying these toothsome treats, the efficient servers stealthily restock your soup spoon with the next bun from the tabletop bamboo steamer. Other house specialties may include red-cooked chicken and braised beef with dried chilies.

Spigolo

Italian ✗✗

C3

1561 Second Ave. (at 81st St.)

Subway: 77 St
Phone: 212-744-1100
Web: www.spigolonyc.com
Prices: $$

Dinner nightly

Set on a generic corner of Second Avenue, Spigolo is more than a simple neighborhood gem. The façade is easily spotted by its wide-open windows, pretty planters, and red awning; likewise, the staff is all ease and warmth. A tiny copper bar offers a cheerful perch to observe the scene—local denizens mingle at bare tables amid polished cork floors and food-themed art.

In the back, a glass-enclosed window lets you peek into the kitchen where the action is palpable. They are in the midst of creating the likes of chewy *bucatini* coated with a spicy squid ink marinara, stocked with slivers of cuttlefish. Dining alfresco is epic, especially if it includes nibbling on spinach agnolotti shimmering in a ricotta purée, trailed by a dense dark chocolate cheesecake.

Sushi of Gari ✿

C3

402 E. 78th St. (bet. First & York Aves.)

Subway: 77 St
Phone: 212-517-5340
Web: www.sushiofgari.com
Prices: $$$

Dinner nightly

Sushi of Gari

The look of this Upper East Side *sushi-ya* may seem typical; the food is anything but. Of Chef Gari's local empire, this is the flagship and *the* place to find sushi prepared with trademark creativity and tremendous skill. The room is efficiently served but always packed. Scoring a reservation can be tricky, so plan on booking in advance.

Be sure to sit at the counter, where each morsel goes straight from the chef's hand to your mouth, just as it is prepared. Furthermore, the excellent omakase includes very interesting creations. The quality of fish is always outstanding, as is the chef's interplay of flavors and textures resulting in a truly original dining experience. Oysters may arrive wrapped in nori or simply baked in their shells. Tuna tartare is placed over a tempura-fried rectangle of nori with toasted pine nuts. Goldeneye snapper is paired with black truffles. Toro may be chopped with marinated daikon or simply barbecued. Unusual and delicious are the hallmarks of any meal here, no matter what may come. The fish imported from Japan is of extraordinary quality, so be sure to explore the extensive array.

Neighbors take note: Sushi of Gari offers a booming takeout business.

Sushi Sasabune

Japanese

C3

401 E. 73rd St. (at First Ave.)

Subway: 77 St
Phone: 212-249-8583
Web: N/A
Prices: $$$

Lunch Tue – Fri
Dinner Tue – Sat

Ignore the unremarkable interior; this kitchen is worthy of high praise. Absolute deliverance is inherent to a fine meal here, as patrons are regaled with blackboard signs that read, "Trust me." Indeed, this is a place where customers find mounted warnings of "No Spicy Tuna, No California Roll" as reminders that the sushi chefs are in charge. Trust *us* that it will be good.

There are no missteps once the omakase-only procession begins, preceded by the commands, "soy sauce" or "no soy sauce." Expect such gems as mackerel sashimi drizzled with ponzu sauce; nigiri of delicate amberjack on warm rice zinged by *yuzu kosho*; or a cooked trio of crisped fluke fin, butter fish, and sea eel.

For a speedier affair, Sasabune Express offers sushi by the piece.

Sushi Seki

Japanese

B4

1143 First Ave. (bet. 62nd & 63rd Sts.)

Subway: Lexington Av - 59 St
Phone: 212-371-0238
Web: N/A
Prices: $$$

Dinner Mon – Sat

Beloved Sushi Seki fills up nightly with a devoted following that represents a cross section of city life: neighborhood families, business colleagues, novices looking to broaden their horizons, and even celebrity chefs enjoying a late night snack. Although the décor of this well-worn sushi den doesn't make much of an impression with its dark carpeting, simple furnishings, and unadorned walls, what goes on behind the counter is truly special.

The menu offers enjoyable appetizers and cooked fare, but sushi is where Seki shines. The original special recipe platter serves up a stellar nigiri array—rich salmon topped with warmed tomato; butter-sautéed scallop; tuna with tofu cream; and silky *amaebi*—as well as a crunchy- creamy- and spicy-shrimp tempura roll.

Tanoshi

Japanese ✕

1372 York Ave. (bet. 73rd & 74th Sts.)

Subway: 77 St
Phone: 646-727-9056
Web: www.tanoshisushinyc.com
Prices: $$$

Dinner Tue – Sat

Tanoshi must be appreciated for its simplicity. The menu is focused on omakase (though a few à la carte options are also offered) and seating is limited to three rounds nightly, enabling just a select number to partake in impressive sushi at good value. The small room is tidy and diners are seated in front of a tempting counter.

Chef Toshio Oguma sources excellent fish and presents a distinctive style of sushi that incorporates loosely packed, warm rice seasoned with red *akazu* (sake lees vinegar). For a modest charge, the deluxe menu reveals a bevy of skillfully knifed, seasonal specialties brushed with house-blend soy. Think Kona amberjack; Hokkaido sea scallop; firefly squid; and torched King salmon. Finish off with ginger and shrimp miso soup.

Taste

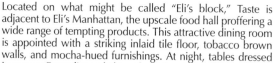

American ✕✕

1413 Third Ave. (at 80th St.)

Subway: 77 St
Phone: 212-717-9798
Web: www.elizabar.com
Prices: $$

Lunch & dinner daily

Located on what might be called "Eli's block," Taste is adjacent to Eli's Manhattan, the upscale food hall proffering a wide range of tempting products. This attractive dining room is appointed with a striking inlaid tile floor, tobacco brown walls, and mocha-hued furnishings. At night, tables dressed in orange Frette linens lighten the rich palette.

The impressive menu focuses on seasonality and simplicity in offerings like grilled Mediterranean sardine crostini with piquillo pepper hummus; or North Carolina chicken with horseradish Yukon Golds and savoy cabbage. If offered, a slice of the famous lemon meringue cake is a must. For home indulgence, order a whole cake in advance.

Breakfast and lunch are self-service, with many items priced by the pound.

Tiella

B4

Italian ✗✗

1109 First Ave. (bet. 60th & 61st Sts.)

Subway: Lexington Av - 59 St
Phone: 212-588-0100
Web: www.tiellanyc.com
Prices: $$

Lunch Tue – Sat
Dinner nightly

Although this forgotten stretch of First Ave, steps from the Roosevelt Island Tramway and Queensboro Bridge, is busy and unattractive, Tiella's Southern Italian specialties and classic hospitality are reason enough to seek it out. This neigborhood fave is housed in a room as slender as a train car, outfitted with espresso-tinted wood furnishings set against ivory walls and exposed brick.

Tiella draws its name from the petite pans used to produce wood-oven pizzas that are characterized by a uniquely delicate crust. Toppings are fresh and balanced, as in the *Caprese* with creamy mozzarella, sweet cherry tomatoes, and fragrant basil. An inventive pasta listing, several *secondi*, and starters such as a *bellisima* block of eggplant *Parmigiana* complete the menu.

Untitled 🕲

B3

American ✗

945 Madison Ave. (at 75th St.)

Subway: 77 St
Phone: 212-570-3670
Web: www.untitledatthewhitney.com
Prices: 🍴🍴

Lunch Wed – Sun
Dinner Fri

Operated with aplomb by the Union Square Hospitality Group, this daytime dining showstopper is ensconced within the Whitney Museum of American Art. This beautifully designed space includes a granite-framed cellar that is flooded with light and furnished with white oak tables, as well as an inviting dining counter facing a blackboard wall listing local ingredients.

Untitled's all-day menu offers breakfast items well into the afternoon. Griddled faves may include huckleberry pancakes; grilled cheese with add-ons such as mushrooms or avocado; and burgers washed down by a chocolate egg cream or boutique roasted coffee. Zingy items might reveal a chicken- ginger- and lime soup; or an artfully constructed smoked trout BLT spread with spiced mayonnaise.

Tori Shin ⌘

B4

Japanese ✕✕

1193 First Ave. (bet. 64th & 65th Sts.)

Subway: 68 St - Hunter College

Phone: 212-988-8408

Web: www.torishinny.com

Prices: $$

Dinner Tue – Sun

Atsushi Kono

The exterior is so quiet that it is not immediately clear what you are about to enter—a dedicated *yakitori-ya*, packed to the gills with savvy diners. Inside, the intoxicating aroma of charcoal, smoke, and searing meat is sure to be your first welcome. The mood is never loud (as many solo diners prefer the counter), but lively by dint of the busy chefs, searing away their range of ingredients.

While the idea of grilled chicken seems simple, if not primal, this kitchen embraces a variety of techniques and has wonderful control over heat (note the fanning of charcoals or careful placement of livers on the cooler side of the grill). This results in skewers that are perfect in flavor, texture, and temperature. The quality here is distinct and dishes are particularly authentic.

Some offerings like thin slices of cold duck breast with shiso leaf and ponzu let the pristine ingredients speak for themselves. Other dishes draw attention to skill with sublime results like a special of chopped chicken meatballs wrapped in duck skin, accompanied by soy sauce with an egg yolk for dipping. The chicken "oysters" are basted and perfectly charred but so tender that they arrive almost quivering.

Uva

C3

Italian

1486 Second Ave. (bet. 77th & 78th Sts.)

Subway: 77 St
Phone: 212-472-4552
Web: www.uvawinebar.com
Prices: $$

Lunch Sat – Sun
Dinner nightly

A few steps away from Lusardi's is this charmingly laid-back and more boisterous member of the family, whose delectable menu is a siren song for focussed diners. The amber-hued neighborhood beacon is packed nightly and whimsically embellished with grape references.

In deftly combining fine ingredients, Uva's kitchen produces an extensive array of plates that shines a light on the Italian table. There's plenty to nibble on, say a host of dressed breads that include *carta de musica condita* (paper-thin Sardinian flatbread), or the likes of quivering *burrata* studded with marinated peppers, fava beans, and basil. Heartier still are the secondi, which may bring *vitello gratinato*—tender veal crowned by whipped eggplant and pecorino.

Wa Jeal

C2

Chinese

1588 Second Ave. (bet. 82nd & 83rd Sts.)

Subway: 86 St (Lexington Ave.)
Phone: 212-396-3339
Web: www.wajealrestaurant.com
Prices:

Lunch & dinner daily

Specializing in the heated fare of the Sichuan province, Wa Jeal is spicing up the Upper East. The upscale room is comfortable with an uncharacteristically cozy atmosphere and gracious service.

The menu offers popular lunch specials and an array of regional favorites, but for a much more distinctive experience dive into the chef's menu, with its assortment of cold or hot appetizers and specialties that demonstrate the kitchen's complexity and strength. Dishes are both fresh and tantalizing, as in poached chicken dressed with soy, crushed dried red chili, and sesame oil boasting the unique, sensational tingle of Sichuan pepper; a mung bean jello salad that is at once cool and spicy; and lean strips of camphor tea-smoked duck boasting a salty-sweet allure.

Yefsi Estiatorio

C3

Greek ✕✕

1481 York Ave. (bet. 78th & 79th Sts.)

Subway: 77 St
Phone: 212-535-0293
Web: www.yefsiestiatorio.com
Prices: $$

Dinner nightly

Squeeze in, grab a seat, and watch as plates fly out of the kitchen fast and furious to keep up with the demand of ravenous Yorkville residents who are counting their lucky stars for this new and tasty resident.

Chef Christos Christou hails from Cyprus, trained at the International Culinary Institute, and has headed stalwarts like Molyvos and Milos. His menu offers an array of meze like *feta sto* fourno, baked sheep's milk cheese set atop roasted eggplant; or *garides me fasolia* comprised of chopped jumbo shrimp tossed with gigante beans sauced with mastic-accented tomato purée. Expect such entrées as grilled fish or baby lamb chops with roasted lemon potatoes.

Plastered walls inlaid with gleaming wood beams and cherry wood tables furnish the cheery room.

The sun is out – let's eat alfresco! Look for 🛖.

Upper West Side

Proudly situated between two of Manhattan's most celebrated parks, home to venerable Lincoln Center, and the beloved Museum of Natural History, the family-friendly Upper West Side is one of the city's most distinct neighborhoods. It has a near-cultish belief in its own way of doing things—whether it's because they boast some of *the* best cafés namely **Épicerie Boulud** that flaunts everything from heart-warming breakfasts, sandwiches, and soups, to coffee, pastries and *gelati*; or that life here means constantly tripping over music fans (often destined for the classically rich Metropolitan Opera), these residents cannot imagine being elsewhere.

First and foremost, the Upper West Side is a neighborhood for strolling. Its sidewalks are lined with quaint brownstones, frequently featured in cherished flicks as well as in primetime TV shows. Imagine rambling apartments filled with bookish locals arguing with equal gusto over the future of opera, or whether **Murray's** carries the best sturgeon. If a scene from *Hannah and Her Sisters* comes to mind, you are beginning to understand this area. What is on offer at **Indie Food and Wine** are delightfully simple sandwiches that deliver ample pleasure to film- and theater-lovers alike. These may be book-ended by lush chocolates from **Mondel** or baked madeleines at **La Toulousaine**.

Medley of Markets

This enthusiasm extends to all aspects of life—particularly food. For shopping, the **Tucker Square Greenmarket** is popular and anchored on West 66th Street (or "Peter Jennings Way"). Equally celebrated is the original **Fairway**, filled with reasonably priced gourmet treats. Intrepid shoppers should brave its famously cramped elevator to visit the exclusively organic second floor.

No visit to this nook is complete without **Zabar's**—home of all things gourmet and kosher—to ogle their olives and grab a few knishes. Another coveted haunt that cradles everything is **The Kosher Marketplace** (www.thekoshermarketplace.com). If planning an Italian-themed evening, visit Cesare Casella's **Salumeria Rosi**. This local darling offers an excellent choice of cured meats as well as tasty bites. Finally, get your sweet fix on at famous and frequented **Levain**'s—if not for its legendary chocolate chip cookie, then for a thrilling spectrum of baked treats from Valrhona chocolate rolls to delicious raisin sticky buns. Of course, one of **Magnolia**'s (many) outposts is sure to gain a quick cupcake following. Too much sugar? Grab a "Recession Special" savory snack at legendary **Gray's Papaya**—the politically outspoken (check the window slogans) and quintessentially Upper West hot dog chain.

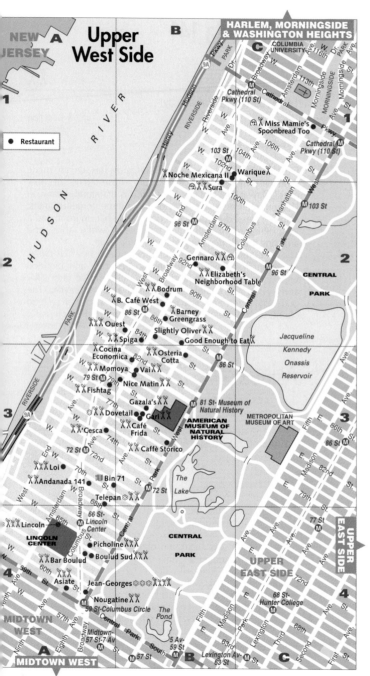

Upper West Side

● Restaurant

NEW JERSEY

HUDSON RIVER

COLUMBIA UNIVERSITY

Miss Mamie's Spoonbread Too

Cathedral Pkwy (110 St)

Noche Mexicana II
Warique
Sura

103 St

Gennaro
Elizabeth's Neighborhood Table
Bodrum
B. Café West
Barney Greengrass
Ouest
Slightly Oliver
Spiga
Good Enough to Eat
Cocina Economica
Osteria Cotta
Momoya
Vai
Nice Matin
Fishtag
Gazala's
Dovetail
Garí
Cesca
Café Frida

CENTRAL PARK

Jacqueline Kennedy Onassis Reservoir

81 St-Museum of Natural History
AMERICAN MUSEUM OF NATURAL HISTORY
METROPOLITAN MUSEUM OF ART

Caffè Storico

72 St

Loi
Andanada 141
Bin 71
Telepan

The Lake

Lincoln
LINCOLN CENTER
Picholine
Bar Boulud
Boulud Sud
Asiate
Jean-Georges
Nougatine
59 St-Columbus Circle

66 St-Lincoln Center

CENTRAL PARK

The Pond

UPPER EAST SIDE

68 St-Hunter College

MIDTOWN WEST
Midtown-57 St-7 Av
57 St
5 Av-59 St

Lexington Av-63 St

Andanada 141

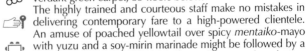

Manhattan ▶ Upper West Side

Spanish XX

A3

141 W. 69th St. (at Broadway)

Lunch & dinner daily

Subway: 72 St
Phone: 646-692-8762
Web: www.andanada141.com
Prices: $$

Despite his youth, Chef Manuel Berganza has already made a culinary mark in his native Spain. Those talents are now on display at this fantastic spot and his inaugural American kitchen. The restaurant is divided into three gorgeous areas: a sunny, glassed-in solarium; comfortable bar up front; and a long dining room with tufted banquettes, white tables, and arresting murals depicting matadors in pursuit.

The ambitious menu highlights inventive dishes like *pastel de cabracho*—meaty scorpion fish poached and blended with aromatics, cream, and tomato, all steamed until silky and topped with cauliflower foam and eggplant "caviar." The pure taste of fresh fish is in every bite of *bacalao al pil pil* (cod confit) served over creamed chickpeas and spinach chips.

Asiate

Contemporary XXX

A4

80 Columbus Circle (at 60th St.)

Lunch & dinner daily

Subway: 59 St - Columbus Circle
Phone: 212-805-8881
Web: www.mandarinoriental.com
Prices: $$$$

The Mandarin Oriental hotel's glass façade is not merely one of the more striking buildings of New York, but also houses one of its most exceptional restaurant locales, Asiate. Money was clearly no object when commissioning the Chihuly dragons (for the hotel's lobby and bar); meanwhile, luxe silks drape the semi-private leather booths and framing views make Central Park seem like a verdant green carpet, 35 floors below.

The highly trained and courteous staff make no mistakes in delivering contemporary fare to a high-powered clientele. An amuse of poached yellowtail over spicy *mentaiko*-mayo with yuzu and a soy-mirin marinade might be followed by a perfectly creamy artichoke risotto with *stravecchio* cheese, sweet Asian pear, and chopped black truffles.

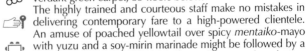

394

Bar Boulud

A4

French XX

1900 Broadway (bet. 63rd & 64th Sts.)

Subway: 66 St - Lincoln Center
Phone: 212-595-0303
Web: www.danielboulud.com
Prices: $$$

Lunch & dinner daily

The birth of Bar Boulud ensured Chef/owner Daniel Boulud's compelling foothold in this quarter of Manhattan. As its name attests, the "bar" pours sizeable and rare bottles in the airy, warm-toned dining lair. To further tease wine pundits, the room—narrow and deep with a rounded ceiling—mimics a barrel's inside, decked with abstract images of wine spills. Whether you nestle into a booth or bar stool, be sure to begin with an impeccable charcuterie plate. It may even wholly consume you, but do save room for thrills like *lapin garigue*, tender rabbit layered with fragrant herbs and carrots; followed by sautéed Quinault sturgeon. Close the deal with *tanin*, an intense dark chocolate tart filled with cocoa mousse that will keep you lilting well into the night.

Barney Greengrass

B2

Deli X

541 Amsterdam Ave. (bet. 86th & 87th Sts.)

Subway: 86 St (Broadway)
Phone: 212-724-4707
Web: www.barneygreengrass.com
Prices:

Lunch Tue – Sun

New York's venerable "Sturgeon King" has earned its title and position as an Upper West Side institution.

In addition to serving breakfast and lunch until 5:00 P.M., they do double duty as a vibrant carry-out business and now take Internet orders. The place is darling, whether eating in or taking out; the deli sandwiches—piled high with pastrami or homemade egg salad, and served with a big, bright, crunchy pickle—are among the best in the city.

Their food is the real thing so order a heaping plate of sturgeon, house-cured gravlax, or clear, flavorful bowl of matzoh ball soup at this Formica-clad jewel and take a trip back in time. Service without ceremony but unique NY attitude makes a trip to Barney Greengrass an authentic and essential experience.

B. Café West

B2

566 Amsterdam Ave. (bet. 87th & 88th Sts.)

Subway: 86 St (Broadway)
Phone: 212-873-0003
Web: www.bcafe.com
Prices: $$

Lunch Sat – Sun
Dinner nightly

It used to be that finding a good spot along this stretch was like looking for a needle in a haystack. Well, needle found! B. Café West (the original "East" is on the Upper East Side) is now a go-to spot. This postage stamp of a restaurant stands out for its charming style, seemingly endless selection of Belgian-only beers, and delicious comfort food that is authentic and satisfying. The rustic, faux traditional style may feel a bit cliché, but no one seems to mind.

First, choose from their impressive beer list (you can't go wrong), then slurp some *moules* swimming in savory broth, and crunch those addictively crispy frites. From beef croquettes to smoked ham-wrapped endive with béchamel and Gruyère, this is Belgian comfort food to the hilt.

Bin 71

A3

237 Columbus Ave. (bet. 70th & 71st Sts.)

Subway: 72 St
Phone: 212-362-5446
Web: www.bin71.com
Prices: $$

Lunch & dinner Tue – Sun

Is it a wine bar? Espresso bar? Italian *assaggini* (small plates) joint? It's all three, and more. This buzzy block boasts a snazzy little number on its hands, where locals can nibble on the likes of Jonah crab *raviolo* before skipping over to Lincoln Center for a night of culture. Charm oozes at every corner, from the flower-topped marble bar, to the dark wood stools, to the French doors that open up onto sparkly Columbus Avenue.

The solid selection of wines would excite any oenophile— over thirty are offered by the glass, and double that by the bottle. Try gnocchi with beef and veal Bolognese studded with carrots, celery, cream, and smoky pancetta; or the heavenly pork, beef, and lamb meatballs stewing in a sumptuous sauce of white wine and lemon.

Bodrum

B2

Turkish ✗✗

584 Amsterdam Ave. (bet. 88th & 89th Sts.)

Subway: 86 St (Broadway)
Phone: 212-799-2806
Web: www.bodrumnyc.com
Prices: $$

Lunch & dinner daily

This Upper West Side Turkish restaurant is the very definition of a cozy and comfortable neighborhood spot. Regulars pack the place throughout the day for its inviting, Mediterranean feel; warm-weather sidewalk seating; and the delicious, well-priced fare.

Though not a traditional feature of Turkish cuisine, there's a wood-burning oven for thin, crafty pizzas, which are a popular choice among chatting locals. The bulk of the appealing menu features traditional Turkish specialties like crunchy and fresh shepherd salad with a smattering of sumac, and grilled chicken *Baharat*. Flavorful and healthy dishes keep the neighborhood coming back for more, as do the lunch and dinner specials that are as light on the wallet as they are on the waistline.

Boulud Sud

A4

Mediterranean ✗✗✗

20 W. 64th St. (bet. Broadway & Central Park West)

Subway: 66 St - Lincoln Center
Phone: 212-595-1313
Web: www.danielboulud.com
Prices: $$$

Lunch & dinner daily

Chef Daniel Boulud indulges his authentic yet modern Mediterranean flair here at Boulud Sud. The decadent menu finds its influences in all sides of the sea from Morocco to Turkey to Italy and back again. Packed and lively, the dining area is designed with the airy spaciousness of vaulted ceilings, long striped banquettes, and natural lighting.

The semi-open kitchen deftly creates delicacies like homemade lemon-saffron linguine mingled with shaved bottarga, dandelion leaves, and cuttlefish so beautifully cooked that it melts on the tongue; or crispy duck duo with aromatic Marsala jus, spring vegetables, and duck confit pastries. Sicilian sabayon is an extraordinary and foamy lemon concoction with bergamot gelato-stuffed tartlets and green tea ice cream.

Café Frida

Mexican

B3

368 Columbus Ave. (bet. 77th & 78th Sts.)

Subway: 81 St - Museum of Natural History   Lunch & dinner daily
Phone: 212-712-2929
Web: www.cafefrida.com
Prices: $$

Sporting bright fuchsia walls, quaint wrought-iron chandeliers, and cozy wooden tables, this pretty little hacienda manages to be festive, classy, and rustic all at the same time. Add in the fluffy handmade tortillas; fresh organic produce; and intricate Mexican specialties, and you'll think you've died and gone to Puebla.

The gorgeous spectrum of homemade margaritas and a serious tequila list only lulls you deeper into the dream. Café Frida's menu, served up by a friendly and knowledgeable staff, might reveal a fragrant and comforting chicken soup bobbing with tender white hominy, potatoes, and tomatillo; or *enchiladas suiza*, stuffed with juicy shredded chicken and draped in a tart tomatillo purée and cool lick of *crema*.

Caffè Storico

Italian

B3

170 Central Park West (at 77th St.)

Subway: 81 St - Museum of Natural History   Lunch & dinner Tue – Sun
Phone: 212-485-9211
Web: www.caffestorico.com
Prices: $$

Philadelphia restaurateur Stephen Starr can sniff out an opportunity better than a hound chasing summer truffles. And voila: his Caffè Storico is born to the freshly revitalized New York Historical Society. Lovely and bright, the space is flooded with natural light bouncing from white walls to marble tables laid bare, as if to match that glorious, windowed sculpture arcade.

Brass chandeliers seem as if they are suspended in thin air, but all eyes remain firm on the open kitchen, preparing the likes of silky *baccalà mantecato* laced with caperberries. Wonderfully thick sourdough spread with some of the city's best liver pâté and trailed by *garganelli* enrobed in cauliflower purée and studded with *bottarga* showcase a successful marriage of ingredients.

'Cesca

Italian ✗✗

A3

164 W. 75th St. (at Amsterdam Ave.)

Subway: 72 St
Phone: 212-787-6300
Web: www.cescanyc.com
Prices: $$

Lunch Sun
Dinner nightly

Tucked into 75th Street, just off Amsterdam Ave., the sexy 'Cesca keeps perfect company with a spate of new condos that were built into this Upper West Side nook over the last few years. The space is stylish and sprawling, with dark, low-ceilings, deep brown velvet banquettes, and iron chandeliers; while the waitstaff is attentive, professional, and eager to please. Everyone is in good spirits at 'Cesca, it would seem.

But how's the food, you wonder? Not wildly innovative, but very fresh and very well-made. Witness a luscious *minestra* studded with cubes of sweet, aromatic *cotecchino*, chard, chickpeas, tomato, and herbs; chewy orecchiette humming with homemade lamb sausage, pecorino, and rainbow Swiss chard; and tender, slow-roasted Long Island duck.

Cocina Economica

Mexican ✗

B3

452 Amsterdam Ave. (bet. 81st & 82nd Sts.)

Subway: 79 St
Phone: 212-501-7755
Web: www.cocinaeconomicamexico.com
Prices: $$

Lunch & dinner daily

Delicious and genuine Mexican fare is served with good cheer here at Cocina Economica. Bedecked with brightly painted walls, Mexican artifacts, and rustic wooden tables, this vibrant little oasis is a welcome addition to the neighborhood.

Nibble on *antojitos* (street snacks) like *pan de elote con aguacate*, cornbread stuffed with creamy avocado, steamed in corn husks; or the delicate, almost flaky vegetable empanadas, piping hot and filled with *huauzontle* and oozing Oaxaca cheese, presented alongside pumpkin-seed *mole* for dipping. Desserts can be absolute standouts as in their chocolate tart, cut into a dense wedge, studded with toasted walnuts and pecans, served with a scoop of house-made sour cream gelato, all sprinkled with granola.

Dovetail

American XX

 B3

103 W. 77th St. (at Columbus Ave.)

Subway: 81 St - Museum of Natural History
Phone: 212-362-3800
Web: www.dovetailnyc.com
Prices: $$$

Lunch Sun
Dinner nightly

© Nathan Rawlinson

Just a stone's throw from Central Park and the Museum of Natural History, Dovetail is situated in a largely residential neighborhood. The slender room feels mature and serious, with dark carpeting, wood-lined walls, and steel columns. The bar is a lovely, quiet option for solo dining.

Driven largely by Chef John Fraser's distinct personality, the menu is a concise list of ingredient-driven fare that can be enjoyed either as a prix-fixe or chef's tasting. Dishes are beautifully colorful as in silky ravioli filled with a mix of wild greens slicked with butter and topped with crisped chorizo, a medley of carrots, and dried white grapes. A rustic vegetable consommé in a Mason jar is actually a bouquet of autumn vegetables in lustrous vegan broth seasoned with ginger and vanilla. Excellent monkfish is cut into medallions to highlight the golden brown caramelization and lobster-like interior, then dressed with mustard-flecked sauce and set atop lentil purée, wilted endive, and braised radishes.

Sunday nights bring a playful and wallet-friendly three-course meal, which ends with sundaes like "it's the great pumpkin, John Fraser!" with pumpkin ice cream, caramel, gingerbread, and white chocolate.

Elizabeth's Neighborhood Table

American 🍴🍴

B2

680 Columbus Ave. (at 93rd St.)

Subway: 96 St (Broadway)
Phone: 212-280-6500
Web: www.elizabethsnyc.com
Prices: $$

Lunch & dinner daily

Sadly, the northernmost reaches of the Upper West Side lack a definitive character. Call it dreary or ho-hum, but it's typically not a nabe that is worthy of sticking around too long. That is until last year's arrival of Elizabeth's Neighborhood Table. Whitewashing with a picket fence-feel, Elizabeth's looks like it would be more at home on beautiful Cape Cod. Inside, butcher-block tables, aquamarine walls, and vivid artwork lend a classic New England vibe. The menu is as all-American as apple pie. The kitchen has a solid farm-to-table focus tinged with nostalgia—think of mac and cheese with manchego and white cheddar; steamed mussels with whole grain mustard aïoli and white wine; or plump, perfectly sweet pork chops with garlic mashers and braised red cabbage.

Fishtag

Seafood 🍴🍴

A3

222 W. 79th St. (bet. Amsterdam Ave. & Broadway)

Subway: 79 St
Phone: 212-362-7470
Web: www.michaelpsilakis.com
Prices: $$$

Lunch Sat – Sun
Dinner nightly

Refined, charismatic, and comfortable, this sliver of a restaurant instantly feels like an iconic bit of New York, with thanks to its classic location tucked amid limestone townhouses. The smartly designed space features a speckled marble bar for dining, earth-toned and exposed brick walls, and an array of seating options (try to snag that large corner booth, if you can).

The menu may seem confusing in its organization of lightest to heaviest dishes, but lets diners take control—with the help of competent and intuitive servers—in choosing an array of seafood delights. Substantial appetizers might include a *skordalia* brandade "melt" with smoked eggplant and tomato confit. The grilled branzino stuffed with headcheese is a longstanding marvel.

Gari

B3

Japanese XX

370 Columbus Ave. (bet. 77th & 78th Sts.)

Subway: 81 St - Museum of Natural History   Lunch & dinner daily
Phone: 212-362-4816
Web: www.sushiofgari.com
Prices: $$$

There is something especially rich and satisfying about dining at Gari—a confluence of minimalist design, elegant food presentation, and sublime cuisine. Neighbor to the Museum of Natural History, this terrific Columbus Avenue outpost is the second of five in the growing Gari kingdom. The space here is bright and simple, with blonde wood furnishings, exposed brick, and hardwood walls.

Have a seat at the counter to watch the masters at work (though try not to jump when they shout "*irasshaimase!*" to welcome entering guests). The omakase could include miso-marinated red snapper topped with strips of crispy seaweed; chopped toro balanced with salty-sweet pickled radish; or deep-red maguro topped with the chef's subtle but beguilingly complex tofu sauce.

Gazala's

B3

Middle Eastern XX

380 Columbus Ave. (at 78th St.)

Subway: 81 St - Museum of Natural History   Lunch & dinner daily
Phone: 212-873-8880
Web: www.gazalasplace.com
Prices: $$

This is Gazala Halabi's second creation (Hell's Kitchen holds the original) but kid sister is quite the hit. Ample, well-run, and attractive, Gazala's churns out tasty Middle Eastern eats with an eye toward Druze specialties. Set in a notable building across from the venerable Museum of Natural History and Central Park, Gazala's has become its own destination.

Focus is clearly on the food in this two-fold dining space, with a tiny kitchen set front and center. A slim room features a communal table, while a larger, sun-lit room has wood tables laden with wafer-thin *sagg*, an ideal vessel for scooping up smoky baba ghanoush. A sesame seed-crested *mankosha* pie is unique and rich with spinach and goat cheese, while dense date cookies are plain outstanding.

Gennaro

665 Amsterdam Ave. (bet. 92nd & 93rd Sts.)

Subway: 96 St (Broadway)
Phone: 212-665-5348
Web: www.gennaronyc.com
Prices: $$

Dinner nightly

Gennaro is as true as a trattoria can be in NYC. This comfortable space is a master of consistency, despite having expanded the dining room to include a wine bar. Its décor is delightfully unchanged and the pasta dishes remain hearty and delicious. The bench is still parked out front and for good reason—Gennaro gets seriously crowded and patrons are glad for a seat.

The casual setting features golden yellow walls hung with ceramic plates and rustic wood shelves displaying wine bottles. Daily specials are a great complement to their homemade menu of *involtini di pesce spada* (swordfish stuffed with breadcrumbs and pine nuts atop peppery arugula); silky *orechiette* with broccoli rabe and sharp provolone; and tiny cannoli filled with rich ricotta cream.

Good Enough to Eat

520 Columbus Ave. (at 85th St.)

Subway: 86 St (Broadway)
Phone: 212-496-0163
Web: www.goodenoughtoeat.com
Prices: $$

Lunch & dinner daily

The title pretty much says it all—it's good enough to eat here, all right, and you could do so from morning 'till night if you wished. This family-friendly comfort food haven offers breakfast, lunch, and dinner (not to mention takeout), and the Upper West Side locals, for one, can't get enough of Chef/owner Carrie Levin's simple, but mouthwatering renditions of tender, home-cooked meatloaf; flaky fish and chips; and crunchy stacks of buttermilk-fried onion rings.

Bounded by a white picket fence and flaunting a façade painted with black-and-white cow spots, this brand-new, super fun, and crowded "barn" exudes a homey atmosphere that matches its food. Add a little frost on the window, and dream that you've returned to your country home for the holidays.

Jean-Georges ✿ ✿ ✿

A4

Contemporary ✗✗✗✗

1 Central Park West (bet. 60th & 61st Sts.)

Subway: 59 St - Columbus Circle   Lunch & dinner daily
Phone: 212-299-3900
Web: www.jean-georges.com
Prices: $$$$

© 2012 Francesco Tonelli

Vibrant, glamorous, and very New York, this is one of the city's favorite places to see and be seen. Yet there is an easiness here among servers who are smooth and naturally pleasant, despite the Trump Tower's surrounding opulence. Bay windows, fixtures inspired by Columbus Circle's constant whirl, and curving banquettes make the dining room elegant, if sober.

Chef Jean-Georges Vongerichten's menu is solidly rooted in French techniques with an Asian twist. There is a devilish pleasure in the details, perhaps beginning with the buttery-warm brioche with duck foie gras that melts in the mouth, sour dried cherries, crunchy candied pistachio, and white port gelée. Line-caught turbot is served in a surprising, tangy, and perfectly balanced green chili and chervil vinaigrette. A premium cut of Wagyu beef is finished *au gueridon* before your very eyes, and served with a knockout combination of sherry vinegar and powerful, dark *mole*.

Desserts feature generous tastings of green apple gelée with *tatin* compote and crème fraîche; pomegranate sorbet with a red wine syrup; poached pear with rose whipped cream, passion-caramel sauce, and crushed nuts; or a cocoa pudding softly spiced with cardamom.

Lincoln ✓

A4

Italian · XXX

142 W. 65th St. (bet. Amsterdam Ave. & Broadway)

Subway: 66 St - Lincoln Center
Phone: 212-359-6500
Web: www.lincolnristorante.com
Prices: $$$$

Lunch Wed – Sun
Dinner nightly

Manhattan ▶ Upper West Side

Iwan Baan

It is almost better to miss the entrance, and wind your way through the stunning Lincoln Center Plaza to find this very modern restaurant. Once inside, clever design plays into every aspect of dining, from the vibrant bar scene and operatic views of the kitchen to the rear dining room—sedate, intimate, and ultra-luxurious. Beneath that slanted wood ceiling, find deep leather banquettes, swanky booths, and wide tables placed away from the din of the bar.

Chef Jonathan Benno's menu is always appealing, creative, and new—a different region of Italy is highlighted each month. House-made pastas are always a standout, whether served as black squid-ink *gigli neri* with Florida shrimp, *bottarga*, and *peperonata*; or luscious *spaghettoni* with sweet crab, green onion, and melting uni. Even more rustic, family-style dishes are elegantly updated here, as in the beautifully seasoned and slow-cooked *porchetta*, served over a powerful balsamic-cherry purée that balances the rich meat. The accompanying polenta is downright extravagant. Come dessert, the fabulous *tartufo alla nocciola* with hazelnut Genovese, salted caramel, chocolate meringue, gelato, *gianduja*, and zabaglione is worth every calorie.

Loi

Greek

208 W. 70th St. (bet. Amsterdam & West End Aves.)

Subway: 72 St   Dinner nightly
Phone: 212-875-8600
Web: www.restaurantloi.com
Prices: $$$

Greek TV personality, cookbook author, and restaurateur, Maria Loi, is a known powerhouse. At her eponymous spot, this favorite chef gives her homeland's cuisine an upscale kick, while maintaining a comforting touch. The airy, elegant main room evokes the country's gorgeous landscape through white leather booths, bright lighting, and colorful photo murals of the Corinthian Gulf. Back-lit wine walls and stunning floral arrangements complete the sophisticated scene.

Dig into delights like sea urchin accompanied by crispy pita chips; baked goat cheese croquets topped with fig and apricot compote; tender grilled octopus with capers, chickpeas, almonds, and fresh herbs; or the *psari se krousta alatiou*—fresh whole fish baked in a sea salt crust.

Miss Mamie's Spoonbread Too

Southern X

366 W. 110th St./Cathedral Pkwy. (bet. Columbus & Manhattan Aves.)

Subway: Cathedral Pkwy/110 St (Central Park West)   Lunch & dinner daily
Phone: 212-865-6744
Web: www.spoonbreadinc.com
Prices:

This venerable Morningside Heights institution doesn't coast on its reputation as a homey Southern haven just north of Central Park. The food is as good as ever, the atmosphere is easygoing and welcoming, and the music is soulful yet unobtrusive.

Fresh and expertly made classics rule the menu, but the daily specials board offers gems that should not be ignored. Here, find the likes of crazy chicken, perfectly fried and juicy with a generous helping of three sides and gravy. The smothered pork chops are tender and wonderfully tangy; the yams are soft and spicy; and the banana pudding is the stuff of dreams. Sit back and soak in a super-sweet iced tea or the Spoonbread punch and relax—food made with such care can take its time getting to your table.

Momoya

B3

427 Amsterdam Ave. (bet. 80th & 81st Sts.)

Subway: 79 St
Phone: 212-580-0007
Web: www.momoyanyc.com
Prices: $$$

Lunch & dinner daily

For a glimpse of the sushi-making prowess, slip into a seat at the sexy, white marble counter and watch these pros do their thing. Blond woods, cream leather booths, slate floors, sultry lighting, and careful orchid arrangements combine subdued masculinity with feminine touches at Momoya, a cool yet bright little spot with a second outpost in Chelsea.

Start off with warm mushroom salad tossed in yuzu-soy vinaigrette, or a special tuna roll done up with grilled yellowtail and almonds. Try the cold soba, bobbing in fragrant broth with spicy tempura rock shrimp; or the tender, flaky miso cod atop wilted, yuzu spinach. The *matcha*-dusted *mille* crêpes, delicately layered with green tea ice cream and cream anglaise, are a triangular slice of heaven.

Nice Matin

Mediterranean ✕✕

B3

201 W. 79th St. (at Amsterdam Ave.)

Subway: 79 St
Phone: 212-873-6423
Web: www.nicematinnyc.com
Prices: $$

Lunch & dinner daily

So well-loved is this local favorite that Nice Matin has gained an everyday roster of ladies lunching, freelance junkies, and stroller-pushing moms. It paints a lively scene on a cold, rainy day, luring everyone in with their warm, worn-in, pseudo-French vibe and years of popularity. In keeping with its easy style, the brasserie also boasts a massive Mediterranean menu coupled with soft prices and a big-time wine list.

The service is not spot-on, but with round-the-clock diners nibbling away on exquisitely simple plates of poached leeks topped with egg mimosa or crunchy beets kissed with *chevre*, it's easy to feel the love. A grilled herb-marinated chicken and arugula sandwich is massive, but blissful when paired with their thin, crispy frites.

Noche Mexicana II

B1

842 Amsterdam Ave. (at 101st St.)

Subway: 103 St (Broadway)
Phone: 212-662-6900
Web: www.noche-mexicana.com
Prices: $$

Lunch & dinner daily

Sequels are usually better known for missing the mark rather than hitting it, but Noche Mexicana II bucks the trend. This pearl known for its fluffy tamales moved to bigger and brighter digs, closing its original some blocks north. These higher reaches of Amsterdam Ave. aren't the prettiest, but once inside this bright, upbeat spot, you'll never look back.

Moist cornmeal tamales with succulent pork and green *mole* sauce; spicy *camarones Mexicana*; tempting *guajilio* chili with tender chicken—you can't go wrong with any of these. Other surefire hits include *tingas*, *taco cesina* (preserved beef), and the *pipian de pollo*, shredded chicken served with toasted pumpkin and sesame seeds and cooked with jalapeño and *guero* chile peppers...*muy bueno*!

Nougatine

A4

1 Central Park West (at 60th St.)

Subway: 59 St - Columbus Circle
Phone: 212-299-3900
Web: www.jean-georges.com
Prices: $$

Lunch & dinner daily

Prestigiously set on the ground floor of the Trump International Hotel, Nougatine proves to be nothing short of lavish. The fresh look is clean and contemporary, bathed in light reflected from its large, unencumbered windows—a world away from the crowded plazas and blaring cabs outside.

Minimalist touches like plush leather banquettes, gleaming light fixtures, and a brushed metal bar convey gentility, making Nougatine an otherworldly spot to rest your weary, globetrotting feet over an aperitif or quick bite. A bowl of verdant green pea soup crested with crispy croutons and Parmesan foam is an elegant standout among other items like succulent skate with aromatic black beans; or a dense slice of sour cream cheesecake with passion fruit compote.

Osteria Cotta

Italian

513 Columbus Ave. (bet. 84th & 85th Sts.)

Subway: 86 St (Broadway)
Phone: 212-873-8500
Web: www.cottanyc.com
Prices: $$

Lunch Sat – Sun
Dinner nightly

Osteria Cotta is a reminder that neighborhood restaurants are a precious thing: comfortable, unpretentious, affordable, and ready to welcome a spontaneous visit. The charming interior is warm with wood beams, wrought-iron bannisters, and brick walls that seem so barnyard-chic that you might just forget quite where you are.

The Italian menu may feature an excellent assortment of *verdure*—all wonderfully balanced and full of flavor—as in classic Sicilian sweet-and-sour caponata teeming with *pignoli*. Every taste is good and right in a tender pork chop fanned over grilled yellow squash and zucchini; roasted cauliflower with pickled *peperoncini;* or spaghetti *pomodoro* with chunky, herb-flecked sauce. Their gelato is smooth, creamy, and memorable.

Ouest

Contemporary

2315 Broadway (bet. 83rd & 84th Sts.)

Subway: 86 St (Broadway)
Phone: 212-580-8700
Web: www.ouestny.com
Prices: $$$

Lunch Sun
Dinner nightly

Ouest is not sexy; it is sultry. But in this area, baby, you've got to have more than looks to last. This particular nook may not swarm with important eateries, but Ouest's elevated and serious cuisine has made it a magnet for celebrities, media moguls, and locals for more than a decade. The slender front bar is adored for sipping; under its grand ceiling lamps are red leather banquettes packed with eager guests.

Bustling with capable servers, the large back dining room is a masculine yet elegant, balconied space. From here, the open kitchen presents plates of silky cauliflower custard beside buttery lobster knuckles; sumac-crusted tuna with a white bean purée and red pepper compote; and a distinctly flavorful peanut butter-chocolate bombe.

Manhattan ▶ Upper West Side

409

Picholine

Mediterranean 🍴🍴🍴

A4

35 W. 64th St. (bet. Broadway & Central Park West)

Subway: 66 St - Lincoln Center   Dinner Tue – Sun
Phone: 212-724-8585
Web: www.picholinenyc.com
Prices: $$$$

Picholine's subtle exterior belies the superior cooking and rich flavors that await inside. Propitiously set near Lincoln Center, this luxe stomping ground of theatergoers remains unchanged...and thankfully so. The grand dining room is undeniably lavish, with meticulously carved moldings and crystal chandeliers. The bar, set among flowers, is an ideal spot for a pre-show cocktail. Smart servers cater to the affluent crowd and are eager to please.

Dishes retain classic appeal while embracing a more contemporary style, as in perfectly prepared agnolotti in a pleasant bath of *bottarga* and squash blossom pesto; their signature cheese course is a storied favorite. Supremely sweet endings include a roasted peach "melba" served with raspberry-yogurt sorbet.

Slightly Oliver

Gastropub 🍴🍴

B2

511 Amsterdam Ave. (bet. 84th & 85th Sts.)

Subway: 86 St (Broadway)   Lunch & dinner daily
Phone: 212-362-1098
Web: www.slightlyolivernyc.com
Prices: $$

Slightly Oliver is a welcome departure from the usual suspects on this stretch of Amsterdam Avenue. Rife with playful drinks, this gastropub's "Commonwealth-inspired" menu also promises to lift your spirits amid the homey space featuring faux bookshelves, low lights, and high tables.

Cozy duos head up a few stairs to romantic booths shrouded in lace curtains. An "apothecary style" bar—featuring a glass-enclosed area packed with distilling elements—is truly unique. The menu meanders, but an informed staff deftly steers you through such good pub grub as puffy flatbreads spread with figs and artichokes. Cool beginnings (roasted butternut squash tossed with frisée) or big plates (flaky steak and kidney pie) are ace when followed by a soft malva pudding.

Spiga

Italian

200 W. 84th St. (bet. Amsterdam Ave. & Broadway)

Subway: 86 St (Broadway)
Phone: 212-362-5506
Web: www.spiganyc.com
Prices: $$$

Dinner nightly

Fantastically authentic Italian is what diners expect at Spiga, the intimate little spot Upper West Siders are lucky to have. Jazzy tunes float through the romantic dining space, replete with distressed brick walls, dark wood tables, shelves of wine bottles, and Italian-speaking servers. The menu is as sophisticated as it is delectable.

Its offerings range from plump grilled scallops over fava bean purée drizzled with a balsamic vinegar reduction, to pan seared duck breast topped with cherry compote and nestled into a mound of sweet potato purée with a side of Brussels sprouts. The pastas are an absolute must, as in lasagna layered with artichokes, béchamel, and Parmesan sauce; or potato and beet gnocchi with melted Taleggio and basil pesto.

Sura 😊

Thai

2656 Broadway (bet. 100th & 101st Sts.)

Subway: 103 St (Broadway)
Phone: 212-665-8888
Web: www.surathaikitchen.com
Prices: 😊😊

Lunch & dinner daily

Sura brings a dose of heat to the spice-challenged Upper West Side. The interior is unexpectedly upmarket with a smoky slate grey palette and shimmering accents. In contrast, white marble-topped tables line the slender setting and the neat culinary presentations enhance the stylish air.

Sura's outstanding preparations indicate that this kitchen is much more serious about its representation of Thai cuisine than many of its ilk. Indulge in standouts such as fresh and flavorful duck *larb*; or blue crab-studded fried sticky rice with egg and scallion. The *khao soi*—slender egg noodles bathed in a house-crafted rich and aromatic coconut curry topped with a peak of crunchy fried noodles and pickled mustard leaves—is a technically superb specialty.

Telepan ❀

A m e r i c a n ✗✗

A3

72 W. 69th St. (bet. Central Park West & Columbus Ave.)

Subway: 66 St - Lincoln Center
Phone: 212-580-4300
Web: www.telepan-ny.com
Prices: $$$

Lunch Wed — Sun
Dinner nightly

Alan Batt

Telepan rests on a quiet, residential block, steps from tony Central Park West. After a warm greeting, the staff leads you into the inviting, intimate, and understated dining rooms. Two sections fall on either side of a curved bar and spotlight light wood floors, pale sage walls, and linen-lined ceiling pendants. Plush U-shaped booths accommodate larger parties, while the front area feels like a snug alcove. Soft tunes in the background complement the urban vibe. An attractive mural of heirloom tomatoes conveys the farm-to-table philosophy practiced in this stellar kitchen.

Ingredient-driven dishes reflect a very American style, as in a beautifully poached egg set over neat piles of frisée with crisp, meaty mushrooms and a powerful mustard vinaigrette. House-made pastas may be twirls resembling spaetzle mingling with smoked Brussels sprouts enriched with egg, and impeccably balanced by a showering of pecorino; or cavatelli coated with luscious pork *Bolognese bianco*.

The finale here is a sweet demonstration of pastry chef talent, as in a layered rectangle of peanut butter and chocolate *gianduja* over fluffy sponge cake with peanut-brittle ice cream and angular cuts of huckleberry gelée.

Vai

Mediterranean

429 Amsterdam Ave. (bet. 80th & 81st Sts.)

Subway: 79 St
Phone: 212-362-4500
Web: www.vairestaurant.com
Prices: $$

Lunch Sat –Sun
Dinner nightly

Happily, Vai is back in the neighborhood, after having lost its former 77th Street digs. The new space is thankfully bigger, but maintains the same alluring style with bare, dark wood tables, brown leather seating, and a curved marble bar illuminated in sultry candlelight. Potted flowers and framed mirrors add a lovely touch.

Jean-Georges alum, Vincent Chirico, continues to lead the charge in the kitchen, firing up dynamite *assaggi* for the small plate-loving crowd. Get on board with sautéed Gulf shrimp atop root vegetable *soffritto*, herbs, and smoky chorizo; pan-roasted Arctic char, flanked by sweet onion confit and drizzled in warm pancetta vinaigrette; and green and white asparagus topped with snowy shavings of *ricotta salata* and truffle essence.

Warique

Peruvian

852 Amsterdam Ave. (bet. 101st & 102nd Sts.)

Subway: 103 St (Broadway)
Phone: 212-865-0101
Web: www.wariquenyc.com
Prices: $$

Dinner nightly

Warique is located in the *way* Upper West Side–you'll need to travel until you hit the triple digits–but this casually comfortable restaurant is worth the trek if only for their stick-to-your-ribs comfort food from Peru.

While some of the classic hits (tripe, braised intestines, guinea pig) are missing here, rest assured as Warique doesn't miss a beat when it comes to delivering knock-your-socks off flavors. The *causa Peruana*, a mix of mashed potatoes, avocado, and shrimp, is doused in a hell-breathing sauce of *aji amarillo*, while those who seek less spicy, but amazingly delicious, should opt for the juicy and tender *pollo a la brasa* (chicken with crispy skin dripping with sweet fat) served with *salchipapa* (fries studded with deep-fried sausage).

Ivo M. Vermeulen/The New York Botanical Garden

The Bronx

The Bronx

The only borough attached to the mainland, the Bronx is marked by contrasts. Although abandoned apartment buildings and housing projects once overran the borough's south section, private foundations and grassroots movements are successfully revitalizing these areas. Grand mansions and lavish gardens still characterize the northern areas of Riverdale and Fieldston; and with such a plethora of organic farms cropping up (Green-Up is a program run by the New York Botanical Garden and organizes tours of these lush lands), it is no wonder that this borough is now a hotbed of culinary gems. Even **Sabatino Tartufi**'s tantalizing truffles have arrived on the scene. Finally, the Bronx Botanical Garden has many garden- and food-related classes which are hosted by top chefs including Lidia Bastianich.

BELMONT

Hispanics, African-Americans, Irish-Americans, West Indians, and Albanians comprise much of the current population. Though a host of Italians once settled in the Belmont area, today they reside as shop proprietors. Thanks to the 19th century journalist John Mullaly, who led a movement in the late 1800s to buy and preserve inexpensive parcels of land, 25 percent of the Bronx today consists of parkland. This includes Pelham Bay Park, with its sandy Orchard Beach. Once here, step into pizza paradise—**Louie and Ernie's**—for a slice of heaven. Beyond, City Island is a gem of a coastal community with its quaint inns and seafood spots. During the summer, stroll down City Island Avenue, and into **Lickety Split** for a scoop of ice cream. Belmont's most renowned street and Italian food mecca, Arthur Avenue, lures everybody from far and wide. Tear into warm, freshly baked breads from **Terranova** or **Addeo**—the choices are plenty. Dive into a ball of warm and creamy mozzarella at **Joe's Deli** (open on Sundays!). The pistachio-studded mortadella from **Teitel Brothers** or *salumi* from **Calabria Pork Store** are also perfect salt licks.

Gourmet Getaway

Don't forget to check out **The Arthur Avenue Retail Market**, a covered oasis built by Mayor LaGuardia to prevent pushcart vendors from crowding busy streets. The dwindling vendors inside sell quality Italian pasta, homemade sausage, olive oil, notorious heroes, heirloom seeds, and hand-rolled cigars. Although the Belmont section is now mainly known as Little Mexico and Ecuador, it has a world of Eastern European treats. Visit **Tony & Tina's Pizza**, but skip the Italian stuff. Instead, devour Albanian or Kosovar *burek*—these flaky rolls are packed with pumpkin purée and are *sine qua non*. **Gustiamo**'s warehouse will delight with simple Italian specialties including a variety of regional oils and vinegars, pastas and rice, San Marzano tomatoes, and other appealing items. In the same vein, **Honeywell Meat Market** (their butchers in particular) can teach newbies a thing or two about breaking down a side of beef. South Bronxite's will revel in **Xochimilco Family Restaurant**, Equadorian delights like *bollon de verde* at **Ricuras**, while others may take themselves out to a ball game at the Yankee Stadium and snack from **Lobel's** cart (the ultimate butcher shop).

Comfort Foods

The Eastchester, Wakefield, and Williamsbridge sections of the Bronx cradle a number of communities and their tasty eats and treats. The spicy, smoky tidbits of the Caribbean have become a local staple. Visit Vernon's **New Jerk House** for mouthwatering jerk chicken, and end with something sweet from **Kingston Tropical Bakery**. Craving some more Italian fare? Drop by **G & R Deli** for big flavors in their many homemade sausages or rich meaty sauce sold by the quart. End at **Sal & Dom's** for some deliciously flaky *sfogliatelle*. Note to Eastern food fans: authentic Asian food has officially arrived in the Bronx and Cambodian delights abound at the exotic **Phnom Penh-Nha Trang Market** across the street. Meanwhile, the classic hamburger craze continues uptown at the **Bronx Ale House**. If yearning for a beer with your meaty treats, **Jonas Bronck's Beer Co.** and **Bronx Brewery** are always frolicking with diverse selections.

A Latin Affair

A distinctive blend of Latin American hangouts populates the South Bronx, with the largest concentration hailing from Puerto Rico. On Willis Avenue, Mott Haven's main drag, bright awnings designate Honduran diners, Mexican bodegas, and Puerto Rican takeout. **The Clock Bar** complete with tasty martinis is certainly a welcome addition here. Vital to New York's food business is **Hunts Point Food Distribution Center**, a 329-acre complex with a mass of food wholesalers, distributors, and food processing businesses. This vast complex also includes **The Hunts Point Meat Market**, **Hunts Point Terminal Produce Market**, and **The Fulton Fish Market**, a wholesale triumvirate where the city's restaurateurs and market owners come to pick their goods. Such delicious browsing can only lead to a bigger appetite, which should be whetted at **Mo Gridder's BBQ**—a classic haunt that radiates potent doses of unique Bronx flavor.

RIVERDALE

Riverdale may not be known for its culinary gems, but it continues to comfort local clusters at **S&S Cheesecake** and the primped **Mother's Bake Shop**, famed for their traditional *babkas* and challahs. **Skyview Wines** carries a rare selection of kosher wines, thereby completing your sweet escapade with a touch of spirit. Hop, skip, and a jump from the last stop on the 1 line, follow your nose (cause it always knows) to **Lloyd's Carrot Cake** for one or several slices of their divine carrot cake.

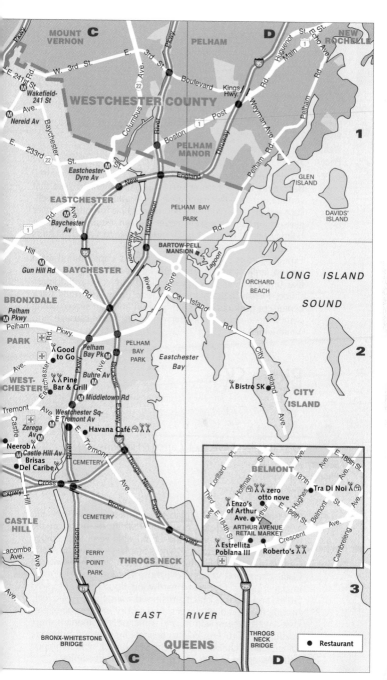

MOUNT VERNON **C**
PELHAM
NEW ROCHELLE **D**

W. 3rd St.
E. 3rd St.
Boulevard
Kings Hwy.

Wakefield-241 St
Nereid Av
E. 233rd St.

WESTCHESTER COUNTY

Eastchester-Dyre Av
EASTCHESTER
Baychester Av

PELHAM MANOR

Post
Boston
New
England
Hutchinson

PELHAM BAY PARK

GLEN ISLAND
DAVIDS' ISLAND

1

Gun Hill Rd
BAYCHESTER

BRONXDALE

Pelham Pkwy
Pelham
Pelham Pkwy.

PARK

BARTOW-PELL MANSION

Lagoon

LONG ISLAND SOUND

ORCHARD BEACH

2

WEST-CHESTER

Good to Go
Pine Bar & Grill
Pelham Bay Pk
Buhre Av
Middletown Rd
Westchester Sq-E Tremont Av

PELHAM BAY PARK

Eastchester Bay

Shore
City Island

Bistro SK

CITY ISLAND

Tremont
Castle
Zerega Av
Havana Café
Neerob
Castle Hill Av
Brisas Del Caribe

CEMETERY

Throgs Neck Expwy

Cross
Bronx Expwy

CASTLE HILL

Hutchinson
FERRY POINT PARK

CEMETERY
THROGS NECK

acombe Ave.

BELMONT

Lorillard Pl.
Hoffman
Third Ave.
Arthur Ave.
187th
E. 186th St.
Hughes
Belmont
E. 188th St.

zero otto nove
Tra Di Noi
Enzo's of Arthur Ave.
ARTHUR AVENUE RETAIL MARKET
Estrellita Poblana III
Roberto's
Crescent
Cambreleng Ave.

3

BRONX-WHITESTONE BRIDGE
EAST RIVER
QUEENS
THROGS NECK BRIDGE

C
D

● Restaurant

419

Beccofino

Italian

 5704 Mosholu Ave. (at Fieldston Rd.)

Subway: Van Cortlandt Park-242 St   Dinner nightly
Phone: 718-432-2604
Web: N/A
Prices: $$

An easy, neighborhood darling that is never taken for granted, Beccofino is that earnest sort of Italian-American spot that genuinely cares that each dish is to your liking. The well-kept setting feels charming and no detail is forgotten—water glasses and breadbaskets never remain empty. Strings of holiday lights, exposed brick, and life-sized French posters fashion a rustic bistro look.

Expect starters like cremini mushroom caps stuffed with shrimp, crab, scallops, and garlicky breadcrumbs; or pastas like braised beef ravioli with diced eggplant and tomato sauce. Hearty entrées might include the wonderfully thick center-cut pork chop, served bone-in and pan seared along with sautéed onions, hot cherry peppers, sweet sausage, and white wine.

Bistro SK

French

273 City Island Ave. (bet. Carroll & Hawkins Sts.)

Subway: N/A   Lunch Sat – Sun
Phone: 718-885-1670   Dinner Tue – Sun
Web: www.bistrosk.com
Prices: $$

City Island locals have a place to call their own at Bistro SK, a sweet mom-and-pop operation making its home in the former Tree House (note the unmovable remnant, a huge glass encased tree trunk). Owners Stephane Kane and Maria Caruso run this delightful French bistro, which flaunts its Gallic charm and stands above those seafood spots that draw in day-trippers. Distressed hardwood floors, flower-topped tables, and sconces on cream-striped walls give a rustic feel.

Among the decadent classics, find savory *moules marinières* kissed with parsley, saffron, and garlic; or French onion soup, oozing with Gruyère. Wintry delights include a mushroom, spinach and cheese-stuffed chicken breast with whipped potatoes, apple-brandy sauce, and braised vegetables.

Brisas Del Caribe

Puerto Rican 🍴

1207 Castle Hill Ave. (bet. Ellis & Gleason Aves.)

Subway: Castle Hill Av
Phone: 718-794-9710
Web: N/A
Prices: 💰💰

Lunch & dinner daily

Fresh, hot, and tasty should be this Bronx native's mantra, set amid a vibrant neighborhood dotted with culinary delights. Boasting years of success, Brisas remains popular among hungry groups who pack its quarters day and night. A steam table laden with Puerto Rican food is in constant motion as the ladies behind the counter plate your order. Towards the back, walls are decked with beach scenes, glossy mirrors, and serve as an ideal backdrop for families tucking into fragrant *arroz con pollo* studded with pigeon peas and served with fried plantains; or tantalizing *chivo guisado*, a garlicky goat stew with fluffy rice and beans.

Seal this savory deal with a sweet *bizcocho Domincano*— vanilla cake layered with pineapples and topped with buttercream.

Ceetay

Asian 🍴

129 Alexander Ave. (at Bruckner Blvd.)

Subway: 3 Av - 138 St
Phone: 718-618-7020
Web: www.ceetay.com
Prices: $$

Lunch Mon – Fri
Dinner nightly

Beyond the proliferation of neighborhood juice stands, find a more sophisticated sip along with fresh, inventive Asian food in a pleasing ambience at Ceetay. The setting is tiny yet handsome with reclaimed wood, metal accents, and a handcrafted bar that sits only 30. Its location just a short drive from Hunts Point means that this is a stop for serious seafood. The sushi bar is a two-chef affair churning out the likes of a Kawasaki roll stuffed with crabmeat, avocado, scallions, and a smear of mayo; or a wonderful assortment of striped bass, *shiro maguro, ebi,* and uni. Other items on offer roam through Asia and may reveal such stylistic or regional inflections as brown rice tossed in a fragrant masala of onions, peppers, carrots, and yellow squash.

El Nuevo Bohío

Puerto Rican

B2

791 E. Tremont Ave. (at Mapes Ave.)

Subway: West Farms Sq - E Tremont Av
Phone: 718-294-3905
Web: www.elnuevobohiorestaurant.com
Prices:

Lunch & dinner daily

Fixed on a prominent corner and strutting windows tempting passersby with hunks of glistening pork, El Nuevo Bohío is hard to miss. Well-liked by its nearby Puerto Rican community, the front room is minimally adorned with a steam table, prep area (counter laden with authentic dishes), and cash register that is packed with orders at the ready. Snag a seat in the back for friendly table service. Bright walls are flooded with framed photos, and tables are filled with pride thanks to the authentic menu.

Succulent *pernil* heavy on the garlic is roasted until crisp on the outside, juicy on the inside. *Pastelles*, traditional bundles of starchy yucca and rich pork stew; and an array of *sopas* from rice and shrimp to cows' feet, round out the daily offerings.

Enzo's of Arthur Ave

Italian

D3

2339 Arthur Ave. (bet. Crescent Ave. & 186th St.)

Subway: Fordham Rd (Grand Concourse)
Phone: 718-733-4455
Web: N/A
Prices: $$

Lunch & dinner daily

With its old-fashioned tiled floors, bistro tables, and pressed-tin ceiling, this offshoot of the original Enzo's might look like your average red-sauce joint, but Enzo's takes comfort cooking to a new level.

Yes, it's informal with casually dressed Fordham students here for everyone's favorite cavatelli with broccoli rabe and spicy sausage, but others come from afar, to shop and sate themselves on some of the city's better clams oreganata. Owner Enzo DiRende (whose father co-founded legendary Dominick's) improves every standby with his devotion to sourcing from local vendors—a smart thing when your 'hood is teeming with killer Italian markets. Fresh, crusty ciabatta, delish cured meats, and the vanilla-scented cheesecake are all made around the corner.

Estrellita Poblana III

Mexican

 D3

2328 Arthur Ave. (bet. Crescent Ave. & 186th St.)

Subway: Fordham Rd (Grand Concourse) Lunch & dinner daily
Phone: 718-220-7641
Web: www.estrellitapoblanaiii.com
Prices: 💰💰

Set against the milieu of the lively Belmont section in the Bronx, this third outpost of the Estrellita family has become an integral member of the diverse community. Fuchsia walls, three huge stars (III) set inside the coffered ceiling, and baby blue accents decorate the small, comfy room. Not only is it friendly and big-hearted, but the food is appetizing yet affordable. This is all ideal for nearby Fordham students and locals craving some *caliente* with their Coronas.

Tamales may only be available on weekends, but thick, spicy *pancita* (beef tripe soup); wonderfully warm *pozole* made with salty pork; and specials like *bistec* featuring citrus-marinated strips of rib eye sautéed with tart cactus and spicy *pico de gallo* are just as desirable.

Good to Go

Italian

C2

1894 Eastchester Rd. (near Morris Park Ave.)

Subway: E 180 St (& bus BX 21) Lunch & dinner daily
Phone: 718-829-2222
Web: N/A
Prices: $$

 With its friendly vibe and plates of belly-pleasing comfort, Indian Village locals love Good to Go. Smack in the heart of bustling Eastchester Road and surrounded by teaching hospitals and commercial enterprises like Starbucks and Dunkin' Donuts, it brings a welcome bit of warmth to the landscape. The lively interior sports exposed brick, caramel-colored walls, and chocolate brown tables glowing under soft track lighting.

Italian-American classics are tasty and well done, as in baked clams—the chopped mollusks tossed with garlicky breadcrumbs, hot chili flakes, and parsley. The decadent *lasagna rustica* is made with heaping layers of meatballs, ricotta, pecorino, mozzarella, and meat sauce, and is sure to keep neighborhood denizens satisfied.

Havana Café

C2

3151 E. Tremont Ave. (at LaSalle Ave.)

Subway: N/A
Phone: 718-518-1800
Web: www.bronxhavanacafe.com
Prices: $$

Lunch & dinner daily

Located in the Schuylerville section of the Bronx, Havana Café is a welcoming, well-run, and comfortable find. Beyond the cream-colored façade, palm trees, and outdoor dining, find a charming interior decked with a dark wood bar and marble-topped tables. Quaint posters, tropical fronds, and lazy ceiling fans evoke a sense of old Havana.

Don't be surprised to see that every single table is probably topped with their wonderful "Cuban pizza" flatbread, served on a wooden plank and topped with fat, sweet shrimp and a garlicky piquillo pepper sauce. More traditional but equally tasty dishes include mounds of tender-juicy braised flank steak piled high on fluffy rice and beans, or pork sautéed with caramelized and crispy tobacco-onions.

Jake's Steakhouse

B1

6031 Broadway (bet. Manhattan College Pkwy. & 251st St.)

Subway: Van Cortlandt Park-242 St
Phone: 718-581-0182
Web: www.jakessteakhouse.com
Prices: $$$

Lunch & dinner daily

Got baseball on the docket but beef on the brain? This multi-level, 126-seat Bronx steakhouse might be one of the best-kept secrets for Yankees fans headed north after the game. Located across from Van Cortland Park, just off the last stop of the 1 train, Jake's Steakhouse offers superior steaks for reasonable prices, in a warm, masculine interior.

Kick things off with the tender house crab cake, chockablock with fresh lump meat; and then move on to the star of the show—a hand-selected, wet-aged slab of premium T-bone, sliced off the bone and laced in natural beef jus. Any cut can be gussied up with melted Gorgonzola, crunchy frizzled onions, and port wine sauce, but with steak this good, you might not need the bells and whistles.

Joe's Place

B3

1841 Westchester Ave. (at Thieriot Ave.)

Subway:	Parkchester
Phone:	718-918-2947
Web:	www.joesplacebronx.com
Prices:	$$

Lunch & dinner daily

The Bronx loves its hometown heroes: J. Lo, Dave Valentin, Sonia Sotomayor, and Joe Torres. Who? If you have to ask, you're not from the Bronx. That's because Torres owns one of the top spots in the Bronx for delicious Puerto Rican/Dominican food.

From children to Congressmen, everybody's here, and Joe chats up all of them. This place draws regulars who come to catch up with the jovial proprietor and for the classic dishes. Begin with *sopa de pollo*, that lovely hot mess of chicken and noodles that tastes just like *papi* ordered. Move on to the *mofongo* with shredded pork and a mash of deep-fried green plaintains. *Pastelillo* is a flaky, crusty triumph and the *bacalao guisado*, a flavorful cod stew with pimiento-stuffed olives and capers, is a surefire hit.

Liebman's

A1

552 W. 235th St. (bet. Johnson & Oxford Aves.)

Subway:	231 St
Phone:	718-548-4534
Web:	www.liebmansdeli.com
Prices:	

Lunch & dinner daily

Some things never change (phew!) and Liebman's is definitely one of those things. This iconic kosher deli has been stuffing sandwiches and ladling bowls of matzoh ball soup for over 50 years. Residents wax poetic about the place, but it's nothing special, just a true-blue deli. Walk in and it's like a Smithsonian set for a Jewish deli—a neon sign in the front window, the grill roasting hot dogs, and meat slicing machines.

The food is classic and soulful as in stuffed veal breast, potato latkes, pastrami and tongue sandwiches on nutty rye bread paired with tangy pickles...and even that old standby—noodle pudding. Order to-go, or take a load off and grab a seat at one of the booths. Just don't forget about that bowl of "cure-all" matzoh ball soup.

Mexicosina

A3

503 Jackson Ave. (at E. 147th St.)

Subway: E 149 St
Phone: 347-498-1339
Web: www.mexicosina.com
Prices: 💰

Lunch & dinner daily

Anyone looking for a bright spot to impress some adventurous friends with a food odyssey should head here—and it's closer to Manhattan than you probably realize. Just two blocks down from the original, this new space is larger yet personalized with whimsical figurines and Mexican artifacts that beam with cultural pride and warmth.

The food remains just as delicious, authentic, and inventive as the original. A thick, complex seafood stew brims with sweet shrimp, catfish, fingerling potatoes, grilled onions, and spicy-smoky-sweet red chili broth. Quesadillas wrap funky *huitlacoche*, charred corn, and habanero sauce for a combination that is as bright as the sun and hot as hell. The intensely fresh corn tortillas are absolutely worth the extra buck.

Neerob

C2

2109 Starling Ave. (bet. Odell St. & Olmstead Ave.)

Subway: Castle Hill Av
Phone: 718-904-7061
Web: N/A
Prices: 💰

Lunch & dinner daily

The Bangladeshi community may be based in Queens, but the Bronx now boasts one of their most authentic eateries. Neerob's room is sunny yet conveys a fast food feel with bright lights and clunky furnishings. And while the country itself may be some 50 years young, its cuisine (laden with influences from West Bengal) exudes distinct flavors and seasonings.

On the steam table, find delicacies that celebrate garlic, green chilies, and mustard with spice levels that can seem unrelenting. Dishes include *chandal*, a yellow lentil soup steeped in cumin and ginger; or *gura mas*, pan-fried fish soaked in greens and mustard oil. Fish *illish* or a series of dishes called *bharthas* (maybe the mashed roasted eggplant?) seem to inspire exuberance among the diners.

900 Park

Italian

B2

900 Morris Park Ave. (at Bronxdale Ave.)

Subway: Bronx Park East
Phone: 718-892-3830
Web: www.900park.com
Prices: $$

Lunch & dinner daily

The Bronx

900 Park is an easy place to return to regularly. The food is neither fancy nor innovative, but brings those soul-satisfying comforts that we all seek. Myriad seating options make it a great choice for couples settling into the lounge with its roaring fireplace, as well as larger groups gathering in the elevated dining room for platters of hot antipasto. White leather chairs, cotton panels, and rustic tables lend a breezy, calming feel.

The Italian and Italian-American specialties might begin with a classic bowl of *stracciatella*, combining chicken broth and spinach strewn with beaten eggs. Ridged tubes of manicotti are filled with ricotta and pecorino cheese, cooked in a meaty Bolognese, and then topped with rich béchamel for an outstanding dish.

NYY Steak

Steakhouse

A3

1 E. 161st St. (in Yankee Stadium)

Subway: 161 St - Yankee Stadium
Phone: 646-977-8325
Web: www.nyysteak.com
Prices: $$$$

Yes, it's tucked inside Yankee Stadium, but you won't find any ballpark franks here. Instead, this steakhouse hits it out of the park with its traditional décor mixed with serious Yankee pride (the autographed walls are Kodak worthy).

You don't need to don a pinstriped suit but definitely skip the Sox, since this place is Yankee heaven. Even the steaks are branded with the interlocking NY. There's certainly plenty of room—these tender, dry-aged, and perfectly seared steaks are monsters but oh-so-good. Sides like lobster mac and cheese and onion rings are home runs and the A+ wine list will have you yelling "beer not here!" A natural during games (when tickets are necessary), NYY Steak keeps the party going only during ticketed events.

427

Oregano Bar & Bistro

Latin American ✗✗

A1

3524 Johnson Ave. (bet. 235th & 236th Sts.)

Subway: 231 St
Phone: 347-843-8393
Web: www.oreganolb.com
Prices: $$

Lunch Sat – Sun
Dinner nightly

Oregano Bar & Bistro's arrival on the scene seems to have brought about many smiles. Adorned with brass, bistro chairs, red-and-blue banquettes, antique mirrors, and a stunning carved wood bar, it is no wonder that locals love it. Large French doors open to the sidewalk decked with potted plants and invite pedestrians to this room abuzz with cocktail-loving cliques.

Add that to the live music, and it's a party complete with hefty portions of French-Latin fare. Expect the likes of *poitrine de poulet à la moutarde*, nicely charred chicken pieces finished in a mustard sauce tinged with tarragon; *paella maison* deliciously loaded with tender strips of duck, seafood, and vegetables; or an intensely rich and moist rum cake swept with a thick layer of icing.

Pine Bar & Grill

Italian ✗✗

C2

1634 Eastchester Rd. (at Blondell Ave.)

Subway: Westchester Sq - Tremont Av
Phone: 718-319-0900
Web: www.pinebargrill.com
Prices: $$

Lunch & dinner daily

Run by the Bronx-based Bastone family (also of the steadfast Pine Tavern), this bi-level stunner is a local favorite. Muted yellow walls showcase black and white photos of the borough's celebrated and lesser known spots, while leafy plants and bright flowers pop against a backdrop of dark wood tables, stairs, and floors.

As testament to the rapidly diversifying local population, the offerings now include Latin influenced delights alongside their wonderfully old-fashion Italian classics. Sample clams casino stuffed with pecorino, breadcrumbs, parsley, and shallots, topped with crispy bacon; or a perfect baked ziti marinara. Then move onto Baja fish tacos and pernil "our way" with roasted, tender pork, fried sweet plantains, and rice with pigeon peas.

Riverdale Garden

Latin American 🍴🍴

B1

4576 Manhattan College Pkwy. (at Broadway)

Subway: Van Cortlandt Park-242 St
Phone: 347-346-8497
Web: www.newriverdalegarden.com
Prices: $$

Lunch Sun
Dinner nightly

As you walk up curving 242nd Street toward this tucked-away Bronx gem, listen for strains of Cuban jazz wafting through the night air. Follow it to the newly renovated Riverdale Garden, where you can throw back a *Cuba libre* or a mojito at the roomy bar (special prices on Havana Thursdays), then escape to the unexpected and leafy tranquility of the back garden terrace.

Charmingly folksy service delivers Afro-Latin treats like tender African stuffed chicken, wrapped around sweet plantain and Serrano ham; or the *Rabo*, a Cuban oxtail stew accompanied by steamed yucca and a bright lime- cilantro- and garlic-*mojito* sauce. You may want to skip dessert and opt for another round of mojitos to sip as you savor the sweet fact that you're not in Manhattan anymore.

Roberto's

Italian 🍴🍴

D3

603 Crescent Ave. (at Hughes Ave.)

Subway: Fordham Rd (Grand Concourse)
Phone: 718-733-9503
Web: www.roberto089.com
Prices: $$

Lunch Mon – Fri
Dinner Mon – Sat

This highly regarded Bronx favorite is most luminescent when its patriarch (Roberto Paciullo) stands sentry. Leading into a spanking clean dining room, the dark wood bar serves an opulent parade of grappas. The tables exude country chic—dark, supple, and bare. Bathed in gentle candlelight, Roberto's seduces crowds into prolonging their Italian love affair, even after scouring Arthur Avenue's treats.

Keeping company with classic Italian-American food in this rustic yet elegant space are a gramophone, tasteful paintings, and velvet drapes. Specials like breaded octopus may not star every night, but *radiatore* pasta tossed with grilled lamb and pecorino; thin swordfish steaks marinated in lemon and herbs; and ricotta-rich cannolis are solid standards.

Taqueria Tlaxcalli

Mexican

B2

2103 Starling Ave. (bet. Odell St. & Olmstead Ave.)

Subway: Castle Hill Av	Lunch & dinner daily
Phone: 347-851-3085	
Web: N/A	
Prices: 🥜	

The exterior may not impress, but the heart of this very sweet little Mexican spot is inviting enough to draw a constant and very diverse stream of locals. Behind the counter set along the narrow space, the smiling staff is machine-gun quick as they prepare each order. Thoughtful details abound, from the fuchsia ribbons that wrap napkins and colorfully painted tortilla baskets to the professional servers who are quick to help anyone not fluent in Spanish.

Made-to-order guacamole is a requisite starter, before exploring delicious *sopas*, *carnitas*, and *tortas*. The humbly named soup of the day may be a surprisingly sophisticated shellfish reduction with tender shrimp, earthy root vegetables, and spicy-smoky chipotle. Tacos are excellent and very generous.

Tra Di Noi 🙂

Italian

D3

622 E. 187th St. (bet. Belmont & Hughes Aves.)

Subway: Fordham Rd (Grand Concourse)	Lunch & dinner Tue – Sun
Phone: 718-295-1784	
Web: N/A	
Prices: $$	

Tra Di Noi could just happily bask in the overflow from nearby Arthur Avenue. Instead, it is a place where dining is about more than just food; your satisfaction is paramount, and the exceptional lasagna may haunt you. The dining room is humble and immaculate, with crimson walls, decorative accents and frescos.

While the name ("between us") invokes a sense of familial commitment or secrecy, Tra Di Noi draws all and sundry for its solid cooking. Sample the fluffy *gnocchi di patate* in tomato-basil sauce; or carrots, celery, and cannellini beans all cooked to a deliciously creamy whole in *pasta e fagioli*. Look for specials like *muscoletti di vitello*, a hearty veal stew with white wine and rosemary. Homemade cannoli are a sweetheart treat offered daily.

zero otto nove

D3

Italian ✗✗

2357 Arthur Ave. (at 186th St.)

Subway: Fordham Rd (Grand Concourse) Lunch & dinner Tue – Sun
Phone: 718-220-1027
Web: www.roberto089.com
Prices: $$

A powder blue, circa 1960s Fiat 500 set on the sidewalk marks the entry to this Italian icon. If that doesn't clue you in to the genius present here, make your way through wood-framed doors, past a snug bar filled with handsome revelers, into an ample dining room flaunting high ceilings, skylights, and enticing aromas.

In the kitchen, the chefs hover over hearty, rustic dishes inspired by Salerno. Most start with pizza, but the *antipasto* featuring stuffed peppers with eggplant, zucchini, and cauliflower is equally tasty. Tender rings of *calamari alla peperonata* sautéed with peppers and studded with olives; or *pasta al forno*, baked rigatoni layered with a meaty ragù, béchamel, *soppresata*, and mozzarella are classics done with expertise and authority.

Feast for under $25 at all restaurants with ⊜.

Peter L. Wrenn/MICHELIN

Brooklyn

Brooklyn

Forage Brooklyn's trellis of neighborhoods and discover an exciting dining destination characterized by mom-and-pop stores, ethnic eateries, and trendy hot spots. Credit the influx of enterprising young chefs—many trained at Manhattan's top restaurants—for ushering in a new level of dining, while sedate establishments maintain the borough's rugged authenticity. The sustainable food movement has taken root as eco-conscious communities expand, and local artisans gain popularity for their high-quality, handcrafted goods. Locavores, want to support your neighbor's garden? Check out the handy website (www.eatwellguide.org) which offers a citywide directory of "green" gastronomy—family farms, farmers' markets, et al.

WILLIAMSBURG

Williamsburg, traditionally an Italian, Hispanic, and Hasidic neighborhood, is now home to hipsters and artists. Here in "Billyburg," artistic food endeavors abound: find upscale diners in former factories, and an artisan chocolate line handcrafted from bean to bar at **Mast Brothers Chocolate**. Be sure to bring a big appetite to **Smorgasburg**, Williamsburg's open-air, all-food market held on the waterfront from spring through fall. If interested in learning how to pickle, bake a great pie, or ferment kombucha, sign up for a cooking class at the **Brooklyn Kitchen**.

Over on Metropolitan Avenue, cute takeout shop **Saltie** offers a short yet delish list of tempting sandwiches and sweets, to be chased down by a cuppa' at **Blue Bottle Coffee Co. Pies 'n' Thighs** has returned to comfort with heaps of down-home goodness.

Inspired by the art of butchery, **Marlow & Daughters** boasts locally sourced meats, house-made sausages, and a delightful spectrum of artisanal dry goods. If meat and cheese are your daily staples, a visit to the boutique pizzeria **Best Pizza** is a must. In keeping with the mien of this neighborhood, and even if their space may appear disheveled (slate-topped tables are scattered throughout), patrons still adore and come in droves for their two varieties—a sliced cheese pizza with pickled veggies, and a sliced white pizza with creamy mozzarella and ricotta. For smoky, sticky, barbecue satisfaction, there's longtime favorite **Fette Sau** and recent infatuation **BrisketTown**; while over in burgeoning Gowanus, **Fletcher's Brooklyn Barbecue** adds to the borough's ever-evolving food scene. Get dessert at **Four & Twenty Blackbirds**, a cute bakeshop that churns out incredible pies.

DUMBO

Besides DUMBO's ace views, stroll down cobblestoned Water Street and into **Jacques Torres** for a taste of chocolate heaven. Bordering Prospect

Park, verdant Park Slope boasts blocks of tony trattorias and cafés, catering to an army of stroller-rolling parents. The **Park Slope Food Coop** is a member operated and owned cooperative selling locally farmed produce, fair trade products, grass-fed meat, free-range poultry, and more. It is the largest of its kind in the country, and membership is offered to anyone willing to pay a small fee and work a shift of less than three hours each month. Carroll Gardens, a historically Italian neighborhood, proffers family-owned butchers and bakeries along Court Street. **D'Amico** is solely for coffee-lovers and **Caputo's** has sandwiches worth the wait. As Court Street blends into family-friendly Cobble Hill, find **Staubitz Market**, the friendliest butcher around. Continue the stroll to Atlantic Avenue with its Middle Eastern goodies at **Sahadi's** and **Damascus Bakery**.

RED HOOK

On Brooklyn's waterfront rests vibrant Red Hook, attracting action with its large spaces and low rents. Industrious residents are transforming the aged piers and warehouses into cool breweries, bakeries, and bistros. Speaking of which, the **Red Hook Lobster Pound** is a cherished hangout for lobster lovers, but if in the mood for a sweet treat, head to **Baked**, **Steve's Authentic Key Lime Pie**, or **Cacao Prieto**'s— courtesy of the Prieto family whose very own Coralina Farms provides the cacao for their chocolates and spirits. The **Red Hook Farmer's Market** features

produce grown on the Red Hook Community Farm. Both ventures are operated by Added Value, a mentoring organization that teaches the urban youth how to till, sow, and harvest. On weekends from May through October, the hugely coveted trucks and tents that line the Red Hook Ball Fields cater to hordes of New Yorkers in the know with their range of homemade Latin American and Caribbean street food.

The Global Highway

Saunter to Fort Greene for a taste of African delicacies: Ethiopian at **Bati's** and South African at **Madiba**. Land at Sunset Park, and you will be tantalized by the Mexican flavors as you bite into a *pambazo* from **Tacos Xochimilco**. Slightly south, Mexico meets China, and this fusion is best expressed in rare culinary offerings. Sidewalks teem with vendors steaming tofu and fishmongers selling offbeat eats—bullfrog anyone? In a flock of kosher restaurants, **Di Fara** is an unusual pizzeria, and every few weeks **North Carolina Country Store** delivers to its locals an array of Southern staples. At the end of Brooklyn, Brighton Beach is best known for its borscht and blintzes. Linger around for Eastern European cooking (maybe at the Ukranian *bijou* **Café Glechik**?), or for an alfresco snack to tote—**Gold Label International Food** is beloved for its crusty breads and moist dumplings. And there is no confusing the Chesapeake with Sheepshead Bay, but the famed **Randazzo's Clam Bar** will provide you with a similar stellar seafood experience.

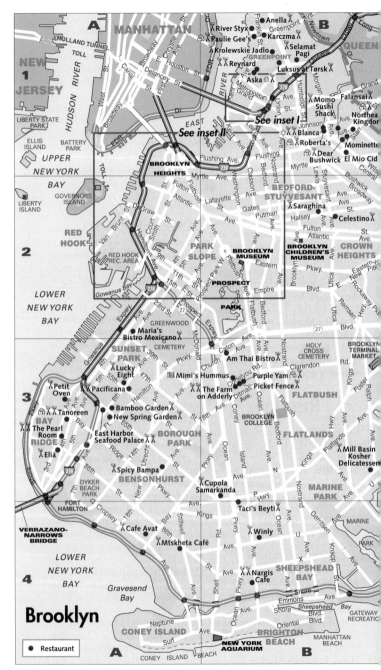

Brooklyn

A

MANHATTAN

HOLLAND TUNNEL
TOLL

NEW JERSEY

LIBERTY STATE PARK

ELLIS ISLAND

BATTERY PARK

UPPER NEW YORK BAY

GOVERNORS ISLAND

LIBERTY ISLAND

RED HOOK

LOWER NEW YORK BAY

HUDSON RIVER

Holland Tunnel

Broadway

Canal St.
E. Houston St.
Delancey St.

West St.
FDR Dr.

EAST RIVER

See inset II

BROOKLYN HEIGHTS

Myrtle Ave.
Flushing Ave.

Atlantic Ave.
Lafayette Ave.
Gates Ave.
Putnam Ave.

De Graw St.
Court St.
Smith St.
Hamilton Ave.
Van Brunt St.

RED HOOK REC. AREA

Gowanus Bay

9th St.
11th St.
15th St.
23rd St.

PARK SLOPE

BROOKLYN MUSEUM

PROSPECT PARK

Prospect Park W.
Flatbush Ave.

GREENWOOD CEMETERY

SUNSET PARK

39th St.
47th St.
Fort Hamilton Pkwy.
5th Ave.
6th Ave.
7th Ave.
8th Ave.

● Maria's Bistro Mexicano ✕

✕ Lucky Eight
✕ Pacificana

● Bamboo Garden ✕
● New Spring Garden ✕

✕ Petit Oven
✕✕ Tanoreen

BAY RIDGE

✕✕ The Pearl Room
● Elía ✕

East Harbor Seafood Palace ✕✕

BOROUGH PARK

65th St.
Ridge Blvd.
3rd Ave.
4th Ave.
5th Ave.
14th Ave.
New Utrecht Ave.

✕ Spicy Bampa

BENSONHURST

86th St.
Bay Pkwy.
Cropsey Ave.
18th Ave.
Kings Hwy.
Stillwell Ave.
Bay Pkwy.

DYKER BEACH PARK

FORT HAMILTON

VERRAZANO-NARROWS BRIDGE

LOWER NEW YORK BAY

Gravesend Bay

✕ Cafe Avat

✕ Mtskheta Café

✕✕ Nargis Cafe

CONEY ISLAND

Neptune Ave.
Surf Ave.
CONEY ISLAND BEACH

B

✕ River Styx
✕ Paulie Gee's
✕ Krolewskie Jadlo
✕✕ Reynard

Franklin St.
Greenpoint Ave.
EDR Dr.

GREENPOINT

● Anella ✕
✕ Karczma
✕ Selamat Pagi

● Luksus at Tørsk ✕

Aska ✕

Newtown Creek

QUEENS

Manhattan Ave.
Humboldt St.
Union Ave.
Metropolitan Ave.
Grand St.
Morgan Ave.
Grand Ave.

✕ Momo Sushi Shack
✕ Falansai

Johnson Ave.

● Northea Kingdor

See inset I

✕✕ Blanca
● ✕ Roberta's
● ✕ Dear Bushwick

Flushing Ave.
Bushwick Ave.
Myrtle Ave.

● Mominette
El Mio Cid

BEDFORD-STUYVESANT

Nostrand Ave.
Classon Ave.
Bedford Ave.
Washington Ave.

Lewis Ave.
Stuyvesant Ave.

Broadway
Bushwick Ave.
Central Ave.

✕ Saraghina
● Celestino ✕

Halsey St.
Fulton St.
Atlantic Ave.
St. John's Pl.

BEDFORD-STUYVESANT

BROOKLYN CHILDREN'S MUSEUM

CROWN HEIGHTS

Eastern Pkwy.
Utica Ave.
New York Ave.
Rochester Ave.

Eastern Pkwy.
Empire Blvd.
Bedford Ave.
Flatbush Ave.

(27)

Church Ave.
Caton Ave.
Ditmas Ave.
Cortelyou Rd.
Coney Island Ave.
Ocean Pkwy.
McDonald Ave.

● Am Thai Bistro ✕

Mimi's Hummus 🏛
✕✕ The Farm on Adderly

● Purple Yam ✕
✕ Picket Fence

FLATBUSH

HOLY CROSS CEMETERY

BROOKLYN TERMINAL MARKET

Foster Ave.
Kings Hwy.
Flatlands Ave.
Ralph Ave.

BROOKLYN COLLEGE

FLATLANDS

● ✕ Mill Basin Kosher Delicatessen

MARINE PARK

Nostrand Ave.
Gerritsen Ave.
Flatbush Ave.
Avenue U
Kings Hwy.

Ocean Ave.

● Cupola Samarkanda

✕ Taci's Beyti

● Winly

MARINE PARK

Shore Pkwy.
Knapp St.

SHEEPSHEAD BAY

Emmons Ave.
Sheepshead Bay Rd.
Shore Blvd.

GATEWAY RECREATI

BRIGHTON BEACH
MANHATTAN BEACH

NEW YORK AQUARIUM

Oriental Blvd.

● Restaurant

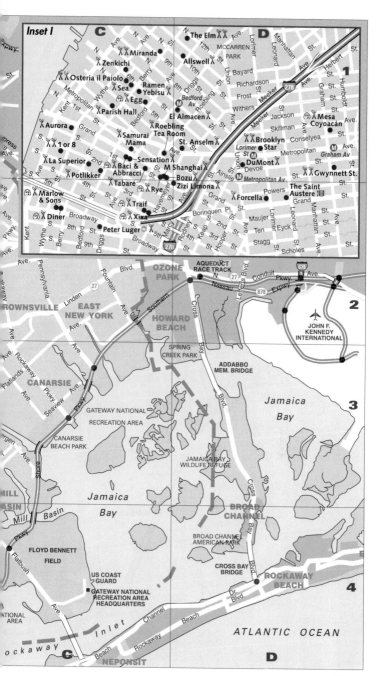

Inset I

The Elm

Miranda
Zenkichi
Osteria il Paiolo
Sea
Ramen
Yebisu
Egg
Parish Hall
Aurora
Samurai
Mama
1 or 8
La Superior
Potlikker
Baci &
Abbracci
Tabaré
Marlow
& Sons
Diner
Peter Luger

MCCARREN PARK

Allswell
Bayard
Richardson
Frost
Withers

Bedford
Av
El Almacen
Roebling
Tea Room
St. Anselm
Sensation
M Shanghai
Bozu
Rye
Zizi Limona
Traif
Xixa

Jackson
Skillman
Lorimer
St
DuMont
Devoe
Ainslie
Metropolitan Av
Grand
Borinquen Pl.

Mesa
Coyoacán
Conselyea
Metropolitan
Graham Av
Gwynnett St.
The Saint
Austere
Forcella

OZONE PARK
AQUEDUCT RACE TRACK
Nassau

BROWNSVILLE
EAST NEW YORK
HOWARD BEACH
SPRING CREEK PARK
ADDABBO MEM. BRIDGE

JOHN F. KENNEDY INTERNATIONAL

CANARSIE
GATEWAY NATIONAL RECREATION AREA
CANARSIE BEACH PARK
MILL BASIN
Mill Basin
FLOYD BENNETT FIELD
US COAST GUARD
GATEWAY NATIONAL RECREATION AREA HEADQUARTERS
NATIONAL AREA

Jamaica Bay

JAMAICA BAY WILDLIFE REFUGE

Jamaica Bay

BROAD CHANNEL
BROAD CHANNEL AMERICAN PARK
CROSS BAY BRIDGE
ROCKAWAY BEACH

Inlet
Rockaway
NEPONSIT
Beach
Channel

ATLANTIC OCEAN

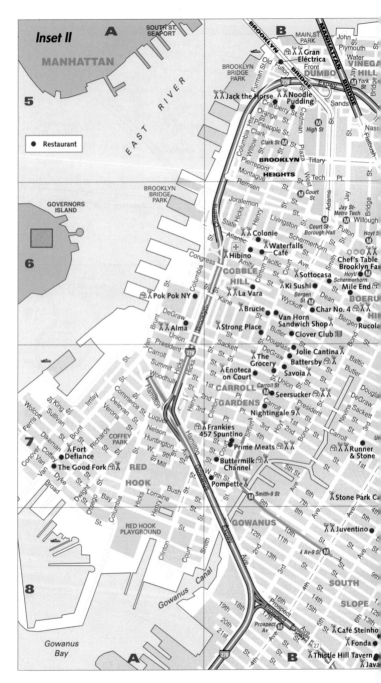

Inset II

MANHATTAN

A

SOUTH ST.
SEAPORT

B
MAIN ST.
PARK

John St.

Plymouth St.

Water St.

VINEGA
HILL

BROOKLYN
BRIDGE
PARK

Gran
Eléctrica

DUMBO

York
St.

Nass

EAST RIVER

Jack the Horse

Noodle
Pudding

Sands St.

• Restaurant

5

High St

GOVERNORS
ISLAND

BROOKLYN
HEIGHTS

Flatbush

BROOKLYN
BRIDGE
PARK

Court
St

Jay St-
Metro Tech

Bridge

6

Colonie

Waterfalls
Café

Court St-
Borough Hall

Willough

Hoyt S

Hibino

Chef's Table
Brooklyn Fa

Mile End

COBBLE
HILL

Sottocasa

Hoyt

Schermerhorn

Pok Pok NY

La Vara

Ki Sushi

BOERU

Char No. 4

Rucola

Alma

Brucie

Van Horn
Sandwich Shop

Strong Place

Clover Club

HI

Jolie Cantina

The
Grocery

Battersby

Enoteca
on Court

Savoia

CARROLL
GARDENS

Seersucker

Nightingale 9

Frankies
457 Spuntino

Prime Meats

Fort
Defiance

COFFEY
PARK

Runner
& Stone

The Good Fork

RED
HOOK

Buttermilk
Channel

Pompette

Stone Park C

RED HOOK
PLAYGROUND

GOWANUS

Juventino

4 Av-9 St

7

SOUTH

8

SLOPE

Gowanus
Bay

Gowanus Canal

Prospect
Av

Café Steinho

Fonda

Thistle Hill Tavern

Java

438

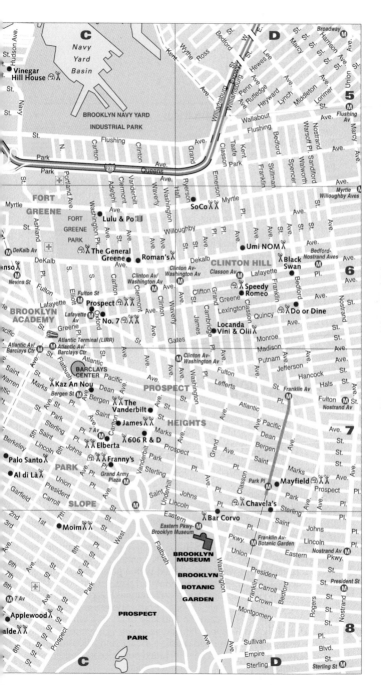

439

Al di Là

Italian

248 Fifth Ave. (at Carroll St.)

Subway: Union St
Phone: 718-783-4565
Web: www.aldilatrattoria.com
Prices: $$

Lunch & dinner daily

This Park Slope fixture serves up delectable Venetian-inspired cuisine in an unbeatably charming setting run by husband-and-wife team Emiliano Coppa and Chef Anna Klinger.

Church pew seating, a blown glass chandelier, and a scattering of whimsical touches dress the high-ceilinged room where local folk and foodies from afar dine on shaved wintry white vegetables—celery root, parsnip, cauliflower, and endive—tossed with champagne vinaigrette, a vibrant hit of black pepper and *Castelmagno* cheese; or pastas such as dense and chewy ricotta *cavatelli* dressed with Parmesan, lemon, wilted radicchio, kale, and crowned by a dollop of whipped ricotta.

Their latest addition, Lincoln Station, is the perfect spot to pick up a picnic basket for a day in the park.

Allswell

Gastropub

124 Bedford Ave. (at N. 10th St.)

Subway: Bedford Av
Phone: 347-799-2743
Web: www.allswellnyc.com
Prices: $$

Lunch & dinner daily

Allswell's menu changes nightly and offers solid, often vibrant cooking that would be an attraction all its own, even if the chef weren't known for having previously manned the stoves at the Spotted Pig. This comfortable Williamsburg tavern boasts walls embellished with a patchwork of vintage wallpaper framed by polished wood slats, a communal table prettied with flowers, and a wall-mounted blackboard menu. Small plates might range from showcasing seasonal vegetables, as in cardoon and kale toast, to a whole grilled quail slicked with red chili and rosemary vinaigrette, perched atop a nest of shredded purple cabbage and batons of green garlic. Larger entrées have included pork *piccata* doused with lemon and caper-sparked butter sauce.

Alma

A6

Mexican

187 Columbia St. (at Degraw St.)

Subway: Carroll St
Phone: 718-643-5400
Web: www.almarestaurant.com
Prices: $$

Lunch Sat – Sun
Dinner nightly

It might be a hassle to get to Alma via public transportation, but this contemporary Mexican charmer is well worth the hike to its increasingly food-savvy Carroll Gardens-meets-Red Hook Brooklyn neighborhood, with priceless views of lower Manhattan and area ship yards.

Duck into the Degraw St. entrance (the Columbia St. entrance takes you through B61, their rollicking bar), and head upstairs. There, a sangria jar welcomes you to the whimsically appointed dining room with wide-plank floors and enormous rooftop dining area (covered in winter). After you start with a generous helping of the guacamole chockablock with avocados, move on to *hongos*—pan-fried, thickly sliced mushrooms with caramelized onions, chili, and *hoja santa* leaves, topped with Oaxaca.

Am Thai Bistro

B3

Thai

1003 Church Ave. (bet. 10th St. & Stratford Rd.)

Subway: Church Av (18th St.)
Phone: 718-287-8888
Web: www.amthaibistro.com
Prices:

Lunch & dinner daily

Despite the many flourishing Thai restaurants in the city, the choices in this gentrifying nook of Brooklyn are few. So, when this sweet and attractive spot showed up, people took notice. The decor is spare with dark walnut tables and a dash of modern Asian accents, but toward the back, a festive spirit looms large via fuchsia lights set against a silver background tracing an outline of Thailand in gold.

The traditional, well-crafted menu may unveil the likes of *yum yum* shrimp tossed with pickled garlic, peanuts, fish sauce, and fresh herbs that deliver a spectrum of sour, sweet, tart, and pungent flavors; fluffy bistro *roti* with massaman curry; or grilled *e-sarn* pork—crunchy, decadent, and deliciously offset by a chili-lime glaze.

441

Anella

B1

222 Franklin St. (bet. Green & Huron Sts.)

Subway: Greenpoint Av
Phone: 718-389-8102
Web: www.anellabrooklyn.com
Prices: $$

Lunch Sat – Sun
Dinner nightly

Tucked away in Greenpoint, just a few blocks from the East River, Anella hosts diners in an intimate rough and tumble space boasting a sliver of a dining room, a charming back patio, and a welcoming bar fashioned out of a reclaimed work bench from the Steinway & Sons piano factory.

The kitchen is on display and sends forth a menu of ambitious creations, beginning with a loaf of bread freshly baked and served in a clay flowerpot. Smoke was a recent inspiration as seen in a slice of brisket afloat in a lusciously fluid risotto of spinach and garlic. Other preparations have included seared striped bass paired with lentils and cauliflower that was roasted and whirled into a purée; and a finale of apple *crémeux* atop almond cake sided by rum ice cream.

Applewood

C8

501 11th St. (bet. Seventh & Eighth Aves.)

Subway: 7 Av (9th St.)
Phone: 718-788-1810
Web: www.applewoodny.com
Prices: $$

Lunch Sat – Sun
Dinner Mon – Sat

Skillfully prepared cuisine and a dainty setting reflect the seriousness of Applewood's owners, David and Laura Shea. The pair is committed to promoting the work of organic and local farmers in a changing menu of small plates and entrées dedicated to reflecting the seasons.

The spare yet comfortable dining room, set in a century-old townhouse on a tree-lined street, is furnished with honey-toned wood tables and spindleback chairs. When in use, a working fireplace warms the light-colored room, accented by the work of local artists.

Starters like house-made charcuterie with garlic crostini and stone-ground mustard set the tone for an enjoyable meal that might feature Vermont lamb with French green lentils, Delicata squash, and buttermilk vinaigrette.

Aska ✿

B1

90 Wythe Ave. (at N.11th St.)

Subway: Bedford Av
Phone: 718-388-2969
Web: www.askanyc.com
Prices: $$$$

Dinner nightly

Daniel Krieger

Hatched from 2012's pop-up Frej emerges Aska, a fully formed and thoroughly enticing venue housed in the multi-disciplinary creative space of Kinfolk Studios. Meander through to find the restaurant which has taken up residence in the back.

Inside, an intimate mood is accompanied by a blithe attitude that's very appealing, never off-putting. The bar—displaying libations on the wall and offering a special assortment of small plates—is attended to by a crew that greets you as if you were a long lost friend. Chef Fredrik Berselius' tasting menu is exhibited on hand-crafted pottery with laudable pride. The Swedish native creates a unique procession that's rooted in Scandinavian tradition and respects local provenance. Tastes include plump Rhode Island oysters afloat in cucumber juice studded with drops of rapeseed oil; fried baby squid plated with shaved cauliflower and squid butter; or cold smoked pike buried under grated egg yolk and licked with onion-infused aquavit. A 100-day, dry-aged strip of beef is precisely cooked and paired with roasted sweet beets.

Following that sample of sweet is cardamom ice cream crested with browned butter-whipped cream and a pinch of hazelnut powder.

Aurora

 C1

70 Grand St. (at Wythe Ave.)

Subway: Bedford Av
Phone: 718-388-5100
Web: www.auroraristorante.com
Prices: $$

Lunch & dinner daily

This charming trattoria has long been a popular dining choice for residents of this dynamic stretch of Williamsburg. Stocked with wood furnishings, the rustic brick and plaster room is dressed up with vintage knickknacks and features a pretty ivy-covered outdoor area that doubles the seating capacity of the corner setting.

Aurora's enjoyable Italian cuisine speaks to the power of simplicity with minimally dressed market greens, expertly prepared pastas, and roasted meats. One can't go wrong with a meal of plump house-made sausage with lightly sautéed broccoli rabe and pickled Calabrian pepper; silky agnolotti stuffed with ricotta, spring peas, and fresh mint; or *affogato* with chocolate crumb-coated vanilla gelato, all offered at impressive value.

Baci & Abbracci

 C1

204 Grand St. (bet. Bedford & Driggs Sts.)

Subway: Bedford Av
Phone: 718-599-6599
Web: www.baciny.com
Prices: $$

Lunch Sat – Sun
Dinner nightly

This upbeat Williamsburg eatery features Italian cuisine with a wholehearted emphasis on pizza. With more than twenty permutations of pies baked in their wood-burning oven from Naples, these smoky-chewy crusts may be the foundation for sauce and freshly made mozzarella, or even *focaccia tartufata*—two thin layers filled with *robiola* cheese and topped with truffle oil. Beyond this, the adept kitchen also boasts homemade bread, enjoyable pastas, and an impressive short list of *secondi* like juicy lamb chops with a crisp potato-rosemary crust.

The intimate space sports a contemporary design framed by a concrete floor, sleek furnishings, and glazed-tile accents. A charming little patch of backyard makes an especially popular setting for weekend brunch.

Bamboo Garden

Chinese

 A3

6409 Eighth Ave. (at 64th St.)

Subway: 8 Av
Phone: 718-238-1122
Web: N/A
Prices:

Lunch & dinner daily

This bustling establishment confirms that there is impressive dim sum to be found in Brooklyn. The large setting may look a bit tattered but it is clean and boasts a generous number of large, round, linen-draped tables; during the day the space is jam-packed with a gregarious flock of local residents.

The tables are attended to by Cantonese-speaking ladies, dressed in fuchsia blouses and red vests, pushing carts of steaming treats through the hungry hordes. Resist the urge to stock your table all at once; instead, survey the delicacies and pace yourself for a spectrum of fresh, delish dumplings, buns, and pastries. The feast also includes some refreshingly unique preparations (perhaps braised tofu with salted fish?) that steer away from the standard lineup.

Bar Corvo

Italian

D8

791 Washington Ave. (bet. Lincoln & St John's Pls.)

Subway: Eastern Pkwy - Brooklyn Museum
Phone: 718-230-0940
Web: www.barcorvo.com
Prices: $$

Lunch Sat – Sun
Dinner nightly

Bar Corvo brings an inspired Italian menu to this rather bleak Brooklyn stretch. A comfortable marble-topped bar is a great place from which to watch this theatrical show of flaming kitchen burners. However, the exterior is anything but flashy. Peek through glass panes for signs of the deliciousness that waits inside.

Diners line the slim entrance in anticipation of a seat within this outdated yet jaunty nest. Quirky touches like distressed wall paper and floors crafted out of pretty penny tiles serve to elevate the pleasure after a warm salad tossing *farro*, roasted cauliflower, and Brussels sprouts; or ricotta *cavatelli* robust with wild mushrooms. Braised lamb shank with fava beans makes for a fantastic finale of comfort food.

Battersby

B7

Contemporary ✗

255 Smith St. (bet. Degraw & Douglas Sts.)

Subway: Bergen St (Smith St.)   Dinner nightly
Phone: 718-852-8321
Web: www.battersbybrooklyn.com
Prices: $$

This bright spot along well-endowed Smith Street is the domain of Chefs Joseph Ogrodnek and Walker Stern. The intimate space has a homey, fuss-free feel, and tiny open kitchen. Squeeze in and glimpse the team at work in their petite but well-equipped corner.

Battersby's sophisticated cooking offers the likes of an ultra-seasonal mélange of spring peas, comprised of pods, young snap peas, shelled sweet peas, and a thicket of pea greens dressed with a touch of lemon and olive oil, and showered with sweet pecorino. Heartier dishes include *fregola Sarda*, bead-shaped pasta from Sardinia prepared with unctuous bits of tripe braised in tomato and sprinkling of Grana Padano. Come dessert, the rhubarb galette with Stilton and Port ice cream is very, very nice.

Black Swan

D6

American ✗

1048 Bedford Ave. (bet. Clifton Pl. & Lafayette Ave.)

Subway: Bedford - Nostrand Avs   Lunch & dinner daily
Phone: 718-783-4744
Web: www.blackswannyc.com
Prices: $$

This hot spot on an up-and-coming stretch of Bedford Avenue in Bed-Stuy is more than just a neighborhood pub. It has all the makings of a beloved bar—the comfort, warmth, and good vibes—but rocks a fantastic menu to boot. Slip into one of the dark wood booths or hang at a communal table and let the food and beer fest begin.

A good starting place is a bowlful of delectable mussels, plump and cooked in a mustard-cream sauce, served with crispy fries; or perhaps a plate of soul-comforting mac and cheese, with orecchiette and jalapeño. Burger lovers are in for a serious treat: this excellent rendition, made with Piccinini Brothers beef and available with all manner of sides (bacon, avocado, goat cheese, fried egg) is one of the best bets around.

Blanca ✿

Contemporary ✗✗

B1

261 Moore St. (bet. Bogart & White Sts.)

Subway: Morgan Av
Phone: 347-799-2807
Web: www.blancanyc.com
Prices: $$$$

Dinner Wed – Sat

Anthony Falco

Diners bound for Blanca first arrive at Roberta's and receive a fervent greeting—a mere sampling to the uninitiated of what a treat one is in for. Each party is then escorted through the pioneering pizzeria's foodie campus to Blanca's front door. Enter to find an elegant dining experience, enjoyed within a chicly utilitarian space where seating is set along a wide counter facing sparkling equipment and Chef Carlo Mirarchi with his team at the ready. The vibe is not all serious or clinical though: a giant bluefin tuna head is mounted on the wall; diners are welcome to play DJ by choosing the night's beats from a stack of vinyl; and a glass of cider offers a bubbly welcome.

The ever-rotating menu flaunts exquisitely crafted canapés and small plates that combine to form a stellar feast starting with crudo (maybe geoduck clam and Spanish mackerel with slivers of green apple?); followed by a hot and crispy shrimp head. Other standouts reveal grilled oysters capped by seaweed-flecked breadcrumbs; agnolotti with pine nut cream showered with black truffle shavings; and roasted Sasso chicken beside creamy polenta and crowned by a shard of skin so flavorful it may just burst in your mouth.

447

Bozu

Japanese

C1

296 Grand St. (bet. Havemeyer & Roebling Sts.)

Subway: Bedford Av   Dinner nightly
Phone: 718-384-7770
Web: www.oibozu.com
Prices: ⚅⚅

An enticing selection of Japanese tapas—with many pleasing vegetarian options—is buttressed by a gracious staff and laid-back vibe at this upbeat, hip, and tasty spot. The slim wood and brick space is dressed in grey and installed with an L-shaped counter, a row of tables, and back patio. Brings friends and order a lot.

The sushi bar tempts with the *yakko* roll filled with silken house-made tofu and green onion; spicy mushroom roll dabbed with tomatillo puree; and *gunkanzushi* topped with sweet sea scallop and plump salmon roe alongside soy sauce pre-seasoned with wasabi. Cooked dishes bring on the likes of deep fried *gyoza* filled with tomato, and fantastically intense nuggets of fried chicken thigh marinated for 48 hours in garlic and soy sauce.

Do not confuse 🍴 with ✿ ! 🍴 defines comfort, while ✿ are awarded for the best cuisine. Stars are awarded across all categories of comfort.

Brooklyn Star

D1

American ✕✕

593 Lorimer St. (at Conselyea St.)

Subway: Lorimer St - Metropolitan Av
Phone: 718-599-9899
Web: www.thebrooklynstar.com
Prices: $$

Lunch Sat – Sun
Dinner nightly

Hooray for Brooklyn Star 2.0. The demise of the original was gut-wrenching—this hand-built restaurant was razed by a fire in 2010. But, perhaps this is a blessing in disguise? Because a just as alluring incarnation sprouted nearby. The fresh setting heralds diners with a bar and dining room enlivened with a brick red terrazzo floor, eggshell walls, and chunky blonde wood tables topped with hot sauce, pepper vinegar, and wild flowers.

Chef Joaquin Baca's love letter to old-fashioned, down home specialties may reveal a green bean casserole coalesced by mushroom béchamel and showered with buttery crumbs and fried shallots; a hunk of a sandwich—warm bacon-wrapped meatloaf stuffed between thick slices of Pullman bread; and excellent buttermilk biscuits.

Brucie

B6

Italian ✕

234 Court St. (bet. Baltic & Kane Sts.)

Subway: Bergen St (Smith St.)
Phone: 347-987-4961
Web: www.brucienyc.com
Prices: $$

Lunch Sat – Sun
Dinner nightly

Despite the tough guy name, this local canteen proudly claims the distinctly female touch of Chef/owner Zahra Tangorra. The pleasantly thrown-together space seats a diverse selection of patrons, many with kids in tow. Step in to find a smattering of tables, copper-topped dining counter, and shelves lined with canned products, jars, and bottles.

Old-world inspiration combines with new-world sensibility and results in product-driven, mostly Italian creations like *tagliatelle* with Brussels sprouts, tomato butter, and house-made *burrata*. Then, savor the brined and barbecued chicken basted with earthy stout- and maple syrup-enriched sauce.

Try the chef's signature lasagna service: drop off your empty pan and pick it up filled and ready to feed a crowd.

Buttermilk Channel

B7

American

524 Court St. (at Huntington St.)

Subway: Smith - 9 Sts.

Phone: 718-852-8490

Web: www.buttermilkchannelnyc.com

Prices: $$

Lunch Sat – Sun
Dinner nightly

The talented duo of Doug Crowell and Chef Ryan Angulo have steered this lovely spot from new kid on the block to a charmer that Brooklynites are proud to call their own.

Pale yellow walls and a chic, simple décor are ideal for unwinding with a brew at the bar before moving back to the seating area to dig into their array of clever fare. Expect the likes of barbecued oysters, gently warmed yet still slurpable, seasoned with green onion, bits of smoked bacon, and a splash of Worcestershire. Equally impressive is the pan-roasted East Coast flounder, served whole, dressed with lentils, and a chunky pistachio vinaigrette. Also find a rotating list of such lovely daily specials as Monday's $28 prix-fixe, Friday's lobster, and tasty vegetarian options.

Cafe Avat

A4

Central Asian

2158 Bath Ave. (bet. Bay 29th St. & Bay Pkwy.)

Subway: Bay Pkwy

Phone: 718-676-4667

Web: N/A

Prices:

Dinner Mon – Sat

At this immaculate little outpost, sweet and hospitable Café Avat valiantly serves the Central Asian cuisine of Uzbekistan and Kyrgyzstan (where the original location is going strong). The décor is limited to ceramic-tiled floors, a wood-framed window overlooking Bath Avenue, and tables arranged with *very* spicy condiments. Its greatest feat may be authenticity— note the refrigerator stocked with Central Asian sparkling waters.

Even if the flat-screen looping music videos is distracting, keep your focus on *manti*, steamed mutton dumplings served with chopped dill; and pliable, golden Uzbek-style round breads filled with cumin-spiced ground lamb. *Chim-cha* is a spicy cabbage salad that should be joined with shish kebabs for a match made in heaven.

Café Steinhof

B8

422 Seventh Ave. (at 14th St.)

Subway: 7 Av (9th St.)
Phone: 718-369-7776
Web: www.cafesteinhof.com
Prices:

Lunch Tue – Sun
Dinner nightly

Austrian flavors abound at this winsome Park Slope café. Dominating the space is an affable bar, where a selection of beers on draught, generously measured libations, and fruit brandies are poured; and any of these would be a fine accompaniment to the traditional and hearty Central European cooking. Dark wood furnishings and old-timey signage promoting Austrian provisions hung on the walls frame the space. The scene is more laid-back during the day but just as enjoyable.

Small plates and house specialties, imbued with old-world relish include the likes of golden chicken consommé with crêpe slivers and chives; black sausage strudel; tender bread dumplings with wild mushroom fricassee; and chicken in paprika-seasoned cream sauce.

Celestino

B2

562 Halsey St. (at Stuyvesant Ave.)

Subway: Utica Av
Phone: 347-787-3564
Web: N/A
Prices: $$

Dinner Tue – Sun

Those on Brooklyn's culinary vanguard know about Celestino and its trailblazing owner Massimiliano Nanni, but the secret is now getting out. Not many would pick this seemingly out-of-the-way spot in Bed-Stuy with its barely burgeoning restaurant scene, but one bite and naysayers are forgotten.

The whitewashed brick walls sparsely decorated with lobster traps and fishing nets suit the concise, piscine-focused menu. Italian servers shuck oysters at the bar and shuffle dishes that begin with simple and classic plates of prosecco-marinated sardines, tender cuttlefish over creamy polenta, and spaghetti topped with mussels in a white wine broth. Light and delicious crêpes are ingenious when filled with a wonderfully unique and rich seafood ragù.

Char No. 4

American ✕✕

B6

196 Smith St. (bet. Baltic & Warren Sts.)

Subway: Bergen St (Smith St.)
Phone: 718-643-2106
Web: www.charno4.com
Prices: $$

Lunch Fri – Sun
Dinner nightly

This discreet 19th century row house is neither notoriously beautiful nor polished, yet it is a truly welcome spot to Cobble Hill. The long, backlit bar is focused on service and the wall of Bourbon and brown spirits that it displays.

The dining room has comfy booths towards the back, tiny tables for two, and a fierce pride in its Southern fare. This is a serious home to smoked meats, so try their thinly sliced, house-cured lamb pastrami: a little smoky, a little sweet, served with coriander aïoli and enhanced with pickling spice. For dessert, the baked Macoon apple kissed with nutmeg and cinnamon and paired with Fontinella ice cream is heavenly. Brunches here are near legendary, as are Mardi Gras, the Kentucky Derby, and other special events.

Chavela's

Mexican ✕

D7

736 Franklin Ave. (at Sterling Pl.)

Subway: Franklin St
Phone: 718-622-3100
Web: www.chavelasnyc.com
Prices:

Lunch & dinner daily

Behold the gorgeous, sea-green dome perched on a sparse corner of Franklin Avenue, directly above the wrought-iron entrance that leads into this lively gem of a spot. Inside, a burst of colorful Mexican tiles blanket the dark wood bar, where antique candle chandeliers dangle from high tin ceilings. Exposed brick and deep red walls showcase ceramic butterflies, iron mirrors, and gold window hangings.

Perfectly made Mexican classics are the name of the game here at Chavela's, which has emerged as a neighborhood treasure. Scrumptious *papas con chorizo*—corn tortillas stuffed with potato, chorizo, shredded cabbage, pickled jalapeños, and *crema fresca*—are a good starting place. Or try the *sopa de tortilla*, a robust soup of chicken and tomatillos.

Chef's Table at Brooklyn Fare ✿ ✿ ✿

Contemporary ✗✗

B6

200 Schermerhorn St. (bet. Bond & Hoyt Sts.)

Subway: Hoyt-Schermerhorn
Phone: 718-243-0050
Web: www.brooklynfare.com
Prices: $$$$

Dinner Mon – Sat

Raymond E. Trinh

On a gritty Brooklyn block known for its parking lots, find one of the city's best restaurants. On the one hand, it is a tiny steel and copper kitchen adjacent to a gourmet grocery store. On the other, Chef César Ramirez is the one preparing your extraordinary and very memorable food. Even those who have been here before should return to witness its dramatic and upscale evolution into a culinary destination. Today, it is complete with more staff and a sommelier pouring champagne into flutes so delicate that they might shatter from the bubbles.

The food continues to surprise with refinement, creativity, and a head-spinning array of fish that is among the finest to be found in the country. Sea urchin arrives straight from Japan to your plate, set between rich brioche and a slice of black truffle. Here, bouillabaisse captures the essence of French technique. Seafood-centric items highlight dragon fish, *hiramatsu*, rudder fish, jawfish...and the very exclusive list goes on. Dessert may look like a golden pound cake, but is in fact frozen chocolate malt, as light and fleeting as air.

With every course and every year, this restaurant is not only getting better—it is skyrocketing.

Clover Club

210 Smith St. (bet. Baltic & Butler Sts.)

Subway: Bergen St (Smith St.)
Phone: 718-855-7939
Web: www.cloverclubny.com
Prices: $$

Lunch Fri – Sun
Dinner nightly

A former shoe store is now an atmospheric Smith Street rest stop that fashions a spot-on vintage vibe with mosaic tiled floors, glove-soft leather banquettes, and pressed-tin ceilings dangling etched-glass pendants that glow as warmly as single malt. The glossy mahogany bar (furnished with leather-upholstered bar stools) is overseen by natty bartenders artfully shaking and pouring a stellar selection of libations like the namesake Clover Club—a mixture of gin, dry vermouth, lemon, and raspberry syrup.

An excellent menu of savory bites is a perfect counterpoint to such liquid indulgences, with herb-marinated hanger steak over toasted baguette spread with horseradish cream, duck fat-fried potato crisps, oysters on the half-shell, or American caviar service.

Colonie

127 Atlantic Ave. (bet. Clinton & Henry Sts.)

Subway: Borough Hall
Phone: 718-855-7500
Web: www.colonienyc.com
Prices: $$

Lunch Sat – Sun
Dinner nightly

Colonie is energetic, hip, and total fun. Step inside this whimsical haven to find Brooklyn style-hounds sipping drinks at the zinc-topped bar, among cherry blossoms branches and tufts of greenery sprouting from brick walls. Behind the scene, find owners who are old pals from working at Public and Chef Bryan Redmond's menu.

Start with an egg salad crostini with smoked beef marrow and drizzled with excellent veal jus; feather-light ricotta *gnudi* with basil chiffonade, Niçoise black olive "dirt," and cubed tomato sauce; or go for the tender pan-seared pork chop with pickled celery jus. Find pure perfection in the warm and sticky date cake drizzled with dark caramel syrup, served with crème fraîche as ice cream and maybe a side of foie gras-filled donuts.

Cupola Samarkanda

Central Asian

B3

1797 McDonald Ave. (at Ave. P)

Subway: Avenue P
Phone: 718-375-7777
Web: N/A
Prices: $$

Lunch & dinner daily

To say that this feels like a glitzy invention by Tony Manero—the star character from *Saturday Night Fever* with a fancy for Brooklyn discos—is surely no exaggeration. Nor is it an exaggeration to claim that here you'll find some of the most memorable *manti* in the city. The lights are flickering, the keyboard wants tuning, and the back-up singer is wobbly, but this is precisely what makes Cupola Samarkanda so desirable, bizarre, and fun.

Among the local Georgians, Uzbeks, and Azerbaijani denizens, this gem offers perfect bites of home in the form of *cheburek*, plump, subliminal layers of flaky dough filled with cheese; and *geez-beez*, a classic sauté of tender, shining liver served in a "bowl" of cracker-like dough and crowned with onion rings.

Dear Bushwick

Contemporary

B1

41 Wilson Ave. (bet. George & Melrose Sts.)

Subway: Morgan Av
Phone: 929-234-2344
Web: www.dearbushwick.com
Prices: $$

Lunch Sat – Sun
Dinner nightly

This slim and snug spot debuted as an ideal option for visitors craving a taste of Bushwick's indie scene. Find it easily by looking for a horse's head protruding above a door. Inside, it is warm and lovely, with a long bar down the middle, hanging birdcages, and pressed-tin ceilings. Solo diners land upon a narrow, comfy ledge, which is perfect for a bite and beverage.

Accentuating the vintage vibe are portraits of men in mustaches who seem to be contemplating diners as they devour hardboiled eggs in a pool of glistening horseradish butter. Or, try a refreshing and dainty dish of baby artichokes "crudo" with farmhouse cheddar and mushrooms. Finish with a scoop of rich chocolate pâté crowned with sea salt, pink peppercorns, and crème fraîche.

Diner 🐶

C2

American ✗

85 Broadway (at Berry St.)

Subway: Marcy Av
Phone: 718-486-3077
Web: www.dinernyc.com
Prices: $$

Lunch & dinner daily

Do not let Diner's impossibly hip crowd and rather ramshackle setting deter you. Beneath all that plaid are ordinary folk who appreciate the restored 1920s Kulman Diner setting and a delightfully unfussy kitchen that knows how to make a perfect block of head cheese. Originally founded by the pioneering restaurateurs and publishers of *Diner Journal*, this establishment has been run with heart and personality since 1998.

Grass-fed steaks and burgers are a mainstay, but the bulk of the impressively prepared menu is inspired by the season and changes daily. The kitchen uses spot-on technique in dishes such as rabbit confit salad with rabbit pâté toast; or lamb steak with charred leek purée, fennel potato salad, and horseradish crème fraîche dressing.

Do or Dine 🐶

D6

Contemporary ✗

1108 Bedford Ave. (bet. Lexington Ave. & Quincy St.)

Subway: Bedford - Nostrand Avs
Phone: 718-684-2290
Web: N/A
Prices: $$

Dinner nightly

It's like the mafia of Michelin-starred runaways at Do or Dine, where made men from The Modern and Daniel have decamped to slum it, Bed-Stuy-style. Finding this place will try the patience of a saint, but here's a hint: look for the awning heralding West Indian takeout. This renegade establishment is bedecked with decoupage tabletops, black and white mosaic tile floor, and a disco-ball spinning above.

The "one fish two fish" charred sardine starter pitched with capers, toasted hazelnuts, and mizuna; and "pork renderloin," cooked in duck fat, fanned across sweet- and sour-braised red cabbage and paired with roasted apple ensconced in wasabi marshmallow are just two examples of the *buonissima cucina* that emerges from the tiny kitchen.

DuMont

American X

D1

432 Union Ave. (bet. Devoe St. & Metropolitan Ave.)

Subway: Lorimer St - Metropolitan Av	Lunch & dinner daily
Phone: 718-486-7717	
Web: www.dumontrestaurant.com	
Prices: $$	

DuMont—which got its name from a salvaged neon sign for the pioneering television network—epitomizes its neighborhood's relaxed, edgy, and creative vibe. The multi-room space is warm and comfortably worn, with dark wood tables topped in brown paper, vintage tile floors, and leather seating handmade by the late owner, Colin Devlin. There is also a backyard with elevated seating called "the treehouse." DuMont fuels Billyburg hipsters clamoring for near-addictive comfort food. Favorites may include lamb meatballs with braised Tuscan kale; roasted chicken with red wine sauce; and of course the DuMac and cheese, *radiatore* pasta in a blend of cheeses studded with bacon. Brunch keeps weekends groovy.

For a quick burger and a beer, try nearby DuMont Burger.

East Harbor Seafood Palace

Chinese XX

A3

714-726 65th St. (bet. Seventh & Eighth Aves.)

Subway: 8 Av	Lunch & dinner daily
Phone: 718-765-0098	
Web: N/A	
Prices: $$	

Come for dim sum to this behemoth that rocks with joyful chatter and gleeful moans from tables devouring impressive morsels. *Cha siu bao* (barbecue pork buns); *cha siu soh* (barbecue pork puff pastry); *zha liang* (fried crullers wrapped with *cheung fun* skin); and other treats are stocked on steaming carts that constantly circulate the room.

However, come sundown the setting is sparsely occupied. But that shouldn't deter you from making dinner here a consideration; quite the contrary in fact. The warm welcome is genuine and suggestions are forthcoming when requested. They may reveal tender stir-fried beef tossed with long beans and cashew nuts; or a succulent sea scallop gently steamed in its shell and topped with chopped garlic-studded glass noodles.

457

Egg

American ✗

135 N. 5th St. (bet. Bedford Ave. & Berry St.)

Subway: Bedford Av   Lunch daily
Phone: 718-302-5151
Web: www.pigandegg.com
Prices: 😋

Boasting that famously laid-back Brooklyn personality, old-fashioned Southern soul, and a daily breakfast that lasts until 6:00 P.M., Egg's slender dining room seems to serve as a remote office for Williamsburg's work-from-home set. We may never know how many bestsellers were conceived here, while downing cups of sustainably-grown coffee or doodling with crayons provided on the paper-topped tables. On weekends, the wait for a table can be lengthy—jot your name on the flipchart stationed outside and be patient.

Days here begin with house-made granola, braised-duck hash, or fresh-baked buttermilk biscuits (perhaps the city's best), slathered in sawmill gravy flecked with pork sausage crumbles, or a vegetarian option with pan-seared mushroom gravy.

El Almacen

Argentinian ✗

557 Driggs Ave. (bet. N. 6th & N. 7th Sts.)

Subway: Bedford Av   Lunch Sat – Sun
Phone: 718-218-7284   Dinner nightly
Web: www.elalmacennyc.com
Prices: $$

This Argentinian grill is a carnivore's delight with its menu of meaty entrées from the grill (*de la parrilla*) like the *parrillada* featuring hearty ribeye and chorizo with truffle fries; or the "kitchen" offerings (*de la cocina*) which might include malbec-braised short ribs with sweet potato purée and Brussels sprouts. These hearty creations are best followed by *dulce de leche* in one of its several guises.

El Almacen, which means general store in Spanish, boasts a dark, rustic, and atmospheric setting replete with creaking wood furnishings, shelves of bric-a-brac, and cast iron skillets mounted on a brick wall. The bar is inviting, amply stocked with wine bottles, and set against a backdrop of creamy white tile warmed by the candlelit room.

Elberta

C7

Southern 🍴🍴

335 Flatbush Ave. (bet. Park & Prospect Pls.)

Subway: 7 Av (Flatbush Ave.)
Phone: 718-638-1936
Web: www.elbertarestaurant.com
Prices: $$

Lunch Sat – Sun
Dinner Tue – Sun

Equal parts modern speakeasy, Southern flare, and cozy hospitality comprise this Prospect Heights charmer. Named for the soulful jazz singer, Elberta's vibe is approachable yet stylish. The interior is clean and linear with stenciled wallpaper, dark woods, and steel touches set beneath dangling filament bulbs.

Chef Kingsley John and team fire up a delectable menu of Southern-inspired dishes, perhaps beginning with an amuse of outstandingly thick and creamy carrot-curry soup to showcase their intense culinary chops. Sample the likes of delicate jerk-fried oysters with sour-sweet pickled mango; or molasses glazed NY strip steak over smoked cauliflower purée and green beans with red wine reduction that is as delicious as it is technically perfect.

Eliá

A3

Greek 🍴

8611 Third Ave. (bet. 86th & 87th Sts.)

Subway: 86 St
Phone: 718-748-9891
Web: www.eliarestaurant.com
Prices: $$

Dinner Tue – Sun

Oh my, Mykonos? Nope, it's Bay Ridge, but Eliá's weathered plank floors and whitewashed walls decorated with wooden shutters will have you convinced otherwise. And that's before you have even seen the charming backyard patio.

This sure isn't a weak Greek with plenty of top-of-mind classics (grilled shrimp, octopus) and a few newbies (house-made ravioli filled with shredded braised lamb) thrown in for good measure. Appetizers, like the tender pork ribs marinated in ouzo and roasted with Greek spices, are large enough to count as entrées, but with so many tempting choices, don't stop there. Definitely go for the pan-seared sheep's cheese *saganaki*, doused with a shot of ouzo for (ta-da!) flaming fun. Who doesn't love dinner and a show?

The Elm

Contemporary XX

C1

160 N. 12th St. (bet. Bedford Ave. & Berry St.)

Subway: Bedford Av   Dinner nightly
Phone: 718-218-1088
Web: www.theelmnyc.com
Prices: $$$

Chef Paul Liebrandt has crossed the river to this new dining room of Williamsburg's King & Grove hotel. The Elm is a spacious, elegantly crafted terrain blending wood, concrete, and glass to beget a jaunty effect—further augmented by poised, versed servers that put the staff at some longstanding gastro temples to shame.

Rousing à la carte preparations recently brought powdered *jamón*-dusted raw kanpachi; and foie gras *torchon* dressed with spiced strawberry gelée and Thai long pepper-studded brioche. Chicken Kiev-style is a feast for two composed of garlic butter-stuffed roulade, tempura wings, and dark meat croquettes, grandly paired with a cloud of *pommes aligot*.

Based on the talented chef's history, the evolution here should be fascinating to behold.

El Mio Cid

Spanish

B1

50 Starr St. (at Wilson Ave.)

Subway: Jefferson St   Lunch & dinner daily
Phone: 718-628-8300
Web: www.elmiocidrestaurant.com
Prices: $$

In contrast to the popular tapas spots sweeping the city, this is an old guard Iberian stalwart, deep in the heart of Bushwick. The interior bears a Mediterranean sensibility, with idyllic murals of the Spanish countryside, dark wood tables, and huge vessels of refreshing sangria.

The best way to explore this menu is through the tapas, salads, and daily soups rather than entrées. The Spanish tortilla is an old-timey classic of crisp potatoes and fluffy eggs, sliced into perfect, warm triangles. Their soups can be exceedingly fortifying, as in the traditional Galician bowl of gently smoked pork, white beans, and collard greens. Interesting desserts include bread soaked in spiced wine with vanilla ice cream; or poached pear and raspberry coulis.

Enoteca on Court

Italian

B7

347 Court St. (bet. President & Union Sts.)

Subway: Carroll St

Phone: 718-243-1000

Web: www.enotecaoncourt.com

Prices:

Lunch & dinner daily

From the folks who run the old-school but freshly revived Marco Polo Ristorante located just next door, comes this fresh-hearted take on *la cucina Italiana*. The wine bar-inspired room dishes out wood and brick details and serves as a cozy spot in which to enjoy a long line of snacks that include Italian cheeses, panini, and *marinati* (olives, roasted peppers, or eggplant).

The wood-burning oven is used to prepare the majority of offerings that highlight baked pastas; *carciofo ripieno* (stuffed artichokes); and an array of pizzas topped with a regionally influenced composition of ingredients. The *spiedini* are worthy of consideration—meaty skewers filled with the likes of house-made sausage, onions, and peppers, finished with red wine reduction.

Falansai

Vietnamese

B1

112 Harrison Pl. (at Porter Ave.)

Subway: Morgan Av

Phone: 347-599-1190

Web: www.falansai.com

Prices: **$$**

Lunch Tue – Fri
Dinner Tue – Sun

This wonderfully fresh Vietnamese kitchen gives you reason to trek out to Bushwick—or is it East Williamsburg? Bay Area transplants listen up: Chef/owner Henry Trieu who once cooked at The Slanted Door has arrived and he's here to stay. Falansai's serene home—highlighting aqua walls and orchids lining the windowsills—is a pretty respite from the 'hood's grit. Find the likes of *bánh mì*, crusty baguettes slathered with black olive pâté, fermented mustard greens, green papaya slivers, and crunchy veggies; or excellent shrimp summer rolls served with a velvety peanut sauce.

For more redolence, order the *ca kho*, catfish fillets cooked in a claypot filled with an ambrosial broth scented with burnt sugar and stocked with red pepper, carrots, and green onions.

The Farm on Adderley

B3

1108 Cortelyou Rd. (bet. 12th St. & Stratford Rd.)

Subway: Cortelyou Rd	Lunch & dinner daily
Phone: 718-287-3101	
Web: www.thefarmonadderley.com	
Prices: $$	

Lots of love flows from breakfast to dinner into this trailblazing Ditmas Park hot spot, where streams of devotees and a whip-smart team with a soaring vision and eco-conscious philosophy keep the place humming. The welcoming digs are decked in exposed brick, wood-paneled walls and simple bare tables, while the sweet outdoor garden is punched up with murals and greenery.

Try homemade *tagliatelle*, lightly coated with a creamy pesto of mushrooms, walnuts, and Parmesan; the signature Farm burger, topped with cheddar, on a toasted English muffin alongside fries and pickles; or the fantastic pan-roasted fluke with baby carrots, spinach, and cumin-butter. End with a chocolate-banana upside down cake decked with caramel and cooled down with coconut sorbet.

Fonda

B8

434 Seventh Ave. (bet. 14th & 15th Sts.)

Subway: 7 Av (9th St.)	Lunch Sat – Sun
Phone: 718-369-3144	Dinner Tue – Sun
Web: www.fondarestaurant.com	
Prices: $$	

Bright colors and bold artwork adorn this cheery Park Slope favorite for creative Mexican cooking. The staff radiates hospitality, and speaking of warmth, when the sun is out, the tiny dining room is augmented by seating out back, which regulars know is *the* place to be.

Fonda's menu is endowed with a skilled spin, evident in items like a refreshing salad of diced watermelon and cucumber embellished with mild yet creamy *queso fresco* and the crunch of crushed *pepitas*. A lighter take on *chile rellenos* reveals roasted poblanos stuffed with spinach, raisins, and pine nuts, and dressed with a tomato-chipotle sauce and knob of epazote-seasoned goat cheese.

Chef Roberto Santibañez lets Manhattan in on the fun at his well-loved offshoot in the East Village.

Forcella

D2

Pizza ✗

485 Lorimer St. (bet. Grand & Power Sts.)

Subway: Lorimer St - Metropolitan Av
Phone: 718-388-8820
Web: www.forcellaeatery.com
Prices: 😊😊

Lunch & dinner daily

A domed wood-fired oven with glossy black tiles is the heart of Williamsburg's Forcella, where pizza falls under three headings: *rosse, bianche,* and *fritte*. In addition to puffy, smoke-imbued disks topped with the likes of imported tomatoes, house-made mozzarella, and fresh basil, some of Forcella's 'zas take a dip in hot oil for a distinctive take on the familiar.

The *montanara* is fried before being decked and baked as a traditional Margherita, while the fully-fried *ripieno classico* stuffs a belly-busting pocket with ricotta, mozzarella, and *soppressata*. *Pizza alla carbonara* for brunch or *alla Nutella* for dessert demonstrates the versatility of everybody's favorite Italian export.

New locations have popped up on the Bowery and Park Avenue South.

Fort Defiance

A7

American ✗

365 Van Brunt St. (at Dikeman St.)

Subway: Smith - 9 Sts (& bus B77)
Phone: 347-453-6672
Web: www.fortdefiancebrooklyn.com
Prices: $$

Lunch daily
Dinner Wed — Mon

Young, likeable, and very resilient (with no thanks to Hurricane Sandy), Fort Defiance proves that a place named for a Revolutionary War fort, focusing on deviled eggs and a handful of daily specials, makes for a great Southern tavern (of sorts). Then again, those spectacular cocktails, like The Pundit with coffee-infused Scotch, make everything all the warmer. The gamut of beers on tap is equally impressive.

Meals might seem progressively delicious, beginning with beautifully crisped sweetbreads set on a bed of parsnip purée with meaty shiitake mushrooms, fried capers, and a sweet Marsala *demi-glace*. Great skill and care is evident in the wonderfully spiced skate fried in a cornmeal crust with fresh cranberry bean ragout and buttery spinach.

Frankies 457 Spuntino

Italian ✗

457 Court St. (bet. 4th Pl. & Luquer St.)

Subway: Smith - 9 Sts
Phone: 718-403-0033
Web: www.frankiesspuntino.com
Prices: 🍷🍷

Lunch & dinner daily

The ever-expanding empire of Frank Castronovo and Frank Falcinelli (the Franks) has its origins in this hands-down Carroll Gardens favorite.

Loosely translated as "snack", the menu of this home-styled Italian spot offers a selection of deliciously fuss-free fare. Headliners include fresh salads like shaved Brussels sprouts pocked with diced Castelrosso cheese and slicked with the house's golden-hued olive oil; the signature meatballs studded with pine nuts and raisins; and sublime pastas like sweet potato-filled ravioli in Parmesan broth.

Cooking is initially done in the basement kitchen, but dishes are finished upstairs behind stacks of charcuterie and crusty breads gracing the utterly charming brick-lined and wood-furnished space.

Franny's 🎿

C7

Italian ✗✗

348 Flatbush Ave. (bet. Sterling & St. John's Pls.)

Subway: Grand Army Plaza
Phone: 718-230-0221
Web: www.frannysbrooklyn.com
Prices: $$

Lunch & dinner daily

The wait is over: Franny's new location is finally up and running. Despite the bigger digs, the queue for a table has barely shortened. A voracious crowd is still the norm, but no matter. Grab a cocktail at the bar and strike up a conversation with a new best friend.

While patio dining is a thing of the past, Franny's now offers a lower level area that doubles as private party room. Upstairs, feast your eyes on the open kitchen equipped with two wood-burning ovens used to produce the majority of the menu. Feast on a succulent assortment of charred snow peas, roasted broccoli with garlic and sunflower seeds, and orecchiette with velvety *borlotti* beans. And then there's that pizza—which is just as puffy, tender, light, and delicious as ever.

Ganso

Japanese

C6

25 Bond St. (bet. Fulton & Livingston Sts.)

Subway: Nevins St
Phone: 718-403-0900
Web: www.gansonyc.com
Prices: 😊

Lunch & dinner daily

A welcome sight amid the sneaker stores and pizza joints peppering the commercial stretch known as Fulton Mall, this sleek newbie is an indication that things may be changing in downtown Brooklyn. Inside, gorgeous wood booths and tables sit atop stone floors while the open kitchen is visible through encased glass. Thank cookbook author and owner Harris Salat for taking the plunge.

Thanks are also due to Chef Rio Irie for his killer menu. Ramen is all the rage here, so get slurping on one of five varieties from spicy miso with braised pork to the "stamina" with chicken *chashu*, onion, Napa cabbage, and garlic bubbling in a soy-chili broth. Also sample Japanese "soul" food snacks like pillow-soft steamed buns filled with kimchi and sweet-savory pork belly.

The General Greene

American

C6

229 DeKalb Ave. (at Clermont Ave.)

Subway: Lafayette Av
Phone: 718-222-1510
Web: www.thegeneralgreene.com
Prices: $$

Lunch & dinner daily

Despite the fact that this sounds like Grandpa's pet-name for his antique tractor, The General Greene is a space that nicely straddles rusticity and hipness while serving three satisfying meals a day. Everything seems cool here, if perhaps a bit aloof, from the perfectly ambient lighting, comfy banquettes, and leather bar stools to that highly prized espresso machine and free WiFi for your iPad.

The menu has a classic Southern slant, as in a warm haricot vert salad tossed with dates, almonds, and orange segments with an extra chive-buttermilk biscuit; or mac and cheese melting Vermont cheddar, Gruyère, and Parmesan over cavatelli. The savory ham-and-Gruyère bread pudding is custard-like and brutally addictive. Homemade cookies seem to fly out the door.

The Good Fork

A7

391 Van Brunt St. (bet. Coffey & Van Dyke Sts.)

Subway: Smith - 9 Sts (& bus B77)
Phone: 718-643-6636
Web: www.goodfork.com
Prices: **$$**

Lunch Sat – Sun
Dinner Tue – Sun

A Red Hook pioneer and adored destination, The Good Fork is truly worth the excursion to this vibrant and food-centric neighborhood. The setting has a rarified intimacy and regardless of where you sit, inside or out, diners are adeptly coddled and cared for. Framed in honey-hued wood veneer and hand-built by Ben Schneider, the dining room is reminiscent of a train car from a bygone era.

His classically trained wife, Sohui Kim, keeps the kitchen wheels churning as it gleefully trots the globe and flaunts a deliciously diverse sensibility. Try the grilled squid packed tight with quinoa, dressed with refreshing mango salsa, and sauced with silken squid ink as a starter. Entrées include roasted local chicken gently kissed by a fermented black bean sauce.

Gran Eléctrica

B5

5 Front St. (bet. Dock & Old Fulton Sts.)

Subway: High St
Phone: 718-852-2700
Web: www.granelectrica.com
Prices: **$$**

Lunch Sat – Sun
Dinner nightly

Located blocks from the riverfront in DUMBO, Gran Eléctrica epitomizes tech-savvy *nouveau* Brooklyn. They may not take reservations, but that isn't a problem, as the helpful staff keeps the tables turning. Settle into their lovely bar, savor a zesty margarita (some rave over the "beet" version), or just take in the vaguely European, shabby-chic décor, mixing modern with a bit of kitsch.

Whether seated in a cozy dining nook or in the lush outdoor garden, start with a tomato-based seafood *coctel* spiked with jalapeño and lime. Then, perhaps move on to a classic *gordita*, a light and crisp tortilla shell encasing strips of decadent *chicharrón*, *crema*, and *queso fresco*. Vibrant flavors come alive in crunchy, spicy, and tangy pickled vegetables *en escabeche*.

The Grocery

B7

American 🍴

288 Smith St. (bet. Sackett & Union Sts.)

Subway: Carroll St
Phone: 718-596-3335
Web: www.thegroceryrestaurant.com
Prices: $$

Dinner Tue – Sat

There's plenty to love about Smith Street's quintessential neighborhood restaurant. Open for over a decade, The Grocery's longevity is commendable. And justly so— the quaint space framed by sage green walls is an always welcoming scene, though regulars know to make a beeline for the luxuriant backyard when the weather warms.

Co-chefs Charles Kiely and Sharon Pachter attend to the kitchen and take turns venturing out into the dining room to chat up the devoted clientele. The vibe is unmistakably cordial. Sit back and relish the facile cooking that renders appetizing items like a salad of sautéed squid, shaved fennel, and kalamata olives dressed with a lemon-scallion vinaigrette; or tender and flavorful slow-roasted duck with red wine sauce.

Gwynnett St.

D1

Contemporary 🍴🍴

312 Graham Ave. (bet. Ainslie & Devoe Sts.)

Subway: Graham Av
Phone: 347-889-7002
Web: www.gwynnettst.com
Prices: $$

Dinner nightly

This ambitious Williamsburg dining room is spaciously arranged and boasts exposed brick, wood-framed mirrors, and prominent wine storage—all the requisite hallmarks of comfortable sophistication. The fine-tuned service team adds a hint of formality, which feels refreshing.

A recent chef change has kept the kitchen steadily turning out an exciting menu. A lovely seasonal starter of satin-smooth chilled potato soup, poured tableside, is garnished with smoked mussels, slivered green olives, and vermouth gelée. Entrées have included visually striking and incredibly tender chicken breast, brined and dusted with hay ash, presented with fermented black bean purée, fried garlic chips, and baby turnips. Desserts follow suit with creative flourishes.

Hibino

B6

333 Henry St. (bet. Amity & Pacific Sts.)

Subway: Borough Hall
Phone: 718-260-8052
Web: www.hibino-brooklyn.com
Prices:

Lunch Mon – Fri
Dinner nightly

This Cobble Hill treat is demure in appearance, but the warm welcome provided by a gaggle of female servers is a fitting prelude to the hospitality that will unfold. Once seated, a small blackboard is brought tableside where guests peruse the list of *obanzai* (Kyoto-style tapas). The evening may bring marinated and fried chicken thigh with tartar sauce; *chikuzen ni* (simmered chicken); or roasted oysters with spicy gazpacho. The menu items change daily but their tastiness remains constant.

Hibino's regional dedication is also evident in its offering of Osaka's traditional *hako* sushi. This box-pressed sushi dish might be served as a layering of excellent quality rice, shiso, *kanpyo* (preserved gourd), and fresh salmon.

The menu is pared-down at lunch.

Jack the Horse

B5

66 Hicks St. (at Cranberry St.)

Subway: High St
Phone: 718-852-5084
Web: www.jackthehorse.com
Prices: $$

Lunch Sun
Dinner nightly

Jack the Horse is named after a lake in Minnesota. If that doesn't tell you how much the chef loved fishing, their seafood bounty will. Brooklyn Heights boasts oldtime dining gems and this younger statesman follows suit. Featuring exposed brick walls decked with quaint clocks and bookshelves, banquettes overflowing with pillows, and a soundtrack belting the classics, this American tavern is loved for its tasty treats and quenching cocktails—note the syrups, tinctures, and bitters.

The scene is blithe with windows overlooking a historic street. Crowds cackle over plates of oysters paired with wakame and a sweet chili sauce; slow roasted duck posed atop fluffy *farro* and anise-tinged sorrel; or steamed persimmon pudding with cinnamon crème anglaise.

James

American

C7

605 Carlton Ave. (at St. Marks Ave.)

Subway: 7 Av (Flatbush Ave.)
Phone: 718-942-4255
Web: www.jamesrestaurantny.com
Prices: $$

Lunch Sat – Sun
Dinner nightly

A Prospect Heights fixture, James is charming, upscale, and comfy. Whether here for Monday Burger night featuring a classic lamb, slow-roasted pork, or lentil burger, or simply to sample this solid American food, James romances you with a Dutch Lucite chandelier, pressed-tin ceilings, tufted leather banquettes, and silver bowls of fragrant citrus.

A feast here includes a parade of such fresh creations as *cavolo nero* mingling red quinoa, smoked almonds, *ricotta salata*, and poached egg; and an expertly prepared Berkshire pork chop with ribbons of fat and creamy beans. Husband-and-wife team, Chef Bryan Calvert and Deborah Williams, recently launched their cheesecake venture Cecil & Merl—these ricotta-based loaves come in mango among other flavors.

Java

Indonesian

B8

455 7th Ave. (at 16th St.)

Subway: 7 Av (9th St.)
Phone: 718-832-4583
Web: N/A
Prices:

Dinner nightly

Java's little corner in Park Slope has been an enduring first choice for the exotic eats of Indonesia since 1992. Tiny yet tidy, the space is brightened by golden drapery, native artwork, and the smiles of a friendly staff wearing batik aprons.

Although Java has recently come under new management, the kitchen is as good as ever. A nibble from the bevy of fried appetizers is certainly recommended, but don't forget the mouthwatering *sate*—charred skewers of chicken, meat, or seafood brushed with *kecap manis* and topped with diced tomato and crispy fried shallots. The array of saucy, simmered options includes *sambal goring udang*: excellent batter-fried shrimp doused in turmeric-tinted coconut milk infused with lemongrass, ginger, and basil.

Jolie Cantina

B7

241 Smith St. (at Douglass St.)

Subway: Bergen St (Smith St.) Lunch & dinner Tue – Sun
Phone: 718-488-0777
Web: www.joliecantina.com
Prices: $$

Fans of the old Jolie, which stood for years on Atlantic Avenue, will remember a graceful Mexican accent that worked its way onto the menu of classic French specialties. And now, as one can gather from the re-christened moniker, a full-on Mexican spirit is at play in this fresh location on a Cobble Hill corner. The kitchen's skilled fusion yields creations such as velvety black bean purée poured over gently poached lobster pieces and cassis-red onion chutney; duck confit enchiladas; or soothing *chilaquiles* glammed up by honey-tinged tomatillo salsa and nuggets of king crab. If dessert is not your thing, opt for the cheese plate stocked with curds procured from neighboring cheesemonger Stinky Brooklyn in lieu of the *churros y dos salsas dulces*.

Juventino

B8

370 5th Ave. (bet. 5th & 6th Sts.)

Subway: 4 Av - 9 St Lunch daily
Phone: 718-360-8469 Dinner Tue – Sun
Web: www.juventinonyc.com
Prices: $$

This lovely storefront feels like a transplant from a seaside New England town. The sundrenched space dons natural wood tables lined with aged newspapers and cheery flower arrangements, while white shelves stocked with an impressive collection of cookbooks stretch across the walls.

The delightful menu includes crispy cornmeal-crusted oysters with wilted greens and a Verdicchio-Sardo cream sauce; a salad tossing Nebrodini mushrooms, whole grains, and explorateur cheese in pumpkin seed vinaigrette; and meatballs mixing veal, beef, pork, and *sardo* cheese simmered in six-hour tomato sauce. Brunch highlights Mexican favorites like *huevos rancheros* and chorizo breakfast sandwiches. Be sure to try the freshly baked biscuits, made in house, Monday-Friday.

Karczma

Polish ✗

136 Greenpoint Ave. (bet. Franklin St. & Manhattan Ave.)

Subway: Greenpoint Av
Phone: 718-349-1744
Web: www.karczmabrooklyn.com
Prices: 🍷

Lunch & dinner daily

Located in a slice of Greenpoint that still boasts a sizeable Polish population, Karczma offers a lovely old-world ambience that may belie its age (opened for five-plus years) but perfectly matches its very traditional, budget-friendly menu. Hearty offerings may include peasant-style lard mixed with bacon and spices, or the plate of Polish specialties that heaps on pierogies (three varieties, steamed or fried, topped with sliced onions and butter), kielbasa, potato pancakes, hunter's stew, and stuffed cabbage. Grilled plates can be prepared for two or three, while others, like the roasted hocks in beer, could easily feed as many.

The charming, farmhouse-inspired interior is efficiently staffed with smiling servers in floral skirts and embroidered vests.

Kaz An Nou

Caribbean ✗

53 6th Ave. (bet. Bergen & Dean Sts.)

Subway: Bergen St (Flatbush Ave.)
Phone: 718-938-3235
Web: www.kazannou.com
Prices: $$

Dinner Tue – Sun

This tiny, dark, and lovable mom-and-pop outfit sprang up amid the Barclays Center construction. The name aptly means "our house" in Creole. The Caribbean-themed space is filled with red tables, comfy banquettes, bright walls hung with artwork, and touches that couldn't be more inviting.

The mouthwatering menu represents the roots of husband and wife team, Sebastien Aubert (who hails from Guadeloupe) and Michelle Lane. Stop in to sample the likes of mashed sweet plantains mixed with basil béchamel and topped with a melting layer of Emmentaler cheese. Specialties include the *dombré crevette*, a traditional dish of insanely spiced little dumplings, deeply flavored and smoky shellfish broth, sweet shrimp, and vegetables. The spicy chocolate cake is a must.

Ki Sushi

B6

Japanese

122 Smith St. (bet. Dean & Pacific Sts.)

Subway: Bergen St (Smith St.)
Phone: 718-935-0575
Web: N/A
Prices: $$

Lunch Mon – Sat
Dinner nightly

Count sushi among Smith Street's wealth of dining options. At Ki, the quality of fish and talented kitchen offer plenty to please. Its devoted fans are here to relish the raw and the cooked in this Zen-chic space fitted-out with a gently flowing wall of water and potted plants.

The cheerful sushi team works from a counter stocked with a tempting array of pristine fish. The sushi and sashimi are excellent, as is the whimsical and visually appealing maki, like the Fashion Roll of chopped tuna, jalapeño, and yuzu *tobiko* wrapped in slices of raw scallop. Dishes like rock shrimp tempura drizzled with a creamy spiced mayonnaise emerge from the small kitchen located in back.

The friendly and attentive service adds to the charm of this Boerum Hill favorite.

Krolewskie Jadlo

B1

Polish

694 Manhattan Ave. (bet. Nassau & Norman Aves.)

Subway: Nassau Av
Phone: 718-383-8993
Web: www.krolewskiejadlo.com
Prices:

Lunch & dinner daily

Krolewskie Jadlo ("king's feast" in Polish) sits in a Greenpoint enclave that was once home to a large number of Polish immigrants. Although the size of the community has decreased through the years, the area still thrives with a distinct Eastern European soul.

The room is pleasant and routinely packed with crowds basking in the enjoyable authenticity. The Polish plate brings all one could hope for in a hearty old-world platter: cabbage rolls stuffed with ground beef and braised in tart tomato sauce; pan-fried potato pierogi; and a link of smoky kielbasa. Other items are just as tasty, like the pounded pork shoulder steak, grilled and brushed with honey, and served with pickled cabbage and beets.

A second outpost is located in Ridgewood, Queens.

La Superior

C1

✗

295 Berry St. (bet. S. 2nd & S. 3rd Sts.)

Subway: Bedford Av
Phone: 718-388-5988
Web: www.lasuperiornyc.com
Prices: 🍪🍪

Lunch & dinner daily

Truly a superior taqueria, this south of the border fave located on Williamsburg's south side proffers a lip-smacking selection of inexpensive tacos made from high quality ingredients and filled with deliciousness. Expect the likes of shredded chicken in a cloak of lush *mole negro*, or turkey escabèche topped with pickled red onion on a black bean purée-slathered tortilla. A rainbow of margaritas—tamarind, *guayaba*, and hibiscus—or a Cube Libre made with Mexican Coca-Cola washes down this most satisfying array that also includes snacks like street-style quesadillas and made-to-order guacamole.

The restaurant's name is scrawled tattoo-like across its painted brick façade, alluding to the carefree décor within, made up of chile red walls and movie posters.

La Vara

B6

✗✗

268 Clinton St. (at Verandah Pl.)

Subway: Carroll St
Phone: 718-422-0065
Web: N/A
Prices: $$

Lunch Sat – Sun
Dinner nightly

Alex Raij and Eder Montero are the dynamic duo behind this hip, tapas-style restaurant that blends Moorish, Jewish, and Spanish influences with terrific results. By virtue of a pretty façade of picture windows framed in slate blue-painted wood frames, La Vara invites you to come inside and sample away. From the *berenjena con miel*—fried eggplant drizzled with sweet honey and served with salty cheese—to braised chickpeas and spinach in a savory broth; or a tender stuffed rabbit loin, plates are very well-crafted and exude huge flavor. Artichokes served with aïoli; smoky cumin-roasted lamb; and creamy cuttlefish strips in a milky almond-based broth are other instances of how the kitchen keeps it coming at this warm and vibrant spot.

Locanda Vini & Olii

Italian

D6

129 Gates Ave. (at Cambridge Pl.)

Subway: Clinton - Washington Avs   Dinner nightly
Phone: 718-622-9202
Web: www.locandany.com
Prices: $$

Ensconced in a restored century-old pharmacy, Locanda Vini & Olii is trimmed with a weathered white tiled floor and rustic furnishings. See-through cabinets stocked with colorful glass and curios flank the room and the kitchen is fronted by the original pick-up window.

The cooking here stays the course and continues to delight with the likes of *pappa al pomodoro*—slick, almost fluffy bread and tomato soup; silky, parsley-flecked *fazzolettini* with shrimp and fish ragù; and grilled duck breast, rich in flavor and pleasantly fatty, simly sauced in pan juices and served with a dollop of cold shallot marmalade. A light-textured coffee *budino* is perfectly chilled and boldy flavored with a pool of thick and rich caramel sauce.

Lucky Eight

Chinese

A3

5204 Eighth Ave. (bet. 52nd & 53rd Sts.)

Subway: 8 Av   Lunch & dinner daily
Phone: 718-851-8862
Web: N/A
Prices: ☜☜

Eat well for a Cantonese song at Lucky Eight, though first you'll need to find it buried among Chinese pastry shops, grocers spilling goods onto the sidewalk, and the throng of pedestrians populating this stretch of Eighth Avenue south of Sunset Park.

Everything is small and bustling. A front counter proffers the menu to go, while those who dine in are swiftly greeted, ushered to a table (or empty seat), and presented with a laminated menu displaying an array of dim sum that is a departure from the standard set (think fish skin dumplings and pork knuckles). The Cantonese line-up offers barbecued meats over rice; a savory tangle of noodles like *e-fu* tossed with XO sauce and dried scallops; and vegetables like *choi sum* steamed to emerald green.

Luksus at Tørst

 Contemporary ✕

615 Manhattan Ave. (bet. Driggs & Nassau Aves.)

Subway: Nassau Av   Dinner Tue – Fri
Phone: 718-389-6034
Web: www.luksusnyc.com
Prices: $$$

Luksus is the secreted back room locale of Greenpoint's new beer den Tørst. Here, Chef Daniel Burns presents his tasting menu to über-foodies kept out of view from the craft beer-downing throng as they feast in a lumber bedecked room brightened by colorful artwork.

A wafer of dehydrated and fried country ham dusted with vinegar powder provides a rollicking kickoff to a parade of creations that recently brought radish shaved over sweet razor clam, melted bone marrow, and cucumber juice; as well as seared lamb breast paired with cool potato-and-lamb's tongue salad dotted with mustard seeds and melon. Wine is not offered, but that hardly matters since the beer pairing curated by Danish brewmaster Jeppe Jarnit-Bjergsø is extraordinary to say the least.

Lulu & Po

 American

154 Carlton Ave. (at Myrtle Ave.)

Subway: DeKalb Av   Lunch Sun
Phone: 917-435-3745   Dinner nightly
Web: www.luluandpo.com
Prices: $$

 On the approach, Lulu & Po isn't quite charming—its sits a bit beyond Fort Greene Park's historic brownstones and closer to the hardscrabble storefronts—but it is a great find for a consistently tasty selection of small plates. The interior features an open kitchen, the huge image of a bright, happy rooster, and ample windows to make the diminutive space seems larger. The room remains packed; watch as those tables for two manage to accommodate three. Or even four.

Impeccably timed plates might begin with grilled pizza dough topped with basil purée and homemade ricotta. Move on to try warm corn tortillas served with tender roasted bone marrow augmented by a parsley-caper salad and *sriracha*; or slices of pickled beef tongue with a red pepper-herb emulsion.

Brooklyn

475

Maria's Bistro Mexicano

Mexican

 A2

886 Fifth Ave. (bet. 37th & 38th Sts.)

Subway: 36 St   Lunch & dinner daily
Phone: 718-438-1608
Web: www.mariasbistromexicano.com
Prices: $$

Head to Sunset Park for some great Mexican cuisine—those who call this vibrant Brooklyn pocket home consider themselves lucky to have such a bright spot in the neighborhood. The cozy space, complete with backyard seating, pops with color and is warmed by the genuinely hospitable light cast by Maria herself.

Dig into a hearty bowlful of *pozole* or tortilla soup before delving into appetizing preparations like a thick-cut grilled pork chop with *salsa roja Oaxaqueño* or *enchilada mi bandera* topped with a trio of sauces. The *chile poblano* combo is a delicately fried one-two punch: one plumped with a savory combination of cheeses, the other stuffed with a beguilingly sweet mixture of chicken, almonds, diced plantains, and apple.

Marlow & Sons

 Gastropub

C2

81 Broadway (bet. Berry St. & Wythe Ave.)

Subway: Marcy Av   Lunch & dinner daily
Phone: 718-384-1441
Web: www.marlowandsons.com
Prices: $$

  This always enticing dusky den is manna for the denizens of Williamsburg's gastronomes who come for a taste of Marlow & Sons deliciously fuss-free fare at breakfast, lunch and dinner. In the front, find strong coffee and sweet treats as well as some interesting sundries. The back room presents a minimally worded carte that offers lunchtime sustenance like a refreshingly chilled yellow squash purée revved up with curry powder and a swirl of yogurt—the perfect antidote to a hot summer afternoon—or smoked trout, a salad-y composition of silken infused fish with warm potato wedges and creamy dill dressing.

Dinner features the succulent, bronze-skinned brick chicken, a menu mainstay as well as oysters, cheeses, and an oft-changing list of specials.

Mayfield

American ✗✗

D7

688 Franklin Ave. (bet. Park & Prospect Pls.)

Subway: Park Pl
Phone: 347-318-3643
Web: www.mayfieldbk.com
Prices: $$

Lunch Sat – Sun
Dinner nightly

Mayfield (named for R&B legend) has rightfully earned each one of its many devotees. Expertly run by co-owners Chef Lev Gewirtzman and Jacques Belanger, this Southern-inspired, elegant, and hip eatery combines a sexy art deco style, soul-stirring soundscape, and unapologetic, expertly made cuisine. Inside, distressed brick walls and sleek tiles outfit the space, while brass mermaid door handles keep the look very playful.

Try the buttermilk-fried quail, dainty, bone-in, and supremely tender, paired with honey dipping sauce, served alongside cornmeal spoonbread and ultra-porky collards. Then, move on to the pork chop saltimbocca, charred and juicy, served with savory-sweet *farro* salad, caramelized onions, and grilled red radicchio.

Mesa Coyoacán

Mexican ✗

D1

372 Graham Ave. (bet. Conselyea St. & Skillman Ave.)

Subway: Graham Av
Phone: 718-782-8171
Web: www.mesacoyoacan.com
Prices: $$

Lunch Wed – Sun
Dinner nightly

Not that Brooklyn is wanting for exciting dining options, quite the opposite exactly, but Chef Ivan Garcia's tempting establishment has been greeted with open arms, and mouths. The Mexico City native ruled the roost previously at Barrio Chino and Mercadito, and has now settled into this glass-fronted slab where wolfish appetites are sated.

It's not just the swank interior, fitted out with richly patterned wallpaper, snug banquettes, and communal tables, but the mouthwatering Mexican food that makes this place such a jewel. Partake in tacos, perhaps the *carnitas*—braised Berkshire pork D.F.-style stuffed into handmade tortillas; or a choice from the *platos fuertes* that include *enchiladas de mole*, made from the chef's secret family recipe.

Mile End 🐶

Deli ✗

B6

97A Hoyt St. (bet. Atlantic Ave. & Pacific St.)

Subway: Hoyt-Schermerhorn
Phone: 718-852-7510
Web: www.mileendbrooklyn.com
Prices: 🪙🪙

Lunch daily
Dinner Wed – Sun

The star of the show at this gem of a spot is Montreal-style smoked meat: pasture-raised brisket that is spice-rubbed, then cured, oak-smoked, steamed, and finally hand cut onto slices of mustard-slathered rye. It's a revelatory sandwich, exactingly prepared, and has few peers in the city. Dinner brings further competition for your appetite with the likes of *poulet Juif*, a tantalizingly smoky, bronze-skinned chicken with wilted escarole and warm schmaltz-enriched vinaigrette. The petite room is rarely quiet. Beyond the handful of tables, there is a dining counter facing the white-tiled kitchen, accented with a blackboard of specials and treats such as Hungarian shortbread. To enjoy the goodness at home, walk up to the sidewalk window for takeout.

Mill Basin Kosher Delicatessen

Deli ✗

B3

5823 Ave. T (bet. 58th & 59th Sts.)

Subway: N/A
Phone: 718-241-4910
Web: www.millbasindeli.com
Prices: $$

Lunch & dinner daily

This thirty nine-year-old Brooklyn treasure is as old-school as it gets, and though it's a bit of a trek to Mill Basin, anyone looking for a real Jewish deli won't think twice. Part deli counter, part artsy dining room, and part party hall, Mark Schachner's beloved spot serves up all the classics from beef tongue sandwiches to gefilte fish.

The wildly overstuffed sandwiches (all served with homemade pickles and coleslaw) are a homerun, as in the pastrami, which is steamed not once but twice, leaving the meat juicy yet hardly fatty. Dive into a Rueben—an open-face and intense pile of juicy corned beef, Swiss cheese, and tart sauerkraut on toasted rye bread, topped with a Russian dressing. The pastrami eggroll is a serious, cultish favorite.

Mimi's Hummus

B3   M e d i t e r r a n e a n

1209 Cortelyou Rd. (bet. Argyle & Westminster Rds.)

Subway: Cortelyou Rd   Lunch & dinner daily
Phone: 718-284-4444
Web: www.mimishummus.com
Prices: 💰💰

Mimi's still whips up a mean hummus that is just as creamy and delicious as ever, not to mention complete with a variety of tasty toppings—even mushrooms! But owner Avi Shuker has expanded his mini operation to include an adjoining Middle Eastern market and The Castello Plan—an inviting bar located two doors down, complete with live music, and named for the first map of New York.

Drop by the original for joyful banter with the über friendly staff along with an Iraqi sandwich piled with fried eggplant and boiled egg; roasted beet salad with an avalanche of onion and parsley; or well-spiced lamb stuffed into bright red peppers. Large windows, wood panels, and a bustling kitchen create an industrial aspect, while maintaining a sleek tone throughout.

Miranda

C1   F u s i o n   ✕✕

80 Berry St. (at N. 9th St.)

Subway: Bedford Av   Lunch & dinner Wed – Mon
Phone: 718-387-0711
Web: www.mirandarestaurant.com
Prices: $$

The cuisines of Latin America and Italy join for a splendid union at this Williamsburg trattoria, run by husband-wife team Sasha and Mauricio Miranda. The pretty space is illuminated with jewel-toned votives and boasts a cement floor inlaid with oak, straw seat chairs, and exposed brick. Beyond this, the chef puts her impressive experience to work in the open kitchen.

The house-made pappardelle is a perfect example of Miranda's unique approach: the wide delicate strands of pasta cling to bits of slow-cooked lamb in a dark, earthy, *mole* tasting of dried chiles, sweet spices, and bitter chocolate. Other items may include grilled baby octopus with avocado and jalapeño; and roasted pork tenderloin with tomato and cumin-scented Arborio rice.

Moim

Korean ✗✗

C8

206 Garfield Pl. (at Seventh Ave.)

Subway: 7 Av (Flatbush Ave.)
Phone: 718-499-8092
Web: www.moimrestaurant.com
Prices: $$

Lunch Sat – Sun
Dinner Tue – Sun

Set among an assemblage of bucolic brownstones, Moim serves a fresh take on Korean cuisine. Like its menu, the setting bears a contemporary vibe in a room of concrete grey and dark wood details. Moim translates as "gathering" and encourages sharing with oversized tables to be topped with any number of plates, small or large.

The kitchen rises above the pack with an array of items that begin with tapas such as stir-fried eggplant, and organic soft tofu in seasoned soy sauce. Small plates are also featured and include puffy steamed buns filled with a mixture of chopped pork and kimchi. Heartier plates and bowls offer the likes of *dak bok-kum*, a Korean-style *pot-au-feu* of rice wine-braised chicken, spicy chili soy, and Korean potato gnocchi.

Mominette

French ✗

B1

221 Knickerbocker Ave. (bet. Starr & Troutman Sts.)

Subway: Jefferson St
Phone: 929-234-2941
Web: N/A
Prices: $$

Dinner nightly

Enter through the swinging wooden doors to discover that the gritty surroundings seem a world away. Inside, Mominette's highly romanticized glow is impossible to ignore—picture wallpaper crafted from sepia-toned newspapers along with risqué photos of women amid vintage chandeliers. Add to that a familial staff and fantastic food...*et voilà*...a fun, energetic, instant favorite!

There is a reason why each newcomer becomes a regular: the food is surprisingly delicious and very authentic. The menu focuses on classics like escargots deliciously baked with tomatoes and garlic; a fresh kerchief of puff pastry filled with tender roast duck infused with wine and tart cranberries; followed by beautifully braised pork tenderloin set atop nutty lentils.

Momo Sushi Shack

B1

Fusion ✕

43 Bogart St. (bet. Grattan & Thames Sts.)

Subway: Morgan Av
Phone: 718-418-6666
Web: www.momosushishack.com
Prices: $$

Lunch & dinner daily

Feeling nostalgic for the days of Manhattan before its Disneyfication? Look no further than this Brooklyn 'hood, where tattooed bike-toting artists rule the roost and graffiti isn't a nuisance, it's an art form. Momo Sushi Shack is packed with hipsters all dancing to a different beat. There's nothing ersatz about its loading dock look, since it's not made to look warehouse-y—it is! Inside is true-blue industrial with cement floors and corrugated steel.

Wagyu beef "sushi" topped with crispy garlic and seaweed and a trio of flavored soy sauces made in-house is scary good. From the minced fresh scallops and the pressed tofu with basil-infused soy sauce, to the cold udon noodles swimming in shiso vinaigrette, it's a total tongue-teasing flavor bonanza.

M Shanghai

C1

Chinese ✕

292 Grand St. (bet. Havermeyer & Roebling Sts.)

Subway: Bedford Av
Phone: 718-384-9300
Web: www.newmshanghai.com
Prices: ⊜⊜

Lunch & dinner daily

Inspired by the cooking of owner May Liu's grandmother, M Shanghai's menu begins with a range of excellent steamed and fried dumplings filled with pork, vegetables, or seafood. A host of other Shanghainese specialties might include *siu mai* stuffed with flavorful sticky rice or double-sautéed pork belly. Even the less regionally specific dishes are intriguing, like the *kung pao* chicken tossed with dried red chillies, whole peanuts, and green onion. Don't forget to order some greens—sautéed morning glory in black tea sauce is gloriously smoky.

Wood flooring and whitewashed brick walls feel contemporary while honey-toned slats above and ceiling lights fashioned from bamboo birdcages lend a distinctly Chinese feel that is attractive and free of kitsch.

Mtskheta Café

X

A4

2568 86th St. (bet. Bay 41st St. & Stillwell Ave.)

Subway: 86 St   Lunch & dinner Thu – Tue
Phone: 718-676-1868
Web: N/A
Prices:

Central Asians have made this nabe their home, and following suit are scores of eateries where these locals can live and play. While their cuisine may not be firmly planted in NYC soil, Mtskheta Café's presence has done much to alter the landscape of food and culture. Inside the dining room, faux exposed brick walls are painted a mossy green and matching the jungle theme are green tablecloths and paper napkins.

If a TV streaming music videos feels gimmicky, the menu written in Russian should relieve all qualms. Let affable servers direct you to the classics, which may include eggplant rolls stuffed with walnut sauce and an eggplant purée; *khachapuri*, creamy pan-fried cheese bread; or *bozbashi*, a mutton and rice soup frilled with fresh onions.

Nargis Cafe

XX

B4

2818 Coney Island Ave. (bet. Kathleen Pl. & Ave. Z)

Subway: Sheepshead Bay   Lunch & dinner daily
Phone: 718-872-7888
Web: www.nargiscafe.com
Prices: $$

This industrial strip is ground zero for Central Asian hot spots, where Nargis Cafe endures as a real treat. Composed of a front bar area and larger, brighter dining room, the entire space is brought together with marvelous Persian rugs and exotic pierced-metal sconces.

Nargis hits a strong stride among the Russian locals for its convivial vibe and unique repertoire of dishes that may include a *bojon* salad of smoky eggplant tossed with garlic, peppers, carrots, and cucumber. Kebabs are taken seriously here, so try the succulent lamb with chopped onion and dill. Uzbek *plov* studded with chickpeas, lamb, and raisins is simple but imperative. For dessert, the honey-sweet *chak chak* is fried but surprisingly light and exquisitely indulgent.

New Spring Garden

Chinese

912 65th St. (bet. Fort Hamilton Pkwy & Ninth Ave.)

Subway: Fort Hamilton Pkwy   Lunch & dinner daily
Phone: 718-680-2289
Web: N/A
Prices: $$

This dim sum palace offers additional evidence that Dyker Heights continues to swell in its slew of Chinese dining. Seating more than 500, the setting inside doesn't break new ground in décor—find fully carpeted floors and bold red-accented walls affixed with gold dragons. And yet, more often than not, every seat is filled and the space rings from the buzz of chatty crowds.

Carts rolling past are stacked with temptations and marvels. Pile your table high with *ngao yuk kao*, beef meatballs flecked with cilantro; sweet and salty braised duck feet; or steamed banana leaf wrapped around sticky rice pocked with mung beans, chicken, dried fish, and lotus nuts. For a sweet and unexpected finish, try the green-tinted pastries filled with durian custard.

Nightingale 9

Vietnamese

345 Smith St. (at Carroll St.)

Subway: N/A   Lunch & dinner Tue – Sun
Phone: 347-689-4699
Web: www.nightingale9.com
Prices: $$

From Arkansas-born Chef Robert Newton, owner of Seersucker located a few doors away, comes this fresh spot where the crew is cooking up delightful Vietnamese food. The chef's passionate, ingredient-driven approach to Southeast Asian cuisine has an unmatchable personality and incorporates items such as Hudson Valley beef, North Carolina peanuts, and Bourbon barrel-fermented soy sauce.

Nightingale 9's dishes have included fried quail served with a bowl of salt, pepper, and lime wedge for a do-it-yourself dipping sauce; green papaya salad with mouthwatering bits of house-dried beef; and fried rice studded with green onion, specks of egg, crispy pork skin, and salty country ham. Finish with a Vietnamese coffee Popsicle crusted in crumbled cacao.

Noodle Pudding

B5

38 Henry St. (bet. Cranberry & Middagh Sts.)

Subway: High St
Phone: 718-625-3737
Web: N/A
Prices: $$

Dinner Tue – Sun

Locals are head over heels in love with this comfort-centric Italian star. The service is sincere; the staff is versed; and the ambience is quaint—Noodle Pudding embodies it all and is a point of pride. Inside this earthy den, kick back and relax to the warm croons of Etta James resounding through terra-cotta floors and a dark wood bar.

With no reservations, arrive early to nab your nook. Like other diners, find yourself sopping up every last drop of *polpo* (tender, chewy octopus in a chunky tomato sauce), or a fresh *sarde* special. The kitchen gets the details right in *rigatoni alla Siciliana* crested with feathers of *ricotta salata*; while *straccetti* (grilled pounded beef served with mushrooms tossed in truffle oil) has been drawing droves for decades.

Northeast Kingdom 😊

B1

18 Wyckoff Ave. (at Troutman St.)

Subway: Jefferson St
Phone: 718-386-3864
Web: www.north-eastkingdom.com
Prices: $$

Lunch & dinner daily

The importance of each ingredient's provenance is more than a policy or marketing ploy here at this Northeast Kingdom of über-local, farm-to-table cooking. Inside, it is cottage-like (if cramped) and charming with vintage chairs, exposed brick, and bare tables. Downstairs, find their wine and cocktail bar. The menu is immersed in sustainability and changes as frequently as the greenmarket offerings. Standouts include burgers with duck-fat fries and pot pies perhaps filled with chunks of Clawhammer Farm pork and meltingly tender root vegetables encased in a buttery and savory pastry crust. Whole animal butchery might be celebrated as the focal point of a multi-course dinner in the feast of a 10-month old pig raised on kale and acorns upstate.

No. 7

American ✗✗

C6

7 Greene Ave. (bet. Cumberland & Fulton Sts.)

Subway: Lafayette Av
Phone: 718-522-6370
Web: www.no7restaurant.com
Prices: $$

Lunch Sat – Sun
Dinner Tue – Sun

Apparently seven is the luckiest number. It's sprouting up all over—there is even a No. 7 Sub sandwich spin-off in the über-hip Ace Hotel. But, this restaurant doesn't look like the corner deli (think distressed mirrors, marble tiles, banquettes, and an open kitchen).

Start with the signature fried broccoli, grapefruit, and black bean hummus appetizer—it's the perfect opener for this slightly offbeat but oh-so-good menu. The General Tso fillet-o-fish sub pairs crispy white fish with cilantro and American cheese, slathers it with a roasted tomatillo-chili mayo, and stuffs it with pickled cabbage into a plush bun. Grab a fork for the comfort of the turkey and goose meatloaf and the bitter bliss of the chocolate and blood orange tart.

1 or 8

Japanese ✗✗

C1

66 S. 2nd St. (at Wythe Ave.)

Subway: Bedford Av
Phone: 718-384-2152
Web: www.oneoreightbk.com
Prices: $$

Dinner Tue – Sun

Taking it's moniker from the Japanese gambling expression that means all or nothing, this atelier of food is a sure thing for an impressive meal. The lofty space features a blank canvas frame accentuated by high-backed white booths surrounding tables set aglow under pendant lamps.

A glass-enclosed kitchen and tempting sushi counter keep the artsy patrons sated with serious raw offerings and unique cooked items. Showing the hands of a skilled team are fluke carpaccio dressed with a bead of ponzu and grapefruit; the *ebisen* maki, wrapped in rice paper and filled with seasoned rice, shrimp, and mango; or steamed *asari* bobbing in a red miso broth. A recent dessert special featured rice flour madeleines filled with red bean paste and dusted with *matcha*.

Osteria il Paiolo

✕✕

C1

106 N. 6th St. (bet. Berry & Wythe Sts.)

Subway: Bedford Av
Phone: 718-218-7080
Web: www.ilpaiolonyc.com
Prices: $$

Lunch & dinner daily

Williamsburg's Osteria il Paiolo rocks a slick and urbane vibe in this hipster 'hood. Step in and find a dark wood bar against a backdrop of polished copper (*paiolo* refers to a copper cooking pot) and linen-covered tables prettied-up by bright flowers. But this is Brooklyn after all, so exposed brick and concrete flooring are part of the deal.

The Italian cuisine bears a northern accent and offers a spectrum of cheeses coupled with homemade jams; house-made pastas like *spaghetti alla chitarra* twirled with a vibrant arugula pesto; and heirloom polenta topped with shrimp and rosemary. For satisfying *secondi*, you can't go wrong by ordering the *osso buco alla Milanese*, classically paired with a dollop of delicious saffron-infused risotto.

Pacificana

✕✕

A3

813 55th St. (at Eighth Ave.)

Subway: 8 Av
Phone: 718-871-2880
Web: N/A
Prices: $$

Lunch & dinner daily

You can thank Sunset Park's growing Asian population for the influx of excellent Chinese restaurants into this far-flung pocket of Brooklyn. Among the best of the lot is Pacificana, a bright, airy restaurant—think vaulted ceilings, jumbo windows, and an open kitchen sporting floor-to-ceiling fish tanks—tucked into a second floor space off bustling Eighth Avenue.

Dim sum carts packed to the gills roll by like temptations-on-wheels and dinner guests tuck into traditional fare like the rich, fragrant South China duck casserole alongside other treats like crispy pork over jelly fish, and tender shrimp dumplings. Chicken with crunchy mustard greens, paired with preserved black beans and a steaming bowl of fluffy white rice is nothing short of heart-warming.

Palo Santo

C7

652 Union St. (bet. Fourth & Fifth Aves.)

Subway: Union St
Phone: 718-636-6311
Web: www.palosanto.us
Prices: $$

Lunch Sat – Sun
Dinner nightly

Nestled among Park Slope's brownstones, Palo Santo's ground floor space feels delightfully homey. Handmade wood furnishings, tiled flooring, and an amber-hued counter set the warmly shaded scene. The kitchen, stocked with neatly arranged produce, is set behind the counter and accented by copper pots and colorful pitchers.

The eclectic Latin cuisine utilizes local ingredients gathered from the Grand Army Plaza Greenmarket as well as those grown in the rooftop garden. The day's *anticuchos* has featured skewers of rich, grilled pork liver dusted with spices; and entrées list a hearty plate of pan-roasted bluefish accompanied by sweet plantain roasted whole in the skin and garnished with shredded cabbage slaw dressed in red wine vinegar and jalapeño.

Parish Hall

C1

109A N. 3rd St. (bet. Berry St. & Wythe Ave.)

Subway: Bedford Av
Phone: 718-782-2602
Web: www.parishhall.net
Prices: $$

Lunch & dinner daily

From the team behind breakfast spot-extraordinaire Egg comes Parish Hall, a delectable addition to this reputedly flavorsome neighborhood. Located merely steps from the Mast Brothers chocolate shop and factory, Parish Hall's concrete floors and white-on-white décor screams industrial-chic.

The menu expertly melds a New York state of mind, an exploratory sense, and the southern leanings of proprietor George Weld. The result is a carte that may reveal a salad of roots and tubers (raw carrots, radish, roasted parsnips, and pickled beets) drizzled with sweet pecan milk; seared Montauk tilefish atop creamy Carolina Gold rice studded with bits of country ham and polished with green garlic broth; or toasted rye cake crowned with frozen maple mousse.

Paulie Gee's

B1

Pizza ✕

60 Greenpoint Ave. (bet. Franklin & West Sts.)

Subway: Greenpoint Av
Phone: 347-987-3747
Web: www.pauliegee.com
Prices: 🍝🍝

Dinner Tue – Sun

Owner Paul Gianonne, aka Paulie Gee, channeled a lifelong love of pizza into this charmingly delicious spot that feels as if it has been around forever. Rustic in appearance, the room's cool concrete and brick are warmed by the glow of the wood-burning pizza oven imported from Naples. From here, Gianonne and son work their magic.

The addictive crust is beguilingly moist and chewy, perfumed with smoke, and adroitly salted. Killer wood-fired pizza dominates the menu with tempting combinations, excellent ingredients, and whimsical names. Offerings may include the Harry Belafontina—fontina, tomatoes, beefy meatballs, cremini mushrooms, and golden raisins. Vegans get respect here, with an added menu of vegan cheese and house-made vegan sausage.

The Pearl Room

A3

Contemporary ✕✕

8201 Third Ave. (at 82nd St.)

Subway: 86 St
Phone: 718-833-6666
Web: www.thepearlroom.com
Prices: $$

Lunch & dinner daily

With its jumbo garden and bright, sun-streaked dining room, this Brooklyn steady is a solid choice year-round. Most days, you'll catch a glimpse of the charming Chef/owner Anthony Rinaldi floating around, working his magic back in the kitchen and out in the dining room.

The Pearl Room is known for its vast seafood spread, and Rinaldi's wheelhouse is intricately designed fish plates like pan-fried, pine nut-crusted lemon sole or ravioli stuffed with Maine lobster, ricotta, and fresh herbs in cream sauce. But don't discount his other offerings—the menu boasts starters like house-made mozzarella with roasted peppers and marinated golden tomatoes, vegetarian and meat dishes ample enough to split, as well as a few tongue-wagging desserts.

Peter Luger ✿

C2

178 Broadway (at Driggs Ave.)

Subway: Marcy Av
Phone: 718-387-7400
Web: www.peterluger.com
Prices: $$$

Lunch & dinner daily

S

Michael Berman

Venerated Peter Luger resides in an expansive space reminiscent of old New York and early German ale houses—an endless line of visitors only serve to reiterate how special a place this truly is. Add to that a series of imposing pane windows, wood-paneled walls, and decorative old steins, and find yourself utterly smitten.

Begin with a thrillingly fresh and full-flavored shrimp cocktail in a rich tomato-based dressing; or smoky bacon slabs, crisp on the outside and nearly sweet on the side. But, what really leaves diners speechless is that delightfully succulent Porterhouse for two, three, or four. These plates of beautifully naked meat seem simple but their marbling is a thing of complexity and perfection, sizzling in drippings. The wedge salad sets a new standard; it is an enormous slice of iceberg with chopped tomato, their own bacon, blue cheese dressing and crumbles. The feast is complete only when sanctified by crispy French fries and creamed spinach. The properly prepped servers are cordial, yet informal and never chatty.

A thick hunk of New York cheesecake, creamy, rich, tart, and served with a mountain of *schlag*, is every bit as classic and marvelous as one may imagine.

Petit Oven

French

A3

276 Bay Ridge Ave. (Ridge Blvd. & Third Ave.)

Subway: Bay Ridge Av   Dinner Wed– Sun
Phone: 718-833-3443
Web: www.petit-oven.com
Prices: $$

Unassuming but worth your attention, this little Bay Ridge site offers a petite, tidy room that is simply done and fills quickly. The ambience here brings a gracious welcome, and the air wears a palpable note of authenticity.

Chef/owner Katarzyna Ploszaj styles her agreeable and refreshingly relaxed cuisine through a classic French lens, with appetizers that may include a novel riff on Greek salad composed of thinly shaved Brussels sprouts mingled with diced feta, a handful of black olives, sliced red onion, and a sprig of fragrant oregano all licked with olive oil and a bright hit of lemon juice. Expect entreés like an impressively cooked duck breast, crisped and rosy, with red onion-ginger marmalade, and duck fat-roasted potatoes scented with thyme.

Picket Fence

American

B3

1310 Cortelyou Rd. (bet. Argyle & Rugby Rds.)

Subway: Cortelyou Rd   Lunch & dinner daily
Phone: 718-282-6661
Web: www.picketfencebrooklyn.com
Prices: $$

This warm, welcoming Ditmas Park family favorite is the go-to spot for some rib-sticking, good old, all-American comfort food. Inside the tiny café, bare wood tables and white chairs perch on well-worn floors, while spring green banquettes, rattan furnishings, and colorful throw pillows add homey touches. On a sunny day, grab a kid-friendly seat in the lovely garden.

Tuck into a tasty plate of farfalle, bursting with juicy jumbo shrimp, crumbled Italian sausage, and fresh herbs in tomato sauce; or the tender, grilled pork chop, with oven roasted butternut squash, fluffy couscous, and applesauce. Swing by on a Thursday night for half-priced bottles of wine, or over the weekend for brunch that includes free-flowing mimosas for all of nine dollars.

Pok Pok NY

A6

127 Columbia St. (bet. Degraw & Kane Sts.)

Subway: Carroll St
Phone: 718-923-9322
Web: www.pokpokny.com
Prices: $$

Dinner nightly

Brooklyn

Lauded for its hugely enjoyable regional Thai cooking, die-hard foodies know to get here early, jot down their name, and start with a fantastic cocktail like the *Khing & I*, mixing Mekhong, lime, and house-made ginger syrup. Tables set with flamboyant vinyl and kitschy picnic-ware fit the quirky mood. Boasting top ingredients is a true, if tamely spiced, papaya salad tossed with dried shrimp; or *hoi thawt*, an elevated street classic of crêpes packed with mussels. *Yam makheua yao*, a smoky eggplant salad bathed in Thai red chillies and fish sauce, is a complex showstopper.

Due to Pok Pok NY's unbridled popularity, this hot spot will soon have new digs rife with expanded delights. An outpost of Andy Ricker's Whiskey Soda Lounge will reside steps away.

Pompette

B7

550 Court St. (at 9th St.)

Subway: Smith - 9 Sts.
Phone: 718-625-2829
Web: www.bistropompette.com
Prices: $$

Lunch Sat – Sun
Dinner Wed – Mon

This newly opened bistro located on the southern edge of Carroll Gardens is fast becoming a neighborhood favorite. Narrow in scale, the space has a perfectly relaxed air. There's a comfortable bar, wood furnishings, and pretty backyard populated by the area's spate of young families.

Classics like cassoulet, hanger steak frites, and bouillabaisse will warm the heart of any Francophile. Other items show a dash of pizzazz, as in grilled octopus salad brightened by yuzu and seaweed aïoli; toasted brioche-crusted striped bass with buttery shellfish sauce and ratatouille; and a tart of raspberries nestled in buttermilk pastry cream. For the kids there's a *menu enfant*, and for the parents, Pompette's wine list offers *vin* by the glass, carafe, and bottle.

Potlikker

 C1

338 Bedford Ave. (bet. S. 2nd & S. 3rd Sts.)

Subway: Bedford Av
Phone: 718-388-9808
Web: www.potlikkerbrooklyn.com
Prices: $$

Lunch Tue – Sun
Dinner nightly

 Despite the down-home handle, Chef Liza Queen's newest venture shows a breadth of inspiration in its menu of well-crafted creations. The relaxed bar is a great spot to chat with the staff while enjoying a beer, and the dining room is bright and welcoming—pistachio green furnishings poised against lemon yellow walls.

In the back, the kitchen is on display and the crew may look intense. But that's for good reason; they're turning out a winning menu. Enjoy the likes of a Dutch baby pancake with goat cheese, raw honey, and fragrant thyme; freshly made cannelloni stuffed with summer squash-studded ricotta; and other big hits such as slow-cooked pork ribs neatly brushed with rhubarb gastrique and sided by a rhubarb-topped corn muffin and tender collards.

Prime Meats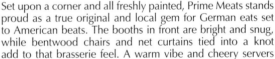

B7

465 Court St. (at Luquer St.)

Subway: Smith - 9 Sts.
Phone: 718-254-0327
Web: www.frankspm.com
Prices: $$

Lunch & dinner daily

 Set upon a corner and all freshly painted, Prime Meats stands proud as a true original and local gem for German eats set to American beats. The booths in front are bright and snug, while bentwood chairs and net curtains tied into a knot add to that brasserie feel. A warm vibe and cheery servers complete the picture.

Hand-crafted sausages and burgers are all the rage here. While the lunch menu is simpler and sandwich-focused, rest assured that their food always has a gutsy edge. Bold flavors shine through in a creamy roasted squash soup; *jagerwurst*, a lightly charred, delicately smoky, and meaty sausage with red cabbage casserole; or Jen's German potato salad tossing waxy potato slices, chopped herbs, and thick bacon lardons in a pickled dressing.

Prospect

American ✗✗

C6

773 Fulton St. (bet. Oxford & Portland Aves.)

Subway: Lafayette Av
Phone: 718-596-6826
Web: www.prospectbk.com
Prices: $$

Lunch Sun
Dinner nightly

The super talented team at Prospect is bringing their A-game to this locality, and getting some well-deserved attention. Inside, the stage is set with sea green walls, tufted gray banquettes, whitewashed brick, and repurposed wood from the old Coney Island boardwalk.

At the kitchen's helm is Chef and co-owner Kyle McClelland whose praise-worthy creations have included spring pea and garlic milk soup studded with lightly fried frog's legs; charred octopus and chorizo salad; or a decadent suckling pig that's crispy on the outside, juicy on the inside, and paired with peanut butter-stuffed dates swaddled in bacon.

Pop in for "Lobster Mondays," a fantastic dinner mingling lobster with Litteneck clams for $8, replete with baked potato and corn-on-the-cob.

Purple Yam

Asian ✗

B3

1314 Cortelyou Rd. (at Rugby Rd.)

Subway: Cortelyou Rd
Phone: 718-940-8188
Web: www.purpleyamnyc.com
Prices: $$

Lunch Sat – Sun
Dinner nightly

Filipino food authorities Amy Besa and Romy Dorotan serve up a deliciously freewheeling array of Southeast Asian treats at this inviting café, named for their homeland's adored tuber. Located in lovely Ditmas Park, a neighborhood extoled for its restored Victorian homes, the interior charms with soothing colors and a view of the kitchen at work.

Filipino favorites abound, as in a chicken *adobo*—the bone-in pieces are browned and braised in a complex-tasting sauce of coconut sap vinegar, coconut milk, and soy sauce. Standouts might include *pancit bihon* made with rice vermicelli stir-fried with roast pork, bok choy, and bean sprouts. Other tasty options depart from the Philippines, such as sweetly spiced goat curry with fresh mango chutney.

Ramen Yebisu

Japanese

126 N. 6th St. (bet. Bedford Ave. & Berry St.)

Subway: Bedford Av
Web: www.ramenyebisu.com
Prices:

Lunch & dinner daily

This anticipated *ramen-ya* adds yet another enticing newcomer to Williamsburg's foodie fold. At Ramen Yebisu, Chef and Hokkaido-native Akira Hiratsuka ladles signature bowlfuls of Sapporo-style ramen, characterized by seafood-infused broth and fresh noodles allowed to ferment for 48-hours. The results are distinct and delicious, as in the *shoyu* (soy sauce) ramen revealing a complex, richly hued broth stocked with roasted pork, bamboo shoots, plenty of green onion, toasted nori sheet, and those uniquely flavored thin noodles. Other options include the house ramen, brimming with shellfish, as well as miso and *shio* (salt)-based soups.

The space is shaded by dark tones and offers a counter and handful of tall tables with metal seating.

Reynard

American

80 Wythe Ave. (at N. 11th St.)

Subway: Bedford Av
Phone: 718-460-8004
Web: www.reynardsnyc.com
Prices: $$

Lunch & dinner daily

Inside Williamsburg's Wythe hotel, find this fun and *très* Brooklyn-chic dining room, thanks to restaurateur Andrew Tarlow (of Diner and Marlow & Sons). The setting's former life as a century-old cooperage is proudly honored in myriad details like original masonry and cast-iron columns. Parchment-colored walls and mosaic-tile floors enhance the throwback mien. Even in the cool light of day, over a bowl of strained house-made yogurt, drizzled in golden honey and topped with granola, Reynard feels sexy.

The kitchen—equipped with a wood-burning oven—produces intriguing creations such as warm olives or red kale tossed with smoked Caesar dressing to snack on while awaiting hake chowder. Hearty entrées include oyster stew or rabbit with whole grain mustard.

River Styx

Brooklyn

Contemporary

B1

21 Greenpoint Ave. (near West St.)

Subway: Greenpoint Av
Phone: 718-383-8833
Web: N/A
Prices: $$

Lunch Sat – Sun
Dinner Wed – Mon

Walk down Greenpoint Avenue and keep walking until you almost hit the East River to reach this newly launched venture. The setting is an undeniably cool combination of raw edges like rough timber ceiling beams, tables embedded with shards of glazed ceramic tile, and an open kitchen installed with a wood-burning oven.

Take a look at the menu and find items like hake with raw almond butter. Sound familiar? This is the handiwork of Chef Dennis Spina, also of Roebling Tea Room. Choose from a tempting lineup and enjoy anchovies sitting by a fire; raviolo stuffed with Taleggio cheese afloat in vibrant green nettle broth; morsels of braised pork dabbed with spicy tomatillo salsa; and vanilla panna cotta sparked by blueberry and black vinegar compote.

Roberta's

Contemporary

B1

261 Moore St. (bet. Bogart & White Sts.)

Subway: Morgan Av
Phone: 718-417-1118
Web: www.robertaspizza.com
Prices: $$

Lunch & dinner daily

Bushwick's love affair with Roberta's seems stronger each year—and for good reason. With its industrial-rustic space, underground Bohemian vibe, homegrown garden, and very own Heritage Radio Network broadcasting from their backyard studio, everything here epitomizes Brooklyn-chic.

Queens native Chef Carlo Mirarchi leads a talented kitchen, which headlines a variety of creatively named pizzas (Cheesus Christ), tasty sandwiches, and a smattering of fresh vegetables harvested from the rooftop garden. Start with a salad of black radishes, organic greens, glazed baby turnips, and diced apples dressed in a delicate sesame vinaigrette. Then, move on to the decadent sliced pork-collar sandwich served on house-made *batard* spread with spicy *gribiche*.

Roebling Tea Room

 C1

143 Roebling St. (at Metropolitan Ave.)

Subway: Lorimer St - Metropolitan Av
Phone: 718-963-0760
Web: www.roeblingtearoom.com
Prices: $$

Lunch & dinner daily

 Roebling Tea Room is the domain of Syd Silver, a former rock musician and tattoo artist, and her self-trained Chef Dennis Spina. The result of their collaboration is a cool, convivial dining hall with plenty of razzle-dazzle on the plate. This festive room is installed with rough-hewn furnishings, metal chairs, and absinthe-green ceramic tile; the picnic table behind the bar is a fun place to hang.

Their eclectic cooking brings grits- and egg yolk-stuffed ravioli slicked with shrimp-infused "flamingo butter" sauce; or strip steak topped in charred, caramelized red onion alongside a decadent cupful of "pourable potatoes" whirled with cream and Gruyère. Come dessert, the flourless chocolate cake is served with puffed wild rice and chilled cream.

Roman's

C6

243 DeKalb Ave. (bet. Clermont & Vanderbilt Aves.)

Subway: Lafayette Av
Phone: 718-622-5300
Web: www.romansnyc.com
Prices: $$

Lunch Sat – Sun
Dinner nightly

Romans is another beloved member of that prolific restaurant family that spawned Reynard, Marlow & Sons... and counting. It's idyllically situated on one of those quaint but never quiet Brooklyn arteries, populated by freelancers, nannies, and parks.

This is a coveted area with sidewalk seating for sipping iced coffee with almond milk. The simple, small interior flickers with candlelight and serves everything its affluent young clientele dreams of finding in an Italian home. House cocktails—one bitter, one sweet—are a memorable start to a meal that might include fresh *maccheroni* with cauliflower, pancetta, and porcini; or perfectly seasoned cannellini beans with *scungilli*. Some wonderfully chosen cheeses augment the pleasant desserts.

Rucola

American   ✗

B6

190 Dean St. (at Bond St.)

Subway: Bergen St (Smith St.)   Lunch & dinner daily
Phone: 718-576-3209
Web: www.rucolabrooklyn.com
Prices: $$

Eat your greens and buy them too at Rucola. This Boerum Hill beauty has a Berkeley-meets-Brooklyn vibe. Inside, it's barn-like, with details like milk bottle chandeliers and Pennsylvania reclaimed wood, but it's really all about the veggies. These streets are lined with enviable, classic townhouses whose residents flock to Rucola, sidle up to a table, and tuck into such heavenly fare as farm fresh zucchini salad served cold with flecks of *ricotta salata*, mint, and cucumbers; or house-made, perfectly cooked shells topped with tomato and shaved *baccalà*. Even the day boat Chatham cod is loaded with greens in all their fresh and crispy glory.

You've been so good and ate all your vegetables, so reward yourself with a slice of that excellent chocolate torte.

Runner & Stone

Contemporary   ✗✗

B7

285 Third Ave. (bet. Carroll & President Sts.)

Subway: Union St   Lunch daily
Phone: 718-576-3360   Dinner Mon – Sat
Web: www.runnerandstone.com
Prices: $$

An innate sense of purpose pervades this serious Gowanus newcomer. The name refers to the two stones used to grind grain, the location is blocks away from where the city's first tide-water grist mill stood, and the dining room is backed by a fantastic bakery headed by an alum of Per Se. The interior boasts walls constructed out of flour sack formed concrete blocks.

The excellent bread and house-made butter is an apt introduction to food that is consistently focused on quality. Find specials like smoked day boat sea scallops arranged with baby arugula, shaved red onion, and citrus; or perfect knobs of red cabbage gnocchi with diced sausage. Unique desserts may feature a chewy rye brownie with whiskey ice cream and buttery caramel.

Rye

American ✗

C1

247 S. 1st St. (bet. Havemeyer & Roebling Sts.)

Subway: Marcy Av
Phone: 718-218-8047
Web: www.ryerestaurant.com
Prices: $$

Lunch Sat – Sun
Dinner nightly

Rye's Classic Old Fashioned—a carefully crafted swirl of liquid amber—is the perfect personification of Chef Cal Elliott's beloved establishment. Like the signature pour (strong, satisfying, and comforting), the mien of this discreetly marked spot follows suit with a space that is anchored by a reclaimed mahogany bar and accented by creaky plank flooring and exposed filament lighting.

The succinct menu boasts adept touches reflecting the kitchen's chops. A recent entrée of skewer-grilled shrimp and scallops dressed with a spicy Thai-inspired vinaigrette and set upon a salad of avocado and grapefruit revealed a highly enjoyable inspiration. For dessert, molten chocolate cake was another classic that was lovingly represented with pistachio ice cream.

The Saint Austere

Contemporary

D2

613 Grand St. (bet. Leonard & Lorimer Sts.)

Subway: Lorimer St - Metropolitan Av
Phone: 718-388-0012
Web: www.thesaintaustere.com
Prices:

Dinner Mon – Sat

Sometimes all one needs is a fine glass of wine and a little snack (or three). For this, The Saint Austere fits the bill nicely. Platings bring on far-flung influences—as in the *banh Mi(lano)*, pork terrine, thinly-shaved mortadella, and house-pickled vegetables sandwiched into a toasted baguette moistened by a chili-flecked dressing. However, the menu's truest muse is a general coupling of Italian and Spanish flavors, such as pork belly *croquetas* accompanied by a dipping sauce of crushed chicken livers; or slow-cooked polenta topped with sweet onions caramelized in sausage drippings.

The spartanly adorned room offers a hospitable bar in addition to three communal tables. And the wine list offers a gently priced selection of mostly European labels.

Samurai Mama

Japanese ✗

C1

205 Grand St. (bet. Bedford & Driggs Aves.)

Subway: Bedford Av
Phone: 718-599-6161
Web: www.samuraimama.com
Prices: 😊

Lunch & dinner daily

Chef Makoto Suzuki (also of Momo Sushi Shack and Bozu) dishes up an appetizing composition of mostly cooked fare at this whimsical Williamsburg gem. The Japanese vibe and flavor are quaint and impressively authentic, and diners tend to partake in preparations that include *konbu dango* (deep-fried seaweed and soybean croquettes); chewy, salty flying fish jerky topped with magenta shards of pickled daikon; or salmon *negi* sushi "taco" cradled in a sheet of toasted nori.

A series of quirky paintings frame the seasonally dressed communal table which may unveil such delicacies as *kinoko tsukejil* "dipping-style" udon, featuring handmade noodles crafted from California-milled flour bobbling alongside rustic wild mushrooms in a rich and complex savory broth.

Saraghina

Pizza ✗

B2

435 Halsey St. (at Lewis Ave.)

Subway: Utica Av
Phone: 718-574-0010
Web: www.saraghinabrooklyn.com
Prices: $$

Lunch & dinner daily

Much more than a pizzeria, Saraghina is a welcomed addition to this rapidly gentrifying area of Bushwick. The multi-room setting is fun and kitschy with old butcher signs, marmalade jars, and restroom signs that read "Women and children, only."

There may be no better start to an autumnal afternoon than a grilled butternut squash, endive, radicchio, and frisée salad with lemon-ginger dressing enjoyed in their foliage-filled back garden. Classic peasant dishes include the *fave e cicoria*, a thick purée of fava beans folded with exceptional olive oil and a nest of wild dandelion greens; while their perfectly charred and puffy pizzas verge on legendary.

Freshly baked breakfast treats and perhaps the most epic espresso in the city also await at Saraghina.

Savoia

Italian

277 Smith St. (bet. Degraw & Sackett Sts.)

Subway: Carroll St   Lunch & dinner daily
Phone: 718-797-2727
Web: www.savoiarestaurant.com
Prices: $$

With its young at-home moms, lunching construction crews, and savvy foreign visitors, all walks of life are drawn to this Smith Street charmer, pastorally furnished with wooden tables and straw-seat chairs. Exposed brick and colorful tiles complement the two-room setting equipped with a wood-burning pizza oven. Fittingly, Savoia devotes a large portion of its menu to manifold pizza offerings made in the Neopolitan tradition. There is also an ample selection of gratifying homemade pastas, like the organic buckwheat *maltagliati* with porcini mushrooms, *bresaola*, and truffle oil; as well as heartier items like the roasted pork chop with eggplant caponata and grilled *orata* with sun dried tomatoes. Affable service adds to Savoia's casual vibe.

Sea

Thai

114 N. 6th St. (bet. Berry St. & Wythe Ave.)

Subway: Bedford Av   Lunch & dinner daily
Phone: 718-384-8850
Web: www.seathainyc.com
Prices:

Peel away the passive greeting at the door, the thumping soundtrack, that lounge-y décor, and Williamsburg's outpost of the multi-branded chain offers a reasonably priced array of tasty Thai standards. The cavernous space pulsates, thanks to its popularity among everyone from young families to after-work groups. The concrete-framed setting is broken up into alcoves arranged around a golden, Buddha-crowned reflecting pool.

The extensive menu boasts an assortment of starters, like Thai sour sausages in green cabbage cups, propped on slivered red onion, toasted peanuts, and fresh ginger. Also find a full range of pick-your-protein noodles, curries, and stir-fries, as well as specialties like crispy whole fish with a tamarind-chili sauce.

Seersucker

╳╳

B7

329 Smith St. (bet. Carroll & President Sts.)

Subway: Carroll St
Phone: 718-422-0444
Web: www.seersuckerbrooklyn.com
Prices: $$

Lunch daily
Dinner Tue – Sun

Chef Robert Newton's Southern stunner does down-home cuisine proud through his commitment to locally sourced ingredients. The perfectly chic room is right at home on Carroll Gardens' competitive restaurant row. Like its moniker, Seersucker fashions a casually dressed-up mien with exposed brick and wooden banquettes in pale shades of grey, a zinc bar, and kitchen displaying jars of pickled produce.

Impressive cooking abounds, as in a cast iron skillet of shredded chicken breast and light, tender dumplings. Also try braised local collards served in mouthwatering potlikker, or chocolate pudding layered with crumbled devil's food cake and Bourbon-whipped cream. Next door, sister spot Smith Canteen offers pastries, sandwiches, and great coffee all day.

Selamat Pagi

╳

B1

152 Driggs Ave. (bet. Humboldt & Russell Sts.)

Subway: Nassau Av
Phone: 718-701-4333
Web: www.selamatpagibrooklyn.com
Prices:

Lunch & dinner Tue – Sun

This curious little café in the far reaches of Greenpoint is owned by the folks behind Van Leeuwen artisanal ice cream. The whitewashed room has limited seating between the wood plank banquette and metal chairs. Dining here is utterly charming, unique, and cheap.

Selamat Pagi means "good morning" in Balinese and greets the 'hood with coffee, pastries, and brunch; but the concise menu of fragrant and flavorful cooking keeps people coming back. Dishes include luscious compositions like *nasi campur*—chopped long bean *lawar* dressed in lime juice, galangal, and toasted coconut, served with prawn crackers, shaved red chili, and Bali fish salad seasoned with turmeric and shallot. For dessert, choose a scoop of sticky black rice or lemongrass ice cream.

Sensation

C1

208 Grand St. (bet. Bedford & Driggs Aves.)

Subway: Bedford Av   Lunch & dinner daily
Phone: 347-335-0063
Web: N/A
Prices:

Sensation hones in on the specialties of Shanghai in a contemporary room that eschews the traditional decorative trappings found in many Chinese spots. The dark grey and burgundy setting offers generously sized tables and a view of the tidy kitchen in back.

These tempting dishes are sure to put a smile on your face, especially if you happen to hail from Shanghai and have a hankering for rich, juicy pork and crab buns—an absolute must. A light touch and fresh flavors typify the cooking here as in neat slivers of tofu sheets tossed with julienned carrot, green onion, and sauced with a mild broth; lightly spiced house-made noodles glistened by fermented soybean paste and studded with diced tofu; or strips of lean pork stir-fried with crunchy wild rice roots.

606 R & D

C7

606 Vanderbilt Ave. (bet. Prospect Pl. & St. Marks Ave.)

Subway: 7 Av (Flatbush Ave.)   Lunch Tue – Sun
Phone: 718-230-0125   Dinner nightly
Web: www.606vanderbiltbklyn.com
Prices: $$

Lush green and earthy colors welcome you into this charming newbie on Vanderbilt Ave. The space is narrow but alluring in front, where it functions as a dairy market and bake shop serving coffee and pastries to a handful of tables. Beyond this, find a bar flanked by mirrors and a bustling open kitchen, where patrons watch the action over a glass of kombucha.

For a more relaxed seat, retreat to the rear made marvelously cushy with espresso-hued tiles, weathered planks, and planter boxes. A kimchi omelette sauced with *sriracha*-infused vinegar reaches epic proportions when paired with a wonderfully fatty and well-seasoned broccoli rabe sausage; while the juicy rotisserie chicken served with watercress and cool yogurt is a signature for good reason.

SoCo

Southern ✗✗

509 Myrtle Ave. (bet. Grand Ave. & Reyerson St.)

Subway: Classon Av
Phone: 718-783-1936
Web: www.socobk.com
Prices: $$

Lunch Fri – Sun
Dinner Tue – Sun

This sleek, always packed SoCo brings down-home sophistication—with Asian flavors and a slightly Nordic aesthetic—to its hipster home at the center of the Clinton Hill-Bed Stuy-Fort Greene triangle. Its cheeky name opposes its sexy, industrial-chic vibe: SoCo is the portmanteau for a viciously sweet liqueur more popular in college dorm rooms than here, among a gorgeous display of backlit bar spirits.

Chef Kingsley John's Southern-fusion menu might begin with pouches of sweet crawfish and collard green dumplings set in a wonderfully spicy coconut green curry. Larger plates of tender short ribs braised in a blissful coconut-molasses-ginger sauce, or jumbo shrimp and lobster knuckles in tomato broth with creamy white cheddar grits will never disappoint.

Sottocasa

Pizza ✗

298 Atlantic Ave. (bet. Hoyt & Smith Sts.)

Subway: Hoyt-Schermerhorn
Phone: 718-852-8758
Web: www.sottocasanyc.com
Prices: $$

Lunch Sat – Sun
Dinner nightly

Harried Atlantic Avenue is home to this refreshingly simple spot, whose terrific Neapolitan-style pies have sent pizza aficionados into a complete a tizzy. Here, Luca Arrigoni makes his magic in a two-ton clay oven imported from Naples—this traditional, wood-burning wonder is set in the tiny, open kitchen. Other accents like bare wood tables and whitewashed brick walls convey a relaxed mood, while the mini bar showcases a selection of killer wines.

Antipasti may include *tonno e ceci*, a zesty concoction of silky tuna, chickpeas, and capers. Pizzas hail from the Napoli—a crispy crust crowned with crushed tomatoes, salty anchovies, and creamy mozzarella—to the verdure with eggplant, sweet caramelized onions, tomatoes, and mushrooms.

Speedy Romeo

D6

376 Classon Ave. (at Greene Ave.)

Subway: Classon Av
Phone: 718-230-0061
Web: www.speedyromeo.com
Prices: $$

Lunch & dinner daily

 Speedy Romeo (named after co-owner Todd Feldman's family's racehorse) is a fun and fab spot located in the far reaches of Clinton Hill. Housed in an old auto parts store, the building's façade (with the shop's name emblazoned in blue) lures from afar. Bypass the nonfunctioning neon "LIQUORS" sign that still hangs over the dark framed door to enter.

Smart and striking, this tavern-meets-roadside grill is fitted with funky industrial-age relics. But, closer scrutiny reveals such solid, inventive dishes as long Italian green peppers stuffed with *soppressata*; or a Casey Moore pizza baked with clams, spinach, and béchamel. Monkfish cheek skewers infused with *puttanesca* flavors display enjoyable twists that bear little likeness to their Italian predecessors.

Spicy Bampa

A3

6920 Eighteenth Ave. (bet. Bay Ridge Ave. and 70th St.)

Subway: 18 Av
Phone: 718-236-8088
Web: N/A
Prices: $$

Lunch & dinner daily

What was once Bamboo Pavilion is now Spicy Bampa. This much more appropriate and enticing handle signals authentic Sichuan fare offered inside this neat spot located in Brooklyn's burgeoning Chinatown. The space remains the same, rather nondescript but gingerly beautified by bamboo-etched wallpaper and pale yellow walls; large tables host hungry families.

Bubbling hot pots are a house specialty and bring trays of soft noodles, succulent meats, leafy greens, and a brew of chili oil steeped with Sichuan peppercorns. Other signatures unveil Chengdu hometown chicken featuring chilled, sliced pieces on the bone dressed with scallions and a smoky red chili vinaigrette; or deep-fried chunks of tender pork chop strewn with smoky cumin and ground fennel seeds.

St. Anselm

 D1

355 Metropolitan Ave. (bet. Havemeyer and Roebling Sts.)

Subway: Bedford Av

Phone: 718-384-5054

Web: N/A

Prices: $$

Lunch Sat – Sun
Dinner nightly

Look to this roughhewn Williamsburg newcomer for a meal of grilled, meaty satisfaction. Loud and proud carnivores, this one's for you.

The perpetually rollicking kitchen embraces grilling as its preferred method of cooking to turn out a commendable bill of fare. Razor clams, sardines, artichokes, or *haloumi* comprise the offering of sizzling "smalls," while "bigs" are founded on cuts of hormone-free meats procured from small ranches, and have included a dinner plate-sized lamb blade steak—scorched, enjoyably fatty, and deliciously salted—topped with a coin of mint-gremolata butter. Other options can include a sweet tea-brined chicken; sides like decadent spinach gratin; or Mason jar of chocolate *pot de crème* topped with *fleur de sel* and whipped cream.

Stone Park Cafe

 B7

324 Fifth Ave. (at 3rd St.)

Subway: Union St

Phone: 718-369-0082

Web: www.stoneparkcafe.com

Prices: $$

Lunch Tue – Sun
Dinner nightly

At this corner location, large windows peer onto Park Slope's vibrant Fifth Avenue thoroughfare and small namesake park, attracting neighborhood couples and families seeking worldly and creative fare.

A three-course, $35 prix-fixe Market menu offers excellent value and admirable cooking. Expect small plates like grilled baby octopus with Spanish chorizo, fingerling potatoes, and preserved lemon; fresh pastas; and hearty entrées such as grilled hanger steak with black pepper spätzle and balsamic-veal reduction.

The light, airy interior has exposed brick, pale sage walls, a long bar near the entrance for pre-dinner cocktails, and a candlelit, sunken dining room with linen-topped tables. Weather permitting, alfresco sidewalk seating is available.

Strong Place

Gastropub 🍴

270 Court St. (bet. Butler & Douglass Sts.)

Subway: Bergen St (Smith St.)
Phone: 718-855-2105
Web: www.strong-place.com
Prices: $$

Lunch Fri – Sun
Dinner nightly

Fronted by a welcoming bar area that is unapologetically devoted to beer (more than 20 labels are served on tap bolstered by an additional selection of fifteen bottles), Strong Place invites everyone to kick back and unwind. The vibe is chill, as chunky wood tables and metal seating render a vaguely industrial look. An open kitchen and raw bar station embellish the amiable atmosphere.

Snacks such as deviled eggs, boiled peanuts, and waffle fries with onion dip serve as perfect partners for a frosty brew; while entrées offer market-focused pub-grub with a French accent. Dishes include fluke carpaccio with shaved fennel and pomegranate seeds, crispy duck leg confit, and a luscious spice-rubbed nugget of pork with black eye peas and baby bok choy.

Tabaré

Latin American 🍴

221 S. 1st St. (bet. Driggs Ave. & Roebling St.)

Subway: Bedford Av
Phone: 347-335-0187
Web: www.tabarenyc.com
Prices: $$

Lunch Sat – Sun
Dinner nightly

Spanish tuna and black olive empanadas, homemade pastas, and the market-driven likes of a summery chilled soup made of cubanelle peppers all deliciously co-exist at the charming Tabaré, where the cuisine of Uruguay headlines the delightful roster. Attractively rustic, the compact dining room is lined by slats of unpolished wood, and provides seating along a colorful fabric-covered banquette. The bar—like the back patio—is an inviting roost.

Tabaré's cooking uses local product and represents the Italian-Spanish influences that color the kitchen's creations. This includes *malfatti*, luscious ricotta dumplings adorned with squash blossoms wilted under a drizzle of hot butter and white truffle oil; or grass-fed skirt steak sided by savory *chimichurri*.

Taci's Beyti

B4

Turkish ✗

1955 Coney Island Ave. (bet. Ave. P & Quentin Rd.)

Subway: Kings Hwy (E. 16th St.) Lunch & dinner daily
Phone: 718-627-5750
Web: www.tacisbeyti.com
Prices: $$

Be prepared to sit among smiling strangers here at Taci's Beyti, where neat rows of tables filled with families and laughing patrons create a comfortable and relaxed atmosphere as waiters spring to and fro, balancing golden, fresh, and fragrant platters. This Midwood favorite serves tasty Turkish bites spun with hearty doses of knowledge and care.

Some of the simplest delights include a perfect shepherd's salad of thinly sliced *kasseri* cheese with fresh cucumbers and tomato; or crisp triangles of feather-light spinach pie. Deep flavors shine through the tangy, sweet-spicy, and delectable pan fried eggplant with tomatoes, peppers, and garlic; and the chopped lamb kabob, grilled and gently seasoned with paprika.

Reserve ahead for weekends.

Talde

C8

Asian ✗✗

369 Seventh Ave. (at 11th St.)

Subway: 7 Av (9th St.) Lunch Sat – Sun
Phone: 347-916-0031 Dinner nightly
Web: www.taldebrooklyn.com
Prices: $$

Headed by Chef Dale Talde, who previously spun his magic at glitzy pan-Asian spots like Morimoto and Buddakan, this fresh venture brings a tasty dose of flavor to a sweet Park Slope corner. It is family-friendly but still rocks a sexy vibe with an abundance of carved wood pieces displayed throughout, high-backed booths, an open kitchen, dining counter, and boisterous ring.

The menu conjures the flavors of China, Japan, Thailand, Korea, and the Philippines for an appetizing mélange that may reveal crispy-chewy pretzel dumplings filled with nuggets of pork and chives, served with tahini-enriched mustard; fried oyster- and bacon-*pad Thai* sided by hot sauce and Filipino-style infused vinegar; or shrimp toast with fried egg and Chinese sausage gravy.

Tanoreen

Brooklyn

A3

Middle Eastern

7523 Third Ave. (at 76th St.)

Subway: 77 St
Phone: 718-748-5600
Web: www.tanoreen.com
Prices:

Lunch & dinner Tue – Sun

In a roomy setting with glassed-in sidewalk dining and jewel-toned sconces, Tanoreen impresses with its extensive menu of Middle Eastern home-style specialties. Chef/owner Rawia Bishara may have started her career with dinner parties, but today she runs this popular foodie destination with her daughter.

Meals graciously commence with a bowl of pickled vegetables and basket of pita and crisp flatbreads topped with *za'atar*. The array of hot and cold appetizers is tempting, but Tanoreen's entrées and grilled preparations command equal attention. Expect baked eggplant layered with lamb, potatoes, tomatoes, and spices; fried fish with tahini dipping sauce; or a combination of grilled chicken, ground and cubed lamb, seasoned with the house spice blend.

Thistle Hill Tavern

B8

Contemporary

441 Seventh Ave. (at 15th St.)

Subway: 15 St - Prospect Park
Phone: 347-599-1262
Web: www.thistlehillbrooklyn.com
Prices: $$

Lunch Sat – Sun
Dinner nightly

In South Slope, this relative newcomer conjures that classic tavern ambience usually found in longtime neighborhood favorites. The corner location is flanked by sidewalk seating for a leisurely alfresco lunch; inside, exposed brick and chocolate-brown wainscoting paint a warm and inviting scene.

Brunch is a mostly savory affair, while evenings might begin with snacks like salt and pepper fries or charred endive with Gorgonzola vinaigrette to go with a house cocktail or beer. Dinners are a hearty expression of seasonal, locally sourced dishes, such as Maine mussels steamed in Brooklyn-brewed pilsner, leeks, Dijon mustard, and tarragon; or braised beef short ribs with smashed fingerling potato salad and pickled horseradish crème fraîche.

Traif

 Contemporary

C2

229 South 4th St. (bet. Havemeyer & Roebling Sts.)

Subway: Marcy Av
Phone: 347-844-9578
Web: www.traifny.com
Prices: $$

Dinner Tue – Sun

Rocking an affinity for pork and shellfish, this rollicking Williamsburg eatery serves up a vibrant array of flavor-packed small plates. The restaurant's moniker translates to "forbidden" in Yiddish, and the extensive menu offers more than 20 eclectic, global creations prepared by Chef/owner Jason Marcus and his team from a sliver of open kitchen that is brightly tiled and equipped with a single Vulcan range.

The team rises to the challenge, sending forth the likes of crispy salt and pepper shrimp with a *sriracha*-spiced salad of pineapple, cucumber, watermelon and Thai basil; Catalan-style black *fideos* with nuggets of octopus, escargot, and drizzles of creamy green garlic sauce; and warm bacon doughnuts with *dulche de leche* and coffee ice cream.

Umi NOM

 Asian

D6

433 DeKalb Ave. (bet. Classon Ave. & Taaffe Pl.)

Subway: Classon Av
Phone: 718-789-8806
Web: www.uminom.com
Prices: $$

Lunch Sat
Dinner Mon – Sat

Tons of fun and quite an adventure, Umi NOM sexes up this drab stretch of DeKalb Avenue, edging closer to Bed-Stuy than to Fort Greene. Just around the corner from the Pratt Institute's lovely campus, Chef King Phojanakong (of Kuma Inn) is giving King's County a taste of his unique Thai- and Filipino-influenced delights.

Classics like *pancit canton* (egg noodles stir-fried with shrimp, chicken, peas, peppers, and fish sauce) share the menu with spicy, mouthwatering mackerel; and outstanding pork sliders with a sweet, peanutty sauce and tart pickles. Get lucky and dine on a day when *adobo* is the special—silky, fatty pork belly rubbed with spices, slowly cooked for three hours, then grilled. Quench your thirst with a refreshing sweet and sour *kalamansi* juice.

The Vanderbilt

C7

570 Vanderbilt Ave. (at Bergen St.)

Subway: 7 Av (Flatbush Ave.)
Phone: 718-623-0570
Web: www.thevanderbiltnyc.com
Prices: $$

Lunch Sat – Sun
Dinner nightly

Relaxed dining with a serious pedigree should be no surprise when Saul Bolton and Ben Daitz are involved. Nothing is stuffy, but each dish is skillfully prepared with much dependability. Servers are engaged and fire up great conversation without ever overstaying their welcome. A long bar is perfect for solo dining, while upholstered seats and weathered-wood panels complete the corner space.

The chef's talents with charcuterie make their kielbasa almost obligatory. The pork belly with grits and fried green tomatoes is outrageously tasty. Weekday happy hour brings a divine roster of cocktails, rum punch, wine, and cheap bites like fried pickles or hushpuppies.

Brooklyn Bangers is their spin-off and creates all the sausages for The Vanderbilt.

Van Horn Sandwich Shop

B6

231 Court St. (bet. Baltic & Warren Sts.)

Subway: Bergen St (Smith St.)
Phone: 718-596-9707
Web: www.vanhornbrooklyn.com
Prices:

Lunch & dinner daily

Emanating a charmingly old-timey appearance and dishing up Southern-inspired fare, this Cobble Hill spot deliciously typifies au courant Brooklyn dining. The menu of hot and hearty sandwiches is fashioned from local ingredients in combinations that feature freshly prepared buttermilk-fried chicken on a sesame-seed bun and North Carolina-style pulled pork. The BLP slathers toasted sourdough slices with pimento cheese, makes a decidedly high-brow substitution of garlic aïoli for plain mayonnaise, then tops it off with crisp bacon and tender butter lettuce.

Side dishes like baked mac and cheese, jalapeño hushpuppies, craft beers, and cocktails round out a down-home menu that tastes even better when enjoyed seated outside in the backyard.

Vinegar Hill House

American ✗

C5

72 Hudson Ave. (near Water St.)

Subway: York St
Phone: 718-522-1018
Web: www.vinegarhillhouse.com
Prices: $$

Lunch Sat — Sun
Dinner nightly

Find this carriage house just steps from the historic Commandant's House and Navy Yard, in a neighborhood that is quickly becoming a beacon for artisans. After its full recovery from Superstorm Sandy, this one-time butcher shop and ever-popular haunt is again as distinguished and delicious as ever.

Packed to the rafters with locals, this "house" boasts quality, sustainable products prepared in a wood-burning oven. A wonderfully broiled grapefruit topped with puffed rice mixed with shrimp paste, or liver pâté topped with pistachios display an inventive mix of global ingredients. Favorites like pappardelle with shad roe and lemon zest, or caramelized pork chops with creamy grits are flooded with flavor.

Big bonus: Hillside resides only doors away.

Waterfalls Café

Middle Eastern ✗

B6

144 Atlantic Ave. (bet. Clinton & Henry Sts.)

Subway: Borough Hall
Phone: 718-488-8886
Web: N/A
Prices:

Lunch & dinner daily

Deliciously uncompromised, made-to-order Middle Eastern food: what's not to love at the Waterfalls Café, a little café that rises above the rush of Arabic diners that cluster along this stretch of Atlantic Avenue? Perhaps the service, which can be a bit stilted and off-the-mark from time to time—that said, you'll soon realize that patience is a mighty big virtue here.

The reward is in the spectacularly creamy hummus; light-as-air falafel, fresh and crackling from the fryer; moist stuffed grape leaves; perfectly-spiced *moujadarra*, spiked with tender caramelized onions; and supremely tender chunks of lamb *shawarma*, served with fresh pita. No alcohol is served, but fragrant teas and Arabic coffee finish the meal and takeout is available.

Winly

Chinese

1217-1221 Ave. U (bet. E. 12th St. & Homecrest Ave.)

Subway: Avenue P
Phone: 718-998-0360
Web: N/A
Prices: $$

Lunch & dinner daily

This is some serious Cantonese dining. And it's where local Chinese diners choose to chow—so take a hint and trek out to this far-flung spot for superb, fresh seafood. The gleaming, two-room dining area sparkles with fish tanks stocked with eel, bass, and other aquatic friends, stopping here on their way to your plate.

The ample menu offers the likes of braised *yee mein* with shiitake, black foot, and white beech mushrooms; sliced pork, mustard greens, and salty duck egg soup; or bean curd stuffed with chopped shrimp, water chestnuts, and egg, served alongside sautéed conch and scallops. Flavorful classics include pork intestines with tangy fermented cabbage.

A bona fide Cantonese affair, this might be a good time to brush up on your language skills.

Xixa

Mexican

241 S. 4th St. (bet. Havemeyer & Roebling Sts.)

Subway: Marcy Av
Phone: 718-388-8860
Web: www.xixany.com
Prices: $$

Dinner Tue – Sun

Chef Jason Marcus' follow-up to Traif (just down the street) is a Mexican-accented romp flaunting the chef's trademark whimsy. The beverage list is arranged by style, so sparkling wines appear under the heading of Liberace and seductive reds like pinot noir under the title Scarlet O'Hara.

As for the food, the extensive menu has fun too. The array offers the likes of *chile rellenos*, served as a mélange of roasted peppers slicked with sweet juices and house-made *burrata*; or grilled carrots *elote*, dressed with honey butter, sprinkles of grated feta, and lime. Their mad scientist version of fish tacos features an *achiote*-rubbed hamachi collar plated with pounded and fried sweet plantain coated with masa, Brussels sprouts slaw, and pickled onions.

Zenkichi

C1

Japanese

77 N. 6th St. (at Wythe Ave.)

Subway: Bedford Av

Phone: 718-388-8985

Web: www.zenkichi.com

Prices: $$

Dinner Tue – Sun

This exceptional Japanese brasserie in Williamsburg bears an utterly unique setting. Pay attention, or you'll miss the entrance—the wood-armored façade is a sly indication of its existence. Step inside and receive warm greetings all around, followed by an escorted journey to your private dining booth on one of the floors above. Each booth is sequestered by bamboo shades, while dark wood and minimal lighting further elevate the sense of intimacy. When you need assistance, ring the tabletop buzzer.

Zenkichi's omakase is a big draw, but items may also be ordered à la carte and highlight house-made tofu drizzled with chilled dashi; *maguro* carpaccio arranged over shredded carrots and dressed with a ginger sauce; or grilled *jidori* chicken with *yuzu kosho*.

Zizi Limona

C1

Mediterranean

129 Havemeyer St. (at S. 1st St.)

Subway: Lorimer St - Metropolitan Av

Phone: 347-763-1463

Web: www.zizilimona.com

Prices:

Lunch & dinner daily

This inviting and low-key café is a luscious addition to Williamsburg's already diverse array of dining options. A trio of skilled partners have come together to highlight the home-style cooking of Israel and Morocco.

The shawarma wrap is a necessary lunchtime indulgence, made with bits of chicken cooked in lamb's fat, spiced with gusto, and wrapped with a spread of incredible hummus, charred red onion, and preserved lemon. Begin with starters like grilled baby eggplant with arugula and feta; or try the hearty 5-hour *bureka* stuffed with slow-cooked oxtail, black olives, and crushed tomato.

Colorful tile lends a distinctive flair to the inviting room embellished with shelves of product for sale such as spices, olive oil, and rosewater.

Queens

Queens

Nearly as large as Manhattan, the Bronx, and Staten Island combined, the borough of Queens covers 120 square miles on the western end of Long Island. Thousands of immigrants arriving here each year make Queens the most culturally diverse county in the country. They all seem drawn to the relatively affordable housing, a familial quality of life, and the tight-knit cultural communities formed by extended immigrant families. Such a unique convergence results in the borough's largely international flavor. Hurricane Sandy may have wreaked much havoc in this borough, yet it continues to allure throngs of New Yorkers who are eager to dine on affordable, ethnic eats.

GLOBAL BUFFET

Stroll through Astoria, a charming quarter of brick row houses and Mediterranean groceries. Discover grilled octopus and baklava at one of the many terrific Greek restaurants; then make your way to Little Egypt on Steinway Street for a juicy kebab; or chow on Czech kielbasas at the local *biergarten*. The iconic Italian *pasticceria*, **La Guli**, has been open since 1937 and dishes out a tandem of cakes, pastries, cookies, and biscuits to everyone's heart's content. Along global lines, **La Boulangerie** in Forest Hills is introducing locals to divine French treats—imagine crusty, piping hot baguettes. And what goes best with beautiful bread? Cheese naturally, available in many selections at **Leo's Latticini** (in Corona). **Terminal C** at La Guardia Airport is now a wonderful food destination with outposts courtesy of Andrew Carmellini, Michael Lomonaco, and many other restauranteurs. On any lazy day, beer-lovers should frequent Astoria's newest beer havens. For an intimate setting with a serious selection, head to **Sweet Afton**; and for the ultimate alfresco experience, **Studio Square** is *the* place. Order a dish from their Garden Grill menu and find yourself in heaven for the rest of the night.

FIERY FLUSHING

Flushing still reigns as Queens' most vibrant Asian neighborhood. Drop in for dim sum, Henan specialties (beef dumplings bobbing in a tangy soup?), or slurp an avocado shake and a savory bowl of hot *pho* like you'd find street side in Saigon. Food vendors at Flushing's mini-malls offer a feast for the ravenous that's light on the pockets with delights from every corner of China. You'll find anything at these stalls including hand-pulled noodles, fiery Sichuan chili oil dishes, Peking duck pancakes, *bings*, and buns in a bustling setting that's right out of a Hong Kong alley. And the Chinese offerings don't stop here. If in the mood for vegetarian kosher

Chinese delights, forge ahead on Main Street to **Buddha Bodai** and savor crispy vegetarian duck, followed by a seaweed sesame roll. Continue the party at **Mingle Beer House** over karaoke and unique brew. Traveling east is the **Queens County Farm Museum**. Considered one of the largest working farms in the city, it supports sustainable farming, offers farm-to-table meals, and is replete with livestock, a greenhouse complex, and educational programs.

ELMHURST

Vivacity and diversity personify Elmhurst, the thriving hearth to immigrants primarily from China, Southeast Asia, and Latin America. The Royal Kathin, a celebration that occurs at the end of Thailand's rainy season, pays homage to the spirit of the monks. The Elmhurst adaptation may lack the floods, but offers a bounty of faithful Thai treats. Whitney Avenue houses a restaurant row with a range of tiny Southeast Asian storefronts. Indulge your *gado gado* craving at **Upi Jaya** and get your *laksa* on at **Taste Good**. Elmhurst spans the globe, so if the powerful and pungent flavors of Southeast Asia aren't your thing, dive into an Argentinean *parilla* for a shift from Asia to the Americas. Jackson Heights is home to a distinct South Asian community. Take in the *bhangra* beats blaring from cars rolling along 74th Street—a dynamic commercial stretch of Indian markets, Bengali sweet shops, and Himalayan-style eateries. Some favorites include Indian tandoor specialties and Tibetan *momos*.

Latin Americans from Colombia, Ecuador, Argentina, Uruguay, Peru, and Mexico also make up a large part of the demographic here. Catering to their tastes, Roosevelt Avenue sizzles with a sampling of enticing taquerias, aromatic Colombian coffee shops, and sweet Argentinean bakeries. The commercial thoroughfare connects several neighborhoods, shape shifting from country to country.

WANDERING THROUGH WOODSIDE

Follow the Avenue west to Woodside, where Irish bars commingle with spicy Thai spots. Once home to a large Irish population, Woodside now shares its blocks with a Thai and Filipino community. The kelly green awnings of decade-old pubs dot the streets, and clover-covered doors advertise in Gaelic. Here **Donovan's** boasts one of the best and juiciest burgers in the city. Alongside is Little Manila, an eight-block stretch of Roosevelt Avenue, where you can find Filipino groceries and diners galore. The opening of **Jollibee**, an ultra-popular fast-food chain, has folks lined up for a taste of home. On Queens Boulevard in Sunnyside (one of the most divergent 'hoods), eat your way through Korea, Columbia, Mexico, Romania, China, and Turkey. In late June, check out The New York City Food Film Festival where food and film lovers gather to view screenings of food films while noshing on a variety of lip-smacking nibbles.

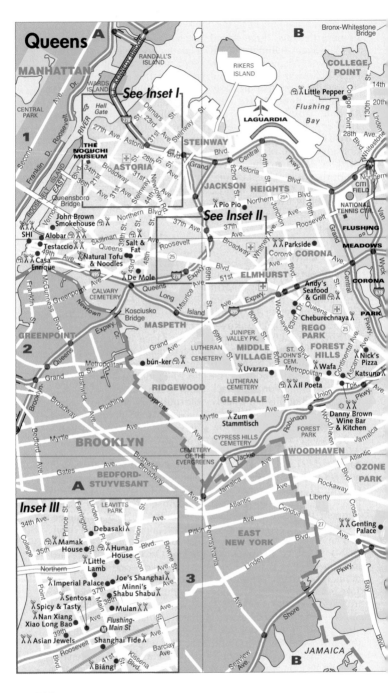

Queens

A   **B**

MANHATTAN

RANDALL'S ISLAND

RIKERS ISLAND

Bronx-Whitestone Bridge

COLLEGE POINT

Little Pepper

Flushing Bay

LAGUARDIA

See Inset I

CENTRAL PARK

Hell Gate

THE NOGUCHI MUSEUM

ASTORIA

STEINWAY

JACKSON HEIGHTS

CITI FIELD

NATIONAL TENNIS CTR

FLUSHING

MEADOWS

Queensboro Bridge

John Brown Smokehouse

SHI

Alobar

Testaccio

Casa Enrique

Natural Tofu & Noodles

Salt & Fat

De Mole

See Inset II

Pio Pio

Parkside

CORONA

CORONA PARK

CALVARY CEMETERY

Kosciusko Bridge

MASPETH

Andy's Seafood & Grill

Cheburechnaya

REGO PARK

GREENPOINT

bún-ker

JUNIPER VALLEY PK.

MIDDLE VILLAGE

ST. JOHN'S CEM.

FOREST HILLS

Nick's Pizza

Katsuno

Metropolitan

Uvarara

Wafa

Il Poeta

LUTHERAN CEMETERY

RIDGEWOOD

GLENDALE

Zum Stammtisch

Danny Brown Wine Bar & Kitchen

BROOKLYN

BEDFORD-STUYVESANT

CYPRESS HILLS CEMETERY

FOREST PARK

WOODHAVEN

CEMETERY OF THE EVERGREENS

OZONE PARK

EAST NEW YORK

Genting Palace

JAMAICA

Inset III

LEAVITTS PARK

34th Ave.

Debasaki

Mamak House

Hunan House

Little Lamb

Imperial Palace

Joe's Shanghai

Minni's Shabu Shabu

Sentosa

Mulan

Spicy & Tasty

Nan Xiang Xiao Long Bao

Asian Jewels

Shanghai Tide

Biáng!

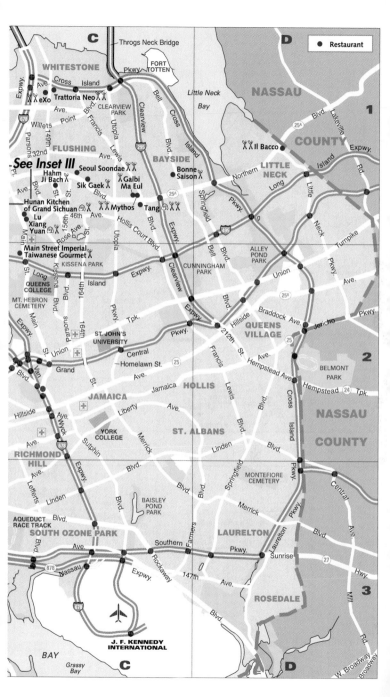

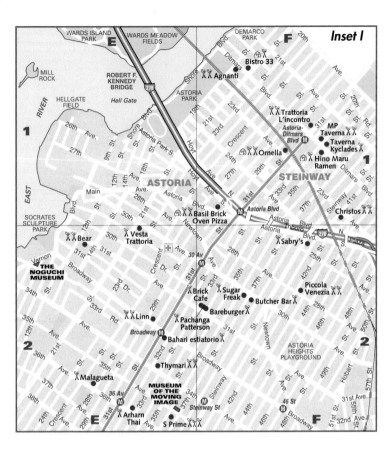

Inset I

WARDS ISLAND PARK
WARDS MEADOW FIELDS

DEMARCO PARK

E

F

MILL ROCK

HELLGATE FIELD

ROBERT F. KENNEDY BRIDGE

Hell Gate

Bistro 33

Agnanti

ASTORIA PARK

Trattoria L'incontro

MP Taverna

Taverna Kyclades

Ornella

Hino Maru Ramen

RIVER

EAST

ASTORIA

STEINWAY

Christos

SOCRATES SCULPTURE PARK

Basil Brick Oven Pizza

Bear

Vesta Trattoria

Sabry's

THE NOGUCHI MUSEUM

Piccola Venezia

Brick Cafe

Sugar Freak

Butcher Bar

Linn

Bareburger

Pachanga Patterson

Bahari estiatorio

ASTORIA HEIGHTS PLAYGROUND

Thymari

Malagueta

MUSEUM OF THE MOVING IMAGE

Steinway St

Arharn Thai

S Prime

Inset II

E

F

Urubamba

Tawa Tandoor

Jackson Diner

Sripraphai

Jackson Hts–Roosevelt Av

Himalayan Yak

Renee's Kitchenette & Grill

Zabb Elee

Engeline's

Payag

Ayada

Chao Thai

Tito Rad's Grill

WOODSIDE

Nusara

BIG BUSH PARK

Uncle Zhou

NEW CALVARY CEMETERY

NATHAN WEIDENBAUM PARK

Taiwanese Gourmet

ELMHURST

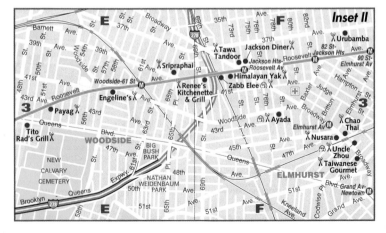

Agnanti

  Greek

19-06 Ditmars Blvd. (at 19th St.)

Subway: Astoria - Ditmars Blvd
Phone: 718-545-4554
Web: www.agnantimeze.com
Prices: $$

Lunch & dinner daily

 This adorable Astoria *taverna* oozes with provincial charm and spins out hearty Greek goodness, all the while boasting killer views of the midtown Manhattan skyline. Inside, ornate linens drape the dining tables, old-world photos hang on terra-cotta walls, and a flickering fireplace intensifies the coziness.

Grab a spot on the partially enclosed, bucolic terrace and fill up on delights like Santorini fava beans mashed with olive oil and topped with chopped red onion, parsley, and dill; a *ntakos* bread salad with tomatoes, olives, capers, and oregano; or *bacalao skordalia* of battered and fried cod topped with a savory potato-and-garlic sauce. The *halvah politiko* is a must try—picture halvah slices dripping with syrup and blueberry compote.

Alobar

 American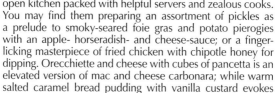

46-42 Vernon Blvd. (bet. 46th Rd. and 47th Ave.)

Subway: Vernon Blvd - Jackson Av
Phone: 718-752-6000
Web: www.alobarnyc.com
Prices: $$

Lunch & dinner daily

Hailed for its inventive cooking and talented butchering, Alobar boasts a vast and deep dining room adorned with antiques and slate floors. Blonde wood ceilings offer a great contrast to worn wood tables, but all eyes are fixed upon the open kitchen packed with helpful servers and zealous cooks. You may find them preparing an assortment of pickles as a prelude to smoky-seared foie gras and potato pierogies with an apple- horseradish- and cheese-sauce; or a finger-licking masterpiece of fried chicken with chipotle honey for dipping. Orecchiette and cheese with cubes of pancetta is an elevated version of mac and cheese carbonara; while warm salted caramel bread pudding with vanilla custard evokes classic Americana infused with an expert Italian twist.

Andy's Seafood & Grill

B2

Chinese

95-26 Queens Blvd. (bet. 63rd Ave. & 63rd Dr.)

Subway: 63 Dr - Rego Park   Lunch & dinner daily
Phone: 718-275-2388
Web: N/A
Prices:

Rising from a diverse pack of Rego Park restaurants is Andy's—a seafood haven and grill that cooks up equally authentic Taiwanese and Sichuan specialties. The owner and staff are warm and engaging, which is helpful as the vast bill of fare requires their navigation. The room feels muted, with beige walls displaying delicate artwork on one side and explosively colored photographs on the other.

Seafood is the star in this menu, but variety can run the gamut. Highlights might include meaty oyster mushrooms tossed with basil and yam noodles; a whole steamed flounder laid on a bed of fragrant pickled *majack* fruit; braised abalone in a soft yet rich oyster sauce; or surprisingly light noodles stir-fried with dry shrimp, ground pork, bean paste, and scallions.

Arharn Thai

E2

Thai

32-05 36th Ave. (bet. 32nd & 33rd Sts.)

Subway: 36 Av   Lunch & dinner daily
Phone: 718-728-5563
Web: www.thaiastoria.com
Prices:

Dishes burst with delightfully refreshing flavor here at Arharn Thai. The small space is bright and clean, arranged with glass-topped tables, decked with artifacts from the motherland, and equipped with two flat screen TVs.

An organized kitchen spins out goodies like *khaum jep*, steamed wonton dumplings stuffed with ground chicken, shrimp, crabmeat, and meaty mushrooms, served with a wonderfully sticky- garlicky- and salty-dipping sauce. The exquisitely tender *gob kra prow* (frog legs) are marinated and fried until golden, then cooked with garlic, chili peppers, onions, coconut milk, and Penang paste. Roasted eggplant arrives white, silky, and sublime, tossed in a light and vibrant salad of citrus-lime sauce, and crowned with flaky dried shrimp.

Asian Jewels

A3

Seafood ✕✕

133-30 39th Ave. (bet. College Point Blvd. & Prince St.)

Subway: Flushing - Main St
Phone: 718-359-8600
Web: www.tunseng.com
Prices: $$

Lunch & dinner daily

Arguably the best dim sum in Flushing, this spectacular gem is an absolute must for anyone seeking serious seafood and very authentic Cantonese cooking. A longtime resident of 39th Avenue, this expansive dining room is outfitted with round, banquet-style tables, bamboo plants, and ornate chandeliers.

Let the feasting begin with memorable crab-and-pork soup dumplings, before moving on to the thrill-inducing dim sum carts. Taste the likes of steamed rice rolls with honey-roast pork; pork spareribs with rice starch and black beans; chicken and ham wrapped in yuba; and poached jellyfish with scallions and sesame. The signature Dungeness crab—steamed and stir-fried with ginger and green onions, served with Japanese eggplant and garlic—is simply outstanding.

Ayada 😊

F3

Thai ✕

77-08 Woodside Ave. (bet. 77th & 78th Sts.)

Subway: Woodside - 61 St
Phone: 718-424-0844
Web: N/A
Prices: $$

Lunch & dinner daily

Bright from the outside and warmly lit indoors, Ayada's warm vibe and friendly, family-run spirit has a knack for making all diners feel at home.

Neon lights work here and glow atop closely spaced dark wood tables. Purists who aren't happy unless they're crying should take the menu's "spicy" selections with a grain of salt, as there is a paltry use of Thai chilies (they're sorely missed in the otherwise delicious crispy catfish salad). But, Ayada boasts an impressive roster of delicious à la carte like the *kang som* sour curry which is redolent of tamarind and lime and tastes as if it were straight out of Bangkok. Sautéed Chinese broccoli with crispy pork, and deep-fried whole red snapper topped with green mango reveal top product and ace technique.

Bahari estiatorio

 E2

31-14 Broadway (bet. 31st & 32nd Sts.)

Subway: Broadway
Phone: 718-204-8968
Web: www.bahariestiatorio.com
Prices: $$

Lunch & dinner daily

 It's all about fresh and traditional Greek classics with a hint of rusticity at this serene Astoria spot. The appealing space sports two airy, wide rooms—one styled in calming whites and blues; the other in rustic tones with exposed brick, a quirky collection of window shutters, and high wood-beamed ceilings.

Check out a few of these must-mentions: *tyrokafteri*—feta cheese and spicy pepper spread, whipped to heavenly creaminess, and served with pita points; or *fasolakia yahni*, string beans cooked in fresh, chunky tomato sauce. Their mousaka is light and deeply flavored, layering eggplant, potatoes, and ground beef with creamy béchamel sauce; and *arni psito* is an exquisitely tender braised lamb served with stewed peas and artichokes in lemon sauce.

Bareburger

 F2

33-21 31st Ave. (at 34th St.)

Subway: 30 Av
Phone: 718-777-7011
Web: www.bareburger.com
Prices: $$

Lunch Sat – Sun
Dinner nightly

This original Bareburger (there are now 13 locations and counting) sits on a well-exposed corner close to bustling Steinway Street. Chandeliers fashioned out of spoons and mini-glass *quartinos* enhance the two dining rooms. On warm days the doors open out to a leafy sidewalk.

The all-American menu serves up a tasty array of all-organic burgers. Choose your patty from the far-reaching selection of beef, turkey, black beans, or even elk. Then pick your bread, anything from brioche to tapioca rice bun, and add succulent embellishments. The habanero express tops your burger with pepperjack cheese, poblano relish, and spicy mayo. Fried sides are bolstered by assorted pickles. Fresh salads and enjoyable sandwiches give the burgers some competition.

Basil Brick Oven Pizza 😀

F1

Italian ✗✗

28-17 Astoria Blvd. (bet. 28th & 29th Sts.)

Subway: Astoria Blvd
Phone: 718-204-1205
Web: www.basilbrickoven.com
Prices: $$

Lunch & dinner Thu – Tue

Astoria now has dibs on some of the best pizza around, thanks to this recently expanded little pizzeria-cum-restaurant. In addition to quadrupling capacity and adding a lovely garden patio, Chef Barbos has augmented the already massive pizza menu with a handful of hearty pastas and entrées.

Masterfully done *pizzucca*, topped with herbed pumpkin walnut sauce, homemade mozzarella, pancetta, and *Parmigiano Reggiano* is a luscious choice. Or, go for *il polpettone*, a wonderfully puffy and golden brown *panino*, stuffed with beef meatballs, tomato sauce, and olive oil. The *lasagna* verde—a unique potato-pesto version topped with mozzarella and a sprinkling of breadcrumbs—is served with pesto, mascarpone, and marinara to reflect the colors of the Italian flag.

Bear

E2

Eastern European ✗✗

12-14 31st Ave. (bet. 12th & 14th Sts.)

Subway: Broadway
Phone: 917-396-4939
Web: www.bearnyc.com
Prices: $$

Lunch Sat – Sun
Dinner Tue – Sun

Tucked away on a side street in vibrant Astoria, Bear may not be an obvious destination for a distinctive meal. But, take the time and look around to find dark glossy walls, fresh flowers, and a host of diners feasting on chef *extraordinaire* Natasha Pogrebinsky's order-in-advance tasting menu. Appearances aside, this place is serious.

Start with a cleverly crafted libation—the St. Dill martini has become a much buzzed about pour—before delving into a carte of items that adeptly parodies old-world foundation with new-world panache. Dinner has yielded smoked fish pâté deviled eggs; Ukrainian-style borscht boosted with vodka and *salo*; and a rich mushroom stroganoff starring slow-roasted mushrooms, deliciously enhanced by garlic and cream.

Biáng!

 Chinese

A3

41-10 Main St. (bet. 41st Ave. & 41st Rd.)

Subway: Flushing - Main St
Phone: 718-888-7713
Web: www.biang-nyc.com
Prices: $$

Lunch & dinner daily

Jason Wang's Xi'an outpost went viral after Anthony Bourdain declared his lamb buns were amazing. That proclamation has since spawned Biáng!, Mr. Wang's latest success story housed amid Flushing's crammed streets. But, Biáng! is a bona fide destination where the vibe is boisterous and the narrow space is moody yet handsome with flattering lights and dark brown walls.

The fantastically funky, regional menu reveals the likes of *má là shuàn níu du*, tripe "cigars" slathered with spicy fermented tofu sauce and chili oil; or *zi rán yáng ròu jia bái ji mó*, succulent and wonderfully messy lamb slices sautéed with cumin and peppers tucked between crisply griddled flatbreads. Unique salads include piney fiddleheads with Sichuan pepper oil and black vinegar.

Bistro 33

 Fusion

F1

19-33 Ditmars Blvd. (at 21st St.)

Subway: Astoria - Ditmars Blvd
Phone: 718-721-1933
Web: www.bistro33nyc.com
Prices: $$

Lunch Sat – Sun
Dinner nightly

Bistro 33 is a sweet and cozy little corner darling, adorned with shelves of books, teapots, and kitchen wares. A picture window frames the view of the street and local artists have painted the original works gracing the walls. Chef and Queens-native Gary Anza keeps himself busy here in Astoria, with Side Door by Bistro 33 and William Hallet, an American bar and bistro, part of his mini-empire. However, his focus never strays far from this charming flagship.

The menu is trimmed by Asian touches, but classic French technique stands out. Revel in duck consommé drizzled with chili oil and filled with chewy soba and leg confit; or gorgeously seared foie gras, indulgently paired with pork belly and chestnut bread pudding but brightened by green olive tapenade.

Bonne Saison

C1

Thai ✕

40-04 Bell Blvd. (at 40th Ave.)

Subway: N/A
Phone: 718-224-6188
Web: N/A
Prices: $$

Lunch Sun
Dinner nightly

Consider it your *bonne chance* to have dined at this bright yet warm restaurant on Bell Boulevard. Steakhouses, wine bars, and barbecue dens may line these streets, but what they lack, Bonne Saison delivers with aplomb. The white interior is set with two rows of tables, a flat-screen, and bustling glass-enclosed kitchen preparing Franco-Thai treats. Quaint sepia photos of France, holiday lights, and a marble floor form most of the ambience, but really, everyone's here for the warm service and superior food.

A bona fide French section in the menu features faithfuls like *filet de bœuf au poivre*, while entrées like tofu with Thai basil sauce; *escargots de Bourgogne*; and tender duck lacquered with tangy tamarind are sure to sate your senses.

Brick Cafe

F2

Mediterranean ✕

30-95 33rd St. (at 31st Ave.)

Subway: Broadway
Phone: 718-267-2735
Web: www.brickcafe.com
Prices: $$

Lunch Sat – Sun
Dinner nightly

This neighborhood *bijou* is beloved for its big flavors and small, rustic space. From lace curtains and weathered floors, to a yellow façade with a "stained" glass pane, everything at Brick Cafe invokes the charming French countryside including its olive-tinted walls set beneath a hand-crafted tin ceiling. It's all very quaint to the point of being precious, but nonetheless appealing.

To match a lovely wine list, the menu highlights such well-made items as cucumber salad tossed with tomatoes, olives, and yogurt; or specials like goat cheese and asparagus-stuffed chicken wrapped in speck, roasted until crisp, and poured with a Parmesan cream set over mashed potatoes. Light and fluffy crêpes filled with berries offer the perfect end to such decadence.

bún-ker 🏵️

A2

46-63 Metropolitan Ave. (at Woodward Ave.)

Subway: Grand St (& bus Q54)
Phone: 718-386-4282
Web: www.bunkervietnamese.com
Prices: 😋😋

Lunch Sat – Sun
Dinner Tue – Sun

Finding bún-ker is tricky and the journey isn't pretty, but this sweet and sunny "coffee shop" shines with a bright yellow façade. Inside, find the owners flitting amid burnt-orange walls, mismatched chairs, and plaid curtains laid atop white-framed windows. Know that this is not simply a spot for cheap eats: bún-ker is skillfully crafting solid Vietnamese food from quality ingredients, and they're here to stay.

Find pure harmony in mushroom *pho* with rice vermicelli and a plate of symphonic herbs and accompaniments. Perfect *banh mi* are filled with melting smoked Gouda and pickled vegetables. *Ca ri ga* (chicken curry with lemongrass and coconut); and *cha cha* (turmeric-bathed fried salmon topped with peanuts and chilies) are both excellent.

Butcher Bar

F2

37-08 30th Ave. (bet. 36th and 37th Sts.)

Subway: 30 Av
Phone: 718-606-8140
Web: www.butcherbar.com
Prices: $$

Lunch & dinner daily

♿

Got grass? That's not a question but rather the cheeky motto of this startlingly delicious smoke joint, as evinced by T-shirts hanging on their walls. Flanked by old-time butcher shops, Butcher Bar aims to pay respect to these nostalgic cleaver-wielding geniuses by showcasing their first-rate finds: ruby red and marbled steaks, sausage links, and thick pork chops. Suitably spartan, the space is simple with mirrors set atop banquettes, bright lights, and a bustling open kitchen. Wood tables are topped with squeeze bottles of "original" and "sweet & spicy" sauces that are best with barbecue treats like a pulled chicken sandwich. Spicy beef chili is a mere teaser before delectable mains like smoked pork belly placed between bread and served with slaw.

Casa Enríque

A2

Mexican 🍴🍴

5-48 49th Ave. (bet. 5th St. & Vernon Blvd.)

Subway: Vernon Blvd - Jackson Av
Phone: 347-448-6040
Web: N/A
Prices: $$

Lunch Sat – Sun
Dinner nightly

Marked by a bright sign and picture windows, it's easy to spot this beacon set steps from the subway. From a warm welcome to a stylish décor, this lively favorite has something for everyone. Keeping revelers quenched is a stainless steel bar, while locals hover around the communal table up front. Sturdy plastic chairs set atop a cement floor gleam with urban flair.

Begin with deliciously fresh guacamole presented in a *molcajete* and a trio of house salsas. Then, luxuriate in glossy bowls of *pozole de mi tia*, roasted red chili-infused broth filled with shredded pork and radish; or *sopes de chorizo*, masa topped with beans and *crema*. *Mole de Piaxtla* featuring dried chilies, almonds, and chocolate is so complex, thick, and rich, it may as well be dessert.

Chao Thai

F3

Thai 🍴

85-03 Whitney Ave. (at Broadway)

Subway: Elmhurst Av
Phone: 718-424-4999
Web: N/A
Prices: 🍛

Lunch & dinner daily

Thanks to the delectable eats, snug setting, and generous spirit, tiny Chao Thai's loyal following makes perfect sense. The LIRR rumbles nearby, but green-painted walls and a lofty window help soothe the setting. In an area teeming with Southeast Asian eateries, Chao Thai thrives as a wonderful destination for die-hard foodies.

Their seemingly silent existence has afforded the kitchen the liberty to create such faithful renditions as a mouth-numbing jungle curry balanced with coconut milk, lemongrass, and rich pork strips. Start with tiny fish cakes (*tod man*) with chili sauce before launching into sour fish stir-fried with a pungent curry paste.

Nearby and larger, Chao Thai Too also parades a deliciously unapologetic use of heat and spice.

Cheburechnaya

B2

92-09 63rd Dr. (at Austin St.)

Subway: 63 Dr - Rego Park
Phone: 718-897-9080
Web: N/A
Prices:

Lunch Tue – Fri
Dinner Sat – Thu

The service can be halting, the halogen lighting is brutal, and the blaring Russian music videos don't exactly scream date-night. But this boisterous Rego Park restaurant's inconveniences fade when the dining room's open grill lights up—crackling and sizzling with juicy kebabs—and gorgeous plates of food start flying out of the kitchen (sometimes all at once). On cold nights, nothing placates like a bowl of chicken soup with *pelmeni*.

Their unique take on kosher food, which caters to the local Bukharan Jewish population, emphasizes roasted meat and hearty, comforting dishes. Every single part of a lamb that can be cooked can be found on the menu (ribs, fat, etc). For a special ending, try the *chak chak*—Chinese noodles bound with honey and aromatics.

Christos

F1

41-08 23rd Ave. (at 41st St.)

Subway: Astoria - Ditmars Blvd
Phone: 718-777-8400
Web: www.christossteakhouse.com
Prices: $$$

Dinner nightly

A dark red awning dips down over windows promising hearty portions of dry-aged beef, while neat hedges line the entrance to this beloved Astoria institution. Inside, a front area serves as both bar and butcher shop, beautifully displaying their range of house-aged chops. Hardwood floors, warm tones, and mahogany tables draped in white linens complete the traditional setting.

But what sets Christos apart from its chophouse brethren is the uniquely Greek influence of the food: *taramosalata* and salads of Greek sausage over *gigante* beans share the menu with standards like roast chicken, lobster, and ribeye. Expertly prepared sides like tart and tender dandelion greens (*horta*) tossed in lemon juice and olive oil bring fresh flavors to steakhouse dining.

Danny Brown Wine Bar & Kitchen ✿

B2

Mediterranean 🍴🍴

104-02 Metropolitan Ave. (at 71st Dr.)

Subway: Forest Hills - 71 Av

Dinner Tue – Sun

Phone: 718-261-2144
Web: www.dannybrownwinekitchen.com
Prices: $$

♿

Gaetano Salvadore

Sitting upon a prominent corner of Metropolitan Avenue, Danny Brown draws passersby through its wooden doors, flanked by large windows. While the site itself is attractive, nearby flower shops and antique stores are equally quaint and festive.

This bright and well-appointed space strikes a sophisticated note from décor to dining. Majestic pieces of art hang languidly on golden yellow walls while muted floors, window treatments featuring seasonal planters, and cushioned seats are reminiscent of classic French country. High ceilings adorned with gently spinning fans and sultry beats fashion a pleasant backdrop.

Delightful starters courtesy of this talented husband-and-wife team may include butternut squash risotto garnished with toasted hazelnuts and enhanced by lacy ribbons of crispy *Parmigiano frico*. Then, move on to a plump fillet of cod sautéed with soft cipollini onions and set atop saffron-clam orzo. An open kitchen in the back seduces diners with tantalizing aromas wafting from a confit of Moulard duck served over crispy potato cubes and charred Brussels sprouts. To finish, the buttery apple tarte Tatin is a cinnamon- and clove-rich classic, glossed with a scoop of *crème sucrée*.

Debasaki

33-67 Farrington St. (bet. 33rd & 35th Aves.)

Subway: Flushing - Main St   Dinner nightly
Phone: 718-886-6878
Web: www.debasaki.com
Prices: $$

Surrounded by chop-shops and industrial outlets, this sexy Korean/Japanese chicken joint in Flushing gets a bit isolated after 8:00 P.M., though those who know where they're headed are in for a treat. Inside, you'll find a slick, stylish interior fitted out with cushy, high-backed striped booths, thumping Korean pop beats, and an intimate back bar that manages to be even darker than the restaurant.

The soups are notable at Debasaki, but it's the chicken that keeps this restaurant packed all hours of the night. Don't miss the deliciously deep-fried *gyoza*; fried chicken wings stuffed with shrimp, corn, cheese, hot peppers, and corn kimchi; boneless barbecue chicken topped with crunchy fish roe; or the tart kimchi fried rice with cheese.

De Mole

45-02 48th Ave. (at 45th St.)

Subway: 46 St - Bliss St   Lunch & dinner daily
Phone: 718-392-2161
Web: www.demolenyc.com
Prices: 🍴🍴

If the words sweet, competent, clean, and Mexican come into mind, you're most likely thinking of this heart-warming haunt for delightful Mexican. Albeit a tad small, with a second dining room in the back, rest assured that De Mole's flavors are mighty, both in their staples (burritos and tacos) and unique specials—seitan fajitas anyone?

This Mexican pearl rests on a corner of low-rise buildings where Woodside meets Sunnyside, yet far from the disharmony of Queens Boulevard. Fans gather here for hearty *enchiladas verdes con pollo*, corn tortillas smeared with tomatillo sauce and *queso blanco*. Crispy chicken *taquitos* are topped with rich sour cream; steamed corn tamales are surprisingly light but filled with flavor; and the namesake *mole* is a must.

Engeline's

E3

Filipino

58-28 Roosevelt Ave. (at 59th St.)

Subway: Woodside - 61 St

Phone: 718-898-7878

Web: N/A

Prices:

Lunch & dinner daily

Admittedly, Filipino cuisine is not for the faint of heart (pig blood, beef hearts, fried chicken skin), but those with a daring spirit or simply longing for a taste of the homeland will do well by visiting Engeline's. This part bakery and part full-fledged restaurant is loved for its top-shelf goods and cadre of amiable staff.

Specialties like the sizzling *sisig*, made with deep-fried pork belly and topped with a just-broken egg; or *rellenong talong* comprising eggplant, pork, and the idea of an omelet are two must-try items. Go for the *pata* and don't be put off by the serrated knife stuck in the middle of this deep-fried pork knuckle. Desserts like cookies steamed in banana leaves and topped with caramel are great to enjoy in-house or to-go.

eXo

C1

Greek

15-16 149th St. (at 15th Rd.)

Subway: N/A

Phone: 718-767-4396

Web: www.exorestaurant.com

Prices: $$

Lunch & dinner daily

Exo, from the Greek word for "outside," is a most apt epithet for the gorgeous garden flanking this very casual and very Mediterranean canteen. The colors and heft of the enclosed area point to a sunny locale. When the clouds part, dine alfresco under the moonbeams.

Settled on a quiet, leafy corner of a bucolic enclave, find eXo's diners relishing, in the garden or rich sunset-yellow dining room, the aromas floating from dishes like lamb roast (they can also bring it home to you); *keftedes*, *halloumi*-stuffed meatballs with *tzatziki*; *horiatiki*, a stellar toss up of vegetables, olives, and feta; or a slow-cooked pork shank with sautéed escarole. On balmy nights, the whole spit-roasted animal is excellent, and perfect for ravenous groups.

Galbi Ma Eul

C1

194-03 Northern Blvd. (bet. 194th & 195th Sts.)

Subway: Flushing - Main St (& bus Q12)   Lunch & dinner daily
Phone: 718-819-2171
Web: N/A
Prices: **$$**

While Flushing has a good number of Korean spots, the lines outside Galbi Ma Eul never seem to fade. Locals and visitors gather here around tabletops equipped with traditional wood-burning charcoal barbecue pits clamoring perhaps for their tantalizing house-specialty, *galbi*—a mountain of perfectly marinated beef short ribs and pork belly with an array of tasty sides. Other than these tabletop feasts, the space itself is nondescript, with large planters and a blaring television.

The menu goes on to offer an excellent second specialty, *agoo jjim*, a gargantuan pot of spicy monkfish stew with spring onions and bean sprouts in a perfect balance of sweet, salty, and spicy flavors. *Banchan* may include octopus in *gochujang* and crab in chili sauce.

Genting Palace

B3

110-00 Rockaway Blvd. (at 110th St.)

Subway: 111 St   Lunch & dinner Wed – Sun
Phone: 718-215-3343
Web: www.rwnewyork.com
Prices: **$$**

This luxe and mod Chinese restaurant is housed in a most unusual space—on the third floor of Ozone Park's Aqueduct Racetrack, a vast entertainment and gambling center. Genting Palace is palatial, sound-proofed, and offers views of the racetrack, making it a mecca for big spenders and moneyed gamers.

The menu is detailed but focuses on Southern China and Canton with tasty dim sum like steamed dumplings filled with shrimp and pork; sticky rice and dried scallops steamed in lotus leaves; or pork spare ribs with a black bean paste. Also find a delicate rendition of shrimp *egg foo young* set in a French *demi-glace*; or pick from a full menu offering poached chicken and vegetables flavored with holy basil, perfectly paired with a seafood-studded fried rice.

Hahm Ji Bach

 Korean

C1

41-08 149th Pl. (bet. Barclay & 41st Aves.)

Subway: Flushing - Main St   Lunch & dinner daily
Phone: 718-460-9289
Web: www.hahmjibach.com
Prices: $$

A healthy assortment of *banchan* (small plates including kimchi and spicy mackerel) is usually a good indicator of a serious Korean restaurant. And you'll find no shortage of them at Hahm Ji Bach—a delicious Korean barbecue joint buried down a nondescript side street in the blossoming K-town that has sprung up near Queens' Murray Hill LIRR station.

The unassuming Hahm Ji Bach won't woo you with it's plain-Jane décor, but scores major points for the patient, oh-so-knowledgable service and masterful Korean specialties. *Daeji bulgogi*, marinated pork ribs in a chili-garlic sauce sprinkled with bright scallions; or *boyang jeongol*, a traditional hot pot of lamb, dumplings, and vegetables swimming in a rich, spicy beef broth are some of the favorites here.

Himalayan Yak

Tibetan

F3

72-20 Roosevelt Ave. (bet. 72nd & 73rd Sts.)

Subway: 74 St - Broadway   Lunch & dinner daily
Phone: 718-779-1119
Web: www.himalayanyakrestaurant.com
Prices:

 From the intricately carved doors and furnishings to the exposed brick and sultry sienna walls lined with masks and miniature yaks, the broadly appealing and exceptionally friendly Himalayan Yak is a place of care, restraint, and dining adventure.

The menu may be best described as Indian-light, a hybrid that draws specialties from several cuisines including Nepali, Indian, Bhutanese, and most heavily Tibetan. Begin a culinary tour with *tsam thuk*, a thick, porridge-like soup served at room temperature, and bobbing with soft cubes of yak cheese; large beef dumplings in a rich, hot, and savory soup of tender greens and diced carrots; or a vegetarian tray which includes pickled mango strips, chutneys, greens, jasmine rice, and Indian pepper "paper bread".

Hino Maru Ramen

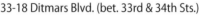
✗

F1

33-18 Ditmars Blvd. (bet. 33rd & 34th Sts.)

Subway: Astoria - Ditmars Blvd   Lunch & dinner daily
Phone: 718-777-0228
Web: www.hinomaruramen.com
Prices: $$

Everybody in this residential neighborhood seems to love Hino Maru Ramen. This Japanese "gastropub" takes its job very seriously, and although the menu is diverse, their ramen promises to rock your world. The décor is nothing flashy, but it is a large, comfy space with hefty seats and serious feasting. A huge blackboard lists daily specials (like astoundingly fresh oysters topped with a *granita* comprised of yuzu, mirin, and dashi); while *hinomaru ramen* is a deliciously dark and stormy staple featuring fiery meatballs in a rich pork broth brimming with garlic and mushrooms. Other items include *miso nasu* (silky eggplant with sweet miso and bonito flakes); or shrimp fried rice studded with pickled red ginger, daikon, and topped with a fried egg.

Hunan House

A3

✗

137-40 Northern Blvd. (bet. Main & Union Sts.)

Subway: Flushing - Main St   Lunch & dinner daily
Phone: 718-353-1808
Web: www.hunanauthentic.com
Prices: 🍜🍜

 This quieter stretch of Northern Boulevard is NY's rising (and reigning) Chinatown and is sure to fire up any spice-seekers willing to brave the trek. Here, Hunan House is a plain but tidy spot serving heartwarming Hunanese fare, and reminding all of its phenomenal complexity. The menu reads like a textbook of this region's cuisine; its authenticity is paramount.

Many dishes, like braised fish head, are seafood-centric, though they often share Sichuan's affinity for chilies. Expect the likes of steamed spare ribs, thick and lean, in a hollowed bamboo branch teeming with a powerful sauce of fermented black beans and red chili oil. White chili-preserved beef is an ingenious dish of dried bean curd and a mix of five-spice and star anise, and beefy broth.

Hunan Kitchen of Grand Sichuan

 C1

Chinese   X

42-47 Main Street (bet. Blossom & Franklin Aves.)

Subway: Flushing - Main St   Lunch & dinner daily
Phone: 718-888-0553
Web: N/A
Prices: 🪙🪙

As New York's Sichuan renaissance continues apace, this pleasant and unpretentious Hunanese spot has popped up on Flushing's Main Street. The look here is tasteful and uncomplicated; the cooking is fiery and excellent.

The extensive menu of Hunan specialties includes the likes of the classic regional dish, pork "Mao's Style" simmered in soy sauce, Shaoxing wine, oil, and stock, then braised to tender perfection. Boasting heat and meat in equal amounts, the spicy-sour string beans with pork expertly combines rich and savory aromatics, vinegary beans, and fragrant pork with tongue-numbing peppercorns. The barbecue fish Hunan-style is a brilliant menu standout.

Smaller dishes, like winter melon with seafood soup, round out an expertly prepared meal.

Il Bacco

 D1

Italian   XX

253-24 Northern Blvd. (bet. Little Neck Pkwy & Westmoreland St.)

Subway: N/A   Lunch & dinner daily
Phone: 718-224-7657
Web: www.ilbaccoristorante.com
Prices: $$

With its dulcet Mediterranean-esque façade, crimson awnings, and rooftop garden, Il Bacco is hard to miss. This Little Neck-by-way-of-Tuscany gem shows off a stylish setting; the fact that it is bolstered by a popular catering operation augments its overall appeal.

This kitchen dutifully honors Italian-American classics with skill and top-notch ingredients. The pizza oven is a beauté that produces perfect pies, while tables pile up with *gamberetti infernali*, shrimp in a drink-worthy sauce of white wine, garlic, and red pepper flakes; or *spaghetti picchi paccu*, tossed with crushed plum tomatoes, basil, and pecorino. *Pollo Gelsomina* is chicken scaloppine beautifully finished with a chunky sauce of mushrooms, artichoke hearts, and roasted peppers.

Il Poeta

Italian ✗✗

B2

98-04 Metropolitan Ave. (at 69th Rd.)

Subway: Forest Hills - 71 Av   Dinner Tue – Sun
Phone: 718-544-4223
Web: www.ilpoetarestaurant.com
Prices: $$

Even if nothing further is said about Il Poeta, let one thing be clear—this family-run charmer knows how to hit Italian specialties out of the park. Perched on a quaint corner and edged with lofty windows, their white curtains contrasted against pink and orange walls seem to capture the soul of Tuscany. The suited staff and vibrant artwork make Il Poeta much more than just a trattoria.

Venerable creations are pitch-perfect, as in calamari *dorati* superbly supple and fried to golden perfection; or outstanding *linguine alla puttanesca con tonno* dressed with tomato sauce studded with tuna, olives, and capers. The *pollo spezzatino* may well resemble the classic *cacciatore*, but is nonetheless stellar starring peppers, sausage, and hints of herbs.

Imperial Palace

Chinese ✗

A3

136-13 37th Ave. (bet. Main & Union Sts.)

Subway: Flushing - Main St   Lunch & dinner daily
Phone: 718-939-3501
Web: N/A
Prices: $$

 Grab a group of your fellow chowhounds and hop the 7 train to Flushing for plates of scrumptious, classic Chinese cuisine. You will need your nosh buddies to help you tackle the ample menu, which is jam-packed with delectable offerings like crunchy snow pea shoots with garlic; flavorful squid with chives; and fragrant preserved meat (sausage) with tart mounds of spinach. But the claim to fame at this frequented spot is the sticky rice and crab...did we say Dungeness? Oh, yes. Juicy, plump, sweet crabmeat served in a leaf-lined steamer with sublime bits of crisp, golden rice, along with black mushrooms, ginger, scallions, and dried shrimp.

Large, banquet style tables dot the dining space where the lively atmosphere brims with a prominently Asian crowd.

Jackson Diner

 F3

37-47 74th St. (bet. Roosevelt & 37th Aves.)

Subway: Jackson Hts - Roosevelt Av   Lunch & dinner daily
Phone: 718-672-1232
Web: www.jacksondiner.com
Prices:

The cultural diversity in this borough rivals a boat-ride through *It's a Small World*. This is particularly true in Jackson Heights, where colorful clothing shops and jewelry boutiques line the streets alongside a stunning array of authentic eateries.

Cue Jackson Diner, with its legendary lunch buffet and real-deal menu, satiating Indian food hankerings of all regions. Warm up with a peppery bowl of mulligatawany soup, brimming with *masala* spices, ginger, almond, coconut, and chicken; or try crab cake *samosas*, stuffed with scallions and potato. Mains include a spicy lamb *biryani*, with cumin, raisins, and whole cardamom, garnished with fried onions and cashews; and *murg tikka palakwala*—tender chicken simmered with spinach, ginger, and cumin.

Joe's Shanghai

A3

136-21 37th Ave. (bet. Main & Union Sts.)

Subway: Flushing - Main St   Lunch & dinner daily
Phone: 718-539-3838
Web: www.joeshanghairestaurants.com
Prices: $$

Ah, Joe's Shanghai, how well you seduce with your deliciously delicate soup dumplings, perhaps with a wad of crab or pork sticking out the top. You may not be large, yet you soar with fans and not a table to spare. Such is the norm at the original Flushing hot spot, which may be a touch dated but is mighty trim and tidy. Two massive flat-screens dominate this room, yet diners remain riveted by the Asian delights churned out of the kitchen.

Swift and sweet servers attend to round and sturdy tables armed with hefty chairs. Robed in matching uniforms, they present the likes of meaty Sichuan beef tendon soup with silky noodles; eggplant and shredded pork glistening with garlic sauce and scallions; and sautéed baby shrimp paired with slices of tangy kidney.

John Brown Smokehouse

A1

10-43 44th Dr. (bet. 10th & 11th Sts.)

Subway: Court Sq - 23 St
Phone: 347-617-1120
Web: www.johnbrownseriousbbq.com
Prices: $$

Lunch & dinner daily

Barbecue fans rejoiced when John Brown moved to a larger home in Hunters Point. While this western tip of Queens is in transition, the food scene is here to stay. Beyond an ample dining room, the simple décor unveils a bustling front area, photos of a bearded man (John Brown?), and an outdoor beer hall featuring live music.

Still, everyone is here for the truly authentic Kansas City-style barbecue and peachwood-smoked treats like rib tips (meat candy, really) with burned ends enticingly seasoned with sugar and ground coffee. Other favorites include kimchi radish, smoky lamb sausage, and *el chupacabra* with roast pork and barbecue sauce—a changing daily special.

If you're craving goat ribs, head to Alchemy, Texas where owner Josh Bowen promises to surprise.

Katsuno

B2

103-01 Metropolitan Ave. (at 71st Rd.)

Subway: Forest Hills - 71 Av
Phone: 718-575-4033
Web: www.katsunorestaurant.com
Prices: $$

Dinner Tue – Sun

In Katsuno's tiny kitchen, find Chef Seo whipping up extraordinarily authentic Kyoto home-style (*obanzai*) cooking. The snug space is simple and clean, with touches of artwork on green walls, and a hidden, semi-private dining room in the back. The setting is modest, but the cuisine soars. Among the delights, discover a supremely delicate and smoky soup with tender baby clams and a fragrant leaf of cilantro bobbing on the surface. The chef's signature squid is always a highlight, pearly white and perfect in texture served simply atop a shiso leaf and side of *natto*. More adventurous eaters will seek the likes of *shiokara* sushi—hailed as a rare flavor for sophisticated palates. Cold *somen* and warm soba noodles round out the menu with hearty satisfaction.

Linn

Japanese   XX

29-13 Broadway (bet. 29th & 30th Sts.)

Subway: Broadway
Phone: 718-204-0060
Web: N/A
Prices: $$

Lunch Fri – Sat
Dinner nightly

Tasty little Linn brings Tokyo via Chelsea to Astoria—enter to find yourself amid an art gallery offering the finest and freshest fish. Simply dressed in dark tile floors and white walls, Linn revolves around its L-shaped bar, as if to ensure that sushi and sashimi are the way to go—oysters mingled with mushroom nigiri are a minute in your mouth, but forever on your mind.

Chef Shigenori Tanaka (who hails from Masa) shines in his handling of such first-rate fish. While most order à la carte, others dive into an omakase that opens with a bowl of dashi brimming with *kombu* and cod flakes, followed by tender pork belly in a sweet mirin glaze. Two cubes of fresh tofu are full of flavor when topped with a plum-soy sauce and caramelized white miso paste.

Little Lamb

Chinese   X

36-35 Main St. (bet. 37th Ave. & Northern Blvd.)

Subway: Flushing - Main St
Phone: 718-358-6667
Web: www.thebesthotpot.com
Prices: ☜☜

Lunch & dinner daily

 Even though English proves challenging for the staff here, that's no reason to fret—especially since "pointing" works just fine at this charming spot for hot pots. Not to be confused with Little Sheep, unique Little Lamb's website handle (the best hot pot!) inspires confidence as does the astonishing roster. Find over 70 varying items to be dunked into bubbling broth, which is available "spicy red," (bobbing with capsicum and Sichuan peppercorns) "non-spicy white," or "half-and-half."

The combos are endless, but it's all a treat: thinly sliced lamb, head-on shrimp, and chewy udon to name a few. Thrill-seekers will devour other unmentionable animal parts; while a refreshing trio of cucumber, bitter melon, and shredded potato is a cool palate cleanser.

Little Pepper

Chinese ✗

18-24 College Point Blvd. (bet. 18th & 20th Aves.)

Subway: Flushing - Main St (& bus Q20A)   Lunch & dinner Fri — Wed
Phone: 718-939-7788
Web: N/A
Prices: 🍲

The exquisite Little Pepper housed in College Point boasts a delicate and faithful rendition of Sichuan cooking. Add that to the fresh and clean interior dressed with marble tiled floors, immaculate white walls adorned with "frescoes" created by the owner's son, and a small service bar, and it is no wonder that this is such a big hit.

But the focus here is surely on their sublime, honest cuisine, which thankfully remains solid. Some irresistible faves include fresh cucumber with mashed garlic sauce; thinly sliced, blanched ox "organs" tossed in an intensely flavorful chili oil; and glass noodles in a heavenly pool of stir-fried pork, scallions, and Sichuan peppercorns. Need some crispy treats? The deep-fried whole fish topped with pickles is bliss.

Lu Xiang Yuan

Chinese ✗

42-87 Main St. (bet. Blossom & Cherry Aves.)

Subway: Flushing - Main St   Lunch & dinner daily
Phone: 718-359-2108
Web: N/A
Prices: 🍲

Exciting and unfamiliar regional Chinese cuisine is flourishing in Flushing. A relative newcomer to this chill stretch of Main Street, Lu Xiang Yuan is firing up outstanding dishes— Quingdao style. The clean but ordinary space and ambience may lack character; yet it is memorable for the food's extraordinary balance and interplay of hot, sour, and sweet tastes.

Subtle smokiness and tangy flavors headline the jaw-dropping selection, featuring the likes of a brilliantly textured mixed-bean jelly with pickled leafy greens, crisp cucumber, and vinegar sauce; or a purple-red Chinese radish and shrimp soup. Pork tendon is toffee-rich and unforgettable. The mountain yam stir-fried with lily bulb, and the silk melon with clam meat are beguiling and elegant.

Main Street Imperial Taiwanese Gourmet

Chinese

59-14A Main St. (bet. 59th & 60th Aves.)

Subway: Flushing - Main St (& bus Q44)   Lunch & dinner daily
Phone: 718-886-8788
Web: N/A
Prices:

 With its impossibly long name and simple, Zen-like interior, this Taiwanese joint isn't trying to woo anyone to Flushing for ambience. You can find that anywhere, after all. It's all about the food at this compact gem sporting a clean space and walls simply adorned with large framed Chinese characters.

Rest assured it's worth it for the stinky tofu alone. The staff speaks little English, but with a dash of ingenuity you'll soon be on your way to exquisite delights like bamboo pork, served together in a hot cast iron vessel with scallions and a mouthwatering sauce; wildly fresh oyster pancakes sporting caramelized edges and a tantalizingly sweet sauce; and tender cuttlefish tossed with minced pork, crunchy Chinese celery, and seared green peppers.

Malagueta

Brazilian

25-35 36th Ave. (at 28th St.)

Subway: 36 Av   Lunch & dinner Tue – Sun
Phone: 718-937-4821
Web: www.malaguetany.com
Prices: $$

For a mainstay that has stood still for many years, Malagueta's Brazilian menu loves to meander north of the country. The captain of the kitchen must clearly be inspired by his homeland, as he pays homage to such authentic items as *feijoada completa*, served on Saturdays only. It may not be the only Brazilian gem in town, but it is one that offers a meal minus the stupefying slices of meat.

The bright walls are judiciously covered with oils and make for excellent views from tables set with flowers and crisp linen. Soft tunes invite one to take time enjoying a classic *caldo verde* soup with chorizo; *corvine com vatapa*, roasted pollock strewn with a spicy shrimp cream sauce and breadcrumbs; or a sweet corn pudding frilled with cinnamon sugar.

Mamak House

Malaysian ✗

A3

35-20 Farrington St. (bet. 35th St. & Northern Blvd.)

Subway: Flushing - Main St   Lunch & dinner daily
Phone: 718-886-4828
Web: www.mamakhouse.com
Prices: ⊜⊜

Mamak House is located on the second floor of a workaday Flushing commercial strip and presents a dining room whose previous incarnation as a Korean joint explains the remnants of prominent barbecue artifacts. Brick walls and an upbeat soundtrack may produce a westernized glint, but make no mistake—the food here is stunningly authentic. This is strictly halal Malaysian cuisine influenced by the country's South Indian immigrants.

The kitchen turns out a tandem of lush items like *sambal ikan*, fish in a tart curry redolent of tamarind; and *mee rebus Mamak*, a mélange of noodles, fried bean curd, and squid draped with a spicy potato-based dressing. Cool off over *ais kacang*—an amazing concoction of shaved ice, grass jelly, creamed corn, and sweet beans.

Minni's Shabu Shabu

Chinese ✗

A3

136-17 38th Ave. (bet. Main & Union Sts.)

Subway: Flushing - Main St   Lunch & dinner daily
Phone: 718-762-6277
Web: www.minnishabushabu.com
Prices: $$

Thanks to a well-deserved face-lift, this always hopping shabu-shabu lair showcases divine food within a lovely setting. The contemporary exterior is a sign of what to expect—a Taiwanese hot pot spot bringing serenity with cool slate floors, tall windows, thick glass doors, and wood beams. A long hallway leads to a sprawling, three-tiered room of white walls and high ceilings.

Packed with families and solo diners, the shimmering expanse keeps the hordes hovering aound a sauce bar of unique condiments. These are a zesty introduction to the spectrum of flavors found in tripe and beef shabu-shabu; a spicy kimchi broth floating with udon noodles and dumplings; or fried pork "chop" presented sliced on a lettuce leaf tinged with a sweet-spicy dipping sauce.

MP Taverna

Greek ✗✗

F1

31-29 Ditmars Blvd. (at 33rd St.)

Subway: Astoria - Ditmars Blvd
Phone: 718-777-2187
Web: www.michaelpsilakis.com
Prices: $$

Lunch & dinner daily

This sprawling, bi-level hot spot has diners and drinkers from all around the city hopping the N or Q line to Astoria. Lively and raucous, the main level is dressed in an urban style of slate walls, steel touches, and wood paneling. The second floor is more luxurious with its ornate chandeliers, leather chairs, and floor-to-ceiling windows.

Brought to you by Michael Psilakis, this outpost is one of three sister locations, all serving up the same tasty menu. Offerings include chopped bulgar salad of dates, green olives, and red onions, studded with pomegranate and pistachio; a hearty mix of grilled lamb sausage, pork tenderloin and chicken basted in oregano and lemon; or fantastic walnut-and-parsnip cake with candied nut rubble and ice cream.

Mulan

Asian ✗✗

A3

136-17 39th Ave. (at Main St.)

Subway: Flushing - Main St
Phone: 718-886-8526
Web: www.mulan-restaurant.com
Prices: $$$

Lunch & dinner daily

Sheltered amid wedding boutiques and Asian pottery shops on the third floor of the Queens Crossing shopping mall, this dazzling spot is one of the prettiest Chinese restaurants around. The chic room is fitted with white high-backed chairs, mahogany wood floors, and silk branches of cherry blossom as window dressings, then partitioned by another seating area smack at its center—a raised platform enclosed within four glimmering water "curtains."

Mouthwatering dishes include coconut soft-shell crab, pan-seared and paired with mango *coulis*; and vegetable fried rice, intriguingly pearly and nutty, with sweet shrimp. Sea bass in a five spice broth with pickled soy beans and mushrooms; and a tender, smoky rack of lamb are favored among the fish and flesh set.

545

Mythos

C1

Greek ✗✗

196-29 Northern Blvd. (bet. 196th St. & Francis Lewis Blvd.)

Subway: N/A
Phone: 718-357-6596
Web: www.mythosnyc.com
Prices: $$

Lunch & dinner daily

Plumb in the heart of Northern Boulevard's stretch of Korean eateries is this Greek favorite for dishes of impeccably fresh fish, grilled to juicy perfection. The welcoming white façade is splashed with a dark blue awning and red paneled doors flanked by oversized windows. The interior is simply done in white linen-topped tables and dark wood floors, with a lower-level private party room.

Start off with *bekri meze*, a warm appetizer combination of crispy codfish served with garlic dip; pan-fried *casseri* cheese; roasted red peppers in wine sauce; and *loukaniko*, grilled Greek sausage. Pair a plate of fresh grilled asparagus, zucchini, and eggplant with a whole grilled porgy, *tsipoura*, that is crispy on the outside and perfectly delicate within.

Nan Xiang Xiao Long Bao

A3

Chinese ✗

38-12 Prince St. (bet. 38th & 39th Aves.)

Subway: Flushing - Main St
Phone: 718-321-3838
Web: N/A
Prices: ⊗⊗

Lunch & dinner daily

Also known as Nan Xiang Dumpling House, it is easily found among a strip of restaurants reflecting the diversity of Flushing's dominant Asian population. Simply decorated, the comfortable dining room features rows of closely set tables and a mirrored wall that successfully gives the illusion of space.

The enjoyable and interesting menu focuses on noodle-filled soups, toothsome stir-fried rice cakes, and the house specialty, juicy pork dumplings. These are made in-house and have a delicate, silky wrapper encasing a flavorful meatball of ground pork or crab and rich tasting broth. Eating the specialties may take some practice, but take your cue from the slurping crowd: puncture the casing on your spoon to cool the dumplings and avoid scalding your mouth.

Natural Tofu & Noodles

Korean ✗

 A2

40-06 Queens Blvd. (bet. 40th & 41st Sts.)

Subway: 40 St
Phone: 718-706-0899
Web: N/A
Prices: $$

Lunch & dinner daily

Natural Tofu & Noodles may appear nondescript, but peek through the large window panes to discover that the kitchen is in full display and perpetually in motion with noodle pulling, sauce ladling, and pots bubbling. A small army of chefs hovers over stoves of aromatic and heartwarming Korean fare.

The long and narrow dining room is modestly embellished with gleaming wood tables. Away from the kitchen's mayhem, diners usually opt for the house-specialty tofu, silky and custard-like, perhaps in a cauldron of fragrant broth with mixed seafood. *Dolsot bibimbap* is a hot casserole of rice topped with a pyramid of minced beef, chicken, and seasoned vegetables enriched with an egg yolk and red chili sauce to taste. Kimchi pancakes are a classic at their best.

Nick's Pizza

Pizza ✗

 B2

108-26 Ascan Ave. (off Austin St.)

Subway: 75 Av
Phone: 718-263-1126
Web: N/A
Prices: ⊜⊜

Lunch & dinner daily

& Pizza couldn't be hotter in New York right now, but this quiet little Forest Hills pie joint was kicking it long before the recent influx of newcomers. Located a stone's throw from the legendary Forest Hills Gardens, a lovely neighborhood featuring stunning Tudor homes, the pizzeria boasts a Norman Rockwell charm, with big glossy windows, a marble pizza counter, and cushy soda shop booths made for dinner with the family.

The menu is straightforward, with pizza, calzones, and a near-perfect cannoli, but don't be fooled by the simplicity. This is some of the city's finest pizza: its perfectly pliant crust is lightly charred, laced with a lick-your-fingers red sauce, and then loaded with toppings like crumbly sausage, fresh prosciutto, or tart anchovies.

Nusara

F3   Thai ✗

82-80 Broadway (at Whitney Ave.)

Subway: Elmhurst Av   Lunch & dinner daily
Phone: 718-898-7996
Web: www.nusarathaikitchen.com
Prices: $$

The surroundings—a multi-use mall anchored by a massive supermarket—leave much to be desired, but step inside Nusara and the busy environs of Elmhurst disappear. The dining room is bright and inviting, and the attractive décor is defined by vibrant photos of fruit from Southeast Asia.

The warm welcome doesn't end there. The menu is filled with traditional Thai hits as well as a few unusual selections thrown in for good measure. Wonderful and flavorsome grilled pork; tender char-grilled Siam chicken; sticky and spicy spare ribs; and fried soft shell crab served with a green mango salad are among the choices. Sweet or sour? Don't choose and get two for one with the roasted duck served beside juicy pineapple, cilantro, red chili, and lime vinaigrette.

Ornella 😊

F1   Italian ✗✗

29-17 23rd Ave. (bet. 29th & 31st Sts.)

Subway: Astoria - Ditmars Blvd   Lunch & dinner daily
Phone: 718-777-9477
Web: www.ornellatrattoria.com
Prices: $$

The walls are warm in color but dressed with vibrant sconces, and the menu is all about tasty, honest Italian-American food. The team behind Ornella clearly has an innate sense of providing the best in Italian hospitality, palpable both here and for those looking to escape to the Viterale's estate in the Catskills for a food-centric weekend.

Knowing that the farm (usually) supplies Ornella its unique batch of herbs and greens, peek at the menu and find yourself craving a taste of everything. Although classic in mien, witness some surprises on the menu like duck meatballs glossed with an orange-brandy reduction; handmade chestnut pasta gliding in a lemon-pistachio pesto; and a thick pork chop with a "pocketful" of mushrooms, prosciutto, and cheese.

Pachanga Patterson

F2

33-17 31st Ave. (at 34th St.)

Subway: 30 Av
Phone: 718-554-0525
Web: www.pachangapatterson.com
Prices: $$

Lunch Sat – Sun
Dinner nightly

For a tasty twist on Mexican classics, pop into Pachanga Patterson, situated on Astoria's 31st Avenue, once known as Patterson. It's a feel-good spot combining exposed brick, red walls, wood tables, artful knickknacks, and strings of twinkle lights. The garden patio is idyllic in summer.

On the menu, the "veggie jenga" tostada is a sinful meal unto itself, piled high with smashed black beans, *queso blanco*, avocado, sweet potato purée, and fried egg. Tacos are a particular treat, whether tucking small mashed lentil cakes, balsamic onions, and velvety peanut sauce into a soft corn tortilla, or stuffed with cubes of ancho-battered pollock and topped with sliced red onion and citrus-habanero sauce. The *paletas* are house-made, delicious and refreshing.

Parkside

B2

107-01 Corona Ave. (bet. 108th St. & 51st Ave.)

Subway: 103 St - Corona Plaza
Phone: 718-271-9871
Web: www.parksiderestaurantny.com
Prices: $$$

Lunch & dinner daily

Set upon a landmark corner beyond the Corona Italian Ice King, Parkside's interior evokes a golden era of Italian-American dining, circa 1978. Waiters don tuxedos, regal archways are the norm, and walls boast classic photos or plaques etched with names of the city's elite above the more desirable tables.

The energy and celebratory atmosphere is contagious, amid linen-topped tables laden with the likes of a thick, earthy lentil soup, or colossal crabmeat cocktail with melted butter and zesty black pepper. Try tender slices of prime steak *pizzaiola* with a chunky-garlicky tomato sauce strewn with herbs, paired with meltingly soft potato croquettes. Finish with a house-made tiramisu served in a glass trifle with powdered chocolate and chewy cocoa bits.

Payag

E3

Filipino

51-34 Roosevelt Ave. (at 52nd St.)

Subway: 52 St
Phone: 347-935-3192
Web: www.payagrestaurant.com
Prices: $$

Lunch & dinner Wed – Mon

The dearth of soulful, authentic Filipino food in the boroughs has been remedied to the tune of one restaurant: Payag. Here, owner Rena Avendula succeeds not just in satisfying hunger, but spirit as well. A *payag* is a simple Filipino hut, and the design of the dining room—airy and bright—is meant to evoke home. Calming touches of sea shells, bamboo, and rattan abound.

The food, which blends Spanish, Chinese, and Malay influences, is equally homey and hearty; portions are gargantuan and carefully presented. The classic Filipino stew, *kare kare*, is full of tender, succulent oxtail and tripe in a peanut based sauce. The crispy *pata*, a deep-fried pig's knuckle, is almost overwhelmingly rich: juicy, crackling skin gives way to the fork-tender pork underneath.

Piccola Venezia

F2

Italian

42-01 28th Ave. (at 42nd St.)

Subway: 30 Av
Phone: 718-721-8470
Web: www.piccola-venezia.com
Prices: $$$

Lunch Mon – Fri
Dinner nightly

Piccola Venezia deserves its landmark status: this old-time idol has been going strong ever since opening in 1973. With Italian-American cooking so rampant in the city, it is wholly refreshing to happen upon a classic of such welcoming comfort. The décor is outdated, but the white tablecloths are clean and crisp. The glasses gleam at the prospect of great wine varietals, and the walls are adorned with watercolors depicting Venetian scenes.

With a distinctly macho mien and crowd, well-versed waiters follow suit. They make you nostalgic for *yota*, a heartwarming bean-and-cabbage soup loaded with bacon; *fusi* swirled in a grappa- mushroom- and Grana-sauce; or *trippa alla Triestina*, succulent tripe in a light tomato sauce served with smashed-fried potatoes.

Pio Pio

Peruvian ✗

84-02 Northern Blvd. (bet. 84th & 85th Sts.)

Subway: 82 St - Jackson Hts
Phone: 718-426-4900
Web: www.piopionyc.com
Prices: ⊜⊘

Lunch & dinner daily

This Peruvian rotisserie chicken joint that spawned a mini-empire is a sprawling, street level operation featuring yellow walls and jumbo photos of everyday life in the motherland. The wood beam-covered lower level replete with a private room and pleasant little garden, is quite fascinating and feels very contemporary

The menu remains blissfully similar with goodies like crispy and flaky empanadas stuffed with sweet, fragrant chicken and a wicked salsa *criolla* (a house specialty that, when it appears on the menu accompanying any dish, should scream "order me"). Enormous in size but filled with flavor, the *arroz con mariscos* is a Peruvian version of paella loaded with scallops, octopus, mussels, and shrimp in a garlicky red sauce flecked with cilantro.

Renee's Kitchenette & Grill

Filipino ✗

69-14 Roosevelt Ave. (bet. 69th & 70th Sts.)

Subway: 69 St
Phone: 718-476-9002
Web: N/A
Prices: ⊜⊘

Lunch & dinner Wed – Mon

Don't come for the setting–a rather utilitarian room located on a stretch of Roosevelt by the Grand Central Parkway overpass–but if you're looking for bang for the buck, you've found it. Renee's is a favorite among Filipinos who come for a taste of their homeland. The fact that you might be the only gringo here is just one more sign that this is the real deal.

Follow the next table's lead and start by slurping one of Renee's signature smoothies. You can't go wrong with classic Filipino staples like chicken *adobo* (in vinegar and soy sauce) and *tinolang manok* (a tart chicken soup with spinach); while items like *paksiw na lechon* (pork in liver sauce) are better suited for the adventurous palate. When you leave, your stomach will be as full as your wallet.

Sabry's

Seafood ✗

24-25 Steinway St. (bet. Astoria Blvd. & 25th Ave.)

Subway: Astoria Blvd
Phone: 718-721-9010
Web: N/A
Prices: $$

Lunch & dinner daily

See that piping hot, fresh pita bread coming out of the oven? It's headed straight to your table with a side of their deliciously smoky baba ghanoush, and a plate of tender grilled sardines dressed with tart vinegar and fragrant oregano.

This comfortable, everyday Egyptian eatery is set smack in the heart of Astoria's "Little Egypt" and serves superbly fresh seafood in a relaxed environment. Try the whole grilled red snapper, cooked in garlic, cumin, red pepper, parsley, and olive oil—tender, aromatic, and delicious. Or give the *taojine* a whirl, a version of a tagine with rich tomato sauce, onions, garlic, cumin, and cardamom, studded with calamari and shrimp.

Note to the drinkers: no alcohol is allowed at this strictly observant spot.

Salt & Fat

Contemporary ✗

41-16 Queens Blvd. (bet. 41st & 42nd Sts.)

Subway: 40 St
Phone: 718-433-3702
Web: www.saltandfatny.com
Prices: $$

Dinner Tue – Sun

This city-wide favorite just keeps getting better. Thank neighborhood native Chef Daniel Yi for his expert vision and execution, as well as his highly skilled staff, both in front and back of the house. The narrow storefront is tidy and warm; the food is contemplative and fun.

Bacon-fat popcorn might be a prelude to the spicy BLT piled with a thick square of beautifully caramelized Berkshire pork bacon, cherry tomatoes, pickled veggies, shredded romaine, and onion on *bao* buns slathered with spicy-sweet mayo. Paired with a smoked porter from upstate New York, the dish is unbeatable. Yellowtail tartare combines a swoosh of yuzu gel, dots of smoky ancho-*sriracha* mayo, and cassava chips to showcase distinct flavors and extraordinary pleasure.

Sentosa

A3

39-07 Prince St. (at 39th Ave.)

Subway: Flushing - Main St

Phone: 718-886-6331

Web: www.sentosausa.com

Prices: ⊜⊜

Lunch & dinner daily

Sentosa is a nirvana of sorts for die-hard Southeast Asian food fans. Set at the base of a building where the foot traffic never ceases, this Malaysian marvel is firmly planted amid Chinese banquet halls and eateries hawking Cantonese roast meats and Vietnamese *pho*. The inside is immaculate, airy, and modern in a muted sort of way with natural light bouncing from teak walls to stone-tiled floors.

The courteous and friendly staff is eager to educate and delight you with any number of dishes from the well-explained menu—from firm and fiery pickled vegetables to the refreshing watermelon juice. Expect *poh piah* packed with jicama, tofu, and bean sprouts; or the ever-authentic *nasi lemak* mingling coconut rice, anchovies, chicken curry, and hard-boiled eggs.

Seoul Soondae

C1

158-15 Northern Blvd. (at 158th St.)

Subway: N/A

Phone: 718-321-3231

Web: N/A

Prices: $$

Lunch & dinner daily

In the heart of Northern Boulevard, among Korean boutiques, groceries and barbecue joints, is Seoul Soondae—New York City's first outpost for this small-chain restaurant.

What gives this delicious gem the edge is its unique regional menu offering a variety of well-made delights. The gargantuan house specialty, *soondae naejang bokeum*, is a rich example: it arrives as a plate of peppery blood sausage, pork intestine, tongue, ears, and a heap of shredded vegetables, all tossed in toasted sesame oil, and ready to be cooked at the table. Other options include fragrant *gamja tang*, pork and potato stew; or *jjol-myun* noodles, served cold and topped with carrots, cabbage, pickled cucumber, bean sprouts, and boiled egg, crowned with a hot and spicy sauce.

Shanghai Tide

A3

135-20 40th Rd. (bet. Main & Prince Sts.)

Subway: Flushing - Main St

Lunch & dinner daily

Phone: 718-661-0900

Web: N/A

Prices: $$

Shanghai Tide may not be new, but it is rising to the top here in Flushing, perhaps leading a new wave of regional restaurants to replace those mélange of general Chinese spots. The space is simply appointed with ropes of twinkly Christmas lights, dark rugs, and well-spaced tables run by a helpful (if slow) staff.

The vast menu is reliably good, but their hot pots have been known to induce much love. Picture huge bubbling pots sitting like centerpieces at each table, filling the restaurant with a spicy sort of aromatherapy, and brimming with marbled meats, mung bean sheets, abalone, prawns, octopus, vegetables... you name it. Beyond this, try silky dried bean curd tossed with soybeans and snow cabbage, or bitter melon with preserved black beans.

SHI

A2

47-20 Center Blvd. (bet. 47th & 48th Aves.)

Subway: Vernon Blvd - Jackson Av

Lunch Sat – Sun

Phone: 347-242-2450

Dinner nightly

Web: www.shilic.com

Prices: $$

SHI makes the most of its extraordinary location with expansive floor-to-ceiling windows that display stellar views of the United Nations and Manhattan skyline. The dramatic dining room alone may literally blow you away. The front lounge offers banquettes, a sleek bar, and crystal chandeliers. In addition to the setting, Asian-American, Chinese, and Japanese specialties attract a steady crowd of affluent professionals and local families.

The menu highlights sentimental favorites, like crab Rangoon combining flaky crab, oozing cream cheese, and scallion in crisp wontons; or Buddhist delight, that wonderful vegetarian ensemble of bean threads, noodles, bamboo shoots, and tofu. Also sample an array of maki like the *tohru* roll filled with eel teriyaki.

Sik Gaek

Korean ✗

C1

161-29 Crocheron Ave. (bet. 161st & 162nd Sts.)

Subway: Flushing - Main St (& bus Q12)   Dinner Tue – Sun
Phone: 718-321-7770
Web: N/A
Prices: $$

When David Chang and Anthony Bourdain have sunk their pincers into some far-flung outer borough joint, you know you're in for a treat. Sik Gaek, a Korean restaurant in Auburndale, is a riot of a place: think corrugated metal roofs, blaring rock music, neon aquariums, and flashing traffic lights, and you will only start to get a picture.

But the fun atmosphere is only the beginning. Kick things off with a piping hot bowl of fish broth bobbing with thin noodles, fish cake, vegetables, boiled egg, and scallions; and then move on to the money shot: an enormous paella-style pan heaped with fresh vegetables, loads of shellfish, and a live—yes, live–octopus, which will probably try to make a run for it. Thankfully, there's not a yellow cab in sight.

Spicy & Tasty

Chinese ✗

A3

39-07 Prince St. (at 39th Ave.)

Subway: Flushing - Main St   Lunch & dinner daily
Phone: 718-359-1601
Web: N/A
Prices:

Spicy & Tasty has found its home in this bustling pocket of Queens, where a dizzying array of restaurants, bakeries, and stores jockey to win the favor of Flushing's booming Asian population. Its local love is clear in the diverse ethnicities scattered across the clean, contemporary, and spacious dining room, as well as in the cuisine—though it does seem to restrain its punchy Sichuan heat for fear of scaring the newbies.

Nonetheless, this food is thoroughly enjoyable. It is likewise fun to watch the warm, knowledgeable staff walk first-timers through steaming plates of dumplings, plump with a spicy red chili sauce and minced meat; broad noodles in a powerful, rich, meaty sauce dancing with scallions and peppers; or a tender and fiery cold tripe salad.

S Prime

Steakhouse

35-15 36th St. (bet. 35th & 36th Aves.)

Subway: 36 Av
Phone: 718-707-0660
Web: www.sprimenyc.com
Prices: $$$$

Dinner Tue – Sat

For all the buzz over Brooklyn, Queens remains in a league of its own. The borough may be loved for ethnic eateries, but innovators and investors have arrived, bringing this true-blue steakhouse with them. S Prime is elegant and masculine, with dark wood, corrugated ceilings, metal-studded columns, and exposed duct work. The staff is attentive, alert, and timely.

On those well-spaced tables, find the likes of perfectly cooked and decadent foie gras with a rich grapefruit reduction. The menu divides sides into the "good" as in mushrooms, and the "bad" like lobster mac and cheese. Of course, the highlight of any meal here is the intensely flavorful and beautifully marbled signature ribeye, carefully dry-aged and prepared to exact specification.

Sripraphai

Thai

64-13 39th Ave. (bet. 64th & 65th Sts.)

Subway: Woodside - 61 St
Phone: 718-899-9599
Web: www.sripraphairestaurant.com
Prices:

Lunch & dinner Thu – Tue

A few years ago, this local favorite set off a critical firestorm for delivering killer, authentic-as-it-gets Thai food, then smartly expanded into roomier digs. In the current space, you'll find a large, elegant dining room with an enormous backyard garden, replete with gurgling fountain.

But with the flood of Westerners hovering like wolves outside the front door, has this beloved Woodside restaurant tamed her fiery ways? She has, but the bland food still remains quite popular regardless of diminished authenticity. The menu may feature bright green papaya salads; tender roasted duck over a bed of greens; fluffy Thai-style frittatas studded with ground pork; or fresh soft shell crab, lightly fried and pooled in a delicious coconut-laced green curry.

Sugar Freak

F2

36-18 30th Ave. (bet. 36 & 37th Sts.)

Subway: 30 Av
Phone: 718-726-5850
Web: www.sugarfreak.com
Prices: $$

Lunch Sat – Sun
Dinner nightly

It's easy to see what's to like about Sugar Freak. This cute and comfortable spot plays up its Big Easy roots at first glance with a wrought-iron façade proudly fixed with a fleur-de-lis in the center. Inside, it's slightly hodge-podge, with its own rendition of recycled-chic (lights fashioned from milk bottles, lots of reclaimed woods, and retro Formica-and-steel high bar tables).

A husband-and-wife team runs the show here, where the menu highlights classic New Orleans-style cuisine (rich crawfish étouffée?) with inventive twists—maybe deviled eggs topped with fried chicken skin? Oh, and with this name, you bet the desserts are good. Diners freak out over the chess pie, a chocolate pie with peanut butter crumble baked in-house inside a Mason Ball jar.

Taiwanese Gourmet

F3

84-02 Broadway (at St. James Ave.)

Subway: Elmhurst Av
Phone: 718-429-4818
Web: N/A
Prices:

Lunch & dinner daily

A spotless semi-open kitchen is one of the first signs that this Taiwanese restaurant is just a little bit different than the other kids. Straddling a corner of Elmhurst, Taiwanese Gourmet is a bright spot on Queens' Chinatown circuit, with jumbo windows flooding the dining room with daylight and beautifully framed ancient warrior gear flanking the walls.

The menu reads minimalist, but the staff can be quite helpful if you approach them with questions. Skip the unimpressive oyster pancakes, and dive into dishes like shredded beef and dried tofu, stir-fried in a complex, dark sauce; a delicate, beer-infused duck hot pot teeming with juju beans and Chinese herbs; or a scrumptious clam and chicken hot pot bursting with flavor from smoky bonito flakes.

Tang

C1

196-50 Northern Blvd. (at Francis Lewis Blvd.)

Subway: N/A
Phone: 718-279-7080
Web: www.gammeeok.com
Prices: $$

Lunch & dinner daily

This 24-hour Northern Boulevard standout is an absolute must-visit for anyone seeking authentic Korean specialties. Connected to an art gallery, Tang has an impeccably cool style, starting with its angled exterior ablaze in beams of yellow light, and an interior done in brick walls and bare-wood tables.

The menu offers a handful of *bibimbap*, tofu dishes, and barbecue platters, as well heavenly soups like *seolleongtang*, made with ox-bone and paired with two outstanding varieties of kimchi—radish and Napa cabbage. But the main attraction is the sensational *jeon*, traditional Korean pancakes grilled to order (weekends and dinner, only). Try the perilla leaf *jeon* stuffed with seasoned pork; or *nok du jeon* of ground mung bean, sprouts, and minced pork.

Taverna Kyclades

F1

33-07 Ditmars Blvd. (bet. 33rd & 35th Sts.)

Subway: Astoria - Ditmars Blvd
Phone: 718-545-8666
Web: www.tavernakyclades.com
Prices:

Lunch & dinner daily

Forget the no-frills surroundings and focus instead on the fantastically fresh fish. This beloved Greek spot has folks happily dining elbow to elbow in a tiny yet lively space where the bustling kitchen is in view and seafaring scenes paint the walls. Quick, straightforward servers may address you in Greek if you look the part—that's just how local it gets here. Grab a seat on the enclosed patio for some serenity and get things going with garlicky and bubbling hot crab-stuffed clams; or the cold, classic trio of powerful *skordalia*, cooling tzatziki, and briny *taramosalata* served with toasted pita triangles. Order a side of *horta* (steamed escarole and dandelion) to accompany a plate of sweet and delicate mullets, served with a side of lemon potatoes.

Tawa Tandoor

Indian ✗

37-56 74th St. (bet. Roosevelt & 37th Aves.)

Subway: Jackson Hts - Roosevelt Av   Lunch & dinner daily
Phone: 718-478-2730
Web: N/A
Prices: $$

There is a very good reason to stop and taste something deliciously unexpected, amid this strip of Indian diners and shops with windows dressed in sumptuous saris and jewelry. The solid Indian menu not only towers above local curry shops but offers fusion dishes honoring the culinary legacy of Chinese immigrants who settled in Calcutta and Bombay eons ago. The narrow, deep room dons dark hues, coffered ceilings, comfy seats, and lures crowds with its lunch buffet. *Aloo tikki chole* with fluffy potatoes, tender chickpeas, and tangy yogurt tossed in tamarind chutney keep regulars happy. Heat-seekers will adore such Indo-Chinese items as *hakka* chili chicken, highly spiced and with the concentrated flavors of star anise, cilantro, ginger, and scallions.

Testaccio

Italian ✗✗

47-30 Vernon Blvd. (at 47th Rd.)

Subway: Vernon Blvd - Jackson Av   Lunch & dinner daily
Phone: 718-937-2900
Web: www.testacciony.com
Prices: $$

Elegant yet rustic, this Roman-inspired *ristorante* is a standout among its Vernon Boulevard neighbors. The bi-level space is filled with high, arched ceilings, distressed brick walls, antique mirrors, and dark wood tables against leather banquettes for a sophisticated vibe. Grab a seat at the fantastic bar, and choose a glass from the ample Frascati wine selection. Comforting, well-made dishes define the food, starting with the likes of marinated artichoke wrapped in thin slices of lamb carpaccio, served over arugula salad. The *gnocco alla romana* baked in rich tomato sauce with basil and Parmesan are light, delicate, and sure to melt in your mouth. Excellent braised oxtail with mushroom ragout and rosemary mashed potatoes is supple and hearty.

Thymari

E2

Greek XX

32-07 34th Ave. (bet. 32nd & 33rd Sts.)

Subway: Broadway
Phone: 718-204-2880
Web: www.thymari.com
Prices: $$

Lunch Sat – Sun
Dinner Tue – Sun

Thymari brings Greek classics back to life in their dainty Astoria home. Drawing you in is an impeccably clean and inviting bar area adorned with plush pillows. Beyond, an archway leads to the main dining room flooded with fuss-free tables, striking photos, and fresh air from wide-open windows.

Shaded with Mediterranean colors, Thymari is the sort of place that fosters relaxation and conversation, perhaps about sweet dolmades filled with rice, apricots, and pine nuts; or sesame-crusted *arahova* feta, pan-fried and topped with strawberry-raspberry compote. The kitchen loves its contemporary twists, patent in *loukaniko*, homemade pork sausage seasoned with fennel, sundried tomatoes, and orange; or flaky baklava soaked in fragrant lavender honey.

Tito Rad's Grill

E3

Filipino X

49-12 Queens Blvd. (bet. 49th & 50th Sts.)

Subway: 46 St - Bliss St
Phone: 718-205-7299
Web: www.titorads.com
Prices:

Lunch & dinner daily

When your breakfast coffee arrives with sardines and garlic fried rice, you'll know you're not really in Queens anymore. The welcome may be frosty and the Filipino-only crowd may wonder if you know what you're in for, but settle into one of the tightly packed tables and be rewarded.

First and foremost, Tito Rad's barbecue specialties are not to be missed. From tuna jaw to supremely tender pork, the barbecue presents the perfect yin and yang flavor combo of salty and sour. Be sure to sample some *menudo*, a pork-based stew, and the spicy tuna belly cooked in coconut milk, served soupy with bits of bitter melon and explosive heat. Tito's delight is the perfect finish with a trio of rich *leche* flan, cassava cake, and *ube*, a dense cake made from purple yam.

Trattoria L'incontro

Italian ✕✕

F1

21-76 31st St. (at Ditmars Blvd.)

Subway: Astoria - Ditmars Blvd
Phone: 718-721-3532
Web: www.trattorialincontro.com
Prices: $$

Lunch & dinner daily

Locals fancy Trattoria L'incontro for proudly dishing out the best in Italian-American cuisine. If you're imagining patrons with tucked napkins clinking glasses and filling the airy room with heartfelt laughter, then you're right on track. The space combines coral walls with frescos depicting a range of idyllic Italian landscapes, and sweet, attentive service.

In the back rests an oven that churns out deliciously blistered pizzas and a long, breathless list of specials. Sample the likes of *portobello in cartoccio* baked with herbs atop a sprightly green salad; or *pollo 4 funghi*, strips of silky chicken tossed with mushroom ragout and a slightly creamy wine- onion- and thyme-sauce. The *pizza al cioccolato* oozing Nutella is worthy of framed accolades.

Trattoria Neo

Italian ✕✕

C1

15-01 149th St. (at 15th Ave.)

Subway: N/A
Phone: 718-767-1110
Web: www.trattorianeo.com
Prices: $$

Lunch & dinner daily

Set on a leafy corner, right off the Cross Island Parkway, Trattoria Neo is a perfect match for its little enclave. Framed by large wooden doors and windows, the inside is cozy and welcoming with wood ceiling beams, Venetian plaster covering columns and walls, and sconces gently lighting the room.

Just as the wrought-iron candelabras recall classic Italy, so does its menu. From the marble bar, expect inventive cocktails to go with *arancini di riso*, saffron rice balls stuffed with ragù Bolognese; or *braciola di maiale*, a huge oven-roasted pork chop with an intense vinegared cherry pepper sauce, paired with buttery potatoes. Wednesday is pasta (and live music!) day so insist on the likes of *stringhetti*, tossed in tomato sauce with fresh basil and Parmesan.

Uncle Zhou

F3

Chinese ✗

83-29 Broadway (at Dongan Ave.)

Subway: Elmhurst Av
Phone: 718-393-0888
Web: N/A
Prices: 💰💰

Lunch & dinner daily

Bare tables, walls adorned with pictures of the food you're about to devour, and a mini mall location don't typically bode well, but what Uncle Zhou lacks in frills, it more than makes up for in flavor.

The food here is incredibly executed. Peruse the menu for perennial favorites like paper-thin beef and hand-pulled noodles laid to rest under a fiery broth flavored with Sichuan peppercorns; or just point to the wall—that big tray of chicken in the photo isn't on the menu but appears mighty flavorful in its chili broth. You can order noodles how you like them (in a brick red soup bobbing with lean slices of lamb); while regulars opt for the whole tilapia, fried to golden perfection and baked with chewy noodles in a zesty sweet and sour sauce.

Urubamba

F3

Peruvian ✗

86-20 37th Ave. (at 86th St.)

Subway: 82 St - Jackson Hts
Phone: 718-672-2224
Web: N/A
Prices: $$

Lunch & dinner daily

Far from the high-end Peruvian cuisine flowing through Manhattan, Urubamba (named for a river in Peru) is rustic, homey, and made to satisfy the soul with its own answer to comfort food classics. Inside, the deep and narrow space feels like a petite hacienda, adorned with wood shutters, a windowed banquette, and whitewashed brick walls covered with Peruvian artefacts and paintings.

Urubamba's delicious *desayuno* is served only on weekends and is adored by its constant crowd. Also find patrons salivating over *cau cau*, cubes of honeycomb tripe stewed in a turmeric-flecked sauce; *chupe de camaron*, a thin shrimp chowder with potatoes, rice, and *choclo*; or traditional *alfajores*, sugar-dusted biscuits filled with thick and decadent *dulce de leche*.

Uvarara

Italian

79-28 Metropolitan Ave. (at 80th St.)

Subway: Middle Village - Metropolitan Av (& bus Q54)
Phone: 718-894-0052
Web: www.uvararany.com
Prices: $$

Dinner Tue – Sun

From its quirky mismatched chairs and gothic arches to the curtain created out of strings of wine corks, Uvarara is intimate, comfortable, and very homey. Tucked away in the quaint, residential neighborhood of Middle Village, this restaurant is the work of the Iadicicco family, who hail from Caserta and have created an authentic atmosphere akin to the *osterie* of their native country.

The kitchen consistently spins out delectable dishes, such as baked gnocchi over butter and *Parmigiano* sauce, with touches of sage and pepper; or broiled portobello mushroom caps stuffed with pork sausage, garlic, cheese, and parsley, topped with toasted breadcrumbs and balsamic reduction. The *basa* fish special arrives flaky and beautifully fried, with a standout lentil salad.

Vesta Trattoria

Italian

21-02 30th Ave. (at 21st St.)

Subway: 30 Av
Phone: 718-545-5550
Web: www.vestavino.com
Prices: $$

Lunch Sat – Sun
Dinner nightly

Vesta is the Roman God of the hearth; in Queens, it is the home to revered Italian delicacies and a unique wine list rife with special blends from Long Island producers. Such local love is undeniably delightful, as is Vesta's simple space with sage-green banquettes, thought-provoking canvases, dark wood floors, and gentle lighting to suit the diminutive room. Maneuvering into your seat may take some effort, but a whiff of their Italianized classics (maybe a soulful chicken soup bobbing with noodles and fennel) and you will be besotted. A thin-crust, whole-wheat pizza slathered with crispy kale, sweet currants, and salty Grana Padano evokes a healthy dictum, while rigatoni tossed in a blue cheese cream and topped with herbed breadcrumbs is pure decadence.

Wafa

B2

Middle Eastern ✗

100-05 Metropolitan Ave. (bet. 70th Ave. and 70th Rd.)

Subway: Forest Hills - 71 Av
Phone: 718-880-2055
Web: www.wafasfood.com
Prices: $$

Lunch & dinner daily

Wafa is loved largely for her delicious and homemade Lebanese cuisine. Having settled into larger quarters, she now sports a lime green décor that is totally rudimentary and wholly suited to her timeless nabe. Flanked by red sauce joints and solid Japanese respites, Wafa is an ideal refuge for those seeking authentic, diverse fare.

Named after her leading lady, Wafa Chami, who can be seen ruling the roost from the open kitchen, Wafa is genuinely warm and bold on authenticity. The kitchen displays a clear grasp of ingredients and flavors when creating a sinfully smoky baba ghanoush infused with lemon and tahini. *Shish tawook* (kebabs) become more enticing when paired with pickles and garlic paste, as does the lamb shawarma doused in pomegranate juice.

Zabb Elee ☺

F3

Thai ✗

71-28 Roosevelt Ave. (bet. 70th & 72nd Sts.)

Subway: 74 St - Broadway
Phone: 718-426-7992
Web: www.zabbelee.com
Prices: ☜☜

Lunch & dinner daily

There is nothing gussied up about Zabb Elee. This tiny Thai storefront is skimpy on style (decked with fluorescent lights and narrow seats where the 7 train roars overhead), but patrons aren't flocking here for its looks. Nope, they're here for really good and truly authentic Thai cooking.

The heat is on at Zabb Elee, where the food isn't dumbed down for blander American palates. It is equal parts sour, sweet, and spicy, though the staff is happy to alter the level of heat. Whether you sink your teeth into marvelously seasoned grilled chicken gizzards with tamarind sauce, or the delightfully sour *esarn* Thai sausage, do ensure you snack on the addictive bits of caramelized pork strewn amid swamp cabbage, or slurp the dreamy broth of the *tom yum* soup.

Zum Stammtisch

German 🍴

69-46 Myrtle Ave. (bet. 69th Pl. & 70th St.)

Subway: N/A
Phone: 718-386-3014
Web: www.zumstammtisch.com
Prices: **$$**

Lunch & dinner daily

Family owned and operated since 1972, this unrelenting success has expanded over the years and recently welcomed Stammtisch Pork Store & Imports next door.

Zum Stammtisch hosts a crowded house in a Bavarian country inn setting where old-world flavor is relished with whole-hearted enthusiasm. The goulash is thick and hearty, stocked with potatoes and beans, but that's just for starters. Save room for *sauerbraten*, *jägerschnitzel*, or a platter of succulent grilled sausages that includes *bratwurst*, *knockwurst*, and hickory-smoked *krainerwurst* served with sauerkraut and potato salad. The *Schwarzwälder Kirschtorte* (classic Black Forest cake) layers dense chocolate cake with Kirsch-soaked cherries and cream, and is absolutely worth the indulgence.

Sunday brunch plans?
Look for the 🥂 !

Jeanine C. Hart/MICHELIN

Staten Island

Staten Island

Unless you live there, chances are that Staten Island is different from the perception. Due to the vast damage incurred by Hurricane Sandy, marinas, shores, and waterfronts remain in shambles. Yet despite the devastation, this will always remain a gateway to the New York Harbor. Then, consider that, in some ways, much of what enters the city has first passed through this most secluded borough. Thus, it is only fitting that the bridge that opened it up and may have ended its previously bucolic existence be named for Giovanni da Verrazano, the Italian explorer who first arrived here in 1524. This is particularly apt, because one of the strongest and most accurate generalizations of Staten Island is that it is home to a large Italian-American population. No self-respecting foodie would consider a visit here without picking up a scungilli pizza from **Joe and Pat's**, or at least a slice from **Nunzio** and maybe **Denino's**, too.

Display of Deliciousness

Beyond this, Staten Island continues to surprise visitors with its ethnically diverse localities. Take a virtual tour of the eastern Mediterranean at **Dinora** and **Nova Food Market** for their olives, cheeses, and freshly butchered meat. Or, visit the old-world Polish delis which seem to comfortably survive on their takeout business and those tasty homemade jams.

Sri Lankan food fans rejoice in the area surrounding Victory Boulevard for its restaurants serving this fiery cuisine—try **New Asha** for its flavorful fish buns. Speaking of South Asia, this area is also home to the culturally rich Jacques Marchais Museum of Tibetan Art. Steps from these Asian thrills, find authentic taquerias as well as the **St. George Greenmarket**, rife with produce grown locally at the borough's very own Decker Farm. Historic Richmond Town also organizes the family-focused festival *Uncorked!*, featuring the best and finest in professional and homemade wine and food, offering recipes of traditional favorites. For rare and mature wines, don't forget to visit **Mission Fine Wines**.

Food, Fun, and Frolic

Keeping all this in mind, it should be of no surprise to learn that the Staten Island of the future includes plans for a floating farmer's market, aquarium, and revamped waterfronts. So sit back and have a drink at one of the bars along Bay Street, and lament the world's myopic view of this much maligned borough. Drive through some of the city's wealthiest zip codes, rife with splendid views of Manhattan and beyond. Whether here to glimpse the world's only complete collection of rattlesnakes at the local zoo; or to seek out the birthplaces of stars such as Christina Aguilera and Joan Baez, a visit to Staten Island is sure to surprise.

Staten Island

• Restaurant

Angelina's

A4

Italian XX

399 Ellis St.

Bus: N/A
Phone: 718-227-2900
Web: www.angelinasristorante.com
Prices: $$$

Lunch & dinner Tue – Sun

Angelina's may live beside a railroad depot, but gauging from its perpetual crowd and packed parking spaces, it is safe to assume that locals and visitors continue to be smitten with this Italian pinup. Poised atop the island's tip, the view from this striking multi-level Victorian home armed with hefty windows is stunning, especially at sunset.

Speaking of day's end, it is also *the* hot spot for live music, stirring drinks, and appealing eats. Grilled asparagus topped with sweet crabmeat and doused in truffle oil is a terrific teaser, chased by hearty helpings of *trenette nere ai frutti di mare*, pasta coated in a chunky tomato sauce studded with shrimp, mussels, and scallops. A delicate *sfogliatella* bursting with ricotta is served hot to sate the soul.

Bayou

B2

Cajun XX

1072 Bay St. (bet. Chestnut & St. Marys Aves.)

Bus: 51, 81
Phone: 718-273-4383
Web: www.bayounyc.com
Prices: $$

Lunch & dinner daily

Southern fare isn't novel to the city, but Cajun food on Staten Island is a whole new realm, which Bayou delivers with its veritable setting and spread. The space may seem a bit bawdy with gold and green accents, but linen-covered tables, luminous mirrors, and luxe chandeliers lend refinement. Live music on weeknights adds fun.

Cajun offerings begin with a wonderfully complex jambalaya, rice tucked with smoky tasso ham, tomato, and sweet shrimp, served with a lemon-basil mayonnaise; or roast beef po'boy with caramelized onions. Blackened catfish is soul-satisfying in every sense, served in a skillet beside a pile of fluffy rice. Bananas Foster with rum and brown sugar are tasty, but turn heavenly when paired with one of the many boozy, rich coffees.

Beso

Spanish ✗

B2

11 Schuyler St. (bet. Richmond Tr. & Stuyvesant Pl.)

Bus: N/A
Phone: 718-816-8162
Web: www.besonyc.com
Prices: $$

Lunch & dinner daily

Well-located? Yes, just off the ferry. Good food? Helpful staff? Of course. Great for both parties and solo diners? You know it. Lovely Beso seems to have it all, including an interior that spotlights quaint accents like antique sideboards and an intricately carved U-shaped bar. While grazing menus are all the rage, the larger dishes (*platos fuertes*) are also worth exploring.

Their tapas selection is vibrant—starting with *fundito*, a richly flavored green chili-tomato sauce topped with melted Mahon cheese and studded with chorizo. Follow with the *elote de cangrejo*, crab cakes with roasted corn over a bracing horseradish aïoli; or flautas filled with roasted mushrooms and melted *cobrales*. Close with sweets like coconut flan cloaked in caramel.

Bin 5

Contemporary ✗✗

B2

1233 Bay St. (bet. Maryland & Scarboro Aves.)

Bus: 51, 81
Phone: 718-448-7275
Web: www.bin5nyc.com
Prices: $$

Dinner Tue – Sun

Bin 5 lives in this unique outer borough, enjoying a culinary upswing with food treasures brimming with action. Amid both residential and commercial structures, Bin 5 is a local favorite for their terrific trifecta of genial service, a charming space, and playful yet consistently flavorful bill of fare.

Under the glint of original tin ceilings and amidst intimate wood tables covered in crisp linen, patrons relish starters like grilled, silky eggplant *rollatini*, wrapped around tart but creamy goat cheese set over an arugula and chopped tomato salad. Larger plates have included penne sautéed with sweet Italian sausage, fennel seeds, tomatoes, and hot cherry peppers; or slices of moist veal scaloppini drenched in a creamy Dijon sauce.

Cafe Luna

A3

Italian ✗✗

31 Page Ave. (bet. Boscombe Ave. & Richmond Valley Rd.)

Bus: 74
Phone: 718-227-8582
Web: www.cafelunanyc.com
Prices: $$

Lunch & dinner daily

Some places are synonymous with ethnic identities: Brighton Beach is known for Russian immigrants; Jackson Heights is an Indian enclave; but nothing says Italian-American quite like Staten Island. Cafe Luna is not only one of the prettiest rooms on the island, featuring ceramics, imported glass accents, and crisp tablecloths; but it also doles out hefty standards.

With its whitewashed-stucco exterior, neon sign, and mini-strip mall locale, this cafe echoes the borough's take-me-as-I-am attitude and is one of the best of the bunch with its homemade pastas and grilled fish. Even seemingly simple items like stuffed artichokes drizzled with olive oil; *anelletti* with meat ragù; or a creamy Italian cheesecake are well-made and boast super-fresh fixings.

Carol's Cafe

B2

American ✗

1571 Richmond Rd. (at Four Corners Rd. & Seaview Ave.)

Bus: 74, 76, 84, 86
Phone: 718-979-5600
Web: www.carolscafe.com
Prices: $$

Dinner Wed – Sat

This is the kind of place that you'd only find in New York and in particular, Staten Island. Carol's Cafe is a local institution and there really is a Carol here. She warmly entreats you to try her Neapolitan-style fried ravioli appetizer filled with ricotta, Parmesan, mozzarella, and salty *soppressata*, before moving on to a hearty plate of rigatoni tossed with wild mushrooms and spinach in a creamy Gorgonzola sauce.

While these are great choices and ideal for sharing, Carol's spin on sautéed broccoli rabe (with the addition of roasted garlic and candied lemon wedges) makes eating your greens a delightful proposition. Quirky selections like Dr. Lou Gianvito's fish (Who is he? Who cares...the dish is great!) add to the charm of this unique mainstay.

Dosa Garden

B2

Indian ✗

323 Victory Blvd. (bet. Cebra Ave. & Jersey St.)

Bus: 46, 48, 61, 66
Phone: 718-420-0919
Web: www.dosagardenny.com
Prices: 🍲

Lunch Tue – Sun
Dinner nightly

The Sri Lankan team at Dosa Garden is giving their South Indian counterparts across the city a run for their money. Inside, towering windows face a bustling street, but melodic tunes and vibrant murals lend balance. This is an impressive place for *dosas* with over nineteen varieties, each prepared-to-order in their small, walled-in kitchen.

Despite its size, the kitchen churns out a knockout feast of heady, complex, fragrant flavors and unique textures as seen in an onion- and chili-studded *utthappam* (rice-and-lentil flour pancake) served with sambar (a fiery lentil soup) and soothing coconut chutney. Some opt for crispy decadence in the *paper masala dosa* stuffed with mustard seed-spiced potatoes. The refreshing salt lassis are an essential pairing.

Enoteca Maria

B2

Italian ✗

27 Hyatt St. (bet. Central Ave. & St. Marks Pl.)

Bus: N/A
Phone: 718-447-2777
Web: www.enotecamaria.com
Prices: $$

Dinner Wed – Sun

Enoteca Maria adeptly conjures images of *bambini* being welcomed home by a comforting meal prepared by *nonna*. Updated and fresh, it is a cut above its neighbors featuring such requisite details as exposed duct work, marble "brick" walls, and a bustling open kitchen—this space could easily land in the Village. A walnut cabinet stocked with wines is a lovely sight and blends perfectly with the aromas wafting from the kitchen.

Expect artichoke-packed *ravioli ai carciofi* simmered in a creamy and lush mascarpone sauce; *insalata di finocchi*, crunchy fennel slices mingled with fruit in champagne vinaigrette; and *involtini di vitello di Giuseppina*, rolls of veal packed with prosciutto, asparagus, and fontina cheese, sautéed in butter and Marsala wine.

Fushimi

B3

2110 Richmond Rd. (bet. Colfax & Lincoln Aves.)

Bus:	51, 81	Lunch & dinner daily
Phone:	718-980-5300	
Web:	www.fushimi-us.com	
Prices:	$$$	

Seeking a quiet space for a one-on-one dinner date? Don't come to Fushimi. This Asian-leaning restaurant should be saved for nights when you want to rev things up. It's sexy and dramatic, if a little bit big on all the decorative bells and whistles. Red, black, and gold dominate the design of the three dining spaces, while the sushi bar is set against a wall covered in shiny river stones.

The food is equally flashy, but well-made and very fresh. Lemongrass hot and sour soup bobbing with shrimp and scallions; crunchy beef *negimaki*; and a crispy duck salad lean more toward Asia, while the cream cheesy-blue crab fajita is fusion all the way. Staten Islanders take their pick from a large, sometimes silly-sounding (the out-of-control roll?) sushi menu.

Giuliana's

B3

4105 Hylan Blvd. (at Osborn Ave.)

Bus:	54, 78, 79	Lunch & dinner daily
Phone:	718-317-8507	
Web:	www.giulianassi.com	
Prices:	$$	

Staten Island may swarm with Italian eateries, but Giuliana's does a masterful job in keeping its kitchen distinct and the patrons loyal. This queen bee rests amid shops, catering halls, and ample competition. The interior is modest and charming, with framed pictures of smiling patrons and a fully stocked bar.

Meals should begin with a taste of their freshly made mozzarella, or perhaps the *carciofi Giuliana,* perfectly seasoned, crispy artichoke hearts with a rich and intensely flavored Gorgonzola sauce. Sesame seed-crusted tuna in a balsamic jus is served with sautéed spinach and a restrained kiss of garlic. Sunday suppers featuring a traditional Southern Italian *ragù del macellaio* simmered with meatballs and *braciole,* are a draw in their own right.

Lakruwana

B2

Sri Lankan ✗

668 Bay St. (at Broad St.)

Bus: 51, 76
Phone: 347-857-6619
Web: www.lakruwana.com
Prices:

It might be New York's most Italian-American borough, but Staten Island is home to countless Sri Lankan joints. Up until recently though, enjoying this country's food meant hunkering down in eateries that looked more like bodegas. No more: with the relocation of Lakruwana, the Sri Lankan food scene here has officially arrived.

The over-the-top space is filled with wood masks, clay pots, and gold plaques, but the meticulously prepared food brings you home. Don't miss fish *lamprais*—banana leaf pouches of aromatic and nutty yellow rice laced with silky fish, cashews, and hard boiled egg; a moist fish croquette blending potato, onion, and mint served with a pepper sauce; or string hoppers, frilly pancakes of rice flour and coconut milk paired with curry.

Maizal

B2

Mexican ✗

990 Bay St. (bet. Lynhurst & Willow Sts.)

Bus: 51, 81
Phone: 347-825-3776
Web: www.maizalrestaurant.com
Prices: $$

Lunch & dinner Tue – Sun

Amid a wealth of Italian options, lovely Maizal is a sweet, attractive, and welcomed addition to this corner of the city. Large, solid wood tables, a marble-topped bar, bright walls, seasonal flowers, and semi-open kitchen in the back fashion a very comfortable atmosphere. Live, contemporary music on weekends enhances the fun of dining here.

Begin with a refreshing salad mingling fennel, crispy bacon, and manchego; or intensely spicy and "angry jalapeños" stuffed with gooey goat cheese and served alongside grapes and mango for sweet, contrasting flavors. Look for daily specials like tacos stuffed with deliciously seared skirt steak, pickled onions, and creamy slaw. The roast lime chicken may sound simple, but is beautifully arranged, silky, and supple.

Nove'

A3

Italian

3900 Richmond Ave. (bet. Amboy Rd. & Oakdale St.)

Bus: 59, 79
Phone: 718-227-3286
Web: www.noveitalianbistro.com
Prices: $$$

Lunch Tue – Sat
Dinner Tue – Sun

Hipsters stay clear—Nove' is an ardent, old-school *ristorante* where couples of a certain age are as well-dressed as the staff and reservations are long-standing. The space is ornamented yet never gaudy, and makes a bold statement with burnt-orange walls, carved wood moldings, and pocket doors separating the warm lounge from the main dining room. Elegant custom cabinets are arranged with fine wines for pairing.

Tasty offerings begin with incredibly tender calamari rings tossed with bits of sweet red pepper, arugula, fennel, and *peperoncini* dressing; or *sacchettini*, beggar's purse pasta, filled with a blend of cheese, pears, and greens in a brown butter-and-sage sauce. Their veal chop *grottino* with spring pea-and-leek risotto is an original classic.

San Rasa

B2

Sri Lankan

226 Bay St. (bet. Hannah St. & Victory Blvd.)

Subway: 51
Phone: 718-420-0027
Web: www.sanrasa.com
Prices:

Lunch & dinner Wed – Mon

San Rasa may require both a ferry ride and an open mind, but this authentic Sri Lankan favorite is absolutely worth it—and absolutely delicious. Conveniently situated just a short walk from the ferry landing, this ace location doesn't exactly mind its appearence (the décor can seem busy with odd gadgets and carved items; the views nonexistent). Focus on the smells and tastes of the feast before you.

Ideally, go with a group to explore the menu and savor the likes of *lamparis*, banana leaf purses filled with fragrant yellow rice and silky chicken. *Appams*, made from flour and coconut milk, are best for sopping up a fiery goat curry infused with turmeric, chilies, and cumin seeds. The Sunday lunch buffet is an extraordinary bargain for intrepid foodies.

Vida 😊

American ✗

B2

381 Van Duzer St. (bet. Beach & Wright Sts.)

Bus: 78   Dinner Tue – Sat
Phone: 718-720-1501
Web: www.vidany.com
Prices: $$

Run by owner Silva Popaz, whose infectious warmth and delightful dishes keep regulars coming back for more, Vida is a truly enchanting local haven. The bright and immaculate room is hung with stunning artwork (which is not for sale). Menu items can be found on an easel, and the friendly staff is dedicated to high-quality hospitality.

From the menu, nosh on the likes of batter-fried eggplant rolled with tart goat cheese, and baked in chunky tomato sauce with mozzarella and herbs; decadent gumbo of smoked sausage, shrimp, and chicken; and organic brown rice and braised lentil cake topped with tahini and spinach, set over grilled portobello mushroom. Satiate the sweet craving with bread pudding, oozing with cinnamon and nuts and served with ice cream.

Zest

French ✗✗

B2

977 Bay St. (bet. Lynhurst & Willow Sts.)

Bus: 51, 81   Dinner Tue – Sun
Phone: 718-390-8477
Web: www.zestaurant.com
Prices: $$

Whether seated inside or out, the surroundings are verdant and lush here at Zest. The outdoor garden is a perfect destination for warm nights, while the elegant interior glows with goldish hues and is outfitted in dark woods, vintage vases, blown glass touches, and handsome greenery.

Begin with a tasty vegetable terrine, layering creamy goat cheese, roasted artichoke, eggplant, zucchini, red peppers, fine herbs, and presented with garlic aïoli. The veal tenderloin Cordon Blue is richly stuffed with ham and Gruyère, drizzled with red pepper sauce, and then fanned over potato gratin and a trio of vegetables. Specials may include dill and vodka-cured gravlax over micro arugula alongside silver-dollar potato pancakes and horseradish-spiked sour cream.

● Where to **Eat**

Indexes

Alphabetical List of Restaurants

N

Indexes ▶ Alphabetical List of Restaurants

Restaurants by Cuisine

American

Alobar	✿	✕✕	521
Back Forty		✕	49
Bareburger		✕	524
BG		✕✕	267
Black Swan		✕	446
Blue Hill	✿	✕✕	136
Blue Smoke		✕	97
Boathouse Central Park		✕✕	362
Brooklyn Star		✕✕	449
Burger & Barrel		✕✕	319
Buttermilk Channel	✿	✕	450
Carol's Cafe		✕	572
Casellula		📖	271
Char No. 4	✿	✕✕	452
Clinton St. Baking Company	✿	✕	205
Clover Club		📖	454
Colicchio & Sons		✕✕✕	19
Community Food & Juice		✕✕	189
Cookshop		✕✕	19
Corner Social		✕✕	189
Craft		✕✕✕	102
Diner	✿	✕	456
Dovetail	✿	✕✕	400
DuMont		✕	457
Dutch (The)		✕✕	322
Egg	✿	✕	458
Elizabeth's Neighborhood Table		✕✕	401
Farm on Adderley (The)		✕✕	462
508		✕✕	324
Five Points		✕✕	146
Fort Defiance		✕	463
44 & X Hell's Kitchen		✕✕	278
Four Seasons (The)		✕✕✕✕	234
Garden Café		✕	191
General Greene (The)	✿	✕	465
Good		✕	147
Good Enough to Eat		✕	403
Gotham Bar and Grill	✿	✕✕✕	148
Grocery (The)		✕	467
Harry's Steak & Cafe		✕✕	83
Harvist		✕✕	192
Hill Country Chicken	✿	✕	108
Home		✕	151
Jack the Horse		✕✕	468
James		✕✕	469
J.G. Melon	✿	✕	372
Kitchenette		✕	346
Lambs Club (The)		✕✕	285
Landmark Tavern		✕✕	285
Lulu & Po		📖	475
Marc Forgione		✕✕	349
Market Table		✕✕	160
Mayfield	✿	✕✕	477
Maysville		✕✕	115
Murray's Cheese Bar	✿	✕✕	166
New Leaf Café		✕✕	195
Norma's		✕✕	296
Northeast Kingdom	✿	✕	484
North End Grill		✕✕✕	85
Northern Spy Food Co.	✿	✕	71
No. 7	✿	✕✕	485
Odeon (The)		✕✕	351
Parish Hall		✕	487
Picket Fence		✕	490
Potlikker		✕	492
Preserve 24		✕✕	211
Print		✕✕✕	302
Prospect	✿	✕✕	493
Red Cat (The)		✕✕	27
Redhead (The)		✕	75
Red Rooster		✕✕	196
Reynard		✕✕	494
Rucola		✕	497
Rye	✿	✕	498
Rye House		✕	121
Seersucker	✿	✕✕	501
606 R & D		✕	502
Speedy Romeo	✿	✕	504
St. Anselm		✕	505
Taste		✕✕	387

Contemporary

Indexes ▶ Restaurants by Cuisine

Indexes ▶ Restaurants by Cuisine

Indexes ▶ Restaurants by Cuisine

Cuisines by Neighborhood

MANHATTAN

Chelsea

American

Colicchio & Sons	ⅩⅩ	19
Cookshop	ⅩⅩ	19
Red Cat (The)	ⅩⅩ	27
Tipsy Parson	ⅩⅩ	30

Asian

Chop-Shop	Ⅹ	17

Chinese

Legend Bar & Restaurant	Ⅹ	24

Contemporary

Americano (The)	ⅩⅩ	16
Foragers City Table	ⅩⅩ	23
Trestle on Tenth	ⅩⅩ	30

Fusion

Morimoto	ⅩⅩⅩ	25

Indian

Bombay Talkie	ⅩⅩ	17

Italian

da Umberto		ⅩⅩ	21
Del Posto	❀	ⅩⅩⅩⅩ	22
Le Zie 2000		ⅩⅩ	25
Ovest Pizzoteca		Ⅹ	26
Pastai		ⅩⅩ	27

Japanese

Naka Naka	Ⅹ	26

Latin American

Coppelia	Ⅹ	20

Mexican

Crema	ⅩⅩ	20
Rocking Horse Cafe	Ⅹ	28

Pizza

Co.	Ⅹ	18

Seafood

Cull & Pistol	Ⅹ	21

Spanish

El Quinto Pino	▤	23
La Nacional	Ⅹ	24
Salinas	ⅩⅩ	28
Socarrat	Ⅹ	29
Tia Pol	▤	29
Txikito	Ⅹ	31

Vegan

Blossom	ⅩⅩ	16

Vietnamese

Cô Ba	㊐	Ⅹ	18

Chinatown & Little Italy

Chinese

A-Wah		Ⅹ	34
Bo Ky		Ⅹ	34
Dim Sum Go Go	㊐	Ⅹ	35
Fuleen Seafood		Ⅹ	36
Golden Unicorn		Ⅹ	36
Grand Harmony		Ⅹ	37
Great N.Y. Noodletown		Ⅹ	37
Nom Wah Tea Parlor		Ⅹ	40
Oriental Garden		Ⅹ	41
Peking Duck House		Ⅹ	42
Royal Seafood		Ⅹ	43
Shanghai Café		Ⅹ	44
Shanghai Heping		ⅩⅩ	44

French

Parigot	Ⅹ	41

Gastropub

Brinkley's	Ⅹ	35

Indexes ▶ Cuisines by Neighborhood

Indexes ▶ Cuisines by Neighborhood

Indexes ▶ Cuisines by Neighborhood

Indexes ▶ Cuisines by Neighborhood

Starred Restaurants

*W*ithin the selection we offer you, some restaurants deserve to be highlighted for their particularly good cuisine. When giving one, two, or three Michelin stars, there are a number of elements that we consider including the quality of the ingredients, the technical skill and flair that goes into their preparation, the blend and clarity of flavours, and the balance of the menu. Just as important is the ability to produce excellent cooking time and again. We make as many visits as we need, so that our readers may be assured of quality and consistency.

A two or three-star restaurant has to offer something very special in its cuisine; a real element of creativity, originality, or "personality" that sets it apart from the rest. Three stars – our highest award – are given to the choicest restaurants, where the whole dining experience is superb.

Cuisine in any style, modern or traditional, may be eligible for a star. Due to the fact we apply the same independent standards everywhere, the awards have become benchmarks of reliability and excellence in over 20 countries in Europe and Asia, particularly in France, where we have awarded stars for 100 years, and where the phrase "Now that's real three-star quality!" has entered into the language.

The awarding of a star is based solely on the quality of the cuisine.

❀❀❀

Exceptional cuisine, worth a special journey

One always eats here extremely well, sometimes superbly. Distinctive dishes are precisely executed, using superlative ingredients.

❀❀

Excellent cuisine, worth a detour

Skillfully and carefully crafted dishes of outstanding quality.

❀

A very good restaurant in its category

A place offering cuisine prepared to a consistently high standard.

Bib Gourmand

This symbol indicates our inspectors' favorites for good value. For $40 or less, you can enjoy two courses and a glass of wine or a dessert (not including tax or gratuity).

Under $25

Indexes ▲ Under $25

Brunch

Late Dining

Notes

Notes

YOU ALREADY KNOW THE MICHELIN GUIDE, NOW FIND OUT ABOUT THE MICHELIN GROUP

The Michelin Adventure

It all started with rubber balls! This was the product made by a small company based in Clermont-Ferrand that André and Edouard Michelin inherited, back in 1880. The brothers quickly saw the potential for a new means of transport and their first success was the invention of detachable pneumatic tires for bicycles. However, the automobile was to provide the greatest scope for their creative talents. Throughout the 20th century, Michelin never ceased developing and creating ever more reliable and high-performance tires, not only for vehicles ranging from trucks to F1 but also for underground transit systems and airplanes.

From early on, Michelin provided its customers with tools and services to facilitate mobility and make travelling a more pleasurable and more frequent experience. As early as 1900, the Michelin Guide supplied motorists with a host of useful information related to vehicle maintenance, accommodation and restaurants, and was to become a benchmark for good food. At the same time, the Travel Information Bureau offered travellers personalised tips and itineraries.

The publication of the first collection of roadmaps, in 1910, was an instant hit! In 1926, the first regional guide to France was published, devoted to the principal sites of Brittany, and before long each region of France had its own Green Guide. The collection was later extended to more far-flung destinations, including New York in 1968 and Taiwan in 2011.

In the 21st century, with the growth of digital technology, the challenge for Michelin maps and guides is to continue to develop alongside the company's tire activities. Now, as before, Michelin is committed to improving the mobility of travellers.

MICHELIN TODAY

WORLD NUMBER ONE TIRE MANUFACTURER

- 69 production sites in 18 countries
- 115,000 employees from all cultures and on every continent
- 6,000 people employed in research and development

Moving
for a world

Moving forward means developing tires with better road grip and shorter braking distances, whatever the state of the road.

CORRECT TIRE PRESSURE

RIGHT PRESSURE

- Safety
- Longevity
- Optimum fuel consumption

-0,5 bar

- Durability reduced by 20% (- 8,000 km)

-1 bar

- Risk of blowouts
- Increased fuel consumption
- Longer braking distances on wet surfaces

forward together
where mobility is safer

It also involves helping motorists take care of their safety and their tires. To do so, Michelin organises "Fill Up With Air" campaigns all over the world to remind us that correct tire pressure is vital.

WEAR

DETECTING TYRE WEAR

MICHELIN tyres are equipped with tread wear indicators, which are small blocks of rubber molded into the base of the main grooves at a height of 1.6 mm. When tread depth is the same level as indicators, the tyres are worn and need replacing.

Tyres are the only point of contact between vehicle and the road, a worn tyre can be dangerous on wet surfaces.

NEW TIRE

WORN TIRE
(1,6 mm tread)

The photo shows the actual contact zone on wet surfaces.

Moving forward
means sustainable mobility

By 2050, Michelin aims to cut the quantity of raw materials used in its tire manufacturing process by half and to have developed renewable energy in its facilities. The design of MICHELIN tires has already saved billions of liters of fuel and, by extension, billions of tons of CO_2.

Similarly, Michelin prints its maps and guides on paper produced from sustainably managed forests and is diversifying its publishing media by offering digital solutions to make travelling easier, more fuel efficient and more enjoyable!

The group's whole-hearted commitment to eco-design on a daily basis is demonstrated by ISO 14001 certification.

Like you, Michelin is committed to preserving our planet.